REPORT ON THE SANITARY CONDITION OF THE

LABOURING POPULATION OF GREAT BRITAIN

Edwin Chadwick in 1848

Report on

THE SANITARY CONDITION

OF THE LABOURING POPULATION OF GT. BRITAIN

by
Edwin Chadwick
1842

edited with an introduction by

M.W.FLINN

EDINBURGH
at the University Press

© EDINBURGH UNIVERSITY PRESS 1965
One George Square, Edinburgh 8
United States and Canada
Aldine Publishing Co.
64 East Van Buren Street, Chicago 5
Australia and New Zealand
Hodder & Stoughton Ltd.
429 Kent Street, Sydney
425 Little Collins Street, Melbourne
41 Shortland Street, Auckland

Printed in Great Britain
by T. & A. Constable Ltd. Edinburgh

PREFACE

The task of preparing this edition of Edwin Chadwick's best-known report has been immensely facilitated by the existence of two first-class studies of his life and work.[1] Both these works tell the story of the events leading up to the Public Health Act of 1848 in ample detail. To avoid unnecessary repetition, much of this detail has not been recapitulated in the *Introduction* to this edition, only a brief summary of the narrative being given. For the same reason, it is unnecessary to burden the *Introduction* with anything more than essential biographical material. As a consequence, it has been possible to devote more attention to some broader aspects of the birth of the public health movement in Britain.

Annotations to the *Report* itself have been restricted, for the most part, to the identification, wherever possible, of the printed sources. Chadwick, it will be seen, drew upon a wide range of official, unofficial, and foreign sources. Although some of the material he collected specially for the *Sanitary Report* was published separately in the two volumes of *Local Reports*, or as appendices to the main *Report*, much of it never found its way into print. Most of the passages quoted by Chadwick in the *Report* which have not been identified in print (and annotated below accordingly) may be assumed to have been drawn from such unpublished sources. It will be noticed that there are a number of quotations from material published by the Children's Employment Commission. The reports of this Commission were published in 1842 and 1843, after the publication of the *Sanitary Report*. The material was almost certainly made available to Chadwick, before publication, by Dr Southwood Smith, who was a member of the Commission, or by Dr Charles Barham, who prepared an important report for the Commission.

The original edition of this *Report* included a large number of appendices, one or two town maps, and some illustrations of model cottages. These have all been omitted from this edition, but full details are given in footnotes of any references to them in the text of the *Report*. The pagination of such references, as well as of references to the prefix to the *Report*, refers to the original 1842 edition. Cross-references to the main text of the *Report* use the page numbers of the present edition. Chadwick's original footnotes may be distinguished from my own editorial footnotes by the use of conventional symbols (asterisk, etc.) and arabic numbers respectively.

I would like to take this opportunity to thank Professor S. B. Saul and Dr T. C. Smout for reading through the typescript of the *Introduction*, and for making a great many helpful comments and suggestions; Dr A. S. Milward for valuable assistance in checking some French bibliographical references; Dr W. H. Chaloner for reading the proofs of the *Report* and eliminating many small errors; and the Wellcome Trust for a generous guarantee which has made possible the publication of this edition in its present form.

M. W. Flinn, Edinburgh, September 1964

[1] S. E. Finer, *The Life and Times of Sir Edwin Chadwick* (1952);
R. A. Lewis, *Edwin Chadwick and the Public Health Movement, 1832-48* (1952).

CONTENTS

INTRODUCTION
[*page* 1]

I. The Roots of the Sanitary Idea
The deterioration of public health conditions p. 3
The contribution of the medical profession p. 18
Statistical studies p. 26
Reformers and administrators p. 29
Laissez-faire or state intervention p. 38

II. The Sanitary Report
The making of the Report p. 43
The issues of the Report p. 58
The Report and sanitary reform p. 66

THE SANITARY REPORT
[*page* 75]

I. General condition of the residences of the labouring classes where disease is found to be the most prevalent p. 80

II. Public arrangements, external to the residences, by which the sanitary condition of the labouring population is affected p. 99

III. Circumstances chiefly in the internal economy and bad ventilation of places of work; workmen's lodging-houses, dwellings, and the domestic habits affecting the health of the labouring classes p. 167

IV. Comparative chances of life in different classes of the community p. 219

V. Pecuniary burdens created by the neglect of sanitary measures p. 254

VI. Evidence of the effects of preventive measures in raising the standard of health and the chances of life p. 276

VII. Recognised principles of legislation and state of the existing law for the protection of the public health p. 339

VIII. Common lodging-houses the means of propagating disease and vice p. 411

IX. Recapitulation of conclusions p. 421

INDEX
[*page* 427]

ABBREVIATIONS USED IN FOOTNOTES

B.M.Add.MSS.	British Museum, Additional Manuscripts.
Econ. H. R.	Economic History Review.
Finer	S. E. Finer, *The Life and Times of Sir Edwin Chadwick* (1952).
J.R.S.S.	Journal of the Royal Statistical Society.
Lewis	R. A. Lewis, *Edwin Chadwick and the Public Health Movement, 1832-48* (1952).
Local Reps. E. & W.	Reports on the Sanitary Condition of the Labouring Population of England (1842).
Local Reps. Scot.	Reports on the Sanitary Condition of the Labouring Population of Scotland (1842).
P.R.O.	Public Record Office.
San. Rep.	Report on the Sanitary Condition of the Labouring Population of Great Britain (1842).
P.P.	Parliamentary Papers.

Except where another source is quoted, all letters referred to in footnotes are in the Chadwick Collection in the library of University College, London.

INTRODUCTION

On 9 July 1842, at the height of a summer marked by perhaps a greater incidence of unemployment, destitution, and social protest than any other in the nineteenth century, Edwin Chadwick, Secretary to the Poor Law Commission, presented to the House of Lords his *Report on the Sanitary Condition of the Labouring Population of Great Britain*, the product of three years' vigorous work. The *Report's* ultimate outcome was the Public Health Act of 1848, by which, for the first time, the British Government charged itself with a measure of responsibility for safeguarding the health of the population. Although an unconscionable time elapsed between the presentation of the *Report* and the passing of the Act; though the Act itself was a poor shadow of the measure Chadwick and other 'sanitary' reformers had worked for; and though the early history of state action in the sphere of public health was to be chequered, to say the least, a beginning had been made.

The compilation of the *Report* was wholly the work of Chadwick. When it came to publication, the three Poor Law Commissioners who were nominally responsible for its production were unwilling to accept responsibility for so radical a document, and the compromise solution of issuing it over Chadwick's name alone was adopted. Yet there were two senses in which the *Report* was not wholly Chadwick's work. Readers of the following pages will quickly observe that much of the *Report* is devoted to direct and extensive quotation from the contributions of a small army of local investigators. More significantly, the *Report* was the culmination of a movement that had been gathering momentum long before Chadwick gave it the benefit of his prodigious energy. Indeed, to ascribe the *Report* and its consequences solely to the genius of a single reformer, however considerable his influence may have been, would be to over-simplify the course of events, and to do injustice to the memories of other men with voices perhaps less strident and compelling than Chadwick's, but whose patient and devoted labours laid the foundations on which Chadwick's enduring edifice was subsequently built.

Chadwick himself was deeply affronted by any suggestion that he was not the sole author of public health reform. When, in 1848, a suggestion was made that some of the credit should go to Southwood Smith, one of his closest collaborators, he was up in arms immediately. In a letter to Southwood Smith, he wrote:

Surprise has been excited on the part of many persons by statements recently made in your behalf, which charge the Government with injustice towards you, and with implications on myself, which if I do not notice, I must appear to admit. Dr Gavin[1] is reported to have stated at a public meeting that there could be no doubt that you were the originator of sanitary reform. Again, it is stated, that you first directed public attention to

---

1. Hector Gavin, a leading member of the Health of Towns Association (see below, pp. 68-9).

the subject. Further, it is set forth in your behalf, that you occupy the same position in relation to Sanitary reform that Mr Rowland Hill occupied in relation to postage reform. Believing these allegations to be untrue, and the charges founded upon them to be unjust, I think it incumbent upon you to disclaim them.

I must aver, that the sanitary measures now in progress had strictly and exclusively an official origin; that they arose as a consequence, tho' an indirect and perhaps an accidental one, of measures directed by the Government in 1832, namely the enquiry into the administration of the poor laws; that in the course of some investigations with the view to discriminate the causes of pauperism, excessive sickness and its preventible causes, were suggested by the circumstances which appeared in the course of that enquiry and are noticed as one of the topics of examination in my report laid before Parliament with others: (*Selections*, 1833); that afterwards, under the administrative Commission in 1838, when a heavy amount of claims to relief appeared, as a consequence of the prevalence of an epidemic, I felt it my duty to call the attention of the Commissioners to a large proportion of these cases, and recommend a special investigation of them. Up to that time, I am unaware of any public agitation whatsoever upon the subject, and I am warranted in saying that in directing the inquiry, the Commissioners were influenced by the circumstances which appeared before them in the course of the business of the day, and by no representations of yours, or, that I am aware, of any person whatsoever . . .[1]

Some allowance ought clearly to be made for the emotional strain under which Chadwick was labouring when he drafted this letter. His indignation—not entirely unjustified—at being denied credit for results, however meagre, of ten years of dedicated labour, led him into two errors. On a purely factual plane, he was over-stating his own early interest in the public health question: the ample report which he wrote in 1833 ('my report laid before Parliament with others . . . in 1833') contains only two short paragraphs that have any bearing on the relationship between preventable 'excessive sickness' and poverty, and the recommendations with which he concluded this report made no reference to this aspect of the problem.[2] Nor, it might be added, since Chadwick fixed as his starting-point of public health reform the initiation of the poor law enquiry in 1832, did the famous *Report* of 1834, the joint work of Chadwick and Nassau Senior, give any hint that at that stage the Commissioners recognised preventable ill-health as a cause of poverty.[3] More serious, however, was the misconception, understandable in an official mind, that the ultimate involvement of the state in the field of public health 'had strictly and exclusively an official origin'.

---

1. Chadwick to Southwood Smith, n.d., but probably 1848. This is a draft of a letter, and there is no evidence that it was actually sent. It must nevertheless accurately mirror Chadwick's feelings on this question.
2. Edwin Chadwick, 'Report from London and Berkshire', *Extracts from the Information received by His Majesty's Commissioners as to the Administration and Operation of the Poor Laws* (1833) p. 316.
3. It is only fair to add, however, that though the correlation between insanitary conditions and poverty did not find its way into the main report, some of the many volumes of evidence which supported the 1834 *Report* contained material relating poverty to poor public health conditions.

Taking the short view, Chadwick was right, of course. The 1838 enquiries of Drs Kay, Arnott and Southwood Smith in London which preceded the sanitary enquiry were directly and exclusively initiated by the Poor Law Commission.[1] Yet it is odd that a man with Chadwick's immense breadth of imagination should so seriously have deceived himself into thinking that even he could have taken the decision to set the three doctors to work in a vacuum. He was, of course, as much a symptom of the changing intellectual climate as he was influenced by its consequences. He saw himself as guiding events, rather than being carried along in their tide: he assumed that *he was* the public health movement, and that sanitary reform would have gone by default, at least in the early Victorian era, had he not personally taken it in hand. He lacked the stature to acknowledge how far he had climbed on other men's shoulders.

In the first part of this introduction, some attempt will be made to look beyond the narrowness of Chadwick's version of the genesis of Victorian public health reform by scrutinising the various intellectual strands which converged on Chadwick in the late 1830s. The second part will concern itself much more closely with the details of Chadwick's claim.

I

THE ROOTS OF THE SANITARY IDEA

The deterioration of public health conditions

In general, the social reforms of the nineteenth century were responses to evils which were not only pressing, but growing. This was as true of public health reform as it was of factory, prison, poor law, emigration, local government, and parliamentary reform. Public health in the early nineteenth century was largely a matter of the sanitary state of working-class dwellings. Recent years have seen much difference of opinion between historians over the questions of the changing fortunes of the working class in the late eighteenth century and the first half of the nineteenth century. There is no doubt, however, that there were substantial increases in both aggregate real income and average real incomes during the first half of the nineteenth century.[2] Average incomes, however, tell nothing of the distribution of income, and very few of the participants in this important debate have been able to throw much light on the trends in real income of, say, the bottom fifty per cent, or the bottom twenty per cent of the income scales. Pollard has argued that the known economic changes of the period inevitably demanded some progressive inequality of income distribution[3]; but even if this argument is conceded, not enough is known about *changes* in income distribution to determine with any certainty whether the growth of average real income during the early nineteenth century offset an increasingly unequal distribution

---

1. See below, pp. 43-4.
2. Phyllis Deane & W. A. Cole, *British Economic Growth 1688-1959* (Cambridge 1962) pp. 19-28, 148-53.
3. S. Pollard, 'Investment, consumption and the Industrial Revolution', *Econ. H. R.* 2nd ser. XI (1958) 215-26.

sufficiently to raise the real income of the lowest income groups, or the reverse.

It remains likely, nevertheless, that all but a small, least-fortunate section of the working population—the traditionally-quoted handloom weavers, other workers in declining domestic industries, and, possibly, agricultural labourers—did benefit from the growing wealth of the economy to the extent of a persistent, if slow, increase in the purchasing power of their incomes. But there is more in a standard of living than what money can buy. Living conditions which were increasingly deleterious to health were by no means incompatible with rising real incomes; nor were they even incompatible with 'better' housing, in the sense of bigger and more solidly-built houses. What mattered from the point of view of health was housing densities—the number of houses per acre, and the number of people per house—and the supply of the basic public amenities—water, sanitation, paving and street cleansing. It is important to recognise that historians cannot yet determine—and may never be able to determine precisely—what proportion of the population at any point of the eighteenth or nineteenth centuries lived under housing conditions that were conducive to good, or bad health. But the assumption that there is an automatic correlation between levels of income and public health conditions can at least be avoided. 'High prosperity in respect to employment and wages, and various and abundant food', argued Chadwick, 'have afforded to the labouring classes no exemptions from attacks of epidemic disease'.[1] 'Commerce', echoed Southey, 'sends in no returns of its killed and wounded'.[2]

Most of the more intransigent social problems of this period grew out of the ever-increasing concentration of the population into towns. Some towns expanded during the early nineteenth century at rates that would bring cold sweat to the brows of twentieth-century housing committees. Glasgow's population grew by 37 per cent between 1831 and 1841; Manchester's and Salford's jointly between 1821 and 1831 by 47 per cent; Bradford's in the same period by 78 per cent; while West Bromwich's rose by 60 per cent between the years 1821 and 1831, and a further 70 per cent in the following decade, and Dukinfield's nearly trebled between 1821 and 1831.[3] Such statistics as are available leave some room for doubt as to whether this rapid urbanisation involved, for the country as a whole, more or less overcrowding. The number of people per inhabited house fell, according to the Census Commissioners, between 1831 and 1841; but the fall was not a very large one, and the 1831 figure had been virtually unchanged through all the previous censuses.[4] Chadwick

---

1. *San. Rep.* p. 422.
2. Robert Southey, *Letters from England* (ed. J. Simmons 1951) p. 197.
3. *Population Census*, 1841, *P.P.* 1843, XVIII, 10.
4. The figures were:

Census	Number of people per inhabited house
1801	5·6
1811	5·6
1821	5·7
1831	5·6
1841	5·4

challenged the conclusion of falling density between 1831 and 1841, on the ground that a different definition of 'house' had been adopted in the later census, rendering any comparison invalid.¹ What interested Chadwick far more than any national average of this kind were the extensive local departures from the national averages. The increase in *per capita* income during the first four decades of the century must certainly have produced some improvements in housing densities which are most likely to have increased house-space for those in the upper half of the income scale. Many of these would be upper working-class families who would use the rise in incomes to reduce the number of people per house—a process still going on in the upper working-class in the mid-twentieth century. In this event, the constancy of the national density over the whole period must, as a result, have involved increased crowding of those in the lower income groups. The 1841 Census itself confirms this. Liverpool, for example, with probably more than its share of the lower income ranges, experienced an increase in the number of people per house from 6·4 in 1831 to 6·9 in 1841. It was claimed, on the basis of census data that, while the population of Glasgow had increased by 36·8 per cent between 1831 and 1841, the number of inhabited houses increased only by 18·5 per cent during the same period. 'In Blackfriars parish (Glasgow) alone,' continued the same commentator, 'where there has been little or no building for ten years back, the population has absolutely increased upwards of forty per cent'.² Robert Cowan, Professor of Medicine in Glasgow University, also spoke of 'the rapid increase in the amount of the labouring population without any corresponding amount of accommodation being provided for them'.³

The most serious deterioration in this respect was on an extremely local scale. Chadwick's conviction that overcrowding had been increasing was the fruit of endless investigations of particular streets, courts and tenements. One such street was the subject of an enquiry by the London Statistical Society in 1847. This was Church Lane, in the notorious St Giles district of London. The Society's investigators found that, whereas in 1841 the twenty-seven houses (averaging five rooms) in this street had housed 655 people, by 1847 their inhabitants had increased to no less than 1,095 people. This increase in density from about twenty-four persons per house to just over forty in six years was attributed to 'improvements' in the neighbourhood, which, by pulling down old property to widen streets, had crowded the existing population into the smaller number of remaining houses; and to the Irish famine of

---

1. *San. Rep.*, pp. 188-9. And see Sir John Clapham, *An Economic History of Modern Britain* (Cambridge 1926) I, 546. A further difficulty with these figures is one inherent in all statistics which select isolated years—that of relating the selected years to the short-run trends, in this case the building cycle. Years falling two or three years either side of the census years might conceivably have shown different results.
2. Strang, the Census Superintendent in Glasgow in 1841, quoted by Sir Archibald Alison, 'Social and moral condition of the manufacturing districts in Scotland', *Blackwood's Edinburgh Magazine*, L (1841) 669.
3. R. Cowan, *J.R.S.S.*, III (1840) 269.

1845-6, which had led to a considerable influx of fresh immigrants into this preponderantly 'Irish' district of London.[1]

Studies of house-building later in the nineteenth century, when more detailed statistics are available, make it clear that, in the short run at least, there was no automatic correlation between trends in demand and supply.[2] Supply fluctuated far more widely than demand, although in the long run, as the Census figures indicate, there was a rough equation between the two factors. Middlesex, for example, apparently experienced a sharp falling-off of new building in relation to population growth in the 1830s,[3] and though the balance may have been restored in the following decade, the pressure on housing was possibly at its most acute just at the moment when Chadwick and his poor law colleagues focused their attention on it.

One symptom of increasing housing density (in terms of houses per acre, rather than of people per house) in the early nineteenth century, which conduced to ill-health, was the spread of back-to-back housing, an innovation of the late eighteenth century, as a regular practice rather than an exception. By the third and fourth decades of the nineteenth century, back-to-back houses were very common in many towns. In 1840 between 7,000 and 8,000 of Nottingham's 11,000 houses were reported to be back-to-back.[4] As early as 1797 it was estimated that 9,000 of Liverpool's population of 63,000 lived in back-to-back houses.[5] There was a similar extension of cellar dwellings, even more injurious to human health.[6]

This sort of population pressure on housing must certainly have been reflected in trends of rents, and one of the more frustrating *lacunae* in the study of nineteenth-century economic and social history is the absence of any statistical study of house-rents. No doubt the problem of defining with any precision over a long period of time the extent of a house, flat, room, or lodging, would make such a study difficult, if not impossible. Under the circumstances, about the only observation that can be made with any degree of certainty is that, square foot for square

---

1. 'Report on the state of the inhabitants and their dwellings in Church Lane, St Giles's', *J.R.S.S.*, XI (1848) 2-3.
2. S. B. Saul, 'House building in England, 1890-1914', *Econ. H. R.* 2nd ser. XV (1962) 131-2.
3. A. K. Cairncross & B. Weber, 'Fluctuations in building in Great Britain, 1785-1849', *Econ. H. R.* 2nd ser. IX (1956) 293-5.
4. *JRSS*, II (1839) 457.
5. James Currie, *Medical Reports* (Liverpool 1797) p. 202.
6. Out of 175,000 persons in Liverpool in 1841, 38,000 lived in cellars (*Report of the Condition of the Hand-loom Weavers*, P.P. 1841, X, 74). Another estimate of the same time gave a figure of only 24,072 (*Report of the Select Committee on Building Regulations and Improvement of Boroughs*, P.P. 1842, X, App. I, p. 133); and another gave 'upwards of 39,000' (*Report of Select Committee on the Health of Towns*, P.P. 1840, XI, p. viii). Estimates of Manchester's cellar population at this period vary widely. One report gave the figure for 1840 as 3,571 (*J.R.S.S.*, III (1840) 7), while another estimated 'nearly 15,000, being 12 per cent of the working population' (*Report of the Select Committee on the Health of Towns*, p. viii).

foot, urban rents for labourers' dwellings were appreciably higher than their rural equivalents—more than double, according to a comparison of average rents in Bedfordshire and the Manchester district.[1] This being so, the substantial increase in the urban proportion of the population in the first half of the nineteenth century must have involved an increased proportionate expenditure on rent from working-class incomes. In a careful study of housing in Leeds, Rimmer has estimated that whereas in the early 1790s the working man spent 5 per cent of his income on rent, by the 1830s wage-earners spent between 10 per cent and 20 per cent in this way.[2] There is probably just sufficient evidence to say that the increasing share of the national income going to rent indicated a steadily mounting pressure of urban population on the supply of housing.[3]

The real measurement of the quality of urban industrial life involves, of course, the widest possible social spectrum. Our understanding of the early nineteenth century has been persistently befogged by partial scrutiny. Some historians have considered trends in real income, because these are the only measurable criteria, as though they are the only valid ones. But, in terms of life itself, it really mattered little how a labourer's wage varied between, say, 12s and 25s a week, if a dwelling-house with water supply, sewers and sanitation, in a paved and drained street—one capable, in other words, of safeguarding a normal span of human life[4]— could not be afforded on *any* income under, say, 30s a week. Other historians have studied housing in terms of bricks and mortar per acre, or people per house, as though a few cubic feet more or less made all the difference. The quality and duration of life are social variables which have always depended upon an almost infinite range of economic and social factors, the most important of which in modern times are levels of real income, the degree of adulteration of food,[5] the quantity and quality of housing, sanitation, paving, sewerage, water supply, open spaces, working conditions, and the public provision of the basic social services, of which education stands at the head of the list. Only some of these factors are capable of statistical measurement, and while the careful and impartial use of such statistical material as is relevant to this historical problem continues to make valuable contribution to the understanding of the social history of this period, it remains true that what is measurable is but a part of the whole.

There was a correlation, at least in the early nineteenth century,

---

1. *San. Rep.* p. 222.
2. W. G. Rimmer, 'Working men's cottages in Leeds, 1770-1840', *Publications of the Thoresby Society*, XLVI, Pt. 2 (1961) 192-4.
3. Rents and dwellings were estimated to receive 5·3 per cent of Gross National Income in 1801, and 8·2 per cent in 1841. (B. R. Mitchell & P. Deane, *Abstract of British Historical Statistics* (Cambridge 1962) p. 366.)
4. 'Normal', that is, by the standards of healthy areas of that age.
5. A factor still seriously under-rated in the study of nineteenth century social history. See John Burnett, unpublished London University Ph.D. thesis, 'The history of food adulteration in Great Britain in the nineteenth century, with special reference to bread, tea and beer', summarised in *Bulletin of the Institute of Historical Research*, XXXII (1959) 104-7.

between overcrowding and disease; but although many medical writers of the first half of the nineteenth century were firmly convinced of a growth in the incidence of epidemic diseases, statistics of any kind bearing on this problem are exiguous in the extreme. There were, indeed, some respects in which a clear case could be made out for a reduction in the incidence of disease in this period. There was no more bubonic plague in Britain: the visitation of 1665 was happily the last. The discovery of vaccination by Jenner had provided the means of conquering smallpox. But so far as other diseases were concerned, there is more evidence in the 1830s and '40s of increase rather than diminution, and even the simple generalisation that the spread of vaccination after 1800 steadily and inexorably reduced the mortality resulting from smallpox requires some modification. Initially, vaccination did its work with astonishing rapidity. In Glasgow, where between 1793 and 1802 smallpox had accounted for 32 per cent of all deaths, it claimed only 9 per cent in the succeeding decade.[1] But the initial enthusiasm for vaccination soon waned, and Cowan detected by the 1830s a resurgence, albeit on a much smaller scale than formerly, of smallpox, which he attributed to a growing neglect of vaccination.[2]

A possible slight increase in the incidence of smallpox was, however, less serious than some other developments. A new and alarming disease, cholera, appeared. Cholera first struck Britain in 1831-32, and returned in 1848-49, 1854, and 1867. Though the cholera epidemics never reached the scale of those of bubonic plague which have left so indelible a mark on the pages of history, they struck down many hundreds of thousands of victims, killing tens of thousands. Cholera struck swiftly and sharply, raising local death rates dramatically if ephemerally. Cholera frightened people. It stirred even the moribund, degraded, unreformed municipal corporations into fits of unwonted sanitary activity. It was the clearest warning of the lethal propensities of the swollen towns of the new industrial era.

But cholera went as quickly as it came: its prevention was relatively simple as soon as its cause in bad water supplies was recognised.[3] Epidemics were brief, memories short, and municipal purses tight. Public health was troublesome as well as expensive, and there was no established tradition of regular preventive action. Cholera was not, in the long run, statistically very significant. But if cholera could be ignored, at least most of the time, typhus and consumption could not. The history of British towns in the first half of the nineteenth century is, to a considerable degree, the history of typhus and consumption. The *Sanitary Report* is mainly concerned with the prevention of typhus. Typhus, commonly called simply 'fever' in this period, was both epidemic and endemic: it was the constant accompaniment to life in the courts, closes

---

1. Robert Cowan, *Statistics of Fever and Smallpox in Glasgow* (Glasgow 1837) p. 31.
2. *Ibid.* In Dundee, for example, in the three years 1837-39, there were 280 deaths from smallpox out of a population of about 59,000. (*San. Rep.* p. 275.)
3. A discovery made by Snow only during the second epidemic in 1848. See John Snow, *On the Mode of Communication of Cholera* (1849).

and wynds; yet serious epidemic outbreaks were also a feature of the disease in this period. Though the fever was not unknown in the eighteenth century and earlier, it was sufficiently uncommon for at least one historian of public health to describe the epidemic of 1818, mistakenly, as 'the first recorded epidemic' in this country.[1] There is little doubt that the epidemic of 1818 was on a more devastating scale than most earlier epidemics in this country: Creighton records a general absence of serious fever epidemics over the whole period from 1770 to 1815.[2]

Epidemics apart, typhus was certainly active on an endemic scale in the first decades of the nineteenth century, and in the eighteenth century as well. Dr Currie recorded an average of over 3,000 cases yearly in Liverpool in the decade 1787-1796.[3] After 1818, however, although typhus retained its endemic character and claimed its annual toll, the disease attracted attention mainly on account of its epidemical nature. Medical writers became interested in its methods of propagation. There were outbreaks in 1826-27, 1831-32, 1837, and 1846.[4] The correlation of these epidemics with periods of bad trade was noted by physicians. Southwood Smith had observed as early as 1830 that 'whatever diminishes the vigorous action of the organs, impairs their functions, and so weakens the general strength of the system, is capable of becoming a predisposing cause of fever'.[5] Richard Millar, the Glasgow professor of medicine, drawing attention to the connection between poverty and susceptibility to disease, observed that typhus 'so often attacks the more indigent portion of our operatives during those periodical suspensions of industry that of late years have caused so much distress among that part of our population'.[6] Robert Cowan described typhus as 'that unerring index of destitution',[7] and Richard Howard asserted that 'it is a matter of notoriety that fever usually prevails extensively during periods of distress and scarcity'.[8]

The trade cycle may account in part for the short-run fluctuations in the incidence of typhus in this period, but its growth in the long run in the second quarter of the nineteenth century was more closely related to trends in living conditions. By the 1830s, the incidence of the disease,

---

1. A. K. Chalmers, *The Health of Glasgow 1818-1925* (Glasgow 1930) p. 3.
2. Charles Creighton, *A History of Epidemics in Britain* (Cambridge 1894) I, 133-67. The one exception was a 'dearth-epidemic' of the war years of 1799-1802.
3. James Currie, *Medical Reports* (Liverpool 1797) p. 204.
4. Charles Creighton, *A History of Epidemics in Britain* (Cambridge 1894) II, 181-98.
5. Southwood Smith, *A Treatise on Fever* (1830) p. 369.
6. Richard Millar, *Clinical Lectures on the Contagious Typhus epidemic in Glasgow and the Vicinity during the Years 1831 and 1832* (Glasgow 1833) p. 11.
7. Robert Cowan, 'Vital Statistics of Glasgow, illustrating the sanatory condition of the population', *J.R.S.S.*, III (1840) 289.
8. Richard B. Howard, *An Inquiry into the Morbid Effects of Deficiency of Food* (1839) p. 38. The correlation was also noticed in a wider European context by August Hirsch (trans. C. Creighton), *Handbook of Geographical and Historical Pathology*, Vol. I (1883) 578-81.

which every medical writer from the 1780s onwards insisted (quite rightly) was the direct product of overcrowded slums and insanitary squalor, was growing steadily. The disease remained endemic, but epidemics became more frequent and intense. 'From 1816, indeed, until the early seventies of the last century', wrote Chalmers, 'the closes and wynds of the City were devastated by recurring epidemics of infectious diseases of several kinds, and of considerable magnitude. Nor did these stand alone; they formed only the higher peaks of an elevated table-land of disease, which was capable of maintaining an annual death rate, oscillating frequently between 30 and 40 per 1,000, and of rising, in occasional years, under the influence of epidemic prevalences, to 46, as in 1832, during the first cholera epidemic; and 56, as in 1846, when typhus fever alone caused a death rate approaching 14 per 1,000, or only a little lower than the average death rate from all causes at the present time'.[1] In Glasgow, possibly the filthiest and unhealthiest of all the British towns of this period,[2] typhus became steadily more menacing. Whereas in the first fifteen years of the nineteenth century, less than 10 per cent of the patients admitted to the Royal Infirmary suffered from typhus, in the next fifteen years typhus patients accounted for between 31 per cent and 36 per cent of total admissions, and in the first half of the 1830s, for exactly half of the admissions.[3]

There is a wide range of social attitudes and responses to different kinds of diseases: much depends upon the social class they afflict, upon whether they are commonly epidemic or endemic, and upon the nature of the diseases themselves. Cholera was swift, dramatic, highly lethal while it lasted, and extremely contagious: it struck terror into the minds of the middle and upper classes who ruled the cities and the country, and accordingly led, as no other disease did in the first half of the nineteenth century, to immediate, vigorous, administrative action. Cholera constituted a more direct threat to the wealthier classes because it was a water-borne disease, and these classes enjoyed more liberal access to a supply of water than did the inferior classes. Typhus, on the other hand, 'might not inaptly be termed the *poor man's disease*'[4]: it was the product of squalor, insanitation and overcrowding, a perquisite of working-class housing. It was less frequently a feature of middle- and upper-class society. But because the disease was frequently lethal; because, even when not fatal, it was always serious; and, more important, because it acquired a sharply epidemical character in the early nineteenth century, it dominated the lives and work of doctors practising in working-class districts. While cholera had briefly galvanised otherwise moribund corporations into temporary frantic activity, typhus stimulated in the

---

1. A. K. Chalmers, *The Health of Glasgow 1818-1925* (Glasgow 1930) pp. 2-3.
2. 'It might admit of dispute, but, on the whole, it appeared to us that both the structural arrangements and the condition of the population of Glasgow was the worst of any we had seen in any part of Great Britain.' (*San. Rep.* p. 99.)
3. Robert Cowan, *Statistics of Fever and Small-pox in Glasgow* (Glasgow 1837) p. 9.
4. Millar, *Clinical Lectures*, p. 11.

medical profession concern, investigation, and indignation. All three reactions were to assist in the slow process of defeating the disease.

As killers, however, both cholera and typhus were dwarfed by tuberculosis; and tuberculosis scarcely stirred the imagination of any social group in this period. It was so much a part of life, so inevitable, so little understood, that it was accepted mutely. Tuberculosis takes many forms, and there was little diagnostic precision in this period. What may well have been tuberculosis was very frequently diagnosed as another disease; medical assessments of the extent of tuberculosis almost certainly under-estimated the incidence and fatality of the disease, rather than the reverse. In spite of this tendency, tuberculosis was still estimated by contemporaries to be the most lethal disease of the nineteenth century, and probably of several centuries before. In the early nineteenth century it may have accounted for one-third of all deaths. A London physician, Robert Willan, found that, out of 246 of his patients who died in the two years 1795 and 1796, 77 (31·4 per cent) died from pulmonary consumption. This corresponded very closely to the proportion for the whole of London in 1796, as indicated by the Bills of Mortality (5,264 deaths from pulmonary disease out of a total of 17,648).[1] In 1839, according to the first analysis by the Registrar-General, identifiable consumption alone accounted for 17·6 per cent of all deaths.[2]

Tuberculosis thrives in deprived bodies: its allies are undernourishment, debilitation, unventilated living and working accommodation, and squalor. Until the end of the nineteenth century, it was almost exclusively an urban disease. Logically, then, the significant increase during the first half of the nineteenth century in the proportion of the population of Britain living and working in the urban environments favourable to the spread of tuberculosis must have led to an increase in its incidence and morbidity. At least one historian of the disease takes this view, believing the fate of the Brontës, Shelley, Keats, Chopin, Paganini, as well as Mimi of *La Bohème*, to be a fair reflection of the health of society at this time.[3]

It is unlikely that this apparently reasonable belief will ever be corroborated by satisfactory statistics. On the basis of information in the London Bills of Mortality, Brownlee showed that the proportion of all deaths due to tuberculosis in London rose throughout the eighteenth century, reaching a peak in the half-century between 1780 and 1830, and falling steadily thereafter.[4] The Registrar-General's returns starting in 1837, however, show very little decline in deaths due to tuberculosis in the first few years of registration, and some recent investigators believe that the effective turning-point in the mortality due to tuberculosis came in 1847.[5]

---

1. Robert Willan, *Miscellaneous Works* (1821) pp. 198-9.
2. See table reproduced below, pp. 76-7.
3. R. & J. Dubos, *The White Plague* (1953).
4. J. Brownlee, *An Investigation into the Epidemiology of Phthisis in Great Britain and Ireland*, Medical Research Council, Special Reports Series, No. 18 (1918) Table XXV.
5. T. McKeown & R. G. Record, 'Reasons for the decline of mortality in England and Wales during the nineteenth century', *Population Studies*, XVI (1963) 113.

Whatever the precise timing, there was clearly a rise and fall in a long epidemic of tuberculosis in Britain. 'Epidemic diseases, like empires, rise, decline and fall.'[1] The slow course of this disease, sometimes afflicting its victims for decades, means that the epidemic cycle must be of far longer duration than that of most other diseases. Thus the historians of tuberculosis prefer to regard the decline of tuberculosis in the second half of the nineteenth century as 'the ebb of a long epidemic wave', rather than as the necessary and inevitable result of public health measures or dietetic improvements.[2] It remains clear that, whether rising, constant, or falling, the incidence of tuberculosis was extremely high in the 1830s and that tuberculosis was overwhelmingly the most important single cause of death.

Thus, while there have been no outbreaks of bubonic plague since the seventeenth century, and while it has been said of the high mortality of 1741-42 that 'the age of massacre by epidemics was over',[3] there are nevertheless grounds for believing that increasing urban overcrowding and insanitation was producing, by the early decades of the nineteenth century, a renewed flowing of the tide of disease. How far was this reflected in the trend of death rates?

For the last dozen years, demographic historians have been debating the causes of the unmistakable rise in the rate of growth of population in the eighteenth century. Though they have been tending recently to show more interest in changes in the birth rate as the most important variable in this acceleration,[4] some informed contemporaries were convinced that the most significant demographic trend of the eighteenth century was a marked fall in the death rate. Using statistical evidence from an enormous sample of government annuities, tontines, and service pensions, John Finlaison, the gifted and conscientious actuary at the National Debt Office of the Treasury, showed increases of between 20 per cent and 35 per cent (varying with age-groups) in the expectation of lives between the early eighteenth century and the early nineteenth century.[5] Joshua Milne, actuary to the Sun Life Assurance Society, calculated that the mortality rate in Northampton, which between 1710 and 1780 had been estimated to average 35·7 per 1,000, fell to 20·4 in the first decade of the nineteenth century, and to 19·6 in the second.[6] A

---

1. Dubos, *The White Plague*, p. 18.
2. Introduction by the Medical Research Council to Brownlee, *An Investigation into the Epidemiology of Phthisis*.
3. J. D. Chambers, 'Population change in a provincial town: Nottingham, 1700-1800', in L. S. Pressnell (ed.), *Studies in the Industrial Revolution* (1960) p. 110.
4. H. J. Habakkuk, 'English population in the eighteenth century', *Econ. H. R.* 2nd ser. VI (1953) 117-33; J. T. Krause, 'Changes in English fertility and mortality, 1781-1850', *Econ. H. R.* 2nd ser. XI (1958) 52-70.
5. *First Report of the Select Committee on the Laws respecting Friendly Societies*, P.P. 1825, IV, App. B.1, pp. 125-6.
6. *Second Report of the Select Committee on the Laws respecting Friendly Societies*, P.P. 1826-7, III, 65. The figure of 35·7 for 1710-80 may well, however, be inaccurate. It was taken from the unreliable actuarial calculations of Dr Richard Price.

reduction of the death rate would not, of course, preclude a subsequent increase in the birth rate: indeed, there are obvious ways in which these two trends are automatically interrelated.

In the present context, the important fact is that national death rates were falling at least until the beginning of the nineteenth century. Towards the end of the eighteenth century, however, this downward tendency in the death rate was beginning to be affected by two other demographic trends: first, for an increasing proportion of the population to live in towns, probably, in this early phase of urbanisation, at an accelerating rate; and second, for urban death rates constantly to be substantially higher than rural death rates. The first trend is obvious enough to require no illustration beyond what the early censuses unmistakably revealed. The second assertion, however, calls for some scrutiny of such figures as are available.

Whereas, according to calculations made for the Friendly Societies Committee in the 1820s, the national death rate in the decade 1811-1820 was 19·3 per 1,000, in Leeds it was 20·9, in Carlisle 23·7, in Birmingham 25·1, and in Liverpool, 26·0.[1] William Farr noticed in 1840 that diseases incidental to childhood were twice as fatal in the town districts as they were in the country. He estimated the mortality in country districts in the period 1831-39 to have been 18·2 per 1,000, compared with a rate of 26·2 per 1,000 for town districts.[2] Even within towns, there were substantial variations in death rates. It was estimated in 1840, that while the death rate in the suburb of Broughton, Manchester, was 15·8 per 1,000, nearer to the town centre in Ardwick the rate was 28·6, and in 'inner Manchester' the rate rose to 35·2, more than twice that of the middle-class districts.[3] Similarly in Edinburgh in the early 1860s, while the death rate in the exclusively working-class district of Grassmarket was 32·5 per 1,000, in the middle-class suburb of Grange the rate was 13·8.[4]

In spite, in other words, of the general tendency of the national death rate to decline, an ever-growing section of the population was being subjected to the less favourable demographic environment of the towns. This, in itself, might not have been sufficient to offset the general downward tendency of the death rate; but there is some evidence that, in the early nineteenth century, the already relatively high death rates in towns began to move upwards to an extent sufficient to halt the decline in the national death rate, and even, for a short time, to reverse it. Some Glasgow figures illustrate this trend. Ignoring the exceptionally high years of 1832 (the cholera epidemic, when a death rate of 49·1 per 1,000 was recorded) and 1836 (when typhus drove the death rate up to 37·5), the Glasgow death rate rose from an average of 28·6 over the whole of the 1820s, to 30·6 in the 1830s. If the two epidemic years are included—

---

1. *Second Report of the Select Committee on the Laws respecting Friendly Societies, P.P.* 1826-7, III, 74.
2. *Third Annual Report of the Registrar-General* (1839-40) pp. 98-9.
3. *Report of a Committee of the Manchester Statistical Society on Bills of Mortality* (Manchester (?) 1842) p. 16.
4. H. D. Littlejohn, *Report on the Sanitary Condition of the City of Edinburgh* (Edinburgh 1865) pp. 15, 18.

and it was the very increase in the frequency and intensity of epidemics that was at the root of the rising mortality of this period—the rate had risen to 34·2 in the 1830s.[1] This retrograde trend evidently continued until at least the late 1840s, after which improved and more widespread public health activity began to remove the more obvious sources of disease.

The resurgence of national mortality rates in the first half of the nineteenth century cannot, of course, be substantiated unequivocally by sound statistical evidence. The early censuses of population were simply enumerations which do not permit the calculation of trends in birth and death rates. The registration of births and deaths began only in 1837, and there are consequently no relevant official statistics before that date. Nevertheless, it was the Census Commissioners in 1831 who first[2] drew attention to the upturn in national mortality rates: they estimated that while the rate for 1816-20 had been 17·6 per 1,000, ten years later it had risen to 18·5.[3] Probably no person knew more about demographic trends in this period than William Farr, Compiler of Abstracts to the Registrar-General. He joined with Finlaison in believing there to have been a marked reduction in the death rate during the eighteenth century. But 'since 1816', he wrote in 1849, 'the returns indicate a retrograde movement. The mortality has apparently increased.'[4]

It is not possible, at least from the statistical material at present available, to date this upturn in mortality rates with greater exactitude than to say that it appears to have occurred during the first two or three decades in the nineteenth century; it was, in any case, from its nature, an extremely gradual movement. Until this time, medical, economic, and environmental forces had slowly, though probably not regularly, depressed the national death rate for perhaps one hundred years to an extent sufficiently great to offset the increasing, though still relatively small, concentration of population in the comparatively lethal environment of towns. But thereafter the solid accumulation of disease-carrying filth in the urban growth of the Industrial Revolution gradually began to offset these improvements, and, in the end, to more than offset them. The 1830s and 1840s saw the appearance of a kind of Malthusian bogey, not, in the terms commonly linked with Malthus, of the positive check of famine—economic advance took care of that; but of retribution by disease. The population of this country was beginning to exceed its capacity—or willingness—to house itself healthily.

There is no inconsistency between this postulated increase in the death

---

1. Robert Cowan, *Statistics of Fever and Small-Pox in Glasgow* (Glasgow, 1837) p. 7. These, of course, are crude death rates, and may reflect, to some extent, a changing age-composition of the population.
2. With the exception of John Finlaison, who already in 1829 had shown from actuarial sources that, for the younger age-groups, there was a turn to rising death rates during the war period from 1793-1815. (*Report by John Finlaison, P.P.* 1829, III, 66-7.)
3. *Comparative Account of the Population of Britain, 1831, P.P.* 1831, XVIII, 15. Their estimates for earlier periods were rates of 20·8 for 1796-1800, and 19·6 for 1806-10.
4. William Farr, *Vital Statistics* (1885) p. 150.

The deterioration of public health conditions

rate and the continued rapid growth of the population. The rate of growth of population did, as it happens, reach its maximum in the second decade of the nineteenth century, falling slightly thereafter, but there are good grounds for believing that birth rates remained high.[1] Chadwick himself was satisfied that, in the conditions of early nineteenth-century towns, birth rates moved directly with death rates, a view supported by one of the best informed of nineteenth-century sociologists, William Alison,[2] as well as by the greatest of vital statisticians, William Farr.[3]

One school of thought attributed the rising incidence of disease in the first half of the nineteenth century quite simply to the Irish immigration. Several witnesses before the Irish Poor Inquiry of 1836 stressed the role of the Irish in disseminating disease. 'The Irish in Birmingham are the very pests of Society', said one, 'they generate contagion.' And the Commissioners themselves concluded that, 'from the filthy conditions of the bedding, the want of the commonest articles of furniture, the uncleanly habits of the inmates themselves, and the numbers which, without distinction of age or sex, are closely crowded together, they [the Irish] are frequently the means of generating and communicating infectious disease'.[4] The President of the Manchester Statistical Society in 1859 went so far as to assert, with reference to the typhus epidemic of 1846-7, that 'its dissemination and virulence were co-extensive, not with the prevalence of nuisances, but rather with the current of Irish immigration so remarkable in that year'.[5] This explanation of the spread of typhus has found favour with at least one influential medical historian.[6] The chronology and geography of the 1817-18 epidemic substantiated the belief that Irish immigrants were the means of diffusing the disease.[7] Typhus was a deficiency disease which struck hardest in times and regions of famine: its home in this era was, above all, in Ireland.[8]

The great weight of medical opinion, nevertheless, preferred to attribute the resurgence of disease to increasing overcrowding and lack of sanitation. As early as 1797, Dr Currie of Liverpool had observed that typhus infection arose from 'a want of cleanliness and ventilation'.[9]

---

1. Glass has shown, for example, that birth rates remained virtually unchanged from 1841 to 1880, quinquennial averages fluctuating only between a minimum of 34·8 per 1,000 and a maximum of 35·8. (D. V. Glass, 'A note on the under-registration of births in Britain in the 19th century', *Population Studies*, V (1951-2) 85.)
2. W. P. Alison, *Observations on the Management of the Poor in Scotland and its Effects on the Health of Great Towns* (Edinburgh 1840) p. 98.
3. *Fourth Report of the Registrar-General* (1840-41) p. 143.
4. *Report of the Poor Inquiry (Ireland) Commission*, App. G, 'Report of the State of the Irish Poor in Great Britain', *P.P.* 1836, XXXIV, pp. 6, xi.
5. T. S. Ashton, *Economic and Social Investigations in Manchester, 1833-1933* (1934) pp. 52-3.
6. August Hirsch (trans. C. Creighton), *Handbook of Geographical and Historical Pathology*, Vol. I (1883) 556-8.
7. Review article on epidemic fever in *Edinburgh Medical and Surgical Journal*, XIV (1818) 531.
8. R. Hare, *Pomp and Pestilence* (1945) p. 96.
9. James Currie, *Medical Reports* (Liverpool 1797) p. 214.

Commenting on an early epidemic of 1806 in Dublin, the physicians there asserted that 'we have many reasons for supposing that fever is often generated by causes independent of contagion, namely by the concurrence of filth, bad air, and accumulated animal effluvia...'.[1] 'Typhus so generally makes its first appearance', wrote another experienced doctor in 1833, 'as well as rages with its highest intensity, in the narrow, airless, and crowded lanes, and alleys, of our great cities.'[2] A group of doctors petitioned the House of Commons as early as 1834 on the subject of the state of London's sewers, and drew attention to the adverse effects on public health of defective sewerage.[3] Dr Yule, the physician to the public dispensary in Edinburgh, believed that 'on the whole, it appears that typhus fever is a disease originating from the re-absorption of a specific poison expelled from the human body, even in a state of health, allowed to accumulate not only in jails, ships, hospitals, etc., but in the close and crowded dwellings of the people'.[4] It was, however, principally the famous reports of Doctors Kay, Arnott and Southwood Smith to the Poor Law Commission in 1838, to which reference is made below, that most emphatically fixed the blame for the spread of disease on squalid urban conditions.

Somewhat paradoxically, the deterioration of urban public health conditions in the second quarter of the nineteenth century went hand-in-hand with an increased attention to public health and sanitation by some local authorities. The work of the bodies variously known as 'Police', 'Lighting', or 'Paving' Commissions, or more generally as 'Improvement' Commissions, is well known, and calls for no additional comment here.[5] Local Boards of Health sprang into existence on the occasion of the more severe epidemics, such as the typhus outbreak in Manchester of 1795-6, and the cholera epidemic in many large towns in 1831-2.[6] A long series of Building Acts endowed local authorities with limited powers of regulation over the quality, design, and location of buildings. Liverpool secured such Acts in 1825, 1839, and 1842, and London in 1774.[7] It was a local Building Act of 1846 which authorised the Corporation of Liverpool to appoint the nation's first local Medical Officer of Health.[8] But

---

1. *First Report on the Object and Effects of the House of Recovery in Cork Street, Dublin, by the Physicians to that Institution* (Dublin 1806) p. 9.
2. Richard Millar, *Clinical Lectures on the Contagious Typhus* (Glasgow 1833) p. 10.
3. *Report of the Select Committee on Metropolis Sewers*, P.P. 1834, XV, 52-63.
4. J. Yule, *Observations on the Cure and Prevention of the Contagious Fever* (Edinburgh 1818) p. 23.
5. See S. & B. Webb, *Statutory Authorities for Special Purposes* (Vol. IV of *English Local Government*), chap. IV. For a full study of the work and achievements of one such commission, see A. Redford and I. S. Russell, *The History of Local Government in Manchester* (1939) I, chaps. IX-XIV.
6. E. P. Hennock, 'Urban sanitary reform a generation before Chadwick', *Econ. H. R.* 2nd ser. X (1957) 113-20; and see W. H. Chaloner, 'Manchester in the latter half of the eighteenth century', *Bulletin of the John Rylands Library*, XLII (1959) 56.
7. *Report of the Select Committee on Building Regulations and Improvement of Boroughs*, P.P. 1842, X, 133.
8. W. M. Frazer, *Duncan of Liverpool* (1947) pp. 35-6.

The deterioration of public health conditions

the local Boards of Health were disbanded, on the waning of the epidemics, with even more haste than they had been constituted, while the improvement commissioners too often concentrated their attention solely on the middle-class districts of their towns, leaving the greater number of streets inhabited by the poorer classes wholly without essential services.[1] However valiantly the improvement commissioners might struggle to cope with the flood-tide of urbanisation—and few of them struggled very valiantly—they were fighting losing battles. Constitutionally, financially, administratively, technically, and ideologically ill-equipped to cope with the frightening immensity of the task in the field of public health alone, they seldom touched more than the outer fringes of the problem. For every step they took forward, they fell back two.

The most fundamental weakness of the improvement commissions was constitutional. The constitutional history of local government took its most decisive turn in 1835 with the passing of the Municipal Corporations Act. Thereafter, those boroughs which took advantage of its provisions to fit themselves out with a local government worthy of the name were tolerably armed to cleanse the Augean stables of their working-class housing districts. Many set to work energetically and effectively from the 1840s; others were tardier, and many small towns and large industrial villages had to wait another generation or more for the establishment of local government authorities capable of tackling, and authorised to spend money on, matters relating to public health. That proportion—a relatively small one—of the population fortunate enough to be served by a modern apparatus of local government after 1835 was reasonably assured of a steady reduction in preventable mortality. Although the first generation governed by the new municipal corporations might still die normally in its forties, its sons could live into their fifties, and its grandsons into their sixties. For these town-dwellers the need for national legislation and centralised administrative supervision on the lines attempted after 1848 was less urgent. But it is important to notice that the work of the new corporations was only beginning in the 1840s, and could hardly pay dividends in the shape of reduced mortality until the following decades. The problem, then, was still unsolved while Chadwick was at the Poor Law Commission. For the great bulk of the population outside the new corporate boroughs the need was for administrative reform of any kind, local or national.

If the decline of the death rate had continued after the first decade of the nineteenth century, it is just possible that existing institutions and existing policies might have been able to cope with the social problems of urban development. But the earlier reduction of mortality was itself the means of releasing upon the hapless cities a flood of immigrants from the surrounding countryside which inflated the subsequent difficulties beyond all hope of solution under existing regimes. However, so inured were the men of the eighteenth and early nineteenth centuries to the toll of disease, to the shortness of the span of urban human life, that they were unlikely to be moved by only a slight rise in the death rate, which, in any case, was not easily detectable in the short-run fluctuations pro-

---

1. *San. Rep.* pp. 115, 125, 166.

duced by epidemics. It would take time. But the pressure grew remorselessly, each fresh epidemic giving the screw a sharper twist. In Glasgow, for example, whereas the fever epidemic of 1836-7 pushed the death rate up to 41 per 1,000, that of 1847 drove the rate up to 56·4 per 1,000.[1]

The contribution of the medical profession
The economic and social background to the public health question of the first half of the nineteenth century has been sketched in at some length because, in the long run, it was the progressive deterioration of living conditions in the cities which, above all, stimulated action within the small group of men aware of the situation. But because this kind of mill grinds slowly, it might not necessarily have produced for several decades the kind of reformation which, thanks to Chadwick's efforts, subsequently transformed British town life within barely two generations. The timing of the beginning of operations was the product of many other factors.

Perhaps the most significant of these other factors was the rise during the late eighteenth and early nineteenth centuries in both the numbers and professional skill of medical practitioners. Even in the mid-nineteenth century, qualified doctors were very few in number, and many, possibly a majority, of the inhabitants of this country lived their lives without ever meeting a medical man. There was, of course, a considerable periphery of ill-qualified practitioners, but the value of the work of these apothecaries in changing the course of national mortality rates may be doubted. Although in the late eighteenth century both the English and Scottish universities possessed medical schools, most produced very few graduates, while the value of the medical training at Oxford and Cambridge which, even in the late eighteenth century, involved 'no patients, no clinical lectures, which are the *sine qua non* of a medical education',[2] must have been negligible. Although the colleges of physicians and surgeons contributed in this period to the increase in the number of skilled practitioners, there can be little doubt that the best doctors were trained in the medical schools of the Scottish universities, and that, of these, Edinburgh led by a long way. There was, it is true, some small augmentation of the supply from Leyden and other universities abroad, but many of those from Britain who studied overseas were already medical graduates of Edinburgh or other universities. In the late eighteenth century, Edinburgh was training pitifully small numbers of medical graduates—213 in the whole of the 1770s, 280 in the 1780s, and 394 in 1790s. Thereafter there was a dramatic increase in the production of doctors at Edinburgh, rising to a peak in the 1820s, when 1,139 graduated.[3] In 1828 the Edinburgh medical school was supplemented by University College, London, where the medical school was one of the most important faculties from the start.

---

1. A. K. Chalmers, *The Health of Glasgow, 1818-1925* (Glasgow 1930) p. 3.
2. B. Hamilton, 'The medical profession in the eighteenth century', *Econ. H. R.* 2nd ser. IV (1951) 148.
3. *List of Graduates in Medicine in the University of Edinburgh from 1728 to 1866* (Edinburgh 1867).

Whether more doctors inevitably meant better health is another question. Until fairly recently it was customary to assume, without going very deeply into details, that it did. Indeed, the common interpretations of the demographic changes of the eighteenth and early nineteenth century depended very largely on this assumption. Recently, however, some disbelief has been cast on this assumption. McKeown and Brown, in a now famous article,[1] insist that there were no medical advances in the eighteenth century likely to reduce the death rate more than marginally; that all surgery in that period was highly lethal, so that the more surgery there was, the higher would mortality become; that institutional confinement was associated with far higher maternal death rates than was domiciliary confinement on account of the higher risk of puerperal infection, so that the spread of lying-in hospitals involved an increase rather than a reduction of the death rate; and that the eighteenth- and early nineteenth-century hospitals spread infection, thus increasing a patient's prospect of dying from a disease other than the one he entered a hospital to have cured. They quote with approval Florence Nightingale's dictum that the first requirement of a hospital was 'that it should do the sick no harm', and conclude that 'the chief indictment of hospital work at this period is not that it did no good, but that it positively did harm'. It followed that not until the basic principles of bacteriology were understood (a development of the last quarter of the nineteenth century) could any reduction of the death rate through the work of doctors and hospitals be expected.

Most of this is undoubtedly true, but it does not point out that not all successful medical treatment in this period depended upon advances in medical knowledge. Much could be accomplished by the application of some very elementary medical principles not unrecognised even in the late eighteenth century. If hospitals were places where infection was spread, they can hardly have been more infectious than the squalid and insanitary dwellings described at length in the *Sanitary Report* and elsewhere from which their patients were being temporarily removed; and it is hard to believe that decent bedding, relatively fresh air, regular food, sympathetic nursing, and even the ministrations of the relatively ignorant doctors of the period, would not go some way towards assisting recovery. 'The condition of the working class', wrote Kay in 1834, 'has been much ameliorated by the promptitude with which medical assistance has been afforded to them. The mortality of large towns has diminished, and considerable subtractions have been thus made from the great sum of misery which is the inheritance of man.'[2] These simple applications of charity and the minimum desiderata of decent human existence not normally achieved by the lower range of urban dwellers can only have done good. Applied to infants—the age-group subject at this period to the highest mortality rates—in Foundling Hospitals as well as in fever and general hospitals, they may well have exercised a

---

1. T. McKeown & R. G. Brown, 'Medical evidence related to English population changes in the eighteenth century', *Population Studies*, IX (1955) 119-41.
2. J. P. Kay, *Defects in the Constitution of Dispensaries* (Manchester 1834) p. 5.

major effect on death rates. More important, there were active doctors like John Haygarth of Chester who were advocating and practising, at the turn of the century, such elementary principles of hospital hygiene as the opening of sickroom windows and doors, the removal and washing of dirty and infected clothing, and, most significantly, the isolation of fever patients.[1] The separation of fever patients into fever wards of general hospitals was begun about this time, as was the establishment of separate fever hospitals in the big towns, and the disinfection of the houses from which fever patients had been removed. It is hard to accept, furthermore, that the establishment of dispensaries was a retrograde step. These were widely set up from the last few years of the eighteenth century, and by offering, generally free of charge, a combination of the services performed in the twentieth century by the general practitioner's surgery, the out-patients' clinic of a hospital, and the dispensing chemist, they must have helped materially the cause of preventive as well as of curative medicine. The doctors of this period may have had little new to offer their patients; but not everything they offered was useless, and many more patients were being brought into contact with medical services of one kind or another. Some of the medical provisions of this period may have been harmful, but it is hard not to believe that much of it was beneficial. If it is conceded that the doctors did more good than harm, the really significant feature of the medical history of the late eighteenth and early nineteenth centuries is that a much wider section of the population was securing access to their services. It may be argued that it was only the urban population to which this applied: the urban population, however, was already sufficiently great for this to affect the national death rate significantly. Moreover, the urban classes newly receiving these benefits were just those suffering from high mortality rates most susceptible to reduction.

The same period—the last few years of the eighteenth century, and the early nineteenth century—also saw some remarkable advances in naval and military medicine which had important repercussions in the civil field. Whereas, according to one statement, in 1782 one man in 3·3 of the total strength of the Navy was sent to hospital during the year, in 1829 it was only one man in 8·9.[2] The conquest of scurvy and the reduction of the incidence and fatality of infectious fevers was the result of the work of military doctors like Pringle and Lind. It owed little to specific advances in medical knowledge, but much of the extension of discipline into the field of personal hygiene, diet, and the use of soap on board ship and in camp. As early as 1781, Sir Gilbert Blane made a series of recommendations to the Board of Admiralty which, he claimed, were the means of bringing about 'a total change in the state of the health of the Fleet'. He attributed the appallingly high sickness rate to:

---

1. John Haygarth, *A Letter to Dr Percival on the Prevention of Infectious Fever* (1801) p. 73 ff.
2. Sir Gilbert Blane, *A Brief Statement of the Progressive Improvement of the Health of the Royal Navy at the End of the Eighteenth and Beginning of the Nineteenth Century* (1830) p. 11; and see his *Observations on the Diseases of Seamen* (1785).

1st. The neglect of cleanliness, ventilation, and dryness in the interior economy of ships.

2ndly. The want of the supply of an article which it had been found, by the most unequivocal experience to be infallible in preventing and curing scurvy, one of the most destructive scourges, and the most peculiar to the sea service, of any class of disease. The remedy alluded to is the juice of lemons or lime.

3rdly. The abuse of spirituous liquors, not merely as the most common means of intemperance, but as the habitual beverage of seamen, even when diluted. . . .

4thly. The want of adequate nourishment and comfort for the use of the sick and convalescent on board of their own ships.

5thly. The want of proper bedding and of soap. . . .

6thly. The want of a gratuitous supply of medicines, as well as necessaries to the surgeon, in order to enable them to cure as many as possible without sending them to hospitals.

7thly. As hospitals are, to a certain degree, indispensable at the principal stations, especially for the relief of ships in which contagious diseases prevail, new regulations of them in point of space, separation, ventilation, and cleanliness, were also recommended.[1]

This kind of common sense paid royal dividends. More important, as the news of its success began to filter through to civil practice during the early decades of the nineteenth century, its precepts became gradually the stock-in-trade of more and more civil practitioners. The contrast between the sort of hygiene which was reducing the lethal nature of service in the armed forces and that prevailing increasingly in the towns persuaded growing numbers of the medical profession to join in the chorus of protest of which the *Sanitary Report* was merely one expression.

That a growing proportion of the population was benefiting from the increasingly effective care of the medical profession in the early nineteenth century is thus reasonably certain. But in spite of this beneficial trend, it is equally certain that disease was winning the race. The doctors were fighting a losing battle against rising ill-health. They remained far too few in number, and were far too ill-equipped technically to do more than touch the fringes of the problem. The real relevance of the medical developments of this period for the early history of public health was less their immediate impact on death rates than their contribution to a growing awareness of the correlation between dirt and disease. And this very awareness itself fathered another tendency of the utmost importance. This was a steadily increasing involvement of members of the medical profession in social questions, and hence in the hurly-burly of the struggle over social policy. The *Sanitary Report* itself owes its origin proximately to the social work of the famous trio of doctors—Arnott, Kay, and Southwood Smith; while William Farr, whose contribution to the movement is discussed below, was attracted to his chosen field through his medical training. More than any other social group, the doctors of the nineteenth century were responsible for stirring the social conscience. So great, in the aggregate, was the share of the medical profession in the campaign for public health reform, that it is tempting

---

1. Blane, *op. cit.* pp. 21-2.

to look rather more closely at the springs of their passionate advocacy of a cleaner and healthier Britain. For it is certain that there was more to it than merely the ardent insistence of medical purists for cleanliness and sanitation for its own sake. It was largely because such medical aims were inspired by more deeply held social convictions that the doctors generated spontaneously a public health movement, and were able to feed it with an inexhaustible supply of persuasive statistical and descriptive material.

Since many of the practising doctors of this period, and, in particular, a high proportion of those active in the early public health movement, were graduates of Edinburgh University, it is possible that one clue may be found there. Three broad classes of social reformers appear to have emerged from Edinburgh University in the first half of the century: first, a group of aristocratic, mainly Whig, politicians, which includes Lords Lansdowne, Russell, Brougham, and Palmerston; second, a group of civil servants, who, as factory, health, and educational inspectors, played major roles in the extension of public work in their respective spheres: they included Leonard Horner and James Stuart, factory inspectors; Gavin Milroy, Hector Gavin, and James Smith, health inspectors; and Peter Reid and J. D. Morell, education inspectors; and third, a group of pre-eminent socio-medical reformers, including James Phillips Kay, Peter Gaskell, and Doctors Percival and Ferriar.[1] Of the first group, one at least—Lord Palmerston—went to Edinburgh specifically to sit at the feet of the then professor of moral philosophy, Dugald Stewart. During his year in Edinburgh, Palmerston lodged with Stewart, and kept very full notes of his lectures on Political Economy.[2] Stewart's claim to distinction lies primarily in his extraordinary success as a lecturer, and in his personal influence on others. He delivered the University course of lectures in Political Economy between 1800 and 1810. While he was particularly anxious to avoid the stigma of radicalism, he does not appear to have been wholly successful in doing so,[3] and, whether he would have liked it or not, his analysis of the social and economic system of the day was the starting-point of many a reformer's career.[4] Sir Samuel Romilly, the great law reformer, referred to 'my old and excellent friend, Dugald Stewart',[5] while Lord John Russell's admiration prompted him to sing his praises in inferior verse.[6] Lord Jeffrey, later of the *Edinburgh Review*, attended the lectures on Political Economy in 1802. Small wonder that Sir James Mackintosh wrote of Stewart that 'his disciples were among his best works'.[7]

---

1. See David Roberts, *Victorian Origins of the British Welfare State* (Yale University Press, New Haven 1960).
2. H. C. F. Bell, *Lord Palmerston* (1936) I, pp. 6-10. Lord Palmerston's notes on Dugald Stewart's Lectures in Political Economy, London Museum MS. 28; Edinburgh University Microfilm, M. 136.
3. See his letter to Lord Craig, 20 February 1794, Edinburgh University MS. DC.6.11, fols. 113-15.
4. The lectures are published in Vol. VIII of the *Works* of Dugald Stewart (1854-60).
5. Edinburgh University MS. DC.6.11., f.16.   6. *Ibid.*, f.11.
7. Stewart, *Works*, VIII, p. ix.

One disciple, pre-eminently, nurtured the seeds of social reflection which Stewart sowed in such fruitful soil in the first decade of the century. This was William Pulteney Alison (1790-1859), whom Stewart hoped would succeed him in the Chair of Moral Philosophy. Alison, however, chose a more practical career. Entering Edinburgh University in 1803, he first studied for an arts degree, before turning to medicine. He was an enthusiastic admirer of Stewart, and his earliest published writing was an article defending Stewart's philosophy.[1] Alison carried his interest in social questions with him into the medical school, where as Professor of Medicine from 1820 to 1856[2] he passed on to several generations of students some of the lessons he had learnt as Physician to the New Town Dispensary. The fruits of twenty-five years' social work in some of the worst social conditions of Britain were embodied in his classic document on the relief of poverty, which was the major influence behind the reform of the Scottish poor law in 1845.[3] Alison was one of Chadwick's major sources for Scottish material for the *Sanitary Report*, and he may be considered to occupy a similar position in Scotland in relation to poor law and public health reform to that held by Chadwick in England.

Between them, Stewart and Alison spanned over seventy years of the life of Edinburgh University, leaving their mark on the minds of many of the major social and medical reformers of the late eighteenth and early nineteenth centuries. One characteristic which distinguishes the medical writers of the early nineteenth century from those of the eighteenth century is their greater willingness to set medical problems in a wider social context, and there are good grounds for believing that the teaching at Edinburgh was at least one of the factors in this widening of the medical horizon.[4]

Whatever the source of the intensely human concern of a growing circle within the medical profession for social welfare, its role in laying the foundations of subsequent social policy is unmistakable. It was the doctors who were the first to see that sheer poverty was the underlying cause of squalor and ill-health. Richard Howard, with years of experience in the Manchester slums behind him, observed that 'in persons labouring under an impaired state of health from deficiency of food, there is a remarkable susceptibility to the effects of contagion. . . . The destitute are [fever's] most frequent victims'[5]; while Richard Millar, with a like background in Glasgow, wrote: 'Typhus so generally makes its first appearance, as well as rages with its highest intensity, in the narrow, airless, and crowded lanes, and alleys of our great cities, the well known

---

1. *Blackwood's Edinburgh Magazine*, II (1817-18) 57-65, 159-65.
2. He held the Chair of Forensic Medicine from 1820 to 1821, that of the Institutes of Medicine from 1821 to 1842, and that of the Practice of Medicine from 1842 to 1856.
3. W. P. Alison, *Observations on the Management of the Poor in Scotland and its Effect on the Health of Great Towns* (Edinburgh 1840).
4. D. Guthrie, *Scottish Influence on the Evolution of British Medicine* (1960).
5. Richard B. Howard, *An Inquiry into the Morbid Effects of Deficiency of Food* (1839) p. 38.

habitations and resort of mendicity and indigence.'[1] As far back as the 1770s, Lettsom had hinted at a link between poverty, urban squalor, and disease. 'Great cities', he wrote, 'are like painted sepulchres; their public avenues, and stately edifices seem to preclude the very possibility of distress and poverty; but if we pass beyond this superficial veil, the scene will be reversed.'[2]

This extension of the medical horizon opened up new possibilities in the study of diseases and epidemiology. Doctors began to probe into the social origins of disease with a new insight. In Dublin, a group of doctors anticipated, as early as 1806, many of the conclusions of the *Sanitary Report*. After investigating conditions in Plunket Street, Dublin, whose thirty-two houses contained 917 inhabitants, they reported that 'a great proportion of the lower classes live in lanes and back yards. The houses through the Liberty in general are unprovided with privies, or the privies are choked up. The lane, therefore, is frequently the deposit of all the filth of the adjacent buildings. If the attention of the scavengers is seldom directed to the streets of the Liberty, still more neglected are those recesses, which in fact, are hardly ever cleansed; the constant respiration of air thus tainted, must gradually weaken the powers of life; and if diseases be not the immediate consequence, the system is at least fitted for the reception of contagion whenever it presents itself.'[3] Other doctors stressed particular black-spots. Ferriar, who observed that 'the mean lodging-houses ... are the principal nurseries of febrile contagion', anticipated one of Chadwick's points of attack,[4] as did Walker, who may be credited with initiating the movement for the reform of the metropolitan burial grounds.[5] In a long and comprehensive study, which anticipated something of Booth's work later in the nineteenth century, Thackrah studied the occupational incidence of ill-health,[6] while in 1801 Willan, and in 1819 Bateman, made special studies of London's diseases.[7]

Vague generalities, however eloquently expressed, tended to cut very little ice in the early nineteenth century. Realising that the first need was for more precise information on the subject, a number of the most active medical reformers turned their attention to detailed local surveys. This was an immensely important approach, since until the late 1830s, when the Registrar-General first started publishing annual reports, there was a complete absence of the statistical basis for satisfactory investigation on

---

1. Richard Millar, *Clinical Lectures on the Contagious Typhus* (Glasgow 1833) p. 10.
2. J. C. Lettsom, *Medical Memoirs of the General Dispensary in London* (1774) p. x.
3. *First Report on the Object and Effects of the House of Recovery in Cork Street, Dublin by the Physicians of that Institution* (Dublin 1806) p. 25.
4. John Ferriar, *Medical Histories and Reflections* (2nd edition 1810) I, 172.
5. G. A. Walker, *Gatherings from Grave Yards* (1839).
6. C. T. Thackrah, *The effects of the Principal Arts, Trades and Professions ... on Health and Longevity* (1831).
7. Robert Willan, *Reports on the Diseases of London, particularly during the Years 1796, 97, 98, 99 and 1800* (1801); Thomas Bateman, *Reports on the Diseases of London* (1819).

a national scale. Moreover, it was as a consequence of careful, detailed and revealing local reports that the *Sanitary Report* itself was ultimately commissioned in the late 1830s.

The pioneer of local epidemiological studies was John Haygarth of Chester (1740-1827). In 1774 he carried out a census of Chester's population, to which he added a survey of the incidence of disease over the previous ten years. It is of some interest that the average annual mortality of 25 per thousand which he estimated for the period 1765-73 (one appreciably higher than the national average for the early nineteenth century), proved, as he said, 'Chester to be healthy in such an uncommon degree as will astonish those who are best acquainted with the general state of mortality in large towns'.[1] Haygarth was amongst the first to recognise the importance of isolating fever patients in hospitals, a principle which he advocated in print together with other sensible doctrines concerning fresh air and cleanliness.[2] His pioneer efforts were followed in the next decade by those of John Heysham, an Edinburgh graduate, at Carlisle. Heysham is best known for his 'Carlisle life table', which was widely used by Friendly Societies and actuaries for the following forty years. His actuarial work, however, was only a by-product of his study of disease in Carlisle. His conclusions, inevitably, were those of the *Sanitary Report* of sixty years later. Disease, he said, 'is the offspring of filth, nastiness and confined air, in rooms crowded with many inhabitants.... I think we may without much hesitation pronounce that the occasional cause of it is *human effluvia*, which has been generated in some little dirty confined place, of which there are great numbers in Carlisle and every other large manufacturing town.'[3]

There were medical writers like John Roberton, who commented at some length on the defective sanitation of particular towns,[4] and others, who, after making some attempt to assess the problem quantitatively, were able to pin down the cause of disease more accurately to particular housing conditions and localities under particularly unfavourable economic circumstances.[5] The best-known product of this school, which provided perhaps the most fruitful quarry for social reformers in the

---

1. John Haygarth, 'Observations on the population and diseases of Chester in the year 1774', *Philosophical Transactions*, LXVIII, Pt. I (1778) 131-54.
2. John Haygarth, *A Letter to Dr. Percival on the Prevention of Infectious Fevers* (1801).
3. John Heysham, *An Account of the Jail Fever or Typhus Carcerum as it appeared at Carlisle in the year 1781* (1782) pp. 24, 31. And see Henry Lonsdale, *The Life of John Heysham, M.D.* (1870).
4. John Roberton, *A Treatise on Medical Police* (Edinburgh, 2 vols. 1809). He examined causes of diseases in Edinburgh in Vol. II, 223-93, and in London in Vol. II, 295-347.
5. E.g. William Moss, *Medical Survey of Liverpool* (1784); James Currie, *Medical Reports* (Liverpool 1797); John Clark, *A Collection of Papers intended to promote an Institution for the Cure and Prevention of Infectious Diseases in Newcastle and other populous Towns* (Newcastle 1802); Robert Cowan, *Statistics of Fever and Smallpox in Glasgow* (Glasgow 1837), and 'Vital statistics of Glasgow, illustrating the sanatory condition of the population', *J.R.S.S.*, III (1840) 257-92.

1830s and 1840s, was James Kay's classic study of the Manchester slums of 1832.[1] By the time of the first cholera epidemic in 1831-32, sufficient was known generally about the interconnection of disease with housing conditions to produce immediately an immense outpouring of literature drawing attention, place by place, and street by street—at times, house by house[2]—to the origin and diffusion of the epidemic by insanitation and poverty.[3]

Statistical studies

The proliferation of local studies bore fruit not merely through the sheer weight of evidence in influential but uninformed quarters, but also through the diffusion of the right blend of science and humanitarianism in all professional arenas, administrative and legal, as well as medical and political. But all these studies suffered from one fundamental weakness: their appeal was emotional rather than intellectual; they lacked the broad statistical basis, without which they could so easily be dismissed as exaggerated, untypical, or unimportant. The need for such quantification had been felt and expressed since the late eighteenth century: Bentham had been outspoken on the need for a far greater range of official statistics than were available to his generation.[4] Malthus's acute observations on the relationship between population and resources played an important part in the decision to take the first census of population in 1801. For whatever reason, this enthusiasm for quantification was intensified in the 1830s, a decade which witnessed the rapid and widespread growth of a serious interest in statistical studies.

It is never easy to explain the sudden emergence of a new intellectual movement, but it is possible that the urge for statistical enquiry which flared up in the 1830s stemmed from the actuarial work sponsored by friendly societies, life assurance societies, and the National Debt Office of the government. Until the 1820s these bodies relied, to their detriment, on the antiquated Carlisle and Northampton tables. The parliamentary enquiries of the 1820s (to which reference has already been made) led, mainly through the work of Finlaison, to a complete revision of the actuarial basis of all forms of life assurance. In the process, for the first time, accurate information concerning the duration of human life was made available. The reality was sufficiently disturbing to stimulate the quest for more information and for the social facts underlying the bare figures. Not all of those who felt the need for an extension of statistical studies, however, shared the desire that these studies should take a sociological direction. Whewell, the Master of Trinity, who was President of the British Association in its early years, deprecated the

---

1. James P. Kay, *The Moral and Physical Condition of the Working Classes* (1832).
2. For example by Henry Gaulter, *The Origin and Progress of the Malignant Cholera in Manchester* (1833) pp. 7-8.
3. Some of it is reviewed by Asa Briggs in 'Cholera and society in the nineteenth century', *Past and Present*, No. 19 (1961) 76-96.
4. Mary P. Mack, *Jeremy Bentham: an Odyssey of Ideas, 1748-1792* (1962) pp. 235-40.

extension of statistical enquiries 'into regions where they would touch on the mainsprings of feeling and passion'. This attempt to suppress the statistical study of social problems led to the breaking-away from the British Association of those interested in this aspect of statistical enquiry, and to the creation, in 1834, of the Statistical Society of London.[1] The new body very quickly got down with the utmost vigour to the prosecution of enquiries, both local and national, into aspects of public health, population, incomes, employment, housing, education, and religion. The London society was neither the first nor the last of its kind.[2]

An important branch of these new statistical studies—'vital statistics'—was created and dominated for several decades by William Farr. Born in Shropshire in 1807, Farr trained as a doctor in Paris and London, and went into practice in London in 1833. He very early showed an interest in public health matters,[3] but his real interest lay in the field of population statistics. An authoritative article on 'Vital Statistics' in McCulloch's *Account of the British Empire* in 1837[4] laid the foundations not only of a new science, but also of Farr's own reputation, and in the following year, through the influence of Sir James Clarke, he secured the appointment as Compiler of Abstracts to the newly-established office of the Registrar-General, at a salary of £350 per annum. Thomas Lister, the first Registrar-General, was a brother-in-law of the Home Secretary, Lord John Russell, and, from the start, Farr was the effective head of the new small department. Though Farr's remuneration was substantially increased as time went on, it is to the discredit of Victorian governments that he was never appointed to the nominal headship of the department that owed everything to his genius, though the post became vacant more than once during his long career there.

The establishment of the office of Registrar-General in 1837 marks a major turning-point in the history of public health, as well as of demography in Britain.[5] For the first time, the accurate measurement of birth

---

1. B. K. Gray, *Philanthropy and the State* (1908), Appendix to chap. II, 'The origin of the Royal Statistical Society'. This attitude did not apparently subsist for long in the British Association, for in 1840 the Statistical Section made a grant of £100 to a powerful committee, which included Robert Cowan, W. P. Alison, and Edwin Chadwick, for an enquiry into vital statistics (*J.R.S.S.*, III (1840) 211).
2. See T. S. Ashton, *Economic and Social Investigations in Manchester 1833-1933* (1934).
3. William Farr, 'Lecture on hygiene or the preservation of the public health', *The Lancet*, I (1835-6) 240-5.
4. William Farr, 'Vital Statistics', in J. R. McCulloch, *A Statistical Account of the British Empire* (1837) II, 567-601.
5. There has never been a satisfactory account of the origin of civil registration in this country. It tends to be commonly assumed that the Act of 1836 was the product of Chadwick's interest in public health questions, or, alternatively, that it was a necessary supplement to the Factory Act of 1833 to authenticate the ages of factory children. Yet the question had been opened at least as early as 1833, and it seems much more likely that the *Report of the Select Committee on Parochial Registration* (*P.P.* 1833, XIV), to which,

and death rates became possible. When the Registration Act was under discussion in 1836, Chadwick had succeeded in securing the insertion of a clause requiring registration of the cause of death, as well as the mere fact of death. One of Farr's first steps after his appointment was to draw up a classified list of causes of death—what he called a 'statistical nosology'—as a guide to the medical profession when registering deaths.[1] For the first time the public health movement was to be armed with trustworthy information concerning the relative importance of different types of diseases causing death. And this could now be set beside the splendid statistical background provided by the Registrar-General's basic returns—the age distribution at death, local variations in the incidence of disease, local variations in mortality rates, and, as time went on, trends in these important indices. This kind of detailed statistical information was to become the starting-point of the invaluable work of the local Medical Officers of Health in the second half of the nineteenth century. Its principles and concepts were the basis of a series of detailed local studies by the early Medical Officers, of which Henry Littlejohn's famous and revealing study of Edinburgh in 1865 is a classic example.[2]

One of the first uses Farr made of his new statistical information was to set a norm of mortality for the period, which he drew from an average of the mortality rates in 'healthy' areas of the country. Setting this beside the less healthy districts, he was able to show, in a particularly vivid way, the actual cost in terms of lives, of defective public health arrangements. Of Manchester in 1846, for example, he wrote: 'How pitiful is the condition of many thousands of children born in this world! Here, in the most advanced nation of Europe—in one of the largest towns of England—in the midst of a population unmatched for its energy, industry, manufacturing skill—in Manchester, the centre of a victorious agitation for commercial freedom—aspiring to literary culture—where Percival wrote and Dalton lived—13,362 children perished in seven years over and above the mortality natural to mankind.'[3] Of the City of London, he stated that 'the plain truth is, that one day with another, 134 persons die daily in London: that the great majority are untimely deaths —children, fathers, mothers, in the prime of life; and that at least 38 die

---

inter alia, Finlaison gave evidence, and which recommended unequivocally 'that a new national system of Registration should be attempted', was a major step towards civil registration. A desire by non-conformists to establish some form of legally-valid registration of births, deaths, and marriages independent of the Church of England seems to have been the principal motive behind the appointment of this Select Committee. Its report, like Finlaison's calculations, appears to have been largely ignored by historians of British population in the eighteenth and early nineteenth centuries. Further investigation into the origin of this Select Committee might throw some light on the inauguration of civil registration in 1837.

---

1. *First Annual Report of the Registrar-General* (1839) pp. 92-100.
2. H. D. Littlejohn, *Report on the Sanitary Condition of the City of Edinburgh* (Edinburgh 1865).
3. *Ninth Annual Report of the Registrar-General* (1846) p. 29.

daily in excess of the rate of mortality which actually prevails in the immediate neighbourhood. 38 persons are destroyed every day in London by local causes.'[1]

But more important even than the mere provision of the essential statistical basis for public health reform, and more remarkable because of his position as a civil servant, Farr both digested and propagated the lessons of his statistics. Perhaps this was because his own route to vital statistics had been via the medical profession; more likely it was because he was fired by an intense spark of humanity absent from so many of the class who were his immediate superiors. But whatever the cause, the *Annual Reports* of the Registrar-General became the vehicle for the expression of passionately-held personal views, for propaganda directed against the opponents of public health reform, and for agitation for state intervention in a new field, to a degree that would send cold shivers down the spine of a modern civil servant. A single example must suffice to illustrate the tone of his contribution—in a place at once unusual and effectual—to the campaign for legislation: 'This disease-mist, arising from the breath of two millions of people, from open sewers and cesspools, graves and slaughter-houses, is continually kept up and undergoing changes; in one season it is pervaded by cholera, in another by influenza; at one time it bears smallpox, measles, scarlatina, and whooping-cough among your children; at another it carries fever on its wings. Like an angel of death, it has hovered for centuries over London. But it may be driven away by legislation. If this generation has not the power to call the Dead up from their graves, it can close thousands of graves now opening. The poisonous vapour may yet clear away from London—and from all the other towns of the kingdom:—some of the sunshine, pure water, fresh air, and health of the country, may be given to the grateful inhabitants of towns by the parting voice of the Legislature.'[2]

Reformers and administrators

It would be pleasant to be able to include among those forces which contributed to the movement for public health reform in its early years the work of the humanitarians and philanthropists. There is, however, little evidence that the great men of this group, who contributed so nobly to the abolition of slavery, to the reform of the factories, and to many other fields of social work in the nineteenth century, showed any serious interest in the public health question. The reasons for this are obscure. Perhaps it was that so few of them were brought into direct contact with the evils that resulted from neglect of central and local government in this field. Perhaps, according to a recently expressed view, the social reforms taken up by the evangelical philanthropists were subsidiary to their main purpose of propagating the evangelical way of life. In this view, social reforms were selected partly for their appeal to the humanitarian instinct, partly for their innocuousness to the existing social structure of the country, but above all with the purpose of attracting into the evangelical fold those whose conservatism had so far kept them

---

1. *Tenth Annual Report of the Registrar-General* (1847) p. xv. 2. *Ibid.*, p. xvii.

away from the paths of 'true religion'.¹ While the abolition of the slave trade and of slavery within the British Empire fitted these requirements exactly, the cause of public health did not. To the ladies of polite society there was nothing appealing about sewers and privies.

If there was little inspiration from a source so traditionally linked with the progress of social reform in the nineteenth century, a major obstacle to advance on the public health front was removed in 1830 by the appearance of a government not as innately hostile to administrative reform as its predecessors. Major measures in the realm of local government and parliamentary reform, factories and the poor law indicate that the Whig administration of 1830-41 at least did not start from the attitude that nothing could reasonably be done about anything. Moreover, there were in the ranks of the Whig ministry some men whose attitude towards public health reform might be even more positive than this. Lord John Russell, Lord Lansdowne, Lord Brougham, and Lord Palmerston each, at some phase of his career, displayed, to greater or lesser degree, an enthusiasm for social reform. Yet the image inspired by the phrase 'Whig reformers' should not be accepted too uncritically. The ministry was Whiggish before it was reforming, and in spite of their group of major reforms, the Whigs were far from possessing an overweaning ambition to set the social and economic troubles of the country to rights. For the Whigs, above all, were landowners, and believed that the duties of government began with the safeguarding of the rights of property and in minimising government expenditure; they were, in any case, far too closely concerned with the twin problems of balancing the budget and the preservation of law and order, to have much thought, energy or time to spare for less pressing social problems of a long-term nature like public health. There was, in short, no correlation one way or the other between Whiggism and an interest in public health reform, and if, in the event, it fell to the lot of Whig governments to initiate Chadwick's enquiry and to pass the first Public Health Act in 1848, these are coincidences which require explanation in other terms.

The Whig ministry of 1830-41 was not the first government to be pushed into a programme of reforms from behind, but it was perhaps among the earliest administrations in which a programme of reform was initiated more by its own professional administrators than by 'public opinion' or even a rudimentary party machine. Recent studies have brilliantly illustrated how, for example, a persistent and quite unprincipled group of free traders in the ranks of the senior staff at the Board of Trade made use of official positions to engage extensively in propaganda and other forms of political pressure for Free Trade;² and how, on a more philanthropic plane, a small group of underpaid emigration officers in the Colonial Office laboured untiringly, and ultimately successfully, for effective amendment to the regulations governing emigrant shipping.³ The highly unorthodox, if praiseworthy, use of the

---

1. Ford K. Brown, *Fathers of the Victorians* (Cambridge 1961) pp. 106-15.
2. Lucy Brown, *The Board of Trade and the Free-Trade Movement, 1830-42* (Oxford 1958).
3. O. MacDonagh, *A Pattern of Government Growth, 1800-60* (1961).

Annual Reports of the Registrar-General by William Farr as vehicles of public health propaganda has already been mentioned, while the part played by the factory inspectors appointed under the 1833 Act in subsequent factory legislation is now well authenticated.[1] Much the same situation prevailed in the spheres of prison and educational reform.

Though such an outcome was clearly no part of the original intention of those responsible for the initial reforms, it is now quite clear that the Emigration Acts of 1828 and 1835, the Factory Act of 1833, the education grant of that year, and, most of all, the Poor Law Amendment Act of 1834, all brought into being a small group of professional administrators whose access for the first time to the real facts illuminating the nature of the problems with which they were grappling fired them with an earnest determination to improve and extend the regulations which were their principal weapons in the fight against social evils. Each of these civil servants in his turn discovered that the problem was far more acute and widespread than the original legislators had envisaged, and that the existing powers were utterly inadequate to enable them to handle their work effectively. They immediately became the leading voices in the campaign for more effective state intervention firstly in their own fields, and later, as the ramifications of social evil yielded to their persistent prodding, in other, related fields. The foundations of effective government action in the basic social and economic spheres were laid by such civil servants as Leonard Horner and Thomas Howell in the factories; James Kay-Shuttleworth and Joseph Morell in the schools; Frederick Hill in the prisons; Seymour Tremenheere in the mines; Lieutenant Low and T. F. Elliot in emigrant shipping; and, above all, by Edwin Chadwick in the Poor Law Commission. The beneficent influence of some of these early civil servants—inspectors, secretaries, and assistant commissioners—pervaded more than their own specialised sectors. Tremenheere, commissioner of mines from 1843 to 1854, served on endless commissions, wrote some major reports, and roamed freely over the whole range of social administration. Edwin Chadwick, nominally Secretary to the Poor Law Commission from 1834 to 1847, and Public Health Commissioner from 1848 to 1854, also played a major part in the reform of factories, the police, and labour in early railway construction, as well as in public health, water supply, burial grounds, and the relief of poverty.[2]

The connection between poverty and disease being so pronounced in the 1830s, it was inevitable that, of all the departmental breeding-

---

1. M. W. Thomas, *The Early Factory Legislation* (Leigh-on-Sea 1948).
2. David Roberts, *Victorian Origins of the British Welfare State* (Yale University Press, New Haven 1960), offers the first systematic enquiry into the background and achievements of this group of civil servants. And see R. K. Webb, 'A Whig Inspector', *Journal of Modern History*, XXVII (1955) 352-64. For a hypothetical systematisation of their work in the process of social reform, see Oliver MacDonagh, 'The nineteenth-century revolution in government: a re-appraisal', *Historical Journal*, I (1958) 52-67; and a criticism of this article by H. Parris, 'The nineteenth-century revolution in government: a reappraisal reappraised', *Historical Journal*, III (1960) 17-37.

grounds of social reform, the Poor Law Commission should yield the richest harvest. The clamour against the principles according to which the New Poor Law was administered has tended to obscure much of what was valuable in the post-1834 administration. Not the least of these virtues was the heightened role in the new administration of the medical profession. In the latter days of the Old Poor Law, it was becoming increasingly common for parishes to make contracts with surgeons and apothecaries, while the Poor Law Amendment Act of 1834 specifically authorised Justices of the Peace to order 'outdoor' medical relief.[1] The consequence of these developments was the appointment of salaried medical officers to virtually every one of the new Poor Law Unions. The medical officers were not, at first, it is true, regarded as part of the main framework of poor law administration, but their functions were quickly integrated, and by 1847 it was possible for the Board to formulate an administrative code of regulations governing the work of union medical officers.[2] It is hardly possible to over-estimate the value of the work done by the medical officers in the service of the poor law in the 1830s. Almost every page of the *Sanitary Report* bears ample testimony to their hard work, conscientiousness, experience, medical commonsense, and compassion. Their knowledge and experience of the factors affecting the lives, work, and health of the working class provided an inexhaustible mine from which the fires of agitation and propaganda might be stoked.[3] They included in their number some of the most distinguished authorities on urban disease of the period—Richard Baron Howard of Manchester, William Duncan of Liverpool, and Charles Barham of Truro. Of more immediate relevance to the production of the *Sanitary Report*, the Poor Law authorities secured the services in the 1830s of the great trio of reforming doctors—James Kay, Neil Arnott, and Southwood Smith. It was the reports of these three doctors on conditions affecting public health in certain districts of London in 1838, which initiated the wider enquiry described in the *Sanitary Report*. But they had all three already been active in this field for some years. Their established reputations led to their being invited to make the surveys reported on in 1838. In the late 1830s they were the natural leaders of the movement for public health reform.

Like so many of the other leading figures in the movement for sanitary reform, James Phillips Kay (1804-77) studied medicine at Edinburgh. He first practised in Manchester, where he was physician to the Ardwick and Ancoats Dispensary in the 1820s. The experience gained while working among the Manchester poor equipped him with a thorough knowledge of the realities of disease and poverty, and imbued him with a

---

1. 4 & 5 William IV, c. 76, sec. 54.
2. M. Greenwood (the elder), *The Law relating to the Poor Law Medical Service and Vaccination* (1901) pp. 11-12.
3. For a survey of the work of the Poor Law medical officers, see Ruth G. Hodgkinson, 'Poor law medical officers of England, 1843-1871', *Journal of the History of Medicine and Allied Sciences*, XI (1956) 299-338; and *First, Second and Third Reports of the Select Committee on Poor Law Medical Relief*, P.P. 1844, IX.

quiet determination to do all in his power to help in the process of improvement. The rest of his life was devoted to the twin causes of the health and education of the labouring poor. His strong convictions concerning the interaction of poverty and bad housing first drove him into print in an obscure medical journal in 1830,[1] and it was only two years later that he produced his terrible indictment of the manufacturing society of his day.[2] As a founder member of the Manchester Statistical Society, he contributed further to the phase of detailed enquiry which must precede reform.[3] His work and influence in Manchester were, however, cut short when, in 1834, he accepted an invitation to become one of the new Assistant Poor Law Commissioners. Here he operated in a very different environment, for the area to which he was allocated was rural East Anglia. In view of his previous castigation of the conditions under which the manufacturing classes of the North of England lived, it is odd that one of his first actions in Norfolk was to organise the mass-migration of many thousands of the Norfolk poor—the unwanted residue of rural over-population—to find employment in the manufacturing districts of the North. It was in Norfolk, too, that he first turned his attention to the education of the poor. He had always believed that the absence of an adequate education was at the root of most of the sufferings of the poor. 'Some prejudiced men,' he wrote in 1832, 'accustomed to examine only one side of the shield, are hence eager to attribute all the evils suffered by the poor, solely to their ignorance or moral deviations. On the contrary, not only do they suffer under the pressure of extraneous grievances, but even those which immediately flow from their own habits, may often be traced to the primary influence of the imperfect institutions of society on their character—to the combined effects of an untutored ignorance, bad example, uncountered by a system of moral instruction—and the desperate straits of a perverted spirit battling with hunger and toil.'[4] But his efforts to promote the education of the pauper child in Norfolk were hampered by being forced to operate within the limits of poor law finance, and Kay was soon attracted to London, to assist the Central Commission with enquiries into the nature and problems of poverty in the Metropolis. His first enquiry was into the growing poverty of the Spitalfields weavers in 1837,[5] and in the following year, in collaboration with Neil Arnott, he produced the seminal report on the causes of fever in London.[6] By now, however, his heart lay in education rather than public health, and, on his appointment to the Secretaryship of the Privy Council's Committee on Education in 1839,

---

1. J. P. Kay, 'Physical condition of the poor', *The North of England Medical and Surgical Journal*, I (1830-31) 220-30.
2. J. P. Kay, *The Moral and Physical Condition of the Working Classes* (1832).
3. J. P. Kay, 'Defects in the constitution of dispensaries', *The Manchester Statistical Society*, 1834.
4. *The Moral and Physical Condition of the Working Classes*, p. 6.
5. 'Distress among Spitalfields weavers', *Third Report of the Poor Law Commission* (1837) pp. 142-9.
6. 'Prevalence of certain physical causes of fever in the Metropolis', *Fourth Report of the Poor Law Commission* (1838) pp. 103-29.

C

he turned his back on fifteen invaluable years in the service of public health reform.[1]

Of his collaborator in the report on the health of London, Neil Arnott (1788-1874), less is known. Alone of the three poor law doctors, he has not yet attracted a biographer. Arnott was a friend of both Bentham and John Stuart Mill, and it was in their company that he first made the acquaintance of Chadwick and Southwood Smith. He became Chadwick's family physician.[2] The foundation of his ideas on sanitary hygiene was undoubtedly laid during his four years' service as a ship's surgeon with the East India Company. In civil practice he acquired a reputation as an authority on the heating and ventilation of houses. After his initial work for the Poor Law Commission in London in 1838, he turned his attention to his native Scotland, and contributed two papers to the volume of Scottish reports which supplemented the main *Sanitary Report*.[3] He was a member of the Health of Towns Commission of 1843.

Of the three, it was probably Southwood Smith (1788-1861) whose medical experience carried the greatest authority, and who, in the long run, contributed most to the cause of sanitary reform. Born in Somerset in 1788, he studied medicine at Edinburgh. After a few years in general practice in Yeovil, he came to London in 1820.[4] There he quickly found a niche in Bentham's circle, and it was he who delivered the famous lecture over Bentham's body before it was handed over, as Bentham had wished, to the anatomists.[5] As physician to the London Fever Hospital he was familiar with disease and its urban background. He had started writing about public health matters as early as 1825, and was a well-established authority in this field by the time that the Poor Law Commission took up the question in 1838.[6] It was as an authority on disease, and as a friend of Chadwick's from the days when Bentham was alive that Southwood Smith was invited to contribute to the Poor Law Commission's preliminary enquiries in 1838. His three papers of 1838 and 1839 presented a vivid and horrifying proof of the interconnection of insanitation and disease in London's East End.[7] Southwood Smith colla-

---

1. Frank Smith, *Life of James Kay-Shuttleworth* (1923).
2. Rachel Chadwick to Charles Babbage, n.d., B.M.Add.MSS. 37,200, f. 82.
3. 'Report on the fevers which have prevailed in Edinburgh and Glasgow', *Local Reps. Scot.*, pp. 1-13; and 'Remarks on Dr W. P. Alison's "Observations on the generation of fever" ', *ibid.*, pp. 34-40.
4. C. L. Lewes, *Dr Southwood Smith: a Retrospect* (Edinburgh 1898).
5. Southwood Smith, *A Lecture delivered over the Remains of Jeremy Bentham* (1832).
6. His early writings on public health include 'Contagion and Sanitary Laws', *Westminster Review*, III (1825) 134-67; *A Treatise on Fever* (1830); and *The Philosophy of Health* (2 vols., 1835-7).
7. 'Report on some of the physical causes of sickness and mortality . . . exemplified in the present condition of Bethnal Green and Whitechapel districts', *Fourth Report of the Poor Law Commission* (1838) pp. 129-39; 'Account of a personal inspection of Bethnal Green and Whitechapel', *ibid.*, pp. 139-53; and 'Report on the prevalence of fever in twenty metropolitan unions or parishes during the year ended the 20th March 1838', *Fifth Report of the Poor Law Commission* (1839) pp. 160-71.

borated with Chadwick in the 1838 reports, and, though the relationship never appears to have been easy,[1] and on one occasion came near to breaking-point, he nevertheless collaborated with Chadwick again for six years on the Central Board of Health of 1848-54.

In the short run, however, the crucial contribution was Edwin Chadwick's. There is little evidence that his interest in public health questions was anything other than minimal before 1838. It might not be fanciful to suggest that even in 1838 his enthusiasm took that direction at least partly because his inability to work with his three commissioners, and they with him, prevented him from filling his time in a normal manner with the routine work of the Poor Law Commission, leaving him to assuage his restlessness by probing matters marginal to the duties he was officially employed to perform. It might be thought that the opportunity of reviewing the reports on Friendly Societies in the 1820s to which Finlaison had made such notable contributions would have set up some train of reflection on factors affecting trends in mortality rates; but his early *Westminster Review* article on this theme offers no serious indication of the absorption that was later to make and break his public career.[2] On the other hand, the brief spell of acting as amanuensis to Jeremy Bentham produced the interesting proposals for a Health Ministry charged with 'the preservation of the national health'.[3]

Between the death of Bentham in 1832, and 1838, Chadwick's life was so completely filled with factory and poor law reform as to leave little time for investigations, or even reflections, in other fields. Yet, just as these were years when medical and statistical opinion was moving most swiftly towards state action, so they were the years when experience in other legislative fields was repeatedly bringing Chadwick face-to-face with the basic facts of poverty and disease in Britain. During the mid-thirties he took virtually no account of what was being done elsewhere in the sphere of public health, nor did the toilers in that field raise their heads for a moment to glance at the figure on the horizon. In 1838, however, the various separate strands that had hitherto constituted the public health movement converged—not so much converged, perhaps, as were drawn together by Chadwick; for Chadwick was a born leader who rose swiftly and inevitably to the forefront of every movement he embraced.

The year 1838, then, was an important turning-point in the history of the public health movement. Although its roots stretch back fifty years, the movement was, before 1838, unorganised, leaderless, and, in a legislative sense—the only sense that mattered in the long run—aimless. Essential foundations had been laid, pre-conditions established, but, important as these were, effective action was missing. This was what Chadwick supplied.

That Chadwick was the ultimate instrument of success was due in a large measure to his rugged determination, to his humanitarianism, and

---

1. The half-dozen draft letters to Southwood Smith in the Chadwick Collection at University College, London, are all in a formal tone, and begin 'Dear Sir'.
2. 'Life Assurances', *Westminster Review*, IX (1827-28) 384-421.
3. Jeremy Bentham, *Constitutional Code*, in *The Works of Jeremy Bentham*, ed. John Bowring (Edinburgh 1843), IX, 443-5.

to his skill as a sociologist. Chadwick has not hitherto ranked very high in the annals of sociology: he was less interested in academic enquiry for its own sake than in social revelation as a means to a legislative end. In the face of the charge that he predetermined conclusions, and selected only confirmatory evidence, Chadwick's claims to the parenthood of modern sociological investigation have been brushed aside in favour of his successor, Charles Booth,[1] a view which owes something to the partiality of some of the earlier investigations in which Chadwick played a leading part: the Factory Commission of 1833, and the Poor Law Commission of 1834. These enquiries, the legislation based on them, and the determination with which their basic principles were ruthlessly pursued to their logical conclusions by Chadwick himself, laid the foundations of much of his subsequent unpopularity. The Factory Commission was consciously established as a corrective to Ashley's Committee of 1832-3: in parading a great deal of medical evidence attesting the innocuousness of factory labour to the health of young children, the 1833 Commission was doing neither better nor worse than Ashley's Committee, but it was certainly not offering a model of impartial empiricism. Nor can the Poor Law Commission of enquiry be more easily excused by circumstances. It was obsessed by a single aspect of what was, in reality, an exceedingly complex social problem. To have tackled successfully the problem of poverty and its relief was probably far beyond the wit and resources of the early nineteenth century: for possibly fifty years before the Commission began its investigations the pressure of a surplus rural population prevented wages from rising to levels which even local Overseers thought adequate.[2] Nevertheless, few commissions of enquiry, before or since, have so determinedly closed their eyes to most of the facts. The Commission as a whole, and Chadwick in particular, was only interested in the supposed ill effects of the allowance, or 'Speenhamland' system. These aspects of the Old Poor Law were pursued with characteristically Chadwickian thoroughness, and the ensuing legislation designed above all to suppress this single perversion.

In extenuation of this undeniable partiality, however, it ought to be observed that the Factory Commission Report of 1833, for all its bias, presented a remarkably balanced conclusion—'calm and dispassionate in tone', as one historian of factory reform has written, 'and revealing clearly the logical and scientific attitude with which its authors had approached their task'.[3] Even more important, the resulting Factory Act of 1833, though falling short of the demands of the Ten-hours Movement, took the crucial step of appointing the inspectors, the real authors of most subsequent legislative extension in this field. And to consider the Poor Law Report or the Act of 1834 in isolation is to do a serious injustice to Chadwick. As one of his biographers has recently shown, the deterrent embodied in the 1834 act was only a part of a much wider scheme by Chadwick for the treatment of poverty. Consideration of the

---

1. T. S. Simey, *Charles Booth* (1960) p. 242.
2. See Mark Blaug, 'The myth of the Old Poor Law and the making of the New', *Journal of Economic History*, XXIII (1963) 151-84.
3. M. W. Thomas, *The Early Factory Legislation* (Leigh-on-Sea 1948) p. 51.

preventive measures he would have liked to supplement the purely repressive ones was swept aside by Lord Melbourne in his haste to get reform of the poor law into the statute book.[1] Nevertheless, even making all possible allowances, both of Chadwick's early ventures into the field of social enquiry offer fairly extreme examples of partiality and predetermination. Chadwick was still raw, inexperienced, and obsessed, like most other social, political, and economic theorists of his day, with the belief that all problems were amenable to determinable laws or principles. However, he was young enough yet to learn, and the sanitary enquiry was to be one of his most effective teachers.

It is quite probable that when Chadwick started work on the sanitary enquiry in 1839, his approach was little different from the earlier enquiries in 1832-4. The problem in 1839 was excessive expenditure on poor relief; its solution he saw quite simply as the authorizing of expenditure for the removal of 'nuisances', supplemented by some quite conventional legislation in the shape of a Building Act.[2] His circular letter to the Assistant Commissioners at the start of the enquiry made it clear that, apart from some possible side effects—'the publication of successful examples [of cottage design] may be useful in stimulating to the voluntary adoption of them'—the only legislative measure he contemplated was a general Building Act.[3] With this only very mildly doctrinaire background, Chadwick set to work for the next three years. The results of his own investigations and those of his hundreds of helpers came as a profound revelation to him—and, no doubt, to many others. As he read, investigated, discussed, and corresponded more widely during the years of enquiry, new questions, new angles, and new horizons opened to him. He followed up each of these with single-minded ardour, and in the process, modern sociology was born. If, at the start of the enquiry, Chadwick had little more in mind than a repetition of the established routine of illustrating yet another 'precognised' principle by the assiduous selection of evidence, before long the evidence being brought to light by the sanitary enquiry was sweeping him along with it to new frontiers of enquiry. 'I may observe', wrote Chadwick later in life, overlooking his earlier aberrations on the Factories and Poor Law Commissions, 'that in my service I have never followed any one, not even Bentham, but have deduced my conclusions not even from Bentham's, but solely from close and important collections of evidence.'[4] The results of nearly three years' work, when considered, tabulated, and arranged, went far beyond the original conception. Chadwick had gained a new measure of sympathy with, and a far greater insight into the nature of social problems. However, while it is easy for the historian to discern how different was the Chadwick of 1842 from the Chadwick of 1834, contemporaries may be excused for assuming that they were still dealing with the same man.

---

1. Lewis, pp. 18-19.   2. For building acts, see *supra*, p. 16.
3. *San. Rep.* p. xiii. This view is confirmed by Chadwick's letter to Lord John Russell of 21 June 1838 quoted below, p. 45.
4. Edwin Chadwick, *On the Evils of Disunity in Central and Local Administration* (1885) p. 2.

Laissez-faire or state intervention

Chadwick's approach to sanitary reform involved a very substantial extension of the powers of both local and central government. Few subjects so easily sparked off the flames of controversy in the nineteenth century as the question of the role of the state in economic and social development. This was a major issue of immediate relevance to the kind of solution to the public health problem to which the *Sanitary Report* pointed. It requires careful consideration.

From the historical point of view, two issues are involved: first, the question of whether there was any unanimity of authoritative opinion regarding the appropriateness of state intervention in social and economic affairs; and, second, whether such opinion actually influenced parliament's decision to act or not to act in specific matters. Both these issues have suffered in the past from woeful over-simplification, and it has only recently become clearer that neither can be dismissed in simple, straightforward generalisations.

The over-simplification that a *laissez-faire* philosophy inhibited state intervention was first made in the middle decades of the nineteenth century by bitter opponents of *laissez-faire* like Carlyle, Dickens, and Kingsley. Literary licence may excuse their over-simplification to some extent. On the other hand, Dicey, who dressed this generalisation up in academic garb early in the new century, dignifying it with a lawyer's authority, had less excuse. *Law and Public Opinion in England during the Nineteenth Century* was a political pamphlet which has unfortunately been mistaken for good history for half a century. Dicey's work has undoubtedly been a major influence on the historical interpretation of the social and economic policy of the nineteenth century, but it is distorted by two basic misconceptions: his equation of Benthamism with individualism, and his insistence that the period between 1825 and 1900 could be neatly divided, at about 1865-70, into a period of individualism, and one of collectivism. His purpose in imposing this pattern on the nineteenth century was to prepare the ground for an attack on collectivism, which he saw as an ugly growth of his own lifetime; but in allowing his political enthusiasm to get the better of his historical judgment, he laid a trail which has misled historians for almost half a century.

The assumption that Benthamism, one of the most powerful influences on nineteenth-century thought, and certainly the mainspring of Chadwick's energy, could be identified with individualism, or *laissez-faire*, rested on a simple reversal of the facts; and, as soon as historians ceased to be mesmerised by the audacity of this switch and turned to read Bentham for themselves instead of accepting Dicey's version of Bentham, the record was straightened.[1] 'Bentham's principles', writes

---

1. J. B. Brebner, '*Laissez-faire* and state intervention in nineteenth-century Britain', *Journal of Economic History*, VIII (1948) Supplement, 59-73; Henry Parris, 'The nineteenth-century revolution in government: a reappraisal reappraised', *Historical Journal*, III (1960) 17-37; L. Robbins, *The Theory of Economic Policy* (1952).

his most recent biographer, 'contrast vividly with the doctrines of laissez-faire.'[1] The cabinet he proposed in the *Constitutional Code*, for example, equates remarkably closely with that of the era of vigorous state intervention of the mid-twentieth century. Of immediate relevance to the movement for public health reform was the proposal for a Health Minister to be charged with 'the preservation of the national health'.[2]

Nor were the other classical economists, the founders of the 'dismal science' of political economy attacked by Carlyle and Dickens, as rigorously anti-interventionist as is frequently supposed. There were, in truth, few advocates of the unmitigated free-for-all which Dickens and Carlyle supposed was primarily responsible for the social evils they so fiercely reprobated. The father of the classical economists, Adam Smith, had specifically advocated the provision by the government of 'certain public works and certain public institutions, which it can never be for the interest of any individual, or small number of individuals to erect and maintain',[3] and his successors encouraged to a greater or lesser extent the intervention of the state in matters relating to factory conditions, the relief of poverty, trade unions, education, and health.[4] In a famous passage of a report often cited as the canonic embodiment of the principle of *laissez-faire*, the arch-priest of non-intervention, Nassau Senior, examined living conditions in the great towns. Accepting the horrifying descriptions of the three doctors in their reports of 1838 as essentially accurate, Senior asked 'What other result can be expected, when any man who can purchase or hire a plot of ground is allowed to cover it with such buildings as he may think fit, where there is no power to enforce drainage or sewerage, or to regulate the width of streets, or to prevent houses from being packed back to back, and separated in front by mere alleys and courts, or their being filled with as many inmates as their walls can contain, or the accumulation within and without, of all the impurities which arise in a crowded population?' He concluded that 'with all our reverence for the principle of non-interference, we cannot doubt that in this matter it has been pushed too far. We believe that both ground landlord and the speculating builder ought to be compelled by law, though it should cost them a percentage of their rent and profit, to take measures which shall prevent the towns which they create from being the centres of disease'.[5] Senior, of course, was also the co-author with Chadwick of the New Poor Law which instituted a powerful central government department that was the model for many subsequent vehicles of state intervention.

The political economists of the first half of the nineteenth century were, in short, too intelligent and too well informed to advocate out-and-out *laissez-faire*. They were constantly being brought up short by

---

1. Mary P. Mack, *Jeremy Bentham: an Odyssey of Ideas, 1748-1792* (1962) p. 297.
2. *The Works of Jeremy Bentham* (ed. J. Bowring, Edinburgh 1843) IX, 443-5.
3. Adam Smith, *Wealth of Nations* (ed. E. Cannan, 1904) II, 184-5.
4. See Robbins, *op. cit.*, Lecture III, *passim*.
5. *Report of the Commissioners on the Condition of the Hand-loom Weavers*, *P.P.* 1841, X, p. 73.

the realities of the economic system in which they worked and thought, and were only too conscious of the clash between the logic of pure theory and the demands of social morality. They did not invariably, as is so often asserted, insist on the priority of the former claim. Genuflections in the direction of theoretical principles were more frequently the signal for acceptance of the need for state intervention in some particular quarter. John Stuart Mill's famous chapter on 'the grounds and limits of the *laissez-faire* and non-interference principle' in his *Principles of Political Economy* of 1848 was perhaps the most explicit recognition of this dichotomy. Most of this chapter is devoted to the delineation of wide fields in which he recognised that departures from the basic principle of non-interference must be sanctioned.

Another common error, however, has been the assumption that the classical economists were the only effective influence on social and economic policy in the early and mid-nineteenth century. This is a curiously perverse view, since it ignores powerful voices like those of Bentham, Chadwick, the social novelists, many by no means inarticulate members of the medical profession, the humanitarians, the Christian Socialists, and most sections of the many working-class movements. There was, in short, nothing approaching a concensus of opinion concerning *laissez-faire* and state intervention, even in the very narrow social sector represented by governments, parliament, and the press. In practice, the ears of ministers were assailed by a confused babel of voices rather than bewitched by the soft whisper of a single plea for inaction.

Bombarded by this battery of conflicting advice, how did nineteenth-century governments react? How right was Dicey in distinguishing so sharply between periods of individualism and collectivism? The questions are better answered if a distinction is made which Dicey did not attempt—between economic and social policy. In the economic sphere, some case can be made out by reference particularly to the free trade movement that a policy of economic freedom was consciously pursued. Outside the field of commerce, the case is less clear-cut. There never had been, in any case, any real tradition of the regulation of manufacture and labour. The tinkering of pre-nineteenth century governments in these sectors had only touched the fringes of industrial development. Many major industries were almost wholly unaffected by 'mercantilist' regulations, so that the absence of intervention in these spheres in the nineteenth century carries no implication of a conscious policy of abstention from economic regulation. Agriculture was affected in the early nineteenth century as in the two preceding centuries by a very positive measure of state regulation, the corn laws. And again it would be an over-simplification to ascribe the repeal of the corn laws in 1846 to a simple victory of *laissez-faire* policy. It was the triumph of the interests of one group over those of another; and who can doubt that, if a duty on corn had suited the interests of the manufacturers, they would have fought as tenaciously as did the landed interest for the retention of the corn laws? The banking system and the note issue were subjected in 1844 to the fairly rigorous measure of control of the Bank Charter Act, while the same year witnessed the second attempt by the legislature to assert some control over the growing railway system, an act which went so far as to provide for the ultimate nationalisation of all railways subsequently authorised. An Act of 1817 authorised substantial government loans for public works, the express intention of which was to raise the level of employment,[1] while the Poor Law Amendment Act of 1834 authorised Boards of Guardians to promote large-scale migration of labour.[2] The catalogue of interventionist measures of the period of so-called *laissez-faire* could be extended much further. What is important is that when economists or statesmen of this period spoke about non-intervention in the economic sphere, they were really concerned with commercial institutions. They believed unquestioningly in the self-regulatory mechanisms of the price system and the gold standard. They were prepared to fight to the last ditch to preserve the commercial and banking sectors against government interference, but, if pushed, were not really unwilling to let the state into other sectors.

In the social sphere, on the other hand, it is scarcely possible to accept the existence of a systematic *laissez-faire* policy at all. The factory and passenger Acts, and the Poor Law Amendment Act which reinforced the Settlement Laws and aimed to facilitate emigration as well as internal migration, were only the beginnings of a crescendo of state regulation of social problems. And by authorising local government authorities—at first through the establishment of improvement commissions, and later through the Municipal Corporations Act of 1835 and subsequent local private acts—to perform a wide range of local services, governments implicitly accepted the principle of local government intervention under the authority of the central government. The long series of private enclosure, turnpike, canal, and railway acts implies the acceptance by parliament, through the exercise of its powers of granting or withholding such statutory authority, of responsibility for social and economic development. That this responsibility was often exercised laxly is beside the point. The overwhelming proportion of the vast mass of early and mid-nineteenth-century legislation was concerned with social and economic affairs.

Nevertheless, John Stuart Mill's view that 'the only purpose for which power can be rightfully exercised over any member of a civilized community, against his will, is to prevent harm to others'[3] received wide general acceptance amongst the politically important classes. But Mill himself had been obliged to admit many exceptions to a *general* theory of *laissez-faire*,[4] so that, in practice, the real issue in the nineteenth century was not simply whether or not governments should intervene in social and economic affairs, but how much, in which directions, and through which channels. The question of the extent of state intervention depended largely on the willingness of the economically wealthy and powerful groups to tax themselves, to reduce their incomes by restrictive legis-

---

1. M. W. Flinn, 'The Poor Employment Act, 1817', *Econ. H. R.* 2nd ser. XIV (1961) 82-92.
2. A. Redford, *Labour Migration in England, 1800-1850* (Manchester, 1926) pp. 84-101.
3. J. S. Mill, *On Liberty* (1859) p. 15.
4. J. S. Mill, *Principles of Political Economy* (1848) Book V, chap. IX.

lation or to restrict their freedom of social, economic, or political action.

The problem of the media of government regulation raised the issue of central versus local control. Contemplating the woeful and wilful failure of local government in the public health field, Chadwick insisted that only the concentration of effective power in the hands of the central government would achieve the desired social ends. Though he elevated this axiom to the level of a principle, it was only because he saw no hope in the existing Commissioners of Sewers, vestries and closed corporations, or even in the new municipal corporations after 1835. There was some justification for this viewpoint: these old local government bodies were corrupt and hopelessly inefficient; but had he been able to see what the new corporations, which evolved after the Act of 1835, were able to achieve in the late nineteenth and twentieth centuries, even he might well have changed his attitude. From his point of view, it was a tragedy that the first experiment in centralisation had been the New Poor Law: the environment of a happier medium than the New Poor Law might well have softened rather than fortified the entrenched hostility to effective central control.

It no longer seems possible to acknowledge *laissez-faire* as the sole or even the first principle of social and economic policy in the early nineteenth century. A very wide range of social and economic issues were raised, debated, and made the subject of legislation by the parliaments of this period. Those whose interests were likely to be protected by these measures gave enthusiastic support: those whose interests were threatened, opposed them, and if, in doing so, they invoked the 'principle' of *laissez-faire*, they were only grasping at a perfectly legitimate straw in the circumstances. Thus the campaign for sanitary reform was not opposed by an immutable and unchallengeable principle; it was faced instead with a powerful opposition whose economic and political interests might be threatened by measures likely to reduce some incomes or diminish local autonomy. Chadwick and his supporters had to arm themselves, therefore, against the spurious use of economic and political theory which was merely the first line of defence of a group of opponents very well aware of the real nature of the threat.

One of the difficulties involved in a precise chronology of the history of political ideas of the kind presented by Dicey, is that it seldom accommodates all the facts. Dicey's turning-point from *laissez-faire* to state intervention came in the late 1860s; Chadwick's public health campaign and the resulting legislation took place in the 1840s. The timing of the sanitary enquiry was, of course, governed far less by any shift of public opinion of the kind that Dicey had in mind, than by the convergence of the several economic and intellectual trends discussed above. In particular, short-run economic fluctuations were of great relevance. It was more than a coincidence that the years 1838-42, when the *Sanitary Report* was being conceived and prepared, were perhaps the most seriously depressed years of any in the nineteenth century. The suffering and deprivation commonly associated with 'the Hungry Forties' might with much greater accuracy be ascribed to the period 1838-42 than to the whole decade of the forties. In spite of the determined stringency of the Poor Law Commissioners, there was a rise in the expenditure on poor relief in 1838 as unemployment mounted, accompanied by the inevitable increase in fever cases. If the documentary evidence be taken at its face value, it was Chadwick's concern for economy in the face of a rising demand for poor relief expenditure which persuaded him in the first place to publicise some facts about the economic consequences of neglect of elementary public health precautions.

II

THE SANITARY REPORT

The making of the Report

The immediate starting-point of Chadwick's sanitary enquiry was the expenditure in 1838 of public money by some poor law unions on the removal of 'nuisances', which may be taken to mean accumulations of human and other refuse believed to be the direct cause of disease. This disease, in its turn, was the cause of increased expenditure on poor relief. The unions in question had acted on the principle that the expenditure of £1 on elementary public health precautions could be made to save a probable subsequent expenditure of £10 in poor relief. But government auditors work according to the letter rather than the spirit of the law, and these items of expenditure by Boards of Guardians, on matters—public health—statutorily *ultra vires*, were disallowed. Had any record survived of which Boards of Guardians were concerned it might have been possible to test the interesting hypothesis that the Guardians concerned were acting on Chadwick's official or unofficial instructions—that the affair, in short, was deliberately contrived in order to justify the employment of medical experts on an enquiry to be made under the auspices of the Poor Law Commission. For it is reasonably certain that Chadwick by now wished to assume the leadership of the public health movement; and, since he was dependent upon the Poor Law Commission for his livelihood, and since, unlike any other branch of local or central government, the Poor Law Commission operated a unique, nation-wide network of social and medical intelligence, it was desirable for the public health movement to be directed and controlled from Somerset House. Already, in 1837, Chadwick had written to Farr to air a proposal for a Registry of Epidemics to work under the Poor Law Commissioners. Farr thought little of it, believing that anything of value in this branch of national statistics could be handled adequately by the Registrar-General's office; but, he added, with a thrust that could hardly have been wasted on Chadwick, 'It is quite natural in them [the Poor Law Commissioners] to desire the addition to their patronage and power.'[1]

Whether the affray with the auditors was accidental or contrived, on 18 April 1838 the Home Secretary, Lord John Russell, taking the disallowed expenditure into account, appears to have gone so far as to have considered the introduction of a Bill to permit such expenditure to be defrayed from the rates. Before doing so, however, he asked for an opinion on the matter from the Poor Law Commissioners. The Com-

---

1. William Farr to Chadwick, 13 February 1837.

missioners immediately ordered small-scale enquiries in London into the relationship between urban conditions and disease. The results of these enquiries, together with a report from the Commissioners, was presented to the Home Secretary on 14 May 1838. This report was published as an appendix to the *Fourth Annual Report* of the Poor Law Commissioners, and, although signed by the three Commissioners, bears all the signs of having been written by Chadwick. Indeed, apart from Chadwick, there were few administrators of that time capable of assembling and presenting the material in so short a time. The Report itself was very brief—a mere ten pages—but it made its principal point effectively enough in drawing attention to the need to 'avert the charges on the poor-rates which are caused by nuisances by which contagion is generated and persons reduced to destitution'. To illustrate the prevalence of these 'nuisances', the Commissioners reported that they had 'directed local examinations to be made . . . by Dr Arnott, by Dr Southwood Smith, and by Dr Kay'. Three reports by the three doctors were published as Supplements to the Report.[1] These three surveys were supplemented in the following year by an additional report on the health of London by Southwood Smith.[2]

There was very little in any of these surveys that had not been fairly common currency amongst some sections of the medical profession for the previous fifty years. The details of open sewers, stagnant pools of liquid refuse, insanitary privies, and the stench of under-ventilated, overcrowded tenements were vivid. Though similar descriptions might be found in the writings of any one of a score or more of doctors of this period, this was one of the earliest occasions when such unimpeachable evidence was publicised officially. More important, these surveys were the first occasion on which the government had formally employed fully-qualified medical men to gather factual information as a prelude to possible parliamentary action. The Reports of the Poor Law Commission were widely circulated and far more generally read than the reports of some of the earlier commissions whose enquiries had skirted the fringe of this subject.[3] Southwood Smith's later report in the Fifth

---

1. Supplement No. 1, 'Report on the prevalence of certain physical causes of fever in the Metropolis, which might be removed by proper sanatory measures', by Neil Arnott and James Phillips Kay (pp. 103-29); Supplement No. 2, 'Report on some of the physical causes of sickness and mortality to which the poor are particularly exposed, and which are capable of removal by sanatory regulations; exemplified in the present condition of the Bethnal Green and Whitechapel districts, as ascertained on a personal inspection by Southwood Smith, Physician to the London Fever Hospital' (pp. 129-39); Supplement No. 3, 'Account of a personal inspection of Bethnal Green and Whitechapel, in May, 1838, with a supplement', by Southwood Smith (pp. 139-53).
2. 'Report on the prevalence of fever in twenty Metropolitan Unions or parishes during the year ended the 20th March, 1838, by Southwood Smith'. Appendix C, No. 2, to *Fifth Annual Report of the Poor Law Commissioners* (1839) pp. 160-71.
3. E.g. the *Factories Inquiries Commission*, 1833; and the *Poor Inquiry (Ireland) Commission*, 1836.

Poor Law Report, following Farr's example at the Registrar-General's office, made generous and effective use of statistical material.

The Commissioners' letter which enclosed the first batch of sanitary surveys was debated in the House of Lords in May 1838. No action ensued, however, and in June Chadwick sought to keep the fires smouldering by writing to the Home Secretary, Lord John Russell, recommending that 'it would be worthy of your Lordship to bring in a Bill for an Act of the nature of the Building Act to regulate the future dwellings of the labouring classes, providing that none should be built without provision being made for proper drainage, and the width of streets . . .'.[1] The Home Secretary was not, apparently, stirred to action, and in the following year, after the original attack in the Fourth Report had been reinforced by Southwood Smith's article in the Fifth Report, Blomfield, the Bishop of London, moved in the House of Lords that an enquiry be made into the sanitary condition of the labouring class.[2] The Poor Law Commissioners were ordered to undertake such an enquiry.[3]

At this time—the early autumn of 1839—Chadwick was still nominally Secretary to the Poor Law Commission. Since the inauguration of the Poor Law Commission in 1834 there had been serious friction between the three central Commissioners and their secretary: the new Poor Law was administered in its early years against a background of undeclared internal warfare. But the sanitary enquiry in 1839 offered the possibility of at least a temporary solution: Chadwick was tacitly released from his duties as Secretary to the Commission, and left free to devote his whole energies to the enquiry. The Secretary's duties were taken over by the Assistant Secretary, George Coode.

Chadwick had been at work for about six months, when a member of the House of Commons, Robert Aglionby Slaney, secured the appointment of a Select Committee to investigate the health of towns. Slaney was an enthusiast for public health reform, and was impatient of the slow grinding of Chadwick's extra-parliamentary mills. His committee reported later in 1840.[4] During the London enquiries of 1838, one of Chadwick's mild converts to the sanitary cause had been Lord Normanby. In September 1839, Normanby succeeded Lord John Russell at the Home Office. This was a bad moment for anybody to take over the Home Office, and for twenty-one months Normanby attempted to grapple simultaneously with Chartism and with the storm of protest which was meeting the Poor Law Commission's attempts to enforce the New Poor Law in the North of England. Normanby, for all his predisposition in favour of Chadwick, was brought face to face with the

---

1. Chadwick to Lord John Russell, 21 June 1838.
2. Blomfield had, of course, been a colleague of Chadwick's on the Poor Law Commission of 1833-4, and, according to Sir John Simon (probably well acquainted with both), Blomfield's action was undertaken at Chadwick's suggestion. (Sir John Simon, *English Sanitary Institutions* (1890) p. 187n.)
3. Because the enquiry was initiated in the House of Lords, the *Sanitary Report* was ultimately published as a House of Lords paper. This is a contributory factor in the relative rarity of copies of the 1842 Report.
4. *Report of the Select Committee on the Health of Towns*, P.P. 1840, XI.

staggering unpopularity of the New Poor Law. In the battle that was fought out, during his tenure of the Home Office, between the advocates of some relaxation of the rigidity of the New Poor Law and Chadwick, Normanby was little more than a spectator; but, as hostility to the New Poor Law contributed to the downfall of the Whig government in the summer of 1841, he could hardly be expected to have retained his enthusiasm for Chadwick and his ideas.

In spite of the change in his personal attitude to Chadwick, Normanby had not lost his interest in sanitary reform. He accepted eagerly the recommendations of Slaney's committee and, early in the session of 1841, introduced a Building Bill based on these recommendations. Chadwick, already at loggerheads with Normanby over the interpretation of the Poor Law Act of 1834, was understandably annoyed at being brushed aside in this manner over the public health question. He believed, rightly, that Slaney's investigations were superficial, and that the proposed Bill was inadequate and ill-considered. Not being a man to conceal strong feelings, in February 1841 he endeavoured to persuade Normanby to drop his Bill to clear the way for measures which would follow the publication of the *Sanitary Report*. This was the last straw for Normanby: he refused to give up his Bill, and ordered Chadwick to abandon his work on the *Sanitary Report*.

There the matter would presumably have rested had Normanby continued in office, but the Whig ministry had already outlived its useful life, and Normanby's Bill died with Melbourne's government in June. The new Home Secretary in Peel's government which took office in June 1841 was Sir John Graham. One of Graham's first actions was to show his hostility to Chadwick by passing him over in filling a vacant Commissionership at Somerset House, nominating instead Sir Edmund Head, a former Assistant Commissioner and himself a contributor to the *Sanitary Report*. To keep Chadwick quiet, however, in November 1841 Graham ordered him to resume work on his *Sanitary Report* and to have it ready for presentation when Parliament met in February 1842. Amazingly, Chadwick achieved this, only to have Lewis, one of the three Commissioners (for the *Report* was officially the work of the Commission), refuse to publish it. After much discussion, in the course of which Chadwick refused to modify the *Report*, a compromise solution was reached. The *Report* would be presented under Chadwick's own name, and not over the signatures of the Commissioners. By dissociating themselves from one of the most incisive and influential documents of the nineteenth century, the three Commissioners stepped out of the pages of history and left Chadwick to receive the plaudits alone. The *Report* was published by the Poor Law Commissioners as Chadwick's work on 9 July 1842.

The *Report* relied for its effect on the principle of selecting certain clear lines of attack, and supporting each thrust with a mass of vivid and unimpeachable evidence. Thus, from the outset, Chadwick's first task was the assembly of material. No source was to be left unexplored, and the coverage was to be as extensive as the means permitted. Although the debate on sanitary conditions had hitherto been conducted principally in the context of the larger industrial towns, Chadwick extended

The making of the Report

his survey to towns of all types and sizes, to rural villages, both agricultural and industrial, as well as to rural labourers' cottages and remote miners' lodging-houses. At first the aim of the enquiry was simply to extend the original metropolitan surveys of 1838 to the wider context of England and Wales, but Chadwick very soon set in motion its extension to Scotland. He visited Edinburgh, where he had several friends, about Christmas-time 1839, soon after starting work on the *Report*. Doubtless as the outcome of his visit, one of these friends was able to inform him in January 1840 that a petition had been sent from the City of Edinburgh praying that 'the enquiry instituted by the Poor Law Commissioners into the causes of disease in the large towns of England and Wales may be extended to Scotland'.[1] The petition was successful. This was a valuable gain, since there was an active body of enthusiastic supporters at work in Edinburgh and Glasgow, and some of the most telling evidence in the final *Report* related to Scottish conditions. When some of the local reports on which the principal *Report* was based were published separately later in 1842, it was possible to devote a whole volume to Scottish reports.[2]

In the first instance, the machinery of the Poor Law was utilised. A circular letter from the Poor Law Commission was addressed to all Assistant Commissioners setting out in some detail the nature of the information Chadwick wanted from them.[3] Most of the Assistant Commissioners contributed individual reports which were published in full, separately, in the volume of local reports for England and Wales.[4] For much of their information the Assistant Commissioners made use of the Poor Law medical officers. There were probably well over one thousand of these at the time of the enquiry, and they, too, were circularised at the outset, asking them to pass on to the Commissioners 'any information which you may have gained in the course of your medical experience, as to the conditions of the inmates of tenements in which diseases have occurred'.[5] W. J. Gilbert, for example, the Assistant Commissioner who reported 'On the sanitary state of the counties of Devon and Cornwall', quoted from the written testimonies of twenty-one district medical officers. Alfred Power, dealing with the central and northern parts of Lancashire, employed information from thirty-seven local medical officers. The Assistant Commissioners also, in their turn, circularised local relieving officers, clerks to Boards of Guardians, and many Guardians themselves. The correspondence with the Board of one Assistant Commissioner, for example—William Day, Assistant Commissioner for North Wales and Shropshire—enclosed completed questionnaires from relieving officers of the unions of his area.[6] Boards of Guardians were asked to submit reports on the sanitary condition of the labouring population of their districts. As some passages in the *Report* show,[7] any points in these reports which appeared to Chadwick to have particular significance were taken up by him, and further details sought by letter.

---

1. Sir William Drysdale to Chadwick, 6 and 13 January 1840.
2. *Local Reps. Scot.*
3. Prefix to *San. Rep.* pp. xi-xiii.
4. *Local Reps. E. & W.*
5. Prefix to *San. Rep.* p. xiv.
6. P.R.O., M.H.32/12, 15 January 1840.
7. *San. Rep.* pp. 323-5.

The questionnaires Chadwick issued to these Poor Law officers left nothing to chance. There is, amongst the Chadwick Papers, a 'Memorandum as to the enquiries on the Sanitary Condition of a Town Population'. It is undated, and although it appears to have been written at some time after the publication of the *Sanitary Report*, it offers an instructive illustration of his systematic approach to the compilation of a local survey. The key is to be found in the opening sentence: 'The most compendious mode of coming at the worst conditioned districts of a town will be. . . .' The investigator is recommended to seek out the schools where the sickly or stunted children could be picked out and asked where they live. He should then visit their homes, 'putting the questions in the form annexed'. Poor Law medical officers should be questioned, and information sought from physicians of fever hospitals, the officers of dispensaries and medical charities, friendly societies, sick clubs, and the local Registrars. When the investigator has found out in this way precisely 'where deaths occur from fever and where the population young as well as old are in the lowest sanitary condition', he should make descriptions of the neighbourhood of the houses (inside and outside), paying particular attention to drainage, sewers, and street cleansing. There was a detailed questionnaire to be used to elicit statistical information from friendly societies.

The material from Poor Law sources provided a solid foundation for the *Report*, but it was only a beginning. Chadwick's circle of personal acquaintances was already extensive, and there were many whose expert knowledge and experience could be tapped profitably. The Poor Law administrative network did not extend to Scotland, and full reliance had to be placed on unofficial sources there. To make matters worse, civil registration, which since 1837 had provided so valuable a statistical basis for the reform movement in England, also did not extend to Scotland.[1] But there were compensations. The Edinburgh University medical school had long been a centre which had radiated enthusiasm for public health reform. Its principal figure, William Alison, launched in 1840 one of the most effective attacks on poverty and urban squalor in his *Observations on the Poor Law in Scotland*. The medical school at Glasgow, led by the professor of forensic medicine, Robert Cowan, was a powerful ally. J. H. Burton, an Edinburgh lawyer, journalist, and historian, was a close friend of Chadwick, and brought to the aid of the movement his valuable knowledge of the Scots administrative background. The Provosts of all Scottish burghs were circularised for information concerning the health of their citizens, and the state of the streets, sewers, and working-class housing.[2] Similarly, all 'Dispensary Surgeons and Medical Practitioners' in Scotland were approached with a substantial questionnaire.[3] Distinguished citizens like William Chambers offered the services of their pens,[4] while ministers of the Kirk, who were

---

1. Civil registration of births, marriages, and deaths began in Scotland only in 1855.
2. Appendix to prefix of *San. Rep.* pp. xvi-xvii.　　　3. *Ibid.* pp. xvii-xx.
4. 'Report on the sanitary state of the residences of the poorer classes in the Old Town of Edinburgh', by William Chambers, *Local Reps. Scot.* pp. 155-8.

at this moment busy on the sociological surveys of their parishes for the *New Statistical Account of Scotland*, were sometimes well informed. There is a splendid contribution to the *Report*, for example, from the Rev. G. Lewis of St David's, Dundee.[1] In the main, however, the Scottish survey was compiled from the reports of doctors. One of these, by Dr Scott Alison, on the small East Lothian mining town of Tranent, was a notable piece of sociological research,[2] and was drawn upon liberally by Chadwick in the compilation of the final *Report*.

The practice of approaching knowledgeable individuals, which was the only means of collecting material in Scotland, proved to be a valuable supplement to the use of official sources in England. A good example of fruitful co-operation of this kind was the contribution of the Cornish doctor, Charles Foster Barham. Barham not only submitted a careful report on conditions in the town of Truro,[3] he also made a valuable study of the working conditions in the Cornish copper-mines, drawing particular attention to the beneficial effects on miners' health of elementary welfare provisions by their employers.[4]

Several prison superintendents were approached with a view to making a comparison between the health of prisoners and that of the working class under normal conditions. The sort of information Chadwick sought from this quarter is illustrated by a letter to Thomas Burgess, the Superintendent of a prison in Birmingham. 'Do you think', he wrote, 'you could get from any data of sick clubs or benefit societies in your neighbourhood composed of adults, or by the aid of your medical officers, or from any other source of information of a comparison of the average health of the prisoners, with the average health as shown by the average sickness and mortality of the labouring classes living in the vicinity? The object of the information is to ascertain as closely as may be done what are the effects of regularity of diet, cleanliness and ventilation upon the prisoners in the gaol: and this information is sought to determine to what extent the health of the labouring classes might be increased if their habitations were made as cleanly and dry, and they were as well ventilated and warm as the prison cells: if their diet were as regular and their persons as cleanly.'[5] In the event, Burgess was apparently not very helpful, for the final *Report* included no material relating to Birmingham prisons. But with characteristic thoroughness, Chadwick also approached other prison officers in Scotland and Salford, and their information enabled him to make the desired

---

1. *San. Rep.* pp. 272-6.
2. 'Report on the sanitary condition and general economy of the labouring population in the town of Tranent and neighbouring district, in Haddingtonshire', by Dr S. Scott Alison, *Local Reps. Scot.* pp. 78-130.
3. 'Report on the sanitary state of the labouring classes in the town of Truro', in *Local Reps., E. & W.* pp. 16-36.
4. *San. Rep.* pp. 262-3, quoting from 'Report by Charles Barham on the employment of children and young persons in the mines of Cornwall and Devonshire', *Report of the Children's Employment Commission*, Part I, *P.P.* 1842, XVI, App. E.
5. Chadwick to Thomas Burgess, 29 October 1841.

comparisons in the *Report*.[1] James Smith of Deanston in Stirlingshire, the celebrated authority on land drainage, was approached, as were several other model employers. Chadwick secured from him drawings and plans of labourers' cottages, and asked that he 'might perhaps delegate to your medical man the business of furnishing an account . . . of the sanatory condition of the population as compared with the condition of the population residing in dwellings of the common order'.[2]

In another instance, a private individual was consulted to verify and confirm the details of a report drawn up by one of the Assistant Commissioners. William Langton of Manchester was sent a report by Charles Mott for his comments. Langton was, on the whole, very critical—'a strange, incoherent collection of matter, some good, no doubt, but a great deal of it is very wide of the mark and little to the purpose—altogether ill-digested and certainly not well reasoned'. He disagreed with Mott's assertion that 'moral degradation' was the principal characteristic of the labouring classes, but concluded that 'progress has certainly been made since 1832 when Kay wrote, but we are still deplorably defective in respect of the condition of streets and drainage in the poorer parts of the town, and Mr Mott has not badly described them in his 3rd page'.[3] It seems that Chadwick heeded these warnings, and, in the event, Mott's published report[4] included no material relating to Manchester, which was covered by a separate report from the distinguished doctor and public health worker, Richard Baron Howard.[5] Nevertheless, some of Mott's remarks on Manchester housing, for all Langton's objections, found their way into the *Sanitary Report*.[6]

For a report on the state of Leeds, Chadwick originally approached a leading doctor in the city, Dr Williamson. But before Williamson had produced anything, Robert Baker, a doctor and sub-inspector of factories in Leeds, had come forward with a 'Sanatory Map of Leeds'.[7] Chadwick was fascinated by the possibility of illustrating with the aid of a map the correlation between disease and the poorest class of housing, and accepted this contribution. There were few people so well-informed as Baker on the subject of working-class housing in Leeds, for he had been commissioned by a Statistical Committee of Leeds Corporation in 1838 to undertake a house-to-house survey of the town.[8] On hearing of this competition, Williamson 'resigned his task . . . on the ground that [Baker] applied to make the report, and that [Baker's offer] had been

---

1. *San. Rep.* pp. 279-80.
2. Chadwick to James Smith, 17 November 1841.
3. William Langton to Chadwick, 17 March 1841.
4. 'Report on the state of the residences of the labouring classes in the manufacturing districts of Lancashire, Cheshire, Derbyshire and Staffordshire', *Local Reps. E. & W.* pp. 232-56.
5. 'Report on the prevalence of diseases arising from contagion and certain other physical causes amongst the labouring classes in Manchester', *Local Reps. E. & W.* pp. 294-336.
6. *San. Rep.* p. 336.
7. Robert Baker to Chadwick, 28 December 1840.
8. W. G. Rimmer, 'Working men's cottages in Leeds, 1770-1840', *Publications of the Thoresby Society*, XLVI, Part 2 (1961) 197.

accepted without mentioning it to him, which he thinks an act of discourtesy'.[1] Baker was thereafter given the task of compiling the report on Leeds. He accepted reluctantly, saying that he had 'given up all idea of such a thing', that he was 'somewhat unprepared', and that he had 'no leisure but in the night'.[2] When, in November 1841, after Graham had ordered Chadwick to present the report by February, and Baker had still not submitted his report, Chadwick chivvied him in fairly sharp terms: 'In respect of Leeds we shall be in an awkward position unless you complete your report in time. It is known that you have undertaken it; it will be unavoidably known that you have failed to accomplish what has long since been accomplished by medical men of other towns ... Liverpool, Manchester and Birmingham, and fault will also be found with us for having so managed as to dispense with the services of Dr Williamson.'[3] Baker completed his report: amply supplemented by statistical material from the Registrar-General's office, it was printed in full in the volume of *Local Reports*,[4] and was drawn on liberally by Chadwick in the final *Sanitary Report*.

In the single instance of Birmingham, rather than delegate the task of compiling a report to an individual doctor, a Committee of Physicians and Surgeons was set up. Their report, too, was printed in full in the volume of Local Reports, and contributed substantially to the *Sanitary Report*.[5]

In these ways, a very considerable labour force of reporters was mobilised. Including Poor Law Assistant Commissioners, medical officers, clerks, receiving officers, guardians, individual doctors, factory inspectors and other miscellaneous experts, and the provosts of all the Scottish burghs, probably upwards of two thousand individuals were approached for information. Many of these, of course, ignored the appeal, but the majority submitted something. There were endless statistical tables, drawings and plans of labourers' cottages, sanitary maps of towns, and a large number of written reports ranging from a few lines to fifty or sixty printed pages. To stiffen the written reports, Chadwick had full access to, and made good use of, statistical material from the Poor Law Commission's and the Registrar-General's offices.

Not content with this flood of written evidence, Chadwick went out into the country to study conditions at first hand. 'I have myself examined the condition of the most important localities on which the report is made,' he wrote to the Earl of Spencer.[6] He was in Edinburgh very shortly after starting work on the *Report* in December 1839, and returned to Scotland later to undertake an extensive tour which included a close inspection of the Edinburgh Old Town wynds in the company of

---

1. Chadwick to Robert Baker, 19 January 1841.
2. Robert Baker to Chadwick, 7 February 1841.
3. Chadwick to Robert Baker, 6 November 1841.
4. 'Report on the condition of the residences of the labouring classes in the town of Leeds in the West Riding of York', *Local Reps. E. & W.* pp. 348-409.
5. 'Report on the sanitary state of the labouring classes in the borough of Birmingham', *ibid.*, pp. 192-218.
6. Chadwick to the Earl of Spencer, 2 February 1842.

Dr Arnott, a tour of Glasgow's working-class housing districts, and a visit to the model factory housing scheme of James Smith at Deanston in Stirlingshire. There is also evidence of visits to Manchester,[1] Dumfries, Leeds,[2] Macclesfield,[3] and Leicester.[4] On occasion, when Chadwick toured personally in quest of information, he took and recorded evidence in question-and-answer form in the manner of commissioners of enquiry. Instances of this procedure may be found in the *Report* on pages 167-71, 192-3, 213-14, 343.

When not travelling, writing letters, or drafting the *Report*, Chadwick was reading widely. It is clear from the *Report* that he was familiar not only with the standard works of his field going back as far as Pringle, Lind, and Mead, but that he missed little in the way of obscure local studies. In a similar way, he was able to draw extensively on his very ample knowledge of the blue books of the 1820s and 1830s. Equally important, his command of the relevant British material was reinforced by an extensive acquaintance with comparable European work. The *Sanitary Report* bears ample testimony to a very considerable familiarity with the whole field of European thought and work in this field, but it is to French developments that Chadwick paid particular attention. It was asserted about this time—though it may be disputed—that French practice was in advance of British in the sphere of public health.[5] More important in the present context, however, is the fact that the twenty years before the publication of the *Sanitary Report* witnessed a great outpouring in France of literature on sanitary questions which acted as a major influence on Chadwick's thinking.

The French lead in this field has been attributed to the advanced nature of French social theory in general in the first half of the nineteenth century, and to the experience and international contacts acquired by French physicians during the Napoleonic Wars. Whatever the cause, there was a body of systematic research and writing in the field of public health already in existence before Chadwick set to work. The two principal authorities were A. J. P. Parent-Duchâtelet (1790-1836), an authority on sewerage and industrial hygiene, and Louis René Villermé (1782-1863), with a long list of publications dealing with prison reform, medical statistics, industrial health, and epidemiology. Both were editors of what must have been the first journal in the field of public health—the *Annales d'Hygiène*, started in 1829—and both influenced and inspired Chadwick to imitate their achievements in England. As a result of the study of continental and American sources, the *Report* is liberally sprinkled with evidence from many parts of the world, as well as with illustrations of the efficacy of particular measures of sanitary improve-

---

1. *San. Rep.* p. 304; Chadwick to James Smith, 17 November 1841.
2. *San. Rep.* p. 75. 3. *San. Rep.* pp. 75, 343.
4. *Leicester Chronicle*, 19 August 1843, quoted by A. Temple Patterson, *Radical Leicester* (Leicester 1954) pp. 336-7.
5. In 1829, one David Johnston of Edinburgh described French public health regulations as superior to those of Great Britain. See E. H. Ackerknecht, 'Hygiene in France, 1815-48', *Bulletin of the History of Medicine*, XXII (1948) 130.

ment which had at some time been put into practice in one country or another.

There is ample evidence in his correspondence that, when finally ordered in November 1841 to present his *Report* in the following February, Chadwick intensified his efforts, bombarding innumerable correspondents with urgent requests to submit material promised earlier. And the refusal of the Commissioners to publish the *Report* as it stood in February 1842, which delayed eventual publication until July, gave Chadwick a further respite which he put to considerable use.

The collection of material was taken up with renewed vigour. On the one hand, dated material in the *Sanitary Report* indicates its insertion at this late hour,[1] while, on the other hand, fresh queries were sent out to contributors, seeking further information on points of importance. To Charles Barham, the Cornish doctor who had already supplied valuable material relating to the Cornish miners, Chadwick wrote: 'I am informed that in some public document you have noticed the habit of workmen in the mines using the warm water from the engines as a bath. The subject is mentioned in the draught of a sanatory report before the Commissioners but not so fully as might be. It is only mentioned as a suggestion. Can you oblige me by informing me . . .', and there followed a string of questions on the practice.[2] There were now available proof copies of the *Report*, which facilitated the work of amendment and improvement. Copies were sent to some of the principal contributors. Dr James Mitchell, for example, who had submitted a report on the conditions in the Pennine miners' lodging-houses, writing to thank Chadwick for a proof copy, commented: 'Intellectual intercourse with you has been the chief source of my happiness for the last eighteen years. . . .[3] I have been much edified with what little I have been able to read of the Sanitary Report, and tomorrow I hope to get through it. I have not observed yet Sunderland, the worst town in England which I have seen yet. . . . If you want a description of the town it is worth taking pains to get it.'[4] Dr Barham in Camborne was sent proofs of a portion of the *Report*, with the request, '. . . If there are any other points that occur to you as desirable from your local knowledge in reference to the portions respecting places of work or labourers' residences or any other point that may occur to you on reading over from p. 73, we should be obliged to you for it.'[5] Experts in particular aspects of the *Report's* subject-matter were invited to comment on what had been written. Griffith Davies, for

---

1. E.g. *San. Rep.* p. 213.
2. Chadwick to Charles Barham, 3 March 1842. The description on p. 318 of the *San. Rep.* was presumably Dr Barham's answer to this request.
3. C.f. the traditional view of Chadwick's 'contempt for the medical profession'.
4. James Mitchell to Chadwick, 12 March 1842. The suggestion does not appear to have been taken up by Chadwick, for Sunderland is one of the few larger towns in the country not mentioned in the *Report*. This is an odd exclusion, in view of the fact that it was in Sunderland that cholera first broke out in this country in 1831.
5. Chadwick to Charles Barham, 18 March 1842.

example, an Actuary to the Guardian Assurance Office, on being sent proofs, offered some detailed comments on comparative life tables,[1] while Anthony Strutt, of the well-known Derby family of benevolent industrialists, was asked to comment on a passage dealing with 'the circumstances arising from the union of the condition of landlord and tenant, and of employer and labourer in the same pair of persons'.[2] Charles Babbage, the economist and statistician, was asked at a very late hour to comment on the section dealing with comparative expectations of life.[3]

Finally, proof copies were sent to distinguished men of letters. Carlyle agreed to 'annotate' a copy, but had not received it by the end of March, and doubted whether his suggestions could be made in time.[4] Surviving correspondence with John Stuart Mill indicates that he played a not insignificant part in the final re-drafting. In April, Mill commented acidly to Chadwick: 'I have read through your report slowly and carefully. I do not find a single erroneous or questionable position in it, while there is the strength and largeness of practical views which are characteristic of all you do. In its present unrevised[5] state it is, as you are probably aware, utterly ineffective from the want of unity and of an apparent thread running through it and holding it together. I wish you would learn some of the forms of scientific exposition of which my friend Comte makes such superfluous use, and to *use* without *abusing* which is one of the principal lessons which practice and reflexion have to teach to people like you and me who have to make new trains of thought intelligible.'[6] Chadwick evidently took this sermon to heart, for two months later Mill wrote again in rather less critical, though hardly less patronising, vein: 'I have read the whole report carefully through again. The defects of arrangement are now corrected and I have nothing to suggest except that it be carefully revised by yourself or some other person to correct the numerous typographical errors and occasional ungrammatical sentences. I think it all excellent and shall be glad to write about it for any newspaper as you suggest.'[7]

When, after almost three years of intensive labour, the *Report* was finally published in July 1842, Chadwick was well aware that this was not the end of his labours, but only the beginning. He had never made the mistake of assuming that the *Report* was an end in itself. The end, to which it was a principal, but certainly not the only means, was a substantial measure of public health legislation along lines suggested in the *Report*'s conclusions. In July 1842, Chadwick set himself systematically and vigorously to the task of laying the foundations of legislation.

---

1. Griffith Davies to Chadwick, 11 January 1842.
2. Chadwick to Anthony Strutt, 15 February 1842.
3. Chadwick to Charles Babbage, 3 June 1842, B. M. Add. MSS. 37, 192.
4. Thomas Carlyle to Chadwick, 23 March 1842.
5. After two and a half years' work on the *Report*, and within three months of its publication, this remark, coming from someone of Mill's stature, must have been a bitter pill for Chadwick to swallow.
6. John Stuart Mill to Chadwick, (?) April 1842.
7. John Stuart Mill to Chadwick, Thursday, 8 (June?) 1842.

The making of the Report

The purpose of the *Report*, of course, was to influence opinion, and Chadwick's task therefore, in the first place, was to ensure that as wide a range of opinion as possible was influenced by the *Report*. Since the original motion by Bishop Blomfield which had initiated the enquiry in 1839 had been introduced in the House of Lords, the *Report* was a House of Lords paper. Thus, in its official form, the *Report* became at birth a scarce document. Aware of this limitation, Chadwick, however, took a step for which he himself had created a precedent with the Poor Law Report of 1834: he arranged for the separate publication of the *Report* in quarto form, far less bulky and unmanageable than the folio of official parliamentary papers. A very large edition of the quarto *Report* was ordered, though how large it is now impossible to say. An unconfirmed tradition puts it at as many as 100,000, but the only firm information on the subject suggests an appreciably lower figure. Writing from a much closer acquaintance with the age, Sir John Simon reported that 10,000 copies were sold or given away.[1] In a letter to Lord Brougham written little more than a fortnight after the actual publication of the *Report*, Chadwick claimed that 'upwards of 20,000 copies of the Report have been sold'.[2] To this should be added the copies distributed free by the Commission—in the first two months 'more than 3,000 copies' were despatched by the Poor Law Commission clerks.[3] All that can be said with any certainty is, in Chadwick's words, that its sale was 'much higher than anything [at the King's Printers] that has yet been sold'.[4] In September, Chadwick had enquiries made with a view to advertising the *Report* in *The Times* and *The Morning Chronicle*.

Copies were automatically sent to every Board of Guardians. In addition, almost every person who could conceivably be interested in furthering the cause of public health received one. Six copies were sent, for example, to the College of Engineers at Putney, for the use of students.[5] J. H. Burton, the Edinburgh journalist who acted very much as Chadwick's agent for Scotland, wrote in September saying, 'If it were not asking too much, I think I might give away to advantage one or two more copies of your report. I remarked to you that its good effect would be (as much almost as by legislation) created by its private influence....'[6] Harriet Martineau wrote to acknowledge that 'it is owing to the fascination of your Report that my acknowledgment is not under my own hand. It arrived safe yesterday evening and kept me up far too late to my detriment today, which I tell you merely as the strongest proof of your having sent me a very acceptable present.'[7] A copy was sent to the Archbishop of Dublin, together with a note from Chadwick explaining that 'my main reason for sending you the Report was that I believe that the physical evils therein described as existing in the English towns and

---

1. Sir John Simon, *English Sanitary Institutions*, p. 196.
2. Chadwick to Lord Brougham, 24 July 1842.
3. Frederick Purdy to Chadwick, 13 September 1842.
4. Chadwick to Macvey Napier, 11 October 1842, B. M. Add. MSS. 34, 623, fol. 175.   5. Butler Williams to Chadwick, 22 November 1842,
6. J. H. Burton to Chadwick, 29 September 1842.
7. Harriet Martineau to Chadwick, n.d.

depressing the moral condition of the inhabitants, exist to a greater extent and as I conceive are likely to have a still more depressing effect on the condition of the town population of Ireland'.[1] Joseph Paxton, the future architect of the Crystal Palace, but at this time occupying the humbler position of landscape gardener to the Duke of Devonshire, wrote to thank Chadwick for his copy, saying that he found it contained 'many subjects (most ably treated) in which I take a very great interest, especially those of cottage gardening, cottage economy, and dwellings for the labouring poor. We have created a number of cottages in this place for the peasantry; but being in the vicinity of a Ducal palace they are not only comfortable, but highly ornamental—and not suitable for general purposes.'[2] An effort was made to interest Charles Dickens in the *Report*. The approach was made through Dickens's brother-in-law, Henry Austin. Austin (1812-61) was himself an important figure in the early public health movement. While employed by Robert Stephenson on the Blackwall Railway he had been 'deeply impressed with the miserable conditions of the dwellings of the working class in the suburbs through which the railway was carried, and with the belief that many of the evils he saw could be remedied by sanitary knowledge and legislation based upon it'. Austin, who contributed propaganda for the public health movement at this time,[3] was active in the establishment of the Health of Towns Association in 1844,[4] and became its first Honorary Secretary.[5] In September 1842, Chadwick wrote to Austin: 'I think Mr Hickson mentioned to me that Mr Dickens is your brother-in-law. I perceive it announced in the newspapers that he has in preparation notes of his tour in North America. . . . I have directed a copy of the report to be sent to you and I should be obliged to you if you would present it to him as a mark of my respect. . . . Yet I hope he had opportunities of visiting the residencies of the working classes; and observing as in the case of the Irish the effects of habits which seem independent of political motivations, for I am informed they carry with them their wretched and filthy hovels and their pig styes with them into whatever part they settle. . . . I hope he who has so well exposed parochial administration[6] will do something better than that inaccurate observer and rash generaliser de Tocqueville, and not countenance the mischievous falsehood of mob flatterers that special qualification for administration is unnecessary or that the capacity for it is intuitive. . . . Mr Dickens will have possession of the ear not only of America but of Europe, and whatever he may say on the importance of a better and scientific attention to the structural arrangements for promoting the health and pleasure and moral improve-

---

1. Chadwick to Joseph Peacocke, Archbishop of Dublin, n.d.
2. Joseph Paxton to Chadwick, 30 September 1842.
3. Henry Austin, 'Metropolitan improvements', *Westminster Review*, XXXVI (1841) 404-35.
4. See below, pp. 68-9.
5. I am indebted to Mr Philip Collins for these notes on Austin. The quotation above is taken from a Memorial to Lord Palmerston, 1862, signed, *inter alia*, by Dickens, Shaftesbury, and Chadwick, in P.R.O. T.1/6486 B.
6. In *Oliver Twist* (1837-8).

The making of the Report

ment of the population cannot fail to produce extensively beneficial results.'[1] Dickens's response must have disappointed Chadwick: his treatment of the sanitary question in *American Notes* was cursory in the extreme, and bore the impression of a trivial afterthought. 'Much of the disease which does prevail', wrote Dickens unenthusiastically, 'might be avoided if a few common precautions were observed.' But, he added, 'there is no local legislature in America which may not study Mr Chadwick's excellent Report on the Sanitary Condition of our Labouring Classes with immense advantage'.[2]

The customary vehicle for propaganda in this period was the quarterly review. Newspapers, though prepared to notice the publication of important documents like the *Sanitary Report*, indulged normally in less discursive comment than their counterparts might today. Nevertheless, Chadwick sent a copy to the editor of *The Times*, and both this paper and *The Morning Chronicle* carried leading articles on the subject.[3] Even before the *Report* appeared, Sir Archibald Alison, brother of William Pulteney Alison, had published an article on the 'Social and moral condition of the manufacturing classes in Scotland' in *Blackwood's*.[4] Chadwick set great store on getting an article in a Tory journal like the *Quarterly* on the grounds that if he published an article in 'the Westminster or any leading Radical publication that it may not tend by instinctive aversion to compel the Quarterly into any opposite course'.[5] He succeeded handsomely in this endeavour, and the *Quarterly* carried a long and extremely sympathetic review of the Report by R. Head in the spring of 1843.[6] Another article was placed in the less important *Tait's*.[7] Sending a copy of the *Report* to Macvey Napier, editor of the *Edinburgh* and Professor of Conveyancing in the University of Edinburgh, Chadwick enquired 'whether it would not be desirable to have an early article upon the subject.... If you should be of opinion that an article on this subject is desirable, I could write you one, if no one else could be got, less upon the report than upon the subject.'[8] But being extremely busy at that time, Chadwick suggested that the Rev. Elwell, of Bath, be approached to write the article. Elwell, who had contributed some valuable notes on the sanitary condition of working-class housing in

---

1. Chadwick to Henry Austin, 7 September 1842.
2. Charles Dickens, *American Notes* (1842) I, 304-5.
3. John Wilson to Chadwick, 31 August 1842; *The Times*, 29 August 1842; *The Morning Chronicle*, 30 August 1842.
4. *Blackwood's Edinburgh Magazine*, L (1841) 659-73. For the attribution of the authorship of this article, see F. W. Fetter, 'The economic articles in 'Blackwood's Edinburgh Magazine', and their authors, 1817-1853; Part II', *Scottish Journal of Political Economy*, VII (1960) 225.
5. Chadwick to J. H. Burton, 12 February 1841.
6. *Quarterly Review*, LXXI (March 1843) 417-53. For the attribution of the authorship of this article, see F. W. Fetter, 'The economic articles in the *Quarterly Review* and their authors, 1809-1852', *Journal of Political Economy*, LXVI (1958) 167.
7. A substantial review of the *Sanitary Report* in *Tait's Edinburgh Magazine*, IX (1842) 649-60.
8. Chadwick to Macvey Napier, 28 July 1842. B.M. Add. MSS. 34, 623, fol. 44.

Bath,[1] was, however, ill, and Chadwick wrote again to Napier, concluding that 'unless I hear from you in the course of a week . . . I must submit an article to you.'[2] But either Chadwick remained too busy, or Napier was uninterested, for no article appeared in the *Edinburgh* on the subject of the *Sanitary Report*.

The issues of the Report

The *Sanitary Report* devoted the greater part of its space to establishing four major axioms. These were built up with an immense wealth of detail, and, although it was no part of Chadwick's intention to delineate with any precision a future course of legislative action, were intended to drive the reader on irresistibly to the desired legislative frame of mind. The four points may be summarised as follows. A lengthy first section (Chapters I-IV) aimed to establish the correlation between insanitation, defective drainage, inadequate water supply, and overcrowded housing, on the one hand, with disease, high mortality rates, and low expectation of life, on the other. This major section comprised half the *Report* and established inexorably the essential basis of fact. It is counter-balanced by a chapter (VI), to which Chadwick attached much importance and directed a great deal of patient research, devoted to the salutary results of the provision by employers and landlords of improved, sanitary dwellings for their employees and tenants. Chadwick was able to show how, by assuming the role of benevolent patriarchs, employers might favourably influence the morals as well as the health of their dependants.

A second axiom concerned the *economic* cost of ill-health. This was, of course, the starting-point of the enquiry. Undoubtedly it was intended at the outset that this should have been the mainstay of the *Report*. In the event, it became swamped by so many other basically humanitarian issues, that it was dismissed with a single chapter of barely twenty pages (Chapter V). The facts about the number of widows and orphans, and of the causes of widowhood and orphanage, were easily established, of course, but the relegation of this point to so insignificant a part of the *Report* is an interesting measure of the metamorphosis of Chadwick's own approach to the sanitary question over the four years between first raising the question and the submission of the *Report*.

The drift of his attitude may be gauged by the far greater importance he attached in the *Report* to his third axiom—the *social* cost of squalor and bad housing. No longer so seriously concerned with the £ s d of neglect, three years of enquiry had impressed on him the infinitely more serious damage inflicted by insanitation on morals and habits. In many ways, this section (the second half of Chapter III) constitutes one of the most valuable contributions of the *Report* to the advance of social policy. Although many medical writers had been making these points for long enough beforehand, Chadwick's unequivocal statement of the interaction of bad and inadequate housing with intemperance, immorality,

---

1. *San. Rep.* pp. 141-2, 146.
2. Chadwick to Macvey Napier, 11 October 1842. B.M. Add. MSS. 34, 623, fol. 175.

The issues of the Report

bad spending, as well as disease, represents a major breakthrough in social thinking. It was, indeed, no less than a complete reversal of the traditional middle-class attitude which ascribed the miserable circumstances of the poor to defects of character. It is, indeed, also a far cry from Chadwick's own assumption of eight years earlier in the Poor Law Report that poverty and the consequential resort to the parish were evidence of shortcomings of character which could only be cured by a deterrent poor law.

Chadwick's fourth point concerned administration. He devoted the whole of the long Chapter VII to demonstrating the inherent inefficiency of the existing legal and administrative machinery. This was an essential stage in his argument in view of his conviction that the only hope of sanitary improvement lay in radical administrative departures. For his aim was no less than the erection of an administrative framework to deal with public health matters on lines closely parallel to those which he himself had earlier designed, built and operated for the poor law. He was conscious that the wedge of centralisation, the thin end of which had been driven in in 1834, would be resisted with all the vigour and fanaticism which landowners, commissioners of sewers and police in several hundred boroughs, vestries, and privately-owned water companies, could muster. Though he could not expect to prevail overnight against emotion and self-interest, it was essential to make a start by the provision of a sound, factual foundation.

To this basic framework, Chadwick added some miscellaneous subsidiary points. The first section of Chapter III is a study of the role of ventilation in places of work, and almost certainly reflects the influence of Dr Arnott, whose special qualification to assist in the sanitary enquiry was an expertise in this particular field. Secondly, Chapter VIII investigates the condition of common lodging-houses. This was, of course, merely one aspect of the housing problem, and one of peripheral importance only; but the lodging-houses catered then for a proportionately far more numerous vagrant population than their equivalents do today, and they uniformly offered glaring examples of the extremes of squalor and insanitation. Thirdly, mention ought to be made of one of the more curious bees in Chadwick's bonnet: his enthusiasm for the use of untreated sewage as a field manure. The persistence with which he pursued this idea detracts in no small measure from the value of the *Report*, a persistence which is the harder to understand in view of the widespread condemnation of the practice by most of the competent medical authorities in Edinburgh, where its possibilities had most impressed Chadwick. No doubt it was the economics of this method of sewage disposal which so fired his imagination. He firmly believed that the sale of urban sewage to farmers in the neighbourhood of towns would wholly pay for the cost of sewerage, although it is only fair to add that Chadwick planned for the removal of sewage from the towns not in solid form, but by suspension in water (a method by which he assumed the noxious gases would not be allowed to escape), and for its distribution to agricultural land in liquid form. It must be remembered that at this time there were still no effective techniques for the scientific disposal of sewage. In Edinburgh, the low-lying Holyrood meadows were gravity-fed with the sewage of the old town, and while the productivity and economic value of these few acres of pasture benefited appreciably, the dwellings in the vicinity, which included Holyrood Palace, the official residence of the monarch when in Scotland, suffered from the stench. This is said to be why Queen Victoria would not stay at Holyrood during her visit to Scotland in 1842 (the first royal visit to Scotland for twenty years), preferring to accept the hospitality of the Duke of Buccleuch at Dalkeith instead. Yet so strongly did Chadwick feel about this aspect of sewage disposal that he was prepared to assert that the principal benefit of the extension of the enquiry to Scotland[1] had been to permit him to make use of this invaluable experiment as an example.[2] Believing that he held here the clue to the solution of problem of urban sewerage, Chadwick pursued his enquiries for several years after the publication of the *Report*.[3] His obstinacy on this point permitted him, of course, to evade one of the major problems raised by the sanitary enquiry—how to dispose of urban sewage. Until the invention of chemical and other methods of the treatment of sewage,[4] the only known alternative was to pour it into rivers. It would have been an improvement to have advocated the siting of sewage outfalls at points below towns, rather than in or above them, but to Chadwick the emptying of sewers into rivers anywhere seemed like pouring away liquid gold.

Finally—a point which should be observed by all who criticise Chadwick for his supposed hostility to doctors and engineers—Chadwick insisted on the engagement of properly qualified, professional men in all public employment in the field of public health. That Chadwick's personal relationships appear to have been at their poorest with doctors, confirms a widely-accepted view of his contempt for that profession. This hostility to doctors has been seen as part of a wider distrust of all professionalism. 'The most important improvements in the arts and sciences', he wrote in 1828, 'have been made, not by the "regularly educated practical men", but by persons trained up to other pursuits.'[5] Too much should not be read into this: he was himself a lawyer dabbling in almost every aspect of government except law, and in most professions in the early nineteenth century the gap between professional and amateur levels of competence was far narrower than it is in the twentieth century. This alleged hostility to the medical profession should first of all be seen against the background of the fact that a high proportion of all the people with whom Chadwick worked after 1838 were doctors. If he was going to have differences of opinion, there was a high mathematical probability that these would be with doctors.

Chadwick was not, in fact, hostile to doctors or engineers as such: he was sickened by the squandering of public money in purchasing the services of ill-qualified quacks. While the medical profession was not

---

1. See above, p. 47. 2. *San. Rep.* pp. 421-2.
3. E.g. correspondence with Sir William Fairbairn, 10 November 1842; and with the Earl of Spencer, 8 February 1843.
4. See A. Redford and I. S. Russell, *The History of Local Government in Manchester* (1940) II, 377-401.
5. Edwin Chadwick, 'Life assurances', *Westminster Review*, IX (1827-28) 392.

The issues of the Report

entirely blameless in this respect, the main weight of his criticism in this direction fell on the engineers. This period was, of course, the very infancy of the professional organisations within the field of engineering, and Chadwick's criticism was not without a great deal of justification. But it is important to notice that Chadwick's approach was wholly professional, in that he laid such great stress on proper and adequate qualifications for skilled men in public employment. Only the highest professional standards, he argued, were good enough for the service of the public. Many of his friends, and most of his collaborators, were doctors. The *Sanitary Report* itself is substantially derived from the reports of scores of medical men up and down the country: it is, in fact, a remarkable example of intensive collaboration and conformity of views between medical men and civil servants.

From the letter to Southwood Smith quoted at the beginning of this introduction it could be said that Chadwick seems to have been afraid of other people receiving the credit that he felt belonged to him. It was possibly this streak of vanity which gave the impression of contempt for professionals, especially doctors; he may have subconsciously felt that they would steal his thunder. He may also have recognised that all the doctors in the world could not have obtained the reforms which he as a civil servant was able to bring to fruition. Such a feeling—that they were puppets in his hands—may have given rise to his ambivalent attitude to doctors, and may explain, if not justify, the common assumption of his hostility to the profession.[1]

On the whole, the *Report* consciously eschewed making explicit recommendations, preferring to leave the facts and conclusions, skilfully presented, to speak for themselves. The first conclusion-cum-recommendation was fundamental. It was so sensible that its subsequent universal adoption has obscured its radical nature at the time. Appreciating that the principal obstacle in the past to the removal of solid refuse and sewage from streets and privies had been the sheer expense of the hand labour involved, Chadwick recommended its removal by suspension in water, to be conveyed in glazed, circular-bored drains. Most of the sewers of the early nineteenth century were large, square, brick-built tunnels. Lacking an adequate flow of water, and containing too many angles and corners, they easily became blocked. They were efficient only in distributing sewage gases over wider areas, while it was not unknown for them to be used unofficially for human burials. It was the failure of all but a small minority of civil engineers to come round to Chadwick's views about sewerage which was a principal cause of his hostility to that profession, in this case with some justification.

The disposal of refuse and sewage by suspension in water, Chadwick believed, would reduce the cost of removal to one-twentieth or less of that of removal by hand labour. But it presupposed the existence of an adequate water supply. In most towns this was lacking, and Chadwick therefore gave urgent priority to the provision of an ample water supply.

For the rest, with one important exception, Chadwick left details of

---

1. I am indebted to Dr T. C. Smout for raising the point discussed in this paragraph.

necessary legislation purposely vague by the use of such phrases as 'by appropriate arrangements', and 'the attainment of these and the other collateral advantages . . . are within the power of the legislature'.[1] The exception concerned the appointment of district medical officers 'with the securities of special qualifications and responsibilities to initiate sanitary measures and reclaim the execution of the law'. So far as administration was concerned, Chadwick's recommendations were vague and imprecise. The construction and maintenance of the necessary sewers he thought should be entrusted to those already nominally performing this function. This was a strangely feeble recommendation, in view of the fierce criticism to which he had subjected, for example, the metropolitan commissions. His proviso that the new commissions should include in them 'the chief elected officers of municipalities, and other authorities now charged with the care of the streets and roads or connected with local public works', hardly met his own criticism of the existing commissions. He was insistent, however, that national uniformity was essential: all parts of the country should have the benefit of the improved public health arrangements. He attacked particularly the practice of exempting Scotland from reforming legislation, citing the exemption of Scotland from the recent measures relating to civil registration (1837) and vaccination (1840). He failed to understand the motives that underlay Scottish resistance to government from Whitehall, which were powerful enough to have Scotland excluded from the Public Health Act when it finally reached the statute book in 1848.

It was scarcely to be expected that in drafting so comprehensive a report, Chadwick would be able to avoid stumbling into considerable areas of controversy. Although there were many such unresolved conflicts of opinion, three major ones ought to be mentioned here. The first of these concerns the method of diffusion of disease. This was central to the whole theme of the *Report*. Chadwick, in common with many members of the medical profession of his day, accepted the miasmatic theory, according to which, to put it crudely, smells generated disease. Disease was widely believed to be generated in the miasma given off by decaying organic matter. 'I think it tolerably evident', wrote Ferriar, 'that the contagion may be propagated by an impression on the olfactory nerves.'[2] 'The immediate, or the exciting cause of fever', wrote Southwood Smith, 'is a poison formed by the corruption or the decomposition of organic matter. Vegetable and animal matter, during the process of putrefaction, give off a principle, or give origin to a new compound, which, when applied to the human body, produces the phenomena constituting fever.'[3] Though few questioned this theory in the 1830s and '40s, the subsequent development of bacteriology has shown this explanation to be utterly misconceived. Although a 'germ' theory had been evolved as early as 1546 by the Veronese, Hieronymus Fracator, in his study *De Contagione*, his work was subsequently forgotten, and it was not until the 1870s and '80s that the bacilli of disease were isolated and

1. *San. Rep.* p. 424.
2. John Ferriar, *Medical Histories and Reflections* (1810 edition) I, 279.
3. Southwood Smith, *A Treatise on Fever* (1830) pp. 348-9.

The issues of the Report

identified, and the bacteriological causation of disease irrefutably established.[1] Nevertheless, even before Chadwick's day, the miasmatic theory was modified by some understanding of contagion. Although there might be some difference of opinion as to the *origin* of infection, common observation made it apparent that, given its existence, disease spread from person to person as a result of contact or contiguity. It was not until the second cholera epidemic of 1848 that John Snow's painstaking investigation demonstrated that disease could be transmitted by water.[2] Thus, Chadwick and his medical colleagues were working in utter darkness so far as the propagation of disease was concerned, and they are not to be blamed for basing their conclusions on an entirely erroneous theory. Yet their error was not fatal: miasma might not actually convey germs from a diseased to a healthy body; but in the absence of an exact and accurate knowledge of the means of infection, it was not a bad guide. The eradication of miasma—not entirely achieved even by the mid-twentieth century—was a sound instinct, and could do nothing but good.

While unable to refute the miasmatic theory with a more correct germ theory, Professor Alison in Edinburgh was at pains to point out the limiting implications for social policy of the former school of epidemiological thought. He quarrelled with the assumption that, 'by removing all such causes of vitiation of the atmosphere, contagious fever may be arrested at its source, and thus all the evils resulting from it be prevented'.[3] While not actually opposing measures to remove the sources of miasma, which he described as 'putrescent animal and vegetable matters, and ... excretions from the human body, accumulated and corrupting', he did not believe that these alone would go far to reduce disease. 'There is no reason whatever for believing that the contagious fever which has prevailed more or less extensively in Edinburgh for the last 25 years has any such origins, or can be suppressed by any such measures.'[4] Alison was rather overstating his case here, but his case was a point of principle of some importance, and it raised the second controversy which ought to be reviewed here. In a strongly-worded article printed in the *Local Reports, Scotland*, referring to the 1838 and '39 reports by Arnott, Kay, and Southwood Smith on the East End of London, Alison expressed his surprise 'at finding that the old doctrine of fevers in this climate originating in the effluvia from putrescent animal substances, had been recommended on so respectable authority to the attention of the Poor Law Commissioners'.[5] As Alison pointed out, it was perfectly possible to have smells which did not necessarily produce disease. There was more disease in winter, he said, when the smells were least. Since he was unable to offer any very precise or convincing explanation of the 'generation of fever', he had to content himself—as indeed also had the supporters of the miasmatic theory—with a consideration of pre-disposing factors alone. Among these, it was his view that poverty did most to

---

1. See R. Hare, *Pomp and Pestilence* (1954) pp. 125-8.
2. John Snow, *The Mode of Communication of Cholera* (1849).
3. W. P. Alison, 'Observations on the generation of fever', *Local Reps. Scot.* p. 13.   4. *Ibid.*, p. 13.   5. *Ibid.*, p. 21.

pre-dispose a person to fever. Poverty enfeebled the human frame 'by deficient nourishment, by insufficient protection against cold, by mental depression, by occasional intemperance, and by crowding in small ill-aired rooms'.[1] The experience of earlier epidemics in Ireland, and among Irish immigrants in England and Scotland confirmed this correlation. 'It is not asserted', he wrote elsewhere, 'that destitution is a cause adequate to the production of fever (although in some circumstances I believe it may be such); nor that it is the sole cause of its extension. What we are sure of is, that it is a cause of the *rapid diffusion* of contagious fever, and one of such peculiar power and efficacy, that its existence may always be presumed, when we see fever prevailing in a large community to an unusual extent.'[2] From this reasoning, it followed that Alison's proposals for the reduction of fever gave high priority to 'a more liberal and better-managed provision against the destitution of the unemployed, or partially or wholly disabled poor'.[3] At this time, Alison was fighting on two fronts: the greater part of his energies was directed into the struggle for a reform of the Scottish poor law, and in this effort the correlation between disease and destitution was a valuable ally.

As one of the miasmatists criticised by Alison, Arnott was given the task of replying. With a conscious superiority that ill became an expatriate Scot, he asked how it was that, if Alison's theory was correct, although as a result of the New Poor Law there was virtually no destitution in England, there was nevertheless still a great deal of fever in London.[4] In equating the New Poor Law with the disappearance of destitution, Arnott was clearly deluding himself. But it was not difficult for him to re-establish the connection between dirt which gave off an 'effluvium', and disease; and he concluded, very sensibly, that 'the real difference between Dr Alison and the London reporters is small indeed'. While both parties to the dispute were wrong in failing to know about the habits of bacteria, they were right in drawing attention to certain pre-disposing factors. They quarrelled only because they did not understand the true causes of 'the generation of fever'. Nevertheless, Alison was too powerful a figure to be brushed aside; but his insistence that the answer to the public health problem lay with the improvement of the poor law could hardly be expected to cut much ice with Chadwick so soon after 1834, however apposite it might be for Scotland. Chadwick's method of handling the controversy—to publish Alison's paper together with Arnott's reply in the Scottish volume of *Local Reports*, and to ignore Alison's viewpoint altogether in the *Sanitary Report*—was probably well gauged.

The third controversial issue touched on in the *Sanitary Report* involved Chadwick not so much in taking sides in a debate in which there had been a clear-cut difference of opinion, as in adopting a positive

---

1. W. P. Alison, 'Observations on the generation of fever', *Local Reps. Scot.* p. 25.
2. W. P. Alison, *Observations on the Management of the Poor in Scotland* (Edinburgh 1840) p. 19. 3. *Local Reps. Scot.* p. 14.
4. Neil Arnott, 'Remarks on Dr W. P. Alison's "Observations on the generation of fever" ', *Local Reps. Scot.* pp. 34-9.

stance in a field in which there had previously been a great deal of vague and confused thinking. This concerned the relationship between the birth rate and levels of income. Malthus, undoubtedly the principal figure in this field of study, had warned against the ultimate inevitability of the 'positive check' to population growth of famine and disease, and recommended as preferable the 'preventive check' of birth control by 'moral restraint', by which he meant avoidance of early marriage. In indicating that whereas nature tended to solve the population problem by regulating the death rate, man could solve it better by regulating the birth rate, Malthus focused attention on the determinants of the birth rate for the labouring classes. The two extreme positions in this discussion, which might be labelled 'optimistic' and 'pessimistic', were, on the one hand, that the rise of income, by stimulating people's acquisitive instincts, would lead to a desire to reduce the size of families; and, on the other hand, that greater wealth to the masses of the labouring population would simply be dissipated in larger families.

The 'optimistic' view was perhaps most clearly expressed by William Alison in his *Observations* of 1840, which, in spite of some points of disagreement, must have constituted one of the major influences on Chadwick's mind when compiling the *Sanitary Report*. 'I assert then, with confidence', wrote Alison, 'that all experience teaches, not only that unrelieved suffering is quite ineffectual to teach prudence or moral restraint to the poor, but that it has uniformly the very opposite effect; and, on the other hand, that the natural effect of well-timed and well-directed public charity is not only to relieve suffering, but to *prevent degradation*, and so to support and strengthen the only check on excessive population which either policy or humanity will allow us to contemplate. *It is not the fear of lowering, but the hope of maintaining or bettering their position, which really constitutes that preventive check, and that hope is continually maintained among the poor, by the certainty of assistance in distress, in circumstances where it would otherwise have been extinguished in despair.*'[1] This view has subsequently won fairly widespread acceptance, and, so far as British demographic history is concerned, has been invoked to explain the sharp fall in the birth rate in the late nineteenth century.[2]

In the *Sanitary Report*, Chadwick accepted Alison's views. Assuming a positive correlation between destitution and disease, he stressed that 'in the districts where the mortality is the greatest the births are not only sufficient to replace the numbers removed by death, but to add to the population', adding that 'the ravages of epidemics and other diseases do not diminish but tend to increase the pressure of population'.[3] Farr, with

1. W. P. Alison, *op. cit.* p. 98.
2. *Report of the Royal Commission on Population* (1949) pp. 38-41.
3. *San. Rep.* pp. 369-70. For a discussion of Chadwick's position, and of some of the foreign influences on him, see D. E. C. Eversley, *Social Theories of Fertility and the Malthusian Debate* (Oxford 1959), pp. 200-2. It is only fair to add that the views of Chadwick, Alison and Farr in this question have a respectable ancestry in Britain as well as abroad, not least in the study by Alison's brother, Sir Archibald Alison, *The Principles of Population and their Connection with Human Happiness* (Edinburgh 1840, 2 vols.).

a wider statistical experience, stated even more explicitly: 'Experience has proved that the births almost invariably increase when the mortality increases; and it will be seen that where the mortality is greatest, the births are most numerous, and the population is increasing most rapidly.'[1]

The relevance of this argument was clear enough. Every means of raising the standard of living of the poor would contribute to reducing the birth rate and to diminishing the rate of growth of population. Such a reduction, by allowing the increase of food supplies to overtake that of population, would further raise the standard of living, and so on. It was a powerful argument in support of sanitary reform. Insanitation could be shown to breed disease; disease, in its turn, was the prime source of poverty; and poverty encouraged high birth rates. Defective public health, in short, deprived society of the 'preventive check', and invoked the operation of the 'positive check'.

The Report and sanitary reform

The marked absence of specific recommendations for legislation in the *Sanitary Report* goes some way towards explaining the long delay in securing parliamentary action. As a result of the difficulties with Lord Normanby in 1841, the completion of the *Report* had been delayed, and its publication in mid-July was not well timed. Parliament was rapidly thinning out as the session drew to its conclusion, and Chadwick could scarcely expect the *Report* to have much impact on Members primarily interested in getting out of London for the summer. The *Report*, in any case, had been commissioned by the House of Lords, and was of no immediate concern to the Commons. Thus, although it was politely noticed and complimented by the principal dailies, and was reviewed at some length, as has been shown above, by selected quarterlies, its immediate impact on Parliament and the Press was negligible.

This apparent failure had no doubt been anticipated by Chadwick. Well-timed publication combined with artful publicity might perhaps have produced results, but the enthusiasm stirred by such a nine-days' wonder evaporates as quickly as it is generated and might well have been fatal to the cause. The widespread distribution of copies coupled with assiduous propaganda work laid much firmer foundations. The price of ultimate success was patience and—after three long years of unremitting toil—more hard work.

Thus, apart from inspiring some local authorities immediately to initiate their own sanitary reforms,[2] the publication of the Report led to

---

1. *Fourth Annual Report of the Registrar-General* (1840-41) p. 143.
2. For example, Leicester (see A. Temple Patterson, *Radical Leicester* (Leicester 1954) pp. 336-40), and St Helens (T. C. Barker & J. R. Harris, *A Merseyside Town in the Industrial Revolution: St. Helens, 1750-1900* (Liverpool 1954) pp. 336-40). Glasgow appointed an Inspector of Cleansing with wide powers early in 1843 (J. B. Russell, *Public Health Administration in Glasgow* (ed. A. K. Chalmers, Glasgow 1905) p. 15). The *Report* was even held to have inspired action in Hamburg, while copies were demanded also in Bremen and Berlin (William Lindley, Hamburg, to Chadwick, 25 October 1842).

no action in 1842. In the following year, Peel's government appointed a royal commission to investigate the Health of Towns under the chairmanship of the Duke of Buccleuch. At first sight, this looks like delaying tactics, but to interpret the Buccleuch Commission in this light is to misunderstand the nature and purpose of the *Sanitary Report* which was primarily to make a case for reform. Though the broad directions of that reform were suggested in the *Report*, the full details were not, and Chadwick no doubt hoped, possibly expected, that, as had occurred with the Poor Law reform of 1834, he would be entrusted with the drafting of the legislative details which would follow naturally and inevitably from the publication of the *Report*. Moreover, although the *Sanitary Report* had made an unequivocal case for reform, it also served as a warning to many potential opponents whose principles or interests were threatened by the kind of action proposed by Chadwick. This opposition would expect to be given a hearing before action was taken. Finally, the *Sanitary Report* had touched on some major points of controversy. Chadwick had not hesitated to take sides in these controversies, and whether he was ultimately shown to have been right or not, Parliament in the 1840s might be excused for its reluctance to accept a single opinion, no matter how well informed, and for preferring to subject his *obiter dicta* to wider scrutiny. The role of the Health of Towns Commission was thus to substantiate by more systematic and widespread survey the accuracy of Chadwick's axioms, and to point more precisely to the details of any necessary legislation. In this way, the 1843 Commission was a logical and reasonable extension of Chadwick's work.

Under all these circumstances, Chadwick himself could clearly not expect to be a member of the new commission. Nevertheless, he had every reason to be pleased that its members were to include Arnott, Southwood Smith, Smith of Deanston, Lyon Playfair (the Scottish chemist), two engineers suggested by himself (Captain Denison and Robert Stephenson), and R. A. Slaney of the 1840 Committee. As one of Chadwick's biographers has observed, 'the sanitary cause was safe with these men'.[1] But although Chadwick was not a member of the commission, it was important to him that the Commission's conclusions should support and amplify those of his *Sanitary Report*. And since, unlike the Sanitary enquiry, the Health of Towns Commission would be accessible to opponents of sanitary reform, great effort would be necessary to ensure that the 'right' views triumphed in the Commission's deliberations. In practical terms this meant ensuring an ample flow of suitably-prepared witnesses, influencing the Commissioners themselves with all kinds of propaganda, and offering assistance in the compilation of the reports. The Commissioners published two reports. The first, issued in 1844,[2] was largely the work of Chadwick. Sending a copy to the editor of the *Edinburgh Review*, Chadwick observed that, 'though not named in the Commission, the Commissioners having their own occupations to pursue, it was found that the subject could not be mastered, as an incident to others, and I was compelled to attend to it, write their

---

1. Lewis, p. 85.
2. *First Report of the Health of Towns Commission*, P.P. 1844, XVII.

questions, take the examinations, and prepare their report, so that nearly two-thirds of these volumes are in my hand writing, for which I am to get only posthumous credit, if at all'.[1] Following the publication of the first report, and in time to influence the recommendations of the Commission in its second and final report,[2] Chadwick submitted personally to the Duke of Buccleuch the complete draft of a parliamentary public health Bill, together with a lengthy explanatory memorandum. But the Commissioners contrived to preserve a degree of independence, and their final recommendations did not slavishly reproduce Chadwick's scheme.[3]

For the three years between 1842 and 1845, the main focus of the movement for sanitary reform was inevitably the Health of Towns Commission; but it was by no means the only line of attack. While waiting for the Commission to open its enquiries in 1843, Chadwick had got to work on the subject of urban burials, an aspect of public health which should have been included in the *Sanitary Report*, but which Chadwick omitted in deference to W. A. Mackinnon's committee mentioned below. The danger arising to public health from burial grounds in close proximity to urban dwellings was first exposed by G. A. Walker in 1839.[4] The attack was taken up in the Commons by W. A. Mackinnon who in 1842, quite independently of Chadwick, secured the appointment of a Select Committee to investigate this problem. Unwilling to take action on the recommendations of this committee,[5] Graham, Peel's Home Secretary, delayed action by asking for a fuller report from Chadwick. Chadwick's report of 1843, published as a supplement to the Sanitary Report,[6] was possibly his finest piece of work. It ranged more widely and probed more deeply than any of the previous investigations of this subject. It ruthlessly exposed the evils resulting from the exploitation of pride and sorrow by undertakers, as well as the fearful consequences to health of the mismanagement and overloading of urban burial-grounds. Though it led to a series of acts quite distinct from the main body of public health legislation, the report proved a valuable and timely ally in the main campaign for sanitary reform.

In addition to these official activities, Chadwick played an active part in the public campaign. After 1844, agitation was mainly carried on through the medium of the Health of Towns Association. This Association, in which leading parts were played by Lord Ashley, Dr Southwood Smith, and Lord Normanby, conducted propaganda for sanitary reform

---

1. Chadwick to Macvey Napier, 12 October 1844, B.M. Add. MSS. 34, 624, fol. 629. Chadwick's contribution to the work of the Commission is fully described in Lewis, pp. 86-105.
2. *Second Report of Health of Towns Commission*, P.P. 1845, XVIII.
3. For details of the Commission's recommendations and points of difference from Chadwick's views, see Lewis, pp. 103-5.
4. G. A. Walker, *Gatherings from Grave Yards* (1839).
5. *Report of the Select Committee on Improvement of the Health of Towns on the Effect of Interment in Towns*, P.P. 1842, X.
6. *Supplementary Report on the result of a special inquiry into the practice of interment in towns*, P.P. 1843, XII. A quarto edition in the same format as the *San. Rep.* was also published.

The Report and sanitary reform 69

through two principal channels: the public meeting, and the publication of books and pamphlets. Branches were formed in London and the principal towns of the provinces, and great public meetings were tirelessly addressed by the Association's leaders, amongst whom members of the medical profession were prominent.[1] Between the founding of the Association in 1844 and the successful culmination of its campaign with the passing of the Public Health Act in 1848, there was a great outpouring of literature by members which helped to keep the fires of agitation burning brightly.[2] Although he was active behind the scenes in planning and advising the Association, Chadwick deemed it advisable, perhaps having regard to his official position (he was still nominally Secretary to the Poor Law Commission), as well as to the unpopularity which his association with the New Poor Law had brought him, not to take a public part in the Association's activities. In any case, he was a very poor public speaker.

But for all this frenzy of activities, the movement for sanitary reform, even at its height in the mid-1840s, operated within very narrow limits. The Health of Towns Association, for example, was a feeble instrument beside the Anti-Corn Law League, while the readership of blue books, however bountifully distributed, was never extensive. It remained possible for wide sections of the middle class, the only class outside the aristocracy that mattered politically, to be completely unaware that an agitation to improve public health had indeed been set on foot. Access to this wider public was sought belatedly and rather half-heartedly by one or two novelists. Although social novels take a prominent place in the history of mid-nineteenth-century literature,[3] there were probably few of the many fields of social reform they tackled in which they can be said to have initiated a desire for reform.[4] In the great majority of instances, the reforming movements will be found to have more definitely 'professional' roots. The sanitary movement of the 1840s was no exception. There are few, if any, indications in literature before the 1840s that the shortness and brutishness of much of human life owed anything to a lack of sanitation. The subject makes its entry into the pages of novels only after 1842, and then seldom with the depth of feeling which characterised the wholehearted sympathy of some novelists with, say, factory, prison, or educational reform. However, when John Barton (Mrs Gaskell, *Mary*

---

1. For an account of the Health of Towns Association, see Lewis, pp. 111-23.
2. For example, R. D. Grainger, *Unhealthiness of Towns: its Causes and Remedies* (1845); J. H. Curtis, *Advice on the Care of Health . . . and the necessity for the Adoption of Public Sanatory Measures* (1845); Hector Gavin, *Sanitary Ramblings* (1846); W. A. Guy, *On the Health of Towns* (1846); G. F. Ellerman, *Sanitary Reform and Agricultural Improvement* (1846); G. G. Bird, *Observations on Civic Malaria and the Health of Towns* (1848).
3. See Kathleen Tillotson, *Novels of the Eighteen-Forties* (1954) pp. 73-91; and Louis Cazamian, *Le Roman Social en Angleterre, 1830-1850* (Paris 1904).
4. An interesting study of the relation of the work of one social novelist to a particular reform movement has been made recently by Philip Collins in his *Dickens and Crime* (1961).

Barton, 1848) visited the Davenports, he threaded his way down Berry Street, a street which might have been taken straight from the pages of the *Sanitary Report*.[1] Carlyle was less concerned with sanitation than he was with the iniquities of factory employment and *laissez-faire*, and although Chadwick endeavoured to interest him in the subject,[2] his powerful influence was scarcely inclined in this direction. Not surprisingly, Chadwick set greatest store by Dickens; but although Dickens devoted some time and energy to public health propaganda later, in the 1850s and '60s,[3] the sanitary idea failed to fire his imagination in the vital years of the 1840s. The public health movement received some help from the world of literature, but it was never extensive, and came too late to be effective in the early years of the campaign.

After the presentation of the Second Report of the Health of Towns Commission in 1845, events conspired to delay the enactment of a measure based on its recommendations for a further three years. Neither Peel's government, which was in office when the Commission reported, nor Russell's which succeeded it in 1846, showed marked enthusiasm for any kind of a public health measure, let alone anything as vigorous as that contemplated by Chadwick; and both, to Chadwick's disgust, dabbled with minor bills which, if passed, would certainly have stood in the way of effective legislation for many more years. As a writer in the *Westminster* about this time observed, 'If the Reform Bill epoch has been justly called one of action without reflection, the times on which we have now entered are certainly quite as remarkable for inquiry without results.'[4] The Irish famine and the question of the corn laws took overwhelming precedence during 1845 and 1846. At last, in 1847, Lord Morpeth introduced a Public Health Bill, only to have it thrown out by the Commons. For a third time, enquiries into sanitary conditions—back in London this time—were set on foot by a government apprehensive of the eastwards march of a new cholera epidemic across Asia and Europe, anxious at last to destroy the old metropolitan commissions of sewers, but still hesitant to introduce a measure drastic enough to be effective. Chadwick and Southwood Smith, as Commissioners, both joined in this seemingly unnecessary re-writing of what had now long been known of the shortcomings of metropolitan sewerage.[5] This enquiry bore immediate fruit in the creation in 1847 of the Metropolitan

---

1. 1901 edition, p. 46.
2. See above, p. 54.
3. Apart from the well-known preface to the 1858 edition of *Oliver Twist*, most of Dickens's writing on public health matters is to be found in his periodicals, particularly *All the Year Round*, IV (1860) 29-31; V (1861) 390-4, 423-7, 453-6, 470-3, 486-9; VI (1861-2) 137-40, 150-3; XIV (1865) 372-6. (I am indebted to Mr Phillip Collins for these and other references.) Dickens also supported the public health movement in the 1850s by public speaking. (K. J. Fielding (ed.), *The Speeches of Charles Dickens* (Oxford 1960) pp. 127-32.)
4. 'The working classes of Sheffield', *Westminster Review*, XL (1843) 460.
5. *First, Second and Third Reports of Commissioners appointed to inquire whether any and what special means may be requisite for the improvement of the health of the metropolis*, P.P. 1847-8, XXXII.

Commission of Sewers,[1] the precursor of the Metropolitan Board of Works, and through that board, of the London County Council, which gave London, outside the City walls, for the first time an administrative body with powers to pursue a range of public services. Early in the following year Lord Morpeth introduced a revised Public Health Bill which, after a prolonged struggle, but powerfully aided by the approach of cholera, passed into law as the Public Health Act of 1848.

The 1848 Act was thus the culmination of a struggle which had been initiated ten years earlier by the publication of the brief reports by Southwood Smith, Arnott, and Kay in the fourth report of the Poor Law Commission, and in the course of which the publication of Chadwick's *Sanitary Report* in 1842 had been a major milestone. However, much water had flowed under the bridge between 1842 and 1848, and the complex and hotly-debated provisions of the Act were a far cry from the few tentative suggestions put forward by Chadwick in the closing pages of the *Sanitary Report*. Some of the *Sanitary Report*'s main recommendations were absent from the Act. There was no comprehensive national system of 'sanitary', 'sewage', or public health commissions. In their place were local public health boards (which, in incorporated towns, were to be the town councils), which were only to be compulsory in places where the death rate exceeded the arbitrary figure of 23 per 1,000[2]; elsewhere, local boards could only be established upon petition from not less than one-tenth of the ratepayers. Thus, the system of local boards could never hope to be more than partial. Nor were the local boards to be *required* to appoint medical officers; they were merely *permitted* to do so if they wished. Again, the local boards were given powers to undertake any necessary cleansing, paving, sewerage, and water supply, but were not *required* to provide these services. However— an important gain—no new houses were to be built in an area within the jurisdiction of a local board without suitable provision for sewage disposal. Although the *Sanitary Report* had remained tactfully silent on the question of central supervision, Chadwick's faith in the efficiency of unaided local authorities was so slight that a central department with adequate supervisory powers, on the lines of the Poor Law Commission of 1834, had always been the central feature of his scheme. This the Act of 1848 created. But with the exception of those places having high death rates, the new central Board was not endowed with what Chadwick considered would be essential powers of initiating local action. In places already possessing a public health authority—one of the old type of 'improvement', 'police', or 'sewage' commissions (out of 471 towns with more than 5,000 inhabitants, only 175 possessed such statutory authorities)—the central board's powers were limited to approving or disapproving the appointment or dismissal of officials, though there was

---

1. The new Metropolitan Commission of Sewers of 1847 should not be confused with the seven metropolitan commissions of sewers which it replaced. See Lewis, pp. 156-7.
2. This figure, well above the national average for this time, is even more arbitrary than it appears at first sight, since it takes no account of the varying age-compositions of the populations of different places.

scope for voluntary co-operation between local and central authorities. Nevertheless, there was most scope for public health work in those places possessing neither municipal governments nor an existing sewage commission; and where, often as a consequence of this want, death rates exceeded the statutory 23 per 1,000, the central board was endowed with fairly extensive powers.

As has been shown above,[1] one of Chadwick's first actions after beginning work on the sanitary enquiry had been to secure power to extend his investigations to Scotland. The closing paragraph in the *Sanitary Report* was devoted to insisting on the inclusion of Scotland in the benefits of any forthcoming public health legislation. Yet, in the event, the provisions of the 1848 act were not extended to Scotland. Why? In the first place, since the act of 1837 had not extended the civil registration of births and deaths to Scotland, there was no means of ascertaining officially in which places the death rate exceeded 23 per 1,000, and which could, therefore, be required by the central board to set up a local board. Secondly, and more important, the medical profession in Edinburgh was sceptical of the advantages that might accrue from the activities of non-medical bureaucratic bodies. They shared a general Scottish reluctance to submit themselves voluntarily to additional supervision from London, suggesting that, instead of submitting any future Scottish local health authorities to the jurisdiction of the central (London) Health Board, the Poor Law Board of Supervision in Edinburgh (the Scottish equivalent of the London Poor Law Commission which had been created by the Scottish Poor Law Act of 1845) was the most suitable Scottish central authority for public health matters. Thirdly, however, the committee which spoke for the Scottish medical profession in this issue was under the chairmanship of Professor W. P. Alison, and he was not slow to point out that 'although they [the committee] have a high respect for the individual members of the General Board of Health in London, yet the confident expression of opinion which those gentlemen have officially made on several important questions touching the diffusion of epidemic diseases, which the committee regard as very difficult and doubtful—and on which they know that some of the most experienced practitioners in Scotland hold a very different opinion—have by no means tended to increase their expectation of the efficacy of measures, applicable to Scotland, for restraining the diffusion of epidemics, which may proceed from that source'. Thus, the debate on the spread of disease, which had been conducted decorously enough between Alison and Arnott in the pages of the *Local Reports, Scotland* of the *Sanitary Report*, became one of the means of delaying a public health act for Scotland.[2] A Public Health (Scotland) Bill was rejected in 1849, and it was not until 1867 that a Public Health (Scot-

---

1. p. 47.
2. *First* and *Second Reports by the Committee of the Royal College of Physicians appointed to consider any bills that may be brought into Parliament for the improvement of the Health of Towns and the applicability of such measures to Scotland* (Edinburgh 1849). The quotation is from p. 18 of the *Second Report*.

land) Act finally gave the Board of Supervision general supervisory powers in relation to public health in Scotland.[1]

The new Central Board of Health set up by the 1848 Act was to have three members. Chadwick, Southwood Smith, and Lord Ashley were appointed. The story of the Board's activities and tribulations has been well told elsewhere and need not be repeated here. Its life was short: the Act had set an initial term of five years, and in 1854 the Board, for all practical purposes, ceased to exist. But if the demise of the Board terminated Chadwick's official career, it did not bring an end to either local activity in the public health field, or to central government control. Public health work was passed to a newly-created committee of the Privy Council, where, under John Simon as Medical Officer, the foundations of the modern public health service were patiently and carefully laid.

The Act of 1848 constituted a tentative and uncertain start to government action in a major field. The brevity of the life of the Board of Health bears witness to its ineffectiveness in the short run. Nevertheless, it had put a foot through a door which had hitherto defied all attempts at opening, and although the detailed administrative arrangements it laid down were scrapped within half a dozen years, its principle of state responsibility was not discarded. It was this principle which the *Sanitary Report* had sought to establish.

---

1. J. H. F. Brotherston, *Observations on the Early Public Health Movement in Scotland* (1952) pp. 93-6.

REPORT

TO

HER MAJESTY'S PRINCIPAL SECRETARY OF STATE
FOR THE HOME DEPARTMENT,

FROM THE

POOR LAW COMMISSIONERS,

ON AN INQUIRY INTO THE

SANITARY CONDITION

OF THE

LABOURING POPULATION OF GREAT BRITAIN;

WITH

APPENDICES.

Presented to both Houses of Parliament, by Command of Her Majesty,
July 1842.

LONDON:
PRINTED BY W. CLOWES AND SONS, STAMFORD STREET,
FOR HER MAJESTY'S STATIONERY OFFICE.

1842.

REPORT

ON THE

SANITARY CONDITION OF THE LABOURING POPULATION

AND ON

THE MEANS OF ITS IMPROVEMENT

London, May 1842.

GENTLEMEN,—Since my special attention was directed to the inquiry as to the chief removable circumstances affecting the health of the poorer classes of the population, I have availed myself of every opportunity to collect information respecting them. In company with Dr. Arnott I visited Edinburgh and Glasgow, and inspected those residences that were pointed out by the local authorities as the chief seats of disease. I also visited Dumfries. An inspection of similar districts in Spitalfields, Manchester, Leeds, and Macclesfield, and inquiries formerly made under the Commission of Poor Law Inquiry[1], and inspections of the condition of the residences of the poorer classes in parts of Berkshire, Sussex, and Hertfordshire[2], had supplied me with means of comparison. Abandoning any inquiries as to remedies, strictly so called, or the treatment of diseases after their appearance, I have directed the examinations of witnesses and the reports of medical officers chiefly to collect information of the best means available as preventives of the evils in question. On the documentary evidence of the medical officers, and on the examinations of witnesses, aided by personal inspections, I have the honour to report as follows:—

Partial descriptions of the condition of the labouring classes, in respect to their residences and the habits which influence their health, afford but a faint conception of the evils which are the subject of inquiry. If only particular instances, or some groups of individual cases be adduced, the erroneous impression might be created that they were cases of comparatively infrequent occurrence. But the following tabular return made up from the registration of the causes of death in England and Wales, which is the most complete yet attained,[3] will give a suffi-

---

1. As Assistant Commissioner, and later Commissioner on the Poor Law Commission, 1833-4.
2. *Extracts from the information received by His Majesty's Commissioners as to the administration and operation of the Poor Laws* (1833); Edwin Chadwick, 'London and Berkshire', pp. 201-339.
3. This table is the work of William Farr, Compiler of Abstracts in the Registrar-General's office. It was originally published as App. 1 to the *First Report of the Registrar-General* (1839).

The Sanitary Report: Summary

ciently correct conception of the extent of the evils in question, when illustrated by the evidence of eye-witnesses, the medical officers whose duty it has been to attend on the spot and alleviate them. The table comprehends the abstract of the returns of the deaths from the chief diseases, which the medical officers consider to be the most powerfully

COUNTIES	Number of Deaths during the Year ended 31st December, 1838, from									Total Deaths from the four preceding Classes of Diseases	Proportion of Deaths from the preceding Causes in every 1,000 of the Population, 1841	Proportion of Deaths from all Causes of Mortality in every 1,000 of the Population, 1841
	1 Epidemic, Endemic, and Contagious Diseases				2 Diseases of Respiratory Organs		3 Diseases of Brain, Nerves, and Senses	4 Diseases of Digestive Organs	All other Classes			
	Fever: Typhus, Scarlatina	Small-pox	Measles	Hooping Cough	Consumption	Pneumonia						
ENGLAND												
Bedford	155	75	40	66	457	97	304	131	57	1,382	13	22
Berks	204	288	21	86	739	231	467	201	162	2,399	15	25
Bucks	256	85	61	27	575	131	348	152	61	1,696	11	19
Cambridge	231	136	57	90	686	156	318	189	70	1,933	12	21
Chester	592	279	178	87	1,742	366	1,442	421	345	5,452	14	21
Cornwall	443	135	168	491	1,270	342	631	228	124	3,832	11	18
Cumberland	165	188	11	83	562	75	278	169	142	1,673	9	21
Derby	394	77	79	71	905	200	777	268	205	2,976	11	18
Devon	615	460	287	312	1,649	564	1,237	471	298	5,893	11	18
Dorset	137	255	80	58	571	146	380	159	106	1,892	11	19
Durham	347	316	139	304	1,007	362	1,138	274	207	4,094	13	21
Essex	417	460	83	163	1,250	276	782	268	234	3,933	11	19
Gloucester	352	457	440	244	1,395	578	1,142	510	476	5,594	13	20
Hereford	84	83	17	36	333	56	238	62	57	966	8	18
Hertford	160	116	45	48	620	107	453	155	90	1,794	11	20
Huntingdon	61	18	1	17	216	45	140	72	42	612	10	18

The Sanitary Report: Summary

influenced by the physical circumstances under which the population is placed—as the external and internal condition of their dwellings, drainage, and ventilation.

The registration of the causes of death for the year 1838 is selected, as that was the year when the report was made on the sanitary condition of

Kent	955	510	169	214	1,701	564	526	1,650	651	6,940	13	21
Lancaster	2,866	1,628	898	910	8,124	2,660	1,916	7,457	3,231	29,690	18	25
Leicester	273	98	17	70	941	243	154	668	314	2,778	13	21
Lincoln	370	138	29	88	874	248	242	1,090	358	3,437	9	17
Middlesex	4,422	3,359	487	1,749	6,220	3,097	2,334	6,643	2,492	30,803	20	27
Monmouth	328	321	49	91	481	183	78	550	100	2,181	16	24
Norfolk	515	126	63	109	1,388	325	281	793	395	3,995	10	19
Northampton	348	148	36	36	762	192	124	503	212	2,361	12	21
Northumberland	366	149	46	113	715	287	240	709	388	3,013	12	21
Nottingham	222	73	18	80	911	225	201	901	287	2,918	12	20
Oxford	222	81	51	59	655	108	152	389	180	1,897	12	21
Rutland	11	2	—	13	64	14	8	56	28	196	9	17
Salop	213	154	112	138	995	242	168	550	284	2,856	12	21
Somerset	560	710	401	46	1,446	426	373	982	473	5,417	12	21
Southampton	454	164	78	148	1,222	338	331	881	372	3,988	17	19
Stafford	610	249	182	268	1,809	539	419	1,251	597	5,924	12	18
Suffolk	480	325	53	158	1,306	315	184	538	275	3,634	11	20
Surrey	1,348	814	177	565	2,196	978	700	2,325	763	9,866	11	25
Sussex	391	80	159	88	1,047	222	181	863	295	3,326	13	18
Warwick	454	415	153	164	1,495	678	361	978	638	5,336	12	20
Westmoreland	41	40	6	41	248	33	44	154	46	653	12	21
Wilts	246	259	263	140	869	268	212	606	241	3,104	16	20
Worcester	381	305	122	258	990	353	235	645	446	3,735	13	29
York, E.R.	194	92	167	149	725	194	176	1,009	251	2,957	9	21
„ N.R.	123	28	69	114	550	102	135	553	187	1,861	14	17
„ W.R.	1,298	993	799	507	4,253	1,202	848	4,374	1,494	15,768	9	21
WALES												
North	660	575	4	210	1,227	102	223	1,311	198	4,510	13	18
South	1,613	1,004	199	398	1,834	129	277	1,200	380	7,034	14	21
Total, 1838	24,577	16,268	6,514	9,107	59,025	17,999	13,799	49,704	19,306	216,299	14	22
Total, 1839	25,991	9,131	10,937	8,165	59,559	18,151	12,855	49,215	20,767	214,771	14	21

the labouring population in the metropolis,[1] which has served as the foundation of the extended inquiry.

There are no returns, and no adequate data for returns, to show the proportion in which deaths from the several causes above specified occur amongst the population of Scotland,[2] but there is evidence to which reference will subsequently be made tending to prove that the mortality from fever is greater in Glasgow, Edinburgh, and Dundee than in the most crowded towns in England.

The registered mortality from all specified diseases in England and Wales was, during the year 1838, 282,940, or 18 per thousand of the population. These deaths are exclusive of the deaths from old age, which amounted to 35,564, and the deaths from violence, which amounted to 12,055. The deaths from causes not specified were 11,970. The total amount of deaths was 342,529 for that year. In the year following the total deaths were 338,979, of which the registered deaths from old age were 35,063, and the deaths from violence 11,980. The proportion of deaths for the whole population was 21 per thousand.

It appears that fever, after its ravages amongst the infant population, falls with the greatest intensity on the adult population in the vigour of life.[3] The periods at which the ravages of the other diseases, consumption, small-pox, and measles take place, are sufficiently well known. The proportions in which the diseases have prevailed in the several counties will be found deserving of peculiar attention.

A conception may be formed of the aggregate effects of the several causes of mortality from the fact, that of the deaths caused during one year in England and Wales by epidemic, endemic, and contagious diseases, including fever, typhus, and scarlatina, amounting to 56,461, the great proportion of which are proved to be preventible, it may be said that the effect is as if the whole county of Westmoreland, now containing 56,469 souls, or the whole county of Huntingdonshire, or any other equivalent district, were entirely depopulated annually, and were only occupied again by the growth of a new and feeble population living under the fears of a similar visitation. The annual slaughter in England and Wales from preventible causes of typhus which attacks persons in the vigour of life, appears to be double the amount of what was suffered by the Allied Armies in the battle of Waterloo.[4] It will be shown that

---

1. Neil Arnott & James P. Kay, 'Report on the prevalence of certain physical causes of fever in the Metropolis, which might be removed by proper sanatory measures', App. A, Supplement 1, to *Fourth Annual Report of the Poor Law Commission* (1838), pp. 103-29.
2. Returns of the Registrar-General for Scotland were first published in 1855.
3. Robert Cowan's statistics of fever (typhus) in Glasgow showed that the heaviest incidence of the disease was between the ages of 15 and 25. (R. Cowan, 'Vital statistics of Glasgow', *J.R.S.S.*, III (1840), 276.)
4. British killed at Waterloo amounted to 2,136. Allied killed and wounded amounted to 36,590, and if allied casualties bore the same proportion to killed as did the British, then the total allied killed must have been in the region of 7,300. (W. B. Hodge, 'On the mortality arising from military operations', *J.R.S.S.*, XIX (1856), 267.)

diseases such as those which now prevail on land, did within the experience of persons still living, formerly prevail to a greater extent at sea, and have since been prevented by sanitary regulations; and that when they did so prevail in ships of war, the deaths from them were more than double in amount of the deaths in battle. But the number of persons who die is to be taken also as the indication of the much greater number of persons who fall sick, and who, although they escape, are subjected to the suffering and loss occasioned by attacks of disease. Thus it was found on the original inquiry in the metropolis, that the deaths from fever amounted to 1 in 10 of the number attacked. If this proportion held equally throughout the country, then a quarter of a million of persons will have been subjected to loss and suffering from an attack of fever during the year; and in so far as the proportions of attacks to deaths is diminished, so it appears from the reports is the intensity and suffering from the disease generally increased. It appears that the extremes of mortality at the Small-pox Hospital, in London, amongst those attacked, have been 15 per cent. and 42 per cent. But if, according to other statements, the average mortality be taken at 1 in 5, or 20 per cent., the number of persons attacked in England and Wales during the year of the return, must amount to upwards of 16,000 persons killed, and more than 80,000 persons subjected to the sufferings of disease, including, in the case of the labouring classes, the loss of labour and long-continued debility; and in respect to all classes, often permanent disfigurement, and occasionally the loss of sight.

In a subsequent part of this report, evidence will be adduced to show in what proportion these causes of death fall upon the poorer classes as compared with the other classes of society inhabiting the same towns or districts, and in what proportions the deaths fall amongst persons of the same class inhabiting districts differently situated.

The first extracts present the subjects of the inquiry in their general condition under the operation of several causes, yet almost all will be found to point to one particular, namely, atmospheric impurity, occasioned by means within the control of legislation, as the main cause of the ravages of epidemic, endemic, and contagious diseases among the community, and as aggravating most other diseases. The subsequent extracts from the sanitary reports from different places will show that the impurity and its evil consequences are greater or less in different places, according as there is more or less sufficient drainage of houses, streets, roads, and land, combined with more or less sufficient means of cleansing and removing solid refuse and impurities, by available supplies of water for the purpose. Then will follow the description of the effects of overcrowding the places of work and dwellings, including the effects of the defective ventilation of dwelling-houses, and of places of work where there are fumes or dust produced. To these will be added the information collected as to the good or evil moral habits promoted by the nature of the residence. These will form so many successive sections of the report, and will be followed by information in respect to the means available for the prevention of the evils described, and an exposition of the present state of the law for the protection of the public health, and of modifications apparently requisite to secure the desired results.

I
GENERAL CONDITION OF THE RESIDENCES OF THE LABOURING CLASSES WHERE DISEASE IS FOUND TO BE THE MOST PREVALENT

The following extracts will serve to show, in the language chiefly of eye-witnesses, the varied forms in which disease attendant on removable circumstances appears from one end of the island to the other amidst the population of rural villages, and of the smaller towns, as well as amidst the population of the commercial cities and the most thronged of the manufacturing districts—in which last pestilence is frequently supposed to have its chief and almost exclusive residence.

Commencing with the reports on the sanitary condition of the population in Cornwall and Devon, *Mr. Gilbert*, when acting as Assistant Commissioner for those counties, reports, that he found the open drains and sewers the most prominent cause of malaria. He gives the following as an instance of the common condition of the dwellings of the labouring classes in Devon, where it will be observed that the registered deaths from the four classes of disease amounted in one year to 5893 cases.

'In Tiverton there is a large district, from which I find numerous applications were made for relief to the Board of Guardians, in consequence of illness from fever. The expense in procuring the necessary attention and care, and the diet and comforts recommended by the medical officer, were in each case very high, and particularly attracted my attention.

'I requested the medical officer to accompany me through the district, and with him, and afterwards by myself, I visited the district, and examined the cottages and families living there. The land is nearly on a level with the water, the ground is marshy, and the sewers all open. Before reaching the district, I was assailed by a most disagreeable smell; and it was clear to the sense that the air was full of most injurious malaria. The inhabitants, easily distinguishable from the inhabitants of the other parts of the town, had all a sickly, miserable appearance. The open drains in some cases ran immediately before the doors of the houses, and some of the houses were surrounded by wide open drains, full of all the animal and vegetable refuse not only of the houses in that part, but of those in other parts of Tiverton. In many of the houses, persons were confined with fever and different diseases, and all I talked to either were ill or had been so: and the whole community presented a melancholy spectacle of disease and misery.

'Attempts have been made on various occasions by the local authorities to correct this state of things by compelling the occupants of the houses to remove nuisances, and to have the drains covered; but they find that in the present state of the law their powers are not sufficient, and the evil continues and is likely so to do, unless the legislature affords some redress in the nature of sanitary powers. Independently of this nuisance, Tiverton would be considered a fine healthy town, situate as it is on the slope of a hill, with a swift river running at its foot.

'It is not these unfortunate creatures only who choose this centre of disease for their living-place who are affected; but the whole town is more or less deteriorated by its vicinity to this pestilential mass, where the generation of those elements of disease and death is constantly going on.

'Another cause of disease is to be found in the state of the cottages. Many are built on the ground without flooring, or against a damp hill. Some have

I. General Condition of the Residences

neither windows nor doors sufficient to keep out the weather, or to let in the rays of the sun, or supply the means of ventilation; and in others the roof is so constructed or so worn as not to be weather tight. The thatch roof frequently is saturated with wet, rotten, and in a state of decay, giving out malaria, as other decaying vegetable matter.'[1]

The report of *Dr. Barham*, on the sanitary condition of the town of Truro, gives instances of the condition of the town population in that part of the country. He states:

'The perfect immunity from deaths by *febrile* and *acute* diseases, enjoyed by Lemon-street during the long period of three years and a half, is a strong testimony to the value of the breadth of its roadway, the openness of its site, and the judicious construction of the houses; for it has to contend with a great deficiency of sewerage. Fairmantle and Daniell-streets are modern, and are occupied by small traders, and by decent artisans and labourers; the *former* lies rather low, the *latter* is on a considerable elevation; both are fairly drained, and are healthy. Charles, Calenick, and Kenwyn-streets present some of the worst specimens of defective arrangement, rendered worse still by the recklessness of the very poor, which can be met with in Truro. The amount of *pauper sickness* is considerable, the deaths not few. The two latter streets are, in the greater part of their length, but little raised above high-water mark. Passing into *St. Mary's* parish, the proportion of sickness and even of deaths in Castle-street and Castle-hill is, to their extent and population, as great, perhaps, as that of any part of Truro; yet their situation is elevated and favourable. There is, however, no mystery in the causation. Ill-constructed houses, many of them old, with decomposing refuse close upon their doors and windows, open drains bringing the oozings of pigsties and other filth to stagnate at the foot of a wall, between which and the entrances to a row of small dwellings there is only a very narrow passage; such are a few of the sources of disease which the breeze of the hill cannot always dissipate. Similar causes have produced like effects in the courts adjacent to Pyder-street, to the High Cross, and to St. Clement's-streets, and in Bodmin-street and Good-wives'-lane, the situations being all more or less confined. The benefits, on the other hand, derived from open rows, and cottages of a better construction are evidenced in Boscawen and Paul's-row, and St. Clements'-terrace, which are well ventilated, and consequently suffer less from the scanty provision of drains and other conveniences.

'A detailed account of the public sewers is given in the Appendix, and is believed to be nearly, if not quite, complete. Many of these are of recent date, and owe their existence to the alarm excited when the cholera was near at hand. Some of them are made to discharge themselves into the rivers; and such of these as are swept by a stream of water are unobjectionable in themselves. Several others stop short of this desirable termination, and, after collecting filth from various localities, deposit a portion in catchpits here and there, and finally open on the surface, frequently in some street or lane, where a neglected deposit of a mixed animal and vegetable nature is allowed to become a probable source of annoyance or mischief. Much of this incompleteness may be removed (as regards the main lines of sewerage) at no great expense; and it is said to be the intention of the commissioners of improvement to remedy the deficiency, when they are free from the debt with which they are now encumbered. Many of the smaller sewers are, however, much too narrow to be

---

1. *Local Reps. E. & W.*, pp. 8-9. W. J. Gilbert, an Assistant Poor Law Commissioner, was transferred from Devon and Cornwall to Staffordshire before the completion of the *Sanitary Report*.

effective, and some of them are no better than covered drains. But the greatest evils in this department are unquestionably those which spring from the ignorance, cupidity, or negligence of landlords. It is useless to have a good sewer carried through the centre of a street, if the houses at the sides, and still more those situated in courts and lanes adjoining, have no communicating drains; and it is worse than useless to furnish these backlets with the mere semblance of drains—gutters forming pits here and there—then as they approach the street, perhaps slightly covered so as to produce obstruction more frequently than protection, a concentrated solution of all sorts of decomposing refuse being allowed to soak through and thoroughly impregnate the walls and ground adjoining. One or more of these mischievous conditions is to be found in connexion with a large proportion of the older houses in Truro, excepting the better class; and in many of the courts and backlets all these evils are in full operation. I have repeatedly noticed in the country that the occurrence of fever has been connected with *near proximity to even a small amount of decomposing organic matter*; and it is certain that all measures for effecting improvement in the sewerage of streets, the supply of water, and ventilation, may be rendered nearly inoperative for the obviating of the causes of disease, if a little nidus of morbific effluvia be permitted to remain in almost every corner of the confined court; where the poor man opens his narrow habitation in the hope of refreshing it with the breeze of summer, but gets instead a mixture of gases from reeking dunghills, or, what is worse, because more insidious, from a soil which has become impregnated with organic matters imbibed long before; and now, though, perhaps, to all appearance dry and clean, emitting the poisonous vapour in its most pernicious state. Nothing short of the placing in proper hands a peremptory authority for the removal of what is hurtful, and the supply of what is defective, making the exercise of that authority a duty, can remedy the existing evils.

'The houses occupied by the lower orders do not often exceed two stories in height, and it is rare to find families occupying less than two rooms. The more recent additions to the town—I speak of residences of the humbler class—have mainly consisted of rows of moderate cottages, having, the majority of them, gardens in front, and usually containing four rooms, commonly occupied by a single family. Some instances have, however, occurred of the building of a very inferior class of dwellings, which will be hereafter pointed out.

'No interments now take place in the town, the present burying-ground being at the distance of a third of a mile to the north of the church. The slaughter-houses are all, or nearly all, situated in populous parts, and occasionally constitute a decided nuisance. No manufactories exist which can be looked upon as prejudicial from any effluvia to which they give rise. The gas-works and smelting-houses are so placed that no mischievous effects can fairly be attributed to them.'[1]

The state of the dwellings of many of the agricultural labourers in Dorset, where the deaths from the four classes of disease bear a similar proportion to those in Devon, is described in the return of *Mr. John Fox*, the medical officer of the Cerne union, who, remarking upon some cases of disease among the poor whom he had attended, says:

'These cases (of diarrhœa and common fever) occurred in a house (formerly a poor-house) occupied by nearly 50 persons on the ground-floor; the rooms are neither boarded nor paved, and generally damp; some of them are occupied by two families. The up-stairs rooms are small and low, and separated from each other by boards only. Eleven persons slept in one room. The house

---

1. *Local Reps. E. & W.*, pp. 23, 17-19.

I. General Condition of the Residences 83

stands in a valley between two hills, very little above the level of the river, which occasionally overflows its banks, and within a few yards of it. There is generally an accumulation of filth of every description in a gutter running about two feet from its front, and a large cesspool within a few feet behind. The winter stock of potatoes was kept in some of the day-rooms, and generally put away in a wet state. The premises had not been white-limed during three years; in addition to this state of things, the poor were badly fed, badly clothed, and many of them habitually dirty, and consequently typhus, synochus, or diarrhœa, constantly prevailed. No house-rent was paid by the occupants. Many, under more favourable circumstances, were clean and tidy, and if their wages were sufficient to enable them to rent a decent cottage, I have no doubt they would soon regain their lost spirit of cleanliness. In this same parish I have often seen the springs bursting through the *mud* floor of some of the cottages, and little channels cut from the centre under the doorways to carry off the water, whilst the door has been removed from its hinges for the children to put their feet on whilst employed in making buttons. Is it surprising that fever and scrofula in all its forms prevail under such circumstances?

'It is somewhat singular that seven cases of typhus occurred in one village heretofore famed for the health and general cleanliness of its inhabitants and cottages. The first five cases occurred in one family, in a detached house on high and dry ground, and free from accumulations of vegetable or animal matter. The cottage was originally built for a school-room, and consists of one room only, about 18 feet by 10, and 9 high. About one-third part was partitioned off by boards reaching to within three feet of the roof, and in this small space were three beds, in which six persons slept; had there been two bedrooms attached to this one day-room, these cases of typhus would not have occurred. The fatal case of typhus occurred in a very small village, containing about sixty inhabitants, and from its locality it appears favourable to the production of typhus, synochus, and acute rheumatism. It stands between two hills, with a river running through it, and is occasionally flooded. It has extensive water meadows both above and below, and a farm-yard in the centre, where there is always a large quantity of vegetable matter undergoing decomposition. Most of the cases of synochus occurred under circumstances favourable to its production. Most of the cottages being of the worst description, some mere mud hovels, and situated in low and damp places with cesspools or accumulations of filth close to the doors. The *mud floors* of many are much below the level of the road, and in wet seasons are little better than so much clay. The following shocking case occurred in my practice. In a family consisting of six persons, two had fever; the mud floor of their cottage was at least one foot below the lane; it consisted of *one* small room only, in the centre of which stood a foot-ladder reaching to the edge of a platform which extended over nearly one-half of the room, and upon which were placed two beds, with space between them for one person only to stand, whilst the outside of each touched the thatch. The head of one of these beds stood within six inches of the edge of the platform, and in this bed one of my unfortunate patients, a boy about 11 years old, was sleeping with his mother, and in a fit of delirium jumped over the head of his bed and fell to the ground below, a height of about seven feet. The injury to the head and spine was so serious that he lived a few hours only after the accident. In a cottage fit for the residence of a human being this could not have occurred. In many of the cottages, also, where synochus prevailed, the beds stood on the ground-floor, which was damp three parts of the years; scarcely one had a fireplace in the bed-room, and one had a single small pane of glass stuck in the mud wall as its only window, with a large heap of wet and dirty potatoes in one corner. Persons

I. General Condition of the Residences

living in such cottages are generally very poor, very dirty, and usually in rags, living almost wholly on bread and potatoes, scarcely ever tasting animal food, and consequently highly susceptible of disease and very unable to contend with it. I am quite sure if such persons were placed in good, comfortable, clean cottages, the improvement in themselves and children would soon be visible, and the exceptions would only be found in a few of the poorest and most wretched, who perhaps had been born in a mud hovel, and had lived in one the first 30 years of their lives.

'In my district I do not think there is *one* cottage to be found consisting of a day-room, three bed-rooms, scullery, pantry, and convenient receptacles for refuse and for fuel in the occupation of a labourer, but there are many consisting of a day-room and two bed-rooms, constructed with a due regard to ventilation and warmth, pantry, and fuel house, with a small garden and pig-sty adjoining, and the labourers occupying such cottages, generally speaking, are far superior to others less advantageously situated. Their persons and cottages are always neater and cleaner, they are less disposed to frequent the beer-houses or to engage in poaching, whilst their children are generally sent daily to some school, in many instances chiefly supported by the clergyman of the parish. As a corroboration of my opinion, I need only state that I am frequently employed by the labourers in the good cottages to attend their wives during their confinement, and generally receive my guinea before I leave the house, whilst the labourer less favourably situated invariably applies to his parish for medical relief under such circumstances. I think there cannot be a doubt if the whole of the wretched hovels were converted into good cottages, with a strict attention to warmth, ventilation, and drainage, and a receptacle for filth of every kind placed at a proper distance, it would not only improve the health of the poor by removing a most prolific source of disease, and thereby most sensibly diminish the rates, but I am convinced it would also tend most materially to raise the moral character of the poor man, and render him less susceptible to the allurements of the idle and wicked.'

The tenor of much information respecting the condition of many of the labouring classes in Somerset, where the deaths from the four classes of disease were still higher than in the two other counties, and amounted during the one year to 5417, is exhibited in the sanitary report of *Mr. James Gane*, the medical officer of the Axbridge union, who states that:

'The situation of this district where the diseases herein mentioned prevail, is a perfect flat called the South Marsh, in the main road between Bristol and Bridgewater. There are numerous dykes or ditches for the purpose of drainage. The cottages of the poor are mostly of a bad description, frequently mud wall, and often situated close to the dykes, where the water for the most part is in a state of stagnation. Oftentimes not more than one room for the whole family; sometimes two; one above the other; with the really poor, the latter is seldom to be met with, (unless it should happen now and then in a parish where a poorhouse was built a short time before the formation of the Union). A pigsty where the inmates are capable of keeping a pig is frequently attached to the dwelling, and in the heat of summer produces a stench quite intolerable; the want of space however prevents it being otherwise. The regular poor-house (those mentioned above being detached cottages) in most of the parishes in this district are of a much worse description, several large families existing under the same roof, occupying only one room each family, and having but one entrance door to the dwelling; here filth and poverty go hand-in-hand without any restriction and under no control. The accumulation of filth being attributable to the want of proper receptacles for refuse, and the indolent and filthy disposition of the inhabitants, in no instance *have* such places been

I. General Condition of the Residences

provided. The floors are seldom or never scrubbed; and the parish authorities pay so little attention to these houses, that the walls never get white-limed from one end of the year to the other. The windows are kept air-tight by the stuffing of some old garments, and every article for use is kept in the same room. The necessary is close to the building, where all have access, and producing a most intolerable nuisance. In a locality naturally engendering malaria, the diseases with which the poor are for the most part afflicted are, fevers such as are stated in this report and which sometimes run into a low typhoid state. The neighbourhood in general is considered in as good a state of drainage as it will admit of. The occurrence of disease among the poor population is for the most part at spring and autumn, at those times agues and fevers prevail. Smallpox and scarlet fever are met with at all seasons of the year, but prevail as epidemics, the former in spring and summer, and the latter about autumn or the beginning of winter. I attribute the prevalence of diseases of an epidemic character, which exists so much more among the poor than among the rich, to be, from the want of better accommodation as residence, (their dwelling instead of being built of solid materials are complete shells of mud on a spot of waste land the most swampy in the parish, this is to be met with almost everywhere in rural districts,) to the want of better clothing, being better fed, more attention paid to the cleanliness of their dwellings, and less congregated together. The health of persons even where a large family is, and where superior cottage accommodation is afforded to them, is much better generally than others less advantageously situated. The influence over their habits will also be very beneficial, they will be less likely to run to a beer-house with their last penny, the comforts of a home after the toils of the day keeps them by their own fire-side; they become better contented, less liable to disease, make better husbands, better fathers, better neighbours, and with each other better friends. There is a subject which I wish particularly to press on the attention of the Commissioners; the presence throughout the country, and to be found in every parish, of low lodging-houses, where persons of the lowest grade of society, beggars, thieves, and such like, take up a temporary abode in passing from one part of the kingdom to another, bringing with them the seeds of infectious diseases and oftentimes the actual disease itself into a neighbourhood previously in a comparative state of health. I have observed, where persons are living in a locality habitually affected with malaria, that when becoming convalescent from any other disease, are often attacked with ague, more particularly among the poorer classes.

'There is a class of persons called the "second poor," who for the most part are constantly employed throughout the year as farmers' labourers, and who are in much better circumstances than those to whom I have above alluded; they have much better cottage accommodation, their houses being provided with one, sometimes two day-rooms, two bed-rooms, a pantry, and other conveniences for fuel and for refuse, and whose general health and condition is much better than those less advantageously situated. Therefore detached cottages for the poor, with a moderate sized day-room, two or three bedrooms, a pantry, receptacles for refuse and for fuel, with casement windows or some such contrivance for ventilation, will be a blessing to them, and very available sanitary regulations. I know of no better method than is to be seen in all cottages for the economical management of fuel, both in cooking and maintaining a proper temperature of the rooms.'

The following extract from the report of *Mr. Aaron Little*, the medical officer of the Chippenham union, affords a specimen of the frequent condition of rural villages which have apparently the most advantageous sites:

I. General Condition of the Residences

'The parish of Colerne, which, upon a cursory view, any person (unacquainted with its peculiarities) would pronounce to be the most healthy village in England, is in fact the most unhealthy. From its commanding position (being situated upon a high hill) it has an appearance of health and cheerfulness which delight the eye of the traveller, who commands a view of it from the Great Western road, but this impression is immediately removed on entering at any point of the town. The filth, the dilapidated buildings, the squalid appearance of the majority of the lower orders, have a sickening effect upon the stranger who first visits this place. During three years' attendance on the poor of this district, I have never known the small-pox, scarlatina, or the typhus fever to be absent. The situation is damp, and the buildings unhealthy, and the inhabitants themselves inclined to be of dirty habits. There is also a great want of drainage.'

Mr. William Blower, the surgeon of the Bedford union, to whose evidence on the influence of moral causes on the health of the population, we shall again have occasion to refer, states:

'Throughout the whole of this district, there is a great want of "superior cottage accommodation". Most of the residences of the labourers are thickly inhabited, and many of them are damp, low, cold, smoky, and comfortless. These circumstances occasion the inmates to be sickly in the winter season, but I have not observed them to generate typhus, the prevailing form of disease being principally catarrhal; such as colds, coughs, inflammations of the eyes, dysentery, rheumatism, &c. However, when any contagious or epidemic malaria occurs, the cases are generally more numerous.'

Mr. Weale[1] reports instances of the condition of large proportions of the agricultural population in the counties of Bedford, Northampton, and Warwick. The medical officer of the Woburn union states, in respect to Toddington, that:

'In this town fever prevailed during the last year, and, from the state of the dwellings of the persons I called on, this could not be wondered at. Very few of the cottages were furnished with privies that could be used, and contiguous to almost every door a dung heap was raised on which every species of filth was accumulated, either for the purpose of being used in the garden allotments of the cottagers, or to be disposed of for manure. Scarcely any cottage was provided with a pantry, and I found the provisions generally kept in the bed-rooms. In several instances I found whole families, comprising adult and infant children with their parents, sleeping in one room.'

The medical officer of the Ampthill union states:

'Typhus fever has existed for the last three or four months in the parish of Flitwick, and although the number of deaths has not been considerable as compared with the progress of the disease, new cases have occurred as those under treatment became convalescent, and several are still suffering under this malady. The cottages in which it first appeared (and to which it has been almost exclusively confined), are of the most wretched description: a stagnant pond is in the immediate vicinity, and none of the tenements have drains; rubbish is thrown within a few yards of the dwellings, and there is no doubt but in damp foggy weather, and also during the heat of summer, the exhalations arising from those heaps of filth must generate disease, and the obnoxious effluvia tends to spread contagion where it already exists. It appears that most

---

1. Robert Weale, Assistant Poor Law Commissioner.

I. General Condition of the Residences

of the cottages alluded to were erected for election purposes,[1] and have since been allowed to decay; the roofs are repaired with turf dug in the neighbourhood, and the walls repaired with prepared clay, without the addition of lime-washing. Contagious disease has not been remarkable within the Union in any other spot than the one alluded to.'

Messrs. Smith and *Moore*, the medical officers of the Bishops Stortford union, state:
'We have always found the smallest and most slightly-built houses the seats of the lowest forms of disease; and although, during the last year, no epidemic or infectious disease here prevailed, it is but just to state that, generally speaking, the cottages of labourers in this district are small, badly protected from both extremes of weather, badly drained, and low in the ground.'

Mr. J. S. Nott, the medical officer of the Witham union, states:
'As medical officer of my district, I am glad to have an opportunity of recording my opinion of many of the causes of fever that uniformly prevails in the autumn and spring in this neighbourhood. I must first state that the situation of the town is exceedingly low, with two small rivers passing through it, and numerous open sewers intersecting the town and its environs, the effluvia of which is frequently exceedingly offensive, and at all times prejudicial to the general health, and calculated to create, by its malaria, the various kinds of fevers, (typhus and remittent). Part of the town is subject to floods; added to which, the cottages are small and crowded together. A great number of the inhabitants accumulate filth and manure for the purpose of sale. There are also many open slaughter-houses, where the refuse and filth is allowed to accumulate for weeks together without removal; and innumerable pigs are kept and fattened on the back of the premises of a great number of the inhabitants; and altogether it would be difficult to find any town of its size where so little regard is paid to cleanliness and ventilation; but where we do find the exception, roomy and well-ventilated cottages, (and they are but few,) the cases of fever are more manageable, and recover sooner.'

The state of Windsor affords an example that the highest neighbourhoods in power and wealth do not at present possess securities for the prevention of nuisances dangerous to the public health. *Mr. Parker*,[2] in his report on the condition of his district, states:
'With regard to the drainage of the towns in the counties of Buckingham, Oxford, and Berks, it may be observed that there is no town in which great improvements might not be effected. In Reading there are commissioners appointed under a local Act[3] to make provision for cleansing the town and removing nuisances; but their duties do not appear to be performed with due regard to the importance of the trust, for the Board of Guardians of the Reading union, by resolutions entered in their minutes, frequently point out nuisances, and remind the commissioners of the filthy condition of many of the courts and back streets. But extensive as the improvements in the state of the drainage of almost every town in these counties might be, there is no town amongst them in which there is so wide a field for improvement as Windsor, which, from the contiguity of the palace, the wealth of the inhabitants, and the situation, might have been expected to be superior in this respect to any other provincial town. Such, however, is not the case; for of all the towns visited by

---

1. The creation of new 40s. freeholds carrying a vote.
2. W. H. Parker, an Assistant Poor Law Commissioner.
3. 7 Geo. IV, c. 56 (1827).

I. General Condition of the Residences

me, Windsor is the worst beyond all comparison. From the gas-works at the end of George-street a double line of open, deep, black, and stagnant ditches extends to Clewer-lane. From these ditches an intolerable stench is perpetually rising, and produces fever of a severe character. I visited a cottage in Clewer-lane in which typhus fever had existed for some time, and learnt from a woman who had recently lost a child the complaint was attributable to the state of these ditches. Mr. Bailey, the relieving officer, informs me that cases of typhus fever are frequent in the neighbourhood; and observes that there are now seven or eight persons attacked by typhus in Charles-street and South-place. He considers the neighbourhood of Garden-court in almost the same condition. "There is a drain," he says, "running from the barracks into the Thames across the Long Walk. That drain is almost as offensive as the black ditches extending to Clewer-lane. The openings to the sewers in Windsor are exceedingly offensive in hot weather. The town is not well supplied with water, and the drainage is very defective." The ditches of which I have spoken are sometimes emptied by carts; and on the last occasion their contents were purchase for the sum of 15*l.* by the occupier of land in the parish of Clewer, whose meadows suffered from the extraordinary strength of the manure, which was used without previous preparation.'[1]

Mr. Harding, medical officer of the Epping union, states:
'The state of some of the dwellings of the poor is most deplorable as it regards their health, and also in a moral point of view. As it relates to the former, many of their cottages are neither wind nor water tight. It has often fallen to my lot to be called on to attend a labour where the wet has been running down the walls, and light to be distinguished through the roof, and this in the winter season, with no fire-place in the room. As it relates to the latter, in my opinion a great want of accommodation for bed-rooms often occurs, so that you may frequently find the father, mother, and children all sleeping in the same apartment, and in some instances the children having attained the age of 16 or 17 years, and of both sexes; and if a death occurs in the house, let the person die of the most contagious disease, they must either sleep in the same room, or take their repose in the room they live in, which most frequently is a stone or brick floor, which must be detrimental to health.'

Mr. J. D. Browne, medical officer of the West Ham union, states that:
'The cases of typhus (21 cases in the parish of Walthamstow) have occurred periodically in certain localities, arising partly from want of personal cleanliness, and also from being situated near ditches into which putrefactive matter was deposited, such as the privies and pigsties emptying themselves. The medical officer called the attention of the Board of Guardians, vicar, and parochial officers to the subject; and though it was unanimously admitted that the evil was great, and an anxious desire was expressed in vestry to remove the existing evil, yet the case fell to the ground, there being no funds to meet the exigency. The medical officer feels persuaded that a power should be invested in the Board of Guardians or parochial officers to meet such cases.'

Mr. Thomas H. Smith, the medical officer of the Bromley union, states:
'My attention was first directed to the sources of malaria in this district and neighbourhood when cholera became epidemic. I then partially inspected the dwellings of the poor, and have recently completed the survey. It is almost incredible that so many sources of malaria should exist in a rural district. A total absence of all provision for effectual drainage around cottages is the

---

1. *Local Reps. E. & W.*, pp. 94-5.

I. General Condition of the Residences

most prominent source of malaria; throughout the whole district there is scarcely an attempt at it. The refuse, vegetable and animal matters, are also thrown by the cottagers in heaps near their dwellings to decompose; are sometimes not removed, except at very long intervals; and are always permitted to remain sufficiently long to accumulate in some quantity. Pigsties are generally near the dwellings, and are always surrounded by decomposing matters. These constitute some of the many sources of malaria, and peculiarly deserve attention as being easily remedied, and yet, as it were, cherished. The effects of malaria are strikingly exemplified in parts of this district. There are localities from which fever is seldom long absent; and I find spots where the spasmodic cholera located itself are also the chosen resorts of continued fever.'[1]

Passing the metropolis and the adjacent districts, I proceed to the evidence as to the condition of the dwellings of the poorest classes in the midland counties.

The report from Mr. Hodgson and the physicians of the town of Birmingham[2] will be considered a valuable public document, as exhibiting the effect of drainage produced by a peculiarly fortunate situation. The houses, of which I requested drawings, are on the whole built upon an improved plan. This town, it will be seen, is distinguished apparently by an immunity from fever, and the general health of the population is high, although the occupations are such as are elsewhere deemed prejudicial to health.

The following extract from *Mr. Hodgkins*, the medical officer of Bilston, in the Wolverhampton Union, describes the condition of the population of a colliery district:

'Bilston, like Wolverhampton, has not been visited by fever to any extent since the cholera in 1832. The awful destruction which then occurred swept off many of those subjects who might afterwards have been victims of fever; in fact Bilston was, after the cessation of cholera, nearly free from disease of any kind for several months. Influenza has occasionally visited us and swept off a few. Small-pox a few years ago was prevalent, but not very fatal, although many children from negligence on the part of the parents are not vaccinated. Scarlet fever has appeared sometimes, but only in straggling cases. The occupations of the poorer classes are chiefly colliers, labourers, &c., great members of the latter being Irish. The houses of those applying for parochial medical relief which I have visited have been dirty and crowded, the habits of the working classes here being generally improvident and dirty, many parties forming heaps of filth close to their doors; and here, as in Wolverhampton, I am afraid it would require the interference of the law to effect any permanent good. Some years ago a large culvert was carried down the principal street which has made a great improvement in that part, but much yet remains undrained. I would mention a place in High-street especially, near to a court, crowded with Irish, there is a pool of green stagnant water or mud continually; another place called the Berry, behind the King's Arms Inn, and a third in a court in Temple-street, where there appears to be a drain which has been choked up, the stench from which is intolerable.'

Dr. *Edward Knight* gives the following description of the sanitary condition of the town of Stafford:

---

1. *Local Reps. E. & W.*, p. 46.
2. 'Report on the sanitary state of the labouring classes in the borough of Birmingham', by a Committee of Physicians and Surgeons, *Local Reps. E. & W.*, pp. 192-217.

I. General Condition of the Residences

'During the year ending September 29th, 1839, there have been in the fever-wards connected with the Stafford County General Infirmary 76 cases of fever, of which number 10 have died, and the remaining 66 were discharged cured. The far greater part of these cases commenced in the town of Stafford, some being brought to the infirmary in a dying state, which gives a greater rate of mortality. Although the fever-wards are well arranged, and every comfort and attention provided for the patients, there is a general dislike on the part of the poor to be removed to them from their own houses, except in cases of actual necessity.

'Owing to this, and the filthy state of those parts of the town occupied exclusively by the lower classes, as the "Broad-eye," "Back-walls," &c., we have generally more or less of infectious diseases during the autumn and winter months in each year, and although such diseases do not extend their ravages to the more respectable inhabitants, the above form but a very small portion of the cases which occur..

'These parts of the town are without drainage, the houses, which are private property, are built without any regard to situation or ventilation, and constructed in a manner to ensure the greatest return at the least possible outlay. The accommodation in them does not extend beyond two rooms; these are small, and, for the most part, the families work in the day-time in the same room in which they sleep, to save fuel.

'There is not any provision made for refuse dirt, which, as the least trouble, is thrown down in front of the houses, and there left to putrefy. The back entrances to the houses in the principal streets are generally into these, the stabling and cow-houses, &c., belonging to them, forming one side of the street, and the manure, refuse vegetable matter, &c., carried into the street, and placed opposite to the poorer houses; so that they are continually subjected to the malaria arising from that, in addition to their own dirt.

'The sedentary occupation of the working classes (shoemaking being the staple trade of the town), their own want of cleanliness and general intemperance, form, also, a fruitful source of disease. One-half of the week is usually spent in the public-houses, and the other half they work night and day to procure the necessary subsistence for their families. There is a great want of improvement in the moral character of the poor; they can obtain sufficient wages to support their families respectably, but they are improvident and never make any provision against illness. A local Act for the improvement of the town empowers the commissioners to remove nuisances; but no notice is ever taken. The situation of Stafford also offers every facility for an efficient drainage; it is nearly surrounded by a large ditch, in which there might be a running stream of water, well calculated to remove all impurities; but it is always choked up, and in a stagnant state. The river "Sow" is also close to the town. There are not any sewers even in the principal streets, the water being carried off by open channels. In the Lunatic Asylum, which closely adjoins the town, and averages 250 patients, great attention is paid to cleanliness, and we never have any infectious diseases."[1]

In the month of December, 1839, an application was made to the Board for advice and aid to meet the emergencies created by an epidemic which had broken out in the parish of Breadsall in the Shardlow union (Derbyshire). Mr. Senior,[2] the Assistant Commissioner for the district, accompanied Dr. Kennedy to the spot where the fever was prevalent, and that report may be submitted to attention, as containing a picture

---

1. *Local Reps. E. & W.*, pp. 225-6.
2. Edward Senior, an Assistant Poor Law Commissioner.

I. General Condition of the Residences

of the habits of a large proportion of the population of that part of the country, and an exemplification in a group of individual cases of the common causes and effects of such calamities on the labouring population.[1]

The report from Dr. Baker, of Derby,[2] and Mr. Senior's report, comprising the returns from the medical officers of Nottingham, Lincoln, and other rural and town unions within his district,[3] pourtray the sanitary condition of a large proportion of the population included in them.

Proceeding northward, a report from *Mr. Bland*, the medical officer of the Macclesfield union, gives the following description of the state of the residences occupied by many of the labourers of that town:

'In a part of the town called the Orchard, Watercoates, there are 34 houses without back doors, or other complete means of ventilation; the houses are chiefly small, damp, and dark; they are rendered worse with respect to dampness perhaps than they would be from the habit of the people closing their windows to keep them warm. To these houses are three privies uncovered; here little pools of water, with all kinds of offal, dead animal and vegetable matter are heaped together, a most foul and putrid mass, disgusting to the sight, and offensive to the smell; the fumes of contagion spreads periodically itself in the neighbourhood, and produces different types of fever and disorder of the stomach and bowels. The people inhabiting these abodes are pale and unhealthy, and in one house in particular are pale, bloated, and rickety.'[4]

Mr. William Rayner, the medical officer of the Heaton Norris district of the Stockport union describes the condition of a part of the population of that place:

'The localities in which fever mostly prevails in my district, are Shepherd's Buildings and Back Water Street, both in the township of Heaton Norris. Shepherd's Buildings consist of two rows of houses with a street seven yards wide between them; each row consists of what are styled back and front houses—that is two houses placed back to back. There are no yards or outconveniences; the privies are in the centre of each row, about a yard wide; over them there is part of a sleeping-room; there is no ventilation in the bedrooms; each house contains two rooms, viz., a house place and sleeping room above; each room is about three yards wide and four long. In one of these houses there are nine persons belonging to one family, and the mother on the eve of her confinement. There are 44 houses in the two rows, and 22 cellars, all of the same size. The cellars are let off as separate dwellings; these are dark, damp, and very low, not more than six feet between the ceiling and floor. The street between the two rows is seven yards wide, in the centre of which is the common gutter, or more properly sink, into which all sorts of refuse is thrown;

---

1. J. P. Kennedy & E. Senior, 'Report on the sanitary condition of the labouring population of the parish of Breadsall in the Shardlow Union', *Local Reps. E. & W.*, pp. 182-91.
2. William Baker, 'Report on the sanitary condition of the labouring population of the town of Derby', *Local Reps. E. & W.*, pp. 162-181.
3. Edward Senior, 'Report on the condition of the residences of the labouring classes in the counties of Leicester, Lincoln, Nottingham, and Rutland', *Local Reps. E. & W.*, pp. 153-62.
4. *Local Reps. E. & W.*, p. 233. For an account of the compilation of this report and of the subsequent development of public health work in Macclesfield, see C. S. Davies (ed.), *A History of Macclesfield* (Manchester 1961), pp. 176-9.

it is a foot in depth. Thus there is always a quantity of putrefying matter contaminating the air. At the end of the rows is a pool of water very shallow and stagnant, and a few yards further, a part of the town's gas works. In many of these dwellings there are four persons in one bed.

'Backwater-street, the other locality of fever, is proverbially the most filthy street in the town, contains a number of lodging-houses and Irish, who mostly live in dark damp cellars, in which the light can scarcely penetrate.

'It is not to be wondered at that such places should be the constant foci of fevers; there is scarcely a house in Shepherd's-buildings that has not been affected with fever, and in some instances repeatedly: new residents are most liable to be affected, the force of habit, or some other protecting influence seems to render those who have lived there some time less liable to be attacked. The same circumstance has been noticed by others, and M. Louis,[1] who is known throughout Europe, having made this subject one of particular observation, states that it is generally within the first year that new comers take fever, whilst the old inhabitants who are equally exposed to the same exciting causes escape.'

The report of Dr. Baron Howard, on the condition of the population of Manchester,[2] and that of Dr. Duncan, on the condition of the population of Liverpool,[3] will make up a progressive view of the condition of the labouring population in those parts of the country. The Report of one of the medical officers of the West Derby union, with relation to the condition of the labouring population connected with Liverpool, will serve to show that the evils in question are not confined to the labouring population of the town properly so called.

'The locality of the residences of the labouring classes are in respect to the surrounding atmosphere favourably situated, but their internal structure and economy the very reverse of favourable. The cottages are in general built more with a view to the per centage of the landlord than to the accommodation of the poor. The joiner's work is ill performed; admitting by the doors, windows, and even floors, air in abundance, which, however, in many cases, is not disadvantageous to the inmates. The houses generally consist of three apartments, viz., the day-room, into which the street-door opens, and two bedrooms, one above the other. There is likewise beneath the day-room a cellar, let off either by the landlord or tenant of the house, to a more improvident class of labourers; which cellar, in almost all cases, is small and damp, and often crowded with inhabitants to excess. These cellars are, in my opinion, the source of many diseases, particularly catarrh, rheumatic affections, and tedious cases of typhus mitior, which, owing to the over-crowded state of the apartment, occasionally pass into typhus gravior. I need scarcely add that the furniture and bedding are in keeping with the miserable inmates. The rooms above the day-room are often let separately by the tenant to lodgers, varying

---

1. Pierre C. A. Louis, author of *Mémoires, ou Recherches anatomico-pathologiques* (Paris 1823); *Recherches anatomico-pathologiques sur la Phthisis* (Paris 1825); and *Recherches anatomiques, pathologiques et thérapeutiques sur la maladie connue sous les noms de gastro-entérite, fièvre putride, adynamique* (Paris 1829).
2. Richard Baron Howard, 'Report on the prevalence of diseases arising from contagion and certain other physical causes amongst the labouring classes in Manchester', *Local Reps. E. & W.*, pp. 294-336.
3. W. H. Duncan, 'Report on the sanitary state of the labouring classes in the town of Liverpool', *Local Reps., E. & W.*, pp. 282-94.

I. General Condition of the Residences

in number from one or two, to six or eight individuals in each, their slovenly habits, indolence, and consequent accumulation of filth go far to promote the prevalence of contagious and infectious diseases.

'The houses already alluded to front the street, but there are houses in back courts still more unfavourably placed, which also have their cellars, and their tenants of a description worse, if possible. There is commonly only one receptacle for refuse in a court of eight, ten, or twelve densely crowded houses. In the year 1836-7, I attended a family of 13, twelve of whom had typhus fever, without a bed in the *cellar*, without straw or timber shavings—frequent substitutes. They lay on the floor, and so crowded, that I could scarcely pass between them. In another house I attended 14 patients; there were only two beds in the house. All the patients, as lodgers, lay on the boards, and during their illness, never had their clothes off. I met with many cases in similar conditions, yet amidst the greatest destitution and want of domestic comfort, I have never heard during the course of twelve years' practice, a complaint of inconvenient accommodation.'

The following extract from the report of *Mr. Pearson*, medical officer of the Wigan union, is descriptive of the condition of large classes of tenements in the manufacturing towns of Lancashire:

'From the few observations which I have been enabled to make respecting the causes of fever during the two months which I have held the situation of house surgeon to the Dispensary, I am inclined to consider the filthy condition of the town as being the most prominent source. Many of the streets are unpaved and almost covered with stagnant water, which lodges in numerous large holes which exist upon their surface, and into which the inhabitants throw all kinds of rejected animal and vegetable matters, which then undergo decay and emit the most poisonous exhalations. These matters are often allowed, from the filthy habits of the inhabitants of these districts, many of whom, especially the poor Irish, are utterly regardless both of personal and domestic cleanliness, to accumulate to an immense extent, and thus become prolific sources of malaria, rendering the atmosphere an active poison. The streets which particularly exhibit this condition are Ashton-street, Hanover-street, Stuart-street, John-street, Lord-street, Duke-street, Princess-street, and the short streets leading from Queen-street, into Faggy-lane and Princess-street. It may be also mentioned, that in many of these streets there are no privies, or, if there are, they are in so filthy a condition as to be absolutely useless; the absence of these must, necessarily, increase the quantity of filth, and thus materially add to the extent of the nuisance.

'In addition to the streets above mentioned, there are, besides, two other localities, which must be considered as peculiarly fitted for the generation of malaria—I mean the waste land in front of Bradshaw Gate, and also that situated between Greenough's-row and Kerfoot's-row; the latter is one complete pool of stagnant water, mixed with various descriptions of putrifying animal and vegetable matters. Many of the yards and courts in various parts of the town are so built up as to prevent the movements of the atmosphere, and are in a horribly filthy state, in consequence of dunghills which are situated therein being allowed to grow to an immense size, and the water which drains therefrom being permitted to flow over the surface.'[1]

Proceeding northwards, little difference is observable in the condition of the working classes in the ancient towns, where the habitations were

---

1. Dr. Pearson's comments are summarised in the report by Alfred Power (Assistant Poor Law Commissioner), 'On the sanitary inquiry in his late district in Lancashire, etc.', *Local Reps. E. & W.*, p. 264.

crowded for the sake of fortification, and in the manufacturing towns, where the habitations are crowded for the sake of vicinity to the places of work, or from ignorance and inattention, or from the high price of land. We cite the following instances of the condition of the habitations and population in Durham, Barnard Castle, and Carlisle:—

Mr. Nicholas Oliver, Durham, states that:
'The city of Durham, like all ancient cities and towns, is built very irregularly, and surrounded on all sides by the river Wear, which is frequently overflown, and much wooded. These in summer and autumn, by the combined influences of heat, moisture, and decaying vegetable substances, become abundant sources of malaria. The streets are very narrow, and the houses are built so much behind each other that the entrance to a great many of the dwellings is by a passage, lane, or alley, either a steep ascent or descent, where, from a proper want of receptacles and sewers, filth is allowed to accumulate, and there necessarily is a constant emanation of fœtid effluvia. The majority of the houses are very old and in a dilapidated state, several not being weather proof. The great bulk of the working classes inhabit these tenements, and they seldom occupy more than two rooms, many only one, where all that is requisite in conducing to cleanliness and comfort has to be performed.

'The spirit of improvement, which is making such rapid strides in other parts of the country, is here quite dormant. Nothing calls louder for the attention of the constituted authorities than the improvements which might be effected in the habitations of the industrious classes, thereby increasing their health, comfort, and happiness.'

Mr. George Brown, of Barnard Castle, in the Teesdale union, states that:
'The residences of the labouring population within the Teesdale Union, especially in Barnard Castle and the more populous villages, is mostly in large houses let into tenements. At least four-fifths of the weavers in Barnard Castle live in such residences, and about one half of all the other labouring poor in the Union. The tenements which form the residences of the weavers and other labourers in Barnard Castle are principally situate in Thorngage, Bridgegate, and the lower parts of the town, and in confined yards and alleys. The houses are many of them very large. I am told somewhere there are as many as 50 or more individuals under one roof. There is generally, perhaps, one privy to a whole yard (or onset as they term it), embracing five or six houses. From the crowded state of these dwelling-houses, and the filthiness of many of their inmates, disease would undoubtedly arise more commonly than it actually does, but the river Tees flows at the foot of each yard, running alongside of all the houses in Bridgegate. The impurities are thus speedily carried away, and the evils which might otherwise be expected from the effluvia of vegetable and other bodies in a state of decomposition are prevented; besides which, the houses in general being large and the poorer class in the upper stories, they are more protected against cold and damp.'[1]

Mr. Brown, in regard to Barnard Castle, further states, that:
'A surgeon here of great intelligence and practice states that in the town of Barnard Castle he has always found the most obstinate cases of typhus and other epidemics, and also rheumatism, to prevail amongst the houses on the west side of the principal street. These houses slope towards the moat of the old castle, which is not sufficiently drained; and the thick and high walls of

---

1. *Local Reps. E. & W.*, pp. 417-18.

I. General Condition of the Residences

the ruins of the castle retain the damp, and prevent the accession of the western winds to the moat and many of the houses. In the interior of the castle, now used as a garden, there is a stagnant pond which ought to be drained off: this pond is nearly opposite the yards, which are full of the residences of the poorer classes, and called the Swamp. Disease is often found to exist in these yards, and the surgeon I have referred to attributes to it the dampness of the moat (upon or on the margin of which the houses are built) and to the pond before mentioned. All the houses on the west side of the street have one step, and some more, down from the street. I am also told by the same surgeon that very many of the cases of fever and rheumatism which he attends may be fairly traced to the dampness of houses or want of sufficient drainage of the ground previously to building, and their being built below the level of the adjoining ground, by which the moisture is thrown into them.'[1]

Mr. Rowland, of Carlisle, states:

'Though Carlisle abounds with beautiful walks, it generally has them accompanied with filthy putrid gutters, and there seems no mode of compelling any one to clean them out. The city is surrounded with such nuisances; on the south side at the foot of Botchergate, there is a gutter, perhaps a mile long, which conducts the filth of that quarter through the fields into the river Petteril. The stench in summer is very great. The filth seems to accumulate from want of descent, and probably the whole descent is in the first field next Botchergate. If this gutter was paved and descent made regular, I have no doubt it would keep itself clean.'[2]

The following is a brief notice of the condition of the residences of the population amidst which the cholera first made its appearance in this country.[3]

Mr. Robert Atkinson, Gateshead, states, that:

'It is impossible to give a proper representation of the wretched state of many of the inhabitants of the indigent class, situated in the confined streets called Pipewellgate and Killgate, which are kept in a most filthy state, and to a stranger would appear inimical to the existence of human beings, where each small, ill ventilated apartment of the house contained a family with lodgers in number from seven to nine, and seldom more than two beds for the whole. The want of convenient offices in the neighbourhood is attended with many very unpleasant circumstances, as it induces the lazy inmates to make use of chamber utensils, which are suffered to remain in the most offensive state for several days, and are then emptied out of the windows. The writer had occasion a short time ago to visit a person ill of the cholera; his lodgings were in a room of a miserable house situated in the very filthiest part of Pipewellgate, divided into six apartments, and occupied by different families to the number of 26 persons in all. The room contained three wretched beds with two persons sleeping in each: it measured about 12 feet in length and 7 in breadth, and its greatest height would not admit of a person's standing erect; it received light from a small window, the sash of which was fixed. Two of the number lay ill of the cholera, and the rest appeared afraid of the admission of pure air, having carefully closed up the broken panes with plugs of old linen.'

The *Rev. Dr. Gilly*, the vicar of Norham and canon of Durham, in an appeal in behalf of the border peasantry, describes their dwellings as 'built of rubble or unhewn stone, loosely cemented; and from age, or

---

1. *Local Reps. E. & W.*, p. 424. 2. *Ibid.*, pp. 416-17.
3. Cholera first appeared in Britain at Sunderland in 1831.

I. General Condition of the Residences

from badness of the materials, the walls look as if they would scarcely hold together.' The chinks gape in so many places as admit blasts of wind:

'The chimneys have lost half their original height, and lean on the roof with fearful gravitation. The rafters are evidently rotten and displaced; and the thatch, yawning to admit the wind and wet in some parts, and in all parts utterly unfit for its original purpose of giving protection from the weather, looks more like the top of a dunghill than of a cottage.

'Such is the exterior; and when the hind comes to take possession, he finds it no better than a shed. The wet, if it happens to rain, is making a puddle on the earth floor. (This earth floor, by the bye, is one of the causes to which Erasmus ascribed the frequent recurrence of epidemic sickness among the cotters of England more than 300 years ago. It is not only cold and wet, but contains the aggregate filth of years, from the time of its first being used. The refuse and dropping of meals, decayed animal and vegetable matter of all kinds, which has been cast upon it from the mouth and stomach, these all mix together and exude from it.) Window-frame there is none. There is neither oven, nor copper, nor grate, nor shelf, nor fixture of any kind; all these things he has to bring with him, besides his ordinary articles of furniture. Imagine the trouble, the inconvenience, and the expense which the poor fellow and his wife have to encounter before they can put this shell of a hut into anything like a habitable form. This year I saw a family of eight—husband, wife, two sons, and four daughters—who were in utter discomfort, and in despair of putting themselves in a decent condition, three or four weeks after they had come into one of these hovels. In vain did they try to stop up the crannies, and to fill up the holes in the floor, and to arrange their furniture in tolerably decent order, and to keep out the weather. Alas! what will they not suffer in the winter! There will be no fireside enjoyment for them. They may huddle together for warmth, and heap coals on the fire; but they will have chilly beds and a damp hearth-stone; and the cold wind will sweep through the roof, and window, and crazy door-place, in spite of all their endeavours to exclude it.

'The general character of the best of the old-fashioned hind's cottages in this neighbourhood is bad at the best. They have to bring everything with them—partitions, window-frames, fixtures of all kinds, grates, and a substitute for ceiling; for they are, as I have already called them, mere sheds. They have no byre for their cows nor sties for their pigs, no pumps or wells, nothing to promote cleanliness or comfort. The average size of these sheds is about 24 by 16. They are dark and unwholesome. The windows do not open; and many of them are not larger than 20 inches by 16; and into this place are crowded 8, 10, or even 12 persons.'[1]

In a selection of plans and drawings of labourers' dwellings will be found a sketch of a group of hinds' cottages, such as those described by Dr. Gilly.[2]

The progress of the inquiry into Scotland shows the external and internal condition of the poorer classes of the population to be still more deplorable. The condition of a large portion of the labouring population of the smaller towns, and of the rural districts, is displayed in the Report

---

1. William Stephen Gilly, *The Peasantry of the Border: an Appeal on their Behalf* (Berwick-upon-Tweed 1841; 2nd. edition, London 1842), pp. 20-3.
2. This illustration, which is to be found opposite p. 266 in the original edition of the *San. Rep.*, has not been reproduced in this edition.

I. General Condition of the Residences

of Dr. Scott Alison, on the sanitary condition and general economy of the population of Tranent;[1] in the Report of Mr. Stevenson, on the condition of the town of Musselburgh;[2] that of Dr. Sym, on the town of Ayr, to which further reference will subsequently be made.[3]

The description given of the houses of labourers of Lochmaben, by *Mr. Wilson*, surgeon, is one which characterizes a large class of houses throughout Scotland:

'In Lochmaben, they are surrounded by low meadow lands subject to frequent inundations, marshes and lakes, with dunghills and pools of dirty water, in which vegetable substances are soaked for the purpose of making manure on all sides of the dwellings. These houses, similar to the dwellings of the generality of the labouring classes, consist of a building 30 feet in length by 16 feet in breadth within the walls; the floor is formed of clay; ceiling, if any, generally formed by spars of wood laid close together, and covered with dry turf; one front door and two front windows. This building is usually occupied by two families, entering by the same door; the partitions are formed by the back of the beds, which will be best understood by describing them as wooden boxes open on one side; the windows rarely are made to open, so that they are ventilated by the door; but having little fuel, the door must be kept shut to maintain warmth, and the chimneys being badly constructed, the dwelling is often full of smoke. Potatoes are often kept under the beds. There are no proper receptacles for filth attached to the houses.'

The most wretched of the stationary population of which I have been able to obtain any account, or that I have ever seen, was that which I saw in company with *Dr. Arnott*, and others, in the wynds of Edinburgh and Glasgow.

I prefer citing his description of the residences we visited:

'In the survey which I had the opportunity of making in September, 1840, of the state of Edinburgh and Glasgow, all appeared confirmatory of the view of the subject of fevers submitted to the Poor Law Commissioners by those who prepared the Report in London.

'In Glasgow, which I first visited, it was found that the great mass of the fever cases occurred in the low wynds and dirty narrow streets and courts, in which, because lodging was there cheapest, the poorest and most destitute naturally had their abodes. From one such locality, between Argyll-street and the river, 754 of about 5000 cases of fever which occurred in the previous year were carried to the hospitals. In a perambulation on the morning of September 24th, with Mr. Chadwick, Dr. Alison,[4] Dr. Cowan (since deceased, who had

---

1. S. Scott Alison, 'Report on the sanitary condition and general economy of the labouring population in the town of Tranent and neighbouring district, in Haddingtonshire', *Local Reps. Scot.*, pp. 78-130.
2. William Stevenson, 'Report on the sanitary condition and general economy of the labouring classes in the town of Musselburgh, in the county of Midlothian and vicinity', *Local Reps. Scot.*, pp. 130-52.
3. James Sym, 'Report on the sanitary condition of the labouring classes in the town of Ayr', *Local Reps. Scot.*, pp. 214-38.
4. William Pulteney Alison (1790-1859), Professor of Medicine at Edinburgh University 1820-56, author of *Observations on the Management of the Poor in Scotland* (Edinburgh 1840), and of many articles on the causes of destitution and fever in towns. See also introduction, pp. 23, 63-4.

G

laboured so meritoriously to alleviate the misery of the poor in Glasgow),[1] the police magistrate, and others, we examined these wynds, and, to give an idea of the whole vicinity, I may state as follows:—

'We entered a dirty low passage like a house door, which led from the street through the first house to a square court immediately behind, which court, with the exception of a narrow path around it leading to another long passage through a second house, was occupied entirely as a dung receptacle of the most disgusting kind. Beyond this court the second passage led to a second square court, occupied in the same way by its dunghill; and from this court there was yet a third passage leading to a third court, and third dungheap. There were no privies or drains there, and the dungheaps received all filth which the swarm of wretched inhabitants could give; and we learned that a considerable part of the rent of the houses was paid by the produce of the dungheaps. Thus, worse off than wild animals, many of which withdraw to a distance and conceal their ordure, the dwellers in these courts had converted their shame into a kind of money by which their lodging was to be paid. The interiors of these houses and their inmates corresponded with the exteriors. We saw half-dressed wretches crowding together to be warm; and in one bed, although in the middle of the day, several women were imprisoned under a blanket, because as many others who had on their backs all the articles of dress that belonged to the party were then out of doors in the streets. This picture is so shocking that, without ocular proof, one would be disposed to doubt the possibility of the facts; and yet there is perhaps no old town in Europe that does not furnish parallel examples. London, before the great fire of 1666, had few drains and had many such scenes, and the consequence was, a pestilence occurring at intervals of about 12 years, each destroying at an average about a fourth of the inhabitants.

'Who can wonder that pestilential disease should originate and spread in such situations? And, as a contrast, it may be observed here, that when the kelp manufacture lately ceased on the western shores of Scotland, a vast population of the lowest class of people who had been supported chiefly by the wages of kelp-labour remained in extreme want, with cold, hunger, and almost despair pressing them down—yet, as their habitations were scattered and in pure air, cases of fever did not arise among them.[2]

'Edinburgh stands on a site beautifully varied by hill and hollow, and owing to this, unusual facilities are afforded for perfect drainage; but the old part of the town was built long before the importance of drainage was understood in Britain, and in the unchanged parts there is none but by the open channels in the streets, wynds, and closes or courts. To remedy the want of covered drains, there is in many neighbourhoods a very active service of scavengers to remove everything which open drains cannot be allowed to carry; but this does not prevent the air from being much more contaminated by the frequent stirring and sweeping of impurities than if the transport were effected under ground; and there are here and there enclosed spaces between houses too small to be used for any good purpose but not neglected for bad, and to which the scavengers have not access.

'Another defect in some parts of Edinburgh is the great size and height of

---

1. Robert Cowan (d. 1841), Professor of Forensic Medicine at Glasgow University, 1839-41, and author of statistical studies on the incidence of fever in Glasgow.
2. The turning-point in the kelp industry came in 1810-11, but the real decline set in after the abolition of the salt excise duty in 1825. There was very little left of the industry by 1840. See M. Gray, *The Highland Economy, 1750-1850* (Edinburgh 1957), pp. 155-8.

II. Public Arrangements External to the Residences

the houses (some of them exceeding ten stories), with common stairs, sometimes as filthy as the streets or wynds to which they open. By this construction the chance of cleanliness is lessened, the labour of carrying up necessaries, and particularly water for the purposes of purifying is increased; and if any malaria or contagion exist in the house, the probability of its passing from dwelling to dwelling on the same stair is much greater than if there were no communication but through the open air. Illustrating how malaria may be produced, I may state that in making a round of observation with Mr. Chadwick, attended by the Police Superintendent, and others, we visited a house at the back of the Canongate, which in former days had been the chief inn of the city, but now, with its internal court-yard of steep ascent, is occupied by families of the labouring classes. In the court-yard a widow of respectable appearance, who answered some of our questions, occupied a room which appeared on the ground-floor, as seen from the court, but was above a stable, now used as a pigsty, opening to the lower level of the external street. A little while before, on the occasion of the dungheap being removed from the pigsty, two children who lived with her, a daughter and a niece, were made ill by the effluvia from below, and both died within a few days.

'The facts here referred to go far to explain why fatal fever has been more common in Edinburgh than from other circumstances would have been anticipated.'[1]

It might admit of dispute, but, on the whole, it appeared to us that both the structural arrangements and the condition of the population in Glasgow was the worst of any we had seen in any part of Great Britain.

II

PUBLIC ARRANGEMENTS EXTERNAL TO THE RESIDENCES BY WHICH THE SANITARY CONDITION OF THE LABOURING POPULATION IS AFFECTED

I now propose to bring under consideration those parts of the various local reports and communications which most prominently set forth special defects that apparently admit of specific remedies.

The defects which are the most important, and which come most immediately within practical legislative and administrative control, are those chiefly *external* to the dwellings of the population, and principally arise from the neglect of drainage. The remedies include the means for drainage simply, *i.e.*, the means for the removal of an excess of moisture; and

The means for the removal of the noxious refuse of houses, streets, and roads, by sewerage, by supplies of water, and by the service of scavengers and sweepers.

Town Drainage of Streets and Houses

The sanitary effects obtainable by an efficient town drainage, independently of all other measures, is exhibited in various parts of the country by such particular instances as the following:—

Dr. *Baker*, in his report on the sanitary condition of Derby, states: 'At the back of the whole row (on the north side of the street) there runs a

---

1. Neil Arnott, 'On the typhus fevers which have prevailed in Edinburgh and Glasgow', *Local Reps. Scot.*, pp. 8-10.

series of little gardens, each house possessing one, in width equal to the frontage of the house it belongs to, and in length 56 feet. To every five houses there is a pump; and at the bottom of each garden a double privy, answering for two houses, the cess-pool shallow, and open to the air; and to this nuisance many have added a pig-sty, and dung or rubbish heap. The inhabitants of this street are poor people, chiefly silk-weavers, and what are here called framework-knitters or stockingers.

'There are on this (the north) side of the street 54 houses, and between October, 1837, and the latter part of March, 1838, the families inhabiting six adjoining houses in the middle of the row were grievously afflicted with typhus fever, whilst those who dwelt in the remaining 48 houses were comparatively healthy.

'The following list will give at one view the details of this visitation.
'The houses are numbered from the bottom of the hill towards the top.

Number of the House	Name of the Family	Number of Persons ill with Fever	REMARKS
No. 25	Langton	3	Children, all of whom recovered.
,, 26	Dearn	4	Man and wife, the former died.
,, 27	Bailey	1	Man, who recovered.
,, 28	Nettleship	4	Three children, and subsequently their mother. The children, after many weeks, recovered, but the poor mother (who was pregnant), being much weakened by the fever, and long attendance upon her children, died soon afterwards in child-bed.
,, 29	Curzon	5	First a lodger, named Elizabeth Sherwin, (recently confined) and her infant, both died. Then three of Curzon's children, who recovered.
,, 30	Hatfield	1	A girl, who recovered.

'In all 16 persons attacked with typhus fever, of whom five died.[1]

'Here then we have a very interesting subject for investigation; namely, how was it that in a row of 54 houses, uniform in situation, size, and construction, tenanted by the same description of persons, the inhabitants of the six centre houses should have been attacked by a malignant fever, from which those who lived in the 24 houses above and 24 below them altogether escaped?

'By a careful inspection of the whole row I obtained the following information and facts:—That before this street was built, the natural moisture of the land, and any sudden rush of water caused by rain, was carried away by a ditch running down the whole length of the hill, where the present gardens terminate. Also, that in the gardens of the upper 21 or 22 houses this ditch had been filled up; and sinks and drains, communicating with the main sewer, that passes down the middle of the street, had been placed between each garden and the dwelling-house. At this point too there is a brick wall, carried down to the bottom of the garden, and dividing this property from the adjoining, and it is very probable that this wall assisted in checking the spread of the fever from the six infected houses, at which part of the row we have now arrived.

'The state of the premises belonging to these ill-fated houses was as follows:—The ditch already alluded to as passing at the bottom of the gardens was here not filled up; there were not any sinks and drains, and the cess-pools

---

1. This was an unusually high mortality rate: usually 10% or less of typhus cases proved fatal in this period.

II. Public Arrangements External to the Residences 101

were overflowing into the ditch, which, here and there obstructed, formed a succession of foul and stinking pools, from four to six feet wide; whilst the earth of the gardens was perpetually saturated with the offensive moisture exuding from them.

'The want of drains, or their faulty construction, may render any situation unhealthy; nor must it be supposed that because high lands in the open country seldom require draining, that it is therefore little needed in elevated portions of a town, for in the latter there are always dirt and slops that require carrying away from the houses that produce them. And inasmuch as drains in high stituations never get such a thorough washing out by rain and natural moisture as those do which, from being in lower grounds, receive a swollen and accumulated stream, the former require the greater attention to keep them from becoming foul and obstructed: and it is not a little remarkable that three elevated parts of the town of Derby are hardly ever exempt from fever. They are the Burton-road (district No. 2 in the table), Litchurch-street (district No. 3), and Parker's Flats (district No. 12).

'In the latter end of the year 1837 and beginning of 1838, Litchurch-street afforded a striking instance of a situation which promised exemption from malaria and disease, being heavily visited by typhus fever, caused, as I shall show, by the most wilful inattention to drainage.

'Litchurch-street is situated in the southern suburb of Derby, from which indeed, although forming a part of the Derby union, it is separated by intervening fields and nursery-grounds belonging to the General Infirmary. Its course is nearly east and west, running down the side of a gentle declivity. The houses in Litchurch-street have not been built many years; are rather small, but are double houses, having a front and back room on the ground floor, and over these a front and back bed-room.

'Descending the hill to the remaining 24 houses (below those infected), and which, from their standing upon lower ground, might reasonably be expected to have fared worse, I soon discovered from whence their protection came. The land adjoining the Litchurch-street gardens belongs, as I have already stated, to the General Infirmary, and the governors of that institution had eight years before built a wall in the former course of the ditch, before spoken of, which wall extended from the foot of the hill as far up as the house No 24; at the same time they had filled up the ditch, carrying its contents by a drain away from the gardens below and into the nearest public sewer: now reference to the list detailing the amount and progress of the fever on this occasion will show that No. 25 was the first house affected. The connexion therefore between the facts here furnished and the tragedy of the six houses is too obvious to require further comment.

'I shall conclude this part of my subject by adding, that from motives of both humanity and economy, the Board of Guardians and the governors of the infirmary jointly exerted themselves to get rid of so serious a nuisance, that the latter, at an expense of more than 50*l*., extended the wall of separation between Litchurch-street and their own lands, but that, in all other respects, the evil remains now (two years since) as it was then; nor was there found any law that would compel its removal, the place complained of being private property.

'My friend Mr. Harwood, surgeon of the Derby union, informs me that in Canal-street (district 5 of table 1) five sisters in one family were successively attacked with typhus fever, caused by the escape of foul air from a drain.

'It appears that a drain, coming from some neighbouring privies, had been carried so near to the house in which they resided as to form part of the boundary wall of the cellar, which had for some time previous become too offensive to be used.

'Four months elapsed before this family became free from disease; no return of which, however, has taken place since the removal of the drain, which now passes at a greater distance.

'Taken altogether, I think that in large towns (and villages also) there is hardly any source of disease more powerful as to its pernicious influence, or more general as to extent, than defective drainage.'[1]

Mr. John Rayner, the medical officer of the Stockport union, states in his report on the condition of that town:

'There is a street of about 200 yards in length, the houses of which are of excellent construction, with very few exceptions, and without those unhealthy places, viz., cellar dwellings. The upper third of it is unpaved and without sewerage. It is 10 yards wide, and the inhabitants are generally very clean, as respects both their persons and dwellings; and notwithstanding they are, without exception, well fed and clad, fever has gradually prevailed, *but only on the north side* of the street. The situation is not a confined one, neither do the houses differ either as to convenience or cleanliness on this side of it.

'In the 10 houses at the upper end of this street (three of which are untenanted) there has been 21 cases of continued fever. Every house, with three exceptions, has had several cases, in some of them as many as four in number. In one, five cases have occurred.

'Seeing this fact, I examined the adjoining yard and gardens, and found a stagnant pool of water and an open ditch about two feet wide, into which the refuse water from the houses, and from two pigsties, was allowed to accumulate. It is about 15 or 20 yards in length. Adjoining the gable end of one of the untenanted houses were found heaps of ordure and other refuse matters undergoing the process of decay.

'The west end of this street opens into some gardens, where free ventilation may easily take place, and, I have no doubt, has prevented the spread of infection to the south side of it.'

The following is the comparison of the different mortality in a drained and an undrained district, made by *Mr. Crowfoot*, surgeon, of Beccles, one of the most eminent of the medical practitioners in Suffolk. In a letter to Mr. Twisleton, the Assistant Commissioner, he states:

'You are aware that these two towns of nearly equal population are nearly alike as to natural advantages of situation, &c., except that Bungay, having a larger proportion of rural population inhabiting the district called Bungay Uplands, ought to be more healthy than Beccles, which has nearly its whole population confined to the town. About 30 years since, Beccles began a system of drainage, which it has continued to improve, till at the present time every part of the town is well drained, and I am not aware of a single open drain in the place. Bungay, on the contrary, with equally convenient opportunities for drainage, has neglected its advantages in that respect, has one or two large reservoirs for filth in the town itself, and some of its principal drains are open ones. The result you will see is, that Bungay, with a smaller proportion of town inhabitants, has become of late years less healthy than Beccles. I have carefully taken the number of burials from the parish registers of each town for the last 30 years, and dividing them into decennial periods, I have calculated the proportion which the deaths bore to the mean population, between one census and the other, during each 10 years; the only possible source of fallacy is the want of the census for 1841; but in its absence I have supposed

---

1. William Baker, 'On the sanitary condition of the town of Derby', *Local Reps. E. & W.*, pp. 166-8.

II. Public Arrangements External to the Residences 103

the same rate of increase as took place between that of 1821 and that of 1831 for each place. Sinking fractions, the following has been the proportion of deaths to the population in the two towns:—

	Beccles	Bungay
Between the years 1811 and 1821	1 in 67	1 in 69
,, 1821 and 1831	1 in 72	1 in 67
,, 1831 and 1841	1 in 71	1 in 59

You will therefore see that the rate of mortality has gradually diminished in Beccles since it has been drained, whilst in Bungay, notwithstanding its larger proportion of rural population, it has considerably increased.

The Ditchingham Factory[1] may have given a greater increase of population to Bungay than I have allowed for, but, on the other hand, the Roman Catholics and the Independents bury many of their dead in their own ground, which I have not calculated upon. Since writing the above, I have been over to Bungay, to examine more particularly the state of its drainage, which is much worse than I had any idea of. If their population should much increase, their mortality will increase much faster.'

A frightful picture of a considerable proportion of the labouring population of Leeds in respect to sewerage and drainage is afforded by the report of *Mr. Baker,* who gives the following instance of amendment:

'In one of the streets of Leeds where stagnant water used frequently to accumulate after rain, and where there was perpetually occurring cases of fever of a malignant character, a deputation of females waited upon me in my capacity of town counsellor to ask if any remedy could be applied to this nuisance, which they declared was not only offensive but deadly. I directed them to communicate with the owner of the property, and to say that if the grievance was not remedied I should take further steps to enforce it. Never hearing again from the deputation, I presumed that the remedy had been applied, and had forgotten the circumstance until the house surgeon of the fever hospital in 1840, in noticing the localities from whence fever cases were most frequently brought to the institution, remarked that "formerly many cases of malignant fever were brought in from ——— street, but for two or three years there had been none or not more than one or two." '[2]

Mr. John Wright, the relieving officer of the Tamworth union, states, that the following extracts exhibit the condition in which large masses of the population are kept by the neglect of the proper means of town drainage, and of the house cleansing, practicable by means of drains:

'Some of the houses in the back streets and courts of Tamworth, particularly those comprised in Class No. 1, are in a wretched state with respect to the common conveniences of life, being adjacent to stagnant ditches and pools of water, and having only one privy, common to many houses, and hemmed in with piggeries, &c., most of these houses having no back doors, the consequence of which is, that fevers and other disorders, generated by filth and malaria, are very prevalent, particularly in humid weather.'[3]

---

1. A silk-throwing mill of the firm of Grout, Bayliss & Co. For an account of this undertaking, see D. C. Coleman, 'Growth and decay during the Industrial Revolution: the case of East Anglia', *Scandinavian Economic History Review,* X (1962) 122-6.
2. Robert Baker, 'On the state and condition of the town of Leeds in the West Riding of the County of York', *Local Reps. E. & W.,* p. 353.
3. *Local Reps. E. & W.,* p. 235.

II. Public Arrangements External to the Residences

Mr. Elias Barlow, the relieving officer of the Wolstanton and Burslem union, states that:

'The townships of Knutton and Chesterton have been visited with fever for several months; and it still continues its raging influence, particularly in Knutton, the reason of which appears to me to be want of drainage, owing to the houses having been built upon low marshy ground; and also want of ventilation, owing to the houses being too small and having no back doors; it first made its appearance in the lowest class of houses, but has since extended to others.'[1]

The condition of the labouring population of Liverpool, in respect to drainage, is thus described in the report of *Dr. Duncan*:

'The sewerage of Liverpool was so very imperfect, that about 10 years ago a local Act was procured, appointing commissioners with power to levy a rate on the parish for the construction of sewers.[2] Under this Act, which expires next year, about 100,000*l*. have been expended in the formation of sewers along the main streets, but many of these are still unsewered; and with regard to the streets inhabited by the working classes, I believe that the great majority are without sewers, and that where they do exist they are of a very imperfect kind unless where the ground has a natural inclination, therefore the surface water and fluid refuse of every kind stagnate in the street, and add, especially in hot weather, their pestilential influence to that of the more solid filth already mentioned. With regard to the courts, I doubt whether there is a single court in Liverpool which communicates with the street by an underground drain, the only means afforded for carrying off the fluid dirt being a narrow, open, shallow gutter, which sometimes exists, but even this is very generally choked up with stagnant filth.

'There can be no doubt that the emanations from this pestilential surface, in connexion with other causes, are a frequent source of fever among the inhabitants of these undrained localities. I may mention two instances in corroboration of this assertion:—In consequence of finding that not less than 63 cases of fever had occurred in one year in Union-court Banastre-street, (containing 12 houses,) I visited the court in order to ascertain, if possible, their origin, and I found the whole court inundated with fluid filth which had oozed through the walls from two adjoining ash-pits or cess-pools, and which had no means of escape in consequence of the court being below the level of the street, and having no drain. The court was owned by two different landlords, one of whom had offered to construct a drain provided the other would join him in the expense; but this offer having been refused, the court had remained for two or three years in the state in which I saw it; and I was informed by one of the inhabitants that the fever was constantly occurring there. The house nearest the ash-pit had been untenanted for nearly three years in consequence of the filthy matter oozing up through the floor, and the occupiers of the adjoining houses were unable to take their meals without previously closing the doors and windows. Another court in North-street, consisting of only four small houses I found in a somewhat similar condition, the air being contaminated by the emanations from two filthy ruinous privies, a large open ash-pit and a stratum of semi-fluid abomination covering the whole surface of the court.

'From the absence of drains and sewers, there are of course few cellars entirely free from damp; many of those in low situations are literally inundated after a fall of rain. To remedy the evil, the inhabitants frequently make

---

1. *Local Reps. E. & W.*, p. 236.
2. 11 Geo. IV, c. 15, of 1830.

II. Public Arrangements External to the Residences 105

little holes or wells at the foot of the cellar steps on in the floor itself; and notwithstanding these contrivances, it has been necessary in some cases to take the door off its hinges and lay it on the floor supported by bricks, in order to protect the inhabitants from the wet. Nor is this the full extent of the evil; the fluid matter of the court privies sometimes oozes through into the adjoining cellars, rendering them uninhabitable by any one whose olfactories retain the slightest sensibility. In one cellar in Lace-street I was told that the filthy water thus collected measured not less than two feet in depth; and in another cellar, a well, four feet deep, into which this stinking fluid was allowed to drain, was discovered below the bed where the family slept!'[1]

He also states:
'There are upwards of 8,000 inhabited cellars in Liverpool, and I estimate their occupants at from 35,000 to 40,000.'[2]

He adds that:
'In a Report lately made by the Surveyors, appointed by the Town Council to examine the condition of the court and cellar residences within the borough, it is stated that of 2,398 *courts* examined, 1,705 were closed at one end, so as to prevent thorough ventilation. Of 6,571 *cellars*, whose condition is reported on, 2,988 are stated to be either wet or damp, and nearly one-third of the whole number are from 5 to 6 feet below the level of the street.'[3]

Dr. Jenks, in his report on the condition of the town of Brighton, states:
'Owing to the imperfect and insufficient drainage of the town, the inhabitants are compelled to have recourse to numerous cess-pools as receptacles for superabundant water, and refuse of all kinds; and to save the inconvenience of frequently emptying them, they dig below the hard coombe rock till they come to the shingles, where all the liquid filth drains away. The consequence is inevitable; the springs in the lower part of the town must be contaminated.'[4]

But even in Birmingham, which, as will be seen, enjoys almost an immunity from fever in consequence of the fortunate position of the town conferring advantages in respect to drainage, and the good construction of the houses, it appears from the report made by the physicians and surgeons, that the drainage is in many places extremely defective.

'The great sewers of the town open into the Rea, or into the rivulets which discharge their contents into that stream. In some places these rivulets are now covered over and constitute sewers. The present sewers, which are numerous and large, appear to be sufficient to carry off any storms or floods to which the town is liable, and no part of the town is subject to inundations. The principal streets are well drained, but this is far from the case with respect to many of the inferior streets, and to many, or rather most, of the courts, which, especially in the old parts of the town, are dirty and neglected, with water stagnating in them. These require immediate attention, and care ought to be taken that the depth of the main drains is sufficient to drain the cellars

---

1. *Local Reps. E. & W.*, pp. 287-9.
2. *Ibid.*, p. 285.
3. *Ibid.*, p. 285.
4. G. S. Jenks, 'On the sanitary state of the town of Brighton, and of the causes and prevention of fever', *Local Reps. E. & W.*, p. 59.

of the adjoining premises, which is not the case in some parts of the town. It is also important that a system of proper drainage should be enforced at the commencement of the building of any new streets or houses. The want of some regulations in this respect often causes the accumulation of putrid water in ditches and pools in the immediate vicinity of newly-erected buildings. In some parts of the borough, as at Edgbaston, there are but few public underground sewers, and the water from the houses is discharged into the ditches or gutters by the sides of the roads, where it stagnates. In the courts the drains are often above ground, and not covered in, and discharge their contents into the gutters or kennels in the streets. We do not think that much advantage is derived from having small under-ground drains in the courts if the gutters are laid upon a proper slope and are kept in proper repair, for the weirs or grates of small under-ground drains are very apt to be out of order, or to become choked, in which case accumulations of filthy fluids take place above them.'[1]

The inquiry into the sanitary condition of the towns in Scotland shows that similar defects stand equally in need of remedy in that part of the empire. Mr. *Burton*, in his report on the provisions of the Police Act for the city of Edinburgh, observes:

'Until very lately the Cowgate, a long street running along the lowest level of a narrow valley, had only surface drains. The various alleys from the High-street and other elevated ground open into this street. In rainy weather they carried with them each its respective stream of filth, and thus the Cowgate bore the aspect of a gigantic sewer receiving its tributary drains. A committee of private gentlemen had the merit of making a spacious sewer 830 yards long in this street at a cost of 2000*l*. collected by subscription. The utmost extent to which they received assistance from the police, consisted in being vested with the authority of the Act as a protection from the interruption of private parties. During the operation they were nevertheless harassed by claims of damage for obstructing the causeway, and their minutes, with a perusal of which I have been favoured, show that they experienced a series of interruptions from the neighbouring occupants, likely to discourage others from following their example.'[2]

In a communication from *Mr. William Chambers*, he observes:

'Within these few years, the practice of introducing water-closets into houses has become pretty general, wherever it is practicable; but in the greater part of the old town nothing of the kind can be accomplished from the want of drains. There are drains in the leading thoroughfares, but few closes possess these conveniences, and water is also sparingly introduced into these confined situations. You will therefore understand that a want of tributary drains and water is a fundamental cause of the uncleanly condition of the town. Of water of the finest kind there is indeed a plenteous supply, but unfortunately this is a monopoly in the hands of a joint-stock company,[3] and excepting at two or three wells, all the water introduced into the town has to be specially paid for, in the form of a tax upon the rental, by those who use it.'

As in England, the ignorance or neglect upon this matter is not con-

---

1. *Local Reps. E. & W.*, pp. 192-3.
2. J. H. Burton, 'On the state of the law as regards the abatement of nuisances and the protection of the public health in Scotland, with suggestions for amendment', *Local Reps. Scot.*, p. 55. The Edinburgh Police Act was 2 & 3 Wm. IV, c. 37 of 1832.
3. The Edinburgh Water Company, established by 59 Geo. III, c. 116 of 1819.

II. Public Arrangements External to the Residences

fined to the labouring population of the capital. *Dr. Scott Alison*, in his report on the condition of Tranent and the adjacent districts, observes that:

'There is nothing like an efficient system of drainage in Tranent and the other villages in the district. There is a piece of drain here and there, but it is very inefficient. There is not even a sufficient water-course in the main streets of Tranent; and it frequently happens, during and after a heavy fall of rain, that the carriage-road is covered with water, and that some of the lower class of houses are inundated. In a few parts of the town the water-course is covered with stones or flags. These occasionally fall in, and openings are made. These openings are generally left unrepaired, and are not filled up. People frequently get hurt by stepping into them when it is dark. I have myself met with an accident; and serious mischief would very frequently occur did people not pay particular attention to avoid them.'[1]

Dr. Sym, in his report on the sanitary condition of the town of Ayr, states that:

'A good covered sewer traverses the principal streets of the new part of Ayr; but the old part of the burgh, and both Newton and Wallacetown have merely shallow open gutters along the sides of the causeway. These gutters receive all the liquid refuse from the closes and alleys which communicate with the street, and which are generally causewayed in such a way that one side is considerably higher than the other, so as to permit water to find its way to the opposite edge. This sort of drainage might suffice for all useful purposes in our dry sandy soil if we had an adequate establishment of scavengers; but the gutters in many of the streets, and in all the closes inhabited by the poor are so much neglected, that they are never free from the stinking residuum of foul water. In Newton and Wallacetown, the drainage is exceedingly imperfect; indeed, in most streets of the latter it may be said scarcely to exist, and as the surface is very flat, almost the whole of the liquid putrescence and filth which are thrown out from the houses is allowed to filter through the sand, or evaporate in the sun, leaving a most offensive paste at the sides of the streets, and in the passages through the houses. This is the more to be regretted, that the beautiful state of cleanliness of the new part of Ayr, shows with how little labour it might be obviated with the aid of our absorbent soil and free atmosphere. There are some streets, the main street of Newton in particular, which have such inequalities in the causewayed footpaths, and such want of escape by the gutters, that it is impossible to find one's way through them in a dark night, without many a plunge into the filth. There is everywhere sufficient slope toward the river to render drainage perfectly effectual, if properly executed.'[2]

Mr. Forrest, the surgeon, in his account of Stirling, states that:

'The drains or sewers, called in Stirling "*sivers*," are all open and sloping. On the public streets they are, in general, well constructed, but in the closes their construction is so very bad that scarcely any of them run well. The only supply of water, so far as I know, which they receive, is from the heavens. The inhabitants of Stirling, during many months of the year, do not obtain water sufficient for their domestic wants, and they cannot, therefore, have any to spare for their sewers. There is a regularly appointed service of scavengers, but it is inefficient. A few old men sweep the public streets from time to time, and the sweepings thus collected are removed in a cart, without any apparent attention to time or order. Sometimes the sweepings remain on the streets for

---

1. *Local Reps. Scot.*, p. 82.   2. *Ibid.*, pp. 219-20.

II. Public Arrangements External to the Residences

many days. To show how matters of medical police[1] are neglected, I shall state a few facts which are known to every person in Stirling. 1st. The filth of the gaol, containing on an average 65 prisoners, is floated down the public streets every second or third day, and emits, during the whole of its progress down Broad-street, Bow, Baker-street, and King-street, the principal streets in the town, the most offensive and disgusting odour. 2nd. The slaughter-house is situated near the top of the town, and the blood from it is allowed to flow down the public streets. 3rd. The lower part of a dwelling-house, not more than three or four yards from the town-house and gaol, is used as a "midding," and pigsty, the filth being thrown into it by the window and door. 4th. There are no public necessaries; and the common stairs and closes, and even the public streets, are used habitually as such, by certain classes of the community. 5th. Two drains from the castle, convey the whole filth of it into an open field, where it spreads itself over the surface, and pollutes the atmosphere to a very great extent. 6th. A dwelling-house in the Castle-hill, the greater part of which is inhabited, is used by a butcher as a slaughter-house; and some of the butchers kill sheep and lambs in their back shops, situated under dwelling-houses. 7th. The closes where the poor dwell, and where accumulations of filth most abound, are, I may safely say, utterly neglected by the scavengers. In some situations, the ventilation around the residences is good, but in many others, and especially in the closes, it is very bad, and in my opinion, quite irremediable.'[2]

Before quitting this class of instances, it may here be necessary to guard against the conclusion that neglect of drainage is confined to towns, or to numerous and crowded habitations. Similar instances may be presented, even of single and isolated houses, and of small groups of rural cottages, in almost every district. Of this last class of cases I give only one instance, supplied by the evidence of *Mr. J. Thomson*, of Clitheroe:

'Have you not had amongst your own people an instance of pestilence occasioned by the neglect of removable causes of disease?—In the summer of 1839 some remarkable cases of fever occurred in my immediate neighbourhood amongst the inhabitants in my employment, of a small cluster of houses called Littlemoor. The situation of this little spot has always been considered, and justly, as remarkably healthy and agreeable, the soil around it being dry, and not marshy, as the name would seem to imply. It is situated on gently sloping ground, about a mile from the town of Clitheroe, and freely exposed on all sides to the wind. It contained six houses and 21 inhabitants at the time of the fever. The houses are built in three distinct groups, round an irregular area of from 50 to 60 feet square. A single, inadequate, and half-choked-up drain, originally constructed more than 40 years ago, for the only cottager, then existing on the spot, was the only under-ground outlet for the filth, and sink, and surplus water of these habitations; the rest was carried off by a deep and open ditch filled with grass and weeds; this ditch spread out, about 100 yards to the north, into a shallow stagnant pool, in summer green and fœtid; from which was conveyed all the water that could flow during that season past and amongst the cottages at Littlemoor. Into the centre of the open area or yard was poured all the filth of the houses in open channels, and thence, by the above-mentioned under-ground drain, conveyed away. This state of things was bad enough, but was rendered still worse by the erection recently of a pig-

---

1. The word 'police' here is used in the sense of 'regulation'.
2. W. H. Forrest, 'Report on the sanitary condition of the labouring classes of the town of Stirling', *Local Reps. Scot.*, pp. 263-4.

Street and Road Cleansing: Road Pavements

sty, the litter and filth of which not only obstructed the drain, but occasioned a pool of abomination of the most perilous and disgusting nature. At the time I saw it—the commencement of the fever—it was overflowing into the foundation of the principal habitation, and had infected the whole house with its stench, and was making its way by innumerable black and fœtid streams through a small shrubbery, the area of which it wholly covered, into the deep and open ditch. Believing this to be the source of the pestilence, I had the sty instantly pulled down, the filth removed, and a large drain brought up to the centre of the yard, terminating in small covered troughs to each habitation. This was in the middle of August, and from the hour of the removal of the filth no fresh case of fever occurred. The first case was on the 12th of May, and was followed by another in the same house on the 27th. In June there were three cases; and in July six; in August four; in all, 15; of which nine were the resident inhabitants, in a population of 21; and the remaining six, nurses and attendants on the sick, obtained from the immediate neighbourhood. No fever prevailed at the time in Clitheroe. One case was fatal, and the health of a most valuable member of that small community was so seriously affected by the fever as to cause his death in a short time. A visitor and attendant on the funeral of the person deceased at Littlemoor, and who took the fever, died also. This spot has remained, and I doubt not will continue, healthy ever since.

'The medical gentleman, Mr. Garstang, of Clitheroe, who attended the preceding case, has communicated to me the equally striking and instructive statement I subjoin:—At Chatburn, a village to the north of Clitheroe, he was called to attend a patient in fever, in the month of May of the same year 1839. The first object that struck his eye on approaching the house was a long pole, with a bunch at the end, black and filthy from its recent use in forcing a choked-up and inaccessible drain, which passed between and under the gable-ends of two closely contiguous houses, only a few inches apart, one of which contained his patient. From this single case and house Mr. G. ascertained that 11 cases arose, by which means the fever was spread through the country, where it prevailed with great severity, and terminated, in many instances, fatally. There was no fever but what could be traced to this, and no other discoverable source.'

Street and Road Cleansing: Road Pavements

The local arrangements for the cleansing and drainage of towns, &c., generally present only instances of varieties of grievous defects from incompleteness and from the want of science or combination of means for the attainment of the requisite ends. Thus the local reports abound with instances of expensive main-drains, which from ignorant construction as to the levels, do not perform their office, and do accumulate pestilential refuse; others, which have proper levels, but from the want of proper supplies of water do not act; others, which act only partially or by suface drainage, in consequence of the neglect of communication from the houses to the drains; others, where there are drains communicating from the houses, but where the house-drains do not act, or only act in spreading the surface of the matter from cess-pools, and increasing the fœtid exhalations from it in consequence of the want of supplies of water; others again, as in some of the best quarters of the metropolis, where the supplies of water are adequate, and where the drains act in the removal of refuse from the house, but where from want of moderate scientific knowledge or care in their construction, each drain acts like the neck of a large retort, and serves to introduce into the house the

II. Public Arrangements External to the Residences

subtle gas which spreads disease from the accumulations in the sewers.* Other districts there are where their structural arrangements may be completed, and water supplied, and the under drainage in action, and yet pestilential accumulations be found spread before the doors of the population in consequence of the defective construction, and the neglect of the surface-cleansing of the streets and roads. Recently a remonstrance was made to an able and active member of a Commission of Sewers, for taking no steps to extend the drainage in a wretched district of the metropolis. The reply was, a statement, that a drain had been cut through a portion of it, but that it had done no good; and the remonstrant was invited to inspect the district himself, and judge whether, with streets that were unpaved and uncleansed, wet and miry, with deep holes full of refuse, it were possible by any under drainage to remove the evil complained of. Other districts there are in which the Road Commissioners or the Paving Board appears to have done their duty; but the benefit is prevented, and the road is kept continually out of repair by the neglect of the service of scavengers.

All these local defects again are referred back to the defective construction of the Acts of Parliament,—which generally either presume that no science, no skill is requisite for the attainment of the objects, or presume both to be universal,—which in some instances actually prohibit the only effectual mode of drainage, namely, that from the houses into the main-drains; and in others, prescribe cleansing by house-drains without supplies of water; or prescribe the construction of roads independently of drains, and direct the execution of only part of the necessary means, leaving other essential parts to the discretion of individuals.

Between a town population similarly situated in general condition, one part inhabiting streets which are unpaved, and another inhabiting streets that are paved, a general difference of health is observed. The town of Portsmouth is built upon a low portion of the marshy island of Portsea. It was formerly subjected to intermittent fever, but since the town was paved, in 1769, it was noticed by Sir Gilbert Blane,[1] that this disorder no longer prevailed; whilst Kilsea and the other parts of the island retained the aguish disposition until 1793, when a drainage was made which subdued its force.

Such strongly marked effects on the health of the population have followed in many places the complete cleansing of the streets, as are stated by *Mr. Bland*, medical officer of the Macclesfield Union:

---

* See the evidence on this subject taken before the Committee of the House of Commons, on the sewerage of the metropolis; see also the evidence of *Mr. Oldfield*, an extensive builder, *post*.[2]

---

1. Sir Gilbert Blane (1749-1834), naval physician. While serving in the West Indies in 1782-3, he made a series of innovations in respect of diet and sanitary discipline which amounted almost to a revolution in naval health. His principal published work in this field was his *Observations on the Diseases of Seamen* (1785).
2. *Report of Select Committee on Metropolis Sewers*, P.P. 1834, XV. For Mr. Oldfield's evidence, see below, pp. 376-8.

Street and Road Cleansing: Road Pavements 111

'To show the value of police regulations in removing any improper accumulations of foul and putrid matter, where a deadly poison is generated, I have a distinct recollection that, when the cholera appeared in Macclesfield, not only was that fatal disease arrested somewhat in its progress by the active vigilance exercised by the gentlemen in seeing that in their several districts all offending deposits were removed, and all pest-houses cleansed, that for several months after the town had undergone this salutary inspection, and the people made alive to the pernicious effects of the dunghill, fever of the worst or contagious form scarcely appeared in the usual localities, although it was at the autumnal season of the year. I likewise noticed in spring-time following, when the filth had begun to accumulate on the surface in certain parts of the town, a severe return of contagious diseases, fever in all its stages, and a very fatal epidemic small-pox.'

Similar cases were frequently noticed in the reports from Scotland; but when the alarm passed away, the habitual neglect of this description of cleanliness returned.

In the consideration of the evidence about to be submitted as to the condition of the streets on the external condition of the residences of the labouring classes, it should be borne in mind that the external condition of the dwelling powerfully and immediately affects it internal cleanliness and general economy.

The description of a large proportion of the streets inhabited by the working classes in Manchester by Dr. Baron Howard, and those of Leeds by Mr. Baker, those of Liverpool by Dr. Duncan, might be extended to Glasgow and other places. *Dr. Howard* states:

'That the filthy and disgraceful state of many of the streets in these densely populated and neglected parts of the town where the indigent poor chiefly reside cannot fail to exercise a most baneful influence over their health is an inference which experience has fully proved to be well founded; and no fact is better established than that a large proportion of the causes of fever which occur in Manchester originate in these situations. Of the 182 patients admitted into the temporary fever hospital in Balloon-street, 135 at least came from unpaved or otherwise filthy streets, or from confined and dirty courts and alleys. Many of the streets in which cases of fever are common are so deep in mire, or so full of hollows and heaps of refuse that the vehicle used for conveying the patients to the House of Recovery often cannot be driven along them, and the patients are obliged to be carried to it from considerable distances. Whole streets in these quarters are unpaved and without drains or main-sewers, are worn into deep ruts and holes, in which water constantly stagnates, and are so covered with refuse and excrementitious matter as to be almost impassable from depth of mud, and intolerable from stench. In the narrow lanes, confined courts and alleys, leading from these, similar nuisances exist, if possible, to a still greater extent; and as ventilation is here more obstructed, their effects are still more pernicious. In many of these places are to be seen privies in the most disgusting state of filth, open cesspools, obstructed drains, ditches full of stagnant water, dunghills, pigsties, &c., from which the most abominable odours are emitted. But dwellings perhaps are still more insalubrious in those cottages situated at the backs of the houses fronting the street, the only entrance to which is through some nameless narrow passage, converted generally, as if by common consent, into a receptacle for ordure and the most offensive kinds of filth. The doors of these hovels very commonly open upon the uncovered cesspool, which receives the contents of the privy belonging to the front house, and all the refuse cast out from it, as if

II. Public Arrangements External to the Residences

it had been designedly contrived to render them as loathsome and unhealthy as possible. Surrounded on all sides by high walls, no current of air can gain access to disperse or dilute the noxious effluvia, or disturb the reeking atmosphere of these areas. Where there happens to be less crowding, and any ground remains unbuilt upon, it is generally undrained, contains pools of stagnant water, and is made a depôt for dunghills and all kinds of filth.'[1]

Of 687 streets, inspected by a voluntary association in that town, 248 were reported as being unpaved, 112 ill ventilated, 352 as containing stagnant pools, heaps of refuse, ordure, &c.

'The state of some of the streets and courts examined was found by the inspectors abominable beyond description, and exhibited a melancholy picture of the filthy condition and unwholesome atmosphere in which a large portion of our poor are doomed to live.

'As an example I will extract the description given of Little Ireland from the proceedings of the Special Board of Health, which I have been permitted to examine through the kindness of the borough-reeve, John Brooks, Esq.:—

' "The undersigned having been deputed by the Special Board of Health to inquire into the state of Little Ireland, begs to report that, in some of the streets and courts abutting, the sewers are all in a most wretched state, and quite inadequate to carry off the surface water, not to mention the slops thrown down by the inhabitants in about 200 houses. The privies are in a most disgraceful state, inaccessible from filth, and too few for the accommodation of the number of people, the average number being two to 250 people. The upper rooms are, with few exceptions, very dirty, and the cellars much worse, all damp, and some occasionally overflowed. The cellars consist of two rooms on a floor, each nine or ten feet square, some inhabited by ten persons, others by more; in many the people have no beds, and keep each other warm by close stowage on shavings, straw, &c.; a change of linen or clothes is an exception to the common practice. Many of the back-rooms, where they sleep, have no other means of ventilation than from the front rooms. Some of the cellars on the lower ground were once filled up as uninhabitable, but one is now occupied by a weaver, and he has stopped up the drain with clay to prevent the water flowing from it into his cellar, and mops up the water every morning."

'The above description represents as faithfully the present state of this place as it did its condition eight years ago. In addition to the circumstances here mentioned, the unhealthiness of this spot is further increased by its low and damp situation, in a deep hollow, bounded on one side by a filthy and stinking brook, which readily overflows after rain; on another, by a very steep embankment; and on another, by a high wall, which separates it from the gas-works, and surrounded moreover by numerous high factories. * * *

'In the open space in the centre, which was formerly uncovered, numerous pigsties are now erected, which add, if possible, to its insalubrity. All the streets on the west side of the square are blocked up at the end by a high wall, so that each forms a *cul-de-sac*, a mode of construction which precludes the possibility of effectual ventilation. Close to this wall, at the upper end of these streets, are placed filthy and dilapidated privies, with large open cesspools, which are frequently full to overflowing. The present condition of those in Bent and James Leigh-streets are disgusting and offensive beyond description.'[2]

Mr. Baker in his report on the sanitary condition of the residences of the labouring classes in Leeds, thus describes their external condition:

---

1. *Local Reps. E. & W.*, pp. 305-6.
2. *Ibid.*, pp. 307-8.

Street and Road Cleansing: Road Pavements

'The river Aire, which courses about a mile and a half through the town, is liable suddenly to overflow from violent or continued rains, or from the sudden thawing of heavy falls of snow. The lower parts and dwellings, both in its vicinity and in that of the becks, are not unfrequently therefore inundated; and as the depth of the cellars is below the means of drainage, the water has to be pumped out by hand-pumps on to the surface of the streets. In those parts of the town, and particularly where the humbler classes reside, during these inundations, and where there are small sewers, the water rises through them into the cellars, creating miasmatic exhalations, and leaving offensive refuse, exceedingly prejudicial to the health as well as to the comfort of the inhabitants. It was stated, on the authority of one of the registrars, that during a season remarkable for an unprecedented continuation of hot weather, that in one of these localities, the deaths were as three to two, while in other parts of the town, at the same period, they were as two to three. The condition of the Timble Bridge beck is doubtless much worse for drainage purposes than formerly, for the bottom has been raised by continual deposits, until the oldest water-wheel upon it has had to be removed as useless and inoperative; and stepping-stones, once the means of passage over it, are at this moment said to be buried under the accumulation of years, as much as one or two feet in depth. It is quite clear, therefore, that that which was once the main receptacle for the drainage of an entire district is, in its present state, no longer capable of fulfilling that purpose; and that though a considerable amount of drainage might still be effected by it, yet, unless emptied of its superfluous matter, it cannot now be made available for the wants of the entire population on its course.

'In an inundation about the period of 1838 or 1839, which happened in the night, this beck overflowed its boundaries so greatly, and regurgitated so powerfully into petty drains communicating with houses 100 yards distant from its line, that many of the inhabitants were floated in their beds, and fever to a large amount occurred from the damp and exhalations which it occasioned. Of the 586 streets of Leeds, 68 only are paved by the town, *i.e.*, by the local authorities; the remainder are either paved by owners, or are partly paved, or are totally unpaved, with the surfaces broken in every direction, and ashes and filth of every description accumulated upon many of them. In the manufacturing towns of England, most of which have enlarged with great rapidity, the additions have been made without regard to either the personal comfort of the inhabitants or the necessities which congregation requires. To build the largest number of cottages on the smallest allowable space seems to have been the original view of the speculators, and the having the houses up and tenanted, the *ne plus ultra* of their desires. Thus neighbourhoods have arisen in which there is neither water nor out-offices, nor any conveniences for the absolute domestic wants of the occupiers. But more than this, the land has been disposed of in so many small lots, to petty proprietors, who have subsequently built at pleasure, both as to outward form and inward ideas, that the streets present all sorts of incongruities in the architecture; causeways dangerous on account of steps, cellar windows without protection, here and there posts and rails, and everywhere clothes-lines intersecting them, by which repeated accidents have been occasioned. During the collection of the statistical information by the Town Council, many cases of broken legs by these unprotected cellars, and of horsemen dismounted by neglected clothes-lines hanging across the streets, were recorded.

'It might be imagined that at least the streets over which the town surveyors have a legal right to exercise control would be sewered. But this is not the case; of the 68 streets which they superintend, 19 are not sewered at all, and 10 are only partly so; nay, it is only within the three or four years past that a sewer

II. Public Arrangements External to the Residences

has been completed through the main street for two of the most populous wards of the town, embracing together a population of 30,540 persons, by which to carry off the surface and drainage water of an elevation of 150 feet, where, indeed, there could be no excuse for want of sufficient fall. I have seen, in the neighbourhood to which I now refer, an attempt made to drain the cottage houses into a small drain passing under the causeway, and which afterwards had to be continued through a small sewer, and through private property, by a circuitous route, in order to reach its natural outlet, and the water from the surveyors' drain regurgitate into the cutting from the dwellings. It only needs to be pointed out that the sewer which has subsequently been made, and is most effective, is an evidence of the previous practicability of a work so essential to the welfare of the people; but, I may add, that many of the inhabitants of districts a little further distant from the town, where fever is always rife, are yet obliged to use cesspools which are constructed under their very doors, for the want of the continuation of this desirable measure.

'Along the line of these two wards, and down the street which divides them, and where this sewer has been recently made, numbers of streets have been formed and houses erected without pavement, and hence without surface drainage—without sewers—or if under drainage can be called sewers, then with such as, becoming choked in a few months, are even worse than if they were altogether without. The surface of these streets is considerably elevated by accumulated ashes and filth, untouched by any scavenger; they form nuclei of disease exhaled from a thousand sources. Here and there stagnant water, and channels so offensive that they have been declared to be unbearable, lie under the doorways of the uncomplaining poor; and privies so laden with ashes and excrementitious matter as to be unuseable prevail, till the streets themselves become offensive from deposits of this description; in short, there is generally pervading these localities a want of the common conveniences of life.

'The courts and *culs-de-sac* exist everywhere. The building of houses back to back occasions this in a great measure. It is in fact part of the economy of buildings that are to pay a good per centage. In one *cul-de-sac*, in the town of Leeds, there are 34 houses, and in ordinary times, there dwell in these houses 340 persons, or ten to every house; but as these houses are many of them receiving houses for itinerant labourers, during the periods of hay-time and harvest and the fairs, at least twice that number are then here congregated. The name of this place is the Boot and Shoe-yard, in Kirkgate, a location from whence the Commissioners removed, in the days of the cholera, 75 cart-loads of manure, which had been untouched for years, and where there now exists a surface of human excrement of very considerable extent, to which these impure and unventilated dwellings are additionally exposed. This property is said to pay the best annual interest of any cottage property in the borough.'[1]

Mr. Shaw, the medical officer of the Hindley district of the Wigan union, after giving a similar description of the streets of that town, adds:

'The greater number of cases of fever in Ince is in a great degree to be accounted for from the extremely filthy state of those places where it has been worst. Some of the cases were much worse than others, several being of the malignant kind of typhus. Most of the cases happened in Broom-street, in Ince, a very uncleanly place, whole pools of stagnant water, decayed animal and vegetable matter, and many other nuisances of a like description lying in heaps from one end of the street to the other. It is extremely probable a little

---

1. *Local Reps. E. & W.*, pp. 351-3.

attention to these matters would save the inhabitants from many of the diseases with which they are now continually affected.'[1]

Dr. *Waite*, in his report on the condition of the population at Lynn, states:

'I have seen typhus fever rage in families, where the refuse of a market-gardener was suffered to accumulate in a hole, immediately before three or four houses, whilst families at fifty yards distant from it were perfectly free.'

The report by *Mr. Anderson*, solicitor, on the sanitary condition o Inverness, exhibits the external features of the condition in which large proportions of the town population in Scotland are still allowed to remain in respect to all these defects:

'From the very open or porous character of the subsoil, the grounds in and around Inverness are seldom retentive of surface-water; and as there is also a considerable inclination of the plain towards the river, a good *drainage* could be easily procured from almost every part of the town. With the exception, however, of the principal streets or thoroughfares, in which the best houses and shops are situated, there are but few covered common sewers; and in the suburbs generally, and from all the side alleys and closes, rain-water and other accumulations pass away only by means of surface or open drains. Hence among the dwellings of the poorer classes *stagnant pools* very frequently occur, and the drainage in these places, naturally bad enough, is often purposely obstructed by the people, for the purpose of adding to their *dunghill* heaps of middens, which, as manure for their potatoe-grounds, form the chief treasures of the poorer cottagers and labourers. A gas and water company, established some years ago,[2] has afforded a great increase of comfort and cleanliness to the buildings along the main thoroughfares; but to the back closes and suburbs such *luxuries* have not yet been extended, and hence the want of order, decency, and comfort are painfully observable among them. *Water-closets* and *public privies* are both rare, the consequences of which, morally as well as physically, may be easily imagined, and no doubt much infectious disease, if not occasioned, is harboured and perpetuated by the want of them. The disgusting state of all the bye-lanes and roads about Inverness proves what the people must suffer on this account.

'As already stated, the dwellings of the humbler classes are in general only *one* story high, that is, they consist of a ground-floor divided into two or three small apartments, with two or three garret-rooms in the roof above, which is covered externally with turf or straw thatch. Such buildings are often intermixed with houses of a better description, and from being but seldom painted or whitewashed, they have not a cheerful nor cleanly aspect. Most of them are provided with small back courts or gardens, in which a few common vegetables are grown; but their principal value is as stances for *pig-houses* and dunghills, which in many instances are improperly allowed to rest upon or touch the dwelling-houses; while it is not to be disguised that cases exist where the *pig*, the *horse*, and the *cow* all live under the same roof with their owners, and the manure allowed to accumulate there also. It is very common for a labourer's *family* to have only a single apartment, or a room and a closet, while one room is the usual accommodation rented by single persons, and that frequently without a particle of ground attached.

'Amidst such a combination of unwholesome circumstances, it is rather wonderful that malignant fever does not very greatly prevail in this town. It is scarcely ever entirely free of it, and occasionally it breaks out in some of its most contagious and dangerous forms, such as measles, scarlet and typhus

---

1. *Ibid.*, p. 270. 2. By 7 Geo. IV, c. 112 of 1827.

II. Public Arrangements External to the Residences

fever, and sometimes even small-pox, spreading upwards among all classes of the community. The writer is strongly inclined to believe that the comparative healthiness of Inverness, notwithstanding its low and undrained position, is owing chiefly to the salubrity of its climate, as influenced by its situation, and the natural porousness of the soil.'[1]

The Provost of Inverness, at the time the report was made, gives the following description of the town:

'Inverness is a nice town, situated in a most beautiful country, and with every facility for cleanliness and comfort. The people are, generally speaking, a nice people, but their sufferance of nastiness is past endurance. Contagious fever is seldom or ever absent; but for many years it has seldom been rife in its pestiferous influence. The people owe this more to the kindness of Almighty God than to any means taken or observed for its prevention. There are very few houses in town which can boast of either water-closet or privy, and only two or three public privies in the better part of the place exist for the great bulk of the inhabitants. Hence there is not a street, lane, or approach to it that is not disgustingly defiled at all times, so much so as to render the whole place an absolute nuisance. The *midden* is the chief object of the humble, and though enough of water for purposes of cleanliness may be had by little trouble, still as the ablutions are seldom, MUCH filth in-doors and out of doors *must* be their portion. When cholera prevailed in Inverness, it was more fatal than in almost any other town of its population in Britain.'[2]

Such is the absence of civic economy in some of our towns that their condition in respect to cleanliness is almost as bad as that of an encamped horde, or an undisciplined soldiery. Mr. Baker applies to Leeds the observations made by Sir John Pringle in his Treatise on the Diseases of the Army,[3] but they are equally applicable to the districts occupied by the labouring classes wherever this inquiry has been carried:

' "The chief cause of dysentery appears to be the foul straw and the privies; for as soon as we had left that ground on which we had been long encamped the sickness visibly abated." And again he says, "The greatest source of dysenteric affections appears to be the privies." And again, speaking of bad air as producing epidemics, he systematizes the mediate agent thus; "1st, Marsh effluvia; 2ndly, Encampment near trees; 3rdly, The privies and foul straw of a camp; and 4thly, A pent, corrupt, and vitiated atmosphere." '[4]

The discipline of the army has advanced beyond the civic economy of the towns. In the standing orders given and enforced by the late General Crauford[5] there are the following from Article 2, on the interior regimental arrangements on arriving in camp or quarters:

---

1. George Anderson, 'Sanitary Report on the town of Inverness, North Britain', *Local Reps. Scot.*, pp. 304-5.   2. *Ibid.*, p. 310.
3. Sir John Pringle (1707-1782), Professor of Moral Philosophy at Edinburgh University 1734-45, and distinguished authority on military medicine. Although he engaged in some very diverse scientific experiments, his principal work lay in the field of military sanitation and the prevention of dysentery and hospital fever in military camps. His principal published work was his *Observations on the Diseases of the Army* (1752).
4. Pringle, *Observations* (6th ed., 1768), p. 21.
5. *Standing Orders as given out and enforced by the late Major-General Robt. Crauford, for the use of the Light Division . . . serving under his Command in the Army of the Duke of Wellington* (1814, and re-published 1844, 1852 and 1880.)

Street and Road Cleansing: Road Pavements 117

'It must be explained to the men, as a standing order, that when no regular necessaries are made, nor any particular spot pointed out for easing themselves, they are to go to the rear, at least 200 yards, beyond the sentries of the rear guard; all men disobeying this order must be punished.

'The captain of the day and the quarter-master under the commanding officers, are particularly responsible for the cleanliness of the camp of each regiment; and the field officer of the inlying piquet, who is charged with the superintendence of the police, and cleanliness of the camp or quarters of the brigade, will give such orders upon the subject as may be necessary to the captain of the day.'

The towns whose population never change their encampment, have no such care, and whilst the houses, streets, courts, lanes, and streams, are polluted and rendered pestilential, the civic officers have generally contented themselves with the most barbarous expedients, or sit still amidst the pollution, with the resignation of Turkish fatalists, under the supposed destiny of the prevalent ignorance, sloth, and filth.

Whilst such neglects are visited by the scourge of a regularly recurring pestilence and ravages of death more severe than a war, it may be confidently stated that the exercise of attention, care, and industry, directed by science in their removal, will not only be attended by exemptions from the pains of the visitation, but with exemptions from pecuniary burdens, and with promise even of the profits of increased production to the community.

This will appear from an examination of the present mode of removing the refuse from towns, and contrasting it with improved methods; and first with relation to the refuse of the houses:—

It is proved that the present mode of retaining refuse in the house in cesspools and privies is injurious to the health and often extremely dangerous. The process of emptying them by hand labour, and removing the contents by cartage, is very offensive, and often the occasion of serious accidents. But the expense of this mode operates, as the reports from the large towns show, as a complete barrier to all cleanliness in this respect in the dwellings or streets occupied by the labouring classes. The usual cost of cleansing cesspools of a tenement in London is about 1*l*. each time. With a population generally in debt at the end of the week, and whose rents are collected weekly, such an outlay may be considered as practically impossible, and the inferior landlords delay incurring the expense until the nuisance becomes unbearable. In London the expense and annoyance of the cleansing of such places is avoided for years, until they are in the condition described by *Mr. Howell*, one of the council of the Society of Civil Engineers, who has acted extensively as a surveyor in the metropolis:

'I would,' he states, 'instance a recent case in my own parish, where I was called to survey two houses about to undergo extensive repairs. It was necessary that my survey should extend from the garrets to the cellars: upon visiting the latter, I found the whole area of the cellars of both houses were full of night-soil, to the depth of three feet, which had been permitted for years to accumulate from the overflow of the cesspools; upon being moved, the stench was intolerable, and no doubt the neighbourhood must have been more or less infected by it. I should mention, that these houses are letting at from 30*l*. to 40*l*. a-year each, and are situated in a considerable public thoroughfare.

II. Public Arrangements External to the Residences

'I would mention another case, amongst many more in St. Giles's parish: I was requested to survey the dilapidations to several houses in the immediate neighbourhood of High-street, upon passing through the passage of the first house, I found the yard covered with night-soil, from the overflowing of the privy, to the depth of nearly six inches, and bricks were placed to enable the inmates to get across dry shod; in addition to this, there was an accumulation of filth piled up against the walls, of the most objectionable nature; the interior of the house partook something of the same character, and discovering, upon examination, that the other houses were nearly similar; I found a detailed survey impracticable, and was obliged to content myself with making general observations. My duties, as one of the surveyors to a fire-office, call me to all parts of the town, and I am constantly shocked almost beyond endurance at the filth and misery in which a large part of our population are permitted to drag on a diseased and miserable existence. I consider a large portion, if not the whole, of this accumulation of dirt and filth is caused by the bad and inefficient sewerage of the metropolis. I am acquainted with numberless houses in Westminster where the cellars are constantly flooded, and having no drainage, the occupiers are obliged to pump out the water, which, from being stagnant, is foul and offensive. If in the performance of this necessary duty the matter becomes known, they are summoned to the public office and fined 5*l*.; however much, therefore, the evil is felt in permitting the continuance of stagnant water, the alternative of the fine for pumping out is worse; they submit therefore to the lesser evil, and leave the water in the cellars. * * *

'I am quite sure, from much observation, that the occupiers of houses in all neighbourhoods are much influenced in their habits of cleanliness by the facilities afforded for draining, and by the want of carriage and foot-paving in the streets; and it is equally certain that both health and life are frequently sacrificed by the constant damps and unwholesome smell, occasioned entirely by the absence of all means to carry off the impurities, which, in densely populated neighbourhoods, increase with such fearful rapidity.'

It might have been expected, from the value of the refuse as manure (one of the most powerful known), that the great demand for it would have afforded a price which might have returned, in some degree, the expense and charge of cleansing. But this appears not to be the case in the metropolis. It is stated that at present, with the exception of coal-ashes, which are indispensable for making bricks, some description of lees, and a few other inconsiderable exceptions, no refuse in London pays half the expense of removal by cartage. The cost of removal, or of the labour and cartage, limits the general use or deposit of the refuse within a radius which does not exceed three miles beyond the line of the district-post of the metropolis, that is, about six miles. It is stated that, partly from the nature of the holdings, and from other circumstances within this limited district, agricultural improvements are not so great as might be expected where the facilities are so easy for obtaining any quantity of manure. Some idea may be formed of the loss of value of this manure from the metropolis, occasioned by the expense of its collection and removal, from the evidence of a considerable contractor for scavengering, &c., who states, with respect to the most productive manure,—'I have given away thousands of loads of night-soil: we knew not what to do with it.'[1]

---

1. 'Evidence of Mr. John Darke, contractor for cleansing, as to the obstacles to cleansing, and the conversion of the refuse of the Metropolis to productive use', App. 2 to *San. Rep.*, p. 379.

Street and Road Cleansing: Road Pavements

In the parts of some towns adjacent to the rural districts the cesspools are emptied gratuitously for the sake of the manure; but they only do this when there is a considerable accumulation, and any accumulation of any decomposing material which offends the smell is injurious to the health, especially in a town where all miasma is less diluted with fresh air, and where the population is less robust. For the saving of cartage, as well as the convenience of use, accumulations of refuse are frequently allowed to remain and decompose and dry amidst the habitations of the poorer classes. Dr. *Laurie* in his report on the sanitary condition of Greenock, furnishes an example. He says,—

'The first question I generally put when a new case of fever is admitted, is as to their locality. I was struck with the number of admissions from Market-street; most of the cases coming from that locality became quickly typhoid, and made slow recoveries. This is a narrow back street; it is almost overhung by a steep hill, rising immediately behind it; it contains the lowest description of houses, built closely together, the access to the dwellings being through filthy closes. The front entrance is generally the only outlet. Numerous food for the production of miasma lies concealed in this street. I think I could point out one in each close.

In one part of the street there is a dunghill,—yet it is too large to be called a dunghill. I do not mistake its size when I say it contains a hundred cubic yards of impure filth, collected from all parts of the town. It is never removed; it is the stock-in-trade of a person who deals in dung; he retails it by cartfuls. To please his customers, he always keeps a nucleus, as the older the filth is the higher is the price. The proprietor has an extensive privy attached to the concern. This collection is fronting the public street; it is enclosed in front by a wall; the height of the wall is about 12 feet, and the dung overtops it; the malarious moisture oozes through the wall, and runs over the pavement. The effluvia all round about this place in summer is horrible. There is a land of houses adjoining, four stories in height, and in the summer each house swarms with myriads of flies; every article of food and drink must be covered, otherwise, if left exposed for a minute, the flies immediately attack it, and it is rendered unfit for use, from the strong taste of the dunghill left by the flies. But there is a still more extensive dunghill in this street; at least, if not so high it covers double the extent of surface. What the depth is I cannot say. It is attached to the slaughter-house, and belongs, I believe, to the town authorities. It is not only the receptacle for the dung and offal from the slaughter-house, but the sweepings of the streets are also conveyed and deposited there; it has likewise a public privy attached. In the slaughter-house itself, which is adjoining the street, the blood and offal is allowed to lie a long time, and the smell in summer is highly offensive. In two of the narrow closes opposite the market, there is in each a small space not built upon, and that space, being the only spare ground in the close, is occupied by a dunghill; these two closes are notorious as nurseries for fever. I believe it to be a rare occurrence when fever is not to be found in them during any time of the year. Market-street is certainly one of the most filthy and unhealthy streets in Greenock; it is needless to say that many places here and there throughout the town are as bad, indeed, I may state that from the best to the worst locality in the town there is not a street but requires to be subjected to some rigid system for removing away regularly the rubbish and impurities which are constantly exhaling forth so much, and which is indirectly the cause of the yearly increase of so much destitution.'[1]

---

1. W. L. Laurie, 'Report on the general and sanitary condition of the town of Greenock', *Local Reps. Scot.*, pp. 256-7.

Mr. Baker, in his report, gives another instance of the ignorance and carelessness under which the health of the population suffers.

'The contractor for the street sweepings, who is the treator with the Commissioners of Public Nuisances in Leeds, last year rented a plot of vacant land in the centre of the North-east ward, the largest ward in point of population in the township of Leeds, and containing the greatest number of poor, and this year rents, in the East ward, another plot of land, as a depôt for the sweepings from the streets and markets, both vegetable and general, for the purpose of exsiccating and accumulating till they could be sold as manure and carried away. So noisome were these exhalations, that the inhabitants complained of their utter inability to ventilate their sleeping-rooms during the day time, and of the insufferable stench to which both by night and day they were thus subjected.'[1]

The comparatively recent mode of cleansing adopted in the wealthy and newly-built districts by the use of water-closets, and the discharge of all refuse at once from the house through the drain into the sewers, saves the delay and the previous accumulation, and it also saves the expense of the old means of removal. It is most applicable to the poorer districts, because really the most economical, when they are properly sewered and supplied with water. The cost of cheap and appropriate apparatus, and of water for cleansing, it will be proved is a reduction of the mere cost of cleansing in the old method, independently of the cost incurred by the decay of woodwork and deterioration of the tenement which commonly takes place on premises in the condition of those described by Mr. Howell. The chief objection to the extension of this system is the pollution of the water of the river into which the sewers are discharged. Admitting the expediency of avoiding the pollution, it is nevertheless proved to be an evil of almost inappreciable magnitude in comparison with the ill health occasioned by the constant retention of several hundred thousand accumulations of pollution in the most densely-peopled districts.

There is much evidence, however, to prove that it is possible to remove the refuse in such a mode as to avoid the pollution of the river, and at the same time avoid the culpable waste of the most important manure.

A practical example of the money value which lies in the refuse of a town, when removed in the cheapest manner, and applied in the form best adapted to production, viz., by a system of cleansing by water, is afforded in connexion with the city of Edinburgh. In the course of the sanitary inquiry in that city the particular attention of Dr. Arnott and myself was directed to the effects of some offensive irrigation of the land which had taken place in the immediate vicinity of that city. It appears that the contents of a large proportion of the sinks, drains, and privies of that city are conveyed in covered sewers to the eastern suburb of the town, where they are emptied into a stream called the Foul Burn, which passes ultimately into the sea. The stream is thus made into a large uncovered sewer or drain. Several years ago some of the occupiers of the land in the immediate vicinity of this stream diverted parts of it, and

---

1. *Local Reps. E. & W.*, p. 356.

collected the soil which it contained in tanks for use as manure. After this practice had been adopted for a long period, the farmers in the vicinity gradually found that the most beneficial mode of applying the manure was in the liquid form, and they conducted the stream over their meadows by irrigation. Others, perceiving the extraordinary fertility thus obtained, followed the example, and by degrees about 300 acres of meadow, chiefly in the eastern parts of that city, but all in its immediate vicinity, and the greater part of it in the neighbourhood of the palace of Holyrood, have been systematically irrigated with the contents of this common sewer. From some of this land so irrigated, four or five crops a-year have been obtained; land once worth from 40s. to 50s. per acre now lets for very high sums. It is stated by a writer cited as an authority, on behalf of the parties interested:

'That the rent for which some of these meadows are let in small portions to cow-feeders varies on an average from 20l. to 30l. per acre. Some of the richest meadows were let in 1835 at 38l. per acre; and in that season of scarce forage, 1826, 57l. per acre were obtained for the same meadows. * * * The waste land called Figget Whins, containing 30 acres, and 10 acres of poor sandy soil adjoining them, were formed into water meadows in 1821, at an expense of 1000l. The pasture of the Figget Whins used to be let for 40l. a-year, and that of the 10 acres at 60l. Now the same ground as meadows lets for 15l. or 20l. an acre a-year, and will probably let for more, as the land becomes more and more enriched.'[1]

This use of irrigation followed so gradually, that the time of its commencement seems not accurately ascertained, but is known to have been usual near the beginning of the present century. The tanks are still to a certain extent used. The irrigation proceeds from the beginning of April to the middle of September, and it is supposed that the deposits in the tanks are in the interval increased by the quantity of soil not employed in irrigations.

The practice is strongly objected to by the inhabitants as an offensive and injurious nuisance. To Dr. Arnott, who surveyed the district, the process appeared to be, like most offensive processes, unfitted for the vicinity of a town. The miasma from the preparation of the large accumulations of manure in open receptacles near places of public resort or crowded habitations would probably affect the public health injuriously to a greater or less degree. In particular states of the weather it could scarcely fail to engender disease. In the decomposition of substances for manure, deleterious gasses will be evolved, which in particular states of the atmosphere will act with powerful effects on animal life within their reach. But it is at the same time stated, the process of applying manure by irrigation, that is, separated and diluted with water, is considered to be productive of less deleterious gas, of less injurious effects, than by spreading it over fields in a solid form, and allowing it to remain until it is decomposed and separated by the atmosphere and conveyed into the soil by rain. Liebig,[2] the greatest living authority on agricultural chemistry, states that night-soil loses in drying half its

---

1. Anon., *Foul Burn Irrigation!* (Edinburgh 1840), p. 24.
2. Justus Liebig, author of *Organic Chemistry in its application to Agriculture and Physiology* (ed. Lyon Playfair, 1840).

valuable products, that is, half its 'nitrogen,' for the 'ammonia' escapes into the atmosphere. By irrigation, by the diffusion and conveyance of the manure to the plant in the medium of water the escape of the valuable substance as a noxious and injurious gas is diminished.* Whatever extent of loss there is from manures by decomposition when placed on the land in a solid form, and when exposed to the action of the atmosphere, it is stated that there is proportionate gain by holding the material in suspension in water. The simple offensiveness, it may be assumed, is a sufficient ground of exclusion of any process from amidst the habitations of a town population. But at a reasonable distance the use of dung or any other manure would not be forbidden; and the process which is the least injurious, the irrigative, is entitled therefore to a preference. Effective drainage must make way for the conveyance of diluted manures, and consequently for effective irrigation.

The continuance of the practice in Edinburgh of the use of the common sewer for irrigation is defended by the occupiers and owners, on the ground that from the time of its commencement, when it was unopposed, and, as it appears to us, escaped any notice, a legal right has been acquired by them in the manure of the city contained in the Burn, and the present claimants of the right contend that they are entitled to compensation under the Scotch law for any diversion of the stream or of the manure which it contains. The irrigation which has surrounded the palace of Holyrood having, as it is considered, rendered it prejudicial to health, Her Majesty's government, for the protection of this palace as a royal residence, have directed legal process for the trial of the right claimed to the irrigation. The defendants vindicate the measure on the ground of its utility as an agricultural operation, and treat the proposal to divert the contents of the sewers as being in fact a proposal to deprive the city of the milk and butter yielded by more than 3000 milch cows, and the markets of the meat from their carcases; that, in fact, 'the grass, which in virtue of irrigation these meadows produce, supports in Edinburgh 3300 cows, and in Leith 600 cows, during the season.'† We were informed that the parties interested in the lands estimate the com-

---

* Mr. Smith, of Deanston, is of opinion that it would be practicable to distribute such refuse by irrigation without exposure of the surface of the fluid in which it is held in suspension. [James Smith (1789-1850), manager of the Deanston cotton mill in Stirlingshire, but best known for his contributions to the art of agricultural drainage. In 1842, he abandoned his mill and farm at Deanston, and set up in London as an agricultural engineer. He became recognised as an authority on sanitary questions, and was a member of the Health of Towns Commission of 1843.]

† Professor Liebig in his work on the 'Chemistry of Agriculture,' refers to various authorities on the practical value of such refuse, who state that 'human urine is, if possible, more husbanded by the Chinese than night-soil for manure; every farm or patch of land for cultivation has a tank, where all substances convertible into manure are carefully deposited, the whole made liquid by adding urine in the proportion required, and invariably applied in that state.' This is exactly the process followed in the Netherlands.—See 'Outlines of Flemish Husbandry', p. 22. 'The business of collecting urine and night-soil employs an immense number of persons, who deposit tubs in every

pensation that would induce them to discontinue the practice at 150,000*l*.; and a pamphlet written at their instance, in 1840, states this as the sum which the proprietors of the meadows to the west of the city would be legally entitled to (independently of the claims of those in the east) were the practice abolished by legislative authority.[1] The proprietors have had, on several occasions, sufficient influence to frustrate the efforts of the city authorities, to obtain legislative sanction for the removal of the nuisance, and for a more salubrious disposal of it for the advantage of the inhabitants themselves.

The public refuse of cities by the usual course of legislation in local Acts, and by custom, and on all principles which govern the application of the proceeds of such produce belongs to the public, and it may be submitted that, whatever may be the decision in the case of Edinburgh, means should be taken to prevent for the future the acquisition of new rights at the expense of the health and of the conveniences of such large classes of the population. And it may here be observed that it will probably be found, under the circumstances of the increasing population of the towns, and the increasing necessity of keeping open spaces within and around the towns, and of exercising a general control for the beneficial arrangement of new buildings for the public health and convenience, and of securing convenient public walks and places of temperate and healthful recreation for the population—that it is most

---

contd.
house in the cities for the reception of the urine of the inmates, which vessels are removed daily with as much care as our farmers remove their honey from the hives. When we consider the immense value of night-soil as a manure, it is quite astounding that so little attention is paid to preserve it. The quantity is immense which is carried down by the drains in London to the river Thames, serving no other purpose than to pollute its waters. A substance which by its putrefaction generates miasmata may, by artificial means, be rendered totally inoffensive, inodorous, and transportable, and yet prejudice prevents these means being resorted to. If,' says the professor, 'we admit that the liquid and solid excrements of man amount on an average to $1\frac{1}{2}$ lb. daily ($\frac{5}{4}$ lb. of urine and $\frac{1}{4}$ lb. fæces), and that both together contain 3 per cent. of nitrogen; then in one year they will amount to 547 lbs., which contain 16·41 lbs. of nitrogen, a quantity sufficient to yield the nitrogen of 800 lbs. of wheat, rye, oats, or of 900 lbs. of barley.'—(Boussingault) 'This is much more than is necessary to add to an acre of land in order to obtain, with the assistance of the nitrogen absorbed from the atmosphere, the richest possible crop every year. Every town and farm might thus supply itself with the manure which, besides containing the most nitrogen, contains also the most phosphates, and if rotation of the crops were adopted, they would be most abundant.'—Edited by Dr. LYON PLAYFAIR. [Liebig (ed. Playfair), *op. cit.* 2nd. ed. (1842), pp. 185-6. Boussingault's standard work on the chemistry of agriculture, in which (pp. 382-9) he recommends the use of human manure in agriculture, was actually published after the *Sanitary Report*—his *Economie rurale considérée dans ses rapports avec la chimie, la physique, et la météorologie* (Paris, 2 vols. 1843-4; English translation by G. Low, 1845).]

---

1. Anon., *Foul Burn Agitation! Statement explaining the Nature and History of the Agricultural Irrigation near Edinburgh* (Edinburgh 1840), p. 161.

desirable for all these objects that means should be taken to redeem to the crown the fee, or otherwise obtain as early as practicable, and on the terms of proper compensation, lands within and in the immediate vicinity of towns for public use.

If then, in Edinburgh, the contents of the cesspools were carried by adequate supplies of water in drains from the houses into covered sewers, and thence in covered instead of open sewers to the lands at proper distances where it might be distributed as manure by irrigation, it would be a mode of irrigation considered by Mr. Smith of Deanston, and other authorities on drainage and irrigation, whom I consulted, the best that is now apparently practicable, *i.e.*, the best means for removing quickly, and constantly, and the least injuriously, the matters which can only remain for removal by any other process at the expense of the public health; they concur in opinion that it would also be the most productive mode of distributing the manure.

On the scale of the value set upon that portion of the refuse of Edinburgh that has been appropriated for irrigation by the occupiers of the land in the vicinity of the city, the value of the whole of the soil of the city (not one-third of which finds its way into the irrigated meadows), if it were made completely available by an appropriate system of town drainage, would be double or treble the amount, producing an income of 15,000*l.* to 20,000*l.* per annum for public purposes. On the same scale of value it would appear that, in the metropolis, refuse to the value of nearly double what is now paid for the water of the metropolis is thrown away, partly from the districts which are sewered into the Thames, and partly from the poor districts which are unsewered, where it accumulates and remains a nuisance until it is removed at a great expense. It is allowed by Captain Vetch[1], an experienced engineer, and by other authorities, to be the most eligible plan in respect to economy as well as efficiency, wherever the levels were not convenient, or it were desirable to send the refuse over heights for distribution, that the contents of the sewers should be lifted by steam power, as water is lifted in the drainage of the fens, and that it might be sent for distribution, wherever it is required for use, in iron pipes, in the same mode as that in which water is conveyed into towns by the water companies. The estimated expense of this mode of cleansing and removal is about the same as the conveyance of water into towns, *i.e.*, not a tithe of the expense of cartage, as will subsequently be shown.

The comparative economy of conveyance of fluid in pipes has been but little observed, and has only recently perhaps been applied for the purpose of cleansing. The following is an instance of the application of the principle:—A contract was about to be entered into by the West Middlesex Water Company for hauling out from their reservoir at

---

1. James Vetch (1789-1869), educated at Edinburgh University and the Royal Military Academy, Woolwich. Served in the Royal Engineers 1807-24. Mining engineer in Mexico 1824-9 and 1832-5. Engineer on the construction of the Birmingham and Gloucester Railway 1836-40. In 1842 he designed a successful sewerage scheme for Leeds, and in 1843-7 a similar one for Windsor. He served on the Metropolitan Commission of Sewers 1849-53. Published two works on sewerage in 1842.

Street and Road Cleansing: Road Pavements 125

Kensington the deposit of eight or ten years' silt, which had accumulated to the depth of three or four feet. The contractor offered to remove this quantity, which covered nearly an acre of surface, for the sum of 400*l*., in three or four weeks. The reservoir was emptied in order to be inspected by the engineer and directors before the contract was accepted. It occurred to one of the officers that the cleansing might be accomplished more readily by merely stirring up the silt, to mix it with the water; and then if a cut or outlet were made in the main-pipe used for conveying the water to London, that it might be washed out. He accordingly got thirty or forty men to work in stirring up the deposit, and accomplished the work at the cost of 40*l*. or 50*l*. and three or four days' labour, instead of so many weeks; when the directors went to see the basin, to decide upon the contract, the reservoir was as free from any deposit as a house-floor. Since the discovery thus made, the silt has been regularly cleansed out into the common sewers. It is to be observed, in respect to the relative cheapness of the two modes, that the contractor would only have removed the silt to the nearest convenient place of deposit in the immediate vicinity of the reservoir, whereas, in the fluid state, it might be carried at the actual cost of conveying water, as far as it is at present conveyed, and sold with a profit, 12 or 14 miles, and raised to heights of 150 feet, at $2\frac{1}{2}d$. per ton.

By the application of capital and machinery, the cost of conveyance of substances in suspension in a fluid, even at the water companies' prices, may be rendered thirty and even more than forty times as cheap as collection by hand labour and removal by cartage. In the metropolis, where the persons who water the roads may obtain water gratuitously from pumps, the water supplied by stand-pipes by some of the water companies at 1*l*. per 100 tons, is found to be twice as cheap as the mere labour of pumping the water into the cart. By proper hydraulic arrangements heavy solid substances may be swept away through the iron pipes.

These means which science gives of cheapening the cost of the conveyance of refuse from houses, will be available also in extending and completing the cleansing of the towns, of removing the filth which oppresses the poorer districts, and rendering the whole of it available, in the best form, for future use as manure.

The expense of cleansing the streets of the *township* of Manchester is 5,000*l*. per annum. For this sum the first class of streets, namely, the most opulent and the large thoroughfares, are cleansed once a-week, the second class once a-fortnight, and the third class once a-month. But this provision leaves untouched, or leaves in the condition described in Dr. Baron Howard's report, the courts, alleys, and places where the poorest classes live, and where the cleansing should be daily. There are abundance of recommendations to the effect, 'Let it be ordered that the streets be properly cleansed;' but in this instance the cost of cleansing the whole of what is properly the same town, Salford, and the out-townships, would be 8,000*l*. or 10,000*l*. per annum; and such a recommendation, under the existing modes of management, is equivalent to saying, let 20,000*l*. or 30,000*l*. of additional rates be expended, and 40,000 or 60,000 additional loads of refuse be removed. In other large towns, the service and the expense is on a similar scale. At the rate of expense of one large parish, the present cost of cleansing in the metropolis may be estimated at about 40,000*l*. per annum. This expense, however, is generally repaid by the sale of the coal-ashes, which are used in the manufacture of bricks.

Though the refuse of the poorer districts is often taken and sold, the immediate objection to the extension of the services of the scavenger to them is the increase of the immediate expense, which it is practically necessary to consider in detail, although if there were no compensation by the sale of any coal-ashes or house refuse, and if the occupants were required to pay for the cleansing at the rate of one of the opulent parishes in the metropolis, that is at the rate of 4*s*. per house per annum, which would be less than a penny per tenement for the weekly street cleansing; or in the poorer districts, where there are mostly two families to a tenement, a charge of less than one halfpenny per week for cleansing, would be found to be good economy, as one means of diminishing the existing heavy charge of sickness, not to speak of the wear and tear of clothes.

Two-thirds of the usual expense of street cleansing is the expense of cartage, which, with a proper adaptation of the sewers, is wholly unnecessary. The exclusive use of hand-labour in street-sweeping is pronounced by competent judges to be a mere barbarism, and several machines have been invented which demonstrate that by mechanical power, moved by horses, the cleansing may be effected in a far shorter time. Some of these scrape the mud in ridges to the sides, where it remains until it can be lifted and carted away. But this is objected to as inconvenient by the shopkeepers, and the scavengers object that it is no convenience to them, inasmuch as raking it in heaps prevents the evaporation of the liquid, and increases the cartage; and, moreover, that the process of sweeping by hand is as quick as the carts can return for its removal. A machine has been used at Manchester which rapidly and cleanly sweeps the level surfaces of the streets into a cart; but there is still the encumberance of the labour, and cost and delay of carting the refuse to a place of deposit, which may be several miles distant, and returning to reload.[1] The value of a process of street-cleansing is proportioned to the rapidity with which it is performed, but at present it is usually delayed until the sun or the air has done a large portion of the work by the evaporation of the moisture, commonly however to the deterioration of the air of the town and the health, and also to the deterioration of the value of the refuse.

On examining these obstructions to the cleanliness and salubrity of our towns, it became apparent that the expensive and slow process of the removal of the surface refuse of the streets by cartage might be dispensed with, and the whole at once carried away by the mode which is proved, in the case of the refuse of houses, to be the most rapid, cheap, and convenient, namely, by sweeping it at once into the sewers, and discharging it by water.

---

1. For 'Mr. Whitworth's automaton street-sweeping machine', and its use in Manchester, see A. Redford and I. S. Russell, *The History of Local Government in Manchester*, II (1940), 141-2, 163-4.

The sewerage of the metropolis, though it is a frequent subject of boast to those who have not examined its operations or effects, will be found to be a vast monument of defective administration, of lavish expenditure, and extremely defective execution. The general defect of these works is, that they are so constructed as to accumulate deposits within them; that the accumulations remain for years, and are at last only removed at a great expense, and in an offensive manner, by handlabour and cartage. The effect is to generate and retain in large quantities before the houses the gases which it is the object of cleansing to remove. In the course of the present inquiry instances have been frequently presented of fevers and deaths occasioned by the escapes of gas from the sewers into the streets and houses. In the evidence given before the Committee of the House of Commons, which received evidence on the subject in 1834[1], one medical witness stated, that of all cases of severe typhus that he had seen, eight-tenths were either in houses of which the drains from the sewers were untrapped, or which, being trapped, were situated opposite gully-holes; and he mentioned instances where servants sleeping in the lower rooms of houses were invariably attacked with fever. It was proposed as a remedy to prevent the escape of the noxious effluvia by trapping them, but this was refused on the ground of the danger to the men, who must enter the sewers to clean them, from the confined gas. In one of the circulars the reason assigned for allowing the escape of the gas into the streets is that if it were confined in the sewers it might impede the flow of the water. It was then proposed to allow the escape of the noxious gases through chimneys constructed at certain distances. But this was decided to be an experiment, and the Committee did not feel themselves authorized to make experiments. Instances were adduced where it had been found necessary either to trap or to remove gully-holes in the vicinity of butchers' shops, to avoid the injurious effects of the effluvium upon the meat. Similarly mischievous effects of the defective construction and management of the sewers are commonly displayed in the medical reports from the provincial towns, and they have been incidentally noticed in the passages already cited.

It may be mentioned as another instance of the absence of appropriate knowledge that has governed these structural arrangements, that a large proportion of the most expensive sewers are constructed with flat bottoms. In proportion as the water is spread the flow is impeded, and the deposit of matter it may hold in suspension increased. Mr. Roe, a civil engineer, who, much to the honour of the Holborn and Finsbury district of sewers, has been appointed to the care of their sewers, and is perhaps the only officer having the experience and qualifications of a civil engineer, states, that as compared with sewers or drains with bottoms of a semicircular form, those with flat bottoms invariably occasion a larger amount of deposit; and with the same flow of water, the difference of construction occasions a difference of more than onehalf in the deposit which is left. By the common and most expensive form, the drains are apt to be choked up with noxious accumulations;

---

1. Evidence of Peter Fuller before the *Select Committee on Metropolis Sewers*, P.P. 1834, XV, Q. 874.

II. Public Arrangements External to the Residences

by being built with flat sides (instead of with curved sides, which give the strength of an arch) they are apt in clayey and slippery ground to be forced in. The expense of the improved form is nearly one-fourth less than those in general use. *Mr. Roe*, whose evidence, which is corroborated by the evidence of other engineers, is given in the Appendix, was asked:

In respect to the levels, how have you found the sewers?—They appear to have been entirely constructed with reference to the locality, to drain to the nearest outlet, and not on an extended view for the whole district, or with any view to sewerage on a large scale. In the Holborn and Finsbury divisions the Commissioners now adopt a series of levels suited from the lowest outlets to the surrounding districts.

Have you heard of any alterations made in the surrounding districts on the the same principle?—I have heard of none as adopted generally. The City have lowered several of their outlets; and the chairman of the Westminster Commission has had the subject under consideration for some time.

What are the chief effects of the piecemeal town drainage without reference to extended levels?—Chiefly that when new lines of houses are built and require new sewers, either the old sewers must be taken up and re-constructed at a great expense, to adjust them to a new and effective sewerage, or the new sewers, if they are adjusted to the old ones, are deficient in fall, and they have greater deposits.

Does the existing form or system of sewerage answer fully and at the least expense the chief objects of sewerage in house and street cleansing, and the removal of noxious substances?—No, it does not, except where the outlets have been lowered, and the sewers continued at a proper level; great accumulations of deposit are occasioned in the sewers, and from their containing the refuse that was at one time deposited in the cesspools, the deposit is more noxious than formerly; the gas is more considerable, it escapes more extensively into streets and into the houses, where the drains are not well trapped. My opinion is that the general health of the men who work and have been accustomed to the sewers, has become still worse; they are more pale and thin, and lower in general health than formerly. The effect of the noxious gases upon men working in these places is to lower the general health. Since I have had the superintendence of the sewers, the men have encountered about half a dozen accidents by explosions of gas.

But is the health of these men who work in the sewers to be taken as a criterion of the health of persons who are not accustomed to such places?—I have had no means of forming a comparison, though I am of opinion that gases which they encounter without any immediate injury would be very injurious to the health of susceptible persons, or of any persons not habituated to it.

The first prejudicial effect of the defective system, then, is to occasion these noxious accumulations; how are they removed?—Formerly, in the Holborn and Finsbury sewers, and at present, I believe, in all other sewers, the streets were opened at a great expense and obstruction (they are so now, I believe, elsewhere); men descend, scoop up the deposit into pails, which are raised by a windlass to the surface, and laid there until the carts come; it is laid there until it is carted away, sometimes for several hours, to the public annoyance and prejudice. The contract price for removal from the old sewers without man-holes was 11$s.$ per cubic yard of slop removed; where they have man-holes it was 6$s.$ 10$d.$ per cubic yard. This practice also involves injury and expense as respects the pavement; a street may be well paved when it is broken up for the cleansing of the sewers, but the portions of pavements so disturbed are never so well put down again; neither can accidents be effectually guarded against.

By what means may these effects be obviated?—In the Holborn and Finsbury divisions I suggested a plan of flushing the sewers, and of carrying off all the refuse by water. This plan has been adopted, and it is now in operation. The breaking up of the streets is avoided by the formation of side entrances; cast-iron flushing gates are fixed in the sewers; the ordinary flow of water in the sewers accumulates at these gates; the gates are opened, and the force of the water is sufficient to sweep off the deposit; and the system may be further extended.

What is the comparative difference in the expense of construction?—The cost of side entrances and flood-gates, as compared with the cost of man-holes, is from 6*d*. to 1*s*. less per foot lineal of the length of new sewers.

What other expense is attendant on this improved practice?—The main expense is the attendance of a man to shut and open the flood-gates.

The structural expense being lower, is the ultimate expense of cleansing lower also?—Yes; the expense of cleansing the sewers is about 50 per cent. less than the prevalent mode. Our expense of cleansing the sewers was about 1,200*l*. per annum; we save 600*l*. of that, and expect to save more; but to this must be added the saving to the public of the cleansing of the private drains, formerly choked by the accumulations in the sewers. This saving, on a moderate calculation, is found to be upwards of 300*l*. per annum. There is also the diminution of the escapes of gas from the old and continued accumulations.

During what intervals are deposits allowed to remain on the old mode?—The average is in one set of sewers about five years, and in another about ten years.

During which time the public are subjected to all the escapes of gas from the decomposing accumulation?—Exactly so. It could not, however, go on so long but for heavy falls of rain or snow, which occasion partial clearances.

What is the effect of these accumulations upon the private drainage?—That the drains to the private houses are stopped: the first intimation of the foul state of the main sewer arises from complaints of individuals whose drains are affected; the accumulations in the private drains also occasions an expense to the individuals and much annoyance. By flushing the sewers this expense might be, and in Holborn and Finsbury division it is, avoided.

Are there any other defects you have, as an engineer, noticed in the prevalent mode of constructing the sewers?—Yes, the prevalent practice is to join sewers at angles, frequently at right angles; this occasions eddies and deposits of sediment that would otherwise pass off with the water; it injures the capacity of the main sewers by obstructing the current of water along them: I ascertained by experiment that the time occupied in the passage of an equal quantity of water, along similar lengths of sewer with equal falls, was—

	Seconds
Along a straight line	90
With a true curve	100
With a turn at right angles	140

The Commissioners of the Holborn and Finsbury divisions agreed to require that the curves in sewers, passing from one street to another, shall be formed with a radius of not less than 20 feet; it is also required that the inclination or fall shall be increased at the junction, in order to preserve an equal capacity for the passage of water, and of effect in sweeping away the deposit.

When by heavy falls of snow or otherwise the refuse of the streets is carried into such sewers, is there any difficulty in sweeping it away?—None whatsoever.

In what number of years would the saving in cleansing sewers by flushing repay the expense of applying the apparatus to the existing sewers in the Holborn and Finsbury divisions?—In seven years.

Have you any doubt of the practicability of carrying all the surface cleansing of the streets into the sewers, and removing it by conveyance in water, instead of by hand labour and cartage?—I entertain no doubt whatever that it might be done, where there is a good sewer and proper gully-holes and shoots; with a good supply of water these would carry away rapidly all the surface refuse; the experience of the sewerage in the Holborn and Finsbury divisions prove it.

How does it prove it?—At every opportunity the street-sweepers sweep all they can into the gully-holes, and it is swept away without inconvenience.

One practical witness states that the expense of the cartage alone of the refuse from a Macadamised street of half a mile, in the winter time in the metropolis, is 5*l*. weekly. What would be the comparative expense of carrying it away by the sewers?—It would save the whole expense of the cartage; it would be less than the present expense of sweeping and filling into the carts, and if there were a sufficient supply of water on the surface, the work might be conducted with great rapidity.

You are aware that one inconvenience of the existing mode of street cleansing, independently of the great expense, is the length of time during which the wet refuse remains to the public annoyance on the surface, until removed by the slow process of sweeping and cartage?—Yes; and the men would appear to delay for the purpose of the dirt being removed, by being washed by rain into the sewers.

Do you conceive that all the business of street cleansing and house draining might be consolidated advantageously to the public?—Yes, clearly so, and with great economy.[1]

In the evidence of Mr. Oldfield, an experienced builder in the wealthy districts of the metropolis, will be found exemplifications of the mischiefs resulting from the defective modes of opening sub-drains or communications, even from houses of the first class, into the main drains. The state of sewerage and drainage in the larger towns, as described in the medical reports, in its effects of frequent disease and death,—is much worse in the provincial towns. But every step in improvement is an advance in reduction of existing burdens; drainage, *per se*, will be found to be a reduction of an existing charge for the expenses of sickness and mortality; *science*, applied to the improvement of drainage, not only gives it efficiency, but reduces greatly the expense.

The streets in the larger towns commonly display, from the want of science in their construction, similar waste, and equally admit of an improved and scientific arrangement, which will conduce to economy and to improved public health.

The bad condition of the streets in many of the towns is very generally ascribable to pavement being commonly regarded as requisite solely for cart or carriage conveyance, and not as a means of cleanliness. The pavement has therefore been usually confined to the chief streets in which the carriage traffic is considerable. Some of the principal streets even in the metropolis almost justify the description of being 'streams of

---

1. 'Evidence of Mr. John Roe on the practical improvement in sewerage and drainage tried in the Holborn and Finsbury divisions of the Metropolis', App. 1 to *San. Rep.*, pp. 373-7.

mud and filth in winter,' and 'seas of dust' in summer. But attention has of late been directed to the cleansing of the road as a means of removing damp and dirt or dust, which are each found to be injurious. So far as various experiments have yet proceeded in the metropolis, they are stated to be highly favourable to the use of wood as a substance for paving the streets, though perhaps in forms different from those at present in use, with improvements which further experience will suggest. Wood, when pinned together and laid on a firm substratum, appears to be less retentive of wet than most forms of stone pavement, and to possess very considerable advantages over the Macadamised roads for crowded thoroughfares. If it be brought into general use it will have an advantage in removing the granite dust, which medical authorities believe to be much more prejudicial to health, in exciting or aggravating lung diseases, than the public have been aware of. Where there is much dust in the working of close quarries, the effects of it are almost as destructive to the lungs of the operatives as the knife-grinding to the operatives of Sheffield who do not guard against the steel-dust. 'It is scarcely conceivable,' Dr. Arnott states, 'that the immense quantities of granite dust pounded by one or two hundred thousand pairs of wheels working on Macadamised streets, should not greatly injure the public health. In houses bordering such streets or roads, it is found that, notwithstanding the practice of watering, the furniture is often covered with dust even more than once in the day, so that writing on it with the finger becomes legible, and the lungs and air-tubes of the inhabitants, with a moist lining to detain the dust, are constantly pumping the same atmosphere. The passengers by a stage-coach in dry weather, when the wind is moving with them so as to keep them enveloped in the cloud of dust raised by the horses' feet and the wheels of the coach, have their clothes soon saturated to whiteness with the dust, and their lungs of course are charged in a corresponding degree. A gentleman who rode only 20 miles in this way, had afterwards to cough and expectorate for 10 days to clear his chest again.' The imperfection of road cleansing in paved streets at the same time deteriorates the salubrity of the towns, the value of the refuse for production, and the streets themselves. The farmers find that the refuse of the streets, of which horse-dung and other excrementitious substances form so important a part, is valuable in proportion as it is 'fresh.' On a proposition to sweep the streets of a town district oftener, it was stated by some farmers that they would, in that case, give more for the refuse. It is with this description of refuse, as stated with respect to the nightsoil, in proportion as it is allowed to remain in the streets to dry, it loses the gas which gives it value; and the gas which is lost frequently gives to streets the offensive smell perceptible to strangers who have not been familiarised to it, and makes a deleterious addition to the compounds by which the health of the town population is injured. The complete and rapid cleansing of the roads has also its effects on the draught. It is proved experimentally that, 'calling the draught on a broken-stone road 5, that on the same road covered with dust is 8, and that on the same road wet and muddy is 10.'[1] A road should be cleansed

---

1. Sir Henry Parnell, *A Treatise on Roads* (1833), p. 438.

'from time to time, so as never to have half an inch of mud upon it. This is particularly necessary to be attended to where the materials are weak, for if the surface is not kept clean, so as to admit of its becoming dry in the intervals between showers of rain, it will be rapidly worn away.'[1] With the even surface obtainable from the use of wood as a pavement, it is stated that the streets which are now kept wet and dirty whilst the process of cleansing is slowly carried on by the hand, may be rapidly and cheaply swept by sweeping-machines drawn by horses. With the advantage of such a system of sewerage as that described by Mr. Roe, the surface refuse, which continues exposed during a whole week, may be removed every morning before the hours of traffic from all the principal thoroughfares. In the main streets of the towns of considerable traffic, a smooth and firm surface for the carriageway would ensure the advantages of a railroad, in addition to those to the public health from cleanliness. The experience on several portions of smooth road shows that single horses with lighter and less expensive vehicles would suffice where two horses are now required on the common roads; where strong stone pavements are required to resist the shock of heavy vehicles, and heavy vehicles propelled with double power to resist the battering of strong pavements, and the grinding and wear and tear of heavy and dirty roads.

Captain Vetch, the engineer, who is extensively acquainted with the structural economy of towns, observes in a communication on the subject, that:

'The other mode of avoiding the formation of mud is the substitution of wooden pavements; of the success of these I have little doubt, though for the present many failures have occurred, either from the foundation not having been truly and firmly laid, or from the blocks of wood not being massive enough. The greatest objection to wood pavements at present is the slipping of the horses, but this I believe might be obviated. The question, however, at present is to get rid of the street dirt, such as it is; and for that purpose I concur in opinion it would only be necessary in wet weather during rains that the street-cleaner should sweep the dirt into the kennels, and aid the water by stirring the mud, to carry off the material in a state of diffusion; in dry weather, the opening of pipes with hose attached would serve the same purpose as the rains, and at the same time aid the sewerage at the time most required. After a short but heavy fall of rain, the cleansing effect of the water is fully perceived: and if any means could be devised of saving the rain-water that falls on the houses and in the streets, so as to apply it in considerable quantities at intervals, it is probable that the rain-water would be amply sufficient for all the purposes in question.'[2]

Mr. Roe states, that arrangements were made with the water companies for supplies of water for the cleansing of the sewers in the Holborn and Finsbury district, but it was found that the ordinary supplies to the sewers sufficed, and those from the company were not used.

The cleansing of the streets and the removal of the impurities from the

---

1. Sir Henry Parnell, *A Treatise on Roads* (1833), p. 275.
2. 'Communication from Captain Vetch, of the Royal Engineers, on the structural arrangements of new buildings, and protection of the public health', *San. Rep.*, App. 5, p. 390.

habitations appears to have been the subject of considerable attention at Paris of late years. An individual proposed to the administration of that city a mode of cleansing the streets and pavement, by sweeping all the refuse into the sewers which are discharged into the Seine, that had hitherto been daily gathered into heaps and carted away beyond the precincts. The minister of police thought it advisable to take the opinion of the Institute on the proposal. The superiority of the proposed mode of street cleansing was admitted, but the members of the Institute, to whom the subject was referred, having ascertained the quantity of rubbish which was daily collected in Paris, and also the quantity of water which flowed in the Seine during the summer-time, they found that this volume of water was 9600 times greater than the greatest quantity of filth and rubbish collected in the same length of time from the streets of Paris; and they reported as their conclusion, 'that the quantity of dirt which would be thrown into the Seine, compared with the volume of water in the river, would be found to be so extremely small as to be absolutely inappreciable; that it was not from the consideration therefore of insalubrity that the project for cleaning the streets as proposed should be negatived, but solely because by that means there would be lost a quantity of most valuable manure, which was quite indispensable to the agriculture around Paris, and consequently to Paris itself.'[1]

Mr. Roe has furnished me with a calculation made from the flow of water in the Thames, at a neap tide: taking the ebb, and comparing it with the quantity of deposit in the water running from the sewers from the whole of the metropolis (assuming that the sewerage bears the same proportion as the Holborn and Finsbury division), that the proportion of impurities to the volume of water of the Thames is as 1 to 10,100. If the surface cleansing of the streets were added to the ordinary mass of impurity, he calculates that the proportion held in suspension would then be about 1 to 5069. To this must be added the impurities from land-floods, and those from vessels in the river. The amount of impurity discharged from the sewers was calculated from the amount of deposit known to have been formed in several of them. The amount of impurity in the Thames would therefore be, at the least, double the amount of that calculated for the Seine.*

---

* In Paris the greater proportion of the private houses are even now supplied with water only by water-carriers, and the means of the immediate conveyance of refuse, by a system of water-closets communicating through drains to sewers to receptacles for use, could not have been presented to the consideration of the men of science to whom the subject was referred. It appears that in the first class of houses in that city the cesspools were formerly only emptied once in four or five years, and that it is now considered a great improvement that they are emptied twice or thrice a-year. But the offensiveness and the frequent injurious effects from emptying and removing the contents, has led to the proposal of a plan of closed receptacles or removable
If the evils of the pollution of such a stream were much greater, they

---

1. 'Extract from the Report of Fourcroy and others, showing the calculation of the extent of pollution of the Seine from the discharge of the refuse of the streets of Paris', *San. Rep.*, App. 4, pp. 381-2.

would still be found inconsiderable as compared with the perpetual pollution of the air by the retention of ordures and refuse amidst large masses of the population. What has been stated as to the practicability of extending threefold the cleansing of towns, by dispensing with cartage, and using the sewers for the removal of the refuse of the streets, is stated as an advantage, even on the supposition that no use is made of the refuse, and that it is entirely thrown away. But it were a reproach to stop at the advance to this far lesser evil, and to add to the pollution of the streams of the towns, which throughout the country form the chief common sewers, by throwing into them everything that is vile in the towns, *i.e.* everything that is most valuable for increasing the surrounding fertility.

On a full examination of the evidence adduced and of the evidence indicated, it will, I trust, be found to be satisfactorily established; that the houses of towns may be constantly and rapidly cleansed of noxious refuse by adaptation of drains and public sewers; and that with such an adaptation, for one street or one district cleansed at the present expense three may be cleansed by the proposed mode; that the natural streams flowing near towns may be preserved from the pollution caused by the influx of the contents of the public sewers, by the conveyance of all refuse through covered pipes, and that the existing cost of conveyance, by which its use for production is restricted, may be reduced to less than one-fortieth or fiftieth of the present expense of removal by hand labour and cartage;* that these bounties on cleanliness and salubrity on

---

* *contd.:*
tanks, in which the soil may be carted away to the place of deposit for use as manure. The retention, however, of accumulations which can only be constantly removed by means of water, and the want of proper supplies of water laid on in the houses very seriously disparages the salubrity and habits of the population of that city, as well as of the towns in this country where the same practice prevails.

* Mr. John Martin[1], the artist, has endeavoured to direct public attention to the sewerage of the metropolis, and proposed the erection of a grand cloaca maxima, and various architectural works along the Thames, with the meritorious objects of preventing the pollution of the river, and saving the refuse. His plan was to form a canal on each bank parallel to the river, so as to intercept the whole of the sewerage, and convey it to large reservoirs or places of deposit at a distance. His plan for the north bank was a canal, constructed of iron, costing 60,000*l*. per mile, extending from Westminster to the mouth of the Regent's Canal, 'where the grand receptacle should be from which the soil should be conveyed to barges, and transmitted by canals to various parts of the country.'—*Committee on Sewers' Report*, p. 169[2]. The primary objection to

---

1. John Martin (1789-1854), best known for his 'Belshazzar's Feast' (1821). From 1827 he became interested in the question of the metropolitan water supply. See *Gentleman's Magazine*, 1854, I, 433-6.
2. Evidence drawn from a memorandum entitled 'A plan for improving the air and water of the Metropolis by preventing the sewage being conveyed into the Thames . . .' submitted by John Martin to the *Select Committee on Metropolis Sewers*, **P.P.** 1834, **XV**, Q. 2340.

the one hand, and beneficial production on the other, are dependent on skilful and appropriate administrative arrangements. But for the attainment of these objects, and the relief of the worst-conditioned districts, another provision appears to be requisite, namely, appropriate

Supplies of Water

Besides those reports from towns in which a large proportion of their salubrity is attributed to a natural drainage, from the porosity of the soil, or from the undulations of the surface being favourable to the discharge of moisture, as at Birmingham, other reports ascribe a large proportion of the comparative health of the population to advantageous circumstances, in respect to the supplies of water. From such information as that already cited, it will be manifest that for an efficient system of house cleansing and sewerage, it is indispensable that proper supplies of pure water should be provided, and be laid on in the houses in towns of every size, and, it might be added, in all considerable rural villages. No previous investigations had led me to conceive the great extent to which the labouring classes are subjected to privations, not only of water for the purpose of ablution, house cleansing, and sewerage, but of wholesome water for drinking, and culinary purposes.

Mr. *John Liddle*, one of the medical officers of the Whitechapel union, after describing the deplorable condition of the dwellings of the labouring population in that part of London, states, that:

'In connexion with this state of things is the deficiency of water which is not laid on in any of their houses.

'How do they get such water as they use?—They get it for the most part from a plug in the courts. I cannot say whether it is the actual scarcity of water, or their reluctance to fetch it, but the effect is a scarcity of water. When I have occasion to visit their rooms, I find they have only a very scanty supply of water in their tubs. When they are washing, the smell of the dirt mixed with the soap is the most offensive of all the smells I have to encounter. They merely pass dirty linen through very dirty water. The smell of the linen itself, when so

---

* *contd.:*

this plan is that it would send the refuse still further out of the reach of large districts, where it is wanted as manure, to a place where it would only be available to the places for which canal conveyance would be convenient; that it would leave untouched the great obstacle to the use of manure, namely, the cost of removal and application by cartage and hand labour. The construction of the canal would also involve the disturbance of the whole of the wharf property; as originally proposed it involved their entire re-construction, and the erection of a grand colonnade along the banks of the river. For the removal of the refuse, engineers of practical experience agree that the most eligible plan was by various small conduits, not larger, where iron pipes might be necessary, than the pipes used by the water companies in bringing water into the metropolis, at a cost not a fifth, perhaps, of one large canal, and without any disturbance of property. For the application of the refuse as manure, practical experience at Edinburgh, and of irrigation elsewhere, shows that the most effectual mode of distribution for use is by water-meadows or drainage and irrigation combined; forming an unseen, unostentatious, self-acting system of excretory ducts, altogether superseding cartage or hand labour, and conveying the refuse in closed streams, acting constantly and rapidly until they distribute the refuse into the field of production.

washed, is very offensive, and must have an injurious effect on the health of the occupants. The filth of their dwellings is excessive, so is their personal filth. When they attend my surgery, I am always obliged to have the door open. When I am coming down stairs from the parlour, I know at the distance of a flight of stairs whether there are any poor patients in the surgery. Any one who attends on the relief days of the out-door relief may satisfy himself as to the personal condition of these parties.

'Are the courts in which the labouring classes reside, in your district, paved or cleansed?—They are not flagged, they have a sort of pebbles; they are always wet and dirty. The people, having no convenience in their houses for getting rid of waste water, throw it down at the doors. If I cast my eye over the whole district at this moment, I do not think that one house for the working classes will be found in which there is such a thing as a sink for getting rid of the water.

'Then there is not such a thing as a house with the water laid on?—Not one in the poorer places. There is also the want of cesspools; there is only one or two places for a whole court, and soil lies about the places which are in a most offensive condition.

'What is the number of cases which you visit for the administration of medical relief during the year?—During the last year the number of cases was 1560, all of them out-patients.

'Has not a large sewer been recently formed through your district?—Yes, through Rosemary-lane.

'What has been its effect?—Very little as respects the inhabitants of the courts; the landlords are not compelled, and do not go to the expense of making any communication from the courts to the sewer; the courts are in as wet and dirty and in as bad a condition as ever.

'What are the rents paid for these descriptions of tenements?—I am informed, very high rents. I am informed that this description of property pays a better per centage than any other description of property.—My impression is that it pays as much as 20 per cent. in many instances.'

This evidence exhibits the common condition of large masses of habitations, even in the metropolis, where there are so many competing companies.

Mr. Mott states that, in Manchester:

'There are numerous pumps and a plentiful supply of water within a few feet of the surface, to say nothing of the various tanks and cisterns in factories and private dwellings, which in this proverbially rainy district are always abundantly supplied; but, from the nature of the atmosphere, the rain-water is frequently like ink. The Irwell and Medlock rivers run through the town of Manchester; but being receptacles for all kinds of filth and refuse, the water is too impure for general use. In the suburbs of Manchester the water is generally procured through the medium of rain-water cisterns, or from very shallow wells by pumps. In the better class of houses it is generally filtered, but the poorer classes use it without any preparation. The custom is for owners of small cottage property to erect a pump for the use of a given number of houses; this pump is frequently rented by one of the tenants, who keeps it locked, and each of the other tenants are taxed a certain sum per month for the use of it. One poor woman told me she paid 1*s.* per month. The water company[1] give a plentiful supply to small houses at 6*s.* per year, or about half

---

1. The Manchester and Salford Waterworks Company was created in 1809 under 49 Geo. III, c. 192. See A. Redford and I. S. Russell, *The History of Local Government in Manchester* (1940), I, 235-9.

what this woman paid for a precarious supply from the subscription pump. The Stockport Local Act[1] empowers the commissioners of that town to *compel* the cottage owners to provide a good supply of water to their tenants.'[2]

Mr. John Moyle, medical officer of the Truro union, states:
'But few houses are properly supplied with water. In very dry seasons, they have to fetch water from a distance varying from a quarter to $1\frac{1}{2}$ mile.'[3]

This is at present the condition of a large proportion of the houses in Hampstead, Highgate, and Hendon, where water is purchased by the pailful.

Mr. Daniel Antrobus, medical officer of the Audley district, Newcastle union, Staffordshire, says:
'They have seldom a good supply of water, are without *pumps*, and the occupants are obliged to obtain it from stagnant reservoirs or impure springs, situate often at a considerable distance.'

Mr. Henry Cribb, the medical officer of the Dunmow union reports, as a circumstance which is highly injurious to the health:
'The want of good and wholesome spring-water: there being scarcely any pumps for the use of the poor, they are compelled to use water collected from ditches; and I have known it frequently to be not only very impure, but almost in a putrid state.'

The medical officer of the Bishop's Stortford union, states:
'I am of opinion that, in this and most of the rural parishes, complaints often arise from the want of good and wholesome spring-water, there being very few pumps, or even wells, and the poor being compelled to use water collected from ditches and other impure sources; this circumstance, connected with the very imperfect drainage, I think requires strict investigation.'

Mr. Whilpels, the medical officer of the Lexden and Winstree union, states:
'There is a point I deem most worthy of notice, I allude to the deficiency of spring-water. The inhabitants of Salcot Virley and Great Wigborough are compelled to drink pond-water, which is impure, brackish, and most injurious to the constitution. The few who have the means, send for water a distance of four miles; to obviate this evil would be a blessing conferred upon the great mass of the population residing in these parishes.'

Mr. William Blower, surgeon of Bedford, states:
'At Wootton (near Bedford) the labourers are very numerous, and before the passing the Poor Law Amendment Act the greater part of them were dependent for support upon the poor-rates. The land was enclosed and undrained, employment was scanty, and wages were very low; the water was very bad, the inhabitants being principally supplied from pits dug near their houses, and filled by rain in the winter, which in the summer, and particularly in dry seasons, were almost emptied by use and evaporation, leaving only a muddy fluid covered with a green scum, and loaded with aquatic animals and plants. Sporadic typhus prevailed extensively in the summer and autumn, and ague in the winter and spring.

---

1. 6 Geo. IV, c. 68, of 1826.
2. Charles Mott, 'Report on the state of the residences of the labouring classes in the manufacturing districts of Lancashire, Cheshire, Derbyshire, and Staffordshire', *Local Reps. E. & W.*, pp. 251-2.
3. *Local Reps. E. & W.*, p. 10.

II. Public Arrangements External to the Residences

'Since the introduction of the New Poor Law and the enclosure of the land, considerable draining has been effected, employment has been more plentiful, and the wages higher, and many of the labourers have allotments of ground. Typhus has been rapidly diminishing, and this year (1839) there was no case until November, and then only two. This must principally be attributed to the improved state of the parish, and partly, perhaps, this year, to the wetness of the season, by which the water-pits have been kept nearly full, so that the conditions favourable to the generation of malaria have not existed.

'A few wells have been dug lately, and good water has been obtained, and there is every probability if the water-pits were filled up, and more wells dug, and the draining completed, that sporadic typhus and ague, which have so long infested this village, and occasioned so much distress and expense, might be entirely eradicated. A respectable farmer informed me that, in the neighbouring parish of Houghton, a few years ago, his was the only family that used well-water, and almost the only one that escaped ague.'

The state of the supplies of water to the labouring classes in Scotland appears to be similar to that prevalent in the towns and the rural districts of England.

Mr. *William Tait*, surgeon, of Edinburgh, states, in regard to the houses in the High-street, Cowgate, and Canongate:

'The dwellings of the poor are remarkable for their generally uncomfortable appearance, and I attribute this in most instances to a deficient supply of water, necessaries, and such like conveniences. There are no receptacles for filth of any description, and it is either accumulated in the stairs or dwellings themselves, and the stairs are scarcely ever washed. And how can it be otherwise, seeing that the poor have to travel for a considerable distance for water, and afterwards carry it up five, six, or seven stories?'

The Return from Glasgow states that the:

'Sewers or drains are left uncovered, and with no diluting water except the refuse of families and rain-water.'

That:

'There is no scarcity of water if carried into the poorer houses.'

Dr. *Alexander Cuddie*, of Aberdeen, states that the:

'Water is plentiful; but it would be proper to bring it into the houses of the poor as well as the rich.'

Mr. *Forrest*, in his report on the sanitary condition of the population of Stirling, states that in that town:

'The supply of water is often very deficient. There is no water-company, and the water is not conveyed into the houses even of the wealthy inhabitants. In times of scarcity it is no uncommon occurrence to see from 80 to 100 persons waiting at each public well for water; and the scarcity of it is often made an excuse by servants for the neglect of domestic duties. I may therefore with propriety say, that the poor of Stirling are often not properly supplied with water for the purposes stated in the query.'[1]

The *Rev. George Lewis*, the minister of St. David's parish, Dundee, in speaking of drainage, says that:

'Everything in this way is done very imperfectly; drains and sewers are insufficient, and run into the mill-pond.'

---

1. *Local Reps. Scot.*, p. 264.

That there is:
'No water, except what is purchased or taken out of the filthy mill-pond.'

Another informant states:
'The west and south-west suburbs are destitute of water, and have no sewers; the north and east suburbs are also badly supplied with water, and have no drains. Indeed there are only two drains in the town that I know of, and I should think them rather hurtful than otherwise, as there is not water enough to scour them out.'

In answer to the question, whether the residences of the population amidst which contagious febrile diseases arise are properly supplied with water for the purposes of cleanliness of the houses, person, and clothing? Dr. *John Macintyre*, of Greenock, states that:
'Their proprietors or landlords, with a few exceptions, have not properly supplied them with water, although an ample supply of that necessary aid to cleanliness can be cheaply obtained by means of pipes from the Shaws' Water Company.'

Dr. *James Sym* states that:
'There are few wells of good water in Ayr. The water in general is strongly impregnated with lime, and the supply is defective. Strangers find it unpleasant, and I believe horses which have not been used with it are apt to suffer when it is given them to drink.'[1]

Mr. *A. Cochrane* and Mr. *W. J. Thomson*, surgeons, of Arbroath, state:
'That the town is well supplied with *hard* water, but that an abundant supply of soft water might be brought into the town with very little expense from a spring in the neighbourhood.'

The Return from Renfrew states that:
'A plentiful supply of water may be had from the street wells, and also from a burn which runs close to the town.'

Dr. *Henry Douglas*, of Dunfermline, says:
'They are *very inadequately* supplied with water for these purposes.'

The return from Kirkwall, states:
'That water is supplied at public wells: there is no scarcity of water, but it is somewhat hard.'

Dr. *W. B. Ross*, of Tain, in reply to the question whether the town is properly supplied with water? says:
'By no means; the water is very hard, and unfit for most domestic purposes.

Dr. *S. Scott Alison*, in his Report on the sanatory condition of the town of Tranent, furnishes an exemplification of the condition of many of the smaller towns:
'I do not believe there is a house in Tranent into which water is conducted by pipes. There existed great difficulty on many occasions in getting water at all. During the seven years I lived there, the village was, on the whole, extremely ill supplied with water: it was usual for it to be occasionally absent from Tranent altogether. Last summer the supply of water was stopped for several months. The inhabitants suffered the greatest inconvenience from this

---

1. *Ibid.*, p. 216.

cause; they could not get sufficient water to maintain cleanliness of person and clothes; it was even difficult for labouring people to get enough to cook their victuals; and I know that many of the poor were, in consequence, reduced to the practice of using impure and unwholesome water. On these occasions water was carried from a considerable distance from the village. Some went the distance of a mile; some used barrels drawn on carriages; some employed children to bring it in small vessels; and, I doubt not, many went without it, when it was highly necessary, from inability or infirmity to go themselves, and from want of funds to employ another for the purpose. Since the above was written I have learned from a lady, previously resident in Tranent, that, when cholera prevailed in that district, some of the patients suffered very much indeed from want of water, and that so great was the privation, that on that calamitous occasion people went into the ploughed fields and gathered the rain water which collected in depressions in the ground, and actually in the prints made by horses' feet. Tranent was formerly well supplied with water of excellent quality by a spring above the village, which flows through a sand-bed. The water flows into Tranent at its head, or highest quarter, and is received into about 10 wells, distributed throughout the village. The people supply themselves at these wells when they contain water. When the supply is small, the water pours in a very small stream only; and it happens, in consequence, that on these occasions of scarcity great crowds of women and children assemble at these places, waiting their "turn," as it is termed. I have seen women fighting for water. The wells are sometimes frequented throughout the whole night. It was generally believed by the population that this stoppage of the water was owing to its stream being diverted into a coal-pit which was sunk in the sand-bed above Tranent. That pit has been lined with sheets of iron, and the water has lately returned to Tranent in great abundance.'[1]

The observations made by *Mr. Burton*, in his Report, appear to be deserving of attentive consideration. He states:

'I have reason to believe that in many parts of Scotland the want of a good supply of water is one of the most material impediments to the furtherance of cleanly habits among the working people. Besides the immediate evils of a narrow supply, much time is wasted, and many bad habits are acquired by those who have to wait their turn at the wells in a time of drought. Dundee, Stirling, Dunfermline, Lanark, and Arbroath, are all, I believe, imperfectly supplied. The community of Dundee have spent about 30,000*l*. in a contest between the supporters of two contending water-bills; and I understand that an Act[2] which was passed about three years ago has been found incapable of being put in operation. The evil is rendered more serious by the demand for cooling water for the numerous steam-engines, and the article is so precious that it is for these purposes repeatedly re-cooled by exposure and evaporation after it has been heated. I believe that in many of the colliery and manufacturing districts there is inconvenience, amounting to suffering, from want of water. Where there is a positive deficiency of the element on the spot, the means of procuring a supply from another place are so various and so dependent on local circumstances, that nothing but some arbitrary authority, possessed of sufficient funds, could ensure its being obtained in every instance.'[3]

On these and various reports from the medical officers and others in England, as well as from Scotland, in which it is stated in terms similar

---

1. *Local Reps. Scot.*, pp. 87-8.
2. 7 Wm. IV, c. 126, of 1837.
3. *Local Reps. Scot.*, pp. 62-3.

Supplies of Water

to the return from Renfrew, 'that a plentiful supply of water *may be* had from the street wells, and also from a burn which runs close to the town,' it is to be observed, that the economy of a town, or of any considerable collection of habitations, appears to be essentially defective, insofar as it leaves a large proportion of the inhabitants dependent on such a mode of supply.

Supplies of water obtained from wells by the labour of fetching and carrying it in buckets or vessels do not answer the purpose of regular supplies of water brought into the house without such labour, and kept ready in cisterns for the various purposes of cleanliness. The interposition of the labour of going out and bringing home water from a distance acts as an obstacle to the formation of better habits; and I deem it an important principle to be borne in mind, that in the actual condition of the lower classes, conveniences of this description must precede and form the habits. It is in vain to expect of the great majority of them that the disposition, still less the habits, will precede or anticipate and create the conveniences. Even with persons of a higher condition, the habits are greatly dependent on the conveniences, and it is observed, that when the supplies of water into the houses of persons of the middle class are cut off by the pipes being frozen, and when it is necessary to send for water to a distance, the house-cleansings and washings are diminished by the inconvenience; and every presumption is afforded that if it were at all times requisite for them to send to a distance for water, and in all weathers, their habits of household cleanliness would be deteriorated. In Paris and other towns where the middle classes have not the advantage of supplies of water brought into the houses, the general habits of household and personal cleanliness are inferior to those of the inhabitants of towns who do enjoy the advantage. The whole family of the labouring man in the manufacturing towns rise early, before daylight in winter time, to go to their work; they toil hard, and they return to their homes late at night. It is a serious inconvenience, as well as discomfort to them to have to fetch water at a distance out of doors from the pump or the river on every occasion that it may be wanted, whether it may be in cold, in rain, or in snow. The minor comforts of cleanliness are of course forgone, to avoid the immediate and greater discomforts of having to fetch the water. In general it has appeared in the course of the present inquiry that the state of the conveniences gives, at the same time, a very fair indication of the state of the habits of the population, in respect to household, and even personal cleanliness. The *Rev. Whitwell Elwin*, the chaplain of the Bath union, gives the following illustration of the habits of many of the working population even in that city, which is well supplied with water:

'A man had to fetch water from one of the public pumps in Bath, the distance from his house being about a quarter of a mile,—"It is as valuable," he said, "as strong beer. We can't use it for cooking, or anything of that sort, but only for drinking and tea." "Then where do you get water for cooking and washing?"—"Why, from the river. But it is muddy, and often stinks bad, because all the filth is carried there." "Do you then prefer to cook your victuals in water which is muddy and stinks to walking a quarter of a mile to fetch it from the pump?"—"We can't help ourselves, you know. We could not go all that way for it." There are many gentlemen's houses in the same district in which the water is not fit for cooking; and I know that much privation and inconvenience is undergone to avoid the expense of water-carriage. I have often wondered to see the shifts which have been endured rather than be at the cost of an extra pail of water, of which the price was three halfpence. With the poor, far less obstacles are an absolute barrier, because no privation is felt by them so little as that of cleanliness. The propensity to dirt is so strong, the steps so few and easy, that nothing but the utmost facilities for water can act as a counterpoise; and such is the love of uncleanliness, when once contracted, that no habit, not even drunkenness, is so difficult to eradicate.'

In most towns, and certainly in the larger manufacturing towns, those members of a family who are of strength to fetch water are usually of strength to be employed in profitable industry, and the mere value of their time expended in the labour of fetching water, is almost always much higher than the cost of regular supplies of water even at the charge made by the water companies. In Glasgow the charge for supplying a labourer's tenement is 5s. per annum; in Manchester 6s. In London the usual charge is 10s. for a tenement containing two families, for which sum two tons and a half of water per week may be obtained if needed. For 5s. per annum, then, as a water-rate (on which from 10 to 20 per cent. is paid to the owner for collection), each labourer's family may be supplied in the metropolis with one ton and a quarter of water weekly, if they find it necessary to use so much. The ton is 216 gallons, equal to 108 pails full, at two gallons the pail. Thus for less than one penny farthing, 135 pails full of water are taken into the house without the labour of fetching, without spilling or disturbance, and placed in constant readiness for use. Under any circumstances, if the labourer or his wife or child would otherwise be employed, even in the lowest-paid labour or in knitting stockings, the cost of fetching water by hand is extravagantly high as compared with the highest cost of water lifted by steam and conducted through iron pipe sat a large expenditure of capital (the lowest in London is about 200,000l.) and by an expensive management. In illustration of the difference in economy of the two modes of conveyance, I may mention that the usual cost of filtered water carried into the houses at Paris by the water-carriers, is two sous the pailful, being at the rate of 9s. per ton; whilst the highest charge of any of the companies in London for sending the same quantity of water to any place within the range of their pipes, and delivering it at an average level of 100 feet, at the highest charge, is 6d. per ton.

At the highest of the water companies' charges it would be good economy for the health of the labourer's family to pay for water being laid on in the house, to reduce the expense of medicines and loss of work in the family, as indicated by any of the tables of sickness. The cost of laying on the water in a labourer's tenement, and providing a butt or receptacle to hold it, may be stated to be on an average 40s., which will last twenty years.

The experience of the water companies tends to show that the distribution of water directly into the houses where it is wanted, would be good economy of the water. When the supply of water into the houses

Supplies of Water

is stopped by frost, and cocks are, on that occasion, opened in the streets, the supply of water required is one-third greater than usual; as great, indeed, as it is in the heat of summer, when there is a large additional consumption for watering gardens and roads. I would here suggest that it is essential that the water should be charged on the owners of all the smaller weekly tenements, because, where the owner finds it necessary to collect the rent weekly, the smaller collection of rates for longer periods would often be impracticable, and the expense of the collection alone of such small rates weekly ($1\frac{1}{4}d.$ per week) would be more than the amount collected.

The mode of supplying water by private companies for the sake of a profit is not however available for the supply of a population, where the numbers are too small to defray the expense of obtaining a private Act of parliament, or the expense of management by a board of directors, or to produce profits to shareholders; it is, therefore, a mode not available to the population of the country who do not reside in the chief towns. The Poor Law Commissioners have been urgently requested to allow the expense for procuring supplies for villages to be defrayed out of the poor's rates in England, but they could only express their regret that the law gave them no power to allow such a mode of obtaining the benefit sought. The mode of supply by private companies is, however, the subject of complaint in the populous towns, where it is the only mode.

Although there is little probability that regular supplies of water would ever have been obtained without the inducement of salaries to the managers and of returns of interest to the capitalists; although the cost of most of the supplies at the highest is much lower than the labour of fetching water from a pump close to the house, and no valid objection appears against compulsory provisions for water being laid on (*i.e.* for existing charges of labour being reduced) in the tenements of the labouring classes in towns, at the common charge of the water companies: still the appearance of a profit and of dividends on the supply of a natural commodity does, in the new districts at least, furnish pretexts for the objection of the poorer owners and ignorant occupiers to the supposed expense of the improvement which consists in an immediate outlay. Apart from such objections, however, it is a mode of obtaining supplies attended with great inconveniences, which it is desirable to have considered with respect to new improvements. The payment of a dividend for an improved supply of such a commodity will be found as imperfect a measure, even of its pecuniary value, as it would be of the pecuniary value of a good and abundant supply of air and of the light of day. There are numerous indirect effects of the use of such a commodity, of which a pecuniary estimate cannot conveniently be made, as against an immediate outlay. For example, there is little ground left for doubt that the effect of street and house cleansing by means of the supplies of water needed in the worst districts, would occasion considerable reductions in the pecuniary charge of sickness on the poor's rates, but it would be extremely difficult to obtain these results in money to make up, with any pretence to accuracy, a profit and loss account as an undertaking for the outlay. The evidence afforded by the creation and success of a private company proves only that a certain class of persons so far appreciate the advantages of the supply as to be willing to incur such an immediate expense as will cover the cost, and yield a profit to the undertakers; it proves nothing as to the intrinsic value of the service or the commodity, which may be immense to the bulk of the community, and yet not one be found ready to volunteer to defray a portion of the expense. But the expense of the machinery of water companies, as already stated, is disproportioned to the means of the smaller towns and to a large part of the country; and generations may pass away amidst filth and pestilence before the scientific means and the economy of prevention can be appreciated by them. And there are further objections made in towns to the mode of supply itself. One is, that it creates strong interest against all improvements in the quality or the supplies of water; for every considerable improvement creates expense, which is felt in diminution of the dividends of the private shareholders; and so long as a majority of the rate-payers are content with bad water, or deem it hopeless to seek to obtain water of a superior quality, so long as any public clamour will not endanger the dividends, it appears that no amendment entailing considerable expense can be expected. Even where there are convenient unappropriated streams, and a wide field is afforded for competition by a very populous district, the competition of different companies does not necessarily furnish to the individual consumer any choice or amendment of the supplies.

The competition frequently absorbs the profit on the funds that might be available to the competing parties (supposing them disposed to carry out any plans other than those which have for their object the cheapest supply that can be procured), and does not reduce the charge of the supply of water to the public. At one time there were three sets of waterpipes belonging to three different companies passing through the same streets of a large proportion of the metropolis. This wasteful competition of three immense capitals sunk in the supply of one district, for which the expenditure of one capital and one establishment would have sufficed, ended in an agreement between the competing companies to confine themselves to particular districts. The dividends at present obtained by the shareholders of the chief companies in the metropolis on the capital now employed, appears, however, to be only 4, 5, or 6 per cent., but this is on several expensive establishments and sets of officers, which appear to admit of consolidation. The committee of the House of Commons which investigated the subject of the supplies of water in 1821,[1] concluded by recommending a consolidation of the several trusts, but excepting that the competition between them has abated, the expense and waste of separate establishments is still continued, and beyond this the expense of the fixed capital and establishment, charged upon perhaps one-third the proper supply of water.

The private companies are also complained of as being practically irresponsible and arbitrary, and unaccommodating towards individuals. If is a further subject of complaint, as respects supplies by such com-

---

1. *Report of the Select Committee on the Supply of Water to the Metropolis*, P.P. 1821, V.

Supplies of Water

panies, that they are directed almost exclusively to the supplies of such private houses as can pay water-rates; that they are not arranged for the important objects of cleansing of the streets or drains, or of supplying of water in case of fire. I have not been able to observe the extent of foundation for these complaints. Whilst no strong motive for aggressive proceedings by the companies against individuals appears, the existing force of the following statement made by the Committee referred to, which sat in 1821, will be admitted:

'The public is at present without any protection, even against a further indefinite extension of demand. In cases of dispute, there is no tribunal but the boards of the companies themselves to which individuals can appeal; there are no regulations but such as the companies may have voluntarily imposed upon themselves, and may therefore revoke at any time, for the continuance of the supply in its present state, or for defining the cases in which it may be withdrawn from the householder. All these points, and others of the same nature, indispensably require legislative regulation, where the subject matter is an article of the first necessity, and the supply has, from peculiar circumstances, got into such a course that it is not under the operation of those principles which govern supply and demand in other cases.'[1]

Since the period of that report, there has been no legislation on the subject other than that in new Acts, or on the renewal of old ones, clauses have been introduced empowering any individual rate-payer to demand a supply of water.

In some instances legislative permissions have been given to the local authorities to obtain supplies for the use of towns, but the permissions have not been accompanied with the requisite powers to make them available.

Bath, however, is supplied with water under the authority of the local Act of the 6 Geo. III. (c. 70), for paving, &c. which, after reciting that there was a scarcity of water within the city and precincts, and that there were in the neighbourhood of the said city several springs of water belonging to the corporation, enacts that the corporation shall have full power to cause water to be conveyed to the said city from such springs, and gives them authority to enter upon and break up the soil of any public highway, or common, or waste ground, and the soil of any private grounds within two miles of the city, and the soil or pavement of any street within the city, in order to drain and collect the water of the springs, and to make reservoirs sufficient for keeping such water, and to erect conduits, water-houses, and engines necessary for distributing it, and to lay under ground aqueducts and pipes most convenient for the same purpose. The Act vests the right and property of all water-courses leading from the said springs to the city, and also of all reservoirs, conduits, water-houses, and engines, erected or used for the purpose, in the mayor, aldermen, and citizens of Bath. The following extract from a communication from the *Rev. Whitwell Elwin*, who has closely investigated the economy of the poorest classes in that city, thus describes the present state of the supply:

---

1. *Ibid.*, p. 8.

II. Public Arrangements External to the Residences

'Bath is surrounded by hills which pour down a vast quantity of water into reservoirs. Pipes are laid from these reservoirs to every part of Bath, and as the springs from which the water originally rises are as high up on the hills as the roofs of the houses, water can be carried into the attics without the application of a forcing pump: thus no machinery is employed. The only water-works are the pipes which convey the water.

'These reservoirs are the property of different persons, and there are five distinct parties by which particular districts in Bath are supplied. They are the Bath Corporation, the Freemen's Company, the Circus Company, the Duke of Cleveland, and Captain Gunning. There can scarcely be said to be any competition, because the possession of a spring in a particular locality gives a monopoly of the surrounding neighbourhood. But wherever there is room for selection, the supply of the corporation is always preferred. It is often resorted to even where the distance is much greater than to other springs; the supply being more regular, more abundant, and cheaper than the rest, with the exception of that of the Duke of Cleveland, who only provides his own tenants. The corporation supplies more than three parts of the town. There are at present 2184 persons paying water-rates, but the number of houses furnished with water is considerably greater, because courts and rows of cottages have frequently a common cistern. Where this is the case each cottage making use of the cistern pays a rent of 10s. a-year, and where the house has a cistern of its own, 20s. a-year. The charge for the water is in proportion to the rent of the house. The quantity of water supplied is about a hogshead a-day. In summer, when the springs are low, the quantity is not so great. The laying down and repair of the feather, that is the pipe which branches from the main pipe, is at the cost of the tenant.

'In addition to these private supplies the corporation provides five public pumps, which are open to all the inhabitants free of expense.

'The greater part of the cottages in the town itself, but not in the suburbs, make use of the water-works. There is generally a pump in addition, which yields water too hard and bad for domestic purposes.

'The water rents of the corporation for the last year were 3,233l. 2s., the expenses (including salaries, rent for springs, repairs of pipes) 449l. 3s. 3d., thus leaving a profit of 2,783l. 18s. 9d. This sum is applied to the reduction of the borough rate.

'The advantages of this system over private companies appear to me great and incontestable. Here are no expenses for solicitors, or litigation between rival concerns; no collusion between coalescing companies to raise the charges to the utmost amount that the inhabitants will bear; no exorbitant salaries to the variety of officers, which every separate establishment demands. A few watermen, whose united salaries are only 114l. 8s. per annum, is the sole addition to the ordinary corporation machinery. When to this we add that all the profits are for the benefit of the town and not for individuals—that the sum paid in water-rate is thus pretty nearly deducted from the borough rate—we can hardly hesitate to strike the balance. The corporation management, here at least, gives unlimited satisfaction. They are under the direct control of the rate-payers, properly desirous to conciliate their opinion, and are sure to hear of any incivility, which, as they have no interest in protecting it, they are always ready to redress.'

In this instance, however, it is to be observed that the real cost of the water to the corporation is not more than one-seventh their charge to the consumer; consequently, the charge for a supply out of the house may be said to be less than 1s. 6d. per annum; and it will admit of little doubt that if the water were lifted by steam power and carried into every

Supplies of Water

tenement, as it might be, the actual expense need not be doubled; six-sevenths then of the charge, which is about the same as the ordinary charges of water companies, is to be considered as a borough rate, levied in the shape of a water rate, applied doubtless to some other proper public services.

An example is presented in Manchester of the practicability of obtaining supplies for the common benefit of a town without the agency of private companies. In that town gas has for some years past been supplied from works erected and conducted not by the municipality but by a body appointed under a local Act by an elected committee of the ratepayers.[1] This mode of supplying the town was, it appears, violently opposed by private interests; but I am informed that the supplies of gas are of as good or even of a better quality, and cheaper than those obtained from private companies in adjacent towns; that improvements in the manufacture of the gas are more speedily adopted than in private associations, and the profits are reserved as a public fund for the improvement of the town. Out of this fund a fine Town Hall has been erected, whole streets have been widened, and various large improvements have been made; and the income now available for the further improvement of the town exceeds 10,000*l*. per annum, after providing for the expense of management and the interest of the sinking fnud on the money borrowed. There are now in the same districts in the metropolis no less than three immense capitals sunk in competition,—three sets of gas-pipes passing through the same streets, three expensive sets of principal and subordinate officers where one would suffice, comparatively high charges for gas to the consumers, and low dividends to the shareholders of the companies in competition. Where a scientific and trustworthy agency can be obtained for the public, manifest opportunities present themselves for considerable economy on such modes of obtaining supplies. A proposal was made in Manchester to obtain supplies of water for the town in the same manner as the supplies of gas, but the owners of the private pumps, who, it is stated, have the monopoly of the convenient springs, and exact double the charge for which even private companies are ready to convey supplies into the houses, made a compact and effectual opposition to the proposal, contending that the supplies of rain-water (which are sometimes absolutely black with the soot held in suspension), together with that from the springs was sufficient, and the proposal was defeated. These petty interests could not, however, avail against the more powerful interest of a joint-stock company, which was established to procure supplies for the middle and wealthier classes of the town[2].

There appears to be no reason to doubt that the mode of supplying water to Bath and gas to the town of Manchester might be generally adopted in supplying water to the population. Powers would be required to enter into the lands adjacent to the towns on a reasonable compensation to the owners to obtain supplies of water; and, as the management of water-works requires appropriate skill, it would be necessary to

---

1. 5 Geo. IV, c. 133, of 1825.
2. See above, p. 136, n. 1.

appoint an officer with special qualifications for their superintendence. Ordinary service may be obtained for the public, if recourse be had to the ordinary motives by which such service is engaged in private companies. It is not mentioned invidiously, but as a matter of fact, that the majority, not to say the whole, of such undertakings by joint stock companies, are, in the first instance, moved by a solicitor, or engineer, or other person, for the sake of the office of manager of the works, and that the directors and shareholders, and the inducement of profit to them, through the benefit undoubtedly to the public, are only the machinery to the attainment of the object for which the undertaking is primarily moved. If competent officers be appointed and adequately remunerated for the service, there can be little doubt that the public may, as at Bath and Manchester, be saved the expense of the management by the occasional attendance of unskilled directors, and that they may save the expense of dividends, or apply the profits to public improvements, as at Manchester, and moreover avoid the inconveniences and obstructions undoubtedly belonging to the supply of a commodity so essential to the public health, comfort, and economy, by a private monopoly. Bad supplies of water would, I apprehend, generally be less tolerated by the influential inhabitants of all parties from a public municipal agency than from a private company.

Another ground for the recommendation that supplies of water for the labouring classes should be brought under some public authority, is that some care may be taken to prevent the use of unwholesome supplies.

The queries transmitted to the medical officers were directed to ascertain the sufficiency of the supplies for the purpose of cleansing, but the returns frequently advert to the bad effect of inferior supplies upon the health of the population; and it is scarcely conceivable to what filthy water custom reconciles the people. Yet water containing animal matter, which is the most feared, appears to be less frequently injurious than that which is the clearest, namely, spring-water, from the latter being oftener impregnated with mineral substances; but there are instances of ill health produced by both descriptions of water. The beneficial effects derived from care as to the qualities of the water is now proved in the navy, where fatal dysentery formerly prevailed to an immense extent, in consequence of the impure and putrid state of the supplies; and care is now generally excercised on the subject by the medical officers of the army. In the Dublin Hospital Reports, for example, we have the following statement, which is still more important, as showing the extent to which the nature of the water influences health:

'Dr. M. Barry affirms that the troops were frequently liable to dysentery, while they occupied the old barracks at Cork; but he has heard that it has been of rare occurrence in the new barracks. Several years ago, when the disease raged violently in the old barracks, (now the depôt for convicts,) the care of the sick was, in the absence of the regimental surgeon, entrusted to the late Mr. Bell, surgeon, in Cork. At the period in question the troops were supplied with water from the river Lee, which, in passing through the city, is rendered unfit for drinking by the influx of the contents of the sewers from the houses, and likewise is brackish from the tide, which ascends into their channels. Mr. Bell, suspecting that the water might have caused the dysentery,

Supplies of Water 149

upon assuming the care of the sick, had a number of water-carts engaged to bring water for the troops from a spring called the Lady's Well, at the same time that they were no longer permitted to drink the water from the river. From this simple, but judicious arrangement, the dysentery very shortly disappeared among the troops.'—*Dublin Hospital Reports*, vol. iii. 11. Paper by Dr. Cheyne 'On Dysentery.'

Parent du Chatelet[1], the most industrious and able of modern investigators into questions of public health, gives the following instance, which in like manner demonstrates the amount of disease generated solely by the use of bad water, as well as the difficulty of detecting the specific effects produced by it:

'When I visited last year the prisons of Paris with my friend Villermé, who was interested in prisons generally, I was extremely surprised at the proportion of sick in the hospital of St. Lazarus, relatively to the whole population of the prisons. The prison, uniting all the conditions necessary to health as regards its position, construction, the dress and food of the prisoners, who were constantly kept at work, how explain the much greater proportion of sick to what we remark in other prisons of a bad condition, and in which are found united all the apparent causes of unhealthiness?—This, I must confess, has baffled all calculation, and has driven every one to say that there must be a cause for the peculiarity, but that it could not be discovered. I do not despair to have hit upon that cause, and I believe it is to be recognised in the nature of the water drunk by the prisoners. Having tasted it in the wooden reservoir behind the house, which was in bad order, and full of plants of the genus confervæ, I found it had a detestable and truly repulsive taste, a circumstance which does not appear to have been hitherto remarked. Might not the cause, then, be detected in the chemical nature of the water of Belleville and of the neighbourhood of St. Gervais, of which the prisoners drink exclusively? What proves it is the striking resemblance which exists in this respect between the water of Belleville and that in the wells of the entrance-court of the hospital of the Salpêtriere, which both contain a very great proportion of sulphate of lime, and other purgative salts. Now the venerable Professor Pinel and his pupil Schwilgué have remarked for more than 20 years the influence that the water of the wells of which I speak has upon the portion of the population of the hospital who make use of it, and they believe that certain affections connected evidently with locality cannot be attributed to any other cause, and particularly the disposition to chronic diarrhœa which is so often observed in this hospital. It turns out upon examination *that the greater part of the sick who fill the infirmary of the prison of St. Lazarus are brought there for illnesses of the same identical nature.* In the prison they are obliged to have recourse to the water of the Seine to cook the vegetables and other food, an evident proof of the truth, or at least the probability, of all I have just advanced.'

In the metropolis the public owes the analysis of the supplies of water and some improvement of supplies not in their nature essentially bad,

---

1. A. J. P. Parent-Duchâtelet (1790-1826) was one of the principal writers in the French school of sanitary reformers. While his main interest was sewerage, he also wrote about the disposal of dead horses (a major problem in nineteenth-century towns), industrial health, homes for the aged, and the influence of tobacco on health. His principal work in the field of public health was *Hygiène Publique, où Mémoires sur les Questions les plus importantes de l'Hygiène appliquée aux Professions et aux Travaux d'Utilité publique* (Paris 1836).

chiefly to the stirring of speculators in rival companies. But the population of the rural districts, and of the smaller towns, afford no means for the payment of companies, still less any field for pecuniary competition. As in the cases cited, it is to be feared that the knowledge gained for the safety of the health of the soldiers and the prisoners was not proclaimed for the protection of the bulk of the poorest population, who, under existing arrangements, only receive care in the shape of alleviations, when the suffering from disease is attended by the destitution which establishes the claim to relief. The middle classes are exposed to the like inconveniences, and put up with very inferior water, whilst supplies of a salubrious quality might be obtained by extended public arrangements for the common benefit.

It will not be deemed necessary to attempt to develope all the considerations applicable to the subject; and I confine myself to the representation of the fact,—That there is wide foundation for the complaint that proper supplies of water to large portions of the community are extensively wanting—that those obtained are frequently of inferior quality—that they are commonly obtained at the greatest expense when obtained by hand labour—that the supplies by private companies, though cheaper and better, are defective, and chiefly restricted to the use of the higher and middle classes, unless in such inconvenient modes (*i.e.* by cocks in courts), as seriously to impede the growth of habits of cleanliness amongst the working classes. To which I venture to add, as the expression of an opinion founded on communications from all parts of the kingdom, that as a highly important sanitary measure connected with any general building regulations, whether for villages or for any class of towns, arrangements should be made for all houses to be supplied with good water, and should be prescribed as being as essential to cleanliness and health as the possession of a roof or of due space; that for this purpose, and in places where the supplies are not at present satisfactory, power should be vested in the most eligible local administrative body, which will generally be found to be that having charge of cleansing and structural arrangements, to procure proper supplies for the cleansing of the streets, for sewerage, for protection against fires, as well as for domestic use.

Sanitary Effect of Land Drainage

In considering the circumstances external to the residence which affect the sanitary condition of the population, the importance of a general land drainage is developed by the inquiries as to the causes of the prevalent diseases, to be of a magnitude of which no conception had been formed at the commencement of the investigation: its importance is manifested by the severe consequences of its neglect in every part of the country, as well as by its advantages in the increasing salubrity and productiveness wherever the drainage has been skilful and effectual. The following instance is presented in a report from *Mr. John Marshall, Jun.*, the clerk to the union in the Isle of Ely:

'It has been shown that the Isle of Ely was at one period in a desolate state, being frequently inundated by the upland waters, and destitute of adequate means of drainage; the lower parts became a wilderness of stagnant pools, the

Sanitary Effect of Land Drainage 151

exhalations from which loaded the air with pestiferous vapours and fogs; now, by the improvements which have from time to time been made, and particularly within the last fifty years, an alteration has taken place which may appear to be the effect of magic. By the labour, industry, and spririt of the inhabitants, a forlorn waste has been converted into pleasant and fertile pastures, and they themselves have been rewarded by bounteous harvests. Drainage, embankments, engines, and enclosures have given stability to the soil (which in its nature is as rich as the Delta of Egypt) as well as salubrity to the air. These very considerable improvements, though carried on at a great expense, have at last turned to a double account, both in reclaiming much ground and improving the rest, and in contributing to the healthiness of the inhabitants. Works of modern refinement have given a totally different face and character to this once neglected spot; much has been performed, much yet remains to be accomplished by the rising generation. The demand for labour produced by drainage is incalculable, but when it is stated that where sedge and rushes but a few years since we now have fields of waving oats and even wheat, it must be evident that it is very great.

'On reference to a very perfect account of the baptisms, marriages, and burials, in Wisbech, from 1558 to 1826, I find that in the decennial periods, of which 1801, 1811, and 1821, were the middle years, the baptisms and burials were as under:—

	Baptisms	Burials	Population in 1801
1796 to 1805	1,627	1,535	4,710
1806 to 1815	1,654	1,313	5,209
1816 to 1825	2,165	1,390	6,515

'In the first of the three periods the mortality was 1 in 31; in the second, 1 in 40; in the third, 1 in 47; the latter being less than the exact mean mortality of the kingdom for the last two years. (*See Registrar-general's Second Report, p. 4, folio edition.*) These figures clearly show that the mortality has wonderfully diminished in the last half century, and who can doubt but that the increased salubrity of the fens produced by drainage is a chief cause of the improvement.'

Mr. R. Turner, medical officer of the Newhaven union, states:
'The district which has been under my care comprises five parishes, three of which, viz., Kingston, Iford, and Rodmell, are (more especially the two latter) situate in close proximity to marshes, which were formerly for a considerable portion of the year inundated; of late very extensive improvements have taken place in the drainage of these levels, and in consequence of that change, the diseases constantly engendered by marsh miasmata, viz., typhus and intermittent fevers, are not more common than in other districts which present to the eye a fairer prospect of health.'[1]

Mr. G. R. Rowe, medical officer of the Ongar union, observes:
'It is worthy of remark, that in the districts surrounding Chigwell no malignant, infectious, or contagious disease has appeared during my experience of thirty years' occasional residence, and even during the prevalence of cholera not one case occurred. The land is well drained, the situation elevated, and the cleanly habits of the poor, with the benevolence of its residents, have tended much to the prevention of disease, and its amelioration when occurring.'

Mr. W. Sanders, medical officer of the Gravesend and Milton union, states:

1. *Local Reps. E. & W.*, p. 51.

152   II. Public Arrangements External to the Residences

'I beg to leave to suggest how extreme are the beneficial effects of a proper drainage, which shall prevent stagnant water, and its deleterious consequences, accumulating in crowded neighbourhoods. This is exemplified in this town, and also in Tilbury Fort opposite, which is built on a marsh, and where, during the cholera period, then under my care, not a single case occurred.'[1]

Mr. Emerson, one of the medical officers of the Eastry union, states:

'There is, I believe, no locality which has been for some years so exempt from fevers of a malignant and contagious character as the eastern coast of Kent. Accordingly, idiopathic fever, under the form of synochus and typhus, very rarely occurs, and when it does appear, is generally of an isolated kind. Intermittents, also, which fifteen or twenty years since were so generally prevalent in this district, have become comparatively of rare occurrence, and indeed have almost disappeared from the catalogue of our local endemics. This exemption from ague and other febrile epidemics of an infectious nature may be justly imputed to the total absence of malaria, and of all those causes which usually generate an unwholesome and contaminating atmosphere, viz., from the whole district being secured from inundations by the most complete and effectual system of drainage and sewerage. Also, from the exposed state of the country favouring a free and rapid evaporation from the surface of the soil.'[2]

Mr. George Elgar, another of the medical officers of the Eastry union, observes that:

'The parishes forming the fifth district of the Eastry union, are, with one or two exceptions, close to marshes separating the Isle of Thanet from this portion of East Kent, and consequently, during the spring and autumn, the inhabitants are exposed to the malaria therefrom; but for these last few years, owing to the excellent plan of draining, very few diseases have occurred (in my opinion) that can be said to be produced by malaria. There is very little ague, scarcely any continued fevers; and a case of typhus, I believe, has not been known along the borders of the marshes for these last three or four years. Some years back, a great portion of the parishes adjoining these marshes was under water from the end of autumn to the early part of the following spring; then, agues and fevers of all characters prevailed to a very great extent. Although the malaria does not produce diseases of any *decided character*, yet, during a wet spring or autumn, there are always cases of inflammation of the lungs or bowels, and rheumatism, both in acute and chronic forms. The houses in general are good, well drained and well ventilated, having one or two sitting-rooms, as many bed-rooms, sometimes more, scullery, &c., and convenient receptacles for refuse and fuel. The cottages generally are *extremely cleanly*; of course there must be some exceptions, where the occupiers would not be clean and careful under any circumstances.'[3]

Mr. Spurgin, the medical officer of the Dunmow union, states:

'In this district great attention is paid to the cultivation of land, under drainage being much attended to, on which account partly we are not exposed to malaria, neither does ague prevail to any extent. A few cases have occurred, and when they have it has been for the most part in individuals whose systems have been impaired by irregular habits, and consequently the more readily affected by external impressions, as atmospheric vicissitudes.'

Mr. D. R. M'Nab, the medical officer of the Epping union, states that:

---

1. *Local Reps. E. & W.*, pp. 49-50.
2. *Ibid.*, p. 50.   3. *Ibid.*, p. 51.

Sanitary Effect of Land Drainage

'The health of the inhabitants of these two parishes is on the whole highly satisfactory, as will appear by this return, but I would observe that the sanitary condition of two localities would be greatly improved by a little attention on the part of the public surveyors and others to the drains and ditches immediately abutting on the dwellings of the poor inhabitants. I refer more especially to that part of Epping which is denominated the Back-street, and the greater part of which is in the parish of Coopersall. In very wet weather the drains and ditches are flooded; in very dry, on the contrary, they are by the evaporation of the fluids rendered very offensive, and thus almost all our cases of malignant fever are situated amongst those dwellings; if the neighbourhood had been crowded with inhabitants the mischief would have been much greater; and even as it now is, it has been the cause of much fatality among the able-bodied men and women. The same observations are applicable to Ducklane in the parish of Weald, and also at the Gullett, but in the latter case it is principally owing to the carelessness and filth of one or two families, who have thrown all sorts of excrementitious substances around their dwellings, and in the course of putrefaction it has occasionally become pestiferous.

'I may also venture to add the following observation, after twenty-six years' practice in this neighbourhood, that I have scarcely ever had a case of typhus fever in a malignant form without discovering some stagnant drain or overcharged cesspool, or some other manifest cause of malaria in the immediate residence of the patient.'

In the reports given from the parish ministers in the statistical accounts of Scotland[1], the effects of drainage upon the general health of the population are strongly marked in almost every county, expressed in notes made from an examination of the returns. Sutherland—parish of *Rogart*, 'healthy, and a good deal of draining.' *Farr*, 'subject to no particular disease; a deal of draining.' Ross and Cromarty—*Alness*, dry and healthy, 'climate improved by drainage.' It is to be understood that drainage appears to form the essential part of agricultural improvement, which is connected with the improvement of health. Thus the notes from another parish in the same county, *Kilmuir Wester* and *Suddy*, states it as 'healthy; great improvement; scarcely an acre in its original state.' *Rosemarkie*, 'healthy; agriculture much improved.' Elgin—*New Spynie*, 'healthy, much waste reclaimed, much draining.' *Alves*, 'dry and healthy, well cultivated, wood sometimes used for drains.' Banff—*Deckford*, healthy, and people long lived, much draining.' Kincardine—*Fordoun*, 'so much draining that now no swamps: formerly, agues common, now quite unknown.' Angus—*Carmylie*, 'health improved from draining.' Kinross—*Kinross*, 'agues prevalent sixty years ago in consequence of marshes, now never met with.' *Oswell*, 'ague prevailed formerly, but not since the land was drained.' Perth—*Methven*, 'the north much improved by draining.' *Redgorton*, 'healthy; no prevailing disease; ague was frequent formerly, but not since the land has been drained and planted.' *Moneydie*, 'healthy; an immense improvement by draining.' *Abernyte*, 'since the land was drained, scrofula rare and ague

---

1. Sir John Sinclair (editor), *Statistical Account of Scotland* (21 vols., Edinburgh 1791-9); and *New Statistical Account of Scotland* (15 vols., Edinburgh 1845). The *New Statistical Account* was also published serially, starting in 1834, so that most of it was available in print to Chadwick when compiling the *Sanitary Report*.

unknown.' *Monzie*, 'healthy; a good deal of land reclaimed.' *Auchterarder*, 'much draining, and waste land reclaimed—climate good.' *Muckhart*, 'great improvement in agriculture; ague formerly prevalent—not so now.' *Muthill*, 'healthy, much draining and cultivation extended.' And similar statements are made from the rural districts in all parts of the country.

In the course of inquiries as to what have been the effects of land drainage upon health, one frequent piece of information received has been that the rural population had not observed the effects on their own health, but they had marked the effects of drainage on the health and improvement of the stock. Thus the less frequent losses of stock from epidemics are beginning to be perceived as accompanying the benefits of drainage in addition to those of increased vegetable production.

Dr. *Edward Harrison*, in a paper in which he points out the connexion between the rot in sheep and other animals, and some important disorders in the human constitution, observes:

'The connexion between humidity and the rot is universally admitted by experienced graziers; and it is a matter of observation, that since the brooks and rivulets in the county of Lincoln have been better managed, and the system of laying ground dry, by open ditches and under-draining, has been more judiciously practised, the rot is become far less prevalent. Sir John Pringle[1] informs us, that persons have maintained themselves in good health, during sickly seasons, by inhabiting the upper stories of their houses; and I have reason to believe that, merely by confining sheep on high grounds through the night, they have escaped the rot.'

Dr. *Harrison* makes some observations on the effects of imperfect drainage in aggravating the evils intended to be remedied, of which frequent instances are presented in the course of this inquiry:

'A grazier of my acquaintance has, for many years, occupied a large portion of an unenclosed fen, in which was a shallow piece of water that covered about an acre and a half of land. To recover it for pasturage, he cut in it several open ditches to let off the water, and obtained an imperfect drainage. His sheep immediately afterwards became liable to the rot, and in most years he lost some of them. In 1792 the drains failed so entirely, from the wetness of the season, that he got another pond of living water, and sustained, in that season, no loss of his flock. For a few succeeding years, he was generally visited with the rot; but having satisfied himself by experience, that whenever the pit was, from the weather, either completely dry or completely under water, his flock was free from the disorder, he attempted a more perfect drainage, and succeeded in making the land dry at all times. Since that period he has lost no sheep from the rot, though, till within the last two years, he continued to occupy the fen.

'Mr. Harrison, of Fisherton, near Lincoln, has by judicious management laid the greatest part of his farm completely dry, and is now little troubled with the rot, unless when he wishes to give it to some particular animals. His neighbours, who have been less provident, are still severe sufferers by it, nor are their misfortunes confined to sheep alone. Pigs, cows, asses, horses, poultry, hares, and rabbits, become rotten in this lordship, and have flukes in their livers.

---

1. For Pringle, see above, p. 116, n. 3.

Sanitary Effect of Land Drainage

'The late Mr. Bakewell was of opinion, that after May-Day, he could communicate the rot at pleasure, by flooding, and afterwards stocking his closes, while they were drenched and saturated with moisture. In summer, rivers and brooks are often suddenly swollen by thunder-storms, so as to pass over their banks, and cover the adjacent low lands. In this state, no injury is sustained during the inundation; but when the water returns to its former channel, copious exhalations are produced from the swamps and low lands, which are exceedingly dangerous to the human constitution, and to several other animals, as well as sheep.

'A medical gentleman of great experience at Boston, in Lincolnshire, and who is considerably advanced in life, has frequently observed to me, that intermittents are so much diminished in his circuit, that an ounce of the cinchona goes further at this time in the treatment of agues than a pound of it did within his own recollection. During his father's practice at Boston, they were still more obstinate and severe. For my own part, I have declared, for several years, in various companies, that marsh miasmata are the cause of both agues and the rot. And as miasmata are admitted, by the concurring testimonies of medical practitioners in every part of the globe, to be produced by the action of the sun upon low, swampy grounds, I hope this interesting subject will be fully investigated, and effectual plans carried into execution, for the preservation of man, and of the animals which are so useful to him.'[1]

I may here mention a circumstance which occurred at the Poor Law Commission Office, and which with succeeding information tended to direct our attention to the subject of sanitary measures of prevention for the protection of the rates. A medical officer of one of the Unions who came to town for the transaction of some business before the Board, begged to be favoured by the immediate despatch of his business, inasmuch as, from a change of weather which had taken place since his departure, he was certain that he should have a number of cases waiting for him. On being asked to explain the circumstances from which he inferred the occurrence of disease with so much certainty, he stated that within his district there was a reservoir to feed a canal: that they had let out the water as they were accustomed to do in spring time for the purpose of cleansing it; and that whenever such weather occurred as then prevailed during the process, he was sure to have a great number of fever cases amongst the labourers in the village which immediately adjoined the reservoir. It appeared to be, in fact, a case in which the rot was propagated amongst the labourers in the village under circumstances similar to those before cited in which it was propagated amongst the sheep.

The following portions of evidence afford instances of the condition in which a larger proportion of the country remains, from the neglect of general land drainage, than would be conceived from any *à priori* estimate of the amount of prevalent intelligence and enterprize.

Mr. R. W. Martyr, one of the medical officers of the Langport union, thus describes the condition of a large proportion of his district:

'The parishes of Kingsbury and Long Sutton being the district No. 1 B of the Langford union, the population of which amounts to above 3,000; Kings-

---

1. Edward Harrison, *An Inquiry into the Rot in Sheep and other Animals; in which a Connection is pointed out between it and some . . . disorders in the Human Constitution* (1804), pp. 6, 41.

bury, containing 2,000; and Long Sutton 1,000, or thereabouts. Both these parishes are partly surrounded by low meadow land, and are liable to frequent inundations, often covering many thousand acres, and sometimes to a great depth; the level of much of this land being below the bed of the main river or drains, makes it very difficult (when once inundated) in very wet seasons to drain or carry off the immense body of water they often contain.

'These inundations are caused by the banks of the main rivers not being sufficiently strong or elevated, and from the bridges not being capacious enough to carry the immense body of water brought down from the neighbouring hills and country higher up, which, in heavy rains, sometimes takes place so rapidly as to completely overflow the banks in twenty-four hours; but besides the casual or accidental giving way of the banks of the rivers, it is sometimes done by interested persons for the purpose of warding off the mischief from themselves by throwing it on their neighbours.

'When these floods occur in the winter season, and there is but little herbage, or early in the spring, and are followed by dry weather, the surface of the ground becomes dry and healthy, and they are then highly beneficial to the land, and but little prejudicial to the health of the surrounding inhabitants; but when, as is sometimes the case, these floods take place late in April, May and June, and cover hundreds of acres of hay, some cut and some uncut, and which must of course rot on the ground, the affluvia and stench is then often unbearable, and highly prejudicial to the health of the neighbouring villages, and it is sometimes years before the land recovers its healthy state, producing nothing but rank herbage, and causing agues, fevers, dysentery, and numerous other diseases. Many of these evils may, I think, be remedied if the owners of large estates in this neighbourhood would interest themselves in the matter: I am persuaded the increased value of their property would amply repay the outlay necessary for the purpose. When the land is in this unhealthy state, it appears to be equally prejudicial to the animal as the human subject, producing numerous diseases among cattle, particularly among sheep, many farmers losing the whole of their flocks.

'Although much remains to be done to remedy the mischief complained of, yet a considerable improvement has taken place within the last twenty years by enclosing many of the large commons, and by that means partially draining them; and also by enlarging the back drains which carry the water to a lower level into the main river, by which means it is carried off much sooner, and less mischief is done, than if it remained longer on the surface of the land.

'It is stated in a very old history of Somerset, that about 300 years ago, nearly the whole of the inhabitants of Kingsbury, Muchelney, and Long Load, were carried off by a pestilence (without doubt meaning a malignant fever); and that for many years afterwards it was considered so unhealthy that it was inhabited solely by outlaws, and persons of the worst character, a clear proof the country is in a much healthier state now than it was in former times.

'In addition to the more general causes of disease arising from the flat state of the country, and its liability to inundations, are many others of a more local character, and much easier of removal, in the village of Kingsbury; and in many others there are numerous pits or ponds in the winter season filled with muddy water, and, in summer, mud alone: these are often situated in the front or at the back of the cottages, and are receptacles for all manner of filth, and in certain seasons are productive of very serious diseases, and at all times highly injurious to health. Besides the mud pits above mentioned, there is scarcely a cottage that is not surrounded with all manner of filth, oftentimes close to the doors of the inhabitants, very few of the cottages being provided with privies, or if there be any, they only add to the general nuisance from being open and without drains.'

Mr. Oldham, the medical officer of the Chesterfield union, gives the following account of his district:

'Wessington is situated upon an elevation, but the houses are arranged around a green or unenclosed common, upon the surface of which are a great number of small pools, which, for the most part, are stagnant. In the winter season they overflow, and at this season the neighbourhood appears less infected with fever. In the summer months, and greater part of the spring and autumn, they are stagnant, and undoubtedly a fruitful source of malaria; indeed the neighbourhood of Wessington is scarcely ever free from fever at these seasons of the year.

'It perhaps may not be amiss to mention, I have attended a number of persons in the neighbourhood of this common who have been attacked with fever, who were at the same time well fed, and lived in comfortable and tolerably well-ventilated houses.'

He then adduces instances, and proceeds:

'From the facts before mentioned, I am led to conclude that the decomposition constantly going on in these small pools is the source of the malaria, and that the malaria so engendered propagates fever. 1st. Because there are cases of fever in this locality nearly all the year. 2nd. Because paupers, and persons who are better fed, and live in more comfortable and better ventilated houses in the neighbourhood of this green or common, are attacked with the disease, and, I may say, almost indiscriminately. 3rd. Because during the years I have attended the paupers of the district, there has scarcely been a case of fever in the winter season when the pools are overflowed, and the atmosphere is colder, and consequently unfavourable to fermentation and decomposition. In my opinion the only method to remedy this evil would be to drain the common, which is small, and its situation being elevated, would greatly facilitate its drainage. The condition of a few of the smaller and more confined of the tenements might be greatly improved.'

Mr. L. Reynolds, one of the medical officers of the Dore union, thus describes in his report the district where some fever cases occurred:

'Of those cases the six first have occurred on Colston Common, a small marshy spot, never drained, and containing several pools extremely unhealthy, from decaying vegetables that never are removed. This year the same families have been again attacked, and shall be so every year till that nuisance be removed. In a medical point of view, such commons are injurious, and they are extremely expensive to the unions, for they cause fever, asthma, and rhumatism, from their incipient moisture, thus injuring the labouring classes, and heavily taxing the parish.

'The four next have occurred at a place called Toad Ditch: it well deserves the name; it is a collection of badly-built houses, rendered unhealthy from the large ditch, into which every kind of refuse is poured; the removal of that nuisance is imperatively called for. All these houses have one privy in common, but the ditch is the place generally used.

'This district would be much served by enclosing and draining Colston Commons, by keeping the sewers at Kingston clean, and by draining the ditch at Toad Ditch. These are the only removable nuisances of which I have any knowledge.'

Mr. Blick, medical officer of the Bicester union, describes the prevalence of typhus:

'This disease has been very prevalent in this district during the past year, indeed we are never free from it. I think its origin may be traced, in most

158 II. Public Arrangements External to the Residences

instances, to a constant exposure to an atmosphere loaded with malaria, and propagated, in the second place, by contagion, so little attention being paid to prevent its diffusion.

'The malaria alluded to arises from the decomposition of vegetable matter left upon Otmoor (a marsh of about 4000 acres), by the previous winter's flood, and acted upon by the sun, &c., during the summer.'

Mr. J. Holt, the medical officer of the Leighton Buzzard union, reports:

'I have had only 34 cases of remittent and intermittent fevers during the last year, which is a small number in comparison to the amount usually occurring in hot summers. The great prevalence of these fevers at such times is attributable principally to the number of stagnant ponds and ditches which are situated in the very midst of many of the towns and villages of this union, and which, in hot weather, become quite putrid and offensive from the quantity of decaying animal and vegetable matter. I have generally observed that the greater number of these fevers occur in houses situated in the immediate vicinity of these ponds, and have no doubt is the chief cause of nearly all the fevers of this description. The villages to which I more particularly refer are Egginton, Eddlesbon, Cheddington, &c.'

The sanitary effects of road cleansing, to which house drainage and road drainage is auxiliary, it appears is not confined to the streets in towns and the roads in villages, but extends over the roads at a distance from habitations on which there is traffic. Dr. Harrison, whose testimony has been cited on the subject of the analogy of the diseases of animals to those which affect the human constitution, in treating of the prevention of fever or the rot amongst sheep, warns the shepherd that, if after providing drained pasture and avoiding 'rotting-places' in the fields, all his care may be frustrated if he do not avoid, with equal care, leading the sheep over wet and miry roads with stagnant ditches, which are as pernicious as the places in the fields designated as 'rotting-places.' He is solicitous to impress the fact that the rot, *i.e.* the typhus fever, has been contracted in ten minutes, that sheep can at 'any time be tainted in a quarter of an hour, while the land retains its moisture and the weather is hot and sultry.' He gives the following instance, amongst others, of the danger of traversing badly drained roads. 'A gentleman removed 90 sheep from a considerable distance to his own residence. On coming near to a bridge, which is thrown over the Barling's river, one of the drove fell into a ditch and fractured its leg. The shepherd immediately took it in his arms to a neighbouring house, and set the limb. During this time, which did not occupy more than one hour, the remainder were left to graze in the ditches and lane. The flock were then driven home, and a month afterwards the other sheep joined its companions. The shepherd soon discovered that all had contracted the rot, except the lame sheep; and as they were never separated on any other occasion, it is reasonable to conclude that the disorder was acquired by feeding in the road and ditch bottoms.'[1] The precautions applicable to the sheep and cattle will be deemed equally applicable to the labouring population who traverse such roads.

---

1. Edward Harrison, *op. cit.*, pp. 29-30.

Sanitary Effect of Land Drainage

Such instances as the following, on the prejudicial effects of undrained and neglected roads, might be multiplied. *Mr. E. P. Turner*, the medical officer of Foleshill union, in accounting for some cases of fever, states:

'These cases of typhus all occurred in the same neighbourhood, where the road is bad and a dirty ditch of stagnant water on each side of it; the road is generally overflowed in the winter. The disease broke out in the month of October; other cases occurred in the same neighbourhood at the time.'

The nature of the more common impediments which stand in the way of the removal of the causes of disease and obstacles to production described in the preceding, are noticed in the instances following. Others will be adduced when the subject of the legislative means of prevention are stated.

Dr. Traves, on the sanitary condition of the poor in the Malton union, states:

'The whole of the low district above alluded to, and extending into the Pickering union, (known by the name of the Marishes, or Marshes,) has at different times within the last few years been the seat of typhus and other fevers.

'Attempts were made by some of the landed proprietors a few years ago to effect a system of drainage and embankments likely to prevent the inundations of these rivers in wet seasons, but the attempt was abandoned in consequence of the reluctance of certain townships to bear their portion of the necessary outlay, and any partial system of embankment is positively injurious, inasmuch as the water that is let in upon the land at a higher point of the river is prevented returning into the stream again by an embankment at a lower point, so that this water, containing vegetable matters in a state of decomposition, must remain stagnant until evaporated by the sun's rays, or dissipated by the wind; cases of fever occurring under these circumstances have repeatedly come under my observation, as well as that of other medical men familiar with the district, and this fruitful source of disease (in seasons like 1839 more especially) will probably now remain in full force until an Act of the legislature shall effect a change.'

Mr. Thomas Marjoribanks, the minister of Lochmaben:

'No means of any consequence, so far as I am aware, have yet been tried to remedy the evil, the removal of such substances as generate malaria. There are no scavengers appointed for the removal of nuisances. One great mean of preventing the generation of malaria (in my opinion) would be the lowering of the bed of the river Annan, which would to a great extent free the surrounding lands of stagnant water, give greater facilities for draining, improve the system of farming, lessen the risk of damage, and increase the quantity as well as improve the quality of the food which the low lands produce, and in every way conduce to the comfort and cleanliness of the inhabitants. It is computed that in consequence of the flooding of the Annan, damage during the last four years has been done to the amount of 6,000*l.*, and this along only about three miles of its course. The property is very much subdivided, and, in consequence, poverty and want has increased to a great extent among the small proprietors.'

In closing this exposition of the state of the chief external evils that affect the sanitary condition of the labouring population, it may be observed that the experience, on which the conclusions rest as to the principles of prevention is neither recent nor confined to this country.

II. Public Arrangements External to the Residences

That which is new, is the advantages we possess beyond other times, and perhaps beyond all other countries, in capital and practical science for its application. The experience of the advantage of public sewers to the health of a town population is nearly as old as Rome itself. I may refer with M. Du Châtelet[1] to the experience of that city, to illustrate the consequences of neglects, such as are manifest amidst large masses of the community throughout the country, and are partially displayed in the mortuary registers first cited. He gives the details from the treatise *De Adventitiis Romani Cœli Qualitatibus*, by the celebrated Italian physician Lancisi,[2] who deeply studied the sanitary condition of Rome, and wrote several admirable works on the subject, which had the happy effect of inducing the pope to cleanse and drain the city:

'The barbarians of every tribe having several times pillaged and sacked the city of Rome, the acqueducts were destroyed, and the water, spreading into the surrounding plains, formed marshes, which contributed greatly to render uninhabitable the surrounding country.

'The aqueducts existing no longer, the sewers and privies were alike neglected, and produced serious and frequent sicknesses, which were more effectual in destroying the population than the arms of the barbarians. All the historians of these remote times, and particularly St. Gregory, in his Homilies, and the deacon John, in the Life of that saint, give a frightful picture of the city of Rome. The air became so vitiated that plagues and fevers of a malignant character continually carried on their ravages to such a point that Peter Damien, writing in the eleventh century to Pope Nicholas II., to intreat him to accept his resignation, alleged as the pretext the danger he ran every instant of losing his life by remaining in the town.

'It was principally during the abode of the popes at Avignon that all which regards health was neglected at Rome, and some historians have not hesitated to attribute to this negligence the depopulation of the town, which was reduced in a little time to 30,000 inhabitants.

'Things remained in this state to the end of the fourteenth century, an epoch at which the popes, resuming the ancient labours, restored things to their proper condition; a new title to glory of Leo X., who of all the popes was the one who occupied himself with this important object in the most especial manner.

'It is, in part, to these precautions that we are to attribute the rapid increase of the population of Rome, which, from 30,000 souls, reached in a short time to 80,000; and it is a thing worthy of our attention that after the death of this pontiff the population quickly fell to the number of 32,000, because, according to the contemporary authors, everything having been neglected, the first calamities were renewed.

'Happily for Rome this state of things did not continue long, because all successive popes, instructed, it appears, by the experience of ancient times, having carried on immense labours, and constructed fresh sewers, have given to the air of this city the necessary purity.'

Italy presents instances, though comparatively modern, of the removal of disease by land drainage:

---

1. For A. J. P. Parent-Duchâtelet, see above, p. 149, n. 1.
2. Giovanni Maria Lancisi, *Dissertatio de nativis, deque adventitiis Romani coeli qualitatibus, cui accedit historia epidemiae rheumaticae, quae per hyemem anni MDCCIX vagata est* (Rome 1711).

Sanitary Effect of Land Drainage

'At Vareggio,' observes M. Villermé[1], 'in the principality of Lucca, the inhabitants, few in number, barbarous, and miserable, were annually, from time immemorial, attacked about the same period with agues; but in 1741 floodgates were constructed, which permitted the escape into the sea of the waters from the marshes, preventing at the same time the ingress of the ocean to these marshes both from tides and storms. This contrivance, which permanently suppressed the marsh, also expelled the fevers. In short, the canton of Vareggio is at the present day one of the healthiest, most industrious, and richest on the coast of Tuscany; and a part of those families whose boorish ancestors sunk under the epidemics of the *aria cativa*, without knowledge to protect themselves, enjoy a health, a vigour, a longevity, and a moral character unknown to their ancestors.'

The histories of other cities, and particularly of Paris, afford illustrations of the effects of the neglect of public cleansing, which begin in the ignorance and carelessness of the superior officers, and continue in the predominance of ignorance and obscure interests of a multitude in the present day:

'For several years the suppression of an enormous cesspool at Paris near the Barrière des Fourneaux was implored by the inhabitants. Placed under the predominant winds, it was a permanent cause of annoyance to the quarters of St. Germain and St. Jacques. But all petitions were in vain. A singular occurrence brought about the event for which the people had prayed more than 50 years. In a hunting party, the Prince of Conde was carried by a fiery horse towards this same cesspool; finding it impossible to turn the animal, the prince had the presence of mind to throw himself on the ground, but the horse darted forward into the cesspool and disappeared. The next day an order was issued from Versailles, enjoining M. Lenoir, the lieutenant of police, to fill up the cesspool, which was accordingly done.'

A particular evil had attracted the attention of an able minister, who had recourse to the expedient which we have seen recently re-discovered and introduced into practice into one section of the sewerage of London:

'The great sewer of Montmartre being uncovered, and the fall exceedingly small, it was easily choked, and spread infection through all the neighbourhood. Turgot thought that the best method to obtain a ready flow for the muddy waters it received was to wash it by frequent currents. A vast reservoir, capable of containing about 22,000 measures of water, was in consequence established at the opening of the sewer, opposite the Rue des Filles-du-Calvaire. The waters of Belleville were conducted there, together with those of two wells dug in the vicinity. This volume of water was, on certain days, let into the main sewer by means of flood-gates, which could be opened at pleasure. The scouring of the sewer by a current of living water attracted the

---

1. Louis René Villermé (1782-1863) was the leading French authority on public health in this period. (See M. Delabroise, *L. R. Villermé* (Paris 1929).) He has been described as the 'Howard of the French prisons', and was the first to take a statistical approach to public health questions. His principal works in the field of public health include *De la Mortalité dans les divers Quartiers de Paris* (Paris 1826); *L'Influence de l'Aisance et de la Misère sur la Mortalité* (Paris 1828); *Population, Hygiène* (Paris 1829); *Sur les Cités Ouvrières* (Paris 1830); and *Des Epidémies sous les Rapportes de l'Hygiène publique, de la Statistique médicale, et de l'Economie publique* (Paris 1833).

public attention, and produced the most happy results. Shortly the people could dwell on the confines of this ancient ditch without fear of dangerous exhalations. The quarters of the Faubourg Montmartre, of the Chaussée-d'Antin, of the Ville-l'Evêque, and of the Faubourg St. Honoré, became populated. At length the land was so valuable in these different quarters that the possessors of the banks of the sewer demanded and obtained the permission to cover it over at their own expense.'

The mode of cleansing had, however, been before proposed by another minister:

'In the conferences which were held in 1666 and 1667 at the house of the Chancellor Seguier respecting the grand police of the kingdom, a thorough examination was made of the sewers of Paris, which began to multiply. The minutes of these sittings still exist. We see there the opinions given on the subject by each of the members of the commission, and particularly by Colbert, who in the sitting of the 13th of January, proposed, as the best method of cleansing the sewers, to establish several fountains in the quarters where they were necessary, and at the side of each of them a reservoir of 15 measures, which should be let out all at once. Nothing, assuredly, could be better than this proposition. But one thing was wanting to the minister—the water could not be procured.'

But the water, though abundant in the vicinity of Paris, is still wanted, and the cause of the want is thus noticed by M. Du Châtelet[1]:

'Paris possesses an immense mass of water, which can be distributed into every quarter and every house. Does the demand multiply with the pipes? Assuredly not, and one might well be surprised to see the negligence and apathy of proprietors in this respect. Some persons adduce the fact to prove that seven litres of water are sufficient for the inhabitants of Paris, whilst sixty are necessary for London, and still more for Edinburgh. But if we look closer to the conduct of the proprietors, we shall find that it proceeds from calculations well understood. It is the certainty that they will have sooner to empty the cesspools which scares them. This operation, and the expense it often brings with it, influences the venal propensities of the proprietors. Is it likely that they will pay for water of which the inevitable result will be to multiply the number of operations they dread the most, and which increase the expense in an enormous proportion? Thus the actual state of our cesspools, and the mode of emptying them now in use, are, in our opinion, the principal causes which prevent individuals from taking the water, and which retard the period in which the city will receive the interest of the enormous sums that it has devoted, and still devotes daily, to the supply of water.'

It is to be hoped, however, that the legislature will give the powers and direct the means requisite in this country, to furnish to every city in Europe a practical demonstration that by the art of the engineer, the obstacle to improvement, formed by the great expense and annoyance of removing the refuse of houses and streets may be rendered inconsiderable. In Paris the interests of turbulent bodies of men, the water-carriers, and another class of men called the chiffonniers, who live by raking for what they can find amongst the refuse cast into the streets, are opposed to any change which will reduce the charge of imperfect cleansing, and the disease promoted by filth. The general practice in that metropolis is to cast all the rubbish of the house into the street on the overnight, or

---

1. For A. J. P. Parent-Duchâtelet, see above, p. 149, n. 1.

Sanitary Effect of Land Drainage 163

before seven o'clock in the morning, when men attend with carts to sweep it up and remove it. In the night-time, however, the chiffonnier comes with a lantern and rakes amongst the refuse, and picks from it bones, rags, or whatever may have been thrown away by accident, or the carelessness of the servants. The offensive filth of their persons and their occupation, makes them outcasts from other classes of workmen; they sleep amidst their collections of refuse, and they are idle during the day; they are like all men who live under such circumstances, prone to indulgence in ardent spirits; being degraded and savage, they are ready to throw away their wretched lives on every occasion. There are nearly 2000 of the chiffonniers alone in Paris, and they and the water-carriers were conspicuous actors in the revolution of 1830. During the administration of Casimir Perrier the householders had complained of the inconvenient mode of cleansing the streets by large heavy carts drawn by three horses, which, during their slow progress throughout the day, obstruct the public thoroughfares and occasion great inconveniences, especially in the narrow streets.

In the beginning of the year 1834, when the cholera broke out, the attention of the authorities was directed to sanitary measures, and the municipality decided that the cleansing of the streets should be done by contract, by a quick relay of carts of a smaller and more convenient shape, drawn by single horses; and in order to diminish the inconvenience of the presence of these improved vehicles, the contractor was allowed to collect one load for each of his carts on the over-night, which would have led to a practice similar to that of London, where the dust-carts take the refuse direct from the house without any deposit in the streets. But in this arrangement an important interest had been overlooked; the chiffonniers, who were said to have been aided and directed by the owners and men belonging to the superseded vehicles, rose in revolt, attacked and drove away the conductors, broke to pieces the new carts, threw the fragments into the river, or made bonfires with them. Unfortunately at that time the cholera had broken out at Paris. The mobs of chiffonniers which collected on the following day were swollen by other crowds of ignorant, terrified, and savage people, who were persuaded that the deaths from the strange plague were occasioned by poison. 'My agents,' says the then prefet of police, in an account of this revolt, 'could not be at all points at once, to oppose the fury of those crowds of men with naked arms and haggard figures, and sinister looks, who are never seen in ordinary times, and who seemed on this day to have arisen out of the earth. Wishing to judge myself of the foundation for the alarming reports that were brought to me, I went out alone and on foot. I had great difficulty in getting through these dense masses, scarcely covered with filthy rags; no description could convey their hideous aspect, or the sensation of terror which the hoarse and ferocious cries created. Although I am not easily moved, I at one time feared for the safety of Paris—of honest people and their property.' In fact the riot was one of the most dangerous that had been witnessed in that city, and it was not suppressed without great exertions and some loss of life. The anxieties which it occasioned to the minister, Casimir Perrier, and his disgust at the political use made of it, were considered to have con-

II. Public Arrangements External to the Residences

tributed to his death. He was himself attacked with the cholera, and died a few days after. Shortly before his death, when expressing his disgust, he said to the prefet, 'My friend, we are harnessed to a vile carriage.' 'Truly so,' replied the prefet, 'and the ways are dreadfully dirty.' The material ways of the city continued as they were, the prefet seeing that the introduction of the new carts became 'a motive to discontent and collision,' took upon himself to set aside the contract with the contractor, who, he states, received no other compensation for his losses than a permission which he could not use to collect the refuse during the day, and the chiffonniers continue to the present time in the exercise of their wretched vocation at the expense of the public health and cleanliness.

The course of the present inquiry shows how strongly circumstances that are governable govern the habits of the population, and in some instances appear almost to breed the species of the population. Conceiving it probable that the amount of filth left by defective cleansing had its corresponding description of persons, I made inquiries of the Commissioners of Metropolitan Police. From returns which they obtained from their superintendents, it appears that of the class of bone-pickers, mud-rakers, people living on the produce of dung-heaps in mews, courts, yards, and bye lanes insufficient cleansed, 598 are known to the police. From an observation of the proportion of filthy children and adults who appear amidst refuse whenever there are new buildings and an unusual quantity of rubbish, and from other circumstances, I believe that, were the refuse of houses daily cast into the streets in London in the same manner as at Paris, London would soon have as large and as dangerous a population of the chiffonnier class. I am informed by Sir Charles Shaw, the chief commissioner of police at Manchester, that there are 302 of them known within the police jurisdiction of that town also. He complains that they have heretofore been licensed in their occupation; that the children are pilferers, and occupy the attention of the police, and furnish a large quota to the stock of juvenile delinquents and the population of the prisons. I am informed that in Bath there are about 100 of them known; and in other towns and places I have little doubt that they would be found in like proportions, which approach the proportions of the stated numbers of chiffonniers to the population of Paris. These degraded creatures are also found amongst the inmates of the workhouses, and the close identity of their habits with those of the chiffonniers of Paris afford a striking proof of the similarity of the population produced by similarity of circumstances. They are thus described to me by an eye-witness:

'The bone-pickers are the dirtiest of all the inmates of our workhouse; I have seen them take a bone from a dung-heap, and gnaw it while reeking hot with the fermentation of decay. Bones, from which the meat had been cut raw, and which had still thin strips of flesh adhering to them, they scraped carefully with their knives, and put the bits, no matter how befouled with dirt, into a wallet or pocket appropriated to the purpose. They have told me, that whether in broth or grilled, they were the most savoury dish that could be imagined. I have not observed that these creatures were savage, but they were thoroughly debased. Often hardly human in appearance, they had neither human tastes

Sanitary Effect of Land Drainage

nor sympathies, nor even human sensations, for they revelled in the filth which is grateful to dogs, and other lower animals, and which to our apprehension is redolent only of nausea and abomination.'

The following report from one of the superintendents to the Commissioners of the Metropolitan Police describes the manner in which they appear to the police, their moral character, and the efficacy of the means of prevention:

'With reference to the question of the Commissioners as to the means of subsistence of that portion of the population which at present exists by picking bones in the bye-lanes, &c., in the event of those places being properly cleansed, I am of opinion that they would be compelled to adopt some more laborious and useful means of obtaining a livelihood, such as field labour, &c. They are at present an idle, dissolute class, prowling about the stables, yards, backs of premises, and lanes, willing to commit petty felony wherever opportunity presents itself. While it would remove them, on the other hand, the instant removal of filth from the metropolis must prove beneficial to the health of the inhabitants.'

It will then be found to be an ultimately beneficial effect of the removal of the circumstances by the adoption of such modes of cleansing as diminish the prevalent amount of filth or filthy processes, that it will force a change to other occupations of a less degrading character, and diminish the number of persons 'brought up' to them. Any provision of the nature of a poor law may be said to be badly constructed which does not allow the exercise of a discretionary authority to alleviate any severe inconveniences to the poorest classes from such changes. For the sake of preventing the growth of the like misery, it would probably be found a good civic economy to maintain the whole of the existing class in idleness, if idleness were not in itself a curse to them. I mention this, because the parish officers frequently oppose improved modes of paving and efficient cleansing, (as they generally opposed the new police on the ground that it diminished the means of subsistence of decrepit old men as watchmen,) for the avowed reason that it is expedient to keep the streets in their present state of filth in order to keep up the means of employing indigent persons as street-sweepers and sweepers of crossings in removing it.

It is found in the metropolis to be a beneficial result of the increase of the practice of removing night-soil by the self-acting process of water-closets communicating with the sewers, that it prevents the increase of the number of nightmen formerly requisite for the performance of that offensive and dangerous labour, and is in the metropolis diminishing the number.

Yet it should be borne in mind, that until more complete measures are adopted, even the services of such agents are an improvement, and in crowded cities are only neglected at the expense of the degradation of the whole mass of the labouring population. An example is to be found in the state of some districts mentioned by *Dr. Speer*, who in his account of the diseases of the lower orders in Dublin, given in the Dublin Hospital Reports, noticed the fact that the fever cases always came from the filthy districts; and he observes:

'We cannot wonder at the rapidity with which contagion often spreads. Both in and out of doors, it seems facilitated in every way; within doors every article of furniture and wearing apparel is disfigured with filth; every spot seems encrusted with its layers, and the foulest odours abound everywhere. Out of doors, at least in warm seasons, our churchyards, slaughter-houses, and the masses of filth and offal with which our streets and lanes are disgraced, contribute no less to the propagation of contagion. In the larger and better streets, the cleansing is very well attended to, but in the narrow and crowded ones, where the necessity of its removal is infinitely greater, the heaps of filth are truly disgraceful. In some of my visits I have been obliged to wade through masses of filth enough to sicken the stoutest and strongest—masses which have remained undisturbed for months, perhaps for years, and thus generating the most putrid effluvia. We know that vegetables are very dear in our markets. Why? Because our gardens are not sufficiently manured; this manure lies in our lanes and alleys, and only wants collecting; but what would this be compared with the benefits from the purification of our atmosphere which its removal would produce?'

The condition of large rural districts in the immediate vicinity of the towns, and of the poorest districts of the towns themselves, presents a singular contrast in the nature of the agencies by which the health of the inhabitants is impaired. Within the towns we find the houses and streets filthy, the air fœtid, disease, typhus, and other epidemics rife amongst the population, bringing, in the train, destitution and the need of pecuniary as well as medical relief; all mainly arising from the presence of the richest materials of production, the complete absence of which would, in a great measure, restore health, avert the recurrence of disease, and, if properly applied, would promote abundance, cheapen food, and increase the demand for beneficial labour. Outside the afflicted districts, and at a short distance from them, as in the adjacent rural districts, we find the aspect of the country poor and thinly clad with vegetation, except rushes and plants favoured by a superabundance of moisture, the crops meagre, the labouring agricultural population few, and afflicted with rheumatism and other maladies, arising from damp and an excess of water, which, if removed, would relieve them from a cause of disease, the land from an impediment to production, and if conveyed for the use of the town population, would give that population the element of which they stand in peculiar need, as a means to relieve them from that which is their own cause of depression, and return it for use on the land as a means of the highest fertility. The fact of the existence of these evils, and that they are removable is not more certain than that their removal would be attended by reductions of existing burdens, and might be rendered productive of general advantage, if due means, guided by science, and applied by properly qualified officers, be resorted to. The impediments arising from the existing state of the law and of its local administration, form a subject for separate representation.

Before stating the cost in life and money attributable to the noxious causes external to the dwelling, it is desirable to notice other noxious causes, within the recognised province of legislative interference, that appear to be similarly under control, namely, the overcrowding of places where large numbers are assembled together, such as the overcrowding of places of work.

III. Internal Economy and Domestic Habits

III

CIRCUMSTANCES CHIEFLY IN THE INTERNAL ECONOMY AND BAD VENTILATION OF PLACES OF WORK; WORKMEN'S LODGING-HOUSES, DWELLINGS, AND THE DOMESTIC HABITS AFFECTING THE HEALTH OF THE LABOURING CLASSES

The evils arising from the bad ventilation of places of work will probably be most distinctly brought to view, by the consideration of the evidence as to its effects on one particular class of workpeople.

The frequency of cases of early deaths, and orphanage, and widowhood amongst one class of labourers, the journeymen tailors, led me to make some inquiries as to the causes affecting them; and I submit the following evidence for peculiar consideration, as an illustration of the operation of one predominant cause;—bad ventilation or overcrowding, and the consequences on the moral habits, the loss of healthful existence and happiness to the labourer, the loss of profit to the employer, and of produce to the community, and the loss in expenditure for the relief of the destitution, which original cause (the bad ventilation) we have high scientific authority for stating to be easily and economically controllable.

Mr. Thomas Brownlow, tailor, aged 52:

'It is stated that you have been a journeyman tailor, and now work for yourself. At what description of places have you worked?—I have always worked at the largest places in London; one part of my time I worked at Messrs. Allen's, of Old Bond-street, where I worked eight years; at another part of my time I worked at Messrs. Stultze's, in Clifford-street, where I worked four years. At Messrs. Allen's they had then from 80 to 100 men at work; at Messrs. Stultze's they had, when I worked there, about 250 men.

'Will you describe the places of work, and the effects manifested in the health of the workmen?—The place in which we used to work at Messrs. Allen's was a room where 80 men worked together. It was a room about 16 or 18 yards long, and 7 or 8 yards wide, lighted with skylights; the men were close together, nearly knee to knee. In summer time the heat of the men and the heat of the irons made the room 20 or 30 degrees higher than the heat outside; the heat was then most suffocating, especially after the candles were lighted. I have known young men, tailors from the country, faint away in the shop from the excessive heat and closeness; persons, working-men, coming into the shop to see some of the men, used to complain of the heat, and also of the smell as intolerable; the smell occasioned by the heat of the irons and the various breaths of the men really was at times intolerable. The men sat as loosely as they possibly could, and the perspiration ran from them from the heat and the closeness. It is of frequent occurrence in such workshops that light suits of clothes are spoiled from the perspiration of the hand, and the dust and flue which arises darkening the work. I have seen 40*l*. or 50*l*. worth of work spoiled in the course of the summer season from this cause.

'In what condition are these work-places in winter?—They are more unhealthy in winter, as the heat from the candles and the closeness is much greater. Any cold currents of air which come in give annoyance to those who are sitting near the draught. There is continued squabbling as to the windows being opened; those who are near the windows, and who do not feel the heat so much as the men near the stoves, objecting to their being opened. The oldest, who had been inured to the heat, did not like the cold, and generally prevailed in keeping out the cold or the fresh air. Such has been the state of

III. Internal Economy and Domestic Habits

the atmosphere, that in the very coldest nights large thick tallow candles (quarter of a pound candles) have melted and fallen over from the heat.

'What was the effect of this state of the work-places upon the habits of the workmen?—It had a very depressing effect on the energies; that was the general complaint of those who came into it. Many could not stay out the hours, and went away earlier. Those who were not accustomed to the places generally lost appetite. The natural effect of the depression was, that we had recourse to drink as a stimulant. We went into the shop at six o'clock in the morning; but at seven o'clock, when orders for the breakfast were called for, gin was brought in, and the common allowance was half-a-quartern. The younger hands did not begin with gin.

'Was gin the first thing taken before any solid food was taken?—Yes, and the breakfast was very light; those who took gin generally took only half-a-pint of tea and half a twopenny loaf as breakfast.

'When again was liquor brought in?—At eleven o'clock.

'What was taken then?—Some took beer, some took gin again. In a general way, they took a pint of porter at eleven o'clock. It was seldom the men took more than the half-quartern of gin.

'When again was liquor brought in?—At three o'clock, when some took beer and some gin, just the same as in the morning. At five o'clock the beer and gin came in again, and was usually taken in the same quantities. At seven o'clock the shop was closed.

'After work was there any drinking?—Yes; nearly all the young men went to the public-house, and some of the others.

'What were the wages they received?—Sixpence per hour, which, at the full work, made 6s. a-day, or 36s. a-week.

'Did they make any reserves from this amount of wages?—No; very few had anything for themselves at the end of the week.

'How much of the habit of drinking was produced by the state of the work-place?—I should say the greater part of it; because when men work by themselves, or only two or three together, in cooler and less close places, there is scarcely any drinking between times. Nearly all this drinking proceeds from the large shops, where the men are crowded together in close rooms: it is the same in the shops in the country, as well as those in the town. In a rural place, the tailor, where he works by himself, or with only two or three together, takes very little of the fermented liquor or spirits which the men feel themselves under a sort of necessity for doing in towns. The closer the ventilation of the place of work, the worse are the habits of the men working in them.

'You referred to the practice of one large shop where you worked some time since; was that the general practice, and has there been no alteration?—It was and is now the general practice. Of late, since coffee has become cheaper[1], somewhat more of coffee and less of beer has been brought in; but there is as much gin now brought in between times, and sometimes more.

'What would be the effect of an alteration of the place of work—a ventilation which would give them a better atmosphere?—It would, without doubt, have an immediately beneficial effect on the habits. It might not cure those who have got into the habit of drinking; but the men would certainly drink less, and the younger ones would not be led into the habit so forcibly as they are.

'What is the general effect of this state of things upon the health of the men exposed to them?—Great numbers of them die of consumption. "A decline"

---

1. In 1835 the import duties on East Indian and West Indian coffees were equalised, reducing that on East Indian (Ceylon) coffee. Further general reductions were made by the budget of 1842.

III. Internal Economy and Domestic Habits 169

is the general disease of which they die. By their own rules, a man at 50 years of age is superannuated, and is thought not to be fit to do a full day's work.

'What was the average of the ages of the men at work at such shops as those you have worked at?—Thirty-two, or thereabouts.

'In such shops were there many superannuated men, or men above 50 years of age?—Very few. Amongst the tailors employed in the shops, I should say there were not 10 men in the hundred above 50 years of age.

'When they die, what becomes of their widows and children, as they seldom make any reserve of wages?—No provision is made for the families; nothing is heard of them, and, if they cannot provide for themselves, they must go upon the parish.

'Are these habits created by the closeness of the rooms, attended by carelessness as to their mode of living elsewhere?—I think not as to their lodgings. The English and Scotch tailors are more careful as to their places of lodging, and prefer sleeping in an open place. The men, however, who take their pint of porter and their pipe of tobacco in a public-house after their hours of work, take it at a place which is sometimes as crowded as a shop. Here the single men will stay until bed-time.

'Are gin and beer the only stimulants which you conceive are taken in consequence of the want of ventilation and the state of the place of work when crowded?—No: snuff is very much taken as a stimulant; the men think snuff has a beneficial effect on the eyes. After going into these close shops from the open air, the first sensation experienced is frequently a sensation of drowsiness, then a sort of itching or uneasiness at the eye, then a dimness of the sight. Some men of the strongest sight will complain of this dimness; all eyes are affected much in a similar manner. Snuff is much used as a stimulant to awaken them up; smoking in the shops is not approved of, though it is much attempted; and the journeymen tailors of the large shops are in general great smokers at the public-houses.

'Do the tailors from villages take snuff or smoke as well as drink so much as the tailors in the large shops in the towns?—They neither take so much snuff nor tobacco, nor so much of any of the stimulants, as are taken by the workmen in the crowded shops of the towns.

'Do their eyes fail them as soon?—No, certainly not.

'With the tailors, is it the eye that fails first?—Yes; after long hours of work the first thing complained of by the tailors is that the eyes fail; the sight becomes dim, and a sort of mist comes between them and their work.

'Judging from your own practical experience, how long do you conceive that a man would work in a well-ventilated or uncrowded room, as compared with a close, crowded, ill-ventilated room?—I think it would make a difference of two hours in the day to a man. He would, for example, be able, in an uncrowded or well-ventilated room, to do his twelve hours' work in the twelve hours; whereas in the close-crowded room he would not do more than ten hours' work in the twelve.

'Of two men beginning at 20 years of age, what would be the difference in extent of labour performed by them in town shops or in the country?—A man who had begun at 20 in these crowded shops would not be so good a man at 40 as a man working to 50 in a country village; of the two, the country tailor would be in the best condition in health and strength; in point of fact he is so. The difference may be set down as a gain of 10 years' good labour. There are very few who can stand such work as the town shops 20 years.

'The eyes then become permanently injured, as well as fail during the day, in these crowded shops?—Yes, they do. After 45 years of age, the eyes begin to fail, and he cannot do a full day's work.

'Supposing a workman to work in a well-ventilated room, and to be freed from the nervous exhaustion consequent on the state of the place, might he not save at least all that he drinks in the times between his meals, or be enabled to apply it better, if he were so disposed; and, perhaps, the value of the two hours' extra work in the 12, when he is working piece-work?—Yes, certainly he might.

'Taking your account of the average loss by nervous exhaustion and bad habits to be two hours' work for 20 years, and 12 hours daily work for 10 years in addition, supposing him to be employed full time, it would be a loss of the value of 50,000 hours of productive labour (of the value at 6*d*. per hour, 1,250*l*.); or, if he were only in work half a-year, at a loss of 25,000 hours; so that if he were employed the half time at the full wages, or full time at the half wages, such workmen will have lost the means of putting by a sum of not less than 600*l*. to maintain him in comfort when he is no longer able to work?—Yes, I think that would be found to be correct. Very few do save; but I have known some save considerable sums. I knew one man, of the name of John Hale, who saved about 600*l*. He was not one of the most sober men, but he was in constant employment, sometimes at Allen's and sometimes at Weston's, and he was very careful; but he died when he was about 45. I knew another man, whose name was Philip Gray, who used to prefer the smaller shops. He was a man of a very good constitution, and he lived until he was about 70. He was a journeyman all his life, and he had, when he died, more than 1,500*l*., all saved by London journeywork. He used to live in a baker's shop in Silver-street, Golden-square.

'Was he of a penurious disposition?—He associated less with the men than others, and they knew little about him. He was dressed much the same as the rest, but he was much more clean in his person: he was remarkable for his cleanliness, and he was very neat in his person. Both he and Hale were single men.

'Can you doubt that, under favourable sanitary circumstances, such instances would become frequent?—It cannot be doubted. I have known other instances of saving, but those were not of men working on the board: they were mostly of men who had situations in the cutting-rooms.'

Mr. John Fowler:

'You are a tailor, are you not?—I have been all my life a journeyman tailor, and worked in the metropolis; but I have long been superannuated, and now act as collector to the Benevolent Institution for the Relief of Aged and Infirm Tailors.

'That is supported by the masters, is it not?—Yes; the journeymen tailors subscribe, but it is principally supported by masters, who subscribe to it most liberally. Mr. Stultze, for example, has subscribed 795*l*. in money, and is a yearly subscriber of 25 guineas. He has made a present to the institution of the ground for the erection of almshouses, worth about 1,000*l*., and has undertaken to build six houses at his own expense for the reception of 20 poor pensioners. The funds are about 11,000*l*., principally subscribed by the masters.

'Have you belonged to any other society?—I was clerk to a trade society, consisting of upwards of 500 men.

'Have you worked in the more crowded shops?—I have worked at Mr. Allen's, and Mr. William's, of Conduit-street, which was a shop containing about as many men as Mr. Allen's. I have worked at other shops, not so large as Mr. Allen's.

'Have you read Mr. Brownlow's evidence?—Yes, I have.

'How far do the facts generally coincide with your own observations?—Generally they do. I agree with him as to the effects of work in close work-shops, and as to the time a man would last as a workman, under the most

III. Internal Economy and Domestic Habits 171

favourable circumstances, in a well-ventilated place. I do not think the drinking of gin was general, to the extent he mentions; and I think the improvement as to drinking beer, as well as spirits, is now very great; particularly in spirits, since tea and coffee have been so much drank. Of late, as far as my knowledge extends, there is very little beer-drinking in the afternoon. I knew the individuals he mentions as having saved money, and I have known many others do so too. Some of them have become opulent and respectable masters, who were fellow-shopmen with me. I conceive that the establishment of coffee-shops has been of great benefit to the health and morals of the men: it has taken them from the public-house. I have known a very large proportion of men carried off young, and in middle life, by consumption; but, in general, irregular habits were mixed up with the effects of the work in close places. The crowding of the large shops must be considered as occurring only in the season.'

The following is the examination of a tailor in Marlborough, taken by Mr. Grainger:—

Charles Dobson, 58 years old:
'Has been a tailor since he was 16 years old. Has always lived in the country. Has two sons journeymen tailors, who have been employed in London, one seven and the other five years. Formerly employed seven or eight men, who worked with witness in a shop which was very close, so that if there were nine men they could scarcely sit on the board. Although there was very little drinking, they were so much oppressed in the summer, and at other seasons when the candles were lighted, that he has seen the men reel after getting off the board. Used himself, when it was very warm, to feel faint. Attributes these effects to the heat of the shop, arising from the closeness, the stove, and the hot irons; also to the smell of the cloth and the breath of the men. Latterly has worked with fewer hands and in a more open shop; finds his health better, and that he is not oppressed by the work. Has often noticed in this town, where there are a few shops containing, in the summer, 14 or 15 journeymen, that when men go into them who have previously worked in the neighbouring villages, they became pale and unhealthy-looking: attributes this to the heat. His sons have complained to him that their health suffers from working in large shops in London. Has seen many who have gone to London return "looking far worse than when they went." From his experience, thinks that a man may enjoy his health in this business, if he works moderate hours and in an airy shop, where the number is small. Should consider 12 hours, allowing out of them one hour for dinner, moderate: these are the common hours in this part of the country. Has known many men who have worked in the neighbouring villages; they are generally quite as healthy as other people, "does not see any difference." They are more strong and not so chilly as those who work in shops. Has known many upwards of 50, who were quite able to go on with the work; they are only obliged to give it up from failure of sight as they advance in age: "from nothing else." Knew one man in this town who went on till he was 77. Has himself good health.'

I have collected the evidence of several master tailors on the effects of work in crowded or bad ventilated rooms. Some are inclined to ascribe more of the ill health to the habits of the journeymen in drinking at public-houses, and to the state of their private dwellings, but in the main results the loss of daily power—*i.e.*, the loss of at least one-third the industrial capabilities enjoyed by men working under advantageous circumstances—the nervous exhaustion attendant on work in crowds, and the consequent temptation to resort continually to stimulants, which in their turn increase the exhaustion, are fully proved, and indeed generally admitted. I have caused the mortuary registers to be examined, but find that they do not distinguish the masters from the journeymen, and that there are no ready means of distinguishing those of the deceased who have been employed in the larger shops. It is also stated that many who come to work in town and become diseased, return and die in the villages. But in the registered causes of death of 233 persons entered during the year 1839 in the eastern and western Unions of the metropolis, under the general head 'tailor,' no less than 123 are registered as having died of disease of the respiratory organs, of whom 92 died of consumption;* 16 of diseases of the nervous system, of whom 8 died of apoplexy; 16 of epidemic or contagious diseases, of whom 11 died of typhus; 23 are registered as having died of diseases of 'uncertain seat,' of whom 13 fell victims of dropsy; 8 died of diseases of the digestive organs, and six of 'heart disease'; and of the whole number of 233 only 29 of old age; and of these, if they could be traced, we may pronounce confidently that the greater proportion of them would be found to be not journeymen, of whom not two or three per cent. attain old age, but masters. On comparing the mortuary registers in the metropolis with the registers in north-western and the south-western parts of England, where we may expect a larger proportion of men working separately, I find that whilst 53 per cent. of the men die of diseases of the respiratory organs in the metropolis, only 39 per cent. die of these diseases in the remote districts; that whilst five per cent. die of typhus in London, only one per cent. fall victims to it in the country; that whilst in London only 12 in the hundred attain old age, 25 in the hundred are registered as having attained it in the remote districts.

It is due to Messrs. Stultze, the employers mentioned by the first

---

* The spread of the knowledge of the fact that animals are subject to typhus consumption, and the chief of the train of disorders supposed to be peculiarly human, will, it may be expected, more powerfully direct attention to the common means of prevention. The following extract from a report on the labours of the Board of Health at Paris will show the effect of bad ventilation on cattle:—'The *epizootie* are in many respects less serious than the epidemics; nevertheless, as they often affect the animals which serve for the nutriment of man, and that apart from this consideration they may have grave consequences for the public health, they have constantly engaged the care of the council. In 1834, an *epizootie* was reported to the administration which prevailed among the cows of the communes round Paris, and which caused a great mortality. The researches of the council established that this *epizootie* was only a chronic disease, a true pulmonary phthisis, to which has been given the name of *pommelière*, and by which the greater part of the cows had been attacked which fill the stables of the milkmen of Paris and its environs. According to the council, the principal cause of the evil was to be attributed to the vicious regimen to which this species of animal is subjected. It is known that they pass a part of the year in stables perfectly closed, in which the space is not proportioned to the number of inmates, in which the vitiated air renews itself with extreme difficulty, and in which the heat is sometimes suffocating. It is known, also, that they pass suddenly from the food of the stable to pasture, and that in this change they go from the hot and humid atmosphere of the stable to a sudden exposure to the continual variations of the external air. This alterna-

III. Internal Economy and Domestic Habits

witness, to state, that since he worked with them they have made considerable alterations with the view to increase the ventilation of their workshops, and have expressed their desire to adopt whatever improvements may be pointed out to them.

I have been informed that some tailors' workshops at Glasgow have been carefully ventilated, and that the immediate results are as satisfactory as were anticipated, but the change has been too recent to permit any estimate of the effects on the general habits of the workmen.

The preceding case may serve as a general instance of the practical difference of the effects in the saving of suffering as well as of expense, by active benevolence exerted with foresight in measures of prevention, as compared with benevolence exerted in measures of alleviation of disease after it has occurred.

The subscriptions to the benevolent institution for the relief of the aged and infirm tailors, by individual masters in the metropolis, appear to be large and liberal, and amount to upwards of 11,000*l.*; yet it is to be observed, that if they or the men had been aware of the effects of vitiated atmospheres on the constitution and general strength, and of the means of ventilation, the practicable gain of money from the gain of labour by that sanitary measure could not have been less in one large shop, employing 200 men, than 100,000*l*. Independently of subscriptions of the whole trade, it would, during their working period of life, have been sufficient, with the enjoyment of greater health and comfort by every workman during the time of work, to have purchased him an annuity of 1*l*. per week for comfortable and respectable self-support during a period of superannuation, commencing soon after *fifty* years of age.

Of that which in these instances appear to be the main cause of premature disease and death, defective ventilation, it is to be remarked

---

* *contd.:*

tion of food and of heat and cold operates as a powerful cause of disease. But as the evil does not announce itself in a violent manner, as its progress is not very rapid, as there is even a period in the disease in which the animal is disposed to get flesh, the cow-feeder, who knows to what point to keep her, sells her when she is ready to calve. It is in a radius of 30 leagues from the capital that cows of this kind are purchased by the jobbers, who supply the milkmen of Paris. With these last they still hold out a certain number of years, if they are properly cared for, but in general they are kept in stables which are neither sufficiently large nor sufficiently airy, where they are exposed to the same causes which gave birth to the malady. The phthisis arrives insensibly at its last stage, and carries off every year from Paris and its neighbourhood a great number of these cows.' A similar discovery was only lately made as to the effect of defective ventilation on the cavalry horses in some of the government barracks in England; and it is stated, that a saving of several thousand pounds per annum was effected by an easy improvement of the ventilation of the barracks near the metropolis. An agriculturalist had a large number of sheep housed to feed them on mangel wurzel, but a great number of them sickened and died, and he declared that it was the food which had killed them. A veterinary surgeon, however, who happened to be aware of the consequences of defective ventilation, pointed out the remedy,—a better ventilation for the sheep, which were overcrowded. The defect was remedied; the sheep ate well, and throve upon the mangel wurzle.

that until very lately little had been observed or understood, even by professional men or men of science; and that it is only when the public health is made a matter of public care by a responsible public agency that what is understood can be expected to be generally and effectually applied for the public protection. Vitiated air not being seen, and air which is pure in winter being cold, the cold is felt and the air is excluded by the workmen. The great desideratum hitherto has been to obtain a circulation of air which was *warm* as well as fresh. This desideratum has been attained, after much trial, in the House of Commons; but there is reason to believe that, by various means, at an expense within the reach certainly of large places of work, a ventilation equally good might be secured with mutual advantage.

The effects of bad ventilation, it need not be pointed out, are chiefly manifested in consumption, the disease by which the greatest slaughter is committed[1]. The causes of fever are comparatively few and prominent, but they appear to have a concurrent effect in producing consumption. The investigation of the whole of the contributary causes to the production of the immense mass of mortality occasioned by that disease, would be beyond the time or means allowed for the present inquiry; but defective ventilation and defective management in respect to changes of temperature, are causes everywhere apparent amongst the labouring classes. The effects of good ventilation, as a single cause of the prevention or alleviation of disease, are nowhere so clearly manifest as in their effects on hospital treatment. What Dr. Bisset Hawkins states in respect to the sanitary measures necessary to ensure successful treatment in hospitals, may be stated in respect to common dwellings as well as places of work.

'Next to the influence of national causes, the mortality of hospitals is most affected by position and internal economy. These circumstances appear more powerful than even the various merits of practice; and, happily for mankind, they are advantages of a definite nature, easily comprehended, and, of late years, generally demanded. The case was formerly very different, when a singular prejudice or indifference existed in respect to ventilation. At the Leeds hospital no case of compound fracture, nor of trepan, survived. At the Hôtel Dieu, of Paris, compound fractures were also almost always fatal, and few survived amputation[2]. The system which will bear improper air with impunity during health becomes keenly susceptible of its mischief when diseased, and a change of air will often restore where the strictest diet has failed. Mortality is seldom to be assigned to the influence of bad practice, which, probably, does not often destroy life. An accomplished friend made particular notes on the comparative mortality under three physicians in the same hospital; one was expectant, one tonic, and the other eclectic. The mortality was the same, but the length of the

---

1. Diseases of the respiratory organs accounted for 27·9% of all deaths in the last six months of 1837. (*First Annual Report of the Registrar-General* (1839), p. 166.) See also table on pp. 76-7, and Introduction, pp. 11-12.
2. As late as 1874 it was claimed that mortality following all forms of amputation was between 35 and 50%, and following certain forms, as high as 90%. (J. E. Ericksen, *On Hospitalism and the Causes of Death after Operations* (1874), quoted by T. McKeown and R. G. Brown, 'Medical evidence related to English population changes in the eighteenth century', *Population Studies*, IX (1955) 120).

III. Internal Economy and Domestic Habits 175

disorder, the character of the convalescence, and the chances of relapse were very different.

'The earliest statement which we possess of the mortality of our hospitals is in Sir William Petty's work on Political Arithmetic[1], from which it appears, that in the year 1685 the proportion of the deaths to the cures in St. Bartholomew's and St. Thomas's hospitals was about 1 to 7. The annual printed report of St. Thomas's hospital for 1689 is still preserved: the mortality was then about 1 in 10. During the ten years from 1773 to 1783, the mortality at St. Thomas's became still smaller, it was 1 in 14. About the year 1783, some improvements were made with respect to cleanliness and ventilation, and during the ten subsequent years the annual deaths were accordingly still fewer than before, less than 1 in 15. During the ten years intervening between 1803 and 1813 the improvement continued, and the proportion fell to only 1 in 16. The average during the 50 years from 1764 to 1813 was remarkably small, only 1 in 15.'[2]

Parent Du Châtelet notices in the following terms the diminution in the mortality of the Hôtel Dieu from better ventilation:

'The mortality has diminished in the Hôtel Dieu in remarkable proportions. Without saying anything of the enlargement of the windows, of the warm clothing, of a better system of heating the apartments, are we to count for nothing the destruction of all the high houses which surrounded the Hôtel Dieu on every side? In our opinion the pure and dry air which circulates now in every part, the sun which penetrates there, the stoves which have been erected, have as much contributed to its healthiness as the suppression of the amphitheatres of anatomy which were in its neighbourhood.'

The reports of other hospitals present similar and generally corroborative experience. In the space of four years, ending in 1784, in a badly-ventilated house, the Lying-in Hospital in Dublin, there died 2,944 children out of 7,650; but after freer ventilation, the deaths in the same period of time, and in a like number of children, amounted only to 279.

One effect of the attention given to the condition of the workers in the factories has been, that ventilation has been extensively introduced, and with marked effects, on the condition of the workpeople. When I was at Glasgow a striking instance was pointed out to me of the beneficial effects of ventilation when applied to the dwellings of the working classes connected with such establishments. I was informed there was in that city an assemblage of dwellings for their workpeople, called, from its mode of construction and the crowd collected in it, the Barracks. This building contained 500 persons; every room contained one family. The consequences of this crowding of the apartments, which were badly ventilated, and the filth were, that fever was scarcely ever absent from the building. There were sometimes as many as seven cases in one day, and in the last two months of 1831 there were 57 cases in the building. All attempts to induce the inmates to ventilate their rooms were ineffectual, and the proprietors of the work, on the recommendation of Mr. Fleming, a surgeon of the district, fixed a simple tin tube of two

---

1. Sir William Petty, *Political Arithmetic* (1690).
2. *Second Report of the Select Committee on the Laws respecting Friendly Societies*, P.P. 1826-7, III, Appendix G. 3, pp. 94-112.

inches in diameter, into the ceiling of each room, and these tubes led into one general tube, the extremity of which was inserted into the chimney of the factory furnace. But the perpetual draught thus produced upon the atmosphere of each room the inmates were compelled, whether they would or not, to breathe pure air. The effect was that, during the ensuing eight years, fever was scarcely known in the place. The process was apparently defective only in not providing for the appropriate warmth of the air introduced. The cost of remedies previously applied in the public hospitals to the fever cases, continually produced as described in the barracks, were stated by Dr. Cowan[1] to have afforded a striking contrast to the cost of the means of prevention.

Similar defective ventilation and overcrowding in rooms of work, with the addition of the deterioration of the air by the use of candles or gas-lamps at night-work, produce similar effects on the milliners and dressmakers employed at the larger workshops of the metropolis. In a return of the causes of death to the milliners and dressmakers who died during the year 1839, in the unions of the metropolis, in which we have no means of distinguishing those who worked separately or in small numbers, the results were as follows:—

TABULAR STATEMENT of DEATHS from Disease of Milliners and Dressmakers, in the Metropolitan Unions during the year 1839, as shown by the Mortuary Registers.

Age	Number of Deaths	Average Age	Number of Deaths from Consumption	Average Age	Number of Deaths from other Lung Diseases	Average Age
Under 20	6	17	4	18	—	—
20 ,, 30	24	24	17	23	1	23
30 ,, 40	11	34	6	34	1	33
40 ,, 50	2	45	—	—	1	40
50 ,, 60	4	54	1	58	2	55
60 ,, 70	5	64	—	—	—	—
Total	52	32	28	26	5	41

Out of 52 deaths in the year, 41 of the deceased attained an age of 25. The average age of the 33 who died of lung diseases was 28.

It is not doubted by medical witnesses that in this class of cases, as in the case of the tailors, one-third at least of the healthful duration of adult life will be found to have been destroyed by the ignorance of the want of ventilation.

Unhappily, this fatal ignorance as to the requisites of the places of work is as frequently manifested in the over-crowded places of repose. I take an illustration from the answers of *Mr. Isaac Gilchrist*, surgeon of Aberdeen, to the question as to the causes of fever:

'In answering this query, the circumstance that calls for most remark in reference to this district is the over-crowded state of dwelling apartments. Six, eight, and even ten occupying one room is anything but uncommon; and these,

---

1. Robert Cowan, *Statistics of Fever and Small-Pox in Glasgow* (Glasgow 1837), p. 14.

III. Internal Economy and Domestic Habits

too, it frequently happens, are lone women, all employed at the manufactories during the day and huddled together during the night. Fever finding its way into any of these apartments, seldom quits it until every member has been attacked. In some instances of families of eight or ten members, not one individual has escaped the disease. I believe also that deficient cleanliness (to a certain extent the result of poverty) and bad ventilation co-operate with the overcrowded state of the apartments in propagating fever.'

Similar information is frequent from the metropolis and other districts. It is understood, and it may confidently be expected, that the Commissioners and Assistant Commissioners appointed to investigate the employment of young persons employed in large numbers in other manufactures than those now included in the provisions of the Factory Act[1] will investigate more closely than has hitherto been done the sanitary condition of the labourers employed in the mines as well as in other branches of industry. I take the following evidence respecting the condition of the lodging-shops, obtained by *Dr. Mitchell*, one of the Assistant Commissioners, in the course of his inquiries into the condition of the labouring population engaged in working the mines in Durham and Northumberland. He gives the following description of their sleeping places:

'Many of the miners, including young persons and boys, will go three miles and upwards from their own homes in the morning to work in the mines, or to wash the ore, and return again after their work at night. Some miners, who are too far off to be able to go and come in this way, find lodgings for the four nights in the week, and the washers for five nights, at some houses not too far from the mines. The usual price is 6*d.* a-week each, for which sum there is a bed between two of them, leave to make their "crowdy" on the fire in the morning, and they have their potatoes boiled for them in the evening. They bring their provisions in a wallet on the Monday mornings: the miners go back on the Friday, and the washers of ore on the Saturday. But there are many mines, and some of them very large, in remote situations in the Fells, far away from all dwelling-houses, where lodgings might be had, and the proprietors have erected for their miners and washers buildings called "lodging-shops," which I now am about to describe:—

'The first one of them which I visited was about nine miles across the Fell, south from Stanhope. It was a plain building, constructed of sandstone, covered with a coarse slate; and all very substantial. There was no opening or window at either end, nor at the back, nor on the roof. On the front or south side was a door towards the west end, and two windows, one a little above the other. On entering the door, it was seen that the lower part was one room, lighted by one of the windows, and had a great fire burning at the east end. By pacing the floor the length was ascertained to be about 18 feet, and the breadth about 15 feet. Along the one side, that next the window, was a deal table, extending the whole length of the room, and alongside of it was a form, and there were two other forms in the room. All along the other side on the wall were little cupboards, 48 in number, in four tiers above each other; six of the cupboards with the doors off, but the most of the rest carefully locked with padlocks, and in which the several miners had deposited their wallets with their provisions for five days. Throughout the room, more particularly at the end furthest from the fire, were hung from hooks and nails in the joists,

---

1. The Royal Commission on the Employment of Children in Mines and Manufactories, appointed 1842, reported 1842-4.

miners' trousers and jackets to be put on in case of the owners returning wet from their work.

'In addition to the articles already named were the following:—

'One earthen pitcher to fetch water; one tea-kettle; one pan for boiling potatoes; two pans for frying bacon; iron fender, a poker, and shovel; a besom.

'There was a large box in the room secured by a padlock, said to contain the clothes which the masters put on when they come to see the mines.

'On ascending to the upper room by a ladder, it was seen to be a sleeping-room. The dimensions of the floor were of course the same as of the room below. There was no fire-place, which indeed was not wanted, but neither was there any opening into a chimney to produce circulation of air. Along one side of the room were three beds, each six feet long by about four feet and a-half wide, the three beds extending the length of the room; then there were three other beds on the other side, and at the furthest end was a seventh bed extending from the one line of beds to the other. Immediately over these seven beds, and supported on posts, were seven other beds placed exactly in the same way. Of course the person who slept in each of the six beds of the upper tier next the wall could raise his head only a very little way on account of the roof. Each of these 14 beds was intended for two persons, when only few men were employed at the mines, but they might be made to receive three men each, and, in case of need, a boy might lie across at their feet. There was no opening of any sort to let out the foul air, yet from 39 to 40 persons might have slept there, the men perspiring from their work and inhaling the small dust from their clothes floating in clouds. The beds were stuffed with chaff. There were blankets but no sheets. The furniture of the lodging-shops is supplied by the masters. The beds and blankets are supplied by the miners themselves. They are taken home sometimes to be washed. On Friday, when the miners leave, the beds are rolled up to prevent damp. I visited the lodging-shop on Monday morning. The beds had not been slept in for Friday, Saturday, and Sunday nights preceding, yet was the smell most noxious. There was one excellent thing connected with this lodging-shop: there was a small but beautiful stream of water which was conducted across the Fell to this spot, and came through an iron pipe near the door, so that the men had an abundant supply of the pure element. I next went to see another lodging-shop on a large scale. On the ground-floor were five rooms. The first is a blacksmith's shop. Next to it is the cooking and eating-room of the washers of ore; from 20 to 30 men and boys, if so many, were employed. It was locked up, and I did not see it. The upper room, extended over the blacksmith's shop and the cooking room, is the sleeping-room of the washers, men and boys. The next room on the ground-floor is a cooking and eating-room of the miners, exactly like the room of the lodging-shop already described. Adjoining to it is a room in which they hang up their wet clothes. At the end is a stable for the horses which are employed to draw the waggons with ore from the pits. By a ladder close to the wall between the cooking-room and drying-room is an ascent to a room exactly like that in the lodging-house already described, with the same number of beds. One little pipe of about two inches diameter was the only communication with the exterior air. Through the partition wall is an opening into a bed-room, extending over the drying-room and the stable. Across this room extended two beds, leaving a space for passing. Above these two was a tier of two other beds: then at a short interval was a second set of beds, four in number; and further on, a third set similarly arranged, four in number. Thus in the space above the cooking-room, drying-room, and stable, were 26 beds, each intended for two or three men, as it might be, and perhaps more; and the same beds for sets of miners in their turns, as one set came from their work and another went off.

III. Internal Economy and Domestic Habits

'Though the beds had not been occupied for the three preceding nights, the smell was to me utterly intolerable. What the place must be in the summer nights is, happily for those who have never felt it, utterly inconceivable. The medical men are best able to give a judgment on these matters, but for my own part I cannot but believe that these lodging-houses are more destructive than the air of the mines. I should think it no hardship to have to remain 24 hours in a mine, but I should be terrified at being ordered to be shut up a quarter of an hour in the bed-room of a lodging-shop.

'Many miners speak of the horrors of lodging-shops of former days; but the only difference I could learn was, that at many mines there were not now so many men and boys at work, and consequently the lodging-shops were not so crowded. Some mines are not now wrought which formerly had large lodging-shops; for example, Mannergill, of which a miner stated to me that he was one of 120 who lodged in a suite of rooms there; and he declared that the nuisance was much aggravated by the great number.

'In such a dense accumulation of bodies, one man who might be ill was a disturbance to all the rest. The coughing of a few interrupted the sleep of others. Men coming from the mine at 12 o'clock at night, and frying their bacon at the fire below, sent up an odour which added to the already too suffocating smell of the sleeping-room above. The great number was an aggravation of what is intolerable at best.

'The miners showed me a tank through which running water passed, in which they had placed their bottles of milk which they had brought with them for their coffee.

'There was an excellent supply of running water of the best quality, and it was the only beverage which the men had; for they stated that there was no public-house or beer-shop nearer than seven miles, and if there were one, they durst not go into it for fear of being discharged.

'The men all said that their lodging-shop was a fair sample of all the lodging-shops in the country, the only difference being the greater or less number of men lodging in them, which would depend entirely on the state of the mine. I have, however, since seen one refinement of which these men did not seem to be aware, and that was a lodging-shop in which were not only the beds in tiers all round the room, but there also was a bed suspended or swung from the top of the room, which economically filled up a space which otherwise would have been vacant.'[1]

The following is the account given by a miner himself of the lodging-places:—

William Eddy, one of the miners, states:

'I went to work in Greenside four years. Our lodging-rooms were such as not to be fit for a swine to live in. In one house there was 16 bedsteads in the room up stairs, and 50 occupied these beds at the same time. We could not always get all in together, but we got in when we could. Often three at a time in the bed, and one at the foot. I have several times had to get out of bed, and sit up all night to make room for my little brothers, who were there as washers. There was not a single flag or board on the lower floor, and there were pools of water 12 inches deep. You might have taken a coal-rake and raked off the dirt and potatoe peelings six inches deep. At on time we had not a single coal. After I had been there two years, rules were laid down, and two men were appointed by the master to clean the house up stairs twice a-week. The lower

---

1. 'Report by James Mitchell on the Lead Mines, etc. in Durham, Northumberland, and Cumberland', Appendix to *First Report of Children's Employment Commission*, P.P. 1842, XVII, pp. 740-2.

apartment was to be cleaned twice a-day. Then the shop floor was boarded, and two tables were placed in the shop. After that two more shops were fitted up, but the increase of workmen more than kept up with the increased accommodation. The breathing at night when all were in bed was dreadful. The workmen received more harm from the sleeping-places than from the work. There was one pane of glass which we could open, but it was close to a bed-head.

'The mines at Greenside were well ventilated, and in that respect there was nothing to complain of.

'In the winter time the icicles came through the roof, and within 12 inches of the people sleeping in bed. During a thaw, water dropped plentifully into the beds. In the upper beds the person sleeping next to the wall cannot raise his head or change his shirt.'

Joseph Eddy, another workman, states:

'I consider the lodging-shops more injurious to the health of the miners than their work itself. So many sleeping in the same room, so many breaths, so much stour arising from their working-clothes, so much perspiration from the men themselves, it is impossible to be comfortable. Two miners occupy one bed, sometimes three. The beds are shaken once a-week on the Monday morning, when the miners come. Some miners make their beds every night. The rooms are in general very dirty, being never washed, and very seldom swept, not over once a-month. There is no ventilation, so that the air is very close at night.'

It is observed of this particular class of men that they are worn out soon after forty; but a large share of this result may also be ascribed to their places of work. The following is a return of the ages of all the miners who died during one year, including those who slept at their own homes, with those who had been accustomed to sleep at the lodging-shops.

STATEMENT of Deaths from Disease and Accidents of Miners, Colliers, and Pitmen, in the Unions of Cumberland and Westmoreland, and parts of the Counties of Lancaster and Northumberland (Population Census of 1831, 338,273), during the Year ended 31st December, 1839, as shown by the Mortuary Registers.

Periods of Age	Number of Deaths	Average Age
Under 20	37	15
20 ,, 30	39	23
30 ,, 40	27	33
40 ,, 50	27	44
50 ,, 60	23	55
60 ,, 70	32	64
70 ,, 80	17	75
80 and upwards	10	86
Total deaths	212	42

The following is a summary view of the causes of death, from which it will be seen that out of 212 deaths 69 fell from diseases of the respiratory organs, and of these 52 died from consumption, whose average age of death was no more than $36\frac{1}{2}$, and that no less than 58 were destroyed by accidents.

III. Internal Economy and Domestic Habits

STATEMENT of the Causes of Death amongst Miners in the Unions of Cumberland and Westmoreland and parts of the Counties of Lancaster and Northumberland, during the Year ended 31st December, 1839, as shown by the Mortuary Registers.

Cause of Death	Number of Deaths	Cause of Death	Number of Deaths
Disease of Respiratory Organs:		Diseases of the Brain and Nerves	12
Consumption . .	52	Diseases of the Digestive Organs	10
Other Diseases .	17		
Epidemic and Contagious Disease	20	Disease of the Heart . .	2
		Other Causes of Disease .	22
Accidents:		Natural Decay and Old Age .	19
In Mine	37		
Not stated to be in Mine .	21		
Total Deaths . . 212			

In a subsequent portion of this report I shall advert to the state of the health of the miners in Cornwall, as compared by Dr. Barham with the state of the agricultural labourers in the immediate vicinity of the mines.

I would here request attention to a suggestion which appears to me to arise from a consideration of the evils above displayed, (and that will receive further corroboration in the course of this report,) that if there were a regular system of periodical inspection of the places of work or places of large assemblage, it would be attended with great advantage to the lower orders of the community, in which the other classes could not fail to participate.

One most important result of such investigations would be to disabuse the popular mind of much prejudice against particular branches of industry arising from the belief that causes of ill health really *accidental* and removable, and sometimes unconnected, are *essentials* to the employment itself. By pointing out the real causes, warning will be given for their avoidance, and indications extended for the application of more certain remedies. Medical men who see only a few patients of the same occupation at distant intervals; who see them in their own dispensaries or in the hospitals, and who have no opportunities of observing such patients under the varied circumstances in which the disease may have been contracted, are left to mere guesses as to its cause. A working person of any of the classes whose condition I have described, presenting himself with the symptoms of a consumption, the medical man has no means of detecting *the* one of many causes by which it may have been occasioned, and the individual patient himself is more likely to mislead than to inform him. Unless his attention were accidentally directed to it, or unless the medical investigator had himself the means of observing the different personal condition of the different sets of persons following the same occupation in town and in country, it is highly probable that the evidence that the disease is not essential to the occupation would escape him. Thus, between different sets of workmen who work at the same descriptions of work during the same hours, and in the same town, but in well or in ill-ventilated factories a marked difference in the personal condition and general health of the workpeople has been perceived. Great differences are perceptible in the general personal condition of persons working during the same hours in cotton-mills in town, and in cotton-mills in rural districts, where they have not only a purer atmosphere, but commonly larger and more commodious places of abode. The factory superintendents[1] generally state that the workers in the country mills are distinguishable at sight by their more healthy appearance, and by the increased proportions amongst them who have florid complexions. Very lately the attention of the Austrian government was called to the labour of the persons working in the cotton-factories in the neighbourhood of Vienna.[2] One half, perhaps, of the mills are of the ordinary construction of the cotton-mills in England of from thirty to forty years' date, and they work on the average as much as fifteen hours per diem. But it appears that the houses in which the workers live belong to the capitalists who own the mills, many of whom have displayed a desire to ensure, as far as the state of the private residences can ensure, the comfort of those whom they employ, and they have accordingly built for them a superior description of tenements. It is stated that the result of the inquiry conducted by the government physicians was, that the average health enjoyed by the workers in those mills is greater than that of any other class of workpeople in the neighbourhood where the mills are situate, and where the general condition of the population is deemed good; the difference in the general health of the two classes (indicated by the proportions of death —of 1 in 27 of the general population, and 1 in 31 of the manufacturing population), was ascribed to the difference of the residences. My colleagues and myself of the central board of the Factory Commission of Inquiry[3] were fully sensible that the effect of one cause on the health of the working population could not fairly be judged of unless its operation was observed under various circumstances, and unless amongst them the influence of the domestic circumstances, as well as the nature of the work and the place of work, were duly examined. We could not but deem it important that the state of the dwellings of the workpeople, who were the subject of inquiry, should also be investigated; and we gave instructions with that view to the district medical commissioners; but the limited time allowed by Parliament for the investigation, prevented its being made as we desired, a circumstance that, for the sake of the workpeople, is much to be regretted, as great injury is done to them by attention being diverted, as it commonly has been, from the real means of prevention.*

---

* The following were the terms of our instructions to the district medical commissioners of inquiry:—'A given amount of evil is experienced by a class

---

1. Inspectors appointed under the 1833 Factory Act.
2. L. M. von Pacher, 'A Report on the statements of Dr. Mauthner regarding the sanitary condition of the operatives in the new cotton manufacture . . . 1841', *San. Rep.*, App. 22, pp. 432-41.
3. The Royal Commission on the Employment of Children in Factories, appointed in 1833, reported in 1833-4.

III. Internal Economy and Domestic Habits

M. Parent Du Châtelet and M. d'Arcet having presented to the Board of Health of Paris a report on an investigation with a view to discover the physical or medical means by which particular sorts of work might be ameliorated, observe:

'Perhaps it will be said that the task has been already performed, and that several celebrated men, whose works are in the hands of all the world, have preceded us in this career, without leaving to their successors the hope to add anything to what they have published.

'We are assured beforehand that this objection will not be made by our colleagues, who have penetrated into manufactures and have studied their influence with a mind free from prejudice. It is because we have studied the works which treat of the maladies of artisans, and have seen a great number of these workmen in their shops; it is because we have compared books with actual observation; it is, finally, because we have not believed authors on their word, and have subjected them all to a severe verification, that we have seen the insufficiency, nay more, the inaccuracy of the greater part of their assertions.

'This method of proceeding has demonstrated to us that the works of which we speak, far from being the fruit of long observation, have been composed in the silence of the cabinet by men who have only had a casual view of artisans and manufactures; and who, generalizing a few facts presented to them by accident, have singularly exaggerated the inconveniencies of some professions, and attributed to others influences which they are far from exercising.'— *Mémoire sur les Veritables Influences du Tabac sur la Santé des Ouvriers.* Par M. Parent Du Châtelet.[1]

They give, as an illustration, the exaggerated accounts of the manufacture of tobacco, of which the supposed evils are proved to be entirely fictitious, or at best an erroneous application to the manufacture,—of

---

* *contd.:*

placed under peculiar circumstances; a large portion of that evil is shared by other classes not under these peculiar circumstances; to attribute the whole of the evil experienced by the first class to those peculiar circumstances is obviously fallacious. It is conceived that it is only by investigating the subject with this precaution constantly in the mind that it is possible to arrive at a just conclusion. While you carefully observe the effects of labour on the children and the adult workpeople, and report every case in which you conceive it to be excessive, and state the reasons on which you ground that opinion, you are requested to investigate minutely the concurrent causes of ill health. With this view you are requested in every case to examine and report the state of the drains in and about the factory: the state of the neighbourhood of the factory as to dryness or dampness, cleanliness or filthiness: the state of the houses and neighbourhood in which the children and adult workpeople take their meals and exercise (if they leave the factory), and where they sleep: the state of the air within the factory, and which the workpeople usually respire, whether it be fresh or whether it be not fresh, owing to deficient ventilation,—whether it be pure, or whether it be rendered impure by effluvia floating in it, and if so, what the effluvia are: what organs of the body are likely to be injured, and what, from careful examination, you find to be actually injured: the temperature of the air, the highest, the lowest, and the average temperature, and the condition of the air as to dryness or moisture.'

---

1. A. J. P. Parent-Duchâtelet and J. P. d'Arcet, 'Mémoires sur les véritables influences que le tabac peut avoir sur la santé des ouvriers occupés aux différentes préparations qu'on lui fait subir', *Annales d'Hygiène* (Paris, n.d.).

effects which, though incidentally met with in the workmen, were equally common to others of their station. In an abstract of their paper, inserted in the Appendix[1], there is even an enumeration, by eminent physicians, of specific cases of death from the fancied agency of tobacco, but they only show the extent of error produced in this and kindred instances by the previous conviction of the noxious influence of particular circumstances, and by referring all existing maladies to these without further inquiry. If I might add my testimony on this point, derived from my own observations on two of the commissions of inquiry on which I have had the honour to serve, it would be entirely in corroboration of the above statement. On comparing the actual condition of workmen with the medical descriptions of these diseases, and the causes, we commonly found that the results of a cluster of causes are commonly ascribed to one; and in respect to several classes of workmen the real cause, the invariable antecedent, such as defective ventilation, is unnoticed. No persons were frequently more surprised than the intelligent workmen, by the frequent exaggerated accounts of the operations of particular causes upon them, and the erroneous association of effects to causes with which they were known to have no real connexion. For example, in the work of M. Patissier[2], one which is the chief work, and of European authority, on the diseases of artisans, he adverts to the diseases of tailors. His description was read to *Mr. Brownlow*, the tailor, examined upon the subject of the overcrowding of places of work, and the observations of that witness on the statement of M. Patissier are given in answer:

M. Patissier. 'The employment of tailor is one of the most sedentary: seated constantly on a board, his legs crossed, his body stooping forward, this class of labourers exercises no part of the body but the arms, and that only the right one.'

Witness. 'That is not so: there is a good deal of action with the left arm in holding and sewing: in using the iron also there is a good deal of action with the arms and knees, and with the rest of the body. Journeymen tailors are remarked as being full breasted, as compared with other workmen; they carry themselves higher, and the chest is more fully developed; so that the labour has, as compared with much other labour, the effect of opening the chest.'

M. Patissier. 'Their position is particularly injurious to the functions of the viscera of the abdomen and chest. It produces difficulty of digestion, injures the gastric juices, brings on constipation, hemorrhoids, chronic catarrhs of the bladder, and obstructions of the bowels.'

Witness. 'I have never heard complaints beginning with the bowels. The stomach may be out of order; they eat very little solid food, and of course the action of the bowels will not be very good; but as to the effect of the tailors' work on the chest, we do not consider it at all injurious.'

M. Patissier. 'I attended a tailor who every time that he applied himself

---

1. 'Instance by Mm. Duchatelet and D'Arcet of the erroneous medical inferences as to the insalubrity of particular trades', *San. Rep.*, App. 17, pp. 424-6.
2. Ph. Patissier, *Traité des Maladies des Artisans* (extracts from the French translation by A. F. de Fourcroy of Bernardino Ramazzini, *De Morbis Artificum Diatraba*, of which an English translation—*A Treatise of the Diseases of Tradesmen*—was published in 1705.).

III. Internal Economy and Domestic Habits 185

diligently to his work, was attacked with nausea, colic, jaundice, and symptoms that denoted irritation of the liver. I have known, says Stoll, a great number of tailors who have suffered more particularly from diseases of the lungs.'

Witness. 'The only complaints I have ever heard are those arising from the foul air, perhaps the dust arising from cloth is injurious. I have already said that men coming from the country to a town shop will faint, and be obliged to leave it in the afternoon.'

M. Patissier. 'As they are almost constantly in a sitting posture, the body bent, with the head stooping forward, the blood is unequally distributed, and too large a quantity accumulates in the lungs, either because the bowels of the abdomen, compressed by the position of the body, admit of less blood, and which is therefore forced back into the vessels situated above, or because the short respirations of those who are sedentary, prevents the blood which enters the lungs from passing out with sufficient rapidity, by which local plethora in the heart and lungs is produced. In short, tailors are very liable to pulmonary phthisis, hydro-thorax, and haemoptysis, which often accompanies them to a very advanced age. M. Corvisart has observed that diseases of the heart and of the larger vessels are not less frequent amongst this class of artisans. As the posture of the tailor causes the blood to flow into the upper part of the body, the circulation in the lower members is consequently much less active, which explains the emaciation and feebleness of the legs and thighs of this class of artisans, and the peculiar walk which distinguishes them.'

Witness. 'As to the circulation of the blood, I should say that it was more free than amongst persons sitting at a desk; as soon as the journeyman tailor begins to feel warm and swell, he loosens everything that he has on; his coat is off, and his shirt neck is open, if he wears a handkerchief it is very loose; a tailor wears no garters, nothing that can stop the circulation of the blood: the only confinement that arises is from the position, which is certainly sedentary, but he frequently changes it, and puts one leg over the other when they are tired; they also stretch their legs out. Their breathing even in the close shops is not noticed as short.'

M. Patissier. 'Ramazzini says they are very subject to numbness of the thighs, neuralgic sciatica, and lameness.'

Witness. 'The tailors are frequently subject to rheumatism, but that is from going from a hot to the cold open air in the way described. Men who are generally emaciated will have their legs emaciated too: the whole frame goes together, but I have never heard young men or tailors in the middle of life being remarked as deficient in that part of bodily capability. Those whom I have known to be emaciated have been spirit drinkers; the emaciation has been more from spirit-drinking than from the heat of the shop, though one brings on the other. Some years ago there used to be much racing at about five o'clock in the morning in the parks, sometimes amongst the tailors themselves, and sometimes with other runners who had celebrity. The tailors were generally good competitors and more active than other workmen in London. There was one of the country tailors at Faversham who some years ago was considered the first runner in England for a hundred yards. The tailors have certainly a peculiar walk, but all whom I have known to be lame were lame originally. When a lad has anything the matter with him, which occasions him not to be strong enough for anything working on his feet, it is a common thing to say, "Then we must make him a tailor." It is a very frequent thing to send weakly children to be tailors, though it is a bad choice, for the lad has little chance of recovering himself in the town shops, and a more open trade would be better for him. Many tailors go for sailors and soldiers, and they are always thought to be good men. I should think there are many tailors in the guards.'

M. Patissier. 'There is sometimes to be observed on the surface of their skin a psoriform eruption, which by some writers is ascribed to the irritation of the woollen cloth which these artisans are continually handling. Guldner, however, considers that this eruption is produced by their mode of living.'

Witness. 'I never saw or heard of any peculiar eruption on the skin of the tailors, though they perhaps do not attend sufficiently to personal cleanliness. The dye of cloth is sometimes bad, but I never observed any effects from it.'

M. Patissier. 'Tailors are apt to prick themselves with their needles, and these wounds often bring on festerings.'

Witness. 'That is certainly the case; the needle may carry with it some of the dye, and the festering may also be occasioned by the bad state of the body.'

M. Patissier. 'They almost all have decayed teeth, which are destroyed by the habit of biting their thread with them. It is very rare to see a tailor of advanced age with any front teeth.'

Witness. 'That is certainly so: they have many of them bad teeth, but I have not noticed any deficiency of the front teeth.'

M. Patissier. 'Their sight is soon enfeebled by the fine work which they have to execute, often at night by the light of candles. When they work in the evening at open windows, they are liable to be affected by ear-ache, tooth-ache, cold in the head, and sore eyes.'

Witness. 'That is very correct with respect to the tailors in town, but it is not noticed so much with tailors in the country.'

M. Patissier. 'The sedentary life which they lead produces heavy, soft flesh, that has no firmness; they generally are thin in body, legs are spare and feeble, and their complexion rather jaundiced.'

Witness. 'Almost all this will be found to be the effect of habits that have nothing to do with the trade.'

M. Patissier. 'Tailors ought to walk in the open air every evening when their work will admit of it, rub their limbs well with flannel, abstain from all food difficult of digestion, avoid all excesses, and generally every kind of debauchery.'

Witness. 'The men when they leave their shop-boards do not begin rubbing their legs, and do not appear to feel the least want of it. The appetites of men working in shops being bad, they do commonly take food that is easy of digestion, as they cannot do with the coarser food. When a tailor comes from the country he will eat a twopenny loaf and take a pint of coffee for breakfast; but after three or four months working in the close shop getting exhausted, then taking beer and then spirits, his appetite fails him, and I have seen him eat only a small slice of bread and butter, and take half a pint of coffee for breakfast, and his appetite generally fails him. The young men on going back to their work in the country, generally recover their appetites unless disease has taken such root that they cannot recover.'

The evidence of Mr. Brownlow was read to Dr. Weber, who has had under his care between 200 and 300 cases of journeymen tailors who were treated by him, as physician to the St. George's Dispensary, which is much resorted to by those of that class of workmen who reside at the west end of the metropolis. Dr. Weber confirms the general tenor of the evidence as to the medical facts, and especially the general conclusion that the greatest proportion of the diseases to which they are subject arise from circumstances separable from their occupation. The evidence as to the personal condition and habits of the workmen is generally corroborated by several master tailors, who state that the journeyman tailor in the rural district who works singly, or in a well-ventilated apartment, is in person commonly the opposite of the one described by

III. Internal Economy and Domestic Habits 187

M. Patissier; he is described as being a hard worker, but at times a man who is in most village foot races, and not unfrequently the foremost runner, and in games of foot-ball not the last. The journeymen tailors are found amongst the best men in the life guards. In consequence of a strike of tailors, one dragoon regiment had a troop chiefly enlisted from them, and military men state that they greatly distinguished themselves.

If we thus find the crowding of unventilated places of work injurious —in which persons rarely pass more than 12 out of the 24 hours, being free during the remaining time to breathe what air they please—how much worse should we expect the consequences to be of the same fault in workhouses, hospitals, schools, and prisons, in which individuals often pass both day and night in the same apartments, or if in different apartments, still in the same crowd. Accordingly, since the attention of medical men has been sufficiently directed to the subject, the explanation has become complete of many deplorable cases of general ill health and mortality in such places, attributed at first to deficiency or bad quality of food, or to any cause but the true one,—want of ventilation. A striking illustration of this was afforded in the case of a large school for children during the years 1836 and 1837, as recorded in the second volume of the Poor Law Reports[1]. Such general failure of health and such mortality had occurred among the children as to attract public notice and the animadversions of many medical men and others who visited the schools; but by most the evil was attributed chiefly to faulty nourishment; and it was only after the more complete examination, made by direction of the board, and of which the report is published, as above stated, that the diet was found to be unusually good, but the ventilation very imperfect. Suitable changes were then made; and now, in the same space where 700 children were by illness awakening extensive sympathy, 1100 now enjoy excellent health. The defective state of information on the subject of ventilation is frequently shown in reports which assume that apartments containing given cubic feet of space are all that is requisite for life and health, whereas if a spacious drawing-room be completely closed against the admission of air, an inhabitant confined to it would in time be stifled, whilst, by active ventilation or change of air, men working in connexion with diving-machines live in the space of a helmet, which merely confines the head.

In the majority of instances of the defective ventilation of schools, the pallid countenance and delicate health of the schoolboy, which is commonly laid to the account of over-application to his book, is due simply to the defective construction of the school-room. In the dame schools, and the schools for the labouring classes, the defective ventilation is the most frequent and mischievous.

Mr. Riddall Wood, an agent of the Manchester Statistical Society, thus describes some of the crowded schools found in the course of examinations, from house to house, of the condition of the town population in Manchester, Liverpool, Leeds, Hull, and York:

---

1. Neil Arnott, 'Report on the Metropolitan houses for the reception of pauper children', App. C to *Second Annual Report of the Poor Law Commissioners* (1836), p. 489.

III. Internal Economy and Domestic Habits

'I may mention that in one school where the average attendance was, I think, 36, not above eight children were present. Upon my inquiring of the mistress as to the reason, she stated that the remainder of her scholars had been taken with the measles. I perceived a bed in the school-room, upon which lay a child much disfigured by that complaint. Another child of the mistress had died of the measles. I had reason to believe that the contagion had been communicated originally from that child, because the cases of the scholars all occurred subsequently. In a school in Liverpool, having above 40 scholars in average attendance, I found the number diminished to somewhere about 10. On inquiring into this case, I ascertained that it arose from the prevalence of scarlet fever, and the master made this remark: 'It is a very strange thing how this fever should have attacked almost all the children coming to my school, whilst none of my neighbours have got it.' I attributed that to the very crowded state of the school. The room was very low. When the whole of his scholars were in attendance, it must have been excessively crowded. There was no thorough ventilation.

'I found that in many of the schools there were from 20 to (in some cases) nearly 100 scholars crammed into a dirty house or cellar, without air or ventilation, the effluvia from whose breath and clothes was exceedingly offensive, and must, I am sure, be very injurious to the children's health. In most of these place, too, I have found that the ordinary household occupations have been carried on by the old women.'[1]

Another inquirer states, that in the neighbourhood of Bolton he saw 70 scholars cooped up in a badly ventilated room not 12 feet square.

Bad ventilation and overcrowding of private houses

The reports from the great majority of the new unions present evidence of the severe overcrowding of the cottages in the rural districts, and the tenements occupied by the working classes in towns.

From the returns as laid before the public from the commissioners appointed to take the last census, it would appear, however, that the number of houses has more than kept pace with the increase of the population.[2]

From these returns it would appear that the increase of houses even in Scotland has more than kept pace with the increase of population. But this result was so much at variance with the reports and communications from all parts of the country relating to the dwellings of the labouring classes, that if any increase of the proportions of houses to the population had taken place, it must have been in the houses of the middle and higher classes of the community. I learn, however, the fact to be, that whilst in obtaining the previous census, merely the heading was given without any instruction for the officer to fill up the 'number of houses'; on the occasion of taking the last census, the commissioners ordered each separate occupation under the same roof to be returned as a house. In the

---

1. James Riddall Wood made a report to the Manchester Statistical Society on 'The physical and moral condition of Liverpool', but it was not published. (*Report of Select Committee on the Health of Towns*, P.P. 1840, XI, Q. 2142.)
2. These figures were published, after the appearance of the *Sanitary Report*, in the Enumeration Abstract of the 1841 Census of Population, in *P.P.* 1843, XXII, pp. 6-7, but could have been calculated by Chadwick from the Summary Tables published in *P.P.* 1841, II, pp. 8-9.

Scotch towns, and in many of the English towns where it is the custom to let off as separate tenements the flats or floors under the same roof, there will, unless it be explained, appear to have been, as compared with the numbers in the last census, when the buildings and not its subdivisions were returned, an increase of accommodation, when, in reality, there may only have been an increased subdivision of tenements in consequence of an increased pressure of population. The evidence received from every part of the country, from rural districts as well as from towns, attest that the dwellings of large numbers of the labouring population are overcrowded, and from many districts that the overcrowding has increased.

For example, the report of *Dr. Laurie* from Greenock states, that such is the crowding of the population in the town that:

'Toward the east or old part of the town the amount of population crowded into a small space can hardly be credited, the rapid increase of the population has so far overstepped the means of accommodation that not the meanest outhouse remains without its tenants.'

Dr. Walker, one of the senior surgeons to the Greenock Infirmary, also states that:

'The rooms are in most instances small, and frequently far too much crowded. It is not unusual to see ten or twelve human beings occupying a room not as many feet square. The lower classes in these districts are grossly filthy in their persons and dwellings; and even many of our operatives who receive good wages are extremely inattentive to cleanliness, both in person and dwelling.'

In a paper on the causes of destitution in Scotland, by *Professor Alison*, read before the Statistical Society of London, it is stated that:

'From a report on the late census, made to the Lord Provost of Glasgow by Mr. Strang, Chamberlain, (19th July, 1841,) it appears that in the most densely peopled part of the town, (Blackfriars' parish,) the population since 1831 has increased 40 per cent., while the number of inhabited houses has not increased at all; and again, in the Gorbals, "there is an increase in the population of 20 per cent. since 1831," though no new buildings have been erected, and where the great majority of the houses are of the smallest class."—(Watt's Report, p. 11.)[1]

Dr. Scott Alison in his report on Tranent, states:

'In many houses in and around Tranent, fowls roost on the rafters and on the tops of the bedsteads. The effluvia in these houses are offensive, and must prove very unwholesome. It is scarcely necessary to say that these houses are very filthy. They swarm likewise with fleas. Dogs live in the interior of the lowest houses, and must, of course, be opposed to cleanliness. I have seen horses in two houses in Tranent inhabiting the same apartment with numerous families. One was in Dow's Bounds. Several of the family were ill of typhus fever, and I remember the horse stood at the back of the bed. In this case the stench was dreadful. In addition to the horse there were fowls, and I think the family was not under ten souls. The father died of typhus on this occasion. The families of most of the labouring people are crowded, in consequence of the smallness of the apartment. Where there are many children, it is common for

---

1. W. P. Alison, 'Further illustrations of the practical operation of the Scotch system of management of the poor', *J.R.S.S.*, IV (1841), 309.

10 or 12 people to inhabit one apartment, and for four children to lie in one bed, both in health and sickness. When a collier has few or no children, he sometimes takes single men and women as lodgers.'[1]

Dr. Keith says the:
'Crowding is fearful. I have seen six or eight sleeping in one apartment, with every crevice stopped, and have more than once been nearly suffocated by entering the apartment even after several of them were up and out.'

As the information sought from the medical officers and witnesses in the course of this inquiry was chiefly as to the sanitary condition of the population, they might naturally be expected only to notice the overcrowding as one of the causes of ill health; and they do frequently notice the fact of that sense; but the overcrowding is also frequently noticed as a cause of extreme demoralization and recklessness, and recklessness, again, as a cause of disease. The following may be given as examples of the statements in respect to overcrowding in the rural districts in England.

Mr. T. P. J. Grantham, medical officer of the Sleaford union, in reference to the typhus fever in the family of an agricultural labourer, gives the following instance of the overcrowding which is frequent in the rural districts:

'The domestic economy in this house was deplorable; eight persons slept in one small ill-ventilated apartment, with scarcely any bed-clothing; the smell arising from want of cleanliness, and the dirty clothes of the children being allowed to accumulate, was most intolerable. Considering the situation of the house, its filthy state, and the vitiated air which must have been respired over and over again, by eight individuals sleeping in one confined apartment, it is not surprising that this family should have been afflicted with fever, and that of a very malignant type; the mother and one child fell victims to it in a very short time.'[2]

The want of separate apartments, and overcrowding of private dwellings

The following extract from a communication from the clerk to the Ampthill union, pourtrays the effects of this overcrowding on the morals of the population.

'A large proportion of the cottages in the Union are very miserable places, small and inconvenient, in which it is impossible to keep up even the common decencies of life. I will refer to one instance with which I am well acquainted: —A man, his wife, and family, consisting in all of 11 individuals, resided in a cottage containing only two rooms. The man, his wife, and four children, sometimes five, slept in one of the rooms, and in one bed, some at the foot, others at the top, one a girl above 14, another a boy above 12, the rest younger. The other part of the family slept in one bed in the keeping-room, that is, the room in which their cooking, washing, and eating were performed. How could it be otherwise with this family than that they should be sunk into a most deplorable state of degradation and depravity? This, it may be said, is an extreme case, but there are many similar, and a very great number that make near approaches to it. To pursue a further account of this family: the man is reported to be a good labourer, the cottage he held was recently pulled down,

---

1. *Local Reps. Scot.*, pp. 89-90.   2. *Local Reps. E. & W.*, p. 157.

The Want of Separate Apartments

and being unable to procure another, he was forced to come into the workhouse. After being in a short time, they left to try again to get a home, but again failed. The man then absconded, and the family returned to the workhouse. The eldest, a female, has had a bastard child, and another, younger, also a female but grown up, has recently been sentenced to transportation for stealing in a dwelling house. The family, when they came in, were observed to be of grossly filthy habits and of disgusting behaviour; I am glad to say, however, that their general conduct and appearance is very much improved since they have become inmates of the workhouse. I without scruple express my opinion that their degraded moral state is mainly attributable to the wretched way in which they have lived and herded together as previously described. I have been thus particular in my account of this family, knowing it to be a type of many others, and intending it to apply to that part of your letter inquiring respecting the comparative character of the female inmates and children of the two descriptions of cottages in question.'[1]

The *relieving officer* of the Leighton Buzzard union states that, in Leighton:
'There are a number of cottages without sleeping-rooms separate from the day-rooms, and frequently three or four families are found occupying the same bed-room, and young men and women promiscuously sleeping in the same apartment.'

Mr. Blick, the medical officer of the Bicester union, states that:
'The residences of the poor in that part of the district are most wretched, the majority consisting of only one room below and one above, in which a family of eight or ten (upon an average, I should say five), live and sleep. In one of these rooms I have witnessed a father, mother, three grown-up sons, a daughter, and a child, lying at the same time with typhus fever: but few of the adjacent residents escaped the infection.'

Mr. L. O. Fox, the medical officer of the Romsey union, states:
'There is not only a great want of cottages, but also of room in those which now stand. In the parish of Mottisfont I have known 14 individuals of one family together in a small room, the mother being in labour at the time, and in the adjoining room seven other persons sleeping, making 21 persons, in a space which should be occupied by six persons only at most. Here are the young woman and young man of 18 or 20 years of age lying alongside of the father and mother, and the latter actually in labour. It will be asked what is the condition of the inmates?—Just such as might be expected.'

Dr. Gilly, the canon of Durham, whose appeal on behalf of the border peasantry, and description of the sheds into which they are placed have been cited, observes, upon the crowding of these small places, 24 feet by 16, with 8, 10, or even 12 persons:
'How they lie down to rest, how they sleep, how they can preserve common decency, how unutterable horrors are avoided, is beyond all conception. The case is aggravated when there is a young woman to be lodged in this confined space who is not a member of the family, but is hired to do the field-work, for which every hind is bound to provide a female. It shocks every feeling of propriety to think that in a room, and within such a space as I have been describing, civilized beings should be herding together without a decent separation of age and sex. So long as the agricultural system in this district requires the hind to find room for a fellow-servant of the other sex in his

---

1. *Ibid.*, p. 127.

cabin, the least that morality and decency can demand is that he should have a second apartment where the unmarried female and those of a tender age should sleep apart from him and his wife. Last Whitsuntide, when the annual lettings were taking place, a hind, who had lived one year in the hovel he was about to quit, called to say farewell, and to thank me for some trifling kindness I had been able to show him. He was a fine tall man of about 45, a fair specimen of the frank, sensible, well-spoken, well-informed Northumbrian peasantry—of that peasantry of which a militia regiment was composed, which so amazed the Londoners (when it was garrisoned in the capital many years ago) by the size, the noble deportment, the soldier-like bearing, and the good conduct of the men. I thought this a good opportunity of asking some questions. Where was he going? and how would he dispose of his large family (eleven in number)? He told me they were to inhabit one of these hind's cottages, whose narrow dimensions were less than 24 feet by 15, and that the eleven would have only three beds to sleep on; that he himself, his wife, a daughter of 6, and a boy of 4 years old, would sleep in one bed; that a daughter of 18, a son of 12, a son of 10, and a daughter of 8 would have a second bed; and a third would receive his three sons of the age of 20, 16, and 14. "Pray," said I, "do you not think that this is a very improper way of disposing of your family?" "Yes, certainly," was the answer; "it is very improper in a Christian point of view; but what can we do until they build us better houses." '[1]

Mr. Riddall Wood was examined as to the effects of overcrowded tenements on the moral habits observed in the course of his visits from house to house in the various towns he was engaged to examine:

'In what towns did you find instances of the greatest crowding of the habitations?—In Manchester, Liverpool, Ashton-under-Lyne, and Pendleton. In a cellar in Pendleton, I recollect there were three beds in the two apartments of which the habitation consisted, but having no door between them, in one of which a man and his wife slept; in another, a man, his wife and child; and in a third two unmarried females. In Hull I have met with cases somewhat similar. A mother about 50 years of age, and her son I should think 25, at all events above 21, sleeping in the same bed, and a lodger in the same room. I have two or three instances in Hull in which a mother was sleeping with her grown up son, and in most cases there were other persons sleeping in the same room, in another bed. In a cellar in Liverpool, I found a mother and her grown-up daughters sleeping on a bed of chaff on the ground in one corner of the cellar, and in the other corner three sailors had their bed. I have met with upwards of 40 persons sleeping in the same room, married and single, including, of course, children and several young adult persons of either sex. In Manchester I could enumerate a variety of instances in which I found such promiscuous mixture of the sexes in sleeping-rooms. I may mention one; a man, his wife and child sleeping in one bed; in another bed, two grown up females; and in the same room two young men, unmarried. I have met with instances of a man, his wife, and his wife's sister, sleeping in the same bed together. I have known at least half-a-dozen cases in Manchester in which that has been regularly practised, the unmarried sister being an adult.

'In the course of your own inquiry, how many instances, if you were to look over your Notes, of persons of different sexes sleeping promiscuously, do you think you met with?—I think I am speaking within bounds when I say I have amongst my memoranda above 100 cases, including, of course, cases of persons of different sexes sleeping in the same room.

---

1. William Stephen Gilly, *The Peasantry of the Border: an Appeal on their behalf* (1842), pp. 23-6.

'Was it so common as to be in nowise deemed extraordinary or culpable amongst that class of persons?—It seemed not to be thought of. As a proof of this I may mention one circumstance which just occurs to me:—Early in my visitation of Pendleton, I called at the dwelling of a person whose sons worked with himself in a colliery. It was in the afternoon, when a young man, one of the sons, came down stairs in his shirt and stood before the fire where a very decently-dressed young female was sitting. The son asked his mother for a clean shirt, and on its being given to him, very deliberately threw off the shirt he had on, and after warming the clean one, put it on. In another dwelling in Pendleton, a young girl 18 years of age, sat by the fire in her chemise during the whole time of my visit. Both these were houses of working people (colliers), and not by any means of ill-fame.

'During your inquiries were you able to observe any further demoralization attendant upon these circumstances?—I have frequently met with instances in which the parties themselves have traced their own depravity to these circumstances. As, for example, while I was following out my inquiries in Hull, I found in one room a prostitute, with whom I remonstrated on her course of life, and asked her whether she would not be in a better condition if she were an honest servant instead of living in vice and wretchedness. She admitted she should, and on asking the cause of her being brought to her present condition, she stated that she had lodged with a married sister, and slept in the same bed with her and her husband; that hence improper intercourse took place, and from that she gradually became more and more depraved; and at length was thrown upon the town, because, having lost her character, the town was her only resource. Another female of this description admitted that her first false step was in consequence of her sleeping in the same room with a married couple. In the instance I have mentioned of the two single women sleeping in the same room with the married people, I have good authority for believing that they were common to the men. In the case which I have mentioned of the two daughters and the woman where I found the sailors, I learned, from the mother's admission, that they were common to the lodgers. In all of these cases the sense of decency was obliterated.'

Mr. Baker, in his report on the condition of the labouring classes in Leeds corroborates this statement:

'In the houses of the working classes, brothers and sisters, and lodgers of both sexes, are found occupying the same sleeping-room with the parents, and consequences occur which humanity shudders to contemplate. It is but three or four years ago since a father and daughter stood at the bar of the Leeds Sessions as criminals, the one in concealing, and the other in being an accessary to concealing, the birth of an illegitimate child, born on the body of the daughter by the father; and now, in November, 1841, one of the Registrars of Leeds has recorded the birth of an illegitimate child born on the body of a young girl, only 16 years of age, who lived with her mother, who cohabited with her lodger, the father of this child, of which the girl had been pregnant five months, when the mother died.'[1]

The overcrowding of the tenements of the labouring classes is productive of demoralization in a mode pointed out by *Mr. Barnett*, the clerk to the Nottingham Union, who states:

'That the houses are generally too small to afford a comfortable reception to the family, and the consequence is that the junior members are generally in the streets. Girls and youths destitute of adequate house-room, and freed from parental control, are accustomed to gross immoralities.'[2]

---

1. *Local Reps. E. & W.*, pp. 358-9.   2. *Ibid.*, p. 155.

III. Internal Economy and Domestic Habits

Hereafter, when considering the pecuniary means of defraying the expense of sanitary measures, it will be shown how much less of such consequences in most districts than may be supposed is ascribable to absolute poverty or real inability to pay for better accommodation. To obviate even immediate impressions of this description, I might adduce much evidence of the character of the following testimony of *Mr. J. Thomson,* of Clitheroe:

'What is the number of persons whom you have in your employment?—Men, women, and children, between 900 and 1000.

'Are you the owner of any of the tenements where they reside?—Very few; not more than 12 or 15.

'What description of tenements are they?—Houses with two rooms above, two rooms below, and a yard; and letting at a rent of from 7*l*. to 8*l*. per annum. These are occupied by foremen in various departments, and the better description of artisans.

'What wages do this description of persons earn?—Various, from 30*s*. to 3*l*. weekly; averaging, perhaps, 2*l*. weekly; out of which they pay 3*s*. per week for rent.

'What is your experience in respect to the habits of the workpeople in these tenements?—The remark which I have to make is on the very low state of feeling prevalent amongst even a high class of workmen as to decency or propriety. The tenements sufficed for them when they were young, but when the female children become young women, and the boys advance to puberty, and decency requires them to have separate rooms, the usual practice of the parents is to take the young women into their own sleeping-rooms. I have one highly respectable foreman who has one daughter aged 20, and another aged 22, sleeping on each side of the bed in which himself and his wife sleep. The next bed-room is filled with the younger children of both sexes, boys and girls, up to 16 years of age. The earnings of this family must have been 50*s*. per week. The rent they paid was 3*s*. weekly, which was little more than the interest on the money invested. I have remonstrated on the indecency of such habits, and on their bad effects, but the expense of the extra shilling a-week for a house with another bed-room was considered a sufficient answer to my remonstrance. In my own tenements I have built the additional room, and notwithstanding the remonstrances, I have required the additional rent. When they have remonstrated, I have told them of the fact, that the cost of the additional room would only be a beneficial deduction from the money spent in liquor.'

It would require much time and various opportunities of observation to attempt to make an exact analysis of the combined causes, and an estimate of the effect of each separate cause which operate to produce the masses of moral and physical wretchedness met with in the investigation of the condition of the lowest population. But it became evident, in the progress of the inquiry, that several separate circumstances had each its separate moral as well as physical influence. Thus tenements of inferior construction had manifestly an injurious operation on the moral as well as on the sanitary condition, independently of any overcrowding. For example, it appears to be matter of common observation, in the instance of migrant families of workpeople who are obliged to occupy inferior tenements, that their habits soon become 'of a piece' with the dwelling. A gentleman who has observed closely the condition of the workpeople in the south of Cheshire and the north of Lancashire, men of similar race and education, working at the same description of work, namely, as cotton-spinners, mill hands, and earning nearly the same amount of wages, states that the workmen of the north of Lancashire are obviously inferior to those in the south of Cheshire, in health and habits of personal cleanliness and general condition.[1] The difference is traced mainly to the circumstance, that the labourers in the north of Lancashire inhabit stone houses of a description that absorb moisture, the dampness of which affects the health, and causes personal uncleanliness, induced by the difficulty of keeping a clean house. The operation of the same deteriorating influences were also observable in Scotland, and it may be illustrated by several instances which I have met with in the course of my own personal inquiries.

One of the circumstances most favourable to the improvement of the condition of an artisan or an agricultural labourer, is his obtaining as a wife a female who has had a good industrial training in the well regulated household of persons of a higher condition. The following instance of the effect of the dwelling itself on the condition of a female servant when married, was brought to my notice by a member of the family in which they had been brought up. One was of a young woman who had been taught the habits of neatness, order, and cleanliness most thoroughly as regards household work.

'Her attention to personal neatness,' says a lady who is my informant, 'was very great; her face seemed always as if it were just washed, and with her bright hair neatly combed underneath her snow-white cap, a smooth white apron, and her gown and handkerchief carefully put on, she used to look very comely. After a year or two, she married the serving man, who, as he was retained in his situation, was obliged to take a house as near his place as possible. The cottages in the neighbourhood were of the most wretched kind, mere hovels built of rough stones and covered with ragged thatch; there were few even of these, so there was no choice, and they were obliged to be content with the first that was vacant, which was in the most retired situation. After they had been married about two years, I happened to be walking past one of these miserable cottages, and as the door was open, I had the curiosity to enter. I found it was the home of the servant I have been describing. But what a change had come over her! Her face was dirty, and her tangled hair hung over her eyes. Her cap, though of good materials, was ill washed and slovenly put on. Her whole dress, though apparently good and serviceable, was very untidy, and looked dirty and slatternly; everything indeed about her seemed wretched and neglected, (except her little child,) and she appeared very discontented. She seemed aware of the change there must be in her appearance since I had last seen her, for she immediately began to complain of her house. The wet came in at the door of the *only room*, and when it rained, through every part of the roof also, except just over the hearth-stone; large drops fell upon her as she lay in bed, or as she was working at the window: in short, she had found it impossible to keep things in order, so had gradually ceased to make any exertions. Her condition had been borne down by the condition of the house. Then her husband was dissatisfied with his home and with her; his visits became less frequent, and if he had been a day labourer, and there had

---

1. Since these remarks relate to the cotton manufacturing district, it is probable that they should relate to the *South* of Lancashire and the *North* of Cheshire. See p. 329 below, where the same source is even further confused by Chadwick.

been a beer-shop or a public-house, the preference of that to his home would have been inevitable, and in the one instance would have presented an example of a multitude of cases.

'She was afterwards, however, removed to a new cottage, which was water-tight, and had some conveniences, and was built close to the road, which her former mistress and all her friends must constantly pass along. She soon resumed, in a great degree, her former good habits, but still there was a little of the *dawdle* left about her; the remains of the dispiritedness caused by her former very unfavourable circumstances.'

I visited some other dwellings not far from the one above described, and met with another instance of a female who had been brought up as a servant in a well-ordered house, and who, for her station, had received a very excellent religious and moral education. Before her marriage she had been distinguished by the refinement with which she sung national airs, and for her knowledge of the Bible and of the doctrines of her church. Her personal condition had become of 'a piece' with the wretched stone undrained hovel, with a pigsty before it, in which she had been taken. We found her with rings of dirt about her neck, and turning over with dirty hands Brown's Dictionary, to see whether the newly-elected minister was 'sound' in his doctrine. In this case no moral lapse was apparent, but the children were apparently brought up under great disadvantages.

There, however, as in most cases, the internal economy of the houses were primarily affected by the defective internal and surrounding drainage that produced the damp and wet, and thence the dirt against which the inmates had ceased to contend. On inquiry of the male labourers in the district, it appeared that almost every third man was subjected to rheumatism; and with them, it was evident that the prevalence of damp and marsh miasma from the want of drainage, if it did not necessitate, formed a strong temptation to, the use of ardent spirits. With them as with the females, the wretched condition of the tenement formed a strong barrier against personal cleanliness and the use of decent clothes.

In the rural districts the very defects of the cottages which let in the fresh air, in spite of all the efforts of the inmates to exclude it, often obviate the effects of the overcrowding and defective ventilation. It has been observed, that while the labouring population of several districts have had no shelter but huts, similar to those described by Dr. Gilly, as the habitations of the border peasantry, which afforded a free passage for currents of air, they were not subject to fevers, though they were to rheumatism; but when, through the good intentions of the proprietors, such habitations were provided as were deemed more comfortable from excluding the weather effectually, but which, from the neglect of ventilation afforded recesses for stagnating air, and impurities which they had not the means or had not a sufficient love of cleanliness to remove; though rheumatism was excluded, febrile infection was generated. In the towns the access of the wind is impeded by the closeness of the surrounding habitations, and the internal construction of the dwellings tends to exclude the air still more effectually. Were the closed windows opened, it would frequently be only to admit a worse compound, the air from neglected privies, and the miasma from the wet and undrained court or street.

The close pent up air in these abodes has, undoubtedly, a depressing effect on the nervous energies, and this again, with the uneducated, and indeed with many of the educated workpeople, has an effect on the moral habits by acting as a strong and often irresistible provocative to the use of fermented liquors and ardent spirits. Much may be due to the incitement of association of greater numbers of people, but it is a common fact that the same workpeople indulge more in drink when living in the close courts and lanes of the town than when living in the country, and that the residence in the different places is attended with a difference of effects similar to those described in respect to the tailors working in crowded rooms in towns and the tailors working separately or in the country. The workpeople who have fallen into habits of drinking, strenuously allege the impossibility of avoiding the practice in such places; they do, however, drink in greater quantities in such places, and give increased effect to the noxious miasma by which they are surrounded.

Some inquiries from *Mr. Liddle*, the medical officer of the Whitechapel union, as to the condition of the workpeople he visited in such places as he has described, brought to notice another indirect effect of the external as well as the internal condition of the dwelling on their domestic economy and general condition.

It appeared that the persons whom he visited for the purpose of administering medical relief, were men earning, when in work, from 16*s.* to 20*s.* per week, the women earning proportionably. Yet whenever they were subjected to the frequent attacks of sickness which prevailed amongst them, they were in the most wretched destitution: the house was bare of everything; they had no provisions and no credit, and their need for relief was most imminent. In answer to the inquiry how this was to be accounted for, inasmuch as with agricultural labourers who earned little more than half that sum, and paid nearly as much for their food, in visiting their cottages with their ministers, I had commonly observed some store of provisions; Mr. Liddle stated that in such places as those in his district, in such atmospheres, a store of provisions would not keep: everything decayed rapidly, and the workpeople consequently lived 'from hand to mouth.' On inquiring as to this fact from a respectable butcher, accustomed to sell meat to persons living in such situations, he stated that:

'Meat sold on a Saturday night, in hot weather, to poor people, who have only one close room, in which they sleep, and live, and cook, will certainly turn before the Sunday morning; when, if it were kept in the butcher's shop, or in a well-ventilated place, it would be in as good a condition on the Monday morning. There is a great deal of loss of meat in consequence of the want of ventilation and bad condition of the dwellings of the poorer classes. The butter kept in such places sooner becomes rancid, and the bread dry and disagreeable.'

Here, then, we have from the one agent, a close and polluted atmosphere, two different sets of effects; the one set here noticed engendering improvidence, expense, and waste,—the other, the depressing effects of external and internal miasma on the nervous system, tending to incite the habitual use of ardent spirits; both tending to precipitate this population into disease and misery.

The familiarity with the sickness and death constantly present in the crowded and unwholesome districts, appears to re-act as another concurrent cause in aggravation of the wretchedness and vice in which they are plunged. Seeing the apparent uncertainty of the morrow, the inhabitants really take no heed of it, and abandon themselves with the recklessness and avidity of common soldiers in a war to whatever gross enjoyment comes within their reach. All the districts I visited, where the rate of sickness and mortality was high, presented, as might be expected, a proportionate amount of severe cases of destitute orphanage and widowhood; and the same places were marked by excessive recklessness of the labouring population. In Dumfries, for example, it is estimated, that the cholera, swept away one-eleventh part of the population. Until recently, the town had not recovered the severe effects of the visitation, and the condition of the orphans was most deplorable.[1] Amongst young artisans who were earning from 16s. to 18s. a-week, I was informed that there were very few who made any reserves against the casualties of sickness. I was led to ask the provost what number of bakers' shops there were? 'Twelve,' was his answer. And what number of whiskey-shops may the town possess? 'Seventy-nine' was the reply. If we might rely on the inquiries made of working-men when Dr. Arnott and I went through the wynds of Edinburgh, their consumption of spirits bore almost the like proportion to the consumption of wholesome food. We observed to Captain Stuart, the superintendent of the police at Edinburgh, in our inspection of the wynds, that life appeared to be of little value, and was likely to be held cheap in such spots. He stated, in answer, that a short time ago a man had been executed for the murder of his wife in a fit of passion in the very room we had accidentally entered, and where we were led to make the observation. At a short distance from that spot, and amidst others of this class of habitation, were those which had been the scenes of the murders by Burke and Hare. Yet amidst these were the residences of working men engaged in regular industry. The indiscriminate mixture of workpeople and their children in the immediate vicinity, and often in the same rooms with persons whose character was denoted by the question and answer more than once exchanged, 'When were you last washed?' 'When I was last in prison,' was only one mark of the entire degradation to which they had been brought. The working-classes living in these districts were equally marked by the abandonment of every civil or social regulation. Asking some children in one of the rooms of the wynds in which they swarmed in Glasgow what were their names, they hesitated to answer, when one of the inmates said, they called them ———, mentioning some nicknames. 'The fact is,' observed Captain Miller, the superintendent of the police, 'they really have no names. Within this range of buildings I have

---

1. An innaccurate statement. The figure of one-eleventh relates to cases, not fatalities. Out of a population of about 10,000, there were 840 cases of cholera, of which half proved fatal. (*Local Reps. Scot.*, pp. 208-9.)

no doubt I should be able to find a thousand children who have no names whatever, or only nicknames, like dogs.' There were found amidst the occupants, labourers earning wages undoubtedly sufficient to have paid for comfortable tenements, men and women who were intelligent and so far as could be ascertained, had received the ordinary education which should have given better tastes and led to better habits. My own observations have been confirmed by the statement of Mr. Sheriff Alison, of Glasgow, that in the great manufacturing towns of Scotland, 'in the contest with whiskey, in their crowded population, education has been entirely overthrown.'[1] The ministers, it will be seen, make similar reports from the rural districts. On the observation of other districts, and the comparison of the habits of the same workmen in town and country, it will be seen that I consider that the use of the whiskey and the prostration of the education and moral habits for which the Scottish labourers have been distinguished is, to a considerable extent, attributable to the surrounding physical circumstances, including the effects of the bad ventilation. The labourers presented to our notice in the condition described, in the crowded districts, were almost all Scotch. It is common to ascribe the extreme of misery and vice wholly to the Irish portion of the population of the towns in Scotland. A short inspection on the spot would correct this error. Mr. Baird, in his report on the sanitary condition of the poor of Glasgow, observes that 'the bad name of the poor Irish had been too long attached to them'.[2] Dr. Cowan, of Glasgow, stated that 'From ample opportunities of observation, they appeared to him to exhibit much less of that squalid misery and addiction to the use of ardent spirits than the Scotch of the same grade.'[3] Instances were indeed stated to us, where the Irish were preferred for employment from their superior steadiness and docility; and Mr. Stuart, the Factory Inspector for Scotland, states, that 'instances are now occurring of a preference being given to them as workers in the flax factories on account of their regular habits, and that very significant hints have been given by extensive factory owners, that Irish workmen will be selected unless the natives of the place, and other persons employed by them, relinquish the prevailing habits of intemperance.' Dr. Scott Alison, in his report on Tranent, has described the population in receipt of high wages, but living under similar influences, as prone to passionate excitement, and as apt instruments for political discontents; their moral perceptions appeared to have been obliterated, and they might be said to be characterised by a 'ferocious indocility which makes them prompt to wrong and violence, destroys their social nature, and transforms them into something little better than wild beasts.'[4]

It is to be regretted that the coincidence of pestilence and moral disorder is not confined to one part of the island, nor to any one race of the population. The over-crowding and the removal of what may be

---

1. Archibald Alison, *The Principles of Population* (Edinburgh 1840), II, 96.
2. *Local Reps. Scot.*, p. 185.
3. Robert Cowan, *J.R.S.S.*, III (1840), 275.
4. This view is expressed by Alison, though not in these precise words, in *Local Reps. Scot.*, p. 96.

termed the architectural barriers or protections of decency and propriety, and the causes of physical deterioration in connexion with the moral deterioration, are also fearfully manifest in the districts in England, which, at the time to which the evidence refers, were in a state of prosperity.

Mr. Baker, in his report on the condition of the population, after giving an instance of the contrast presented by the working-people living in better dwellings, situated in better cleansed neighbourhoods (to which I shall advert when submitting the evidence in respect to preventive measures), describes the population living in houses:

'With broken panes in every window-frame, and filth and vermin in every nook. With the walls unwhitewashed for years, black with the smoke of foul chimneys, without water, with corded bed-stocks for beds, and sacking for bed-clothing, with floors unwashed from year to year, without out-offices, * * * * while without, there are streets, elevated a foot, sometimes two, above the level of the causeway, by the accumulation of years, and stagnant puddles here and there, with their fœtid exhalations, causeways broken and dangerous, ash-places choked up with filth, and excrementitious deposits on all sides as a consequence, undrained, unpaved, unventilated, uncared-for by any authority but the landlord, who weekly collects his miserable rents from his miserable tenants.

'Can we wonder that such places are the hot-beds of disease, or that it obtains, upon constitutions thus liberally predisposed to receive it, and forms the mortality which Leeds exhibits. Adult life, exposed to such miasmata, gives way. How much more then infant life, when ushered into, and attempted to be reared in, such obnoxious atmospheres. On the moral habits similar effects are produced. An inattention on the part of the local authorities to the state of the streets diminishes year by year the respectability of their occupiers. None dwell in such localities but to whom propinquity to employment is absolutely essential. Those who might advocate a better state of things, depart; and of those who remain, the one-half, by repeated exhibitions of indecency and vulgarity, and indeed by the mere fact of neighbourship, sink into the moral degradation which is natural to the other, and vicious habits and criminal propensities precede the death which these combinations prepare.'[1]

No education as yet commonly given appears to have availed against such demoralizing circumstances as those described; but the cases of moral improvement of a population, by cleansing, draining, and the improvement of the internal and external conditions of the dwellings, of which instances will be presented, are more numerous and decided, though there still occur instances of persons in whom the love of ardent spirits has gained such entire possession as to have withstood all such means of retrieving them. The most experienced public officers acquainted with the condition of the inferior population of the towns would agree in giving the first place in efficiency and importance to the removal of what may be termed the physical barriers to improvement, and that as against such barriers moral agencies have but a remote chance of success.

A gentleman who has had considerable experience in the management of large numbers of the manufacturing population stated to me that in every case of personal and moral improvement the successful step was

---

1. *Local Reps. E. & W.*, pp. 361-2.

The Want of Separate Apartments

made by the removal of the party from the ill-conditioned neighbourhood in which he had been brought up. When a young workman married, he interfered to get him a better residence apart from the rest; and when this was done important alterations followed; but if he took up his abode in the old neighbourhood, the condition of the wife was soon brought down to the common level, and the marriage became a source of wretchedness.

Benevolent persons, viewing the bare aspect of some of the most afflicted neighbourhoods, have raised subscriptions for the purchase of furniture, bedding, and blankets, for the relief of the inmates, but by this pecuniary aid they have only added fuel to the flame; that is, they have enabled the inmates to purchase more ardent spirits. The force of the habit, which is aggravated by misdirected charity, is indicated in the following instances, of which one was mentioned to me by the *Rev. Whitwell Elwin*:

'I was lately informed by a master tailor of Bath that one of his men, who had earned 3*l*. a-week at piece-work for years, had never within his knowledge possessed table, chairs, or bedding. I found the statement on examination to be strictly true. Some straw on which he slept, a square block of wood, a low three-legged stool, and an old tea-caddy, are the complete inventory of the articles of a room, the occupier of which, with only himself and his wife to maintain, was wealthier than many in the station of gentlemen. He had frequently excited lively compassion in benevolent individuals, who, supposing that he was struggling for very existence, furnished him with a variety of household goods, which were regularly pawned before a week was out, and afforded to the superficial observer fresh evidence of the extremity of his distress. The cause of all this is quickly told: the wife was to be seen going to and fro several times a-day with a cream-jug of gin, and to gratify this appetite, they had voluntarily reduced themselves to the condition of savages. I could add numerous instances of a similar kind. Indeed, were a stranger to go through the town, and judge only from the appearance of things, I am convinced that he would select his examples of greatest privation not from the really poor, but from men who were in the receipt of more than 30*s*. a-week. Charity, which when prompted by pure motives, always blesses him that gives, does not always bless him that takes. I am afraid that the indiscriminate adoption of dirt and rags as a test of poverty, especially in a town like Bath, where private charity prevails on an extensive scale, operates as a premium upon ill habits, and as a discouragement to cleanliness, and leads many to affect a vice which was not habitual to them.'

As an instance of that state of voluntary wretchedness which renders all such charity or assistance worse than useless, I may give an incident mentioned to me by *Sir Charles Shaw*, the chief commissioner of the new police force in Manchester:

'A week since,' says Sir Charles, 'I sent an inspector of police to examine a lodging-house. He came back to state that he had never witnessed such a sight. He found in one room, totally destitute of furniture, three men and two women lying on the bare floor, without straw, and with bricks only for their pillows. I observed, that I supposed they were drunk. "Yes," said the inspector; "they were, and I found the lodging-house keeper himself in a tolerable bed, and in another room I found bundles of fine fresh straw. I blamed the man for not giving that straw to his lodgers. He answered, 'I keep that straw for the people who prefer purchasing it to gin: those above stairs preferred the gin.'" It is, I find, a common thing here for lodging-house keepers to have straw for sale.'[1]

In the course of an examination which I took, under the Poor Law Commission of Inquiry, from the late *Mr. Walker*, the stipendiary magistrate of the Thames Police Office, he observed, in respect to cases of apparent destitution:

'Casualties occurring among the indigent or profligate are at all times liable to be represented as cases resulting from the neglect of the proper authorities. Some time ago, in going round the parish of Whitechapel with the churchwardens, during service-time, we entered an old building in Rosemary-lane, for which there was then no owner, the stairs were so dark and ruinous that though it was mid-day we were obliged to have a candle, to enable us to go up to them: the first-floor was the receptacle of every description of filth. We entered one room, in which we found two half-naked dirty children; their mother lay in one corner on some dirty straw, covered only with a sack. There was no furniture nor other articles in the place, except a fagot of wood and a few broken plates, a basket of skate, and some sprats strewed on the floor. This woman was a fish-hawker, a business by which, in all probability, she gained enough to have made her extremely comfortable, but she preferred an alternation of great privation and profligate enjoyment. Had she accidentally died in this state, here would have been a scene of misery, and a case of excitement for the philanthropists! In our district there are other premises under similar circumstances, all of which are tenanted by persons of the very lowest grade; and it is surprising, considering the state in which they live, that unaccountable deaths, having the semblance of starvation, do not take place amongst them. From what I have observed of these places, I am fully convinced that if shambles were built on any spot, and all who choose were allowed to occupy them, they would soon be occupied by a race lower than any yet known. I have often said that if empty casks were placed along the streets of Whitechapel, in a few days each of them would have a tenant, and these tenants would keep up their kind, and prey upon the rest of the community. I am sure that if such facilities were offered, there is no conceivable degradation to which portions of the species might not be reduced. Allow these tubmen no education, and you would have so many savages living in the midst of civilisation. Wherever there are empty houses which are not secured, they are soon tenanted by wretched objects, and these tenants continue so long as there is a harbour for them. Parish officers and others come to me to aid them in clearing such places. I tell the police and the parish that there is no use in their watching these places, that they must board them up if they would get rid of the occupants. If they will give the accommodation they will get the occupants. If you will have marshes and stagnant waters you will there have suitable animals, and the only way of getting rid of them is by draining the marshes.'[2]

---

1. In 1839 the new municipal corporation of Manchester secured the appointment of a Chief Commissioner of Police by 2 & 3 Vic., c. 87. Sir Charles Shaw was the first to hold this post. He appears to have made the statement quoted here in writing to Chadwick. He did, however, subsequently express strong views in print on the condition of the working class in Manchester in a pamphlet, *Manufacturing Districts: Replies of Sir Charles Shaw regarding the Education, and moral and physical Condition of the labouring Classes* (1843).
2. Appendix to *First Report of Royal Commission on the Poor Laws, P.P.* 1834, XXIX, Part III (Evidence collected by Edwin Chadwick), p. 156A.

The Want of Separate Apartments

The *Reverend Whitwell Elwin* observes upon this subject that:

'Those who think that labourers will work for themselves a reform in their habitations very much underrate the effects of habit. A person accustomed to fresh air, and all the comforts of civilized life, goes into a miserable room, dirty, bare, and, above all, sickening from the smell. Judging from his own sensations, he conceives that nothing but the most abject poverty could have produced this state of things, and he can imagine nothing necessary to a cure but a way for escape. A very simple experiment will correct these erroneous impressions. Let him remain a short time in the room, and the perception of closeness will so entirely vanish that he will almost fancy that the atmosphere has been purified since his entrance. There are few who are not familiar with this fact; and if such are the effects of an hour in blunting our refined sensations, and rendering them insensible to noxious exhalations, what must be the influence of years on the coarser perceptions of the working-man?

'All who know the lower classes will testify that the last want felt by the dirty is cleanliness, that their last expenditure is on the comforts of their home. Two winters ago I found a painter whose bed was without blankets, whose room was without furniture, who was destitute even of the ordinary utensils of civilized life, whose floor was covered with worse filth than that of the streets—I found this man at dinner with a roast loin of pork stuffed with onions, a Yorkshire pudding, a large jug of ale, cheese, and a salad. I will undertake to say that half the gentlemen in Bath did not sit down on the Sunday to so good a dinner.

A number of communications simply assign 'intemperance' as the cause of fever, and of the prevalent mortality. Of most of these communications, which it were unnecessary to recite, it may be observed, that when intemperance is mentioned as the cause of disease, as being the immediate antecedent, on carrying investigation a little further back, discomfort is found to be the immediate antecedent to the intemperance; and where the external causes of positive discomfort do not prevail in the towns, the workpeople are generally found to have few or no rival pleasures to wean them from habits of intemperance, and to have come from districts subject to the discomforts likely to engender them. In one of the returns from Scotland it is observed that with the people, whether for a fever, a cold, or consumption, or a pleurisy, whiskey is the universal antidote. The popular belief that fermented liquor or ardent spirits are proper antidotes to the effects of damp or cold has been universal, and has not wanted even medical sanction. Out-door allowances of beer have been prescribed by some medical officers in marshy and undrained districts as the proper preservatives against ague or rheumatism. The Board will now be in a position to urge the importance of facilitating drainage as a means for the protection of the population by the prevention of disease and the inducement to pernicious habits, as well as a source of profitable industry. It is now beginning to be observed in several dangerous occupations that temperance is the best means of withstanding the effects of the noxious agencies which they have to encounter. Amongst the painters, for example, the men who are temperate and cleanly suffer little from the occupation, but if any one of them become intemperate, the noxious causes take effect with a certainty and rapidity proportioned to the relaxed domestic habits. The Inquiry presents many instances of the beneficial effects of the changes of the popular habit of having recourse to fermented liquors or to spirits as necessary protective stimulants. In several of the mining districts, for example, it is an extensive practice to provide for the accommodation of the miners out of the hot mines a room in which they may drink beer as a preservative against the effects of the change to the cold and damp air to which they are about to expose themselves. *Dr. Barham*, in his Report to the Commissioners appointed to inquire into the Employment of Young Persons in Mines and Manufactories, notices an admirable example within the province of voluntary exertion, and the beneficial effects produced by it at the Dolcoath copper and tin mine, Camborne, Cornwall. There the proprietors, besides establishing other easy and economical preventive arrangements, provide a warm room for the miners to change their dresses and take hot meat-soup, which is cheaper, probably, than beer. 'And the men' (says a witness) 'say they never feel cold when they take it. We conceive that there have been much fewer cases of consumption on the club since this practice has been adopted.'[1]

The effects of the noxious physical agencies on the moral condition of the population will receive more full illustration in connexion with the statistical evidence as to their effects, with the evidence on the practical operation of the means of prevention.

Domestic mismanagement, a predisposing cause of disease

The subsequent examples relate chiefly to the effects of general domestic mismanagement as a concurrent cause of disease.

Dr. Baker, in his report on the sanitary condition of the population of Derby, states that:

'There is also another cause of sickness to be found in their houses, and which, like the former, *i.e.*, the external circumstances, is in constant operation: I mean the want of domestic comforts, a want which the wages they earn would, in many instances, enable them to remove if their means were not, as too often happens, expended viciously or improvidently. It is with regret that I speak unfavourably of the poor, whilst my whole aim, in this communication, has been to awaken a sympathy towards those sufferings of which I have been so often a witness. But several years' experience of the habits of the poor, derived from my situation as an hospital physician, and backed by the additional evidence I have obtained by acting for three years as a guardian of the poor in this large town, has, I am sorry to say, served but to confirm me in the opinion I have just now expressed; and in support of which I shall instance the family of the Slaters mentioned at No. 12, in Short-street.

'The earnings of four members of this family were as follows:—

	s.	d.	
The father . . .	14	0	per week, at gardening, &c.
The eldest son, aged 20 .	12	0	„ at a brewery.
Daughter . ⎰ Twins, ⎱ .	6	0	„ at a factory.
Son . . ⎱ aged 18 ⎰ .	9	0	„ at the same factory.
£2	1	0	per week.

---

1. 'Report by Charles Barham on the employment of children and young persons in the mines of Cornwall and Devonshire', *Report of Children's Employment Commission, Pt. I, P.P.* 1842, XVI, Appendix E, p. 838.

Domestic Mismanagement

'The mother of this family, it appears, is left disengaged from all but her household duties and the care of the younger children; the house, nevertheless, is nearly destitute of furniture, and presents a picture of disorder and want. On the other hand, at No. 15, (Briggs) although the husband has for some years past been a weak and ailing man, the family is well ordered and cleanly; and to this fact I mainly attribute the milder and modified form of fever which affected the children.'[1]

The Committee of Physicians and Surgeons at Birmingham, in their report, indicate the powerful operation of depraved domestic habits as a predisposing cause to disease:

'It cannot,' they say, 'be doubted that whilst the arts and manufactures of the place prove in some instances injurious to health, and in a few possibly destructive to life, these evil consequences, as well as hereditary predisposition to disease, are promoted by intemperance, not that intemperance is an infinitely more frequent cause of disease and death amongst the artisans than all the various employments of all the manufactories combined.

'In the expenditure of their weekly earnings, improvidence and thoughtless extravagance prevail to a lamentable degree. The observations upon which this opinion is formed are made upon the habits of the people themselves, confirmed by extensive and recent inquiries among the shopkeepers with whom they deal. Tea, coffee, sugar, butter, cheese, bacon, (of which a great deal is consumed in this town,) and other articles, the working people purchase in small quantities from the hucksters, who charge an enormous profit upon them, being, as they state, compelled to do so to cover the losses which they frequently sustain by bad debts. Huckster dealing is a most extravagant mode of dealing; there were in this town, in 1834, 717 of these shops, and the number has greatly increased since that time. Meat is purchased in the same improvident manner; the working men generally contrive to have a good joint of meat upon the Sunday; the dinner on the other days of the week is made from steaks or chops, which is the most extravagant mode either of purchasing or cooking meat.

'The improvidence of this class of persons arises in many instances from the indulgence of vicious propensities. Drunkenness, with all its attendant miseries, prevails to a great extent, though it is by no means to be regarded as a characteristic feature of the mechanic of this town in particular. It most generally prevails among that class of workmen who obtain the highest wages, but who are often found in the most deplorable and abject condition. The improvidence of which we are speaking is to be traced in very many instances to extreme ignorance on the part of the wives of these people. The females are from necessity bred up from their youth in the workshops, as the earnings of the younger members contribute to the support of the family. The minds and morals of the girls become debased, and they marry totally ignorant of all those habits of domestic economy which tend to render a husband's home comfortable and happy; and this is very often the cause of the man being driven to the alehouse to seek that comfort after his day of toil which he looks for in vain by his own fireside. The habit of a manufacturing life being once established in a woman, she continues it, and leaves her home and children to the care of a neighbour or of a hired child, sometimes only a few years older

---

Though not published until after the appearance of the *Sanitary Report*, Barham's examination of this witness is dated 23 April 1841, and he no doubt made it available to Chadwick in manuscript.

---

1. *Local Reps. E. & W.*, pp. 180-1.

III. Internal Economy and Domestic Habits

than her own children, whose services cost her probably as much as she obtains for her labour. To this neglect on the part of their parents is to be traced the death of many children; they are left in the house with a fire before they are old enough to know the danger to which they are exposed, and are often dreadfully burnt.'[1]

Mr. *Mott's* report on the sanitary condition of the population of his district presents parallel instances of the different economy prevalent amongst these classes:

Contrast in the Economy of Families

1

Cellar in Wellington-court, Chorlton-upon-Medlock; a man, his wife and seven children; income per week, 1*l*. 11*s*.; rent 1*s*. 6*d*. per week; three beds for seven, in a dark, unventilated back room, bed-covering of the meanest and scantiest kind—the man and wife occupying the front room as a sleeping-room for themselves, in which the whole family take their food and spend their leisure time; here the family, in a filthy destitute state, with an income averaging 3*s*. 5¼*d*. each per week, four being children under 11 years of age.

1

In a dwelling-house in Chorlton Union, containing one sitting-room and two bedrooms; a man, his wife and three children; rent 2*s*. 6*d*. per week; income per week 12*s*. 6*d*., being an average of 2*s*. 6*d*. per week for each person. Here, with a sickly man, the house presented an appearance of comfort in every part, as also the bedding was in good order.

2

Cellar in York-street, Chorlton-upon-Medlock; a man—a hand-loom weaver—his wife and family (one daughter married, with her husband forms part of the family), comprising altogether seven persons; income 2*l*. 7*s*., or 6*s*. 8½*d*. per head; rent 2*s*. Here, with the largest amount of income, the family occupy two filthy, damp, unwholesome cellars, one of which is a back place without pavement or flooring of any kind, occupied by the loom of the family, and used as a sleeping-room for the married couple and single daughter.

2

In a dwelling-house, Stove-street, one sitting-room, one kitchen and two bedrooms, rent 4*s*. per week. A poor widow, with a daughter also a widow, with ten children, making together 13 in family; income 1*l*. 6*s*. per week, averaging 2*s*. per head per week. Here there is every appearance of cleanliness and comfort.

3

John Salt, of Carr Bank (labourer), wages 12*s*. per week; a wife, and one child aged 15: he is a drunken, disorderly fellow, and very much in debt.

3

George Hall, of Carr Bank (labourer), wages 10*s*. per week; has reared ten children; he is in comfortable circumstances.

4

William Haynes, of Oakamoore (wiredrawer), wages 1*l*. per week; he has a wife and five children; he is in debt, and his family is shamefully neglected.

4

John Hammonds, of Woodhead (collier), wages 18*s*. per week; has six children to support; he is a steady man and saving money.

5

George Locket, of Kingsley (boat-man), wages 18*s*. per week, with a wife and seven children; his family are in a miserable condition.

5

George Mosley, of Kingsley (collier), wages 18*s*. per week; he has a wife and seven children; he is saving money.

6

John Banks, of Cheadle (collier), wages 18*s*. per week; wife and three children; his house is in a filthy state, and the furniture not worth 10*s*.

6

William Faulkner, of Tean (tape-weaver), wages 18*s*. per week; supports his wife and seven children without assistance.

---

1. *Local Reps. E. & W.*, pp. 217, 210-11.

7
William Weaver, of Kingsley (boat-man), wages 18s. per week; wife and three children; he is a drunken, disorderly fellow, and his family entirely destitute.

7
Charles Rushton, of Lightwoodfields, wages 14s. per week; he supports his wife and five children in credit.

8
Richard Barlow, of Cheadle (labourer), wages 12s. per week; wife and five children, in miserable circumstance, not a bed to lie on.

8
William Sargeant, of Lightwoodfields (labourer), wages 13s. a-week; he has a wife and six children, whom he supports comfortably.

9
Thomas Bartlem, of Tean (labourer), wages 14s. per week; his wife earns 7s. per week; five children; he is very much in debt; home neglected.

9
William Box, of Tean (tape-weaver), wages 18s. or 20s. per week; supports his wife in bad health, and five children.

10
Thomas Johnson, of Tean (blacksmith), wages 18s. per week; his wife earns 7s. per week; three children; he is very much in debt, and his family grossly neglected.

10
Ralph Faulkner, of Tean (tape-weaver), wages 18s. or 20s. per week; supports a wife and five children, three of them are deaf and dumb.[1]

Mr. Harrison, the medical officer of the Preston union, observes that: 'I have known many families whose income has exceeded 100*l*. a-year, who in times of sickness have been in great distress, and even some who have been obliged to have recourse to the parish for assistance. And I am acquainted with several families now of the best paid class of workpeople, whose total weekly earnings will average 2*l*., and in some cases 3*l*. a-week, who, should sickness overtake the head of the family, and some of the principal workers among the children, would be thrown upon the parish. I have been convinced from extensive observation, that the masters of these people have it in their power to improve the condition and happiness of their workpeople beyond what can be effected by any other agency.'[2]

These descriptions are not confined to the English towns. Mr. Jupp and others cite instances from the rural districts. They are similarly prevalent in Scotland. As an example I would refer to the description given by Dr. Scott Alison, of the condition of the highly-paid collier population of Tranent. Take another instance of the condition of the same class, the colliers at Ayr, given by *Dr. Sym*, in his report on the sanitary condition of the population of that town:

'Although the colliers have large wages, they are, from their want of economy and their dissolute habits, uniformly in poverty; and their families, though well fed, are miserably clothed, ill lodged, uneducated, and less industrious than the families of the weavers; the females of which work with great constancy at hand-sewing. The modes of living of these two classes are very different. The weaver is not intemperate, because he cannot afford to purchase ardent spirits, and the nature of his employment prevents him from having those hours of idleness during the day which the collier is so apt to consume in dissipation. He lives on very innutritious food, seldom eats butchers' meat, and the most indigent, who are generally Irishmen, subsist chiefly on potatoes. The collier, on the other hand, indulges to excess in ardent

---

1. *Local Reps. E. & W.*, pp. 238-9.
2. *Ibid.*, p. 275.

spirits, and both he and his family partake of animal food every day. In short, the colliers live better than any of the other labouring classes in Ayr.'[1]

Dr. Scott Alison, speaking of the colliers of Tranent, states that they obtain very high wages. 'A man, his wife, and perhaps two children may earn perhaps 40s. a-week, if industriously employed during that time.' On the subject of appearances of destitution, on which medical men sometimes report, he observes:

'I have had occasion to know that medical men, judging from internal appearances of the dwellings of the labouring classes, are liable to be led into erroneous inferences as to the extent of destitution. The appearance of the place or of the person is no test of the want of means or of the highness or lowness of wages. Filth is more frequently evidence of depravity than of destitution; indeed, in places where the wages or means are really scanty, there is very frequently considerable cleanliness. If a stranger went into the house of a collier, he might exclaim, "What extreme wretchedness and destitution!" when, in fact, on the Saturday they had received 30s., which before the Tuesday had all been squandered. I think medical men, who are not intimately acquainted with the character of people, are often drawn into mistakes.'[2]

The domestic condition of this population admits of a contrast with the condition of individuals of their own description of employment, or with the condition of other classes of miners who receive no higher wages, but whose condition is highly superior, to show that the depraved habits and condition are not the necessary result of the employment. He contrasts the condition of the colliery population of Tranent with the condition of the agricultural labourers in the immediate vicinity of the town:

'With very few exceptions, the condition of the interior of the houses of the hind population is excellent, most pleasing to the eye, and comfortable. These respectable people, in spite of the defective construction of their cottages, manage to throw an air of comfort, plenty, neatness, and order around their homes. I have often been delighted to observe these characteristics, and not less so to mark the co-existence of pure, moral, and religious principles in the inmates, the presence of practical religion and practical morals. When the floor wears away, it is repaired; when the walls lose their whiteness, they are white-washed; and every few days the whole wooden furniture in the house is subjected to thorough cleansing with sand and warm water. The various articles of furniture, and the different household utensils, are kept in places allotted to them; and the earthenware and china well cleaned, are neatly arranged, and made to serve as ornaments to the apartment. The metal spoons, candlesticks, and pitchers for containing milk and water, are well burnished. The milk taken from the cow may be seen set apart in vessels kept in the nicest order; and beside them lie the churning-barrel and strainer. A fire sheds its cheerful influence over the scene; the kettle never wants hot water; and the honest, frugal housewife is ever discharging some household duty in a spirit of placid contentment, attending to her partner when present, or preparing his meals against his return from the fields.

'The external economy of the houses of the hinds is on the whole very good. The ground in front of the cottages is kept clean and free of impurities. The little garden, which is almost invariably connected with the cottage, is kept in good order, and is in general well cultivated.'[3]

---

1. *Local Reps. Scot.*, p. 224. 2. *Ibid.*, p. 96. 3. *Ibid.*, pp. 86-7.

Contrast in the Economy of Families

The like contrast, derived from an intimate knowledge of the population of another class, is presented in the following portions of a report from *Mr. Wood*, of Dundee:

'There are many families among the working classes who are in the receipt of from 15*s*. to 22*s*. per week, who are insufficiently clothed, and irregularly and poorly fed, and whose houses as well as their persons appear filthy, disorderly, and uncomfortable. There are other families among them, containing the same number of persons, whose incomes average from 10*s*. to 14*s*. a-week, who are neatly, cleanly, and sufficiently clothed, regularly and suitably fed, and whose houses appear orderly and comfortable. The former class care little for the physical comfort, and far less for the intellectual, moral, and religious education of their children; in many cases, indeed, they neglect the education of their offspring when it is offered to them gratuitously, and in place of sending them to school, where they might be fitted for the duties and disappointments of life, they send them at a very early age to some employment, where they will earn the poor pittance of 1*s* 6*d*. to 3*s*. a-week. The latter class, on the contrary, are most anxious to give their children a good education: they study to obtain it for them by every means in their power, and they pay for it most cheerfully. The former class again grasp at every benefit which the charitable institutions of the place have provided for the poor. When, for example, medical attendance is given them gratuitously, they not unfrequently despise and refuse it, unless medicines are given them gratuitously also. Whereas the latter description of families are not only ready and willing to pay for medicines when prescribed to them, but they generally manifest much gratitude, and very often present their medical attendant with a small fee.

'Now it is among the former class of families where generally there appears to me to be a deficiency of wholesome food and of warm clothing; where contagious, febrile diseases are most commonly found; and from whence they are most extensively propagated. Fever is no doubt found among the latter. more frugal, and therefore better conditioned families, but seldom of that malignant, contagious character which it invariably assumes among the other class of families. Here, then, we have on the one hand, filth, destitution, and disease, associated with good wages; and on the other, cleanliness, comfort, and comparative good health, in connexion with wages which are much lower. The difference in the amount of their incomes does not account for the difference in the amount of comfort which is found existing among the working classes. The statements just made make known the fact, that above a certain amount, say 12*s*. or 14*s*. of weekly income, wages *alone*, without intelligence and good habits, contributes nothing towards the comfort, health, and independence of the working population.* * * Were I asked how I would propose to relieve such a family, I would say, show them how they may live comfortably within their incomes; let them be taught and trained to habits of industry, frugality, sobriety, cleanliness, &c., and with this 12*s*. or 14*s*. they may live in health and happiness as others in similar circumstances have lived and are now living. The man who maintains himself and his family in comfort on 12*s*. or 14*s*. of weekly income, possesses what he well deserves, happiness at home, and he stands forth in his neighbourhood a noble example of honest independence. I am persuaded that the filth, fever, and destitution in many families is occasioned, not by their small incomes, but by a misapplication or a prodigal waste of a part, in some cases a great part, of their otherwise sufficient wages. Frequently cases are found where, with a want of skill and economy, there is combined the intemperate use of intoxicating liquors, and here the misery may be said to be complete.

'Such is the explanation which I have to offer regarding much of the misery

III. Internal Economy and Domestic Habits

now prevalent, and it is the explanation invariably given by the economical working classes themselves when questioned on the subject. Heads of families, having three or four children, whose incomes average from 14s. to 18s. per week, have assured me that a man with a wife and three or four children can live comfortably on 12s. or 14s. a-week; and they generally account for the misery and destitution existing among families by saying, that many who have good wages reduce themselves to poverty and deprive themselves of sufficient food and clothing by their mismanagement, want of frugality, and drinking practices. Cases of waste and dissipation have been related to me, where the husband having gone to the tippling-house to enjoy his glass and his friend, the wife, knowing this, sent for her bottle and her friend, and enjoyed herself at home. A single visit to one of these spendthrift families, who are in the receipt of good wages, would convince any one that their persons and houses might be far more orderly, clean, and comfortable, were they but half trained to the tastes and habits of household industry, sobriety, and economy.'

The more closely the investigation as to the causes of epidemic disease is carried the more have the grounds been narrowed on which any presumption can be raised that it is generally occasioned by extreme indigence, or that it could be made generally to disappear simply by grants of money.

In the great mass of cases in every part of the country, in the rural districts and in the places of commercial pressure, the attacks of disease are upon those in full employment, the attack of fever precedes the destitution, not the destitution the disease. There is strong evidence of the existence of a large class of persons in severe penury in some places, as in Glasgow, being subject to fever, but the fever patients did not, as a class, present evidence of being in destitution in any of the places we examined. *Dr. William Davidson*, the senior physician of the Glasgow Royal Infirmary, who has written a Treatise on the Sources and Propagation of Continued Fevers, for which the prize instituted by Dr. Thackeray, of Chester, was unanimously awarded at the annual meeting of the Provincial Medical and Surgical Association, states in that treatise, when speaking of the influence of delicacy of constitution as a predisposing cause of fever:

'We have kept a record of the physical habit of the patients admitted into the Glasgow Fever Hospital from May 1st to November 1st, 1839, and the following were the divisions adopted:—

'1. Moderate, by which is meant a person having an ordinary quantity of muscle and cellular substance.

'2. Full or plethoric, having an extra quantity of adipose texture or of blood.

'3. Muscular.

'4. Spare.

'5. Emaciated or unhealthy in appearance.

	Males	Females	Total
Moderate . . .	116	93	209
Full or Plethoric . .	28	73	101
Muscular . . .	44	—	44
Spare	24	41	65
Unhealthy or Emaciated .	2	8	10
			429

'The whole of these 429 cases were characterized by the typhoid eruption, and will therefore be considered as decided cases of typhus. It appears from this table that there were only 10 cases in an emaciated or unhealthy condition; and almost all of them, as far as could be ascertained, were engaged in their ordinary occupations at the time of their seizure. The spare and unhealthy, when added together, only form about 17 per cent. of the whole number.'

He gives two tables of the proportionate numbers of persons admitted, during the year 1839, into the Glasgow Fever Hospital, whose persons were clean or filthy:
'These two tables show that, among 611 cases admitted as continued fever, there were 340 filthy and 271 clean, or about 55 per cent. filthy; that among 395 cases of eruptive typhus, there were 245 filthy and 150 clean, or about 62 per cent. filthy; and that among 48 cases of febricula there were 14 filthy and 34 clean, or about 29 per cent. filthy.'[1]

Amongst the fever patients are found a larger proportion of the highly intemperate than appear to be usually found amongst the labouring classes.

Dr. *Davidson*, in remarking on the influence of intemperance on fever, adduces the following table to show the proportion of temperate and intemperate individuals who were admitted into the Glasgow Fever Hospital from November 1st, 1838, to November 1st, 1839, whose habits could be ascertained with more or less certainty. He states that the eruptive cases only are included:

	Temperate	*A little Intemperate*	*Intemperate*
Typhus (MALES)	125	51	73
Typhus (FEMALES)	76	8	30

I have been informed that those were classed as 'temperate' who never indulged in strong liquors to the extent of inebriety; those a 'little intemperate' who now and again, perhaps at long intervals, drank to intoxication; and those as 'intemperate' who were habitually so—who drank whenever they could get ardent spirits.[2]

He adds:
'In the Glasgow Fever Hospital there occurred 81 deaths from eruptive typhus in individuals whose habits were ascertained, and 34 of these were reported as intemperate, 19 a little intemperate, and 28 temperate. In Dr. Craigie's table of the deaths in 31 fever cases that occurred in the Edinburgh Royal Infirmary[3], there were 15 stated to be irregular or dissipated; only two regular; the habits of the remainder are not stated.

'It is also a singular fact, which has been noticed by several writers, that fever is more fatal among the higher than among the lower classes. Dr. Braken states, in reference to the fever which prevailed at Waterford during the years 1817-18-19, that "it would be difficult to adjust the rates of mortality in the

---

1. William Davidson, *The Sources and Mode of Propagation of the Continued Fevers of Great Britain and Ireland* (1841), p. 62.
2. William Davidson, *op. cit.*, pp. 63-4.
3. David Craigie, 'Clinical report of the cases treated in the Fever-Ward No. 9 of the Infirmary, Edinburgh, during the year 1836-7', *Edinburgh Medical and Surgical Journal*, XLVII (1837), 285-331.

III. Internal Economy and Domestic Habits

upper classes, but it seems probable that one-fourth, or perhaps one-third of all those persons who were attacked with fever fell victims to its power."[1]

'Drs. Barker and Cheyne, in their historical account of the Irish epidemic,[2] state that, "in every part of the country, fever was reported to have been much more fatal amongst the upper than the lower classes." To what is this difference of mortality, so generally remarked by experienced hospital physicians, to be attributed, and which in Ireland seemed to be very remarkable, namely, in the lower classes about one in twenty-three cases, and in the upper classes one in three of four generally, but in other places about one in seven? Can the difference in the mode of living account for this anomaly? as the first live very much on potatoes, while the others use a larger or smaller proportion of animal food; and the lower classes almost everywhere in this country use less animal food and stimulating dishes than those who are more wealthy and in a higher sphere of society.'

In remarking on the supposed influence of fear and the depressing passions in producing fever, *Dr. Davidson*, however, remarks:

'The influence of fear and the depressing passions has also been considered as very powerful in predisposing persons to be affected with typhus contagion. There can be no doubt that fear has a tendency to produce a temporary depression of the physical powers; but, as has been already shown, there is no proof that persons of a naturally spare or weak habit of body, who are generally very sensitive, are more liable to fever than those of an ordinary constitution; this opinion must also be considered hypothetical. Indeed the facts, as far as our inquiries have enabled us to judge, seem to prove that the apprehension of fever, more particularly when it is not epidemic, is very rarely felt until the person is actually seized with the disease; for some cannot recollect of a single circumstance by which they could be exposed to contagion; and a considerable number of those who had undoubtedly been exposed to it were only made aware of the fact when it had been elicited by cross-examination. We are quite aware that cases may be brought forward of sensitive individuals who have been seized with fever soon after visiting a person labouring under the disease; but as this fact can be opposed with at least an equal number of persons who were destitute of fear, and yet caught it after an exposure to contagion, no conclusion whatever can be drawn from them. It must be observed, however, that though there is no proof that persons who are naturally weak in body or of a sensitive disposition are more susceptible of fever than those who are naturally vigorous and robust, yet that, during famine or commercial distress, poverty, by depressing the mind and lowering the physical status from insufficient aliment, does powerfully predispose a community to become affected with fever. This has been already shown in a former part of the essay, and has been again alluded to in order that the distinction might be made between an individual of naturally weak mental and physical stamina, and one who has been reduced to that state by deficient nutriment.'[3]

There appears to be little evidence on one side or the other in support of this last hypothesis, other than such as that cited from Dr. Davidson himself; but it is to be observed that the wet or bad seasons, which

---

1. J. K. Bracken, 'Medical report of the Fever Hospital of the City and of the County of Waterford during the epidemic fever of the years 1817, 1818 and 1819', in F. Barker and J. Cheyne, *An Account of the Rise, Progress and Decline of the Fever lately epidemical in Ireland* (1821), I, 277.
2. Fraser Barker and John Cheyne, *op. cit.* (2 vols., 1821).
3. William Davidson, *op. cit.*, pp. 64-5.

suspend agricultural industry and much labour in the towns, is usually of a character of itself to predispose to disease, if not to produce it; and that it does propagate it amongst all classes, high and low, in proportion to their exposure to it. It appears to be highly probable that the privation attendant on the stoppage of work, by diminishing the means for the purchase of fuel, of soap, &c., and in various ways by inducing lax habits of life, may increase the amount of exposure to and loss from the all-pervading cause.

The preponderant evidence given on this subject by the great majority of the medical officers in England who are accustomed to visit the labouring classes in their own dwellings, is however of the tenor of the following from the medical officer of the Whitechapel union acting in Spitalfields parish.

Mr. Byles, the medical officer of the Whitechapel union:

'What is the number of cases you have had to visit during the year 1841 as a medical officer?—I think the number of cases I have had to visit during each year since the commencement of the Union has been upwards of 2,000 cases of various disease, of which 1,400 were cases out of the workhouse.

'Has the present winter been unhealthy?—I do not think it has; there has been an increase of fever cases during the last month. The number of cases is, however, still below the average of 1838.

'Is there not, however, unusual distress in your district, comprehending Spitalfields and a portion of Whitechapel?—Yes, there is: I believe that more than half the looms are out of work.

'Do you not find that fever attacks in greatest number those who are out of work?—On the contrary, the greatest number of the cases of fever we have are those who fall ill during the time they are in employment. I think they are more attacked when in work, when the windows are closed, and there is no ventilation. Many of them are obliged to work with closed windows, to keep out the moist air, and prevent the dust blowing upon their work. When they are out of work, they are more out of doors looking after work, more in the open air, and that very exercise may be the means of keeping them in health. This observation applies to the weavers. I find that they have generally less fever when they are out of work. The reverse, I think, holds as respects out-door labourers, such as those who work at the docks. When they are out of work, they stand about waiting in the cold, and when cold, they generally take cheap gin, and no food: they catch cold, and on going to their close filthy habitations, their cold is apt to generate fever.

'There was an unusual amount of fever prevalent in Spitalfields and Whitechapel, was there not, in the year 1838?—Yes, there was; in the proportion, perhaps, of more than two to one of the present amount. My last account for the year ending Lady-day, 1842, was about 250 fever cases; it has been as high as 800.

'Did it prevail proportionately amongst the weavers?—Yes, I believe it did.

'Was there any marked or unusual distress at that period?—Not that I remember.

'Do you find in the course of your experience that the diminution of food is followed by fever?—Not as a general cause, I should say. If these two persons, casually exposed to the contagion of fever, the one in full vigour, and with a full stomach, the other with an empty stomach, the person with the empty stomach would be the most obnoxious to its influence. In my experience, however, intemperance is a much more frequent antecedent to fever than destitution or want of food.

'Have you ever observed that habits of intemperance are created by distress of mind?—Such cases may occur, but I have not observed them, and I think it does not operate as a general cause.

'What are the chief remedies which your experience in this district would lead you to recommend for the prevention of fever and contagious diseases?— The promotion of cleanly habits amongst the poor; the promotion of sewerage and drainage; having proper supplies of water laid on in the houses; the removal of privies from improper situations. I could point out in our neighbourhood many houses, and some courts, that ought to be pulled down as wholly unfit for human habitation.

'What is the personal state of the labouring classes in your district?— Generally extremely filthy. I have said that I could almost smell from what street a man came who came to my surgery: I do not think the poor themselves are conscious of it, but the smell to other persons must be extremely offensive. I certainly think that the want of personal cleanliness, and of cleanliness in their rooms, and the prevalence of fever, stand in the relation of cause and effect.

'Your colleague has pointed out that the want of proper and convenient supplies of water is an antecedent to the filth and the fever. Does your experience enable you to concur with him?—My experience entirely agrees with his on that point.'

The late *Dr.Cowan*, of Glasgow[1], and the great majority of the medical officers, assign the foremost place to these physical agencies as antecedents to fever.

The medical controversy as to the causes of fever; as to whether it is caused by filth and vitiated atmosphere, or whether the state of the atmosphere is a predisposing cause to the reception of the fever, or the means of propagating that disease, which has really some other superior, independent, or specific cause, does not appear to be one that for practical purposes need be considered, except that its effect is prejudicial in diverting attention from the practical means of prevention.

Dr. Bancroft, one of the controversialists cited by Dr. Davidson, observes:

'That fever often exists in them' (gaols) 'cannot be denied; but this circumstance can afford no evidence of its being generated therein, any more than the multiplication of vermin in such places could demonstrate the spontaneous generation of these and other insects by the nastiness which favours the deposition and hatching of their eggs.'[2]

Taking the controversy at this point, and admitting the force of this statement, the decision upon it will not alter the practical value of cleanliness, or of its protective effects in prevention, whether it remove an original or only a predisposing cause.

Yet it cannot but be regretted that the enlightened force of the professional opinion should sustain any diminution from an apparent want of unanimity on so important a question as the necessity of removing these causes, whether original or predisposing: that, for example, whilst the fleets were ravaged by fever and disease, men of high standing should have occupied the attention of the public with specula-

---

1. For Professor Robert Cowan, see p. 98, n. 1 above.
2. Edward Nathaniel Bancroft, *An Essay on . . . Yellow Fever, with Observations concerning febrile Contagion, Typhus Fever, Dysentery, and the Plague* (1811), p. 143.

tions on contagion, and infection from the gaols as the original cause, and diverted attention from the means of prevention, cleansing and ventilation, the means by which, as will hereafter be shown, the pestilence was ultimately banished. The main error of those who have ascribed fever to destitution, appears to have been in adopting too hastily as evidence of the fact of destitution, such *primâ facie* appearances as are noticed by Dr. Scott Alison, an error which non-professional experience may correct. In more than one instance where, in a district in which the demand for labour was still great, and the wages high, benevolent gentlemen have propounded similar doctrines, which, being at variance with the known state of the labour-market, I have requested that the names of these fever cases might be given, that their antecedent circumstances might be examined, and the accuracy of the conclusions tested, by officers of experience in such investigations; but I think it right to state the names or means of inquiry have never been forthcoming. In general, medical practitioners and benevolent individuals are extremely liable to deceive themselves and to deceive others, by what they call the evidence of their own eyes. The occurrence of severe destitution is denied as a general cause of fever, not as a consequence. The evidence shows that the best means of preventing the consequent destitution are those which prevent the attacks of fever and other epidemics upon all classes of the community.[1]

By an extract from a report of the late Dr. Currie, of Liverpool, given in the Appendix,[2] it will be seen that at the time he wrote, 1797, when only 9,500 of the population are reported to have lived in cellars, the proportion of fever cases was nearly the same as at present, when the cellar population has risen to 40,000; the disease has been almost as constant as the surrounding physical circumstances of bad ventilation, filth, and damp then pointed out as removable, and the disease has continued in every period of the prosperity of the town in its progress from a population of 77,000 to 223,000 in 1841. So the late Dr. Ferriar, of Manchester, when writing between 30 and 40 years ago,[3] of the state of the population in periods of great prosperity, especially for hand-loom weaving, described the effect of the bad economy of the habitations much as they were described in the year 1829 by Dr. Kay,[4] and as they are described in 1840 by Dr. Baron Howard.[5] *Dr. Ferriar*, when he wrote

---

1. For the controversy concerning the relationship between destitution and the generation of disease, see Introduction, pp. 63-4.
2. J. Currie, 'Typhus fever, the vast amount of, produced among the poor of Liverpool from want of ventilation and cleanliness', *San. Rep.*, Appendix 23, p. 441.
3. John Ferriar, *Medical Histories and Reflections* (1st. edition 1792; 2nd. edition 1810).
4. Kay's descriptions of working-class housing in Manchester were published in 1830 (in *The North of England Medical and Surgical Journal*), and in 1832 (in his *The Moral and Physical Condition of the Working Classes*). See Introduction, pp. 32-4.
5. Richard Baron Howard, 'Report on the prevalence of diseases arising from contagion and certain other physical causes amongst the labouring classes in Manchester', *Local Reps. E. & W.*, pp. 294-335.

to warn the labouring classes as to the choice of their dwellings, stated that:

'The custom of inhabiting cellars also tends to promote both the origin and preservation of febrile infection. But even in them the action of filth and confined air is always apparent when fevers arise. I have often observed that the cellar of a fever patient was to be known by a shattered pane, patched with paper or stuffed with rags, and by every external sign of complete dirtiness.'[1]

The false opinions as to destitution being the general cause of fever, and as to its propagation, have had extensively the disastrous effect of preventing efforts being made for the removal of the circumstances which are proved to be followed by a diminution of the pestilence.

The opinion of the majority of the medical officers of the unions in England on this topic, acting in districts in every condition, might be expressed in the terms used by *Dr. Davidson*:

'It has already been shown that filth and deficient ventilation tend much to spread the contagion of typhus, being almost constant concomitants; and that while it generally affects the whole members, or the large proportion of a family among the lower orders, it rarely spreads in this manner among the better classes of society, who attend more to cleanliness and ventilation. It is quite obvious that an amelioration of the physical condition of the lower orders, in these particulars, would, in proportion as this was effected, diminish their chances of catching the contagion, which would not only operate in lessening directly its diffusion, but by reducing the number of its sources, must tend to lessen the actual quantity of this principle that might be generated in a given time.

'But can this amelioration be effected to any appreciable extent; or, if effected, could it be maintained for any length of time? We fear that little permanent amelioration could be effected without a legislative enactment; for though our philanthropists are very active in their charities during the prevalence of an epidemic, it no sooner subsides than they relapse into a comparative quiescence, and our working population into their former habits of filth and intemperance. And the evil will continue to assail us so long as our cities contain so many narrow and filthy lanes, so long as the houses situated there are little better than dens or hovels, so long as dunghills and other nuisances are allowed to accumulate in their vicinity, so long as these hovels are crowded with inmates, and so long as there is so much poverty and destitution. Why, then, should we not have a legislative enactment that would level these hovels to the ground—that would regulate the width of every street—that would regulate the ventilation of every dwelling-house—that would prevent the lodging-houses of the poor from being crowded with human beings, and that would provide for their destitution? It may be said that this would interfere too much with the liberty of the subject, and no doubt it would be vehemently opposed by many interested persons. In place, however, of being an infringement on the liberty of the subject, it might rather be designated an attempt to prevent the improper liberties of the subject; for what right, moral or constitutional, has any man to form streets, construct houses, and crowd them with human beings, so as to deteriorate health and shorten life, because he finds it profitable to do so? As well ought the law to tolerate the sale of unwholesome food because it might be profitable to the retailer of it.'[2]

But the professional experience and weight of professional testimony

---

1. Ferriar, *op. cit.* (1792 edition), I, 138.
2. Davidson, *op. cit.*, p. 56.

on this subject is not confined to this country. In a report prepared under the superintendence of a commission of the Royal Academy of Medicine at Paris,* appointed to investigate the epidemics prevalent in France, similar general conclusions are announced upon similar evidence adduced, of which we select the following instance:

'If an example,' says the report, 'be necessary to justify this placing of circumstances as cause and effect, we shall find one in the terrible epidemic which desolated the commune of Prades, in the department of Ariège, at the end of the year 1838. Out of 750 healthy and vigorous inhabitants of this commune 310 were attacked with the disease, and 95 died, thus the deaths were 1 in every $3\frac{1}{4}$ cases. The cause of this epidemic, violent and sudden in its nature, and which broke out in all points at once, is not less evident. It proceeded from a sewer, the receptacle of all the water from the neighbourhood, and of the filth which the water brought with it, and of the dead animals of the district. The hot, damp weather which preceded it no doubt augmented the activity of this focus of infection. The first persons attacked were the women employed in washing linen in this pestiferous pool, and the labourers working in the neighbourhood of it. This terrible epidemic recurred three times, which the invalids in their simplicity attributed to the influence of the moon, but which mainly depended upon the wind at certain periods passing over the infected pool, and bringing the miasma in the direction of their dwellings. If for want of sufficient description it is not possible to prove completely the similarity of the epidemic at Prades with the typhus fever, yet it may be inferred from the symptoms, viz. that when the skin was broken deep sores were formed, and that serous abscesses showed themselves in the lymphatic ganglions, that this disease was very similar to the ancient putrid and malignant fevers formerly described by authors, and which are entirely replaced in our *nosology* by the typhoid affection. The physicians of Ariège, in order to prove that the disease was not *contagious*, and to re-assure the inhabitants, lay in the beds from which the invalids had been removed.'

Adverting to the local reports they have received, the Commissioners state—'These reports have awakened in us the sad conviction that many localities are quite devoid of even the most simple ideas on public health; the inhabitants live surrounded by marshes, drains, stagnant pools, manure heaps, without having the slightest idea of the dangers they are incurring. Indeed, many of them blindly speculate in these heaps of infection, increasing the manure which is to enrich their fields at the expense of their health, and often of their lives.'

The Commissioners observe,—'Most of the improvements in public health have been brought about through the experience and science united in our large cities; so much so that now epidemics often come to us from the rural districts. These epidemics are generally much less fatal than formerly, but are still very prevalent even in the wealthiest and the most civilized departments. It would be an important problem to solve, what are the causes which produce these epidemics in the agricultural as well as in the manufacturing counties, as in ancient Normandy and Picardy. One cause is certainly the unhealthiness of the houses. The inhabitants of these districts are, in general, well fed, well clothed, but

* Rapport de la Commission des Epidémies de l'Académie Royale de Médecine pour l'année 1839 et un partie d' 1840. Par M. Brichetan, Secrétaire Rapporteur de la Commission.

ill lodged. We are surprised to find in the midst of a fertile plain wide districts covered with luxuriant vegetation, villages buried in the ground, *smothered* with large trees, and cottages constructed without any art or plan, and almost entirely without windows.' The Commissioners state, further,—'If you wish to have a robust and healthy people, you must have a care for their physical education, their houses, and their modes of living. Do not allow generation after generation to be depressed under the evil effects of recurring epidemics, which must eventually ruin the strongest constitutions, as is seen to be the case in marshy and ill-drained districts, where fevers, *goitres*, and scrofulas constantly prevail.'

In another report made on the proceedings of the Conseil de Salubrité, the diseases prevalent amongst the population in the towns is adverted to:—'We must be like the men so well painted by the Psalmist, to reject such evidence—*eyes have they, and see not*. How shall we explain, or rather to what shall we attribute the difference that is remarked between the mortality of one quarter and that of another quarter of the same town; of one street and that of another street of the same quarter or of the same village; or, lastly, the difference that is observed in this respect between the houses of the same street and those houses which are completely isolated? Misery, it is replied to us, is the cause. Yes, without doubt, misery is a powerful cause; but it is so especially when it is driven back into the most insalubrious quarters, streets, and houses; when it lives habitually in the midst of filth and dirt, that is to say, in the midst of an infected atmosphere; and when there is no misery, or when it exists in the same degree in the quarters, in the villages, in the streets, and in the houses with which the comparison is made; and, stronger still, when poverty is met with precisely there where there is the least mortality; in what is to be found the cause of this difference, if it is not in the insalubrity of the dwelling-places?'[1]

The report on the local epidemics concludes by earnestly recommending to the government—'That sanitary measures be adopted by means of which the constitution of the people may be renewed, and their longevity increased. If this recommendation be fulfilled, we may then hope to see the condition of some of the departments ameliorated, in which now the population is so degenerated that the men seem to diminish in size each time they are measured for the conscriptions.'

Evidence on the mismanagement of expenditure in respect to supplies of food, on mismanagement also in respect to clothing and fuel by the labouring classes, might be added to complete the view of the principal causes of disease prevalent amongst them, but these do not come within the immediate scope of the present inquiry, which has been directed chiefly to the investigation of the evils affecting their sanitary condition, that come within the recognized provinces of legislation or local administration.

The information on the means for the prevention of epidemic disease arising in the common lodging-houses maintained for the accommodation of trampers and vagrants, might also have been considered in

---

1. Quoted by M. Trebuchet, 'Report on the labours of the "Conseil de Salubrité" of Paris, from 1829 to 1839', *San. Rep.*, Appendix 14, p. 415.

IV. Comparative Chances of Life in Different Classes

connexion with the subject of the effects of overcrowding and filth which they strongly exemplify; but it appeared most convenient to consider them apart from the exposition of what may be termed the indigenous evils that afflict the settled inhabitants of the labouring class.

I would now submit for consideration, 1st, the total expense of the present state of things, so far as a proximate view of it can be obtained, on the health, strength, and life of the lower classes of the population. 2nd, a proximate view of the pecuniary expense of such partial remedies as are at present applied or applicable to alleviate the consequences of these preventible diseases.

IV

COMPARATIVE CHANCES OF LIFE IN DIFFERENT CLASSES OF THE COMMUNITY

Very dangerous errors arise from statistical returns and insurance tables of the mean chances of life made up from gross returns of the mortality prevalent amongst large classes, who differ widely in their circumstances. Thus we find, on inquiry into the sanitary condition of the population of different districts, that the average chances of life of the people of one class in one street will be 15 years, and of another class in a street immediately adjacent, 60 years. In one district of the same town I find, on the examination of the registries, the mortality only 1 out of every 57 of the population; and in another district 1 out of every 28 dies annually. A return of the average or the mean of the chances of life, or the proportions of death in either instance, would and does lead to very dangerous errors, and amongst others to serious misapprehensions as to the condition of the inferior districts, and to false inferences as to the proper rates of insurance. With the view of arriving at some estimate of the comparative extent of the operation of the chief causes of sickness and mortality proved to be prevalent, amidst the different classes of society, in the towns where the sanitary inquiries have been made; I have obtained the following returns from the clerks of the several unions acting as superintendent registrars. These returns have, as far as practicable, been corrected by particular local inquiry, and are submitted as the best approximations that can readily be obtained. In all districts, and especially in the manufacturing districts, there is some migration of labourers which would, for the obtainment of perfect accuracy as to the chances of life in particular localities, have rendered necessary an examination of every individual case enumerated. This extent of labour has been considered unnecessary. In the returns from single towns, the numbers of deaths of persons of the first class are too small not to be affected by accidental disturbances, but when large numbers of the like class are taken, the uniform operation of the like circumstances are shown in the like results. It is at present a general defect of the important head of information, 'the occupation of the deceased,' that the deaths of masters are not carefully distinguished from the deaths of journeymen. So far as this error prevails, it will tend to raise the apparent chances of life amongst the labouring classes. In some instances the occupations of the deceased, or of the parents of the deceased, in the case of children,

IV. Comparative Chances of Life in Different Classes

are not described in the registries. With these and possibly with other defects that may have escaped notice, these returns will be received as corroborative of the reports of the medical officers and physicians who have attended and observed many of the individual cases themselves, though not enumerated by them. Had the mortality prevalent amongst workpeople of particular trades and their families been taken, instead of the mean chances of persons of all occupations deriving subsistence from weekly wages, the case of classes with still lower chances would have been presented; but these would have appeared to suggest particular remedies. Such returns of the effects of common evils were therefore taken as appeared applicable to the consideration of common or general means of prevention.

One of the first returns obtained is from *Dr. Barham*, as to the different rates of mortality in Truro:

'The information derived from the registers of deaths and sickness has been arranged in a series of tables. The first gives a return of the condition in life, average ages, and the causes of death, with respect to all who died in Truro from July 1st, 1837, to December 31st, 1840. The occupation of the deceased not being stated in the register, except in the case of adult males, the condition of others has been inferred in the majority of cases from that of the parent or husband, in many from my own knowledge of the parties, and in others from the place of abode or other collateral evidence. Altogether I am confident that the statement is not materially erroneous.[1]

The sum of these several returns was as follows:

No. of Deaths	TRURO	Average Age of Deceased
33	Professional persons or gentry, and their families	40 years
138	Persons engaged in trade, or similarly circumstanced, and their families	33
447	Labourers, artisans, and others similarly circumstanced, and their families	28

In Derby the proportions appear to be as exhibited in the following table:

No. of Deaths	DERBY	Average Age of Deceased
10	Professional persons or gentry	49 years
125	Tradesmen	38
752	Labourers and artisans	21

To compare the chances of life between a crowded manufacturing population and a less crowded rural population, I selected the county of Rutland, because it had been selected as an average agricultural district for a comparison as to its general condition by the members of the Statistical Society of Manchester, and they deputed their agent, *Mr. J. R. Wood*, to make inquiries on an examination from house to house. The following are portions of his examination:

---

1. Charles Barham, 'Report on the sanitary condition of the labouring classes in the town of Truro', *Local Reps. E. & W.*, p. 29.

IV. Comparative Chances of Life in Different Classes

'Amidst what population have you inquired from house to house?—Amidst a portion of the population of Manchester, viz. Pendleton, having a population of about 10,000; I visited every house. In like manner I went through Branstoun, Egleton, and Hambleton, in Rutlandshire, being a rural population of upwards of 1,000, and Hull, having a population of nearly 40,000, exclusive of Sculcoates, Ashton, and Dukinfield. I also went over for the purpose of checking an inquiry into the state of the population of those towns, which had been previously made by another party. In Liverpool I did not go from house to house; I went into a considerable number of the houses amidst the poorer districts. In certain districts of Manchester, though not for the Statistical Society, I did the same. In Birmingham I made many memoranda, and, as far as my limited time would permit, I visited a portion of the population. In York, containing a population of 26,000, I went into every street and court, visiting occasionally, to obtain a general idea of the condition of the inhabitants. York included 23 parishes of small extent, all which I visited.

'What did you find to be the condition of the tenements in the rural districts as compared with the towns you examined?—In Branstoun, Egleton, and Hambleton, being in a rural district, the houses are low, never exceeding two stories; many of them are thatched, and nearly all are built of stone. To each a garden is attached, which is generally of sufficient dimensions to supply the family with vegetables. As there are no cellars, most of the houses have a small dairy or store-room attached, which, however, has not been counted in reckoning the number of rooms in each house. Forty-one per cent. of the dwellings in Branstoun, and 51 per cent. in Egleton and Hambleton I found to be '*well furnished.*' In Manchester and Salford 52 per cent., and in the Dukinfield district 61 per cent., had that character. The proportion reported to be *comfortable* in each district were:—

'In Branstoun . . 50 per cent.
Egleton and Hambleton . 65 ,,
Manchester, &c. . . 72 ,,
Dukinfield . . . 95 ,,

'The word "*comfortable*" must always be a vague and varying epithet, nor is it possible to attach any precise definition to it. In filling up this column I was guided by observing the condition of the dwelling, apart from any consideration of order, cleanliness, and furniture. If I considered it capable of being made comfortable for the tenant, I set it down accordingly; if it were damp, the flooring bad, and the walls ill-conditioned, I reported it uncomfortable. The general appearance of the interior of the houses (in Rutlandshire) indicated thrifty poverty, and instances of the squalid misery so frequent in large towns were here extremely rare. In comparing the physical condition of the people in the three parishes, Egleton and Hambleton appeared to have some slight advantage over Branstoun, while 31 per cent. of the houses in the former parishes contained four rooms only; 17 per cent. in the latter had this advantage. In its amount of sleeping accommodation, also Branstoun is inferior to the neighbouring parishes.

'From a comparison of the tables with those in a former Report, it appeared that in Egleton, &c., 14 per cent. of the families have more than three persons to a bed; Branstoun, 19 ditto; Dukinfield, 33 ditto; and Bury, 35 ditto.

'The rents of the houses in Rutlandshire would appear to be very low compared with those in large manufacturing towns. Not only is the average cost of the former less than half of the latter, but for that diminished cost the dimensions of the houses are double those in large towns, with comforts and conveniences which the latter never can possess.

	£	s.	d.
'Egleton, &c., average yearly rent	2	17	3
Branstoun	3	0	0
Dukinfield, &c.	6	14	0
Manchester, &c.	7	11	8'

But moral causes, inducing habits of sobriety, appear from the report of the Manchester Society to contribute to the general result of the superior condition of the Rutland population, in which the duration of life amongst the lowest classes appears to be nearly as high as amongst the highest classes in Manchester. Wages in Lancashire, it must be premised, were then (in 1837), and, as I am well informed from the payers of several thousand labourers, are now at least double what they are in Rutlandshire. The Society state in their report that it appears:

'That the people do nearly as much for themselves in Rutlandshire as they do in Manchester, notwithstanding the more extensive endowment of their schools.

'In a separate examination of three parishes in Rutlandshire, carried on from house to house, the larger attendance of children at school in that county was confirmed, and it also appeared that the average time of their remaining at day schools was greater than in Lancashire. In Pendleton, near Manchester, one third only of the children appeared to remain at school above five years, and one third remained less than three years; while, in the three parishes of Rutlandshire which were visited, it was found that, of the children who had left school, one half had remained there above five years.

'The teachers generally bear irreproachable characters, which has doubtless much influence on the character and deportment of the population, whose manners appeared exceedingly orderly and respectful.

'In the dame schools it was very gratifying to observe the marked difference in general appearance and order, as compared with schools of a similar class in large towns. The mistresses are almost invariably persons of good moral character, of quiet orderly habits, cleanly in their habitations, decent in their personal appearance, and of respectful deportment. The scholars, too, except in one or two instances, were found clean and tidy, however mean their attire, and generally remained orderly and quiet during the visit. The rod or cane is much less in use than in the towns formerly examined, though it usually forms part of the furniture of the school. The girls were generally found sewing or knitting, and in many schools the boys learn to knit.

'A society for the promotion of industry, supported by subscriptions, exists in the county; and prizes are given to those children, who, according to their age, have performed the most work during the year. This excites a great competition as to which village shall produce the queen of the knitters, or the queen of the sewers, and many ladies in the county consider the Society to have great influence in inducing habits of diligence and order. The moral effect is no doubt good, and a greater interest in the lower class of schools is also thereby created amongst the gentry.

'In conclusion, we may observe that the visitation of the houses of the labouring poor in Rutlandshire, and the observation of their language, manners, and habits, leave a favourable impression with regard to their moral condition. Swearing and drunkenness are far from common, and the general conduct of the people is marked by sobriety, frugality, and industry.'

Mr. Wood was asked:

'You have seen the following returns of the average ages of death amongst the different classes of people in Manchester and Rutlandshire:—

IV. Comparative Chances of Life in Different Classes

	Average Age of Death	
	In Manchester	In Rutlandshire
	Years	Years
'Professional persons and gentry, and their families	38	52
Tradesmen and their families, (in Rutlandshire, farmers and graziers are included with shopkeepers)	20	41
Mechanics, labourers, and their families .	17	38

Bearing in mind the fact that wages are nearly double in Manchester to the average of wages in Rutlandshire, though rents are higher in Manchester: are the different chances of life amongst each class of the population to the extent they are indicated by the returns, conformable to what you would have anticipated from your personal examinations of the houses and observation of the condition of the inhabitants?—They are decidedly conformable to my anticipation in the general results. I apprehend, however, that some allowance must perhaps be made for the very high average age in Rutlandshire, from the circumstance that many of the children or young people migrate from thence to manufacturing neighbourhoods for employment. These would certainly have passed the age at which the greatest mortality takes place amongst children; but we may expect that their migration, as it is a constant migration, might to some extent increase the average age of death or apparent duration of life in Rutlandshire, though not very materially. On the other hand, there is, perhaps, a larger proportion of children in Manchester. The results certainly correspond with my own impressions as to the relative condition of the different classes in the different neighbourhoods.'

In the union comprehending the adjacent manufacturing district of Bolton, the proportions of deaths in the several classes as returned by the superintendent-registrar were as follows in the year 1839:

No. of Deaths	BOLTON UNION	Average Age of Deceased
103	Gentlemen and persons engaged in professions, and their families	34 years
381	Tradesmen and their families	23
2,232	Mechanics, servants, labourers, and their families .	18

It is proper to observe, that so far as I was informed upon the evidence received in the Factory Inquiry, and more recently on the cases of children of migrant families, that opinion is erroneous which ascribes greater sickness and mortality to the children employed in factories than amongst the children who remain in such homes as these towns afford to the labouring classes.[1] However defective the ventilation of many of the factories may yet be, they are all of them drier and more equably warm than the residence of the parent; and we had proof that weakly children have been put into the better-managed factories as healthier places for them than their own homes. It is an appalling fact that, of all who are born of the labouring classes in Manchester, more than 57 per cent. die before they attain five years of age; that is, before they can be engaged in factory labour, or in any other labour whatsoever.

---

1. Peter Gaskell, *The Manufacturing Population of England* (1833), pp. 195-6, confirms this statement.

IV. Comparative Chances of Life in Different Classes

Of 4,629 deaths of persons of the labouring classes who died in the year 1840 in Manchester, the numbers who died were at the several periods as follows:

Under 5 years of age	. . . . .	2,649 or 1 in $1\frac{7}{10}$
Above 5 and under 10	. . . .	215 or 1 in 22
Above 10 and under 15	. . . .	107 or 1 in 43
Above 15 and under 20	. . . .	135 or 1 in 34

At seven, eight, or nine years of age the children of the working classes begin to enter into employment in the cotton and other factories.[1] It appears that at the period between 5 and 10 years of age the proportions of deaths which occur amongst the labouring classes, as indicated by these returns, are not so great as the proportions of deaths which occur amongst the children of the middle classes who are not so engaged. Allowing for the circumstance that some of the weakest of the labourers' children will have been swept away in the first stage, the effect of employment is not shown to be injurious in any increase of the proportion who die in the second stage.[2]

In a return obtained from a district differently situated (Bethnal Green, where the manufactory is chiefly domestic) it appears that of 1,268 deaths amongst the labouring classes in the year 1839, no less than 783, or 1 in $1\frac{4}{7}$, died at their own residences under 5 years of age. One in 15 of the deaths occurred between 5 and 10, the age when employment commences. The proportion of deaths which occurred between 10 and 15, the period at which full employment usually takes place, is 1 in 60 only.

In that district the average age of deaths in the year 1839 was as follows, in the several classes, from a population of 62,018:

No. of Deaths	BETHNAL GREEN	Average Age of Deceased
101	Gentlemen and persons engaged in professions, and their families	45 years
273	Tradesmen and their families	26
1,258	Mechanics, servants, and labourers, and their families .	16

The mean chances of life amongst the several classes in Leeds appear from the returns to the Registrar-general generally to correspond with the anticipations raised by the descriptions given of the condition of the labouring population.

No. of Deaths	LEEDS BOROUGH	Average Age of Deceased
79	Gentlemen and persons engaged in professions, and their families	44 years
824	Tradesmen, farmers, and their families . . .	27
3,395	Operatives, labourers, and their families . . .	19

---

1. Strictly speaking, since 1833 no child under nine ought to enter cotton factory employment.
2. This is a very questionable argument. The very fact that so high a proportion of the working-class children died under five invalidates any comparison of higher age-groups.

IV. Comparative Chances of Life in Different Classes   225

But in Liverpool (which is a commercial and not a manufacturing town) where, however, the condition of the dwellings are reported to be the worst, where, according to the report of Dr. Duncan, 40,000 of the population live in cellars, where 1 in 25 of the population are annually attacked with fever,[1]—there the mean chances of life appear from the returns to the Registrar-general to be still lower than in Manchester, Leeds, or amongst the silk weavers in Bethnal Green. During the year 1840, the deaths, distinguishable in classes, were as follows:

No. of Deaths	LIVERPOOL, 1840	Average Age of Deceased
137	Gentry and professional persons, &c.	35 years
1,738	Tradesmen and their families	22
5,597	Labourers, mechanics, and servants, &c.	15

Of the deaths which occurred amongst the labouring classes, it appears that no less than 62 per cent. of the total number were deaths under five years of age. Even amongst those entered as shopkeepers and tradesmen, no less than 50 per cent. died before they attained that period. The proportion of mortality for Birmingham, where there are many insalubrious manufactories, but where the drainage of the town and the general condition of the inhabitants is comparatively good, was, in 1838, 1 in 40: whilst in Liverpool it was 1 in 31.

I have appended the copy of a map of Bethnal Green,[2] made with the view of showing the proportions in which the mortality from epidemic diseases and diseases affected by localities, fell on different classes of tenements during the same year. The localities in which the marks of death (×) are most crowded are the poorest and the worst of the district; where the marks are few and widely spread, the houses and streets, and the whole condition of the population, is better. By the inspection of a map of Leeds, which Mr. Baker has prepared at my request, to show the localities of epidemic diseases, it will be perceived that they similarly fall on the uncleansed and close streets and wards occupied by the labouring classes; and that the track of the cholera is nearly identical with the tract of fever. It will also be observed that in the badly cleansed and badly drained wards to the right of the map, the proportional mortality is nearly double that which prevails in the better conditioned districts to the left.[3]

To obtain the means of judging of the references to the localities in the sanitary returns from Aberdeen, the reporters were requested to mark on a map the places where the disease fell, and to distinguish with a deeper tint those places on which it fell with the greatest intensity. They were also requested to distinguish by different colours the streets inhabited by the higher, middle, and lower classes of society. They returned a map so marked as to disease, but stated that it had been thought unnecessary to

---

1. *Local Reps. E. & W.*, pp. 283, 285. Duncan estimated Liverpool's cellar population at 'from 35,000 to 40,000'.
2. This map has not been reproduced in this edition.
3. This map has not been reproduced in this edition. For Baker's work in connection with the sanitary map of Leeds, see introduction, pp. 50-1.

distinguish the streets inhabited by the different orders of society, as that was done with sufficient accuracy by the different tints representing the degrees of intensity of the prevalence of fever.

In the Whitechapel union, in which the special investigation which led to the inquiry into the sanitary condition of the metropolis was first directed, the numbers were as follows in the year 1838:

No. of Deaths	WHITECHAPEL UNION	*Average Age of Deceased*
37	Gentlemen and persons engaged in professions, and their families	45 years
387	Tradesmen and their families	27
1,762	Mechanics, servants, and labourers, and their families .	22

To judge of the comparative mortality amongst the average of a town population, I obtained the following returns; the one from the clerk of the Strand union, the other from the clerk of the Kensington union:

No. of Deaths	STRAND UNION	*Average Age of Deceased*
86	Gentry and persons engaged in professions and their families	43 years
221	Tradesmen and their families	33
674	Mechanics, labourers, servants, and their families .	24

No. of Deaths	KENSINGTON UNION	*Average Age of Deceased*
331	Gentlemen and persons engaged in professions, and their families	44 years
348	Tradesmen and their families	29
1,258	Labourers, artisans, and others similarly circumstanced, and their families	26

The remarkable result obtained from the examination of the mortuary registries of the county of Rutland induced me to have them examined for different periods. They have accordingly been examined for three complete years, 1838, 1839, and 1840, and it is found that the same general law of mortality obtains with little variation for each period.

As the climate or soil of that county might possess some peculiarities, I caused an examination to be made of the average periods of death amongst the agricultural population of all the unions in the county of Wilts during 1840. In this examination the registries of deaths in the towns were excluded, and only those of persons included who were described as agricultural labourers, or as farmers and graziers, or as gentry and professional persons resident in the rural districts. The results of this examination are as follow:

No. of Deaths	UNIONS IN THE COUNTY OF WILTS	*Average Age of Deceased*
119	Gentlemen and persons engaged in professions, and their families	50
218	Farmers and their families	48
2,061	Agricultural labourers and their families . . .	33

IV. Comparative Chances of Life in Different Classes

The following table exhibits the mortality prevalent amongst the different classes, partly mining and manufacturing, and partly agricultural, returned by the clerk of the Kendal union:

No. of Deaths	Kendal Union	Average Age of Deceased
52	Gentlemen and persons engaged in professions, and their families	45 years
138	Tradesmen and their families	39
413	Operatives, labourers, servants, and their families	34

The following tables exhibit the results of such returns of mortality as have been made for quinquennial and decennial periods, from an examination of upwards of 25,000 cases for this inquiry. They show in the mean ratios for large numbers of the like class the steady influence of the different circumstances under which each class is placed. The labouring classes, it is generally known, become old the soonest, and the effects of the unfavourable influences in the adolescent and adult stages is shown in the smaller proportions who attain extreme old age, and also in the periods of the deaths of heads of families of this class, by which widowhood is produced. These last will be shown in subsequent tables.

* * *

On comparing the proportion of deaths amongst all classes between one district and another, as well as between class and class, the general influence of the locality becomes strikingly apparent. The difference of mortality between one large district of the metropolis and another is shown in the following tabular view, made up by Mr. Alexander Finlaison,[1] from the superintendent-registrar's weekly returns of the mortality prevalent in the chief registration districts of the metropolis during the different seasons of the year. But the extremes of difference are more strikingly exhibited in smaller districts.

---

1. Alexander Finlaison should not be confused with John Finlaison, Actuary to the National Debt Office.

IV. Comparative Chances of Life in Different Classes

CLASSES	Total No. of Deaths under 20 Years of Age	Proportion of Deaths which occurred at the under-mentioned periods of Age			Proportion of Deaths under 20 Years to Total Deaths
		Between 0 — 5	Between 5 — 10	Between 10 — 20	
Gentry and Professional Persons, Children of					
Manchester	21	1 in 3	1 in 24	1 in 54	1 in 3
Leeds	20	1 in 5	1 in 26	1 in 40	1 in 4
Liverpool	61	1 in 3	1 in 11	1 in 23	1 in 2½
Bath	32	1 in 11	1 in 12	1 in 31	1 in 4½
Bethnal Green	33	1 in 5	1 in 20	1 in 13	1 in 3
Strand Union	21	1 in 6	1 in 29	1 in 29	1 in 4
Kendal Union	15	1 in 7	1 in 26	1 in 9	1 in 3
County of Wilts (Unions of)	25	1 in 9	1 in 40	1 in 13	1 in 5
County of Rutland (Unions of)	4	1 in 4	—	—	1 in 7
Total	232	1 in 5	1 in 19	1 in 19	1 in 3½
Farmers, Tradesmen, and Persons similarly circumstanced, Children of					
Manchester	444	1 in 2	1 in 18	1 in 27	1 in 2
Leeds	425	1 in 2	1 in 18	1 in 18	1 in 2
Liverpool	1,033	1 in 2	1 in 19	1 in 33	1 in 1¾
Bath	78	1 in 4	1 in 24	1 in 30	1 in 3
Bethnal Green	142	1 in 2	1 in 20	1 in 28	1 in 2
Strand Union	99	1 in 3	1 in 20	1 in 25	1 in 2
Kendal Union	47	1 in 4	1 in 35	1 in 14	1 in 3
County of Wilts (Unions of)	54	1 in 7	1 in 27	1 in 15	1 in 4
County of Rutland (Unions of)	174	1 in 3	1 in 30	1 in 17	1 in 3
Total	2,496	1 in 2¼	1 in 20	1 in 23	1 in 2
Agricultural and other Labourers, Artisans, and Servants, Children of					
Manchester	3,106	1 in 2	1 in 22	1 in 19	1 in 1½
Leeds	2,245	1 in 2	1 in 14	1 in 14	1 in 1½
Liverpool	4,004	1 in 1½	1 in 15	1 in 33	1 in 1¼
Bath	508	1 in 2	1 in 19	1 in 18	1 in 1¾
Bethnal Green	908	1 in 2	1 in 15	1 in 30	1 in 1½
Strand Union	367	1 in 2	1 in 14	1 in 23	1 in 2
Kendal Union	186	1 in 3	1 in 19	1 in 11	1 in 2
County of Wilts (Unions of)	954	1 in 3	1 in 21	1 in 14	1 in 2
County of Rutland (Unions of)	293	1 in 3	1 in 18	1 in 18	1 in 2¼
Total	12,571	1 in 2	1 in 17	1 in 20	1 in 1½

* These Tables are compiled from deaths which took place in Manchester during the year 1840; in Leeds during the year 1840; in Liverpool during the year 1840; in Bath during the year 1839; in Bethnal Green during the year 1839; in the Strand Union during the year 1840; in the Kendal Union during the year ended 30th September, 1841; in the county of Wilts during the year 1840; and in Rutland during the three years 1838, 1839, and 1840.

IV. Comparative Chances of Life in Different Classes

Classes	Total No. of Deaths which occurred between 20 and 60	Proportion of Deaths which occurred at the under-mentioned periods of Age				Proportion of Deaths from 20 to 60 to Total Deaths
		Between 20—30	Between 30—40	Between 40—50	Between 50—60	
Gentry and Professional Persons and their Families						
Manchester . . .	13	1 in 18	1 in 14	1 in 18	1 in 18	1 in 4
Leeds	28	1 in 11	1 in 10	1 in 16	1 in 10	1 in 3
Liverpool . . .	34	1 in 46	1 in 15	1 in 23	1 in 9	1 in 4
Bath	29	1 in 29	1 in 24	1 in 24	1 in 12	1 in 5
Bethnal Green . .	21	1 in 25	1 in 17	1 in 25	1 in 14	1 in 5
Strand Union . .	37	1 in 9	1 in 9	1 in 10	1 in 11	1 in 2¼
Kendal Union . .	18	1 in 13	1 in 13	1 in 7	1 in 17	1 in 3
County of Wilts (Unions of) . .	32	1 in 15	1 in 15	1 in 17	1 in 13	1 in 4
County of Rutland (Unions of) . .	7	1 in 14	1 in 14	1 in 14	1 in 28	1 in 4
Total . . .	219	1 in 17	1 in 14	1 in 16	1 in 12	1 in 4
Tradesmen, Farmers, &c.						
Manchester . . .	220	1 in 14	1 in 11	1 in 13	1 in 18	1 in 3¼
Leeds	238	1 in 12	1 in 14	1 in 14	1 in 19	1 in 3½
Liverpool . . .	481	1 in 22	1 in 13	1 in 14	1 in 13	1 in 3½
Bath	109	1 in 11	1 in 7	1 in 9	1 in 9	1 in 2¼
Bethnal Green . .	92	1 in 15	1 in 11	1 in 12	1 in 11	1 in 3
Strand Union . .	71	1 in 16	1 in 22	1 in 10	1 in 9	1 in 3
Kendal Union . .	43	1 in 8	1 in 14	1 in 17	1 in 17	1 in 3
County of Wilts (Unions of) . .	65	1 in 22	1 in 14	1 in 10	1 in 12	1 in 3½
County of Rutland (Unions of) . .	108	1 in 15	1 in 16	1 in 19	1 in 19	1 in 4
Total . . .	1,427	1 in 15	1 in 12	1 in 13	1 in 14	1 in 3½
Agricultural Labourers, Operatives, Servants, &c.						
Manchester . . .	1,149	1 in 16	1 in 14	1 in 18	1 in 17	1 in 4
Leeds	773	1 in 14	1 in 16	1 in 20	1 in 22	1 in 4½
Liverpool . . .	1,205	1 in 17	1 in 18	1 in 17	1 in 24	1 in 4½
Bath	258	1 in 12	1 in 14	1 in 13	1 in 17	1 in 3
Bethnal Green . .	228	1 in 18	1 in 23	1 in 21	1 in 31	1 in 5½
Strand Union . .	212	1 in 13	1 in 12	1 in 13	1 in 13	1 in 3
Kendal Union . .	113	1 in 13	1 in 14	1 in 18	1 in 14	1 in 3¾
County of Wilts (Unions of) . .	492	1 in 13	1 in 18	1 in 18	1 in 19	1 in 4
County of Rutland (Unions of) . .	157	1 in 12	1 in 18	1 in 18	1 in 27	1 in 4
Total . . .	4,587	1 in 15	1 in 17	1 in 18	1 in 20	1 in 4

IV. Comparative Chances of Life in Different Classes

CLASSES	Total No. of Deaths which occurred above 60	Proportion of Deaths which occurred at the under-mentioned periods of Age				Proportion of Deaths above 60 to Total Deaths
		Between 60—70	Between 70—80	Between 80—90	90 and upwards	
Gentry and Professional Persons and their Families						
Manchester	20	1 in 6	1 in 8	1 in 14	—	1 in 2¾
Leeds	31	1 in 7	1 in 7	1 in 13	1 in 79	1 in 2½
Liverpool	42	1 in 7	1 in 7	1 in 34	—	1 in 3¼
Bath	85	1 in 5	1 in 6	1 in 5	1 in 146	1 in 1¾
Bethnal Green	47	1 in 6	1 in 5	1 in 9	1 in 101	1 in 2
Strand Union	28	1 in 7	1 in 9	1 in 22	1 in 86	1 in 3
Kendal Union	19	1 in 17	1 in 7	1 in 6	1 in 52	1 in 2¾
County of Wilts (Unions of)	62	1 in 5	1 in 4	1 in 12	1 in 119	1 in 2¼
County of Rutland (Unions of)	17	1 in 9	1 in 4	1 in 6	1 in 28	1 in 1¾
Total	351	1 in 6	1 in 6	1 in 10	1 in 115	1 in 2¼
Farmers and Tradesmen, and Families						
Manchester	61	1 in 21	1 in 38	1 in 145	1 in 242	1 in 12
Leeds	161	1 in 13	1 in 12	1 in 34	1 in 824	1 in 5
Liverpool	224	1 in 16	1 in 22	1 in 51	1 in 869	1 in 8
Bath	57	1 in 9	1 in 12	1 in 40	1 in 122	1 in 4¼
Bethnal Green	44	1 in 13	1 in 15	1 in 93	1 in 278	1 in 6¼
Strand Union	51	1 in 9	1 in 13	1 in 22	—	1 in 4¼
Kendal Union	48	1 in 6	1 in 10	1 in 13	—	1 in 3
County of Wilts (Unions of)	99	1 in 7	1 in 6	1 in 10	1 in 31	1 in 2¼
County of Rutland (Unions of)	168	1 in 8	1 in 7	1 in 9	1 in 90	1 in 2⅛
Total	913	1 in 12	1 in 14	1 in 29	1 in 122	1 in 5
Agricultural Labourers, Operatives, Servants, &c.						
Manchester	374	1 in 20	1 in 43	1 in 149	1 in 772	1 in 12
Leeds	377	1 in 20	1 in 23	1 in 62	1 in 485	1 in 9
Liverpool	385	1 in 27	1 in 47	1 in 102	1 in 1865	1 in 15
Bath	130	1 in 16	1 in 19	1 in 45	1 in 149	1 in 6¾
Bethnal Green	122	1 in 21	1 in 28	1 in 97	1 in 419	1 in 10¼
Strand Union	95	1 in 12	1 in 23	1 in 84	1 in 225	1 in 7
Kendal Union	114	1 in 11	1 in 9	1 in 15	1 in 207	1 in 3¾
County of Wilts (Unions of)	615	1 in 11	1 in 9	1 in 11	1 in 108	1 in 3½
County of Rutland (Unions of)	227	1 in 10	1 in 8	1 in 10	1 in 75	1 in 3
Total	2,439	1 in 18	1 in 23	1 in 43	1 in 338	1 in 8

IV. Comparative Chances of Life in Different Classes

Seasons	Weeks	West District	North District	Central District	East District	South District	Whole Metropolis	Deaths in the Four Seasons out of 10,000 Persons
Winter	13	2,127	2,588	3,064	3,227	3,542	14,548	78
Spring	13	1,611	2,066	2,264	2,264	2,682	10,887	58
Summer	13	1,486	1,817	2,064	2,220	2,458	10,045	54
Autumn	13	1,518	1,959	2,144	2,476	2,655	10,752	57
Totals	52	6,742	8,430	9,536	10,187	11,337	46,232	247
Population enumerated, 1841		300,705	365,660	373,806	392,496	438,060	1,870,727	
Deaths out of 10,000 inhabitants		224	231	255	260	259	247	
No. of Inhabitants out of which 1 death happened		44·60	43·38	39·20	38·53	38·64	40,464	

The West District comprises Kensington, St. George, Hanover Square, Westminster, St. Martin-in-the-Fields, St. James.

The North District „ St. Marylebone, St. Pancras, Islington and Hackney.

The Central District „ St. Giles and St. George, Strand, Holborn, Clerkenwell, St. Luke, East London, West London, City of London.

The East District „ Shoreditch, Bethnal Green, Whitechapel, St. George-in-the-East, Stepney, Poplar.

The South District „ St. Saviour's, St. Olave, Bermondsey, St. George, Southwark, Newington, Lambeth, Camberwell, Rotherhithe, Greenwich.

The female is most in the house; she is the most regular and temperate in her habits; the male is subject to the influence of his place of occupation—the operative to his workshop, the clerk to the counting-house, and the merchant to crowded places of business. In the following returns made up by *Mr. Farr*, and in others that will hereafter be cited, the mortality prevalent amongst the females is given separately, as probably indicating most correctly the operation of the noxious influences connected with the place of residence:

Mean Annual Mortality of Females in the following Metropolitan districts in the two Years and a half ending 31st December, 1839:[1]

Districts	Annual Deaths 1 in
Hackney	57·87
St. George, Hanover Square	57·05
Camberwell	55·34
Islington	50·03
Rotherhithe	38·58
Clerkenwell	38·54
St. Luke	38·49
Greenwich	38·42
St. George, Southwark	33·77
East and West London	33·50
St. Giles and St. George	33·46
Whitechapel	28·15

1. Figures abstracted from the *Third Annual Report of the Registrar-General* (1841), Table (o), p. 244.

IV. Comparative Chances of Life in Different Classes

Yet it is to be observed that the best and the worst districts present striking instances of extremes of condition in the residences and the inhabitants. In the Bethnal Green and the Whitechapel unions, in which are found some of the worst conditioned masses of population in the metropolis, we also find good mansions, well drained and protected, inhabited by persons in the most favourable circumstances. Immediately behind rows of the best-constructed houses in the fashionable districts of London are some of the worst dwellings, into which the working classes are crowded; and these dwellings, by the noxious influences described, are the foci of disease. These returns are all from large parishes, containing the mean results from all classes. If it had been practicable to give correctly the average rate of mortality prevalent in different classes of streets, the variation of results, it is to be presumed, from the variations of circumstances, would have been much greater. Since the character of the residences of many of the labouring classes, and the condition of their places of work and their habits are known, it is to be considered that where the occupations are duly registered, returns, on the principle of those we have first given of the average age of death amongst particular classes, will afford the most close approximation to accuracy, or the best indications of the extent of the operation of the noxious circumstances under which each of those classes is placed.*

---

* A brief explanation of the construction of tables of mortality may be desirable to prevent misapprehensions by those who are unacquainted with the nature of such evidence. If amongst 4,481 who die each year, as at Leeds, it be found that altogether, man, woman, and child, they have lived 92,734 years, that number equally divided, without distinction of the old and young, gives 21 years as the *average period of life*. The variations of such average periods, as shown by the tables showing the mean periods of death of a whole population, are deemed the best test of its condition and progress. The tables of *proportional mortality* are such as those of Liverpool, where, out of 223,054 inhabitants, 7,435 die; that is to say, one-thirtieth of the ascertained population are swept away every year. Such tables only serve, however, for remote comparison of the condition of different districts, for it will be perceived how large will be the different conditions of two communities having exactly the same proportions of mortality, but in one of which the deaths occur principally amongst the infant population, and the other in which they occur amongst the adults. Thus in all the parishes of Leeds, where the average age of deaths of all who die is 21 years, since the deaths occur chiefly at young ages amongst the labouring classes, the proportions of the population who die annually is only 1 in 37. The average age of death, or the average extent of life to every individual, may go on increasing, and yet the proportions who die remain the same. Hence it is that statistical returns of the proportions of death, which are so generally used, are fundamentally unstable as means of ascertaining the progressive sanitary condition of a population in different countries. The *probabilities of life* at different periods of life on which insurance companies act, are determined by tables of a different construction. To form a table of the probabilities of life at given periods, in 1,000 cases say, the date of the birth in each case is ascertained, and observations are made of how many remain alive at the end of each year at the different periods of life. From the different ages at which that 1,000 have died, it is held to be probable that every other 1,000 persons similarly circumstanced will die. The observations on which tables of this description have been founded have generally been from mixed classes

IV. Comparative Chances of Life in Different Classes

The annexed linear view of the numbers of deaths from the chief diseases during every month of two years in the metropolis will be of interest as showing the influence of the seasons, and especially of the winter, when there is the most cold, wet, and crowding.[1]

In Scotland we have not the advantage of systematized registries of mortality or of the causes of mortality, and we are therefore unable to make the same comparisons as in England[2]; yet so far as the records of the dispensaries serve, they are confirmatory of the returns with respect to the different rates of mortality in differently conditioned districts in England. Thus, in a report from Leith, it is stated that:

'Contagious febrile diseases of all kinds are met with in Leith, particularly typhus, which in certain seasons is prevalent to a great extent. The parts of the town in which it seems to prevail chiefly (so far as can be deduced from the records of the Leith Dispensary for the last five years) are the central and most crowded districts in which the number of cases amongst the poor during the last five years have been in the proportion of 1 to 6 of the whole population, while in other districts not so central in situation, but inhabited by persons of nearly the same class, the proportion has been not above 1 to 13 within these districts. One locality containing a population of 1,579, has produced 433 cases of contagious fevers in general (of which 306 were of typhus) in dispensary practice, within five years, being in the ratio of 1 to $3\frac{2}{3}$ of fevers in general, and 1 to $5\frac{1}{8}$ of typhus to the gross population; of these 433 cases, 130 of all fevers, and 96 of typhus, occurred in the two narrow streets (St. Andrew's-street and Giles's-street) which bound the district to the north and south, the remainder in the narrow lanes and closes communicating with them. These may be regarded as the most unhealthy parts of the town.'

An impression is often prevalent that a heavy mortality is an unavoidable condition of all large towns, and of a town population in general. It has, however, been shown that groups of cottages on a high hill, exposed

---

* contd.:
differently circumstanced, and no observations on a basis sufficiently large, that I am aware, have been made to determine the probabilities of life to any one class of workpeople, or to any one class of professional persons. The three tables of the proportions of deaths at different ages would be of little service to indicate the probability of life at different ages unless we could ascertain with exactness the precise numbers of the classes *living* from which the deaths have occurred. More than half the children of the working classes die, and only one-fifth of the children of the gentry die, before the fifth year of age; and after having attained that age, the *probabilities of life* of the labourer's child might be greater than that of the child of the person of the superior classes; but though we have other evidence that the reverse is the case, we have not the evidence of well-constructed tables of the probability of life at different periods strictly applicable to that class. Though the proportions per cent. of those who die in the higher and in the lower classes approximate in the periods between 20 and 60 years of age, yet we know that the probabilities of life in each class at each period are widely different. The probable duration of life of a miner who had attained 40 years of age may not be, and we have reason to believe is not, half that of the agricultural labourer, not one-third that of a person of the higher ranks who had attained the same period.

---

1. This chart has not been reproduced in this edition.
2. Civil registration was introduced in Scotland in 1855.

to the most salubrious breezes, when cleanliness is neglected are often the nests of fever and disease, as intense as the most crowded districts. The mortuary returns of particular districts (in the essentials of drainage, cleansing, and ventilation, to which it is practicable to make other districts approximate, and that too with reductions of existing charges), prove that a high degree of mortality does not invariably belong to the population of all towns, and probably not necessarily to any, even where the population is engaged in manufactures. The proportion of deaths appears in some of the suburbs of the metropolis (as at Hackney), and of Manchester and Leeds, to be lower than amongst the highest classes in two of the agricultural counties.

It appears from the report of Dr. d'Espine, one of the members of the Council of Health of Geneva, who has examined the records of the mortality prevalent amongst the population *extra muros*, as well as that in the city (which will hereafter be submitted to special notice), that the deaths were in the rural districts 1 in 39·3; whilst in the city they were 1 in 44·7 of the whole of the population in the year 1838. In the poorest and worst conditioned of the rural districts the proportions of the deaths were the greatest. In the year 1837 the deaths were in the poorest of the rural districts 1 in 38·6; in the intermediate district, 1 in 40·8; in the richest district, 1 in 53·2.

In comparison with the very high state of the chances of life in the county of Wilts, the city of Bath presents an example confirmatory of this view. The *Rev. Whitwell Elwin* has supplied the following return of the chances of life amongst the different classes in that city. Out of 1286 cases of death in 1840, the results were as follow:

No. of Deaths		Average Age of Deceased
146	Gentlemen, professional persons, and their families	55
244	Tradesmen and their families	37
896	Mechanics, labourers, and their families	25

The very high average chances of life amongst the middle classes, which is nearly the same as that of the farmers, &c. of the agricultural districts, is the fact adduced as most strongly proving the salubrity of the place.

'In making these returns,' says Mr. Elwin, 'I have thrown out all visitors and occasional residents, and my knowledge of the locality, with the assistance of the clerk of the union, has enabled me to attain complete accuracy with respect to the gentry, and a close approximation to it in the remaining cases. The difference in the ages of these several classes presents to my mind a tolerably exact scale of the difference of their abodes. The large houses, the broad streets, looking almost invariably on one side or other upon parks or gardens or open country, the spacious squares, the crescents built upon the brows of the hills without a single obstruction to the pure air of heaven, give the gentry of Bath that superiority over other grades and other cities which their longevity indicates. And herein, it appears to me, consists the value of the return. It shows that the congregation of men is not of necessity unhealthy; nay, that towns, possessing as they do superior medical skill and readier access to advice, may, under favourable circumstances, have an advantage over the country. The situation of the tradesmen of Bath, inferior as it is to that of the gentry, is better than that of their own station in other places. The streets they chiefly inhabit, though with many exceptions, are wide, and swept

IV. Comparative Chances of Life in Different Classes 235

by free currents of air, with houses large and well ventilated. The condition of the poor is worse than would be anticipated from the other portions of the town. They are chiefly located in low districts at the bottom of the valley, and narrow alleys and confined courts are very numerous. Yet even here we have an unquestionable advantage over most large towns. It was only yesterday that I was expressing my horror to a medical gentleman at some portions of the habitations of the poor, when he replied, that it excited little attention, because they were so much better than what was to be seen in other parts of the kingdom.

'Whatever influence occupation and other circumstances may have upon mortality, no one can inspect the registers without being struck by the deteriorated value of life in inferior localities, even where the inhabitants were the same in condition with those who lived longer in better situations. The average age of death among the gentlemen was as high as 60, till I came, at the conclusion, to a small but damp district, in which numerous cases of fever brought down the average to 54. So again with the shopkeepers, the average was reduced two by the returns from streets which, though inhabited by respectable men, were narrow in front and shut in at the back. The average among the labourers was greatly diminished by the returns from some notorious courts, and raised again in a still higher proportion by districts which appertained rather to the country than the town. Of three cases of centenarians, one of whom had attained the vast age of 106, two belonged to this favoured situation. Not but that great ages were to be found in the worst parts as in the best, or that particular streets did not in a measure run counter to the rule. Still, wherever I brought into opposition districts of considerable extent, I found the law more or less to obtain. Bath is a favourable town to institute the comparison, from presenting such marked contrasts in its houses, and the inquiry being little complicated by the presence of noxious trades, which in some towns would necessarily disturb every calculation of the kind. Even here a colony of shoemakers would bring down the average of its healthiest spot to the age of childhood. My attention was called to this circumstance by the clerk incidentally remarking that more shoemakers were married at his office, and were uniformly more dirty and ill-dressed, than any other class of persons. The proneness to marriage or concubinage in proportion to the degradation of the parties is notorious, and I anticipated from the fact an abundant offspring, afterwards to be carried off by premature disease. Accordingly I went with this view through several of the registers, and the result was, that while the average of death amongst the families of labourers and artisans in general was 24 and 25, that of shoemakers was only 14. Had the shoemakers been excluded from the former average, as for the purpose of this comparison they should have been, the disproportion would be some years greater.

'The deaths from fever and contagious diseases I found to be almost exclusively confined to the worst parts of the town. An epidemic small-pox raged at the end of the year 1837, and carried off upwards of 300 persons; yet of all this number I do not think there was a single gentleman, and not above two or three tradesmen. The residences of the labouring classes were pretty equally visited, disease showing here and there a predilection for particular spots, and settling with full virulence in Avon-street and its offsets. I went through the registers from the commencement, and observed that, whatever contagious or epidemic diseases prevailed,—fever, small-pox, influenza,—this was the scene of its principal ravages; and it is the very place of which every person acquainted with Bath would have predicted this result. Everything vile and offensive is congregated there. All the scum of Bath—its low prostitutes, its thieves, its beggars—are piled up in the dens rather than houses of which the street consists. Its population is the most disproportioned to the accommo-

IV. Comparative Chances of Life in Different Classes

dation of any I have ever heard; and to aggravate the mischief, the refuse is commonly thrown under the staircase; and water more scarce than in any quarter of the town. It would hardly be an hyperbole to say that there is less water consumed than beer; and altogether it would be more difficult to exaggerate the description of this dreadful spot than to convey an adequate notion to those who have never seen it. A prominent feature in the midst of this mass of physical and moral evils is the extraordinary number of illegitimate children; the off-spring of persons who in all respects live together as man and wife. Without the slightest objection to the legal obligation, the moral degradation is such that marriage is accounted a superfluous ceremony, not worth the payment of the necessary fees; and on one occasion, when it was given out that these would be dispensed with, upwards of 50 persons from Avon-street, who had lived together for years, voluntarily came forward to enter into a union. And thus it invariably happens in crowded haunts of sin and filth, where principle is obliterated, and where public opinion, which so often operates in the place of principle, is never heard; where, to say truth, virtue is treated with the scorn which in better society is accorded to vice. I have been rendered familiar with these places by holding a curacy in the midst of them for upwards of a year, and my duty as chaplain to the union, in visiting the friends of paupers or discharged paupers themselves, keep up the knowledge I then contracted.

'I think these facts supply us with important conclusions. Whether we compare one part of Bath with another or Bath with other towns, we find health rising in proportion to the improvement of the residences; we find morality, in at least a great measure, following the same law, and both these inestimable blessings within the reach of the legislature to secure. When viewed in this light, these investigations, so often distressing and disgusting, acquire dignity and importance.'

The suffering and expense of life prevalent in differently situated districts observed in this country, are consistent with the experience of the continent.

In a report prepared by M. Villermé[1], as the reporter of a committee of the Royal Academy of Medicine at Paris, appointed to investigate some statistical data on the mortality prevalent in that city, and the department of the Seine, several tables are given to show the proportions of deaths that occur in each of the several arrondissements. In the table on which the most reliance appears to be placed, the mortality in each arrondissement is exhibited as it occurs in the private residences. In the following table the arrondissements are arranged in the order of the proportions in which the houses are exempted from taxation, on the ground of the poverty of the inhabitants, beginning with the arrondissements where the exemptions are the fewest, where the houses are the largest and most valuable, and proceeding to those where the exemptions are most numerous, and the houses the least in size, as indicated by the value. The average of exempted houses, with slight exceptions, he considers a fair indication of the average condition of each arrondissement as compared with the other arrondissements. In this table I have included a column showing the deaths of persons from each arrondissement who die in the public hospitals and other places appropriated to

---

1. L. R. Villermé, *De la Mortalité dans les divers Quartiers de Paris* (Paris 1826).

IV. Comparative Chances of Life in Different Classes

the care of the sick. These tables perhaps comprise the whole of the mortality that occurs in that capital. I have added the proportions of deaths from cholera in each arrondissement, which followed in the highest and the lowest arrondissements the general law of mortality, with some irregularities in the intermediate arrondissements which I have not seen accounted for:

ARRONDISSEMENTS	Proportion of Tenements exempted from Taxation	Annual Average Value of Tenement	Deaths in Private Houses		Total of Deaths in the House and at the Hospitals		Cholera
			Period from 1817 to 1821	Period from 1822 to 1826	Period from 1817 to 1821	Period from 1822 to 1826	
		fr.	1 in	1 in	1 in	1 in	1 in
3. Montmartre	0·07	425	62	71	38	43	90
2. Chaussée d'Antin	0·11	604	60	67	43	48	107
1. Roule, Tuileries	0·11	497	58	66	45	52	82
4. St. Honoré, Louvre	0·15	328	58	62	33	34	54
11. Luxembourg, &c	0·19	257	51	61	33	39	17
6. Porte St. Denis, Temple	0·21	242	54	58	35	38	62
5. Faubourg St. Denis	0·22	225	53	64	34	42	67
7. St. Avoie	0·22	217	52	59	35	41	34
10. Monnaie, Invalides	0·23	285	50	49	36	36	34
9. Ile St. Louis	0·31	172	44	50	25	30	22
8. St. Antoine	0·32	172	43	46	25	28	36
12. Jardin du Roi	0·38	147	43	44	24	26	35
In all Paris					32	36	

It will be observed that in each table the mortality is the lowest in the three richest arrondissements (1, 2, and 3), and is the highest in the three arrondissements, which are positively the poorest, namely, the 8th, 9th, and 12th. Similar results were deduced from comparisons of the mortality prevalent in streets inhabited by different classes; and from comparisons of the different rates of mortality prevalent amongst persons of the same condition as to income, but residing in houses of favourable or unfavourable construction and situation.

If we could ascertain the rates of mortality formerly prevalent in the separate districts of each large town, it is probable we should find that the improvement in the average chances of life of the whole town has been raised principally by the improved chances in the districts where the streets have been widened, paved, and cleansed, and the houses enlarged and drained; and that the amount of sickness and chances of life in the inferior districts are as little altered as their general physical condition. The present condition of those parts of London where the average mortality is 1 in 28 annually, appears to be not dissimilar to the general condition of the whole metropolis about a century ago, which was said to be about 1 in 20, a rate still to be found in some of the most neglected streets.

Dr. Heberden, in an able paper which he wrote at the beginning of the present century, on the disappearance of several diseases in London, ascribes the fact, and the advance of the public health, to the improvements that have gradually taken place in the widening, paving, and cleansing the streets since the great conflagration. He observes that 'the annual pestilential fever of Constantinople very much resembles that of our gaols and crowded hospitals,' and 'is only called plague when attended with buboes and carbuncles.' He ascribes the exemption to 'our change of manners, our love of cleanliness and ventilation, which have produced amongst us, I do not say an incapability, but a great inaptness any longer to receive it.' The examination of the disease prevalent in the poorer districts, however, raises the question whether they have not, in the 'pestilential fever by which they are ravaged,' any other than a type of the malady from which it is supposed the country is exempted. The fever itself is almost as severe in particular neighbourhoods and in unfavourable states of the weather, as it is stated to be in the bad quarters of Constantinople.[1]

The like improvement in the public health that has followed the slow structural improvements in the best districts of the metropolis has been displayed in Paris, where some of the worst districts which remain in a condition not dissimilar to that in which the whole of Paris is described to have been, in closeness and filth, and where the chances of life have remained nearly in the same low condition. M. De Villermé, in proof of an improvement commensurate with the improvements that have been made in the condition of the streets and houses, and the habits of the inhabitants, cites a curious document of the date of the fourteenth century, namely, the register of a tax levied upon all assessable persons of Paris, when Philip-le-Bel knighted his eldest son, who afterwards succeeded him under the name of Louis the Xth. The persons assessed were housekeepers, manufacturers, merchants, masters of the different handicrafts, master jewellers, master masons, master upholsterers, haberdashers, confectioners, butchers, brewers, wine, corn, and cloth merchants, the heads of houses, amongst whom mortality in the present times would be slight compared with that prevalent amongst the lower classes. From the number of this class who are named and registered street by street by the parish priests, as having died between the date of the assessment and the date when the tax was levied, it appears that 232 out of 6,042 died in thirteen months and a half, during a time which was not remarked for any extraordinary sickness. From hence it is inferred that the general annual mortality in Paris could not be less at the commencement of the 14th century than one-twentieth or a twenty-second part of the whole population; whereas in later times the general mortality has not been known to exceed one thirty-second part. The general mortality, therefore, or rather the mortality of a high and select class, was worse in the 14th century than the mortality in the worst districts in the 19th, where it was 1 in 24.

'But it will be said,' observes M. Villermé, 'how can so dreadful a mortality be admitted to have taken place in a climate so salubrious as that of Paris? I confess that if, in order to justify that statement, I had nothing but the book of assessment of the year 1313, I should not have allowed myself at this distance of time to have made any use of the facts which are found recorded in the book of which I am speaking; but the accounts of the time inform us how much public *hygiène* was then neglected, and that in Paris particularly, the horrible

---

1 . William Heberden the Younger, *Observations on the Increase and Decrease of different Diseases and particularly of the Plague* (1801), p. 87. The passage in question is, in fact, quoted by Heberden from Sir John Pringle, *Diseases of the Army*.

IV. Comparative Chances of Life in Different Classes 239

filth of the streets was insupportable, so much were they encumbered with dirt of every kind.

'Some idea may be formed of the dirtiness of the streets of Paris, towards the end of the fourteenth century, from the words of an ordinance of Charles VI issued in 1388, 'And whereas the pavements of Paris are much injured and fallen into decay, so that in many places no horse or carriage can go without very great danger and inconvenience, and whereas this town has long been, and still is, full of dirt, rubbish, and ordure, which each person has left at his own door, so that it is a great horror, and a great displeasure to all persons of respectability and honour, and a great scandal and shame to this city, and a great grief and prejudice to the human beings dwelling in and frequenting the said city, who by the infection of the stinking mass of filth, have fallen in times past into great illness and infirmities of body, and great mortality.'

'It must be borne in mind (many other facts prove it),' observes M. Villermé, 'that the humble citizens of the present day, artisans for example, are for the most part much better off, as regards air, and those conveniencies which preserve life than persons of much greater wealth were in former times in this capital.' From a passage in Ulpien[1], it is estimated that the chances of life is in ancient Rome as deduced from the experience of a select class was 30 years.

He states, that the first agent to improvement is changing the infected air that they inspired in Paris for air that is pure. In the recent progress of the same change it has been observed there, as in this country, that parts of streets better paved and cleansed are marked by the comparative infrequency of disease.

Yet how much remains to be done is shown by the fact that in Paris, with a drier and more salubrious climate, the mortality is still greater than in London; and that the advantages of which M. Villermé justly speaks so highly, are distributed with extreme inequality, is apparent from his tables, which show that in one district the mortality has diminished to 1 in 52; whilst in another it remains as great as 1 in 26 annually. So we have seen that in London it ranges from 1 in 28 to 1 in 57; and it will be seen that in the township of Manchester, a population of nearly 80,000, one twenty-eighth are swept away annually, whilst, in a favoured suburban district, no more than one sixty-third part die.

I have been favoured by M. Ducpetiaux, the Inspector-general of prisons in Belgium, with the copy of a report on an inquiry similar to the present, into the condition of the labouring population in Brussels. I have submitted an extract from it in the Appendix[2], descriptive of the general condition in which their residences were found. When the proportion which the well-conditioned houses of that city bear to the great mass is considered, it will not excite surprise to those who have traversed the poorer districts to find that the average mortality amongst the whole population was, in the year 1840, 1 in 24. In 1829, it appears to have been 1 in 21.

In illustration of the moral and social effects to be anticipated from measures for the removal of the causes of pestilence amongst the labour-

---

1. Domitius Ulpianus, Roman jurist.
2. 'Extract from the report of the commission appointed by the Central Board of Public Health to ascertain the condition of the dwellings of the working classes in Brussels, and to suggest means for their improvement', *San. Rep.*, Appendix 20, pp. 429-30.

IV. Comparative Chances of Life in Different Classes

ing classes, and for the increase of their duration of life, concurrently with an increase of the population. I refer to the effects experienced in Geneva from the like improvements effected during the lapse of centuries. That city is, so far as I am aware, the only one in Europe in which there is an early and complete set of registers of marriages, births, and deaths. These registries were established in the year 1549, and are viewed as pre-appointed evidences to civil rights, and are kept with great care. This registration includes the name of the disease which has caused the death, entered by a district physician who is charged by the State with the inspection of every person who dies within his district. A second table is made up from certificates setting forth the nature of the disease, with a specification of the symptoms, and observations required to be made by the private physician who may have had the care of the deceased. These registries have been the subject of frequent careful examinations. It appears from them that the progress of the population *intra muros* of that city has been as follows:

In the Year	Inhabitants	Proportionate rate of Increase as compared with 1589
1589	13,000	100
1693	16,111	124, or 24 per cent.
1698	16,934	130, or 30 ,,
1711	18,500	142, or 42 ,,
1721	20,781	160, or 60 ,,
1755	21,816	168, or 68 ,,
1781	24,810	191, or 91 ,,
1785	25,500	196, or 96 ,,
1789	26,140	201, or 101 ,,
1805	22,300	171, or 71 ,,
1812	24,158	186, or 86 ,,
1822	24,886	191, or 91 ,,
1828	26,121	201, or 101 ,,
1834	27,177	209, or 109 ,,

It is proved in a report by *M. Edward Mallet,* one of the most able that have been made from these registries, that this increase of the population has been followed by an increase in the probable duration of life in that city:

	Years	Months	Days	Proportionate rate of Increase as compared with the end of 16th Century
Towards the end of the 16th century the probabilities of life were, to every individual born . .	8	7	26	100
In the 17th century .	13	3	16	153, or 53 per cent.
1701-1750 . .	27	9	13	321, or 221 ,,
1751-1800 . .	31	3	5	361, or 261 ,,
1801-1813 . .	40	8	0	470, or 370 ,,
1814-1833 . .	45	0	29	521, or 421 ,,

IV. Comparative Chances of Life in Different Classes

The progression of the population and the increased duration of life had been attended by a progression in happiness: as prosperity advanced marriages became fewer and later;* the proportion of births were reduced, but greater numbers of the infants born were preserved;† and the proportion of the population in manhood became greater. In the early and barbarous periods, the excessive mortality was accompanied by a prodigious fecundity. In the ten last years of the 17th century, a marriage still produced five children and more; the probable duration of life attained was not 20 years, and Geneva had scarcely 17,000 inhabitants. Towards the end of the 18th century there was scarcely three children to a marriage, and the probabilities of life exceeded 32 years. At the present time a marriage only produces $2\frac{3}{4}$ children; the probability of life is 45‡ years, and Geneva, which exceeds 27,000 in population, has arrived at a high degree of civilization and of '*prospérité matérielle.*' In

---

* It is the practice in Geneva for female servants to delay marriage until they have saved enough to furnish a house, &c. In illustration of this state of things it is stated that in 290 out of 956 marriages, the female was at the time of marriage older than the male. With further advances in prosperity, it is anticipated that age of marriage would again diminish.

† 'Out of 100 deaths in the 16th century, 25·92 were children in their first year; in the 17th century, 23·72; in the 18th century, 20·12; in 1801-13, they were 16·57; and in 1814-33, they were 13·85.' In Liverpool, the number of children which in the year 1840 died under one year of age was no less than 23 per cent., or what it was in Geneva in the 17th century. In the county of Wilts where the proportionate mortality is 1 in 58, the deaths of children in the first year were 16 per cent. Dr. Griffin, in a report on the sanitary condition of the population of Limerick,[1] where the births appear to bear such proportions to the marriages as they appear to have borne in Geneva in the earliest periods, namely, of five children to a marriage, and more in the worst-conditioned districts, makes an important observation on the subject: 'I find that as the poor nurse their own children, there is in general an interval of about two years between the birth of one child and that of the next; but if the child dies early on the breast, this interval will be much shorter; and if this occurs often, there will be a certain number born as it were *for the purpose of dying*; and these being soon replaced, the same number may still be preserved as if there had been few or no deaths, or only the ordinary number.' Of these 55 per cent. died.

‡ The registries in England at present supply no means of distinguishing the migrant population who die in given places; and in each return a small proportion of deaths have been omitted where the station of the party has not been described; but taking as approximations the returns of the ages of all who die, no district examined appears to present so high a probability of life as at Geneva. The average age of all who died in the respective periods before stated appear, from the returns I have obtained, to be in the county of Rutland 39 years; in the Kendal union 36; in the county of Wilts 35 years; in Bath 31; in the Kensington union 30; in the Strand union 28; in the Whitechapel union 27; in Bethnal Green 21; in Leeds 21; in Manchester 20; in Bolton 19; in Liverpool 17. By the Northampton Tables the probability of life in infancy to all born was 25 years; in Carlisle it was 38.

---

1. Daniel Griffin, 'An enquiry into the mortality occurring among the poor of the City of Limerick', *J.R.S.S.*, III (1840), 320.

1836 the population appeared to have attained its summit; the births barely replaced the deaths.

M. Mallet observes, that it is difficult, if not impossible, to distinguish the different causes, and the different degrees of intensity of each of the causes that have tended to produce this result. It is, however, attributed generally to the advance in the condition of all classes; to the medical science of the public health being better understood and applied; to larger and better and cleaner dwellings; more abundant and healthy food; the cessation of the great epidemics which, from time to time, decimated the population; the precautions taken against famine; and better regulated public and private life. As an instance of the effects of regimen in the preservation of life, he mentions that, in an establishment for the care of female orphans taken from the poorest classes, out of 86 reared in 24 years, one only had died. These orphans were taken from the poor. The average mortality on the whole population would have been six times as great.*

An impression of an undefined optimism is frequently entertained by persons who are aware of the wretched condition of a large portion of the labouring population; and this impression is more frequently entertained than expressed, as the ground of inaction for the relief of the prevalent misery from disease, that its ravages form the natural or positive check, or, as Dr. Short[1] terms it, a 'terrible corrective' to the pressure of population on the means of subsistence.

In the most crowded districts, which have been the subject of the present inquiry, the facts do not justify this impression; they show that the theory is inapplicable to the present circumstances of the population. How erroneous the inferences are in their unrestrained generality, which assume that the poverty or the privation which is sometimes the con-

---

* Some consitutions are found which resist vaccine matter. Here and there constitutions appear which resist all the noxious influences by which they are surrounded, and attain extreme old age. Not unfrequently we find the existence of these solitary individuals referred to as proofs of the general salubrity of the very circumstances under which generations have fallen and been buried around them. It is a singular fact, as yet unexplained, that the greatest proportion of centenarians are of the labouring classes; and that instances of them have from time to time appeared amidst the crowded populations in some of the worst neighbourhoods in London, where the average duration of life is the lowest. It is remarked by Mr. Mallet, that in Geneva extreme old age has not participated in the prolongation of life which has taken place in the less advanced ages. In the periods of from 60 to 70 years of age the amelioration is inconsiderable; after 70 years there is no perceptible improvement; after 80 years the aged have indeed a little less probability of life at the present time than they had in the 16th century. Centenarians, who were not rare in the 16th and 17th centuries, now disappear; during the last 27 years Geneva has not produced a single one.

---

1. Thomas Short (1690?-1772), author of *New Observations, Natural, Moral, Civil, Political, and Medical on City, Town, and Country Bills of Mortality* (1750); and *A Comparative History of the Increase and Decrease of Mankind in England and several Countries abroad* (1767).

IV. Comparative Chances of Life in Different Classes 243

sequence,—is always the cause, of the disease, will have been seen from such evidence as that adduced from Glasgow and Spitalfields, proving that the greater proportion of those attacked by disease are in full work at the time; and the evidence from the fever hospitals, that the greatest proportion of the patients are received in high bodily condition. If wages be taken as the test of the means of subsistence, it may be asked how are such facts to be reconciled as these, that at a time when wages in Manchester were 10s. per head weekly on all employed in the manufactories, including children or young persons in the average, so that if three or four members of a family were employed, the wages of a family would be 30s. or 40s. weekly, the average chances of life to all of the labouring classes were only 17 years; whilst in the whole of Rutlandshire, where the wages were certainly not one half that amount, we find the mean chances of life to every individual of the lowest class were 37 years? Or, to take another instance, that whilst in Leeds, where, according to Mr. Baker's report, the wages of the families of the worst-conditioned workers were upwards of 1l. 1s. per week, and the chances of life amongst the whole labouring population of the borough were only 19 years; whilst in the county of Wilts, where the labourer's family would not receive much more than half that amount of wages in money, and perhaps not two-thirds of money's worth in money and produce together, we find the average chances of life to the labouring classes 32 years?

If, in the most crowded districts, the inference is found to be erroneous, that the extent of sickness and mortality is indicative of the pressure of population on the means of subsistence, so is the inference that the ravages act to the extent supposed, as a positive check to the increase of the numbers of the population. In such districts the fact is observable, that where the mortality is the highest, the number of births are more than sufficient to replace the deaths, however numerous they may be.

This fact is shown in the following returns from the eight townships which comprehend Manchester and its suburbs, made by the Statistical Society of that town. But I believe the results would be more strongly manifest if the registration of the births and of the residences of the mothers were complete. I have reason to believe that in the lower districts many births, and especially illegitimate births, escape registration, and that many take place in hospitals and workhouses out of the township; whilst in the better conditioned districts the registration is comparatively accurate. I have caused attempts to be made in several of the worst neighbourhoods in Bath and other places, to ascertain with greater precision the actual number of births; but from the migratory character of the population and other circumstances, the efforts failed to do more than to confirm the impression that many had hitherto escaped registration.

The proportion of mortality in the several townships denotes with little variation the state of the streets and houses, and the condition of the inhabitants. The township of Broughton is inhabited almost exclusively by the upper classes, who are connected with Manchester. The houses are new, spacious, and well built; the site is elevated, and offers

IV. Comparative Chances of Life in Different Classes

great facilities for drainage. The township of Cheetham and Crumpsall is also inhabited for the most part by the upper classes, who live in peculiarly good houses, with a superior natural drainage. There is a proportion of the working population resident in this district whose houses are well built, and also favourably situated for drainage. The condition of the habitations of a large proportion of the labouring population in Manchester has already been described.

It will be observed also that the moral as well as the sanitary influences have a coincidence in the larger proportion of the illegitimate births in the worst conditioned districts. In the best conditioned districts the great majority of illegitimate births belong almost exclusively to the more dissipated of the labouring classes who inhabit them.

Localities	Population		Deaths		Total Deaths of Males & Females	Proportion of Births to Population	Proportion of Illegitimate Births to Total Births
	Males	Females	Males	Females			
			1 in	1 in	1 in	1 in	1 in.
Broughton . .	1,554	2,239	44·40	89·56	63·21	36·82	51·50
Cheetham and Crumpsall	3,963	4,862	45·03	63·14	53·48	34·74	50·80
Pendleton . .	5,109	5,796	40·22	49·96	44·87	52·47	12·58
Chorlton-upon-Medlock	12,551	15,771	30·91	47·79	38·48	26·05	32·93
Hulme . .	12,850	13,969	37·24	38·48	37·87	23·17	24·10
Ardwick . .	4,586	5,320	35·55	34·54	35·00	24·27	34·00
Salford . .	24,762	26,760	27·30	36·69	31·42	22·83	21·90
Manchester .	79,061	84,606	26·61	30·15	28·33	26·79	19·20
Total . .	144,436	159,323	28·84	34·62	31·60	25·74	21·26

In the ten registration districts of Leeds the mortality prevalent in them varies coincidently with their physical condition, and the recklessness and immorality as shown in the proportion of illegitimate births, increases in a greater proportion than the mortality; and in this instance also, as in most others, if the registration were more accurate, the proportion of both legitimate and illegitimate births would be still closer to the deaths in the worst conditioned districts.

Registration Districts	Population	Ratio of Deaths to the whole Population	Ratio of Births to the whole Population	Ratio of Illegitimate Births to Total Births
		1 in	1 in	1 in
Chapeltown . .	4,538	57·7	30·6	74·0
Whitkirk . .	3,194	56·0	29·0	36·7
Kirkstall . .	17,816	45·6	24·8	23·1
Rothwell . .	5,557	45·1	28·2	24·6
Wortley . .	16,185	44·4	24·9	26·0
Holbeck . .	16,668	41·9	25·4	24·3
Leeds, West .	32,286	40·4	28·4	19·2
Hunslet . .	15,784	35·5	24·2	21·7
Leeds, North .	30,465	30·9	23·9	14·3
East District (Kirkgate) . .	24,862	28·8	24·3	20·0
Total of Leeds .	167,355	37·3	25·5	20·1

We have seen that in the lowest districts of Manchester of 1,000 children born, more than 570 will have died before they attain the fifth

IV. Comparative Chances of Life in Different Classes

year of their age. In the lowest districts of Leeds the infant mortality is similar. This proportion of mortality M. Mallet designates as the case of a population but little advanced in civilization, ravaged by epidemics—a population in which the 'influences on the lower ages are murderous, but where the great mortality in infancy is compensated by a high degree of fecundity. It is the case of the population in many large towns, especially in past ages.' But whilst in Manchester, where one twenty-eighth of the whole population is annually swept away, the births registered amount to 1 in 26 of the population; in the county of Rutland, where the proportion of deaths is 1 in 52 of the population, the proportion of births, as shown by an average of three years, (by a registration which I apprehend is more complete than in the lower districts of Manchester,) is only 1 to 33 of the population.

The increase of births after a pestilence has been long observed; the coincidence of an increase of births in a proportion to the high rate of mortality in the worst districts has frequently been noted on the continent. M. Quetelet[1] has observed the fact in several countries, and gives instances from which the following are selected:

Countries	Inhabitants		
	For one Death	For one Marriage	For one Birth
Department of Orne	52·4	147·5	44.8
Department of Finisterre . . .	30·4	113·9	26·0
Province of Namur	51·8	141·0	30·1
Province of Zealand	28·5	113·2	21·9

He states that he had often been tempted to attribute these discrepancies to a faulty census of the population; but more attentive researches had induced him to believe that this state of things is dependent on local causes.

M. Bossi, in the Statisque du Department le l'Ain, gives a striking example of the effect of the locality. With a view to study the influences of locality, he divided the department into four portions; and from documents collected during the year 1812, 1813, and 1814, he obtained the following results:

Inhabitants

	To 1 Death annually	To 1 Marriage annually	To 1 Birth annually
In mountain parishes . .	38·3	179	34·8
On the seaside . . .	26·6	145	28·8
In corn districts . . .	24·6	135	27·5
In stagnant and marshy districts	20·8	107	26·1

1. L. A. J. Quetelet, author of *Recherches sur la Population* (Brussels 1827). For an examination of Quetelet's population theories, see D. E. C. Eversley, *Social Theories of Fertility and the Malthusian Debate* (1959), pp. 195-6

IV. Comparative Chances of Life in Different Classes

Notwithstanding the depression of many districts, and the decrease of health amongst the classes in the manufacturing towns from which a large proportion of conscripts are taken, the annual proportions of deaths appear to have decreased.

In 1784, from researches taken in France under Necker's directions, it appeared that there was:

one birth for every	. . . . . .	25·56 inhabitants
one death for every	. . . . . .	30·02 ,,

From 1816 to 1831 there was:

one birth only for every	. . . . .	32 ,,
one death for every	. . . . . .	39·8 ,,

M. Quetelet's returns show that so far as the present state of information can be relied upon, the same law is observed in general action, not only in provinces but in whole countries throughout Europe. It is confirmed by extensive experience occurring in the new world. The trustworthiness of the registration of births and deaths in Mexico are attested by the examination and use of them by Humboldt[1], and have been the subject of legislative proceedings. The ratios of births and deaths in the province of Guanaxuato have been referred to by Sir F. d'Ivernois[2], in illustration of the position that pestilence does not check the progress of population. A large proportion of the inferior Mexican population are reported to 'have converted the gifts of heaven to the sustenance of disgusting misery.' It is reported of this populace that it is 'half clothed, idle, stained all over with vices; in a word, hideous and known under the name of *leperos*, lepers, on account of the malady to which their filth and bad diet subjects them. Nothing can exceed the state of brutality and superstition to which they have been subjected.'*

---

* *Bibliothèque Universelle*, September, 1831.

In Alexandria, which is a seat of pestilence, where the Arab population leave the ordure before their doors (as we have seen large classes of the lower population do in this country), where the dog is the only scavenger of the animal refuse (as the pig is in many districts in our towns), where those who have died of plague remain unburied for days amidst the abodes of the living (as those who have died of fever often do in the poorest districts in this country),—there, under the more powerful action of a burning sun, disease and death are proportionately rife; and, as shown by some returns of death in 1841, out of a population of 60,000, the deaths were 7,017 (of which 1,165 only were from plague), or more than one-tenth of the population. It is known, however, that in the well-cleansed and best streets, inhabited by the European and fluctuating population, the proportion of mortality is not greater than amidst a similar population in the towns of Europe; but it is stated that the lower population, notwithstanding that it has been decimated by the annual mortality, has, within the last quarter of a century, more than doubled.

---

1. These rates are given in Alexander von Humboldt, *Personal Narrative of Travels to the Equinoctial Regions of the New Continent during the Years 1799-1804* (trans. H. M. Williams, 1826), VI, 130.
2. Francis d'Ivernois, *Sur la Mortalité proportionelle de quelques Populations, considérée comme Mesure de leur Aisance et de leur Civilisation, analysé des quinze Régistres de l'Etat civil en France pour les Années 1817-31* (Geneva, 1834).

IV. Comparative Chances of Life in Different Classes

The fecundity of this population, sunk in the lowest vice and misery amidst the means of the highest abundance, was greater than amidst any other whole population in Christendom;* they stood thus in 1825 and 1826:

	1 in
Deaths	19·70
Births	16·08

They are much mistaken who imagine that a similarly conditioned population is not to be found in this country; it is found in parts of the population of every large town; the description of the Mexican populace will recall features characteristic of the wretched population in the worst parts of Glasgow, Edinburgh, London, and Bath, and the lodging-houses throughout the country.

Seeing that the banana (with the plantain or maize) is the chief food of the inferior Mexican populace, their degraded condition has been ascribed to the fertility of that plant, as the degradation of a large proportion of our population has been ascribed to the use of the potatoe, whereas a closer examination would have shown the fact of large classes living industriously and virtuously chiefly on simple food, and preferring saving money to better living; and that, if a high and various meat diet were the cause of health, industry, and morality, those virtues should stand highest amongst the population of the lodging-houses, for more meat and varied food is consumed in those abodes of pestilence than amongst the industrious population of the village. In Manchester, where we have seen that the chances of life are only 17 years, the proportions and varieties of meat consumed by the labouring classes, are as their greater amount of wages compared with the meat consumed by the labouring classes in Rutlandshire, whose mean chances of life are 38 years.† But I apprehend that the superior health in Rutlandshire is as little ascribable to their simpler food as the greater amount of disease

---

* An English military officer, who has had much practice as an engineer, and who has done much to protect the health of the population of one of the South American towns, by drainage, whose opinion I took on the efficiency of measures for cleansing inferior districts, recently informed me that he should take advantage of a favourable change which had occurred in one of the recent revolutions, to return to South America, and try what he agreed was the most efficient course of proceeding, commencing with the middle classes, by inducing the new government to undertake works for bringing water into the houses of the inhabitants, and adopt the self-acting system of cleansing the poorest districts, and the use of the refuse for distant production, on the principles established in this Report.

The authorities in Hamburgh have applied to Mr. Lindley, the engineer, for a plan for the drainage of that town, and he has recommended for adoption the same principles, and the application of the refuse for agriculture, at a distance from the houses, instead of discharging it into the water which washes the town.

† Dr. Bisset Hawkins, the medical Commissioner in the Factory Inquiry, stated in his Report, 'I believe that most travellers are struck by the lowness of stature, the leanness and paleness which present themselves so commonly to the eye at Manchester, and above all, among the factory classes. I have never been in any town in Great Britain nor in Europe in which degeneracy of form

IV. Comparative Chances of Life in Different Classes

amidst the town population is ascribable to the greater proportion of meat which is there consumed. It is probable indeed that the standard of vitality in Rutlandshire might be raised still higher by improvements in the quality of their food. There are abundant reasons to render it desirable that the food of the population should be varied, but it is shown that banishing the potatoe or discouraging its use, or introducing any other food, will not banish disease.

By means of the last census and the last year's completed registration of deaths and births in England, I am enabled to show that there has been an increase of the population from births alone in those parts of the country where the proportionate mortality is the greatest.

Taking the 42 counties as I find them arranged in Mr. Porter's paper on the census;[1] dividing them into three parts, viz., the 14 counties where there has been the least proportionate mortality, the 14 counties where the proportion of mortality has been the greatest, and the 14 counties where the proportion of mortality has been intermediate, I find the results as to the proportionate increase of births to the increase of deaths to be as follows:

	The annual average Rate of Increase of Population has been per 10,000 persons between 1831 and 1841	Proportion of Births and Deaths to Population in the Year ended June 30, 1840	Proportion of Births and Deaths to every 10,000 Persons in same period	Excess in every 10,000 Persons of Births above Deaths
a. The 14 counties where the mortality has been the least	112	deaths (1 in 54), births (1 in 34),	deaths 184 births 297	113
b. The 14 counties where it has been intermediate.	121	deaths (1 in 48), births (1 in 33).	deaths 208 births 302	94
c. The 14 counties where it has been the greatest	183	deaths (1 in 39), births (1 in 29),	deaths 259 births 348	89

† *contd:—*

and colour from the national standard has been so obvious.'[2] From a return obtained in 1836 and presented to the Manchester Statistical Society, of the cattle passing the toll-gates and the meat sold in the markets, it appeared that the consumption exclusively amongst this population could not be less than 105 lbs. each person annually, man, woman, and child, or 450 lbs. yearly per family of butchers' meat alone, exclusively of bacon, pork, fish, and poultry. The wretched personal appearance of this population was only equalled by that of the Irish population of St. Giles, where the man earned from 14s. or 16s. to 1l. per week, (the wife and child earning something in addition,) but where it is their habit to live chiefly on potatoes and use little meat. The effect of a pure atmosphere, independently of diet, is shown in this population when they go into the country during harvest time. After a fortnight or three weeks' absence, in which they will have had little change of living, except, perhaps, taking less spirits, the whole family return with the hue of health.

---

1. G. R. Porter, 'An examination of some facts obtained at the recent enumeration of the inhabitants of Great Britain, as far as the same have been published by the Census Commissioners', *J.R.S.S.*, IV (1841), 277-87.
2. 'Medical Reports by Dr. Hawkins', p. 3, *Second Report of the Royal Commission on the Employment of Children in Factories*, *P.P.*, 1833, XXI.

IV. Comparative Chances of Life in Different Classes

The following are the proportions of birth and deaths to the population in 1840, and the total rate of increase of population between the years 1831 and 1841:

	Deaths per An. 1 to	Births per An. 1 to	Pop. Incr. per Cent.		Deaths per An. 1 to	Births per An. 1 to	Pop. Incr. per Cent.
Hereford	64	45	2·9	Somerset	48	33	7·8
Dorset	61	34	9·7	Derby	47	35	14·7
Cornwall	59	30	13·4	Northampton	47	29	10·9
Devon	58	36	7·8	Warwick	47	31	19·4
Sussex	55	34	10·0	Hunts	46	28	10·3
Southampton	55	37	12·9	Cambridge	45	28	14·2
Essex	53	35	8·6	Surrey	45	33	19·7
Wilts	53	35	8·2	Bedford	44	26	13·0
York, N.R.	53	38	7·2	Northumberland	44	29	12·2
Rutland	53	30	10·0	Westmorland	43	35	2·5
Suffolk	53	32	6·3	York, E.R.	43	34	14·6
Bucks	52	33	6·4	Durham	43	28	27·7
Lincoln	52	31	14·2	York, W.R.	43	27	18·2
Stafford	51	31	24·2	Chester	43	34	18·5
Norfolk	51	34	5·7	Berks	42	28	10·2
Cumberland	51	35	4·8	Middlesex	42	35	16·0
Gloucester	51	37	11·4	Leicester	40	29	9·5
Salop	50	37	7·2	Monmouth	38	26	36·9
Oxford	50	32	6·1	Nottingham	36	28	10·8
Hertford	49	29	9·6	Worcester	33	20	10·4
Kent	48	35	14·4	Lancaster	32	26	24·7

We here find that in the 14 counties where proportionate mortality has been the least, the 184 deaths in 10,000 persons are made up by the 297 births; hence 113, or more than 1 per cent., is added by new births to the existing population. In the 14 intermediate counties where the deaths on every 10,000 persons increase to 208, there the deaths are again made up by 302 births, and 94, or close upon 1 per cent., are again added to the population. In the 14 counties where the increase of the population is the greatest, the deaths in every 10,000 persons are increased to 259, but here also we find that the births are again sufficient to make up for the deaths; they are 348, and increase the population by 89, or less than 1 per cent.

Hence, if the number of births in each 10,000 persons of the 14 counties where the mortality has been the greatest had taken place amongst every 10,000 persons of the counties, where the mortality has been the least, then the increase of population in these latter by births, instead of being 113, would have been 164.*

I must again observe that the registration of births in the most populous town districts, where the mortality is greatest, is the least perfect. The excess of births over deaths may really be taken to be greater than shown in the returns from the districts where the mortality is the greatest.

The estimated increase of population in England in the year 1840, as compared with 1839, is 190,460. In the same period it appears that the births exceeded the deaths by 143,178. The difference between these two amounts, or 47,282, may be considered as the extent of emigration to

* I have referred to the experience since the year 1801 in France, where the registration of births amongst the migratory population of the crowded districts, where the greatest mortality prevails, is likely to have been as

England, together with the cases of births not registered. To whatever extent emigration takes place from England, there must of course have been a proportionate immigration from other places to make up the increase of population beyond the apparent increase from births.

It is observed in some of the worst conditioned of the town districts that the positive numbers of the natives of the aboriginal stock continually diminishes, and that the vacancy as well as the increase is made up by immigration from the healthier district. In a late enumeration of the settled inhabitants of the labouring classes in the lower parts of Westminster, it appeared that not more than one-third of them were natives of London. If inquiry had been made as to whether their parents were natives, it would probably have been found that still fewer had inhabited the district for more than one generation.

Simple enumerations of the numbers of a population are of themselves but imperfect means for judging of its progression in strength. That is best shown in the increased proportions of the adults, who are of the age and strength and skill for productive industry, in the extended period during which each adult labourer occupies his post.

M. Mallet bears testimony that the experience of Geneva is confirmatory of the important rule, that the strength of a people does not depend on the absolute number of its population, but on the relative number of those who are of the age and strength for labour. It is proved that the real and productive value of the population has there increased in a much greater proportion than the increase in the absolute number of the population. The absolute number of the population has only doubled, in the instance of Geneva, during three centuries; but the value of the population has more than doubled upon the purely numerical increase of the population. In other words, a population of 27,000, in which the probability of life is 40 years for each individual, is more than twice as strong for the purposes of production as a population of 27,000 in which the probability or value of life is only 20 years for each individual.

The important general fact of the proportion of adult physical strength to the increased duration of life, or improved sanitary condition of the individuals, is verified by the examinations of the individuals of different classes. M. Villermé states that the difference of strength between classes such as those in which we have seen that the value of life

---

* *contd.:*
imperfect as in England, but that experience is, on the whole, confirmatory, and proves that in the worst districts the births still exceed the mortality.

	Increase of Population in 35 Years in every 10,000 Persons	Proportion of Births in 35 Years to 10,000 of Population	Proportion of Deaths in 35 Years to 10,000 of Population	Excess of Births over Deaths in 10,000 of Population
5 groups of departments of *lowest* mortality	311	10,705	8,079	2,626
6 groups of departments of *mean* mortality	2,396	12,439	10,044	2,395
6 groups of departments of *highest* mortality	4,190	13,024	12,350	674

IV. Comparative Chances of Life in Different Classes 251

differs, is well known to the officers engaged in recruiting the army, but no one had collected the facts to determine the precise difference. The time allowed to M. Villermé only enabled him to do so at Amiens. The result was, that the men of from 20 to 21 years of age were found the more frequently unfit for the trade of arms from their stature, constitution, and health, as they belonged to the poorer classes of the manufacturing labourers. In order to obtain 100 men fit for military service, it was necessary to have as many as 343 men of the poorer classes; whilst 193 conscripts sufficed of the classes in better circumstances. Analogous facts were observed in the greater part of the towns in France in which he conducted his official investigations.*

In the evidence of recruiting officers, collected under the Factory Commission of Inquiry, it was shown that fewer recruits of the proper strength and stature for military service are obtainable now than heretofore from Manchester. I have been informed that of those labourers now employed in the most important manufactories, whether natives or migrants to that town, the sons who are employed at the same work are generally inferior in stature to their parents. Sir James M'Grigor, the Director-general of the Army Medical Board, stated to me the fact, that 'A corps levied from the agricultural districts in Wales, or the northern counties of England, will last longer than one recruited from the manufacturing towns from Birmingham, Manchester, or near the metropolis.' Indeed, so great and permanent is the deterioration, that out of 613 men enlisted, almost all of whom came from Birmingham and five other neighbouring towns, only 238 were approved for service.

The chances of life of the labouring classes of Spitalfields are amongst the lowest that I have met with, and there it is observed of weavers, though not originally a large race, that they have become still more diminutive under the noxious influences to which they are subject. Dr. Mitchell, in his report on the condition of the hand-loom weavers, adduces evidence on this point. One witness well acquainted with the class states, 'They are decayed in their bodies; the whole race of them is rapidly descending to the size of Liliputians. You could not raise a

---

* In recruiting for the French army, the standard is now fixed at 1·566 metres of height, which is about 5 feet $1\frac{1}{2}$ inches English.
Fifty years ago, however, the standard height was 5 feet 4 inches English.
The English standard is for the Foot Guards 5 feet 6 inches.

	lbs. avoirdupois
The mean weight in Belgium (Brussels and environs) of the man is	140·49
In France (Paris and the neighbourhood) the man is .	136·89
The mean weight of the Englishman (taken at Cambridge), from 18 to 25	150·98
(In coaches it is usually considered that it averages 165 lbs.)	

The mean height of the Belgian male is	. .	5 feet $6\frac{3}{10}$ inches
,, Frenchman	. . .	5 feet 4 ,,
,, Englishman	. . .	5 feet $9\frac{1}{2}$,,

(M. Quetelet and M. Villermé, on the authority of M. Tenon, Annuaire de l'Obs. de Bruxelles, 1836).

grenadier company amongst them all. The old men have better complexions than the young.' Another witness who says there were once men as well made in the weaver trade as any other, 'recollects the Bethnal Green and Spitalfields regiment of volunteers during the war as good-looking bodies of men, but doubts if such could be raised now.' Mr. Duce concurs in the fact of the deterioration of their size and appearance within the last 30 years, and attributes it to bad air, bad lodging, bad food, 'which causes the children to grow up an enfeebled and diminutive race of men.'[1]

This depressing effect of adverse sanitary circumstances on the labouring strength of the population, and on its duration, is to be viewed with the greatest concern, as it is a depressing effect on that which most distinguishes the British people, and which it were a truism to say constitutes the chief strength of the nation—the bodily strength of the individuals of the labouring class. The greater portion of the wealth of the nation is derived from the labour obtained by the application of this strength, and it is only those who have had practically the means of comparing it with that of the population of other countries who are aware how far the labouring population of this country is naturally distinguished above others. There is much practical evidence to show that this is not a mere illusion of national vanity, and in proof of this I might adduce the testimony of some of the most eminent employers of large numbers of labourers, whose conclusions are founded on experience in directing the work of labourers from the chief countries in Europe, e.g., Mr. William Lindley, the civil engineer, engaged in the superintendence of the formation of the new railway between Hamburgh and Berlin, found it expedient to import as the foremost labourers for the execution of that work a number of the class of English labourers called navigators. These were recently employed in pile-driving at wages of 5s. per diem, or more than double the amount of wages paid to the German labourers. The German directors were surprised, and remonstrated at the enormously high wages paid to the English labourers; when the engineer directed their attention to the quantity of work performed within a given time, and showed that the wages produced more than amongst the native labourers. English labourers of the same class have been imported to take the foremost labour in the execution of the railways in progress from Havre to Paris,[2] their work at very high wages being found cheaper than the work even of the Norman labourers. Skill and personal strength are combined in an unusually high degree in this class of workmen, but the most eminent employers of labour agree that it is strength of body, combined with strength of will, that gives steadiness and value to the artisan and common English labourer.

Nor is such experience confined to one branch of industry. In the

---

1. 'Report by J. Mitchell on the East of England', *Reports from the Assistant Hand-Loom Commissioners*, P.P. 1840, XXIII, p. 240.
2. For an account of the employment of British capital and labour on German and French railway construction, see W. O. Henderson, *Britain and Industrial Europe*, 1750-1870 (Liverpool 1954), pp. 64-74, 158-60.

IV. Comparative Chances of Life in Different Classes

heaviest works of the manufactories on the continent the strength and energy of the English artisan puts him in advance of all others.

Mr. J. Thomson, of Clitheroe, in treating of a question affecting the branch of industry, cotton-printing, in England, observes:

'This limited production, in proportion to the hands employed,' in France, 'has a deeper source than in styles which may be varied, and simplified, and changed at pleasure. It is to be found in the character and habits of the people, which cannot be changed or moulded at the will of a task-master; nor can an English day's work be had in France for an English day's wages. In 1814, I saw France before she had time to profit by the industrial skill and improvements of England; again in 1817, and in 1824, when I examined with anxious care, during a prolonged stay, the grounds of the prevailing apprehension, that our manufacturing greatness was declining, and that the cheap labour of France would more than compensate her many disadvantages. I returned home with the conviction, since, and now again confirmed, that the labour of Alsace, the best and cheapest in France, is dearer than the labour of Lancashire. I would not aver that an English workman would perform twice the work of a workman of the same class in France, but of this I feel assured, from frequent personal observation of their habits, and from long and confidential intercourse with their intelligent and enlightened manufacturers, that the advantage is *more than twofold* on the side of England, and that the true result is not to be obtained by comparisons between individuals, or even classes of workmen, but in the comparative aggregate industry of large establishments, or a whole population.

'Of this difference the intelligent witnesses, who gave evidence in 1835, before the French Commission of Inquiry into their prohibitory system, were fully aware, and with some allowances for that natural, excusable, and perhaps commendable nationality on such a subject, they did justice to the superior persevering energy of the English workman, whose enduring, untiring, savage industry, surpasses that of every other manufacturing country I have visited, Belgium, Germany, and Switzerland not excepted.'

The noxious agencies not only impair the strength of the labouring community, but, as will be further shown, they tend also to shorten the period of its exercise. This effect will be more apparent when considering merely the pecuniary burdens of the excess of orphanage and premature widowhood, apart from the loss of protection and the misery which it causes. I shall here only observe, as to the depressing effects assumed from the admitted tendencies of an increase of population, that the fact is, that hitherto, in England, wages, or the means of obtaining the necessaries of life for the whole mass of the labouring community, have advanced, and the comforts within the reach of the labouring classes have increased with the late increase of population. This may be verified by reference to various evidence, and amongst others to that contained in Sir F. Eden's examinations of the wages and modes of subsistence of the agricultural labourers in his day,[1] and we have evidence of this advance even in many of the manufacturing districts now in a state of severe depression. For example, an eminent manufacturer in Lancashire, stated to me in November ultimo—'That the same yarn which cost my father 12*d*. per lb. to make in 1792, all by machinery, now costs only 2*d*. per lb.; paying *then* only 4*s*. 4*d*. per hand wages weekly, *now* 8*s*. 8*d*.

---

1. Sir Frederick M. Eden, *The State of the Poor* (1797), III, App. XII.

or more; yet those wages amounted *then* to 5½*d*. per lb., and notwithstanding the higher wages, *now*, to only 1*d*. per lb.'

The prices of provisions were, during the first period, as high as now, and the cost of clothing 30 or 40 per cent. higher.

V

PECUNIARY BURDENS CREATED BY THE NEGLECT OF
SANITARY MEASURES

The more closely the subject of the evils affecting the sanitary condition of the labouring population is investigated the more widely do their effects appear to be ramified. The pecuniary cost of noxious agencies is measured by data within the province of the actuary, by the charges attendant on the reduced duration of life, and the reduction of the periods of working ability or production by sickness; the cost would include also much of the public charge of attendant vice and crime which come within the province of the police, as well as the destitution which comes within the province of the administrators of relief. Of the pecuniary effects, including the cost of maintenance during the preventible sickness, any estimate approximating to exactness could only be obtained by very great labour, which does not appear to be necessary.

To whatever extent the probable duration of the life of the working man is diminished by noxious agencies, I repeat a truism in stating that to some extent so much productive power is lost; and in the case of destitute widowhood and orphanage, burdens are created and cast either on the industrious survivors belonging to the family, or on the contributors to the poor's rates during the whole of the period of the failure of such ability. With the view to judge of the extent to which such burdens are at present cast upon the poor's rates, I have endeavoured to ascertain the average age at which death befell the heads of those families of children who with the mothers have been relieved on the ground of destitution, in eight of the unions where the average age of the mortality prevalent amongst the several classes of the community has been ascertained.

The workmen who belong to sick-clubs and benefit-societies generally fix the period of their own superannuation allowances at from 60 to 65 years of age. I see no reason to doubt that by the removal of noxious agencies not essential to their trades; by sanitary measures affecting their dwellings, combined with improvements in their own habits, the period of ability for productive labour might be extended to the whole of the labouring class.

The actual duration of the ability for labour will vary with the nature of the work, though there can be little doubt that the variations under proper precautions would be much less than those which now take place. From the information received in respect to the employment of tailors in large numbers, it is evident that the average period of the working ability of that class might be extended at least ten years by improvements as to the places of work alone. The experience which might serve to indicate the extent of practicable improvement is at present narrow and scattered. The chief English insurance tables, such

V. Pecuniary Burdens Created by Neglect

as the Northampton and Carlisle tables[1], are made up apparently from the experience of a population, subject probably to a greater or less extent to the noxious influences which are shown to be removable. By the Carlisle table, however, the probability of life to every person who has attained the age of twenty-one—the age for marriage—would be 40 years, or 40·75. By the Swedish tables[2], which are frequently applied to the insurance of the labouring classes, it would be 38·0. The observations that have been made on the subject, show that marriage improves rather than diminishes the probability of life. Where the duration of life is reduced by the nature of the employment below the usual average, by so much the widowhood may be considered as increased, as also the orphanage of their children. As labouring men generally marry early in life, their wives have ceased to bear children before they have reached fifty, so that the great mass of orphanage may be assigned to the consequence of premature death. The following table shows the average ages at which the deaths occurred of the fathers of the widows' orphan children who are in receipt of relief in the following unions. The average includes the cases of all who died at whatever ages, whether above or below sixty:

Unions	Number of Husbands dying under 60	Average Age at Death	Number of Husbands dying above 60	Average Age at Death	Total Deaths	Average Age
Manchester	718	42	432	69	1150	52
Whitechapel	351	44	239	69	590	54
Bethnal Green	250	44	195	69	445	55
Strand	157	42	63	66	220	49
Oakham & Uppingham	136	45	118	71	257	57
Alston-with-Garrigill	69	45	20	66	89	50
Bath	66	38	1	60	67	39

This premature widowhood and orphanage is the source of the most painful descriptions of pauperism—the most difficult to deal with; it is the source of a constant influx of the independent into the pauperised and permanently dependent classes. The widow, where there are children, generally remains a permanent charge; re-marriages amongst those

---

1. The Northampton table was calculated by Richard Price and published as an appendix to his *Observations on Reversionary Payments* (2nd. edition, 1772). The Carlisle table was calculated by Milne from Heysham's data on Carlisle, and published in his *Treatise on the Valuation of Annuities and Assurances* (1815), II, appendix tables.
2. The Swedish life tables were compiled from data relating to the whole of Sweden and Finland between 1755 and 1776, and were subsequently corrected according to additional data for the years 1775-1795 and 1801-5. They have been printed in many places, but are most conveniently gathered in Bisset Hawkins's article on 'Laws of Human Mortality', in the 4th. edition of the *Encyclopedia Britannica*, which was reproduced as App. G. 3 to the *Second Report of the Select Committee on the Laws Respecting Friendly Societies*, P.P. 1826-7, III, pp. 94-112.

V. Pecuniary Burdens Created by Neglect

who have children are very rare; in some unions they do not exceed one case in twenty or thirty. By the time the children are fit for labour and cease to require the parents' attention, the mothers frequently become unfit for earning their own livelihood, or habituated to dependence, and without care to emerge from it. Even where the children are by good training and education fitted for productive industry, when they marry, the early familiarity with the parochial relief makes them improvident, and they fall back upon the poor's rates on the lying-in of their wives, on their sickness, and for aid on every emergency. In every district the poor's rolls form the pedigrees of generations of families thus pauperized. The total number of orphan children on account of whose destitution relief was given from the poor's rates in the year ended Lady-day, 1840, was 112,000.

The numbers of widows chargeable to the poor's rates was in those unions at that period 43,000. The following abstract of the returns from the eight unions selected (see facing page) exhibit the proportions who become chargeable at different periods of the head of the family.[1]

Of the whole number it appears that upwards of 1746 became chargeable by premature deaths. If the same rule obtains in the other unions, which could only be ascertained by a very long and expensive inquiry, then nearly 27,000 cases of premature widowhood, and more than 100,000 cases of orphanage may be ascribed to removable causes. The chief effects or the chief of the diseases which appear as consequents to the circumstances under which the labouring population of the several districts have been described as living, and under which the fathers of the orphan children above enumerated have died, are set forth in the following table:

TABLE of the Chief Causes of Death producing Widowhood and Orphanage in the undermentioned Unions and Parishes

DISEASES, &c.	Man-chester Union	White-chapel Union	Bethnal Green Parish	Strand Union	Oakham and Uppingham Unions	Alston-with-Garrigill Parish	Bath Union	Total		
	No. of Deaths	No. of Deaths	No. of Deaths	No. of Deaths	No. of Deaths	No. of Deaths	No. of Deaths	No. of Deaths	Average Age of Decease	No. of Orphan
Respiratory Organs	500	212	147	95	69	47	40	1110	51	221
Epidemic, Endemic and Contagious	146	65	73	28	34	9	4	359	46	86
Digestive Organs	60	16	10	10	14	5	3	118	54	18
Nervous	74	41	38	17	25	3	5	203	55	29
Violent Deaths	94	44	20	16	23	13	5	215	46	50
Old Age	84	104	46	13	47	5	—	299	74	5
Other Diseases*	129	68	104	32	36	7	8	384	54	69
Undescribed	63	40	7	9	6	—	2	127	47	17
Total	1150	590	445	220	254	89	67	2815	53	498

* The diseases included under 'Other Diseases,' include the deaths registered from a number of miscellaneous ca too numerous to be specified in the table.

1. In an article of 1844, Chadwick took up this point further, and showed, with reference to the four provinces of Ireland, that there was consistently a higher proportion of widows to total population in towns than in rural districts. For the whole of Ireland in 1841, whereas in rural districts there were 12 widows to every 100 of population over 17 years of age, in urban areas there were 16. (E. Chadwick, 'On the best modes of representing accurately, by statistical returns, the duration of life, and the pressure and

V. Pecuniary Burdens Created by Neglect

Ages	Manchester Union No. of Hus- bands who Died	Manchester Union No. of Or- phan Chil- dren	White- chapel Union No. of Hus- bands who Died	White- chapel Union No. of Or- phan Chil- dren	Bethnal Green No. of Hus- bands who Died	Bethnal Green No. of Or- phan Chil- dren	Strand Union No. of Hus- bands who Died	Strand Union No. of Or- phan Chil- dren	Oakham & Uppingham Unions No. of Hus- bands who Died	Oakham & Uppingham Unions No. of Or- phan Chil- dren	Alston with Garrigill No. of Hus- bands who Died	Alston with Garrigill No. of Or- phan Chil- dren	Bath Union No. of Hus- bands who Died	Bath Union No. of Or- phan Chil- dren	Total No. of Hus- bands who Died	Total No. of Or- phan Chil- dren
20—25	11	20	7	12	2	3	1	4	—	—	1	2	—	—	22	41
25—30	56	126	17	40	9	19	11	19	12	25	5	12	9	28	119	269
30—35	108	317	31	85	25	89	23	70	8	36	4	16	13	52	212	665
35—40	108	333	42	114	40	137	20	69	19	71	6	24	12	52	247	800
40—45	126	361	63	201	40	153	35	81	24	68	12	58	18	84	318	1006
45—50	112	302	61	178	44	105	23	58	19	50	18	84	9	37	286	814
50—55	100	183	78	137	45	107	24	34	30	60	9	30	4	15	290	566
55—60	97	138	51	37	45	54	20	17	24	36	14	11	1	6	252	299
60—65	147	148	87	46	53	35	25	17	26	15	13	4	1	4	352	269
65—70	96	60	48	18	52	17	15	13	32	13	1	—	—	—	238	121
70—75	87	55	54	8	57	7	13	—	22	10	4	—	—	—	247	80
75—80	60	22	25	4	24	7	5	2	11	4	1	—	—	—	137	40
80—85	35	4	17	2	7	8	5	—	—	6	1	—	—	—	76	12
85—90	5	—	7	3	2	—	—	—	1	—	—	—	—	—	14	3
90—95	1	—	2	—	—	—	—	—	—	—	—	—	—	—	4	—
95—100	—	—	—	—	—	—	—	—	—	—	—	—	—	—	—	—
100—105	1	—	—	—	—	—	—	—	—	—	—	—	—	—	1	—
Totals	1150	2069	590	885	445	734	220	384	254	394	89	241	67	278	2815	4985
No. receiving Relief previous to husband's death	199	—	80	—	—	—	37	—	11	—	27	—	—	—	—	—

Total Deaths below 60 years of age 1746

* contd.:
progress of the causes of mortality amongst different classes of the community, and amongst the population of different districts and countries, J.R.S.S., VII (1844), 18.

V. Pecuniary Burdens Created by Neglect

As an example of the mode in which the causes of premature deaths fall, and of the burdens they entail in many districts, I submit a return of the whole of the cases of widowhood on the pauper rolls of the parish of Alston and Garrigill, Cumberland, the parish in which are situate the lodging-houses described in the evidence collected by *Dr. Mitchell*.[1]

ALSTON WITH GARRIGILL PARISH
Number of Widows, and Children dependent upon them, in receipt of Relief in the above Parish; Age of Husband at death; and the alleged Cause of Death

Initials of Widows	Number of Children dependent at the time of Husband's Death	Occupation of deceased Husband	Age at Death	Years' loss by premature Death	Alleged Cause of Death
R. W.	—	Miner	83	—	Decay of nature.
M. S.	—	Tailor	78	—	Natural decay.
M. B.	—	Miner	73	—	Not stated.
M. R.	—	Miner	72	—	Decay of nature.
S. M.	—	Miner	72	—	Decay of nature.
M. T.	—	Mason	72	—	Asthma produced from age.
A. V.	—	Miner	67	—	Asthma produced from working in mines.
M. L.	—	Miner	64	—	Influenza.
A. M.	—	Miner	63	—	Asthma produced from working in the lead-mines.
M. S.	—	Miner	63	—	Natural decline.
J. P.	—	Labourer	62	—	Consumption.
H. T.	2	Mason	62	—	Asthma.
S. H.	2	Miner	60	—	Rupture of blood-vessel.
J. R.	—	Miner	60	—	Asthma produced from working in the mines.
H. L.	—	Miner	60	—	Asthma.
J. P.	—	Miner	60	—	Consumption.
M. T.	2	Miner	60	—	Bursting blood-vessel.
A. C.	—	Joiner	60	—	Jaundice.
E. K.	—	Miner	60	—	Asthma produced from working in the mines.
E. H.	—	Miner	60	—	Cholera.
D. J.	—	Glazier	59	1	Affection of the liver.
N. D.	4	Butcher	59	1	Apoplexy.
M. T.	—	Miner	59	1	Inflammation of the lungs.
H. A.	—	Miner	59	1	Asthma produced from working in the lead-mines, which terminated in consumption.
J. B.	—	Miner	59	1	Asthma ditto.
E. T.	—	Labourer	58	2	Accident by a coal-waggon.
M. P.	—	Miner	58	2	Asthma produced from working in the lead-mines, which terminated in consumption.

1. 'Report by James Mitchell on the Lead Mines, etc. in Durham, Northumberland, and Cumberland', Appendix to *First Report of Children's Employment Commission, P.P.* 1842, XVII.

V. Pecuniary Burdens Created by Neglect

Initials of Widows	Number of Children dependent at the time of Husband's Death	Occupation of deceased husband	Age at Death	Years' loss by premature Death	Alleged Cause of Death
H. T.	—	Miner	57	3	Consumption accelerated by working in the lead-mines.
M. P.	1	Turner	57	3	Consumption.
H. S.	3	Miner	57	3	Influenza, terminating in dropsy.
M. J.	3	Blacksmith	55	5	Asthma.
S. M.	—	Miner	55	5	Inflammation of lungs from cold.
R. W.	—	Miner	55	5	Asthma produced from working in lead-mines.
M. R.	—	Miner	55	5	Asthma from working in the mines.
J. W.	2	Miner	54	6	Pleurisy.
A. F.	—	Miner	54	6	Asthma and rupture of blood-vessel.
J. L.	2	Miner	53	7	Chronic disease of rheumatism.
N. H.	2	Miner	53	7	Asthma produced from working in the lead-mines.
A. S.	—	Miner	52	8	Asthma and bursting blood-vessel.
M. W.	6	Miner	52	8	Asthma produced from working in the mines.
E. W.	5	Miner	52	8	Asthma produced from working in the mines, which terminated in consumption.
J. S.	6	Miner	51	9	Paralysis.
H. P.	9	Quarryman	49	11	Asthma by working in the lead-mines.
H. P.	5	Miner	48	12	Typhus fever.
E. H.	6	Miner	48	12	Killed in lead-mines.
M. A.	7	Miner	48	12	Consumption by bad air in the pit.
J. C.	8	Miner	47	13	Asthma produced by working in the lead-mines.
S. E.	6	Miner	47	13	Consumption produced from a continuance of influenza.
M. T.	8	Miner	47	13	Consumption and asthma.
E. B.	3	Miner	47	13	Affection of the head, caused from an accident received in the mine.
D. R.	—	Miner	46	14	Asthma produced from working in the lead-mines.
E. B.	5	Miner	46	14	Rheumatic fever, which produced inflammation of the brain.
M. S.	5	Miner	46	14	Killed in lead-mine.
M. R.	1	Joiner	46	14	Dropsy.
M. F.	7	Coal Miner	46	14	Explosion of fire-damp in a coal-mine.
L. T.	3	Miner	45	15	Asthma, which terminated with dropsy.

V. Pecuniary Burdens Created by Neglect

Initials of Widows	Number of Children dependent at the time of Husband's Death	Occupation of deceased Husband	Age at Death	Years' loss by premature Death	Alleged Cause of Death
H. P.	3	Miner	45	15	Scarlet fever.
H. Y.	5	Miner	45	15	Consumption, accelerated by working in the lead-mines.
M. S.	2	Miner	45	15	Inflammation of bowels.
M. S.	5	Joiner	45	15	Consumption.
A. S.	6	Miner	44	16	Dropsy.
A. B.	6	Miner	44	16	Asthma from working in lead-mines.
F. C.	5	Miner	43	17	Asthma produced from working in the lead-mines.
M. D.	4	Miner	43	17	Consumption produced from asthma, caused by working in the mines.
H. M.	7	Miner	43	17	Asthma, which terminated in consumption.
A. P.	7	Superintendent	43	17	A fall from the 'horse' in the engine shaft.
P. W.	4	Miner	43	17	Pleurisy.
E. W.	8	Miner	42	18	Consumption and asthma produced from working in the lead-mines.
J. H.	4	Miner	42	18	Consumption.
J. J.	5	Miner	42	18	Pleurisy.
A. J.	2	Miller	42	18	Found drowned.
M. R.	—	Shoemaker	40	20	Injury from fall of a cart.
E. R.	7	Joiner	38	22	Affection of the liver.
J. B.	5	Miner	38	22	Consumption.
A. P.	7	Miner	37	21	Asthma.
E. W.	3	Miner	36	24	Accident in mine, which terminated in consumption.
E. H.	3	Miner	35	25	Killed in coal-pit.
M. L.	2	Miner	35	25	Water of the head.
A. S.	4	Miner	35	25	Income on leg.
S. H.	7	Miner	34	26	Accident in coal-mine.
J. H.	4	Cordwainer	30	30	Typhus Fever.
S. H.	3	Cartman	30	30	Accidental.
E. A.	2	Miner	30	30	Consumption.
M. J.	3	Teacher	29	31	Consumption.
M. R.	3	Miner	29	31	Affection of urinary organs.
A. W.	2	Miner	28	32	Cholera.
M. W.	3	Miner	27	33	Inflammation of bowels.
A. H.	1	Pitman	25	35	Accident at colliery.
J. M.	2	Miner	21	39	Small-pox.
89	242	—	4418	—	
		Average age at death of each below 60 years of age.	45		Total No. of orphans by deaths caused below 60 years of age. 236

V. Pecuniary Burdens Created by Neglect

A complete analysis of the whole of the causes contributory to the premature mortality displayed in this group of cases would be a work of much labour, and would in nowise affect the soundness of the conclusions derivable from other sources, that a large amount, and probably the great mass of it, is preventible.

It would, for instance, be difficult to decide the precise term of years of life cut short by the effects of the lodging-houses, in producing or aggravating other tendencies to consumption; but the information possessed by persons who have made themselves acquainted with the effects of impure air enables them to pronounce with certainty that the habitual exposure of a body of men to such noxious influences must be attended by a diminution of several years of the definite standard of life. Of the 31 deaths of miners below 60 years of age, from diseases of the respiratory organs, enumerated in the above return, a part of the causes may be attributable to their occupation, a part to the external circumstances of residence and connected habits. Now we have examples of the separate advantages attendant on the removal of both causes of disease, I adduce the following information, obtained through Sir John Walsham[1], with relation to the effects of an improvement in the external circumstances of the workmen as to residences.

Captain Harland, the chairman of the Reeth union, York (North Riding), in a communication to Sir John Walsham, states, that he has been anxious to ascertain as correctly as possible, first, the average duration of life among the mining population of the respective parishes in that district, and how far it appeared to be affected by their general habits as well as by the state of their domiciles; and he gives the following results:

By a careful examination of the parish registers, I find that in the last seven years there have died in—

The parish of Marrick . . .	15 miners;	average age,	$47\frac{3}{5}$ years,
The parish of Arkendale . .	70 ,,	,,	$45\frac{19}{35}$,,
The chapelry of Muker, in the parish of Grinton	39 ,,	,,	$45\frac{29}{39}$,,
The remainder of the parish of Grinton, *viz.* Grinton Reeth and Meblecks	40 ,,	,,	$54\frac{39}{40}$,,

Total, 164; general average, $48\frac{13}{164}$ years.

'The prevailing diseases throughout the whole district are bronchial affections and rheumatism, which may generally be attributed to exposure to cold and rain after leaving the close, warm atmosphere of the mine.

'The miners' dwellings in Marrick are small thatched cottages, situated very near their work; they are consequently less exposed to wet and cold on their way home, but (although dry and kept tolerably clean) from the want of room

---

1. Sir John Walsham was Assistant Poor Law Commissioner for the four northern counties of England. His three reports, 'On the state of the dwellings of the labouring classes in Cumberland, Durham, Northumberland, and Westmoreland', were printed in *Local Reps. E. & W.*, pp. 409-44.

and proper ventilation, the inmates are more liable to contagious disorders than the more comfortably lodged miners in the parish of Grinton. In Arkendale the houses are of a somewhat better description, but the drainage is imperfect; the habits of the people filthy and intemperate; cutaneous disorders very common; and they are frequently the victims of typhus and other malignant fevers.

'In the parish of Grinton the houses are of a decidedly superior description. Forty years ago they were mostly thatched with ling or heath; a thatched house is now rarely seen. The miners are all comfortably lodged, generally well clothed, clean, and orderly in their habits; and I have no doubt to these causes may be attributed the great difference between the mortality in this parish and that of Arkendale in the same period.

'In Muker the mortality, in proportion to its population, has been nearly the same as in Arkendale; but many of the miners work occasionally in coal-mines, are more exposed to storms, by reason of their work being at a greater distance from their dwellings; and those dwellings are also of a description inferior to those of the other townships in the parish of Grinton. From these circumstances I infer that the average duration of a lead-miner's life, and his greater freedom from disease, have increased in proportion to the increased airiness and increased convenience of his dwelling.'

I have already referred to the example cited by Dr. Barham of the health of the miners in one mine, the Dolcoath mine, in the parish of Camborne, in Cornwall, where great attention is paid to obviate agencies injurious to the miners. Care is there taken in respect to ventilation in the mines. 'The ventilation in Dolcoath is particularly good, and the men are healthier than in most other mines; there are more old miners.' Care is taken for the prevention of accidents. 'Our ladders,' says one of the witnesses examined by Dr. Barham, 'are about two fathoms and a half in length, generally with staves one foot apart. We use oak staves; old ship oak we find the best. We formerly used the hafts of the picks and other tools, but found these unsafe, the wood being sleepy and flawed, and sometimes breaking off in a moment, without having shown any outward sign of unsoundness. Iron staves, besides being at times very slippery, are apt to be corroded, so as to cut the hand. We have had no accidents on our footways for a long time.' They have introduced the safety fuse, and the witness says:—'Very few accidents now arise from explosions: they used to happen frequently formerly.' Care is taken of the miners on quitting the mines: hence, instead of issuing on the bleak hill side, and receiving beer in a shed, to prevent chill and exhaustion, they issue from their underground labour into a warm room, where well-dried clothes are ready for them, and warm water, and even baths are supplied from the steam furnace, and, in the instance of this mine, a provision of hot beef-soup instead of beer is ready for them in another room. The honour of having made this change is stated to be due to the Right Hon. Lady Basset, on the suggestion of Dr. Carlyon. 'Hence in this mine,' says Dr. Barham, 'we may fairly attribute to the combination of beneficial arrangements just noticed that in Dolcoath, where 451 individuals are employed underground, only two have died within the last three years of miners' consumption, a statement which could not, I believe, be made with truth nor be nearly approached in respect of an equal number of miners

V. Pecuniary Burdens Created by Neglect

during the same term in any other Cornish district.' The sick-club of the mine 'is comparatively rich, having a fund of 1500*l*.'[1]

When 'care' is mentioned as taken for sanitary measures, it is to be remembered that it is care only at the outset, and that when in habitual action the care required is really less, and the measures should be characterized as means for avoiding care and trouble and diminishing pecuniary loss.

The effect of sanitary care in the mines of Camborne is, so far as it has been carried, marked in the following table, made up by Mr. Blee, a medical practitioner in the neighbourhood, from the mortuary registers, showing the average age of death of the population as compared with the average of death in two other adjacent parishes of Illogan and Gwennap, in both of which some beneficent alterations have been made, especially in Illogan, but the works are stated to be new, and the circumstances not so favourable as at Camborne:

TABLE showing the average Ages of Persons dying above 30, and registered, in three years in the Parish of Camborne, in two years in Gwennap, and in one year in Illogan.

	Males		Females	Proportion per cent. of Miners' Deaths by Mine Accidents
	Miners	Not Miners		
Gwennap . .	45	60	64	16
Illogan . .	49	68	64	32
Camborne . .	54	60	63	5

The improvement in Camborne had not reached the residences, where the miners kept pigs, in sties close behind the house, and a dungheap is carefully fostered in a catch-pit adjacent. Dr. Barham, and the medical men practising in the vicinity, attribute to the decomposition of vegetable matter in the 'soaked soil from the receptacles near the dwellings a form of fever which has been hanging about Camborne, and has often passed into the typhoid condition, and has been attended with great prostration of strength.'*

I have obtained through Mr. Baker of Leeds, who, as superintendent of factories, has had good means of making an accurate comparison, the following contrast of the results as shown in the state of mortality amidst the population of two contiguous manufacturing districts employed in similar proportions in the same description of work, and differing only in the state of the atmosphere in which they lived. The districts are in the townships of Great Bradford and Horton, in York-

---

* Where so much independent provision is made, as by clubs, only a part of the consequences of premature deaths appear on the poor's roll. The population of Camborne is less exclusively mining than in Gwennap; but the

1. 'Report by Dr. Charles Barham', *Report of Children's Employment Commission*, *P.P.* 1842, XVI, pp. 740, 837-8. For Cornish mining in the early nineteenth century, see A. K. Hamilton Jenkin, *The Cornish Miner* (1927); and J. Rowe, *Cornwall in the Age of the Industrial Revolution* (Liverpool 1953).

V. Pecuniary Burdens Created by Neglect

shire, both in the parish of Bradford, and contiguous, differing only in elevation and atmospheric influence.

'The town of Bradford lies in a hollow formed by the high land of the surrounding country, a part of which forms the township of Horton, and both populations, in about an equal ratio, are employed in worsted mills, built about the same period of time, in the same kind of architecture, with the same appliances for ventilation and purification in every respect, differing only in comparison as to numbers both of population and mills.

	Population	Births	Deaths
Bradford	34,560	1 in 25·8	1 in 37·3
Horton	17,618	1 in 28·0	1 in 47·0

The difference between the two localities will at once be seen, and can only be accounted for by the difference in atmospheric influences, the former population being resident in ill-conditioned dwellings, without sufficient ventilation; the latter residing in localities which, though undrained in many instances, are yet open to pure air and breezes which never reach the town without the most perfect contamination.

Dr. Barham mentions, as an example of the benevolent foresight which economizes the strength and life of workmen, and perceives that there is a profit as well as humanity in so doing, that at Tresavean a great copper mine in Gwennap, as a substitute for the ladders, before universal, machinery has been erected for the raising and lowering of the miners. This, he states, will be effected at the cost of 2000*l.* at the least, but this sum, it is calculated, will soon be repaid by the saving of the time and fatigue of the men.[1]

---

* *contd.:*
records of pauperism in the office afford marks of a general difference in the condition of the population of the two parishes.

Parish	Ratio of Paupers to the whole Population	Ratio of Widows and Women whose Husbands have deserted them, or are transported, to the whole Population	Cost of Relief per Head on the whole Population
			s. d.
Gwennap	1 in 25	1 in 186	3 2
Illogan	1 in 35	1 in 346	2 2¾
Camborne	1 in 34	1 in 401	2 4¾

---

1. This is a reference to the so-called 'man-engine', by which the miner was lifted on a ladder suspended from the beam of a beam-engine. At the top of each stroke, the miner stepped off the moving ladder on to a fixed platform and waited until the ladder reached the bottom of the stroke before mounting again to be carried up to the next fixed platform. The man-engine at Tresavean was believed to be the deepest in Britain—290 fathoms. See D. H. Tew, 'The Continental origins of the man-engine and its development in Cornwall and the Isle of Man', *Transactions of the Newcomen Society*, XXX (1955-7), 49-62.

V. Pecuniary Burdens Created by Neglect

Such evidence as that above given, and as will be submitted in other instances, will leave little doubt that, by a combination of practicable sanitary regulations comprehending the economy of the residence as well as the place of work, the enormous suffering and waste of life which at present depresses large masses of the working population may be rendered comparatively inconsiderable. The amount of such depression on the mining population, in making it consist of young persons and more transient, is marked in a return prepared by Mr. R. Lanyon, the medical practitioner acquainted with the locality, and which was read at the Polytechnic Society in Cornwall.

On examining the ages of 2145 *men* engaged in mining, it was found that their average age was 30 years, and that the average period they had been engaged in work was 15 years. On examining the condition of 1033 *men*, artisans, agricultural labourers, living and working in the vicinity, it was found that their average age was 40 years, and that their average period of work then completed was 25 years. Of the mining population one-third only had reached 50 years of age, whilst of the non-mining population one-third had attained 70 years of age.

I might submit these two examples, the one as a young and comparatively weak population, the other as a comparatively mature and strong population. The adult mining population of 30 years of age is not, I apprehend, a population advancing to a further stage of maturity, but one kept down by noxious agencies and premature mortality to that limit of age, with no chance for them or for other generations to pass beyond it whilst in this employment, except through the operation of sanitary measures in removing the causes of depression.

The difference in the proportions of ages between a depressed and unhealthy and a comparatively long-lived and strong population, is shown in the following comparative view of the ages of the miners and of the 1033 non-mining labourers who were living and working:

	30 Years of Age and under 40	40 Years and under 45	45 Years and under 50	50 Years and under 55	55 Years and under 60	60 Years and under 70	70 Years and under 80	80 Years and upwards
Miners 1651	772	377	239	125	56	29	1	—
Labourers 1033	695	422	Not given	284	Not given	144	48	7
	Per cent.	Per cent.	Per cent.	Per cent.	Per cent.	Per cent.	Per cent.	Per cent.
Miners	47	23	14	$7\frac{1}{2}$	$3\frac{1}{2}$	$1\frac{1}{2}$	—	—
Labourers	67	41	—	27	—	14	$4\frac{1}{2}$	$\frac{1}{2}$

So that whilst in every 100 men of the younger population of workpeople there would not be 2 men of the experience beyond sixty years of age, not 8 above fifty, or not a fourth passed forty, in the older population there would be 14 beyond sixty, 27 beyond fifty, or a clear majority of mature age, and, it may be presumed, of the comparatively staid habits given by age. Dr. Scott Alison found that the average age of the living male heads of families of the *collier* population at Tranent whose condition he has contrasted with that of the agricultural population, and whose ages he could ascertain, was 34 years; whilst the average age of the living male heads of the agricultural families was 51 years and 10 months. He considers that the like proportions would be found to be more extensively prevalent, and would serve as fair indications of the relative condition of the different populations.[1]

Whenever the adult population of a physically depressed district, such as Manchester, is brought out on any public occasion, the preponderance of youth in the crowd, and the small proportion of aged, or even of the middle-aged, amongst them is apt to strike those who have seen assemblages of the working population of other districts more favourably situated.

In the course of some inquiries under the Constabulary Force Commission as to the proportions of a paid force that would apparently be requisite for the protection of the peace in the manufacturing districts, reference was made to the meetings held by torchlight in the neighbourhood of Manchester.[2] It was reported to us, on close observation by peace-officers, that the bulk of the assemblages consisted of mere boys, and that there were scarcely any men of mature age to be seen amongst them. Those of mature age and experience, it was stated, generally disapproved of the proceedings of the meetings as injurious to the working classes themselves. These older men, we were assured by their employers, were intelligent, and perceived that capital, and large capital, was not the means of their depression, but of their steady and abundant support. They were generally described as being above the influence of the anarchical fallacies which appeared to sway those wild and really dangerous assemblages. The inquiry which arose upon such statements was how it happened that the men of mature age, feeling their own best interests injured by the proceedings of the younger portion of the working classes, how they, the elders, did not exercise a restraining influence upon their less experienced fellow-workmen? On inquiring of the owner of some extensive manufacturing property, on which between 1000 and 2000 persons were maintained at wages yielding 40*s.* per week per family, whether he could rely on the aid of the men of mature age for the protection of the capital which furnished them the means of subsistence? he stated he could rely on them confidently. But on ascertaining the numbers qualified for service as special constables, the gloomy fact became apparent, that the proportion of men of strength and of mature age for such service were but as a small group against a large crowd, and that for any social influence they were equally weak. The disappearance by premature deaths of the heads of families and the older workmen at such ages as those recorded in the returns of dependent widowhood and orphanage must to some extent practically involve the necessity of supplying the lapse of staid influence amidst a young population by one description or other of precautionary force.

On expostulating on other occasions with middle-aged and ex-

---

1. *Local Reps. Scot.* pp. 103-4.
2. *First Report of the Constabulary Force Commission, P.P.* 1839, XIX, p. 82.

perienced workmen on the folly as well as the injustice of their trade unions, by which the public peace was compromised by the violences of strike after strike, without regard to the experiences of the suffering from the continued failures of their exertions for objects the attainment of which would have been most injurious to themselves, the workmen of the class remonstrated with invariably disclaimed connexion with the proceedings, and showed that they abstained from attendance at the meetings. The common expression was, they would not attend to be borne down by 'mere boys,' who were furious, and knew not what they were about. The predominance of a young and violent majority was general.

In the metropolis the experience is similar. The mobs against which the police have to guard come from the most depressed districts; and the constant report of the superintendents is, that scarcely any old men are to be seen amongst them. In general they appear to consist of persons between 16 and 25 years of age. The mobs from such districts as Bethnal Green are proportionately conspicuous for a deficiency of bodily strength, without, however, being from that cause proportionately the less dangerously mischievous. I was informed by peace officers that the great havoc at Bristol was committed by mere boys.

The experience of the metropolitan police is also similar as to the comparatively small proportion of force available for public service from such depressed districts. It is corroborative also of the evidence as to the physical deterioration of their population, as well as the disproportion in respect of age. Two out of every three of the candidates for admission to the police force itself are found defective in the physical qualifications. It is rare that any one of the candidates from Spitalfields, Whitechapel, or the districts where the mean duration of life is low, is found to possess the requisite physical qualifications for the force, which is chiefly recruited from the open districts at the outskirts of the town, or from Norfolk and Suffolk, and other agricultural counties.

In general the juvenile delinquents, who come from the inferior districts of the towns, are conspicuously under size. In a recent examination of juvenile delinquents at Parkhurst by Mr. Kay Shuttleworth[1], the great majority were found to be deficient in physical organization. An impression is often prevalent that the criminal population consists of persons of the greatest physical strength. Instances of criminals of great strength certainly do occur; but speaking from observation of the adult prisoners from the towns and the convicts in the hulks, they are in general below the average standard of height.

Reverting to the observations as to the influence of adverse physical circumstances on the morals of the population, I must here include in the observation the younger portion of the population.

I might adduce the evidence of the teachers of the pauper children at

---

1. This paper cannot be traced. There is no reference to such a paper in Bloomfield's bibliography of Kay's writings (*British Journal of Educational Studies*, IX (1961)). There are, however, some references to problems of juvenile delinquency in Kay's articles, 'On the establishment of pauper schools', and 'Notes illustrative of a previous paper on the training in Schools of Industry of children dependent from crime, orphanage, etc.', *J.R.S.S.*, I (1839).

V. Pecuniary Burdens Created by Neglect

Norwood[1] to show that a deteriorated physical condition does in fact greatly increase the difficulty of moral and intellectual cultivation. The intellects of the children of such inferior physical organization are torpid; it is comparatively difficult to gain their attention or to sustain it; it requires much labour to irradiate the countenance with intelligence, and the irradiation is apt to be transient. As a class they are comparatively irritable and bad tempered. The most experienced and zealous teachers are gladdened by the sight of well-grown healthy children, which presents to them better promise that their labours will be less difficult and more lasting and successful. On one occasion a comparison was made between the progress of two sets of children in Glasgow, the one set taken from the wynds and placed under the care of one of the most skilful and successful infant schoolmasters, the other a set of children from a more healthy town district and of a better physical condition, placed under the care of a pupil of the master who had charge of the children from the wynds. After a trial for a sufficient time, the more experienced master acknowledged the comparative inferiority of his pupils, and his inability to keep them up to the pace of the better bodily-conditioned children.

The facts indicated will suffice to show the importance of the moral and political considerations, viz., that the noxious physical agencies depress the health and bodily condition of the population, and act as obstacles to education and to moral culture; that in abridging the duration of the adult life of the working classes they check the growth of productive skill, and abridge the amount of social experience and steady moral habits in the community: that they substitute, for a population that accumulates and preserves instruction and is steadily progressive, a population that is young, inexperienced, ignorant, credulous, irritable, passionate, and dangerous, having a perpetual tendency to moral as well as physical deterioration.

The group of cases of the mining population from Alston and Garrigill, it appears to me, will, when considered, afford an example of the powerful nature of the physical elements of deterioration. In that district the employers and persons of the higher classes have paid great attention to maintain the means of moral improvement. They have only not been made aware of the practicability or of the importance of sustaining the physical condition of the workpeople, as exemplified in respect to the same description of labourers at Camborne.

The duration of life amongst the mining population of the lead-miners at Alston and Garrigill, and the adjacent district, is about 14 years less than that given by the Swedish tables. Their physical condition was depressed. 'The young men appeared very healthy, but exceedingly few of them,' says Dr. Mitchell, 'were of a large size; and in general it may be said they are of a small size.' He states that in moral condition they are most exemplary:

'The means of education in Alston parish are extensive; there is the grammar-school, the master of which must be acquainted with Latin, but he gives a general education; there is a charity-school, and a school kept by a master on his own account; there is the school of the London Lead Company

---

1. For the Norwood pauper school, see below, p. 274, n. 2.

V. Pecuniary Burdens Created by Neglect 269

at Nenthead, at which other children besides those of their own workpeople are allowed to attend. There is a school at Garrigill Gate, and one at Tynehead, and another at Leadgate; there are also many dame schools and 10 Sunday schools. * * * I procured the catalogues of several libraries, and the books are such as to convey valuable information, and are far superior to most of the works which are found in the catalogues of the institutions called literary and scientific in and about the metropolis.[1] * * * As to the intellectual condition of the people, it is decidedly superior to that of any district of England of which I have any knowledge. The witnesses uniformly manifested a clearness of comprehension of the inquiries made of them, and gave distinct replies, and added of themselves other information bearing on the subject. Almost all of them could sign their evidence, and most of them wrote exceedingly well. * * * The evidence of the employers and the parochial authorities, as well as of the men themselves, fully proves that there is a very general sobriety, and that the contrary practice is exceedingly rare. * * * Offences against property are very rare. It may be doubted whether we may consider it a proof of the honesty of the people, that pigs of lead may be seen lying by the road-sides and in the fells as much exposed as so many stones. There is no magistrate nearer to Alston than a distance of 14 miles. Offences against the law are very rare.'[2]

Instances have been frequently presented in the course of this inquiry of the moral degradation of the children of workpeople, and of the workpeople themselves, who have once been what those miners now are in moral condition; but the cases taken from the pauper roll of the union will serve to show that even a good education will not, of itself, sustain such a body of workmen against the physical causes of depression. The group of cases of widowhood, when considered, will serve to show that the causes in question create the evils of which they are supposed to be natural correctives.

With such an educated class of workmen, the obtainment of a place and the wages of an adult must be the necessary preliminary to a marriage, and unless such place or wages were obtained, the young workman would either remain single or seek employment farther a-field. But we will suppose, for illustration, that a casualty occurs, such as the last death on the list, J. M., where a young miner who has married and has a wife and two children is prematurely swept away by an epidemic at 21 years of age, leaving a widow and two destitute orphan children dependent on poor relations, or on the ratepayers. The first-mentioned, say S. H., then takes the vacant place of work, marries, and is killed at 34 years of age by 'an accident in the mine,' leaving a widow and seven orphan children. This third vacancy in the place of work is occupied by another miner, H. Y., who marries and works until he is 45, when he is killed by 'consumption,' leaving a widow and five children.

Such casualties do not of course actually so fall on any one place of work, but the vacancies so created in different places at the younger periods of life must be and are supplied by new hands coming into the employment, and marrying as a consequence of that employment; and

---

1. For the educational provision of the Alston lead-mining companies, see A. Raistrick, *Two Centuries of Industrial Welfare* (1938), pp. 58-76.
2. 'Report by James Mitchell', pp. 752-3, Appendix to *First Report of the Children's Employment Commission, P.P.* 1842, XVII.

V. Pecuniary Burdens Created by Neglect

the succession will fairly represent the mode in which the vacancies created by the various causes of death displayed in the last table and in the other tables of the causes of premature widowhood and orphanage occur.

In works where the average period of working ability is extended to the natural period of superannuation, which the evidence shows that a combination of internal and external sanitary measures may be expected to give, namely an average of full 60 years, the account for one place would be one superannuated workman and one widow, and a family of four or five well-grown children, who, having received parental care during that period, will probably all have obtained, before its termination, the means of independent self-support. Whereas with a population of only 15 or 20 years of working ability, the same place of work may during the same period have been filled by two generations and one-fourth of workpeople, not one of which has brought all the children dependent on it to maturity or a condition for self-support; and the account of widowhood and orphanage will frequently for the same place of work stand thus:—

Workmen prematurely Dead	Orphan Children	Years' loss of Support
J. M. 1 widow	2	39
S. H. 1 ,,	7	26
H. Y. 1 ,,	5	15

That is to say, three widows instead of one, and three sets of stunted and unhealthy children dependent for such various periods as those above specified, and competing for employment at the same place, instead of one set of healthy children arrived at the age of working ability for self-support. The occupation of the places of work by a comparatively young and procreative population, brought forward by the premature removal of the middle-aged and the aged workers, by the various causes of premature deaths—the acceleration of births by premature deaths in infancy as stated in a preceding note—will, I apprehend, sufficiently clearly account for the generally increased proportions of births in those districts where the rate of mortality is high; and it will scarcely be necessary to give further illustrations of the dreadful fallacy which tends to an acquiescence in the continuance of the causes of pestilence and premature mortality as 'correctives of the pressure of population.'

Though the deaths from accidents bear only a small proportion to the deaths from disease, yet registries show that the scattered deaths from various descriptions of violence amount to an average of about 12,000 yearly, in England and Wales alone, or more than aroused the national attention in the late massacre of the troops of the empire during the war in India.[1] The position which this class of causes occupy, in the production of destitute orphanage and widowhood, is shown in the previous tables; but these do not comprehend the whole of the effects; another class of which appear on examining the causes of pauperism: namely, the injuries which occasion permanent disablement. In an analysis of

---

1. The massacre of Elphinstone's force on the retreat from Kandahar, January 1842.

V. Pecuniary Burdens Created by Neglect

the causes of pauperism, by *Mr. Simkiss*, the auditor of the Wolverhampton union, the cases of which the subjoined is a list were apparent on the pauper roll.

No. of Cases	Previous Occupations of the Paupers	Nature of Accident	Respective Ages
18	Miners	Hurt in mines	21, 23, 27, 30, 34, 34, 40, 40, 43, 44, 47, 49, 50, 50, 51, 53, 60, 60.
2	Ditto	Burnt in mines	40, 60.
1	Locksmith	Lamed by accident	30.
1	Wheelwright	Accident by waggon	69.
1	Single woman	Lost her arm by accident	23.

On examining the individual cases of deaths that are classed as incident to the pursuit of the chief branches of mining or manufacturing industry, or in transport whether by land or water, it has always been satisfactory to find that for the future, by care, the greater proportion of them are preventible. In the case of the mining accidents, one part of them appear preventible by care of the superior managers of the mines—in arrangements over which the individual workman has no control; the other portion, by intelligence and care on the part of the workmen; and this last class of cases again reverts back to the power, and therefore to the means, of imposing responsibility on the employers in the selection of educated and intelligent workmen—of habits of sobriety, and care to qualify them for works of danger. But at present they are, in a great measure, relieved from responsibility by the charge incurred by the want of care being thrown on other funds raised from persons who have as yet no practicable means of protection or prevention. When continued and dreadful losses of life take place, in the face of examples of successful prevention such as might be collected from every part of the country, it is impossible to avoid the conclusion that if the branch of industry were charged with the pecuniary consequences of the losses assumed to be necessarily incident to it, generations would not be allowed to pass away in fear, recklessness, and misery, without the early adoption of those means of prevention which self-interest would then stimulate. A frequent suggestion made upon the view of such casualties is that government inspectors should be appointed to inspect and direct and regulate machinery.

This subject was brought under consideration in the course of the proceedings of the Factory Commission of Inquiry, and it was then agreed that such a measure as that of inspection would only give an imperfect security, and would occasion vexatious interruptions, and that the least objectionable mode of interference, as well as the most efficient and just as a means of prevention, would be to charge a portion at least of the cost of such casualties upon the branch of industry. Subsequent observation, especially of the causes of pauperism, has strengthened my convictions of the soundness of the principle of prevention as stated in our Report, a passage from which I have submitted in the Appendix.*[1]

In illustration of the pecuniary cost of disease, as shown in the cost of remedies in Scotland, there are several documents. The late *Dr. Cowan*, the Professor of Forensic Medicine at Glasgow, gives one in which he states:

'If any arguments were wanting to arouse the community to the investigation of this important subject, they might be drawn from the heavy pecuniary tax which fever entails on the benevolent of our city, from the poverty, misery, and crime which this disease engenders. It is not possible, from the data before me, to give anything like an accurate calculation of the sums spent for the treatment of fever in Glasgow during the last twenty years. The following calculation intentionally falls considerably under the amount, to prevent every suspicion of exaggeration:

	£	s.	d.
1. Cost of the fever hospital	8,566	7	9
2. Temporary hospitals, and maintenance of patients in them	5,000	0	0
3. 21,691 patients at 1*l*. 10*s*. treated at the expense of the infirmary	32,536	10	0
	£46,102	17	9

To this amount fall to be added the expense of treating the poor in their own houses under the district surgeons of the burgh, and any sums expended by the heritors of the Gorbals and Barony parishes for similar purposes. But this sum must have been greatly increased by the demands of pauperism produced by fever, on our poor's-rates, and on the private benevolence of our citizens: for the duration of the disease, and the period of convalescence which must elapse before an individual can resume his work, will average rather more than six weeks; and when to this is added the difficulty of again finding immediate employment, we may safely assume that the 12,895 individuals treated in the fever hospitals during the last seven years, all, with few exceptions, depending on their daily labour and extending the benefit of that labour to others, were out of employment for a period of at least six weeks.'[2]

The *Rev. G. Lewis*, the minister of St. David's parish, Dundee, who has answered the queries issued by the Board, and very powerfully addressed the inhabitants on this subject, in the course of one of his addresses observes that:

'Apart altogether from the waste of human life, and the indescribable suffering and sorrow which annually fall upon the working classes of Dundee from this periodical scourge, and viewed only as a mere matter of profit and loss to the mercantile and monied interest of Dundee, it were easy to demonstrate, that the expenditure of several thousand pounds per annum in

---

* I am informed that regulations on the principle of those we recommended under the Factory Commission for the Protection of Adult Workmen from the consequences of Accidents, are now adopted in the Prussian code, and practically enforced.

---

1. 'Principles of jurisprudence and responsibility for accidents: extract from the First Report of the Commissioners of Inquiry into the Labour of Children in Factories', *San. Rep.*, Appendix 25, pp. 442-4.
2. Robert Cowan, *Vital Statistics of Glasgow* (Glasgow 1838), pp. 13-14.

V. Pecuniary Burdens Created by Neglect

providing the means of cleanliness to this town, in the better cleansing of its streets, but, above all, of its back closes, courts, and lanes, and the clearing away of those pestilential masses of building which lie concealed from view behind the front lines of some of our principal streets, would have been rewarded by a saving to the community of a vast sum, which the ravages of disease and death have been, for the last few years, compelling Dundee to pay in a way its inhabitants think not of. That this may appear, I have brought into one table the number of cases of fever during the last seven years.

'CASES of Fever in Dundee during the last seven years, from 1833 to 1839, inclusive, calculated from the Bills of Mortality according to the proportion of nine cases to each death:

Year	Cases	Deaths
1833	1,188	132
1834	1,521	169
1835	1,179	131
1836	2,673	297
1837	1,881	209
1838	1,773	197
1839	1,593	177
	11,808	1,312

'Thus, in seven years, fever has fallen on much more than a tithe of the inhabitants,—choosing its victims here, as elsewhere, in the manhood of life, and compelling the citizens of Dundee to pay a tax frightful in the amount of personal sufferings and family bereavements.

'But it were a mistake to imagine that the sufferings and death of so many citizens are the only *tithes* which fever has compelled us to pay during the last seven years. Put wholly aside the details of domestic woe and personal suffering which 11,808 cases of fever have introduced into the families of Dundee in these seven years—omit all reckoning of the watching, want, and wretchedness wrapped up in so many cases of acute disease, and the family bereavements implied in these 1,312 deaths—and let us view for a moment our fellow-creatures but as so many machines suspended from work by the derangement or destruction of the human machinery, that we may learn something of the probable money loss incurred by fever in these seven years.

'From Dr. Southwood Smith, the highest authority on these subjects, we learn that fully one-half of the cases of fever occur in the prime of life, when men are most useful either to their families or to society. Deducting then the 1,312 deaths from the whole number of cases, there will remain 10,496 cases of fever, the one-half of whom, at least, were adults,—that is, 5,248 persons in the prime of life, very many of them heads of families, had fever in these seven years. Now, the average period fever detains a patient from work, according to the same authority, is six weeks. Let us take the earnings in health of these adults at the average of 8*s*. weekly; and the loss of wages to these 5,248 adults, by six weeks' fever, amounts to 12,595*l*.; and this, after excluding all under age, and all the deaths. But these cases, whether treated at home or at the infirmary, must be also loaded with the expense of medical treatment, which is estimated in our infirmary reports at 1*l*. to each case, that is, 5,248*l*. must be added to the loss by wages. But 5,248 cases of those under age remain to be accounted for; and, as fever rarely attacks mere children, but chiefly those either in manhood or approaching manhood, we may estimate the loss of their labour at the one-half of the adults, or 6,297*l*. 12*s*., and the expense of attendance and recovery at one-half also, or 2,624*l*.

V. Pecuniary Burdens Created by Neglect

'But how shall we estimate the pecuniary loss of 1,312 deaths? It seems a strange thing to go about estimating the money value of that which money did not give, and cannot restore when taken away; yet as there are those who understand better a profit and loss account than the arguments of religion and humanity, we shall attempt to estimate the money loss of these 1,312 deaths by fever.

'At least one-half, or 656 of these deaths, were deaths of adults, and very many of them heads of families, of which the 337 widows in St. David's parish afford melancholy evidence.'[1]

He then refers to an estimate made by *Mr. M'Culloch*, who, viewing a human being as a productive machine, reared to last a certain time, and to return so much more than he costs, estimates a full-grown workman just arrived at maturity as having 300*l.* of capital invested in him. At the actual cost of maintaining and training a pauper child in England at the school in Norwood,[2] 4*s.* 6*d.* per week, he will have had expended upon him at 21 years of age, 245*l.*, or at 30 years, 350*l.*; but he supposes—

'The money value of these male and female adults to be just the one-half of this, or 150*l.*, which makes the loss, by the premature death of these 656 adults, to be 98,400*l.*; and, if the remaining 656 under the age of maturity, yet approaching it, be taken at the half of the adults, or 75*l.* each, we have a loss of 49,200*l.* more; to which, if we add 1*l.* a-piece, or 1,312*l.* in all, for attendance and medical expenses, the Fever Bill of Dundee, during the last seven years, will stand as follows:

Fever Bill of Dundee from 1833 to 1839

	£	s.	d.
Loss of labour for six weeks of 5,248 adults, at 8*s.* a-week	12,595	0	0
Attendance, medicine at home or infirmary, at 1*l.* each	5,248	0	0
Loss of labour for six weeks of 5,248 under age, at 4*s.* a-week	6,297	12	0
Expense of treatment of the above at infirmary or home, at 10*s.* a-piece	2,624	0	0
Loss by death of 656 adults, at 150*l.* each	98,400	0	0
Loss by 656 deaths under age, at 75*l.* a-piece	49,200	0	0
Treatment of 1,312 cases, at 1*l.* each	1,312	0	0
	£175,676	12	0

Or 25,096*l.* 13*s.* per annum

'The poor, we are told, we shall always have with us, and so with disease and death. Yet the evils, both of poverty and disease, come in very different measures to different communities. As there is a poverty that is self-inflicted, and may be self-removed, so there is a certain amount of disease and annual mortality in every city that is self-inflicted; and the community that does not

---

1. Rev. George Lewis, *A Course of Lectures on the Physical, Educational and Moral Statistics of Dundee* (Dundee 1841), No. 2, 'The filth and fever bills of Dundee', pp. 6-8.
2. The school for pauper children at Norwood was adopted by Kay in 1838-9 as an experimental school to point the way to a general improvement in the system of pauper education. See his report in the *Fifth Annual Report of the Poor Law Commissioners* (1839), pp. 145-60; and Frank Smith, *The Life and Work of Sir James Kay-Shuttleworth* (1923), pp. 57-60.

V. Pecuniary Burdens Created by Neglect

strive, by every available means, to reduce its disease and mortality bills to the lowest sum of human suffering, and the lowest rate of annual mortality, is as guilty of suicide as the individual who, Judas like, takes with his own hands the life God has given, and hurries unbidden into the presence of his Judge. The fever bills of the Scottish towns, contrasted with those of the English commercial towns, declare too plainly that man has not yet done his part in Dundee to avert this scourge of society; and, while fever is undoubtedly to be regarded as the visitation of God, it is also to be regarded as the visitation of God for the sin of neglecting a population fallen in character and habits.

In the following table are given the deaths in Dundee in seven years, and the rate to the population,—supposing the inhabitants in 1831 to have been 45,355 souls, and to have increased about 2000 annually, until 1839, when from bad trade the increase was checked:

Years	Deaths	Population	Proportion of Deaths to the Population
1833	1,482	49,355	1 in 33·3
1834	1,650	51,355	1 in 31·1
1835	1,673	53,355	1 in 31·9
1836	1,923	55,355	1 in 28·8
1837	1,963	57,355	1 in 29·2
1838	1,511	59,355	1 in 39·3
1839	1,763	59,355	1 in 33·7
	11,965	385,485	1 in 32·2

Thus, the average mortality in Dundee, during the last seven years, was 1 in 32 annually. * * * Here, then, in Dundee, the deaths annually are at least one-fourth more than over the rest of Scotland, Glasgow excepted,[1] which seems to surpass Dundee in the waste of human life. If the deaths are a fourth greater, those diseases which are its harbingers must be many times greater than the deaths; and to this extent, at least, it was in the power of human means to have provided a remedy,—to have abated by one-fourth the physical suffering and mortality of Dundee, saved 2,952 persons from fever, and 328 persons from premature death, and reduced by a fourth part the pecuniary loss incurred during the last seven years,—in other words, to have saved 43,919*l*., or 6,274*l*. annually, to the profit and loss account of this city in the single item of fever.

'The statistics of small-pox in Dundee might be added to this bill of charges. It is sufficient, however, to allude to it. Last year, the deaths by small-pox were 77. In 1838, they were also 77; and in 1837, they amounted to 126. The number of cases, of course, must have been many times the deaths; by far the greater number under age and unvaccinated,—a neglect no longer confined to the Irish population.

* * * * * *

'Though I am no medical authority, yet I am sure that I have every medical authority with me when I connect, as foremost amongst the causes of the enormous Fever Bill of Dundee that monstrous Tavern Bill, which last lecture I showed you was the worm in the bud of the happiness and well-being of its working classes. That Tavern Bill, according to the mean of three different estimates, amounts to 21,234*l*. a-year in my parish alone, and to 180,000*l*. a-year to all Dundee. In vain we cry out against the taxation of Government.

---

1. According to Cowan, the average mortality in Glasgow for the period 1831-9 was 1 in 31·986 (or 31·3 per 1,000). (*J.R.S.S.*, III (1840), 266.)

While the words of complaint are on our lips, here is a vice of continual tasting and tippling in strong drink,—a private self-imposed tax, but heavier far than any public tax. It is this besetting sin that has been not only devouring the substance of the poor, but every year sowing the seeds of that enormous Fever Bill which for the last seven years has been taxing us, not only in purse but in person,—compelling every tenth man in Dundee during that period to pay the wages of six weeks' labour, and to suffer all the langour, sickness, and oppression of six weeks' fever, besides the bereaved widows and orphans, and the fatherless and motherless children it has left in Dundee.'[1]

I now proceed to submit the reasons for believing that the immediate expenditure of so much money as would be incurred by the adoption of such of the remedial measures as appear to be available by the agency of any public administration would be sound measures of immediate economy, and of ultimate public gain: and also the grounds for believing that the same conclusion is applicable to the cost of those measures of prevention which, though directly or indirectly controllable by legislative authority, are within the province of private individuals to execute, such as the construction of the dwellings of the labouring classes.

VI

EVIDENCE OF THE EFFECTS OF PREVENTIVE MEASURES IN RAISING THE STANDARD OF HEALTH AND THE CHANCES OF LIFE

On viewing the evidence, which shows that in most situations higher chances of life belong to the middle and higher classes of the population, an impression may be created that the higher standards of health are essentially connected with expensive modes of living. The highest medical authorities agree, however, that the more important means for the protection and advance of the health of those classes must be in still further reductions than those which it is the present tendency in the higher classes of society to make of the use of highly stimulating food. The evidence already adduced with respect to the labouring classes in the rural districts and those living on high wages in towns, will have gone some way to remove the erroneous impression with respect to them, and it admits of proof that a higher standard of health and comfort is attainable for them even at a less expense than that in which they now live in disease and misery. The experience of the effect of sanitary measures in the royal navy may be adduced as evidence of the practicable standards of health consistent with great labour and exposure to weather obtained at a cost not higher than that within the wages of ordinary labourers. The experience of the effects of sanitary measures in banishing spontaneous disease from crowded prisons, offers further evidence of the health obtainable by simple means, under circumstances still more unfavourable.

The prisons were formerly distinguished for their filth, and their bad ventilation; but the descriptions given by Howard[2] of the worst prisons

---

1. Rev. George Lewis, *A Course of Lectures*, pp. 8-11.
2. John Howard (1726-1790), celebrated prison reformer.

VI. The Effects of Preventive Measures

he visited in England (which he states were amongst the worst he had seen in Europe) were exceeded in every wynd in Edinburgh and Glasgow, inspected by Dr. Arnott and myself, in company with the municipal officers of those cities. More filth, worse physical suffering and moral disorder than Howard describes as affecting the prisoners, are to be found amongst the cellar population of the working people of Liverpool, Manchester, or Leeds, and in large portions of the metropolis. As a standard of the progress made in ameliorating the condition of prisoners, I refer to his general statement of the condition in which he found the prisons when he inspected them in England.

'*Water.*—Many prisons have *no water*. This defect is frequent in bridewells and town gaols. In the felons' courts of some county gaols there is no water: in some places where there is water, prisoners are always locked up within doors, and have no more than the keeper or his servants think fit to bring them.

'*Air.*—And as to air, which is no less necessary than the two preceding articles, and given us by Providence quite gratis, without any care or labour of our own; yet, as if the bounteous goodness of heaven excited our envy, methods are contrived to rob prisoners of this genuine cordial of life, as Dr. Hales[1] very properly calls it; I mean by preventing that circulation and change of the fluid without which animals cannot live and thrive. It is well known that air which has performed its office in the lungs is feculent and noxious. Writers upon this subject show that a hogshead of air will last a man only an hour: but those who do not choose to consult philosophers may judge from a notorious fact. In 1756, at Calcutta, in Bengal, out of 170 persons who were confined in a hole there one night, 154 were taken out dead. The few survivors ascribed the mortality to their want of fresh air; and called the place, Hell in Miniature.

'From hence any one may judge of the probability there is against health and life of prisoners crowded in their rooms, cells, and subterraneous dungeons, for 14 or 15 hours out of the 24. In some of those caverns the floor is very damp; in some there is sometimes an inch or two of water; and the straw or bedding is laid on such floors, seldom on barrack bedsteads. Where prisoners are not kept in underground cells, they are often confined in their rooms, because there is no court belonging to the prisons; which is the case in many city and town gaols; because the walls round the yard are ruinous, or are too low* for safety; or because the gaoler has the ground for his own use'. Prisoners confined in this manner are generally unhealthy.

'In Baker's Chronicle, p. 353[2], that historian, mentioning the assize held in Oxford Castle, 1577 (called, from its fatal consequences, the Black Assize), informs us, "that all who were present died within forty hours; the lord chief baron, the sheriff, and about 300 more." Lord Chancellor Bacon ascribes this

---

* An Act made in Ireland the 3rd year of his present Majesty 'for better preventing the severities, &c.', has the following clause:—'Whereas many infectious disorders are daily produced by the confinement of numbers in close prisons, whereunto there is no back-yard adjoining, and the lives of his majesty's subjects are endangered by the bringing of prisoners into public

---

1. Stephen Hales, author of *A Description of Ventilation* (1743); and *A Treatise on Ventilation, part second* (1758).
2. Sir Richard Baker, *Chronicle of the Kings of England from the Time of the Roman Government unto the Reign of King Charles* (1643).

to a disease brought into court by the prisoners; and Dr. Mead[1] is of the same opinion.

'The first of these two authors, Lord Bacon, observes, that "the most pernicious infection, next the plague, is the smell of a jail, when the prisoners have been long close and nastily kept; whereof we have had, in our time, experience twice or thrice; when both the judges that sat upon the jail, and numbers of those who attended the business, or were present, sickened and died."

'Sir John Pringle[2] observes that "gaols have often been the cause of malignant fevers;' and he informs us that in the late Rebellion in Scotland, above 200 men of one regiment were infected with the gaol fever by some deserters brought from prisons in England.

'Dr. Lind[3], physician to the royal hospital at Haslar, near Portsmouth, showed me, in one of the wards, a number of sailors ill of the gaol fever, brought on board their ship by a man who had been discharged from a prison in London. The ship was laid up on the occasion. That gentleman, in his "Essay on the Health of Seamen," asserts that "the source of infection to our armies and fleets are undoubtedly the gaols; we can often trace the importers of it directly from them. It often proves fatal in impressing men on the hasty equipment of a fleet. The first English fleet sent last war to America lost by it above 2000 men. In another place he assures us that the seeds of infection were carried from the guard-ships into our squadrons; and the mortality thus occasioned was greater than by all other diseases or means of death put together."

'It were easy to multiply instances of this mischief; but those I have mentioned are, I presume, sufficient to show, even if no mercy were due to prisoners, that the gaol distemper is a "national concern" of no small importance.'

'*Sewers.*—Some gaols have no sewers or vaults; and in those that have, if they be not properly attended to, they are, even to a visitant, offensive beyond description; how noxious, then, to people confined constantly in those prisons!

'One cause why the rooms in some prisons are so close is the window-tax, which the gaolers have to pay; this tempts them to stop the windows and stifle their prisoners.[4]

'*Bedding.*—In many gaols, and in most bridewells, there is no allowance of *bedding* or straw for prisoners to sleep on; and if by any means they get a little, it is not changed for months together, so that it is offensive and almost worn to dust. Some lie upon rags, others upon bare floors. When I have complained

---

* *contd.:*
streets for air; be it enacted—That every grand jury at the assizes or quarter sessions may be enabled, and they are hereby required and directed to contract either by lease, or to purchase a piece of ground next adjoining the gaol, or as near as conveniently can be had thereto and cause to be erected necessary houses, and a wall sufficient for the security of the said prisoners'.

---

1. Richard Mead, author of *A Short Discourse concerning pestilential Contagion, and the Methods to be used to prevent it* (1720).
2. Sir John Pringle, author of *Observations on the Nature and Cure of Hospital and Jayl-Fevers* (1750); and *Observations on the Diseases of the Army* (1752).
3. James Lind, author of *An Essay on the most effectual means of preserving the Health of Seamen in the Royal Navy* (1757).
4. The window tax was first levied in 1696 to finance the recoinage of that year. It was re-designed in 1766, and augmented substantially in 1784, when it was used to compensate the reduction in the tea duties.

VI. The Effects of Preventive Measures

of this to the keepers, their justification has been: "the county allows no straw; the prisoners have none but at my cost.""[1]

Since Howard succeeded in gaining national attention to the condition of prisoners, the evils of prison management have been removed. A large proportion of the prison population is taken from the worst regulated and most confined neighbourhoods, which have been the subject of examination; and, with the view to judge what might be effected by sanitary regulations, I have made frequent inquiries as to the effects of sanitary measures on the worst class of persons, the larger proportion of whom are taken from the worst neighbourhoods, that is, as to the effects of living in the same atmosphere, on a less expensive diet than that of the general labouring population, but provided with clean and tolerably well-ventilated places of work and sleeping-rooms, and where they are required to be cleanly in their persons.

I have obtained through Mr. Hill, the prison inspector of Scotland, an accurate return of the number of days which the prisoners had been absent from labour on the ground of ill health in the celebrated prison at Glasgow, where the separate system of confinement has been tried (Return No. 1); a similar return from the Edinburgh prison, (No. 2). I also obtained a careful examination of the amount of sickness prevalent amongst the prisoners at Salford prison, (No. 3). The average cost of the diets, (principally vegetable,) at Salford, varied from 1s. 4d. to 1s. 6d. per week; at Edinburgh, 1s. 9d. per week; and at Glasgow, 1s. 7d. per week. *Vide* Appendix.[2]

The medical practitioners, who are well acquainted with the general state of health of the population surrounding the prisons concur in vouching to the fact, upon their own knowledge, that the health of the prisoners is in general much higher than the health almost of any part of the surrounding population; that the prisoners, as a class, are below the average of health when they enter the prisons; that they come from the worst neighbourhoods; that many of them come from the lodging-houses, which, in those towns, as will be shown, are the constant seats of disease; that they are mostly persons of intemperate habits; that many of them come in in a state of disease from intemperance and bad habits; and notwithstanding the depressing influence of imprisonment, the effect of cleanliness, dryness, better ventilation, temperance, and simple food, is almost sufficient to prevent disease arising within the prison, and to put the prisoners in a better working condition at the termination than at the commencement of their imprisonment. At the Glasgow bridewell, the prisoners are weighed on their entrance and at their discharge, and it is found that, on the average, they gained in weight by their imprisonment.* At Edinburgh, there were instances of

---

* Thirty-three males who were imprisoned for six months gained 37 lbs. total weight; five females gained 19 lbs.; twenty-two males confined during twelve months, gained 3 lbs.; eight females, during the same period, gained

---

1. John Howard, *The State of the Prisons in England and Wales* (Warrington, 1777), pp. 12-20.
2. 'Tables of sickness in prisons', *San. Rep.*, Appendix 27, p. 449.

VI. The Effects of Preventive Measures

poor persons in a state of disease committed from motives of humanity to the prison, that they might be taken care of and cured. The tables are to be taken as showing imperfectly the comparative effects of the different circumstances; because, when a labourer is obliged to leave work he loses wages; and it is known of large classes of them, that they often work improvidently and injuriously to their chances of recovery by continuing at work in impaired health too long; the prisoner, on the contrary, by absence on the sick list, gains ease and exemption from slave labour; and the officers have constantly to contend against feigned sickness to avoid task-work and punishment. It should also be noted that a large proportion of the sickness of the prisoners is of a character that is excluded from all tables of insurance, from the benefit societies as being specially excluded from their benefits. The numbers imprisoned at the lower ages, or above 36 years of age, were too few to form any comparison:

	Average Annual Sickness of Male Prisoners in the			Labourers and Operatives			No. 7	No. 8
	No. 1 Glasgow Prison	No. 2 Edinburgh Prison	No. 3 Salford Prison	No. 4 Employed in East-India Company's Warehouses	No. 5 Average duration of sickness per annum of every person employed in Cotton Factories of Lancashire	No. 6 Males of Families in Wynds of Edinburgh		Average Annual Sickness of Members of Benefit Societies in Scotland	Average Annual Sickness of provident portion of Working Classes throughout Great Britain, according to the experience of Mr. Finlaison
AGE	Days & Decimals	Days & Decimals	Days & Decimals	Days & Decimals	Days & Decimals	Days & Decimals	Years of Age	Days & Decimals	Days & Decimals
Under 16 Years	—	—	—	—	3·5	—	—	—	—
16 to 21	3·05	4·01	3·10	4·02	4·42	2·3	18	2·5	5·18
21 to 26	1·83	2·04	1·64	5·40	4·91	5·1	23	3·8	6·75
26 to 31	2·65	2·33	2·72	4·49	6·88	11·0	28	4·6	6·78
31 to 36	2·83	3·10	2·63	4·55	3·85	8·3	33	5·6	6·33
36 to 41	9·00	5·10	·85	5·57	4·13	4·1	38	6·2	7·86
41 to 46	·49	2·75	·51	5·18	5·09	15·1	43	8·8	9·02
46 to 51	—	—	—	5·43	7·18	30·0	48	9·1	11·76
51 to 56	—	—	—	6·80	3·47	16·2	53	14·8	16·77
56 to 61	—	—	—	7·21	12·68	30·4	58	17·8	23·57
61 to 66	—	—	—	10·24	—	42·7	63	20·0	33·22
66 to 71	—	—	—	9·93	—	64·2	68	36·0	61·22
71 to 76	—	—	—	10·60	—	41·0	73	38·6	101·44
76 to 81	—	—	—	12·67	—	83·6	78	70·9	164·72

The total number of male prisoners in the three prisons from which the returns were compiled was 7,328; of which number, in the Glasgow prison there were 1,796, in the Edinburgh prison 1,256, and in the Salford prison 4,276 prisoners. The columns inserted in the above table from the prisons give only the amount of sickness prevalent amongst

---

* contd.:
5 lbs.; seven males in eighteen months gained 24 lbs.; and two females 10 lbs. At Edinburgh also they were weighed, and, on the whole, they gained. See Appendix, statement of the periods of confinement and weight of prisoners at the commencement and termination of their imprisonment.[1] | 1. *Ibid.*, pp. 449-51.

VI. The Effects of Preventive Measures

the males. The returns which are given in full in the Appendix contain the amount of sickness prevalent among the female prisoners also.

The information as to the actual amount of sickness prevalent amongst the labouring classes is at present extremely defective for the purposes of insurance. One of the most authentic tables is that compiled by Dr. Mitchell, from returns we obtained under the Factory Commission of Inquiry, of the experience of sickness amongst the labourers employed by the East India Company in their warehouses in London. The experience was from 2,461 workmen employed during ten years. (Return No. 4).[1]

This is a highly favourable table, inasmuch as the men were, in the first instance, select, nearly as much so as recruits in the army; care was also taken to give men who became infirm such labour as they could perform without exertion; but, above all, they had the benefit of medical advice without any expense, and being thereby induced to make early application, disease was cut short at once on its first appearance. Moreover, they were not allowed to return to work until they had a medical certificate of their cure.

Another table (No. 5) given is one of the amount of sickness experienced by the male operatives in the cotton mills in England, also deduced from the returns directed to be made under the Factory Commission of Inquiry. But these returns do not include the experience of the mills in Manchester, which was not collected by the district commissioners.[2]

The table (No. 6) is that made up by Mr. Tait, surgeon, from his inquiries of the experience of sickness in the wynds of Edinburgh.

The next table (No. 7) is made up from the experience of benefit societies in Scotland, subsequent to the experience tables which were compiled by the Highland Society; but this is the experience of a select class, which appears to me to be too favourable for general use in Scotland.[3]

The next table (No. 8) is one in use by Mr. Finlaison, the actuary at the National Debt Office, prepared from various sources of information. It has been tried by the experience of a large benefit society in Bethnal Green, and the allowance for sickness was found to be low as compared with the sickness occurring amongst the labouring classes in that district.[4]

The account given by Mr. Tait, of his investigation of the sickness which had prevailed amongst 335 persons in 180 families, exhibited in column No. 5, is as follows:

'The parts visited may be considered a fair specimen of the Edinburgh

---

1. *Factories Inquiry Commission, Supplementary Report, Part II*, P.P. 1834, XIX, pp. 47-53. 2. *Ibid.*, p. 59.
3. The table was first printed in *Report on Friendly or Benefit Societies* (Highland Society, Edinburgh 1824), pp. 148-9. It is reprinted in full in *San. Rep.*, Appendix 28, p. 452.
4. There is a table relating to sickness among the labouring classes of London, drawn from the records of a London Friendly Society for the years 1821-7 showing very similar figures to these, in John Finlaison, *Report on the Law of Mortality of the Government Life Annuities*, P.P. 1829, III, p. 62.

VI. The Effects of Preventive Measures

wynds and closes. They consist of Gillon's and Gibb's Closes, Canongate, Blackfriars' Wynd, Bremot's and Skinner's Closes, High Street, and Mealmarket Stairs, Cowgate. The drainage of all these places is bad; the sewers are without exception open, and those in Gillon's and Gibb's Closes being nearly on a dead level, keep these places constantly in a filthy condition. The poverty of the inhabitants who reside in Gibb's Close, especially, is also extreme, five out of seven families living in apartments without furniture. The ventilation in general is also bad: several apartments are so close that it is difficult for a person when he first enters them to breathe. In several instances I had to retreat to the door to write down my notes, as I found the stench and close atmosphere produce a sickening sensation which, on one occasion, terminated in vomiting. Although some of the apartments visited were tidy and clean, in general they were the reverse. It is impossible to conceive or describe the filthy condition of some of them. Many of them were very small, and others rather capacious, considering the quantity of furniture they contained. The diseases mentioned were such as to throw the persons affected out of employment. There were many cases of slight and continued ailment of which no notice was taken. No case of rheumatism was taken down unless so severe as to lay the person entirely off work.

'About 180 families were visited, but only 117 of them had been one year and upwards in their present dwelling: all the cases of sickness occurred between Martinmas, 1840, and Martinmas, 1841, and none of the patients,' *i.e.* of whom any account was taken, 'were under ten years of age,' those under that age being intentionally excluded.

Mr. Hill states, that he has no doubt the results, which will be apparent from the examination of the several tables which are placed in juxta-position, would be corroborated by similar returns obtained from other well-regulated prisons in Scotland. The returns from the prisons in England up to the year 1834-5 (which do not, however, give the days of sickness, but only the number of prisoners attacked with sickness during the period for which the return was made) further corroborate these results. Even in the Milbank Penitentiary, the situation of which is insalubrious, the average annual amount of sickness to the prisoners who are confined two years and a half is only about eight days to each person, which, for the average ages, is little above the standard obtained from the experience of the East India Company's labourers. The sickness amongst the metropolitan police is about $10\frac{1}{2}$ days per annum for each of the force, $2\frac{3}{4}$ per cent. being constantly on the sick-list. The sickness in the army is on the average $14\frac{1}{2}$ days each soldier. Mr. Finlaison informs me he can venture to state, that were any benefit society to use scales of premiums founded on the prison experience, they would inevitably be insolvent in less than three years.

M. Villermé has shown the diminution of mortality that has taken place in the prisons of France, chiefly from stricter attention to cleanliness, ventilation, and diet, to be equally striking.[1] At Lyons, from 1800 to 1806, the annual mortality in the prisons was 1 in 19; from 1806 to 1812, it was 1 in 31; from 1812 to 1819, it was 1 in 34; and from 1820 to 1826, 1 in 43: a similar amelioration has also been remarked in the prisons of Rouen, and some other large towns in that kingdom.

---

1. L. R. Villermé, *Les Prisons telles qu'elles sont, telles qu'elles devaient être* (Paris 1820).

VI. The Effects of Preventive Measures

The following is a summary return of the diseases of the duration of each, amongst the population of the wynds, examined by Mr. Tait:

Nature of Disease	No. of Cases	Average duration of Disease	No. of Deaths	No. of Families visited	No. of Persons visited
		Weeks			
Disease of Lungs	23	5½	1	117	335
Rheumatism	9	9			
Accidents	9	4½			
Erysipelas	3	8			
Inflammation of Throat	3	5			
Fever	15	5¼	1		
Palsy	4	—	1		
Dropsy	1	7			
Disease of Liver	1	—			
Jaundice	1	4			
Carbuncle	1	5			
Affection of Urinary Organs	1	17			
Acute affection of Brain	2	3	1		
Small-pox	2	5	1		
Opthalmia	1	6			
Whitlow	1	3			
Lumbago	2	7			
Eruptive disease	1	9			
Inflammation of Stomach	1	—			
Ague	1	4			
Abscess in Loins	1	5			
Total	83		5	117	335

It may be safely pronounced that if such an amount of sickness were known to prevail in a prison containing between 300 and 400 prisoners, the circumstance would excite public alarm and attention.

Any of the preceding tables of the lower amounts of sickness may be taken as practicable standards of the extent to which it were possible, by the removal of the causes of disease, to bring the health of the labouring population.

I may here observe, that the tables of sickness above referred to exhibit the very unsatisfactory footing on which the means of insurance against sickness and mortality within the reach of the labouring classes are now placed. An artisan of the condition of the East India Company's labourers who insures for an allowance for sickness between the age of 61 and 66 years, which, according to the experience of his own class, would be a period of 10 days, would have to pay for 20 days, or 10 days in excess if he insured on the tables of the experience of benefit societies in Scotland, or 23 days in excess if he insured on tables founded on the experience collected by Mr. Finlaison. On the other hand, were a benefit society composed of members living under depressed circumstances, as in close courts or ill-drained districts, to adopt the table of the experience of the East India Company's labourers, and to take members, living under the circumstances indicated by the Highland societies or Mr. Finlaison's tables, the allowance on such a rate of insurance would be fraught with certain and speedy loss of the funds of the contributors. Having received contributions for an allowance on the chances of 10 days' sickness, they would, upon insurances from the wynds of Edinburgh, have to pay for 40 days. The range of variation in the chances of life in different districts, such as have been shown in the returns from the different towns, exhibiting the mortality amongst the different classes, all present instances of the ruin to which benefit societies are exposed in acting upon tables calculated only for select classes, or on the mean experience of large classes, or of many classes differing widely in their circumstances. The probabilities of life at infancy for the whole population of Liverpool, as deduced from the actual ages of deaths of the whole population, would be 17 years; but on the Northampton tables of probability, payment would be required for the insurance of 25 years at infancy; for 38 years according to the Carlisle table; and if a male, for 37 years, according to the Swedish table[1]. Yet such are the data and their applications on which large masses of savings and property are frequently invested and made dependent in various forms of insurance in benefit societies. The ruin of such societies is, I lament to say, by no means an unfrequent occurrence. The most painful spectacle that is presented in a painful and difficult service is that of a hardworking, industrious labourer, who has lived frugally and saved rigidly, who in his old age is stripped of his savings and reduced to destitution. Once such example is enough to destroy the frugality of a whole village, and of all the labourers to whom it is presented. The necessity of a revision of all the tables which govern the subscriptions to friendly societies and the allowances from them, is strongly suggested by the evidence. It is to be lamented that, before giving tables of sickness or mortality to the members of benefit societies, many of the actuaries who have advised them have made no inquiries as to the condition of the neighbourhoods where the members reside or as to their general circumstances. The best advice to the labourers for the future will, however, be proved to be, that the most safe, economical, and efficient outlay as an insurance, will be in their own contributions, in rates or extra rent where needful for the execution of sanitary measures.

The further example adverted to as to the efficiency of preventive measures, is furnished by the naval medical service.

So dreadful was once the condition of the navy that, in the year 1726, when Admiral Hosier sailed with seven ships of the line to the West Indies, he buried his ships' companies twice, and died himself of a broken heart. Amongst the pictures then presented, as in Anson's Voyages, 1740-44, were those of deaths to the amount of eight or ten a-day in a moderate ship's company; bodies sewn up in hammocks and washing about the decks, for want of strength and spirit on the part of the miserable survivors to cast them overboard. Dr. Johnson, in the year 1778, thus describes a sea life:—'As to the sailor, when you look down from the quarter-deck to the space below, you see the utmost

---

1. For the Northampton, Carlisle, and Swedish life tables, see above, p. 255, nn. 1-2.

VI. The Effects of Preventive Measures

extremity of human misery; such crowding, such filth, such stench!' 'A ship is a prison, with the chance of being drowned,—it is worse, worse in every respect; worse air, worse food, worse company.'[1]

Dr. *Wilson*, in his preface to the Medical Returns, observes that, within the limits of the South American command, the Centurion, exactly a century ago, lost in a few weeks 200 out of 400 men by scurvy. During the years from 1830 to 1836, the British *squadron* employed in South America, lost by diseases of every description only 115 out of 17,254 men. He observes:

'There is no reason to doubt that instead of every second man perishing miserably within a few weeks, the rate of mortality might have been as low as that exhibited in the South American Report, viz., one death annually by disease out of 150 men. Now there was nothing new nor mysterious in the pestilence either as to its origin or its essence: it was not a sudden climatorial influence which could not be resisted nor understood; it was a well-known affection presenting all the signs of utter prostration and pointing to pure debility as its source, the effects principally of scanty, unwholesome, unvarying diet and bad water—partly of inadequate attention to cleanliness, order, and ventilation, and the nearly total neglect of systematic attention to measures for amusing, cheering, and improving the mind with which resulting despondency often co-operated. The remedy therefore would appear to have been self-evident and at hand, not to the commanders of ships and fleets, but to the administration. Information on many points in the animal economy was certainly less exact than it is now, and vague unfounded notions prevailed of necessary relations existing between a sea-life and scurvy. Hence it may be concluded that ignorance rather than inhumanity was the reason why effectual measures were not long before adopted for the prevention of such terrible calamities.'

He observes further that:
In 1779 the proportion dying was 1 in 8 of the employed.
In 1811 the proportion dying was 1 in 32 of the employed.
From 1830 to 1836 the average number dying annually was 1 in 72 of the employed.

But:
'In this calculation, the deaths from all sources are included from wounds, drowning, and all other external causes as well as from disease. From the latter source the deaths were in the proportion of 1 to 85 of the number employed annually. When it is considered that the ratio applies to the whole

---

1. When quoting from blue books, Chadwick's standard of accuracy is extremely high. He obviously relied on memory in quoting these well-known views of Dr. Johnson, and his memory has confused the great doctor's remarks on three separate occasions. On 31 August 1773 (during the tour of the Highlands), Johnson observed: 'Why, sir, no man will be a sailor, who has contrivance enough to get himself into a jail; for being in a ship is being in jail, with the chance of being drowned'. On 23 September of the same year he added: 'The man in a jail has more room, better food, and commonly better company, and is in safety'. Finally, on 10 April 1778 he made the remark first quoted here (accurately) by Chadwick. (James Boswell, *The Journal of a Tour to the Hebrides with Samuel Johnson* (Everyman edition), pp. 103, 203-4; and *The Life of Samuel Johnson* (Everyman edition), II, 196.

service, and therefore includes the most unhealthy sections, the Coast of Africa and the West Indies, it will be admitted, even without reference to former periods, to be very low.'*[1]

The scurvy, once so fatal in the navy, is now almost unknown in men-of-war, whilst it still prevails often to a most serious extent in the mercantile navy where the same care is not taken. It was a popular opinion in the navy, that the use of lemon juice in the grog was a specific against scurvy; but it is stated that the health of seamen has in some instances been advanced by the discontinuance of the grog itself, and the substitution of coffee. Dr. *Nisbett* says, 'I may state generally, that this substance (lemon juice) in the quantities usually issued (one ounce per diem) does not prevent the appearance of scurvy under circumstances favourable to its production; that in increased quantities it appears to have some power of arresting, at least for a time, this disease in its earlier stages, and is thus of great value; but that it is not to be considered an antidote, and that the only cure for this disease is a

---

* It is observed by Dr. Wilson, in reference to the mortality in the navy, that 'the mortality from wounds is inconsiderable compared with that occasioned by disease. Much misconception has prevailed on this subject in the public mind. Deaths in action, by the general excitement attending them, from being published in official despatches and perpetuated in gazettes, make more than a due impression; for it is found, when accurately reckoned, that they are few in comparison with those resulting from ordinary diseases. Sir G. Blane, when writing under the common impression, and without the corrections of figures, alleges that half the mortality in war periods is attributable to wounds received in battle and other external causes; but he gives a very different account when he dismisses unauthenticated notions to deal with numerical facts. He then states, that from 1780 till 1783, though in that period, besides single actions, engagements with forts, &c., the great battle of the 12th of April was fought, the mortality from disease, compared with that from external causes, was as 3 to 1; in 1779, according to his statement, the former was to the latter as 8 to 1.' During the last 41 months of the peninsular war, whilst 24,930 privates died of disease, only 8,899 died of wounds, or were killed in battle. The deaths during the campaign were,—of the privates in battle, 4·2 per cent.; of disease, 11·9 per cent.: of officers, in battle, 6·6 per cent.; of disease, 3·7 per cent. per annum. The average deaths in four battles, Talavera, Salamanca, Vittoria, and Waterloo, were 3·9 per cent. of officers, 2·11 of privates. In the peninsular war there were generally 22½ per cent. of men absent on account of sickness; and a reduction of the proportions of sick to 6 per cent. would have set free 10,000 men from the hospitals to be added to the effective force of the army.—*Official Returns*. The highest increased charge for insurance of military men during the peninsular campaign was 10 guineas per cent. The extra premiums taken on the insurance of military lives on service in India and China are from 3 to 5 guineas per cent., governed, however, by the unfavourable chances of the climate to which the campaign leads, as well as by the increased risks from battle. The extra premiums on naval officers in hostile service is usually from 3 to 5 guineas per cent., governed by the consideration of the climate.

---

1. John Wilson, introduction to *Statistical Reports on the Health of the Navy for the Years 1830-36, P.P.* 1841, Sess. 2, VI, pp. v-vi.

full diet of fresh meat and vegetables;'[1] the preventives being, general and personal cleanliness, ventilation, and liberal supplies of good water, in addition to supplies of wholesome food.

The mortality of the home force ships employed chiefly in harbour duty, &c. (where of course they were not cut off from communication or means of infection from the shore,) in Great Britain and Ireland, gives the rate of mortality obtainable by sanitary means, even now confessedly imperfect especially in ventilation, amongst a male population ranging from 15 to 50 years of age, and may be taken as illustrative of the amount of health attainable on shore.

In 1830 the deaths in the navy from disease independently of external causes were:

	Disease, per 1,000	All Causes, per 1,000
1830	6·0	8·7
1831	11·5	13·4
1832	11·9	14·0
1833	6·3	7·9
1834	4·9	6·7
1835	5·9	7·2
1836	7·5	9·5

Mr. Finlaison has lately calculated that the deaths *on shore* out of 1,000 of the population of 29 years of age may be estimated at about 12 per annum. Mr. Rickman calculated that the deaths at that age in Essex and Rutland would be about $12\frac{1}{2}$ persons per 1,000 per annum: for the metropolis it would be about $15\frac{1}{2}$ deaths. Out of 1,000 workmen in the Government dock-yards, the number of deaths were 15; and hitherto in the metropolitan police force, which is more select than the navy, the number of deaths appear to be about 9 per annum; but about the same number of men is annually invalided from the force. The proportion of deaths amongst the troops appears to be, amongst the household cavalry, 14·5, amongst the dragoons, 15·3, amongst the infantry in depôt, 18·5, and amongst the foot guards, 21·6. Since the Guards have been in Canada the rate of mortality has been reduced to that of other regiments.

The health of the foot guards is believed to be affected by peculiar circumstances.

I may add, as respects soldiers, that by proper care such epidemics as typhus, scarlet fever, are now scarcely known as affecting large groups in the army, and that such an occurrence would denote to the chiefs of the army medical board the existence of some great neglect into which it would be necessary to make inquiry.

Cost to tenants and owners of the public measures for drainage, cleansing, and the supplies of water, as compared with the cost of sickness.

Persons well acquainted with the inferior descriptions of tenements in Manchester state that a large proportion of them change owners in ten years, and that few remain in the same hands more than twenty years;

---

1. William Nisbet, *The Clinical Guide and Practical Pharmacopoeia* (1793), pp. 112-4, deals with the treatment of scurvy, though not in precisely these words.

VI. The Effects of Preventive Measures

and it is observed in other populous districts that this description of property most frequently changes hands. The chief obstacle to the execution of legislative measures for public improvements of tenements of the class in question in such districts has been, that large immediate outlays of capital have been required to be made in an inconvenient manner for permanent improvements, by persons possessing only short or transient interests, to whom no means are given for spreading the charge over longer periods of years to make it coincident with the benefits.

In reference to the structural arrangements which come within the public authority, the majority of professional persons the best acquainted with the description of tenements occupied by the poorer classes, and the importance of getting the work done, agree that it would, on the whole, be the most advantageous course to execute them, by loans paying interest on the security of the rates, and spread the charge over 30 years during which the original outlay should be repaid. This would allow of the annual instalment being charged in fair proportions to the tenant, and to the holders of short interests.

The outlay for the execution of measures which come within the public authority are those, 1, for bringing water on the premises; 2, for applying it to remove refuse by a cheap apparatus; 3, a drain for conveyance of the refuse to the (4) main drains or common sewer.

In the rural districts all these purposes of cleansing may, it is considered, be accomplished by means of a proper use of the rain-water; and that which is here given may be considered as a maximum estimate for *towns*, if the work be properly done by public contract on a large scale.

First Outlay per Tenement	Annual Instalment for Repayment in Thirty Years	Annual Interest, commuted at 5 per cent. on Outlay charged as Rent on Tenant	Weekly Charge to the Tenant, or increased Rent, being the 1-54th part of the sum of the annual instalment and annual interest	Total Outlay on One-third (1,148,282 inhabited houses) of the existing Tenements in England, Wales, and Scotland		
				First Outlay	Annual Instalment for Repayment in Thirty Years	Annual Interest commuted at 5 per cent. on Outlay charged as Rent on Tenant
£ s. d.	s. d.	£ s. d.	d.	£	£	£
Water-tank* and apparatus 10 8 6	6 11	0 6 8	3	11,970,840	399,028	379,687
Sewer 5 12 0	3 9	0 3 6	1½	6,430,379	214,346	203,957
Water —	—	0 5 0	1	—	—	—
Total	10 8	0 15 2	5½	18,401,219	613,374	583,644

* *Vide* Appendix for estimate and detailed specification.[1] From some recent experiments made with the egg-shaped sewers or main drains, it appears that drains of sufficient size might be made at one-third less than the price for sewers in the annexed estimate. In many instances, main drains costing one-half the sum would suffice.

---

1. 'Suggested form of notification to owners or occupiers, for the distribution of the expense of permanent alterations and the avoidance of overcharges on persons enjoying only portions of the benefit', *San. Rep.*, Appendix 29, pp. 453-4.

Cost to Tenants and Owners of Public Measures

The above is a maximum estimate, and if the work be executed systematically by contract for districts, the charge may be so far reduced that it may be taken to include repairs, but if it were executed by each occupier or each owner separately, 15 per cent. must be added to the charge; and if, in addition to the separate charge incurred by neglect of legislative or administrative arrangements there be also incurred the ordinary fees of new surveyors of sewers, and new surveyors of buildings, paid by the ordinary fees, the charge for these structural improvements will be still further increased.

But the supplies of water for all the household purposes at the highest water company's charges, which is 138 pailsful for less than $1\frac{1}{4}d.$, is, in fact, to be considered a reduction of an existing expenditure of labour of fetching water.

The cost of cleansing privies is estimated as an existing charge in the metropolis and many towns of not less than 10s. per tenement annually. If the duty were duly performed the cost would perhaps be double the amount, and be equivalent to the whole of the proposed new expenditure; and taking the new expenditure as being less that charge, there only remains the cost of the new sewerage,—$1\frac{1}{2}d.$ weekly, or 6s. 6d. annually. Supposing this charge of $1\frac{1}{2}d.$ weekly imposed upon the landlord, he will have to set against it the preservation of the tenement from dilapidation by drainage, which of itself would frequently repay the whole outlay. He has also the circumstance to consider that he may get better tenants by the improvement of his houses, and that with such tenants he will have more regular payments of rent. Protracted sickness and protracted losses of employment, and the frequent mortality caused by neglect of cleansing, occasion heavy losses to the owners, and occasion a greater diminution of the returns for such tenements than is commonly apparent.

One obstruction to any amendment by cleansing is occasioned by the circumstance that the laying on the water is considered a tenant's charge, and the lower the class the more fluctuating the tenantry and the greater the reluctance of the tenant, and the less indeed are the means to make any immediate outlay for permanent purposes. To cast any immediate outlay on occupiers of this class, who have scarcely self-control to make reserves of the weekly rents, practically amounts to a prohibition of the work being done. That which will in extensive districts really be a new charge, *i.e.*, sewerage, will fall only at the rate of the $1\frac{1}{2}d.$ per week per tenement, and as most tenements are now occupied in the more crowded districts, this will be a charge to be divided between two families. If it were properly distributed, it is an amount not to be spoken of as serious in the weekly charge.*

---

* As an instance of the little account the manufacturing workpeople have made of such charges, it is mentioned by Sir Charles Shaw that, on the introduction of the new police force into Manchester, he found the workpeople in the habit of paying 6d. per week each to the old watch for calling them up. He put a stop to the practice, as being one which interfered with the regular duties of the police, and as being founded on a habit which might be corrected. The employers, however, complained of the interruption of the practice, and requested that it might be renewed. Sir Charles, considering that 6d. was too

VI. The Effects of Preventive Measures

New charges, for improved house accommodation, as well as for sewerage and house cleansing, may all be submitted as means for the reduction of the existing heavy charges of sickness, and of the loss of work and loss of wages consequent upon sickness. To judge of the extent of the immediate charge of sickness in money and *time*, which is independent of the charge of insurance against premature death, we may select the case of an ordinary family, say of a man at 40, a wife at 30, and two children, who may be represented as equivalent to one child aged 15, the lowest age estimated in the insurance tables, which for an average family is an under estimate. Now to insure these a payment of 10s. per week each during sickness, the charges would be as follows, according to the insurance tables computed by Mr. Finlaison for the guidance of benefit societies.[1]

Age	For an allowance of 10s. per week during sickness, according to the Table constructed by Mr. Finlaison, the Actuary of the National Debt Office	
	Monthly Payment	Single Payment
	£ s. d.	£ s. d.
Man, 40	0 2 11	27 5 2
Woman, 30	0 1 11½	21 0 6
Child, 15	0 1 3¼	14 18 1
Total per family	0 6 1¾	63 3 9
Total annual charge	3 13 9	—
Total weekly charge per family	0 1 5	—

In the course of the Factory Commission of Inquiry in 1834, we ascertained that the wages of upwards of 40,000 employed in the cotton mills, of whom two-thirds were below the adolescent stage, amounted,

---

* *contd.:*
high a charge, offered to allow the police to call up the work-people at 2d. per week each, provided the masters, to save the trouble of the weekly collection, deducted the amount from the weekly wages, and paid it over to the police fund. The answer to the proposal was, that the work-people would sooner pay 6d. of their own accord than have 1d. deducted from their wages by their masters.[2]

---

1. In the form that Chadwick has reproduced it, this table is meaningless, since it does not indicate the age at which the payment of premiums ceases. Two such tables by Finlaison, calculated for premiums ceasing at ages 60 and 65 respectively, are published in the *First Report of the Select Committee on the Laws respecting Friendly Societies*, P.P. 1825, III, App. B.9, Tables XIII and XIV, pp. 150-1.
2. This point is discussed more fully by Sir Charles Shaw in his pamphlet *Manufacturing Districts: Replies of Sir Charles Shaw* . . . (1843), p. 12.

Cost to Tenants and Owners of Public Measures

on the average, to 10s 5d. per week.[1] Up to the beginning of the present year the wages of those in work were not lower. Mr. Finlaison's table, therefore, will best represent the existing pecuniary charge of sickness from the loss of wages to a family in such a district in ordinary seasons of employment. The actual charge of sickness in *time* lost every year, as represented by the experience of the sickness tables before cited, would be as follows:

Age	Experience of the Wynds of Edinburgh	Experience of Benefit Societies in Scotland	Mr. Finlaison	Experience under Sanitary Measures
	Days, &c.	Days, &c.	Days, &c.	Days, &c.
Man, 40	15·1	6·9	9·2	2·75
Woman, 30	11·0	4·2	6·33	2·10
Child, 15	3·5	0·2	5·18	0·17
Total per family	29·6	11·3	20·71	5·02

The experience of the effect of sanitary measures proves the possibility of the reduction of sickness in the worst districts to at least one-third of the existing amount. Amidst classes somewhat better situated, it were possible to reduce the sickness to less than one-third; it were an under estimate to take the probable reduction at one-half. Taking it, however, at one-half, by the new payment of 1½d., or say 2d., weekly for drainage, the occupants of the tenements will save 7½d. of the weekly contribution for an allowance of 10s. per week each during sickness. But the allowance insured to be paid during sickness only replaces the earnings: the sickness, besides its own misery, entails the expense of medical attendance, which, at the usual rate of insurance in medical clubs, would be 5s. or 6s. per annum for such a family. This would also be reduced one-half, making the total family saving at the least 9d. weekly. But the single payment for structural alterations is to be regarded as general, and as a means of affecting the whole of the objects for the whole of the population. For this 2d. each tenement, or 1d. each family, then, they will not only save double the weekly amount, but they will save, in the wear and tear of shoes and clothes, from having a well-drained and well-cleansed instead of a wet and miry district to traverse; they will also save the sickness itself, and each individual will gain a proportionate extension of a more healthy life. In a district where the wages are not one-half the amount above stated, the expenditure for efficient means of prevention would still leave a surplus of gain to the labourer.

These are the chief gains on the side of the labourer; but in general every labourer over and above what he consumes himself, produces enough to repay the interest on capital and cost of superintendence or the profits of the employer. The loss of this extra production is the loss

---

1. The figure is drawn from *Supplementary Report of the Royal Commission on the Employment of Children in Factories*, *P.P.* 1834, XX, 'Tables extracted by Mr. S. Stanway', p. 123. It relates to the average wage of 48,645 persons engaged in cotton manufacture in April-May 1833.

VI. The Effects of Preventive Measures

of the community during the whole time the services of the labourer are abridged by sickness or death. To this loss is to be added, where the labourer has made no reserve, the loss of the cost of his unproductive maintenance as a pauper, and of medical attendance during sickness.

The existing insurance charge, then, represents the existing charge on the labouring classes from the loss of wages consequent on sickness; to which charge might be added the existing additional charge denoted by the insurance on account of the abridged duration of life and more frequent deaths. The aggregate charge for structural improvements, though amounting to so many millions as a first outlay, is still, for the reasons above stated, only a means of obtaining an incalculably greater gain. But it will be shown that the attainment of that gain is dependent on securities for the application of science to the efficient execution of the combined structural means of prevention. If these were to be no better than those in use in the greater part of the metropolis and the towns throughout the country, and the outlay for drainage were to be an outlay for receptacles to serve as the means of accumulating decomposing deposits, and as latent magazines of pestilential gases, to be themselves cleansed from time to time of the accumulations at a great expense, or to be discharged to pollute the natural streams of the country, then the aggregate expenditure would, to the amount of the inefficiency, be an aggregate of so many millions of money spent in waste.

The *immediate* cost of sickness and loss of employment falls differently in different parts of the country, but on whatsoever fund it does fall, it will be a gain to apply to the means of prevention that fund which is and must needs otherwise continue to be more largely applied to meet the charge of maintenance and remedies. Admitting, however, as a fact the misconception intended to be obviated, that the necessary expense of structural arrangements will be an immediate charge instead of an immediate means of relief to the labouring classes;—in proof that they have, in ordinary times, not only the means of defraying increased public rates but increased rents, I refer to the fact that the amount expended in ardent spirits (exclusive of wines), tobacco, snuff, beer, &c., consumed chiefly by them, cannot be much less than from 45,000,000*l.* to 50,000,000*l.* per annum in the United Kingdom. By an estimate which I obtained from an eminent spirit merchant, of the cost to the consumer of the British spirits on which duty is paid, the annual expenditure on them alone, chiefly by the labouring classes, cannot be less than 24,000,000*l.* per annum. If visible evidence of the means of payment were needed I would point to every gin-palace in the metropolis, or to similar places throughout the country, which are chiefly supported from the expenditure of the class of persons who are overcrowded and lodge most wretchedly, and its duty-paying building materials represents a portion of the money available as rent for abodes of comparative comfort. The cost of one dram per week would nearly defray the expense of the structural arrangements of drainage, &c., by which some of the strongest provocatives to the habit of drunkenness would be removed. In illustration of the extent of the means of defraying such expenses, even in some of the poorer districts, I would cite the following statement

Cost to Tenants and Owners of Public Measures 293

of the minister of the parish of Stevenston, in Ayrshire, given in the last statistical account from that parish:
'When the survey by the present incumbent was completed in 1836, the population stood as follows:—

Number of families 833
Number of population . . . . . . 3681.'

The report further states:
'There are in the parish no less than 33 inns, and public-houses, and whisky-shops. A few inns are needed for the accommodation of travellers, and for the transaction of business; but the rest serve as so many decoys to lure and destroy the thoughtless in their neighbourhood. The sale of spirits in grocers' shops has had a most pernicious influence, especially on the female part of the community, who, when there is no danger of detection, are tempted to add a dram to the other commodities puchased. But the most pernicious practice is that of several families clubbing that they may drink together cheaply in one of their own houses; for in this way husbands, wives, and children all share in the debauch, and drunken habits are perpetuated from generation to generation.

'We are grieved and ashamed to mention the sum annually expended in this parish for ardent spirits. We have learned from the excise-officer of the district the quantity sold in it last year; and without taking into account what is bought at a distance for the use of private families, and exclusive also of all that is expended for wine, and ale, and porter, and beer, and calculating at a rate greatly below the retail price the quantity of ardent spirits sold in the parish, it amounts to the enormous sum of 4125*l*.'[1]

This is nearly at the rate of 5*l*. a-year per family for ardent spirits alone. To give another example:

In the town of Bury, with an estimated population of 25,000, the expenditure in beer and spirits is estimated at 54,190*l*., annually, or 2*l*. 3*s*. 4*d*. for each man, woman, and child, a sum that would pay the rent and taxes for upwards of 6,770 new cottages at 8*l*. per annum each. But on an inquiry made from house to house by the agency of the Manchester Statistical Society into the condition of the labouring population of this town, with such an expenditure on one source of dissipation and ill-health, it appeared that of 2,755 of their dwellings examined, only 1,668 were decidedly comfortable; that a smaller number were well furnished; that the number of families in which there were less than two persons sleeping in one bed were only 413; that the number in which on the average there were more than two persons to a bed was 1,512; that the number of families who had not less than *three* persons in a bed and less than four, was 773; that the number of families in which there were 'at least four persons, but less than five persons to one bed,' was 207. There were 63 families where there were at least five persons to one bed; and there were some in which even six were packed in one bed, lying at the top and bottom—children and adults.[2] Similar results as to misapplied means and numbers crowded

---

1. *New Statistical Account of Scotland* (Edinburgh 1845), V, pp. 459, 472-3. For Chadwick's use of material from the *New Statistical Account*, see above, p. 153, n. 1.
2. These figures are drawn from *Report of a Committee of the Manchester Statistical Society on the Condition of the Working Classes in an extensive manufacturing District in 1834, 1835 and 1836* (1838), pp. i, vii.

together would be ascertained from similar inquiries into the state of the population in other districts.

Any measures must commend themselves to public support that would effect in the application of the immense fund expended in ardent spirits alone, a change for assured physical comforts and undoubted moral advantages of the highest order. Admitting the validity of statements often made and seldom proved in ordinary times, but which nevertheless may occur, of classes of labourers reduced to the minimum of subsistence, that their wages will not admit of any change of application, then another set of considerations would arise, namely, whether the increased charges for new tenements, or for improvement of the existing tenements, will not compel an advance of wages, and thence be charged in the cost of the commodity produced? And whether if the trade will not allow such advanced wages, the amount of misery of the labouring classes is not really increased by exemptions or legislative facilities, which allow the trade to be carried on only at the expense of the health, the morality and the comfort of the labourers engaged in it, and also at the expense of the ratepayers in providing against the casualties of sickness and mortality?

These, however, are questions that appear to be less likely to occur practically to any important extent than may be supposed. The general difficulty would apparently be with the habits of the adults, who will, to use the illustration presented in a portion of evidence previously cited, 'prefer the gin' to the best accommodation that can be offered to them.*

Whilst there is such evidence as that above cited to show that there is in ordinary times no real need, there is much evidence to show the impolicy of any exemptions from the payment of properly distributed charges for the requisite public improvement. In general labourers have been losers by exemptions from charges on their tenements, and scarcely in any instance have gained even by exemptions from the payment of their contributions to the poor's rates.

The effect of administrative proceedings on the condition of the dwellings of large portions of the labouring classes, and thence on the condition of the labourers, is, under varied circumstances, adverted to in the local reports on their sanitary condition, and it is shown that the former parochial administration has operated mischievously in degrading the habitations of the labouring classes, or in checking tendencies to improvement.

The mode by which the condition of the dwellings of the labouring classes has been most extensively deteriorated in England, has been by the facility afforded to owners of cottage tenements, usually when acting

---

* The experience of France is precisely similar. In a work of great authority on the lower classes of that country,[1] it is stated that the secret of the existence of so many filthy, infected, and miserable habitations, is simply that the persons who pay two sous for their lodging at night spend ten sous on brandy by day.

1. This is probably a reference to L. R. Villermé, *Sur les Cités Ouvrières* (Paris, 1830).

Cost to Tenants and Owners of Public Measures

as administrators of the Poor Law, to get their own tenants excused from the payment of rates. The legal ground for exemption was, not the value of the tenement, but the destitution or inability of the tenant to pay; but inasmuch as the occupation of a well-conditioned tenement, or of a tenement in advance of others, would be popularly considered *primâ facie* evidence of ability to pay rates, the cottage speculator would not be at the expense to present evidence against the exemption by which he would gain. The general tenor of the evidence is, that the exempted tenements are of a very inferior order, and that the rents collected for them are exorbitant, and such as ought to ensure tenements of a higher quality.

Such residences appear to come in competition very rarely, and, viewed with reference to the place of work, the habitations of the labouring classes in the manufacturing towns extensively partake of the nature of monopolies, and hence the landlord is enabled to exact a price for position, independently of the character or quality of the building, or of the extent of outlay upon it. Where there is any choice, the labouring classes are generally attracted to these tenements by the promise of exemption from the payment of poor's rates, and are deluded into the payment of a proportionately higher rent. (See the evidence on this subject taken before the House of Commons' Committee on the Rating of Cottage Tenements in 1838; Questions 1103; 1106; 1222; 1377; 1403; 1504—7; 1637—8; 1594; 2269; 2271; 3124; 2234—5; 2240; 2279; 3106; 3723—4; 3920; 4054; 4071.)[1]

The depressing effect of such exemptions is illustrated by the effect of their withdrawal, in cases where the inmates were not only excused from the payment of rates, but from the payment of rents, as in the instance of the parish cottages. The sales of cottage tenements held by the parish have formed a part of the business of this Commission since its commencement. The effects of the removal of the exemption from the payment of rent consequent upon the sale are generally described as beneficial. The tenor of the evidence on this subject is conveyed in a communication from the *Rev. Charles Turner*, the chairman of the Tenbury union, quoted in Sir Edmund Head's report:

'Mr. Turner also says, "When the parish property has been sold, a vast improvement in the external appearance of the cottages has taken place, and consequently a higher rent is demanded, and frequently obtained." We thus see one proof, among many, that the sales of parish property which have taken place under the orders of the Commissioners have been beneficial to the public at large; a vast mass of small buildings (amounting, for instance, in the Bromyard union only, to no less than the net worth of 3643*l.*) has been withdrawn from a state of dilapidation and decay and thrown into the market. Money has been expended on it; it has been put into tenantable and proper repair, and all parties have found their interest in the change. To the parish it formerly yielded nothing. The pauper lived on in filth and wretchedness, in a hovel of which he did not dare to complain, because he held it by sufferance; and the community at large were deprived of an opportunity for a profitable outlay of capital on tenements thus kept in mortmain of the worst kind. Such an outlay would not have taken place unless it promised a return, that is to

---

1. *First and Second Reports of the Select Committee on Rating of Tenements,* P.P. 1837-8, XXI.

say, unless the class for whose reception the cottages are fitted could in all probability pay for the improved accommodation. With regard to parties living in their own houses, Mr. Turner says, "There are many poor persons living in their own cottages, which are of a very inferior description, wretchedly comfortless, and have only one floor. They are decidedly worse than those which are rented, both as to accommodation and state of repairs; but these, for the most part, have been built on the waste and unenclosed land." [1]

The mischievous effect of exemptions from rating on the ground of poverty, in bringing down buildings to the exempted scale, and in preventing advances beyond it, is strikingly displayed in Ireland, where all houses not exceeding the value of 5*l.* are exempted from contribution to the county cess. The general consequence is that the farmers' residences throughout the country are kept down to the level of mere cottages or inconvenient hovels, to avoid passing the line of contribution, and only pass it by indulgent or evasive valuations. But the supposed exemption (which, if it be not often made up by increased rent, is a circumstance peculiar to the smaller holdings in that country) —an exemption which no doubt was procured as a boon, was productive of further ill effects to the parties intended to be benefited.* Being kept by the immediate expense and the fear of their share of the tax to thatched roofs, these thatched roofs afforded facilities to incendiarism, since any one might put a cinder in the thatch, and run away without detection; hence it has placed the inmates so far under continued terror in disturbed times, that it would frequently have been worth the expense of putting on a slate roof as a measure of preventive police. The depression of the tenement is practically a depression of the habits and condition of the inhabitants.

I may assume that it has been proved that the labouring classes do possess the means of purchasing the comforts of superior dwellings, and also that they are not benefited by exemptions from the immediate charges wherever requisite to defray the expense of those superior comforts.

I shall now show how little it is in the power of these classes voluntarily to obtain these improvements,—setting aside entirely the consideration of the obstacles arising from depraved habits already formed.

The workman's 'location,' as it is termed, is generally governed by his work, near which he must reside. The sort of house, and often the particular house, may be said to be, and usually is, a monopoly. On arriving at manhood in a crowded neighbourhood, if he wishes to have a house, he must avail himself of the first vacancy that presents itself; if there happen to be more houses vacant than one, the houses being usually of the same class, little range of choice is thereby presented to

---

* A butter merchant informed me that the value of the Irish butter was deteriorated to a greater extent than they were aware of, from its being frequently made in close smoky hovels instead of in clean and well-ventilated dairies, as in England.

---

1. Sir Edmund Head, 'Report on the state of the residences of the labouring classes in the counties of Gloucester, Hereford, Monmouth, Salop, Worcester, Brecknock, and Radnor', *Local Reps. E. & W.*, p. 115.

him. In particular neighbourhoods near Manchester, and in other parts of the county of Lancaster, in some other manufacturing and in some rural districts, instances occur of the erection of improved ranges of larger and better constructed houses for the labouring classes; and, making deduction for the occasional misuse of the increased space by subdividing them and overcrowding them with lodgers, the extent to which these improved tenements are sought, and the manner in which an improved rent is paid, afford gratifying evidence of an increasing disposition prevalent amongst artisans to avail themselves of such improvements. These opportunities, however, are comparatively few, and occur in districts where multitudes continue in the most depressed condition, apparently without any power of emerging from it.

The individual labourer has little or no power over the internal structure and economy of the dwelling which has fallen to his lot. If the water be not laid on in the other houses in the street, or if it be unprovided with proper receptacles for refuse, it is not in the power of any individual workman who may perceive the advantages of such accommodations to procure them. He has as little control over the external economy of his residence as of the structure of the street before it, whether it shall be paved or unpaved, drained, or undrained. It may be said that he might cleanse the street before his own door. By some local acts the obligation to do so is imposed on the individual inhabitants. By those inhabitants who have servants this duty may be and is performed, but the labourer has no servant; all of his family who are capable of labour are out a-field, or in the manufactory or the workshop, at daybreak, and return only at nightfall, and this regulation therefore is unavoidably neglected.

Under the slavery of the existing habits of labourers, it is found that the faculty of perceiving the advantage of a change is so obliterated as to render them incapable of using, or indifferent to the use of, the means of improvement which may happen to come within their reach. The sense of smell, for instance, which generally gives certain warning of the presence of malaria or gases noxious to the health, appears often to be obliterated in the labourer by his employment. He appears to be insensible to anything but changes of temperature, and there is scarcely any stench which is not endured to avoid slight cold.

It would have been matter of sincere congratulation to have met with more extensive evidence of spontaneous improvement amongst the classes in receipt of high wages, but nearly all the beneficial changes found in progress throughout the country are changes that have arisen from the efforts of persons of the superior classes. Inquiries have been made for plans of improved tenements, but none have been found which can be presented as improvements originating with the class intended to be accommodated. In the rural districts, the worst of the new cottages are those erected on the borders of commons by the labourers themselves. In the manufacturing districts, the tenements erected by building clubs and by speculating builders of the class of workmen, are frequently the subject of complaint, as being the least substantial and the most destitute of proper accommodation. The only conspicuous instances of improved residences of the labouring classes found in the rural districts are those which have been erected by opulent and benevolent landlords for the accommodation of the labourers on their own estates; and in the manufacturing districts, those erected by wealthy manufacturers for the accommodation of their own workpeople.

As in England so in Scotland, the most important improvements have been effected through enlightened landlords. The members of the Highland Society, who have made the best exertions for improving the condition of the labouring population in the rural districts, and have offered prizes for the best-constructed cottages and the best plans, competition being open to all parties, got nothing from the lower classes, and only succeeded in exciting the interest of the most intelligent proprietors, and getting improvements effected through their exertions. Mr. Loudon, in an appeal on behalf of the agricultural labourers, lays it down as a primary position that, 'In general, proprietors ought not to entrust the erection of labourers' cottages on their estates to the farmers, as it is chiefly owing to this practice that so many wretched hovels exist in the best cultivated districts of Scotland and Northumberland.'

Employers' influence on the Health of Workpeople by means of improved Habitations

Preparatory to the exposition of the means of protection of the public health provided by the existing law, and of the modifications that appear to be requisite for the attainment of the object in question, I would submit for consideration practical examples of its partial attainment by means of improved dwellings; combined with examples of other improvements effected in the moral condition of the labouring classes, by the judicious exercise of the influence possessed by their superiors in condition.

Throughout the country examples are found of a desire, on the part of persons of the higher class, to improve the condition of the poorer classes by the erection of dwellings of a superior order for their accommodation. These, however, are generally at a cost beyond any return to be expected in the present state of the habits of the people in the shape of rent, or any return in money for an outlay on an ordinary investment of capital. But the instances about to be noticed, though generally originating in benevolence, and without the expectation of a return, do, in the results, prove that in money and money's worth, the erection of good tenements affords the inducement of a fair remuneration to the employers of labour to provide improved accommodation for their own labourers.

Wherever it has been brought under observation, the connexion of the labourer's residence with his employment as part of the farm, or of the estate, or of the manufactory on which he is employed, and as part of the inducement to service, appears to be mutually advantageous to the employer and the employed. The first advantages are to the person employed.

We everywhere find (in contradiction to statements frequently made in popular declamations) that the labourer gains by his connexion with large capital: in the instances presented in the course of this inquiry, of residences held from the employer, we find that the labourer gains by the expenditure for the external appearance of that which is known to be part of the property,—an expenditure that is generally accompanied by corresponding internal comforts; he gains by all the surrounding advantages of good roads and drainage, and by more sustained and powerful care to maintain them; he gains by the closer proximity to his work attendant on such an arrangement, and he thus avoids all the attacks of disease, occasioned by exposure to wet and cold, and the additional fatigue in traversing long distances to and from his home to the place of work, in the damp of early morning or of nightfall. The exposure to weather, after leaving the place of work, is one prolific cause of disease, especially to the young. When the home is near to the place of work, the labourer is enabled to take his dinner with his family instead of at the beer-shop.

The wife and family generally gain, by proximity to the employer or the employer's family, in motives to neatness and cleanliness by their being known and being under observation; as a general rule, the whole economy of the cottages in bye-lanes and out-of-the-way places appears to be below those exposed to observation. In connexion with property or large capital, the labourer gains in the stability of employment, and the regularity of income incidental to operations on a large scale; there is a mutual benefit also in the wages for service being given in the shape of buildings or permanent and assured comforts; that is, in what would be the best application of wages, rather than wholly in money wages.

In the manufacturing districts there is a mutual and large gain by the diminution of the labour of the collection of rents, the avoidance of the risks of non-payment, and also in the power of control for the prevention of disturbances, and the removal of tenants of bad character and conduct.

Surprise is frequently expressed at the enormous rents ranging up to and beyond 20 per cent. on the outlay, exacted by the building speculators in the towns. But when the experience of these descriptions of tenements is examined, it is found that the labour of collecting the rents, and the labour of protecting the property itself against waste from unprincipled tenants, is such as to prove that accommodation given to the disorderly and vicious is scarcely remunerative at any price. The tenants are loosely attached, and large numbers migratory, partly from the nature of their work; and having little or no goods or furniture, they have no obstacles to removal; they frequently, before absconding, commit every description of waste; they often burn shelves and cupboard-doors, and the door itself, and all timber that can be got at for the purpose.* An objection frequently made against laying on the water

---

* In an inquiry, from house to house, into the condition of the labouring population in the parishes of St. Margaret and St. John Westminster, it was found that, out of a total of 5,366 houses, 2,352 were occupied for terms under one year, and that no less than 1,834 had been occupied during periods from one to six months only.[1]

---

1. 'Report of a committee of the Statistical Society of London on the state of the working classes in the parishes of St. Margaret and St. John, Westminster', *J.R.S.S.*, III (1840), 24.

VI. The Effects of Preventive Measures

in houses inhabited by a population addicted to drinking is, that they would sell the receptacles and destroy the pipe, and let the water run to waste, for the sake of the lead. The expense and delay of legal remedies precludes redress for such injuries.

In some of the worst neighbourhoods in Manchester, the whole population of a street have risen to resist the service of legal process by the civil officers. In the course of the Constabulary Inquiry I was informed by the superintendent of the old police of that town, that one of the most dangerous services for a small force was attending to enforce ejectments. This they had often to do, cutlass in hand, and were frequently driven off by showers of bricks from the mobs.[1] The collection of the rents weekly in such neighbourhoods is always a disagreeable service, requiring high payment. This, and the frequent running away of the tenant, and the waste, greatly reduce the apparently enormous rent obtainable from this poorer class of tenants. For all these vices, risks, and defaults of others, the frugal and well-conducted workman who has no choice of habitation, is compelled to pay in the shape of an increased rent; he is most largely taxed in the increased rent, necessary as an insurance for the risks and losses occasioned by the defective state of legal remedies.

All these risks the employer is enabled to diminish or avoid, by selecting his own tenants, and he has the best means of doing so; by reservations of rent on the payment of wages, he saves the labour and risks of collection; nor will the vicious workman so readily commit waste in the house belonging to his employer as in one belonging to a poorer and unconnected owner. The employer has, moreover, the most direct interest in the health and strength of his workpeople.

It is not supposed that these are arrangements which can be universal, or readily made the subject of legislation. At the commencement of some manufactures, the additional outlay may not be practicable. But those manufactures have generally had the greatest success where good accommodation for the workpeople was comprehended in the first arrangements. When, however, a manufactory has been once established and brought into systematic operation, when the first uncertainties have been overcome and the employer has time to look about him, there appears to be no position from which so extensive and certain a beneficial influence may be exercised as that of the capitalist who stands in the double relation of landlord and employer. He will find that whilst an unhealthy and vicious population is an expensive as well as a dangerous one, all improvements in the condition of the population have their compensation. In one instance, of a large outlay on improved tenements, and in provision for the moral improvement of the rising generation of workpeople, by an expensive provision for schools, the proprietor acknowledged to me that although he made the improvements from motives of a desire to improve the condition of his workpeople, or what might be termed the satisfaction derived from the

---

1. Chadwick was a member of the Constabulary Force Commission which reported in 1839, but this evidence, which may have come to Chadwick's notice, was not embodied in any part of the *Report.* (*P.P.* 1839, XIX.)

improvements as a 'hobby,' he was surprised by a pecuniary gain found in the superior order and efficiency of his establishment, in the regularity and trustworthiness of his workpeople, which gave even pecuniary compensation for the outlay of capital and labour bestowed upon them. He stated that he would not, for 7,000*l*., change the entire set of workpeople on whom care had been bestowed for the promiscuous assemblage of workpeople engaged in the same description of manufactures.

I would now submit for consideration, with the view to promulgation for voluntary adoption, instances of the arrangements which have been found most beneficial in their operation on the condition of the manufacturing population.

The most prominent of these instances was pointed out to our attention in the course of the Factory Inquiry, in the habitations connected with the mills superintended by the late Mr. Archibald Buchanan, at Catrine, in Ayrshire. Nearly 1,000 persons are employed in these mills, the places of work are well ventilated and carefully kept; the village where the workpeople live is advantageously situated, and the houses are well built. They are thus described by his son in answer to my inquiries:

'The system that has been pursued here, and which was adopted by my father for the purpose of giving the workers a greater interest in the place, at the same time that it gave them an object to be careful and saving, while it raised them in point of standing and respectability, has been different from that generally acted upon at country works. Instead of our company continuing the proprietors of the dwelling-houses and letting them to the workpeople, my father gave the workers every encouragement to save money, so that they might themselves become the proprietors of a house and small garden, either by making a purchase from the company or fencing ground and building a house for themselves. This plan has been very successful, and many of our people are proprietors of excellent houses with gardens attached, which afford them employment and amusement in their spare hours; and among themselves they have a horticultural society and an annual competition. Though many houses have been sold in this way, a considerable part of the village is still the property of our company, and those that have been built by other parties are in accordance with a plan of streets laid down; and I should say are about equal to the others in comfort and conveniences, it being the interest of the person investing his money to get the best return he can for it; and that he may get his house let and a fair rent for it, he must build as good a house as the tenant can get for the same rent from another. The houses are substantially built of stone and lime, and slated, and are generally of two stories, containing four families, occupying two rooms each. They have generally small plots of garden-ground behind, in which are dungsteads and necessaries, with a space between them and the houses. The village is well supplied with water by spring-wells and pumps in various parts of it; and some of the streets have water conveyed to them in pipes from the aqueduct to the water-wheels that give motion to the works. I cannot, however, very well give any distinct plan or drawing of the dwellings of the work-people, our houses being a good deal mixed with those belonging to others.

'The population of the village, per census taken 30th December last, is 2699, and the number of families 566, so that the proportion of individuals to each family is $4\frac{435}{566}$, and the number employed in the works is 936. The proprietors of houses appoint annually a committee of their number to attend to the repairs of the streets, and the keeping of them clean; and they have a man

VI. The Effects of Preventive Measures

constantly in their employment for this purpose, the expense being defrayed by the feuers assessing themselves according to the rental of their properties.'

These mills were pointed out to our attention during the Factory Inquiry, by Mr. Stuart, the commissioner, who observed that the workpeople, 'more especially the females, are not only apparently in the possession of good health, but many of them (quite as large a proportion as we have seen in any of the extensive well-regulated similar establishments in country districts) are blooming—as unlike as possible to the pale, languid-looking females too frequently to be found in similar works in great cities.'

Mr. Hill, the prison inspector for Scotland, stated that the procurator fiscal, or public prosecutor, reported to him that he had nothing to do in that village; and in his Third Report he thus mentions it:

'There is little crime here, and very few offences of any kind, and it is reported that there is not a single person in the village who is of a bad character. Indeed no person of bad character, or who is in the habit of drunkenness, is allowed to remain in the mills, on which nearly the whole population of the village is directly or indirectly dependent. The few offences which are committed are almost all by vagrants. The inhabitants of Catrine appear to be in the enjoyment of an unusual amount of comfort; they are well clad, live in neat houses, many of them their own property, and look healthy and cheerful; indeed the only person in the village who has reason to be downcast is the medical man, who complains that he has nothing to do.'[1]

Similar effects are manifested in the mills at New Lanark, at the flax-mills near Cupar. These instances would suffice to establish the fact of the very little sickness that is *essential* to the occupation itself. *Mr. Hill* who, by his office, is led to appreciate highly instances of exemption from crime and disorder, exclaims, upon the sight of such establishments,—'Notwithstanding what has been said on the subject of factories, I have no hesitation in declaring that I believe that the workpeople at Catrine, New Lanark, and other similar establishments, form some of the healthiest, happiest, and most moral communities in the world.'[2]

From other examples it appears to be by no means essential to such improvements that the labourers should become proprietors of their occupations. *Mr. Buchanan, jun.*, expresses his concurrence in the general conclusions to which I have arrived of the advantages derived by the labourer from his connexion with his place of work, and says:

'I perfectly agree that a labouring man will generally be found in a state of greater comfort, holding a tenement from his employer, than when left to provide a dwelling of whatever kind he chooses for himself. In our case the proprietors, in the first place, furnished the house, in which the workmen formed habits of cleanliness and comfort, and when by care and economy he had saved as much as enabled him to purchase it, he was advanced a step higher by becoming himself the proprietor, continuing to occupy part of the house himself, and letting the other parts to his fellow-workmen.

'I believe that our people enjoy as good health, and have as many comforts as any of the same class either in the same or any other employment, as their

---

1. *Third Report of Inspectors of Prisons*, IV (Scotland, Northumberland and Durham), *P.P.* 1837-8, XXXI, p. 47.
2. *Ibid.*, p. 7.

appearance will testify; and the generally different appearance of the manufacturing population in towns is to be attributed to the habits of the people themselves, and the way in which they are crowded together, and not to anything in the nature of the employment.'*

The following account which I have received in answer to inquiries from *Mr. Henry Ashworth*, of Turton, near Bolton, with relation to the manufacturing population of that place, is so far characteristic of the progress of a population of more extensive districts, and of the means of their improvement, that I submit it at full length:

'On the early introduction of the cotton manufacture, the parties who entered into it were men of limited capital, and anxious to invest the whole of it in mills and machinery, and therefore too much absorbed with the doubtful success of their own affairs to look after the necessities of their workpeople.

'Families were attracted from all parts for the benefit of employment, and obliged, as a temporary resort, to crowd together into such dwellings as the neighbourhood afforded: often two families into one house; others into cellars or very small dwellings: eventually, as the works became established, either the proprietor or some neighbour would probably see it advantageous to build a few cottages; these were often of the worst description; in such case the prevailing consideration was not how to promote the health and comfort of the occupants, but how many cottages could be built upon the smallest space of ground and at the least possible cost. We find many built back to back, a most objectionable form, as precluding the possibility of any outlet behind.

'People brought together as these were for a living, had no alternative but to occupy such dwellings. Whatever the weekly income, the wife could never make such a house comfortable; she had only one room in which to do all her work; it may be readily supposed the husband would not always find the comfort he wished in such a home. The public-house would then be his only resort. But here the evil does not end; the children brought up in such dwellings knew no better accommodation than such afforded, nor had they any opportunities of seeing better domestic management. Few of the parents in these parts have ever lived as domestic servants, so that it becomes no matter of surprise that the major part should have so little knowledge of improving their social condition even when the pecuniary means are within their reach. It must be allowed that the introduction of manufactures is not justly chargeable with producing the whole of this evil. About this time the old Poor Law was exercising a very pernicious influence upon the labouring classes, by means of inducing both the landowners and farmers to discourage cottage property for fear the inmates should gain parish settlements.[1]

'Cottages were forbidden to be built; some pulled down when empty, and others fell to decay for want of repair; poor people were banished as much as possible from the agricultural districts on account of the burden of parish settlements; even in this county I saw the ruins of two cottages, which I was informed were the two last cottages in the parish.

'Under such depressing causes it is not to be wondered at that we frequently

---

* It appears that the mortality for five years, ending 1839, was in Catrine 1 to 54·20, whilst in Glasgow for the same period it was 1 to 31.

---

1. It is often overlooked that the New Poor Law did not, of course, abolish settlement and removal: it merely extended the area of settlement from Parish to Union. See S. & B. Webb, *English Poor Law History, Part II: The Last Hundred Years* (Vol. VIII of *English Local Government*), pp. 419-35.

received families into our employ who did not know how to conduct (with propriety) a decent cottage in such a manner as to conduce either to the health or comfort of the inmates.

'About twelve years ago we had occasion to introduce a considerable number of families into some new houses; in the course of a few months a most malignant fever broke out amongst them, and went from house to house, till we became seriously alarmed for the safety of the whole establishment. We instituted an inquiry into the state of the houses where the fever first appeared, and found that from the low habits of the occupants, and the ignorance of the proper decencies of life, the cottages were in so filthy a state that it was apparent we should not long be free from a recurrence of the same evil unless we took some active means to effect a change in the habits of these people.

'Although we felt very unwilling to do anything which appeared to interfere with the domestic management of our workpeople, still the urgency of the case at the time seemed to warrant such a step. We therefore ordered an examination of every cottage in our possession, both as regarded cleanliness and ventilation, as well as bedding and furniture.

'The striking difference exhibited in the state of these cottages, the neatness and cleanness of some, the gross neglect of others, appearing to have no relation to the amount of income, convinced us that an occasional repetition of these visits would be essential in order to effect any permanent improvement amongst them.

'These periodical visits have now been continued through a series of years; and as no invidious distinction or selection was ever made, do not appear to have been viewed in the light of an intrusion; a week or two of notice being mostly given, a laudable degree of emulation has been excited as to whose house bedding and furniture should be found in the best order; my brother or myself have occasionally joined in these visits. By these means we were made acquainted with the wants and necessities of the various families in our employ. Having had such opportunity of observing the great inconvenience arising from small dwellings where the families were large, both as regards bed-rooms and living-rooms, few cottages having more than two bed-rooms; and where there were children or young persons of both sexes, the indelicacy of this arrangement was apparent; we therefore concluded to build larger cottages, and make them with three bed-rooms in each. These houses were sought after with the greatest avidity, and families allowed to remove to them as an especial favour; the increase rent of $1s.$ to $1s.$ $6d.$ per week was a small consideration in regard to the additional comfort afforded to a family where the income was from $24s.$ to $50s.$ or $60s.$ per week, as is frequently the case with families employed in manufactories.'

But I am enabled to adduce evidence showing that by structural improvements of the places of work as well as of abode which present the bounty on and security for future adoption, constituted by experience of pecuniary saving, the health of the manufacturing workpeople, now amongst the lowest, may be advanced to the average of health enjoyed by any other class.

On my return from Glasgow, I proceeded to visit and examine the cotton manufactory and machine-making works erected and carried on under the directions of Mr. James Smith, of Deanston, near Stirling, the inventor of the subsoil plough, to whose valuable opinion on the subject of drainage I have already made reference.

The principle of the improvement of places of work, which constituted the chief object of attention at Deanston, was the erection of manufactories in one large flat or ground floor, instead of story piled upon story as in the old mode.

Mr. Smith had constructed a new department of the cotton-mill in one room or flat, which covered about half an acre of ground. The roof was composed of groined arches in divisional squares of 33 feet 6 inches, supported on cast-iron columns, which were hollow, and through which the drainage of the roof was effected. In order to render the roof of the building water-tight, the outer superficies of the arches were covered with a coat of common plaster, over which, when dried, was laid a coating of coal-tar, boiled to a pitchy consistence, and mixed with sand, laid on to a thickness of three-quarters of an inch. Over this was laid a surface of from 12 to 16 inches of garden-soil, which prevents the injurious effects on the pitch of the frost in winter, and the sun in summer.

The height of this large room was 12 feet from the floor to the spring of the arches, and six feet rise, giving a height to the room in which the operatives were engaged of 18 feet. The height of the ordinary rooms in which the workpeople in manufactories are engaged is not more than from 9 to 11 feet. This restricted space arises from various points of economy (now considered to be mistaken) in the old modes of constructing manufactories, which were first erected in towns where land was dear, and in times when the immediate economy of capital was of more pressing importance. The adverse consequences to the operatives are the restriction of space for air; that the heat and effluvia of the lower rooms are communicated to the rooms above; and that the difficulty of ventilating them is exceedingly great, especially in the wide rooms, where it is found to be practically extremely difficult to get a current of fresh air to pass through the centre. The like difficulties have been heretofore experienced in respect to the ventilation of large ships. There is also in the mills of the old construction the additional fatigue of ascending and descending to the higher rooms, and carrying material. To avoid this, in some instances, machinery is resorted to.

The ventilation through the side windows of large rooms is generally found to be imperfect and inconvenient in many of the processes, and annoying to the workpeople from the influx of the air in strong currents. The arrangements for ventilation through the roof of this room appeared to be highly advantageous. The light was brought in from above, through openings eight feet in diameter at the top of each groin, surmounted by domes or cones of glass, at the apex of which there were openings of about 16 inches in diameter, with covers that could be opened or shut at pleasure, to admit of ventilation. The better distribution of the light for the work from these openings was one advantage they appeared to possess over the ordinary mode of getting light from side windows.

The chief arrangements from below for ventilation were made by tunnels 10 feet distance from each other, carried across and underneath the floor of the building, and terminating in the open air on either side. The covers of these tunnels were perforated with holes of about an inch in diameter and 12 inches apart, disposed through the floor so as to occasion a wide and uniform distribution of fresh air throughout the whole building, on the same principle as that adopted for the admission of fresh air through the floor of the House of Commons. In winter time the fresh air admitted was warmed on the same principle, by pipes of hot water, to prevent the inconvenience of the admission of currents of cold air. The whole building was, from its size and arrangements, kept at a steady temperature, and appeared to be less susceptible than other buildings to atmospheric influence. The shaftings for the conveyance of the power were carried through the tunnels, and straps or belts from the shafts rise through the cover of the tunnels, and, by their motion, aid in promoting the circulation of the air. The possibility of fatal accidents from the persons being caught by the straps and wound round the shafts, was by this arrangement entirely prevented. The tunnelling under this arrangement constituted a boxing off of the whole of the shafting. Another advantage from the removal of the driving-straps from above was that the view over the whole room was entirely unimpeded.

Another structural improvement was in the use of a thin flooring of wood over the solid base of stone floors. The floor so arranged affords the solidity of the stone floor, and inconsiderable danger of combustion, whilst the advantages of the wooden surface to the workers were a diminution of swelled ancles and rheumatic affections of the joints, often produced by working bare-footed on stone floors.

There were no entries made from which I could obtain for comparison an account of the amount of sickness experienced by the workpeople in this new room, but it was obvious that the improvement must be considerable, and it was attested by the rosy and fresh countenances of the females and of the workpeople generally. A considerable improvement was manifest in the health of those workpeople who had previously worked in the older and less spacious rooms.

The improvement of the place of work was combined with improvements in the residences of the workpeople. About one-half of the hands employed in the mills resided in houses near the works, which were well drained; the ashes and other refuse was cleared away from the village every morning between six and seven o'clock, and carried to a general dungstead at a distance, for use on their gardens. On inquiry as to the state of the health of the workpeople living in these improved tenements, it appeared that they had not one-half the amount of sickness experienced by the rest of the workpeople who lived in the common ill-regulated houses about a mile distance. The whole population had fewer diseases than any other class of the population in the surrounding country; they presented fewer cases of rheumatism, and there were scarcely any lung diseases amongst them; their general health was decidedly better than that of the adjacent agricultural population.

The chief advantages of the improved arrangements of the places of work were, on the side of the workpeople, improved health; security for females and for the young against the dangers of fatal accidents, and less fatigue in the execution of the same amount of work. But beyond these the arrangement of the work in one room had moral advantages of high value. The bad manners and immoralities complained of as attendant on assemblages of workpeople of both sexes in manufactories, generally occur, as may be expected, in small rooms and places where few are employed, and that are secluded from superior inspection and from common observation. But whilst employed in this one large room, the young are under the inspection of the old; the children are in many instances under the inspection of parents, and all under the observation of the whole body of workers, and under the inspection of the employer. It was observed that the moral condition of the females in this room stood comparatively high. It would scarcely be practicable to discriminate the moral effects arising from one cause where several are in operation; but it was stated by ministers that there were fewer cases of illegitimacy and less vice observable among the population engaged in this manufactory than amongst the surrounding population of the labouring class. The comparative circumstances of that population were such as, when examined, would establish the conclusion that it must be so.

The first expense of such a building is higher than a manufactory of the old construction; but it appeared to possess countervailing economical advantages to the capitalist, the chief of which are,—this same facility of constant general supervision, the increase of the certainty of superintendence, and the reduction of the numbers of subordinate managers, the increase of efficiency of management, and a diminution of its expense. Another advantage arose to the manufacturer in the superior action of the machinery. In mills of the ordinary construction the machinery is frequently deranged in its structure, and put out of order by the yielding and unsteadiness of the upper floors. The machinery erected on the ground floor has a firm basis, and a steady and more durable action. The other advantages presented were, the saving of labour in transporting the material from one process to another, a labour which is often considerable in expense, as well as in inconvenience, in lifting it into the higher rooms; the reduction of the hazard of fire, and consequently in expense of insurance against it, as fire could scarcely take place, and certainly could not rapidly extend in a manufactory so constructed. These several sources of economy Mr. Smith calculated would more than compensate for any increase of ground-rent, even if the building were erected on land costing 1,000*l*. per acre. Mr. Marshall, of Leeds, on consulting with Mr. Smith, has constructed a new manufactory (on the principle of that in Deanston) in Leeds, where ground is valuable.[1] This manufactory covers more than two acres of ground, and is reported to be eminently successful. Power looms are frequently arranged in buildings of one story, and I was informed of another manufactory in Lancashire, nearly as large as that of Messrs. Marshalls, built on one floor, but it did not appear to possess the arrangements for ventilation and warming, and the other arrangements necessary to the complete action of a place of work on the plan of that at Deanston.

Mr. Smith considered that the principle of arrangement for superior inspection and management of a manufactory was equally applicable to agricultural operations, and that it would be proportionately advan-

---

1. This is probably a reference to the single-storey mill built in Marshall Street, Leeds, by Marshalls in 1838. See W. G. Rimmer, *Marshalls of Leeds, Flax-Spinners, 1788-1886* (Cambridge 1960), pp. 202-3.

tageous in the superior ventilation and equality of temperature for cattle, in the avoidance of labour and wet and cold, in removing from one small separate building to another, and in the transport of produce, to have all under one large roof, where the whole direction and inspection of the homestead farming operations are brought under one view.

Of the manufacturing advantages of such arrangements I have had strong testimony: of the advantages of such arrangements to the health and moral and social condition of the workpeople, I could not entertain the slightest doubt. I feel confident that the more closely it is examined, the more clearly will the coincidence which I have endeavoured to trace, of pecuniary interest with the health and the highest physical and moral improvement of the lowest of the labouring classes, be established. Mr. Smith avowed his confidence in this coincidence from his own experience and observation as a practical principle. The improved health of the workpeople was attended by more energy and better labour; by less of lassitude and waste from relaxed attention; by fewer interruptions from sickness, and fewer spare hands to ensure the completion of work. Under the persuasion of the coincidence of interest, he had endeavoured to direct the structural alterations to the promotion of the health of the workpeople; he believed they might be advantageously carried further, and had it in contemplation to make arrangements to promote habitual bathing amongst them. He had, moreover, retained the services of a medical gentleman to inspect the workpeople from time to time, and give them timely advice, and, as far as possible, to prevent disease. He agreed, and had long considered, that it was in the power of the masters of Britain 'entirely to extirpate excessive and habitual drinking. We never,' said he, 'permit a man to come near the works who is in the slightest degree intoxicated, and never permit any one to be absent one day drinking. You never can be well or cheaply served by a dissipated workman. The most skilful workman, the man whose services I can the least spare, must, if he takes to drinking, leave the place. It may occasion immediate inconvenience and even immediate loss, but if the rule be steadily applied, it will contribute to the comfort and the profit of the master as well as of the man.'

The importance of such beneficent influence on the health, the moral condition and respectability of the labouring classes, is so little understood, that I beg leave to submit further illustrations of the value of:

The Employers' Influence on the Sobriety and Health of Workpeople by modes of Payment which do not lead to Temptations to Intemperance.

The power possessed by extensive employers of labour to influence beneficially their labourers, is not however confined to those who stand in the combined relation of employer and landlord. In the course of another inquiry as to the means of preventing crime, it appeared that a large class of crimes and disorders arose from drunkenness. On carrying the inquiry back into the causes out of which the drunkenness arose, they appeared to be extensively removable, and that by the employers of labour. The important influences that belong to this position will be displayed in the effects of alterations in detail in one point of management, namely, the mode of paying wages. The direct sanitary effects may be best displayed in the following evidence of *Mr. Lomax*, an army pensioner, which has been corroborated by superior officers:

'When I was in the Life Guards, 14 or 16 years ago, there was a good deal of ill health prevalent amongst them. Before that time the men received part of their pay weekly, namely, 7s. at the end of the week. With this 7s. they had to provide the food which they required, except their dinner. The ration for dinner was three-quarters of a pound of uncooked meat, a pound of potatoes or vegetables, and a pound of bread. It was found, however, that many of the men spent the whole of the 7s. in a single day in drink or dissipation. During the remainder of the week the men would be on what was called the *crib-bite*, that is, living only on their dinner rations. I knew many of the men who drooped under this system, partly from the excess of drinking or dissipation, and partly from the privation of the necessaries of life and the work they had to undergo. This, again, led them to much temptation. If anything was lost it was amongst this class of men that we looked for it. The crime-book would speak as to the further bad consequences of these habits.

'The plan was then tried of paying the men 1s. each day. Over and above that the men were provided with coffee. It was universally felt that this change was highly beneficial to their health, and it stopped the dissipation, and the consequences of the dissipation.'

The incapacity to apportion their means for temperate consumption (which is not however confined to the working classes) is extensively shown in the mismanagement of the means for procuring food. It is a subject of complaint which frequently appears in the reports, that the ignorance of domestic economy leads to ill health, by the purchase of unsuitable and, and at the same time, expensive food. We have been frequently besought to obtain and promulgate, for popular information, instructions in frugal cookery, and the management of supplies. It is observed by *Mr. Brebner*, the governor of the Glasgow bridewell, where the cost of maintaining the prisoners in health and increased strength is on average only $2\frac{3}{4}d$. per diem, that:

'The regularity of diet in the prisons here is of vast importance, both as to the quantity and the time of serving it up. If the same persons were to get the same amount of food for a whole week, or for a less time, at their own discretion, they would suffer from surfeit at one time, and from long fasting at another. Irregularity of diet is one of the most fruitful sources of disease that occur in civilized life.'

In further illustration of the beneficial influence which employers may often exercise to assail such vices by regulations in detail, I cite the following instances from a communication I have received from *Mr. Edwin Hill*, the inspector of stamping machinery for the Government:

'During a period of nine years (from 1818 to 1827) I was engaged in the superintendence of one of the largest works in the town of Birmingham, consisting of two distinct mills, one employed in rolling copper for the use of braziers and shipwrights, and the other in rolling silver, brass, and other metals. In each mill there was a set of skilled workmen, who undertook the work at fixed prices, and who themselves employed numerous assistants at weekly wages.

'Owing to difficulties in the way of making up the accounts at short intervals, it was the custom for the master to advance weekly to each workman in the silver mill a fixed sum of money (besides advancing a sum to pay the assistants with). The accounts were made up annually, and the balances due to the several workmen then paid. The payments, both weekly and annually, were almost always made not to the men but to their wives. The earnings of the men were considerable, varying from 80*l.* to 180*l.* a-year. The men were, almost without exception, highly respectable in their stations, their families were well provided for, their homes cleanly and not without pretensions to some degree of elegance, and their children sent to school at the sole expense of the parents. Some of them had made considerable accumulations of money, and even become proprietors of houses and land. The workmen employed in the copper mill, on the contrary, had been accustomed to receive the full amount of their earnings at the end of each week, and, after paying their assistants, to divide the surplus. These men were much addicted to drinking and feasting at the alehouse; and, although their earnings were nearly as great as those of the other men, their families were in wretchedness, and the wives obliged to eke out a slender pittance by washing and other laborious occupations. There were also several men employed as millwrights and engineers, at regular and good weekly wages. These men were, almost without exception, steady and respectable, and their families well provided for. About the year 1822 the inconvenience and annoyance, and loss, which arose from the unsteady habits of the second set of men, led me to inquire into the causes of their inferiority to the others, and I was soon led to attribute much of the evil to the great irregularity in the amount of their weekly incomes, which varied from about 10*s.* to 4*l.* 4*s.* per man.

'The effects were as follows:—The men were reckless, trusting to their luck to get "good work," *i.e.*, that which bears a high price in proportion to the required labour. They were enabled to deceive their wives as to the amount of money obtained. They learned the minimum with which their wives could contrive to keep house, and, having learned it, they endeavoured to retain all above this minimum for their own gratifications. Their wives, under the pressure of necessity, picked their pockets, opened their drawers, &c., in search of money believed to be hidden. Their wives actually desired that their husbands might get drunk on Saturday night, because they could the more easily abstract the money from their persons.

'Upon the termination of my inquiries I induced the men, with little difficulty, to receive their money in the way the other men did, viz., by regular weekly advances, rather under their average earnings, with a quarterly or annual settlement; and I took care that the wives should know exactly what their husbands would receive; and from the day the plan commenced, a most decided and permanent improvement took place in the habits of the men, and in the appearance and general comforts of their families. One of the men commenced saving money immediately. This man's savings, as I have lately been informed, now in January, 1841, considerably exceed 1000*l.*; whereas, during the five or six years which he passed in the same occupation before the change of plan, he made no saving whatever.'

Another valuable example of the easy means possessed by employers of preventing the formation of habits destructive to the health and prosperity of workmen, is set forth in the evidence of Mr. Peter Fairbairn, the extensive mechanist of Leeds.

Mr. Fairbairn examined.
'You are a mechanist at Leeds?—I am.
'What number of men do you employ?—Between 500 and 600.
'Have you ever observed any effects produced in the habits of the labouring classes in respect to drinking intoxicating liquors by the mode in which they are paid their wages?—Yes, there are two modes in which wages are most

frequently paid, and both these modes are prejudicial in their effects. The first effect is connected with the place of payment. Some masters pay at the public-house, others pay the men at the counting-house after the work is completed. The effects produced by payment at the public-house are to oblige the workman to drink. He is kept waiting in the public-house during a long time, varying from two to three hours, sometimes as much as five hours. The workman cannot remain in the house without drinking, even if he were alone, as he must make some return to the landlord for the use of the room. But the payment of a number of men occupies time in proportion to their numbers. We find that to pay our own men in the most rapid way requires from two to three hours. The assembled workmen, of course, stimulate each other to drink. Out of 100 men, all of whom will, probably, have taken their quart of porter or ale, above a third will go home in a state of drunkenness— of drunkenness to the extent of imbecility. The evil is not confined to the men; the destructive habit is propagated in their families. At each public-house a proportion of the poor women, their wives, attend. According to my own observation, full 10 per cent. of the men have their wives and children in attendance at the public-house. The poor women have no other mode of getting money to market with on the Saturday night than attending at the public-house to get it from their husbands. They may have children whom they cannot leave at home, and these they bring with them. The wives are thus led to drink, and they and their children are made partakers at the scenes of drunkenness and riot; for there are not unfrequently quarrels leading to fights between the workmen when intoxicated.

'Do not these late hours, consequent on such a mode of payment, also lead them to the inferior markets, and prejudice the domestic economy of the labourer's household?—Yes, they have the less money to purchase with, and must purchase an inferior quality of provisions. I have observed that they do so. They are driven to the inferior shopkeepers who keep open late; and they are also driven to make purchases on the Sunday morning. It is only the inferior shopkeepers or hucksters who will sell on the Sunday morning, and they sell an inferior commodity at a higher price. Then the Sunday morning is thus occupied; the husband, and sometimes the wife, is kept in a state of feverish excitement by the previous night's debauch: they are kept in a state of filth and disorder; even the face is unwashed; no clean clothes are put on, and there is no church attendance and no decency. Indeed, by the pressure of the wants created by habits of drinking, there is soon no means to purchase clean or respectable clothes, and lastly, no desire to purchase them. The man, instead of cleaning himself, and appearing at church on the Sunday, or walking out with his family on the Sunday afternoon in a respectable condition, remains at home in filth, and in a filthy hovel. Of course there are no contributions to sick-clubs under such circumstances; and if the workman has been previously led to join a club, he is almost always in arrear with his contributions, and is ultimately expelled. On the occurrence of the disease to which such habits predispose him, there is nothing but the most abject and complete destitution and pauperism. I have served the office of churchwarden and overseer in Leeds three years, and, having attended the weekly Board where applications for relief are made, I have seen the end of this train of circumstances in the applications for relief from parties who had previously been in the receipt of good and sufficient wages (and even high wages) to have prevented such applications. I have observed the whole train of these consequences in several large works in London as well as in this town.

'Are there not consequences too to the employers themselves, as well as to the rate-payers, in connexion with the habits of labourers thus created?—One consequence of these habits is the loss of time at the commencement of the week, and the comparative inefficiency of the workmen when they do come. The workman who has been absent from drunkenness comes to his work pale, emaciated, shattered, and unnerved. From my own observation in my own branch of manufacture, I should say that the quantity and quality of the work executed during the first day or so would be about one-fifth less than that obtainable from a steady and attentive workman.

'This deterioration, then, in a large number of workmen engaged in a manufactory, may be noted as an important item of saving for the consideration of a provident manufacturer?—Undoubtedly. Another consideration for the master is the fact that such workmen, the most idle and dissolute, are the most discontented, and are always the foremost in mischievous strikes and combinations.

'You have spoken of the consequences of making the public-house a place of payment; what are the comparative effects of making the payments at the counting-house?—A considerable reduction of the evil. Payments to large numbers at the counting-house is still, however, attended with much inconvenience and evil. The payment of the number of men employed at our works (between five and six hundred) would, as I have stated, occupy between two and three hours. This mode of payment, therefore, implies the keeping of a large crowd together during that time. During that time appointments are made of meetings at public-houses to drink that would not otherwise take place. It also generates discontent: it gives an opportunity, by assembling a crowd, for any discontented or mischievous person to operate upon a large mass of people. Formerly the business of my manufactory, and the welfare of the working people, were very seriously interrupted by strikes; and I could not help observing the facilities which such meetings gave to such mischievous persons.

'What is the mode of payment which you have adopted?—I send the pay clerk into each room in the manufactory immediately after the dinner hour, and he pays each man individually. Each man is scarcely taken from his work half a minute. I may observe, that some masters, to save themselves trouble, so as to avoid the inconvenience of getting small change, will pay several men together. This again leads to the public-house, where the men commonly go to get change to divide the money amongst them; I therefore avoid paying any two men together, and subjecting them to temptation as well as inconvenience and cost. Each of my workmen being paid in the shop, without the loss of a minute, may go at once directly home at the time when the work closes. He is thus afforded an opportunity of going at once to the market at an early hour, and is subjected to no factitious inducements to drink, disorder, improvidence, and destitution.

'What is the average time thus saved to each of the 550 workmen in your manufactory, as compared with the more ordinary mode of payment?—About an hour and a half, or half the three hours of payment.

'Then, by this means, instead of bringing 550 persons to the one person, the pay clerk, sending that one person to the 550 persons, you save to them upwards of 800 hours of inconvenient waiting?—Just so.

'How many persons, on the average, have you absent from work on the Monday morning?—Nor more than from four to five, until eight o'clock in the morning; and on the return to work after dinner from one to two persons.

'That is from one to two persons the entire day during the Monday, out of between five and six hundred workpeople?—Yes.

'What number would have been absent on the Monday under the ordinary circumstances?—About 30 per cent., or one-third, would be drunk on the Saturday night; and full 10 per cent. would not make their appearance until the Tuesday morning. Instead of only two absent during the whole of the day,

Employers' Influence: Modes of Payment

I should have more than 50; or, in other words, more than 50 families not only distressed by what is spent in drink, but losing one-sixth of their earnings, and I as a master losing from their deteriorated work on the days when they do return. I beg leave further to observe, that mere education in reading or writing, precepts or preaching, are of very little avail against the temptations to drink held out to working men; and I am confident that if employers could be made to see and attend to their mutual interests, by a little care in the removal of temptations, they might generally prevent the most fruitful cause of disorder, destitution, and pauperism, at least as extensively as I have prevented those consequences to my workmen and their families by the adoption of the means I have described.'

In the course of a report on the sanitary condition of the labouring classes in the town of Lancaster, received from *Dr. De Vitrie*, the effects of an amended practice are thus noticed:

'An excellent example is shown in this neighbourhood by the wealthy manufacturers and tradesmen almost universally paying their men's weekly wages on a Friday evening (or, what is still better, early on Saturday morning) instead of Saturday, thus putting it into the power of all to spend their money to the best advantage at Saturday's market, and obviating the great temptation which formerly existed of spending their earnings, or a large proportion of them, in the public-houses and beer-shops after the termination of the week's labour. It may be said that such parties are as likely to dissipate on a Friday as on a Saturday evening. The propensity I grant may be the same, but there is no intervening day of rest to shake off the effects of intemperance and indulgence, and as workmen must resume their labours on the Saturday, hence it is that such a regulation exercises not only a salutary but a provident influence.'[1]

The *Rev. Whitwell Elwin* observes:

'Where gain was dependant on the growth of better habits, I have seen, with the agency of judicious individuals, encouraging cases of complete reformation: an intelligent engineer in this neighbourhood was about paying off a man whose profligacy had left him without a decent covering, and who often depended for his victuals upon the generosity of his fellow-workmen. He begged hard to be retained, and his master at last consented, on condition that he himself should lay out his wages for the next three months. He provided the man with good lodgings, allowed him tea, sugar, and bread and butter night and morning; meat, and either bread or potatoes, with a pint of beer every day for his dinner; and before the appointed time was up, bought him with the surplus a new suit of clothes. The man was so sensible of the advantage of the change, that he became one of the most thrifty and valuable workmen; and his master has often since tried the same experiment with the same success. If we could collect all the philanthropy and much of the self-interest of the country into wise and profitable channels, we might, I believe in a twelvemonth, do much towards regenerating the most wretched classes.'

One employer of numerous labourers in a well-conducted establishment stated to me that after long experience he found it necessary, for the protection of the workpeople, as well as the efficiency of the establishment, invariably to discharge every workman who was guilty of drunkenness; and that the first visible sign to excite suspicion of the habits of intoxication was the absence of personal cleanliness, then a

---

1. Edward de Vitrie, 'Report on the sanitary condition of the labouring population in the town of Lancaster', *Local Reps. E. & W.*, p. 346.

pallid countenance, on which inquiry was made. Another employer of numerous labourers, *Mr. William Fairbairn*, of Manchester (the brother of Mr. Fairbairn, of Leeds), who has had between one and two thousand workpeople engaged in the manufactories of machinery in the firm of which he is the first partner, stated, in answer to the question:

'What are their habits in respect to sobriety?—I may mention that I strictly prohibit on my works the use of beer or fermented liquors of any sort, or of tobacco. I enforce the prohibition of fermented liquors so strongly that, if I found any man transgressing the rule in that respect, I would instantly discharge him without allowing him time to put on his coat.

'Have you any peculiar grounds for adopting this course?—No; but as respects myself I wish to have an orderly set of workmen; and in the next place I am decidedly of opinion that it is better for the men themselves and for their families.

'Are you aware that it is a prevalent opinion that strong drink is necessary as a stimulus for the performance of labour?—I am aware that that was a prevalent opinion amongst employers of labour, but it is now very generally abandoned; there are nevertheless some foundries in which there is drinking throughout the works all day long. It is observable, however, of the men employed as workmen, that they do not work so well; their perceptions are clouded, and they are stupified and heavy. I have provided water for the use of the men in every department of the works. In summer time the men engaged in the strongest work, such as the strikers to the heavy forges, drink water very copiously. In general the men who drink water are really more active, and do more work, and are more healthy than the workmen who drink fermented liquors. I observed on a late journey to Constantinople that the boatmen or rowers to the caiques, who are perhaps the first rowers in the world, drink nothing but water; and they drink that profusely during the hot months of the summer. The boatmen and water-carriers of Constantinople are decidedly in my opinion the finest men in Europe as regards their physical development, and they are all water drinkers: they may take a little sherbet, but in other respects are what we should call in this country, tee-totallers.

'What is their diet?—Chiefly bread; now and then a cucumber, with cherries, figs, dates, mulberries, or other fruits which are abundant there; now and then a little fish.

'Do they ever use animal food?—Occasionally I believe the flesh of goats, but I never saw them eating any other than the diet I have described.

'Did they appear to eat more than the European workmen?—About the same; if anything, more moderate as respects the quantity.'

I have collected much other information to the same effect. In the Appendix, I have given, as a contrast, an instance of arrangements which tend to promote the habit of drinking, and the consequences, a part of which are met and dealt with by the administrators of relief from the poor's rates, in the shape of claims to relief on the ground of sickness and consequent destitution; and another part of which fall as disorders and crimes to be encountered by the police.[1]

I submit here one important instance of the exercise of a wise influence on the habits of the agricultural population:

In a form of lease used in leasing the Highland property of the Duke

---

1. 'Extracts from evidence on the moral and physical evils which may be created by the mode of hiring and paying workmen', *San. Rep.*, Appendix 30, pp. 454-7.

Employers' Influence: Promotion of Cleanliness

of Sutherland, which appears to be ably devised to ensure progressive improvement, care for the moral welfare of the population is not omitted. The poverty, disorder, and crime engendered by the destructive habit of whisky drinking, fostered by the practice of illicit distillation, is encountered by a clause which provides that if the tenant 'distill whiskey, or shall permit any one to distil whisky, or shall sell or permit the same to be sold on the said premises hereby set, or on any part of the said estate, or shall contravene any of the regulations the said proprietors have established for the management thereof, and that if he or they shall be convicted of any of the said offences before the sheriff, depute, or substitute, or any two of his Majesty's justices of the peace for the said county; then, in either of these events or cases, this agreement shall be, *ipso facto*, void and null, and the said tenant shall be forthwith removable by summary process before the judge ordinary, whereupon decree shall be pronounced upon relevant proof of the fact.'[1]

The lease ensures the improvement of the tenements, and provides that 'no earthen houses or huts are permitted to be built on any consideration.' The one provision is the proper complement of the other; and Mr. Hill gives his testimony to the excellent effect which the support given to the law, and the prevention of whisky drinking, produce on the habits of the population.

Employers' Influence on the Health of Workpeople by the Promotion of Personal Cleanliness

I proceed to another instance of the power of the employers to protect the health, as well as the morals of their workpeople, by influencing their habits of personal cleanliness.

But I shall first submit a few instances of the extent and prevalence of personal uncleanliness amongst whole classes of workpeople.

Mr. John Kennedy, in the course of the examinations of some colliers in Lancashire, asked one of them:

'How often do the drawers (those employed in drawing coals) wash their bodies?—None of the drawers ever wash their bodies. I never wash my body; I let my shirt rub the dirt off; my shirt will show that. I wash my neck and ears, and face, of course.

'Do you think it usual for the young women (engaged in the colliery) to do the same as you do?—I do not think it is usual for the lasses to wash their bodies; my sisters never wash themselves, and seeing is believing; they wash their faces, necks, and ears.

'When a collier is in full dress, he has white stockings, and very tall shirt necks, very stiffly starched, and ruffles?—That is very sure, sir; but they never wash their bodies underneath; I know that; and their legs and bodies are as black as your hat.'

One labourer remembered that a particular event took place at Easter, 'because it was then he washed his feet.' The effects of these habits are seen at the workhouse on almost every one of the paupers

---

1. Since the Sutherland estate acquired a most unsavoury reputation for the eviction of tenants by the thousand for reasons unconnected with distilling, this reference by Chadwick is somewhat tendentious.

admitted. When it is necessary to wash them on their admission, they usually manifest an extreme repugnance to the process. Their common feeling was expressed by one of them when he declared that he considered it 'equal to robbing him of a great coat which he had had for some years.' The filthy condition in which they are found on admission into the hospitals is frequently sufficient to account for the state of disease in which they appear, and the act of cleansing them is itself the most efficient cure. The out-door service of the union medical officers amidst such a population is often most painful and disgusting: *e.g.*—

Mr. J. F. Handley, medical officer of the Chipping Norton union, states in his report:
'When the small-pox was prevalent in this district, I attended a man, woman, and five children, all lying ill with the confluent species of that disorder, in one bed-room, and having only two beds amongst them. The walls of the cottage were black, the sheets were black, and the patients themselves were blacker still; two of the children were absolutely sticking together. It was indeed a gloomy scene. I have relished many a biscuit and glass of wine in Mr. Grainger's dissecting-room when ten dead bodies were lying on the tables under dissection, but was entirely deprived of appetite during my attendance upon these cases. The smell on entering the apartments was exceedingly nauseous, and the room would not admit of free ventilation.'

Such conditions of the population, of habitual personal and domestic filth, are not necessary to any occupation; they are not the necessary consequence of poverty, and are the type of neglect and indolence; this is proved by the example of men engaged in the same occupations with improved habits. The medical officers of the Merthyr Tydvill union, in their returns, represent the health of the colliery population to be very good, a circumstance which is ascribed to their habitual cleanliness.

Mr. J. L. Roberts, surgeon, states:
'The colliers in our district invariably, on their return from the pits in the evening to their houses, strip to the skin, and wash themselves perfectly clean in a tub of lukewarm water, and wipe with towels until the cuticle is dry. The miners are not so particular. I firmly believe that the health of other workmen employed generally about the ironworks is not so permanently good as the colliers; they, generally speaking, not undergoing complete ablution as the colliers do. Generally, the colliers are quite free from any cutaneous disease, or at least not so much affected with psora, &c., as the generality of their fellow-workmen. Cutaneous diseases are frequent amongst children from want of cleanliness.'

In the places of work where there is the greatest need for cleanliness, in every place where there is a steam-engine, hot water, which is commonly allowed to run waste, is already provided in abundance for warm or tepid baths, not only for the workpeople, but, where there are numerous engines, for the whole population. If the same hot water arose at the same heat and abundance from any natural spring, baths would be erected, and medical treatises would be written in commendation of its medicinal virtues, which, the better opinion appears now to be, are ascribable, in the majority of instances, simply to the hot water, and to its application in cases where it had not before been used. Hot or tepid baths are deemed of more importance for the labouring classes in winter than are cold baths in summer, and they might be generally provided for the working classes in the manufacturing districts at a cost utterly inconsiderable.

A few years since a gentleman, observing some ditches in London, in the neighbourhood of the City-road, smoking with clean hot water running away from the steam-engine of a manufactory, directed attention to the waste, and suggested the expediency of using that water to supply public warm or tepid baths. After a time the suggestion was acted upon as a private speculation, and large swimming-baths were constructed; one, with superior accommodation and decorations at 1s.; another, with less costly fittings-up, at 6d. the bath. These were luxurious tepid baths, kept at a heat of 84°. The example appears to have been followed in Westminster by the establishment of similar tepid swimming-baths, where only 3d. is charged to persons of the working-class. As many as 2,000 and 3,000 of this class have resorted to these baths in one day, and the bath at the lowest charge is stated to make the best return for the capital invested in it. Similar establishments are, we believe, in progress in other parts of the metropolis. *Mr. Samuel Greg*, at Bollington, has formed baths for the use of his workpeople, which he thus describes:

'The bathing-room is a small building, close behind the mill, about 25 feet by 15. The baths, to the number of seven, are ranged along the walls, and a screen about six feet high, with benches on each side of it, is fixed down the middle of the room. The cold water is supplied from a cistern above the engine-house, and the hot water from a large tub which receives the waste steam from the dressing-room, and is kept constantly at boiling temperature. A pipe from each of these cisterns opens into every bath, so that they are ready for instant use. The men and women bathe on alternate days; and a bath-keeper for each attends for an hour and a half in the evening. This person has the entire care of the room, and is answerable for everything that goes on in it. When any one wishes to bathe he comes to the counting-house for a ticket, for which he pays a penny, and without which he cannot be admitted to the bathing-room. Some families, however, subscribe a shilling a-month, which entitles them to five baths weekly; and these hold a general subscriber's ticket, which always gives him admittance to the room. I think the number of baths taken weekly varies from about 25 to 70 or 80. We pay the bath-keepers 2s. 6d. and 2s. a-week, and I believe this amount has been more than covered by the receipts. The first cost of erecting the baths was about 80l.'

The feet of the female as well of the male workers in such establishments, who work in the mills without their stockings, are seen coated with the filth of years, for which there is no other necessity than their own habitual indolence. These habits mere admonitions will not always remove from the adult population. A manufacturer in London, who did not care to take this trouble with them, began with his apprentices, and took them several times to the new tepid baths, as a holiday and a reward, until they had experienced the comfort, and had formed a habit, when he left them to themselves, and they paid out of their own pocket-money the small amount necessary to defray the expenses. Where the use of hot or warm water has been given to the work-people, and baths have been provided, they have frequently been defective in some important point. *Dr. Barham* states that the miners, on their ascent to the ground, have commonly only the means of using the hot water from a rivulet on a bleak and exposed situation; in other places, as where bath-rooms are provided, the accommodation for dressing was defective, in being cold and chilling instead of being made warm, as it might be at a very trifling expense. It was only at Camborne, the mine already noticed, that anything deserving the name of proper baths had been erected. Dr. *Barham* observes, in a communication on this subject:

'The security from chill during the ablution, and the abundance and comfortable temperature of the water in the cases mentioned as examples of superior accommodation, have no doubt contributed to a comparative immunity from pulmonary disease and catarrhal affections, which the managers and the men themselves have noticed since this provision has been made.

'The cost of the practice is so inconsiderable as to be unworthy notice. Timber and iron for such purposes are always to be found in our mines among what is no longer fit for its original destination. No charge of any kind is made for the use of these accommodations.

'The owners of steam-engines might always supply hot water, in proportion to the amount of condensation effected, without any extra cost to themselves, when they do not employ the heated water to some purpose of their own. In some mines the warm water is husbanded for the cleansing of the ores, but this is an exceptional case. Generally speaking, there is a great quantity of iron cylinder and other materials convertible to the conveyance of the water, which may be supplied at a very low rate, as unserviceable for engine-work.

'I have thought that steam-engines are not the only sources for the supply of hot water to the public at an insignificant cost. All works in which great heat is employed, or almost all such works, might supply heat to large bodies of water after the fuel has been most economically applied to their own purposes. Smelting-houses, foundries, glass-houses, for instances, have always heat enough to spare for the warming of extensive thermæ. By the use of brick pipes, surrounded by wood or some bad conductor, such heat, first applied to the bottom of large reservoirs, might be distributed over extensive districts, and buildings might be warmed and workshops supplied with warm water for the thorough purification of the labourers, at a very trifling expense. My own opinion is, that a system of *washing* is more desirable as a national habit than a system of *bathing*. The latter is doubtless excellent for bodies of men who are under effectual control, and for the young.'[1]

Employers' Influence on the Health of Workpeople by the Ventilation of Places of Work, and the Prevention of Noxious Fumes, Dust, &c.

In some of the 'dusty trades,' the excessive amount of premature mortality is so great as to justify interference, defensively, as against the charges which, from the neglect of sanitary measures, fall neither upon the employer nor upon the consumer, who directly benefit by the produce of the industry, but upon rate-payers, to whom the manufactory itself may be a nuisance. In the instance of such trades, personal cleanliness is so far a requisite as to justify an additional rate of insurance where it is neglected. Yet the regulations preventive of disease are by no means onerous, either in their cost or their interference with the

---

1. For the circumstances in which Barham passed this information to Chadwick, see Introduction, p. 53.

processes. Some of the noxious manufactures, and especially those in lead, have been the subject of examination by the 'Conseil de Salubrité of Paris,'[1] and the preventive rules they prescribed were as follows:— 1. The establishment of a good ventilation in the workshops or manufactories. 2. Exacting from the workpeople close attention to personal cleanliness; obliging them to wash the hands and face before dining, and before leaving the workshop; forbidding them taking any of their meals in the workshop, and, by reasoning and information, directing their attention to the dangers by which they are surrounded. 3. Employing the practicable means for conducting the processes so as to raise the least dust possible. 4. Boarding off the mills and sieves, so as to prevent the escape of the smaller particles. 5. Requiring of the workmen engaged in the processes where there is lead-dust or any other injurious dust suspended in the air, that they cover the nose and mouth with a handkerchief slightly moistened. 6. Subjecting the workshop to occasional medical inspection, in order to prevent the intensity of any maladies that break out, and with that view to examine the workmen from time to time to detect any symptoms of disease, and to oblige the workman attacked to abstain from work until the medical officer declares that he may resume it without inconvenience. 7. Obliging workmen to wear frocks or blouses, which they should leave in the workshop when they quit work; and these blouses should from time to time be washed. 8. Sending away from the workshop every workman who gives himself up to debauchery or drunkenness. 9. Endeavouring to get the workmen, (*i.e.* workers in lead) to form the habit of drinking every day, on leaving the workshop, a little hydro-sulphuretted water, to neutralize the effects of the lead that may have been taken into the stomach.

All these regulations, with the medical attendance for the purpose of prevention, would be greatly below any charge of insurance to the individual workman for procuring medical attendance and remedies when thrown out of work by sickness.

In some of the trades, scattered instances of attention to cleanliness and measures of prevention are found: for example, amongst the journeymen painters. In answer to a question put by Dr. Mitchell to *Mr. Tomlins*, the clerk to the Painters' Company, whether painters suffer so much as formerly from the disease to which they are peculiarly liable, the clerk says:

'Not so much as formerly. This has been ascertained by a charity administered at Painters' Hall to men labouring under sickness. The men are now more attentive to cleanliness. Formerly they would throw their clothes on their beds and go to their meals without washing their hands. A large proportion of the journeymen now carry a working-dress to their job with them, and when they quit work at night they exchange and put on clean clothes which are free from paint. This applies more particularly to the westward of Temple Bar. One master-painter of my acquaintance, Mr. Thornton, of Doctors'

---

1. For the Conseil de Salubrité de Paris, see M. Trebuchet, 'Report on the labours of the "Conseil de Salubrité" of Paris, from 1829 to 1839', *San. Rep.*, Appendix 14, pp. 409-23; and E. H. Ackerknecht, 'Hygiene in France 1815-48', *Bulletin of the History of Medicine*, XXII (1948), 121.

Commons, keeps a pail of solution of potash in his shop, in which the men wash their hands, and which takes off every particle of paint; and it is worthy of remark that only two men in 20 years have been afflicted with paralysis in his employ. This is taken from 15 men constantly employed on an average for seven years.'

It will suggest itself that another generation of workpeople, and their premature sickness and death, ought not to pass away leaving this practice confined to the painters to the west of Temple Bar, and leaving the beneficent expedient exclusively to the shop of Mr. Thornton, of Doctors' Commons.

In connexion with the instance of the painters, I may give the following from *Mr. James Gibbins*, a manufacturer of colours at the Mile-end road. He was asked—'Are there any peculiar hazards to health connected with the trade?' He replies:

'Arsenic and lead are employed in making colours, and hence injury does arise, but such need not necessarily be the case; but although water, towels, and soap are placed at the use of the men, there is no persuading them to be habitually cleanly. After making or grinding colours, they will not take the trouble to wash their hands, but merely wipe them a little on their clothes, and then will take their bread and meat, by which particles are carried off into the stomach. It is impossible to persuade the men to be more cautious. The lead is much more in use than the arsenic, and on the whole does more harm, as the men are more on their guard against the arsenic.'

The prevalent impression upon such instances would be expressed by such phrases as, 'If men will be so careless, there is no help for it; they must take the consequences:' but they only take a part of the consequences—the sickness; the main part of the consequences are taken by others, especially if they are married, when the premature widowhood and orphanage are sustained by the wife and children, who are maintained at the expense of the relations or of the public. This recklessness is however the result of neglected education, of which the workmen are the victims, and for measures of beneficence such workmen are to be regarded and treated as children, for they are children in intellect. An instance of a beneficial measure of compulsory prevention taken by some employers of labour is mentioned by Mr. John Kennedy, jun., in a report on the condition of some classes of workpeople examined under the Commission of Inquiry into the Employment of Children, not included in the regulations of the Factory Act.[1] Some workmen employed in 'Kyanizing' wood became frequently ill from the fumes created in the process, to which fumes they unnecessarily exposed themselves. Admonitions to care were found to be of no avail, and the employer at length gave notice that he would discharge entirely from employment the first that was attacked with the peculiar illness produced by the fumes of the metal. This threat was acted upon, and no other cases of illness afterwards occurred.

In France, where the diseases by which the working classes are

---

1. 'Report by John L. Kennedy', in Appendix to *Second Report of Children's Employment Commission, P.P.* 1843, XIV, p. B11. Kennedy's report is dated 6 June 1841. An extract from it is printed as Appendix 26 to the *San. Rep.*, pp. 445-8.

afflicted have been investigated by those medical men who have given their attention to the improvement of the public health, the general conclusion has been established of the futility of leaving protective measures to the voluntary adoption of the individual workman. In the course of one of his reports,[1] *M. Duchâtelet* observes, that:

'It appears certain that the greatest part of the attacks of asphyxia which have taken place in the sewers have arisen from the traps being closed. I know that it is now enjoined on the workmen to open these traps while they are at their labour. But do they do this? Assuredly not in by far the majority of cases. Is it not a maxim to render independent of the will and superintendence of men, and above all of workmen, everything which appertains in a notable manner to their preservation? In the grave and learned discussions which have occupied this year (1824) the Academy of Sciences, on the means of preventing the dangers arising from steam-engines, not only all the members of the Commission, but the entire Academy, have been unanimous on the necessity of rendering independent of the workmen the direction of the level of the water in the boilers, and the tension of the steam. It evidently appeared that on this depended the solution of the problem. The same thing is now discussing on the subject of lighting by hydrogen gas.'

I will further adduce parallel examples, drawn from experience, in respect to the condition of the working population in France. It is contained in a treatise by *M. Emile Beres*, on the Means of Ameliorating the Condition of Artisans:[2]

'The condition of the labouring population would be less precarious, and their lives less exposed to accidents of every kind, if more foresight presided over their operations. Employers are often guilty of unpardonable carelessness with respect to the employed. To see their conduct, one would suppose that the men in their service were inert machines, or else that they possessed the power of the Creator to reconstruct broken limbs, to restore exhausted constitutions, or to give life to the dead. Here a deleterious atmosphere, which ought to be carefully purified, is imprudently allowed to be inhaled; there a poison, which ought to be handled with precaution, is allowed to penetrate every pore. Further on, as if man had wings, he is embarked on the most fragile scaffolds. Again, he is inconsiderately left to prosecute dangerous researches which demand the utmost care. It is not thus that we should act when the health and life of human beings are in question. To such neglects how many families owe their poverty and misery!

'There have long existed mills to grind plaster, which have not, nevertheless, prevented the unhappy workmen from being employed, in many places, and even in Paris, to pound it with a wooden club, their bodies bent towards the ground, and thus inhaling it in such quantities that the greatest number of them die young, of pulmonary phthisis.

'The use of the moveable inodorous tanks has been long understood in Paris. It consists in substituting for the tanks of masonry vessels of oak, painted, and strongly hooped with iron, so as to allow neither matter nor smell to escape. They are placed beneath the pipe which conveys the contents of the water-closet, and, when full, are carried away, and replaced by others at every hour of the day, without difficulty, without danger to the workmen, without

---

1. For A. J. P. Parent-Duchâtelet, see above, p. 149, n. 1.
2. Emile Beres, *Les Classes ouvrières. Moyens d'améliorer leur sort sous le Rapport du Bien-être matériel et du Perfectionnement moral* (2nd. edition, Paris 1836).

inconvenience to the inhabitants. Well; not only are the ancient tanks not suppressed in favour of this system, so convenient in all respects, but every day new ones are constructed, though not a year passes in which we do not hear of unhappy men perishing in the process of emptying, suffocated by the gas which escapes in their disgusting operation. Now, if we add to the danger of emptying the receptacles, the nuisance to all the inhabitants of the house, which is infected in its remotest corners, as well as the neighbouring houses of the same street, or even quarter; when we take into account the damage to furniture (especially to things that are gilt) by the escape of sulphureous gas, we shall have the measure of the negligence, I will not say of the proprietors only who maintain such an abuse without any justifiable motive, but even of the authority that suffers it. It is no rare thing, after the emptying has taken place, to see asphyxia produced in the masons who are employed in repairing the walls, or in remedying the infiltrations from the privies.

'There is another method, more recent, and, in all probability, more advantageous, of preventing the inconveniences of the ancient receptacles; it is the system of disinfecting fecal matter, discovered by a learned chemist, M. Payen[1]. Independently of its hygienic advantages, and the procuring a powerful manure, this method comprises a question of human dignity of great value. It is necessary, as far as possible, to take from our fellow men the mischievous necessity to perform labours which invest them with ideas of disgust.

'Since the use of gas for lighting, several accidents have happened. Are they not due, for the most part, to the want of precaution in the directors of these manufactories, who have not sufficiently prescribed to their men the necessary measures of prevention? Should they not all know that one must not run with a candle into a place where there is a stream of gas, as one would go in search of a stream of water? It is this imprudence which commonly occasions the explosions that happen, and which are ordinarily followed by the gravest accidents. Do we not find the same carelessness in our mines, followed by the same catastrophes? It is in vain, therefore, that Sir Humphry Davy applied his genius to the discovery of the safety-lamp! Do not the most ordinary rules of health condemn the ignorance with which the preparations of mercury, of sulphur, of lead, of oxide of copper, &c., are made? In the places, lastly, in which wool, hides, and other animal substances are prepared, why not purify the atmosphere in which the workmen exist with such difficulty? This omission is the more strange, that some centimes of solution of chlorine every day would be sufficient to purify the largest shops.

'I insist strongly on the contents of this chapter, because it reveals one of the deepest plague-spots of the labouring population of towns, and because the remedies that it indicates are neither difficult to discover, nor expensive in their application. With more solicitude and surveillance on the part of the government, with more philanthropy on the part of masters, with more precaution as well as self-love on the part of the workmen, would our hospitals receive so many unhappy beings, and death reap so many victims?'

Employers' Means of influencing the Condition of the Working Population. by regard to respectability in Dress

Besides those means which affect immediately the health and moral condition of the workpeople, others are within the control of their

---

1. This refers either to A. Payen, *Notice sur les Moyens d'utiliser toutes les Parties des Animaux morts dans les Campagnes* (Paris 1830), which, in spite of its somewhat bizarre title, deals with the subject of disinfection; or to Paul F. J. Payen, *De la Fièvre typhoïde* (Paris 1839).

employers which affect the personal appearance, and, through the self-respect, the morality of the population. *Mr. William Fairbairn*, in the course of an examination, adverted to the means of promoting respectability in personal appearance:

'It is always,' said he, 'an indication of looseness of character, and a low standard of moral conduct, to see a mechanic in dirt or in his working-clothes on Sunday. Thirty years' experience leads me to draw a very unfavourable conclusion as to the future usefulness to me, and of success to himself, of any workman whom I see in dirt on a Sunday.

'As a general rule, does the advance of his house keep pace with the advance in condition of the person?—As a general rule, it does. Better personal condition leads to better associates, and commonly to better marriage, on which the improved condition of the house is entirely dependent. It is due to the labouring classes of females in Lancashire and the surrounding districts to state that, in the important household virtue of cleanliness, they are superior to the females of the same class in Scotland.

'Are you aware of what is the condition of their houses. Have you visited them?—I have not made it a practice to visit them, I chiefly judge of their circumstances from seeing them with their wives and families, and their well-dressed and respectable condition on the Sundays. These externals are always indications of greater comforts and respectability at home. I am a strong advocate for dress, and encourage the working men to dress well; if I see any workman in a dirty condition and in his working-clothes in the streets on the Sunday, I do not, perhaps, speak to him then, but on the Monday I tell him that I have been looking over the books, that I find that he has had as good wages as other men who dress respectably, and that I do not like to have any one about me who will not dress well on the Sunday. This intimation has generally had the desired effect.'

Employers' or Owners' Influence in the Improvement of Habitations and sanitary Arrangements for the Protection of the Labouring Classes in the Rural Districts

I would now submit for consideration the evidence collected to show the appropriate means for the improvement of the condition of the labouring classes in the rural districts; and first, as to the effects produced by improved residences:

These are stated in a letter from the chairman of the Bedford union to Mr. Weale, the Assistant-Commissioner of the district, who had been requested by the Board to inquire as to the moral as well as the sanitary effects of improve tenements:

'*Turvey Abbey, January* 4, 1841.

'My dear Sir,—I beg to acknowledge the receipt of your letter of the 1st of January. You there state that, in a Return made to you by the Board of Guardians of the Bedford Union on the sanitary condition of the labouring population, it is reported that, in a few instances, cottages of an improved description have been erected by the employers of labour, the advantages of which have had a salutary influence on the moral habits of the inmates: and you request to know in what particular acts the improvement in moral conduct is displayed.

'I have much pleasure in saying that some cases of the kind have come under my own observation, and I consider that the improvement has arisen a good deal from the parties feeling that they are somewhat raised in the scale of society. The man sees his wife and family more comfortable than formerly; he has a better cottage and garden: he is stimulated to industry, and as he rises in respectability of station, he *becomes aware* that he has a character to lose. Thus an important point is gained. Having acquired certain advantages, he is anxious to retain and improve them; he strives more to preserve his independence, and becomes a member of benefit, medical, and clothing societies; and frequently, besides this, lays up a certain sum, quarterly or half-yearly, in the savings' bank. Almost always attendant upon these advantages, we find the man sending his children to be regularly instructed in a Sunday, and, where possible, in a day-school, and himself and family more constant in their attendance at some place of worship on the Lord's-day. I know of more instances than one where, in consequence of encouragement of the kind above mentioned to the father of a poor family, the children were regularly sent to school, and there became so much improved in character and learning that they are now filling situations of high respectability, (one a confidential clerk in a large mercantile house in London,) and are assisting to support their parents in a manner as delightful as it is creditable.

'A man who comes home to a poor, comfortless hovel after his day's labour, and sees all miserable around him, has his spirits more often depressed than excited by it. He feels that, do his best, he shall be miserable still, and is too apt to fly for a temporary refuge to the alehouse or beer-shop. But give him the means of making himself comfortable by his own industry, and I am convinced by experience that, in many cases, he will avail himself of it.

'Believe me, my dear sir, sincerely yours,

'CHARLES LONGUET HIGGINS.[1]

'*To Robert Weale, Esq.,*
'*Assistant Poor Law Commissioner.*'

The next exemplification is afforded in a letter from the clerk of the Stafford Union:

'*Marston, Stafford, January* 20, 1841.

'Sir,—I beg to acknowledge the receipt of your letter of the 1st instant, as to the Return made by the Board of Guardians on the sanitary condition of the labouring population of this Union, in which it is stated that improved cottages have been erected by landed proprietors for their labourers, and the advantages afforded by such cottages have had a salutary influence on the moral habits of the inmates, and requesting to be informed in what particular acts the improvement in moral conduct is displayed.

'In answer thereto, I will endeavour to illustrate the remark of the Board of Guardians by contrasting the habits, the condition, and prospects of a labourer occupying an improved cottage with the occupier of a cottage of a contrary description. If we follow the agricultural labourer into his miserable dwelling, we shall find it consisting of two rooms only; the day-room, in addition to the family, contains the cooking utensils, the washing apparatus, agricultural implements, and dirty clothes, the windows broken, and stuffed full of rags. In the sleeping apartment, the parents and their children, boys and girls, are indiscriminately mixed, and frequently a lodger sleeping in the same and the only room; generally no window, the openings in the half-thatched roof admit light, and expose the family to every vicissitude of the weather; the liability of the children so situated to contagious maladies frequently plunges the family into the greatest misery. The husband, enjoying but little comfort under his own roof, resorts to the beer-shop, neglects the cultivation of his garden, and impoverishes his family. The children are brought up without any

---

1. *Local Reps. E. & W.*, pp. 128-9.

regard to decency of behaviour, to habits of foresight, or self-restraint; they make indifferent servants; the girls become the mothers of bastards, and return home a burden to their parents, or to the parish, and fill the workhouse. The boys spend the Christmas week's holiday and their year's wages in the beer shop, and enter upon their new situation in rags. Soon tired of the restraint imposed upon them under the roof of their master, they leave his service before the termination of the year's engagement, seek employment as day-labourers, not with a view of improving their condition, but with a desire to receive and spend their earnings weekly in the beer-shop; associating with the worst of characters, they become the worst of labourers, resort to poaching, commit petty thefts, and add to the county rates by commitments and prosecutions.

'On the contrary, on entering an improved cottage, consisting on the ground-floor of a room for the family, a washhouse and a pantry, and three sleeping-rooms over, with a neat and well-cultivated garden, in which the leisure hours of the husband being both pleasantly and profitably employed, he has no desire to frequent the beer-shop or spend his evenings from home; the children are trained to labour, to habits and feelings of independence, and taught to connect happiness with industry, and to shrink from idleness and immorality: the girls make good servants, obtain the confidence of their employers, and get promoted to the best situations. The boys, at the termination of the year's engagement, spend the Christmas week's holiday comfortably under the roof of their parents; clothes suitable for the next year's service are provided, and the residue of wages is deposited in the savings' bank; a system of frugality is engrafted with the first deposit, increasing with every addition to the fund: they are gradually employed in those departments of labour requiring greater skill, and implying more confidence in their integrity and industry, and they attain a position in society of comparative independence.

'I have selected an extreme case to show more fully the advantages derived from improved cottages, and the immoral effects of inferior dwellings, unfortunately too numerous, in this Union.

'I have the honour to be, sir,
'Your obedient servant,
'PETER LOWE.[1]

'*To Robert Weale, Esq.,*
'*Assistant Poor Law Commissioner.*'

Much regret is frequently expressed at the change of condition which has taken place in the cultivation of the soil by farm labourers instead of farm servants living in the house of the farmer, and subject to the household rules at his board; but whatever real ground there may be to regret the change, it appears to be one generally preferred by both parties, and there appears to be no reason to expect that the ancient system will be revived. In the Appendix I have given an examination of the Rev. Thomas Whately, in reference to some frequent and most important mistakes in respect to cottage economy.[2]

The Board agreeing that the most important leading examples of

---

1. *Local Reps. E. & W.*, pp. 129-31.
2. 'Examination of the Rev. Thomas Whateley, Cookham, Berks, on cottage allotments and the keeping of pigs by cottagers', *San. Rep.*, Appendix 12, pp. 403-5.

VI. The Effects of Preventive Measures

improvement were to be expected from the benevolence and public spirit of opulent individuals, requested the assistant commissioners in England to note the most conspicuous improvements of labourers' tenements they have met with in their districts, and procure plans with a view to their promulgation. From these I have selected several examples, and have added several that I have met with in the course of my own inquiries.

Some eligible plans of cottage tenements are thus described in *Mr. Twisleton's* report from Norfolk and Suffolk:

'Although the general aspect of the cottages in Norfolk and Suffolk is pleasing and attractive, I do not think that these counties can be generally cited as abounding with model cottages. Some of the best which I have seen belong to the Earl of Stradbroke, at Henham, near Halesworth in Suffolk; to the Earl of Leicester, at Holkham; and to the Rev. Mr. Benyon, at Culford, about five miles from Bury St. Edmunds. Those of the Earl of Stradbroke are built of brick, roofed with tiles, have four rooms at least, and have all proper conveniences of pantries, cupboards, and out-offices; but, at the same time, as they are principally with only one story, so that the bed-rooms are on the same floor with the parlour and kitchen, such cottages would only be built where land is no object; and they must be considered in the light of luxuries and ornaments. Some of the cottages of the Earl of Leicester, at Holkham, are perhaps the most substantial and comfortable which are to be seen in any part of England; and if all the English peasantry could be lodged in similar ones, it would be the realization of an Utopia. I have obtained from Mr. Emerson, of Holkham, their builder, drawings of the plans and of the elevation of eight of these cottages, which are built of brick roofed with tiles. I herewith transmit them to you, and it will be observed that there are three sets, two of two cottages each, and one of four cottages. Without entering into details respecting all the eight, I will draw your attention to the double cottages of 1819. Each of these has a front room, 17 feet by 12 feet in width, and 7 feet to 7 feet 6 inches high; a back kitchen of the same height, and 13 feet by 9 feet wide, together with a pantry on the same floor. Above these are three bed-rooms which, in different proportions, cover the space already specified for the ground-floor. At a convenient distance behind, each cottage has attached to it a wash-house, a dirt-bin, a privy, and a pig-cot. I may add that the drainage is excellent, that the water is good, that each cottage has about 20 rods of garden-ground, and that the rent, including gardens, is only three guineas a-year. Hence it is not to be wondered at that Mr. Emerson the builder has been enabled to say, in a letter to me: "I have never known in them an instance of fever or any epidemic."

'These cottages are cited as showing what may be done by a landed proprietor who takes as great a pride in his good cottages and farms as others in fine hunters and race-horses, rather than with the least intention of asserting that the example is ever likely to be universally imitated. The cost of building two such cottages is stated by Mr. Emerson to be 220*l*. or 230*l*., which would be 110*l*. or 115*l*. each. Now, although individuals, here and there, may build cottages without regard to the pecuniary return, it may be assumed as incontrovertible, that no class of cottages will be universally adopted which does not command a reasonable interest for the money expended on them. But considering the cost of repairs, and the frequent trouble and uncertainty of obtaining the rents, it will probably not be denied that 6*l*. a-year would be the *minimum* as a remunerative rent for the outlay of 110*l*. or 115*l*. on a cottage. However, the rent of 6*l*. would scarcely be paid by the agricultural population generally at the present wages: for reckoning the rate of wages at 12*s*. a-week

Employers' Influence: Habitations in Rural Districts 327

(which would be high for some parts of the country), very few would be willing, out of that sum, to expend 2s. 3¾d. a-week, or nearly a fifth of their earnings, for the rent of their cottage.

'I would take, therefore, a more attainable standard of excellence in the cottages of the Rev. E. Benyon, at Culford. This is a remarkable village of about fifty cottages, built within the last twenty years by Mr. Benyon de Beuvoir. The outward appearance of them is pretty, and it was this which first attracted my attention to them. They are built with bricks, faced with blue flint-stones, which harmonize agreeably with the blue slate of the roofs. They have each four rooms—two below and two above—with a pantry and a cupboard. I herewith transmit to you plans and drawings of five of these cottages in two sets—one consisting of double tenements, and one of three tenements. It will be observed that the principal room is 14 feet by 12 feet wide, and 7 feet high, which is inferior in size to those at Holkham, and that they have only two bed-rooms, while those at Holkham have three. At the distance of a few feet from each set of cottages there is a wooden building, roofed with tiles, which comprises a space for fuel, and a privy for each cottage, and a common oven. The average cost of the double cottages at Culford is stated to have been 170l., or 85l. each.'[1]

Mr. Loudon, who has paid great attention to the subject of cottage architecture, directs attention to the labourers' cottages, either newly erected, or altered, or improved, on the estate of Gregory Gregory, Esq., at Harlaxton, near Grantham, Lincolnshire.

'The village of Harlaxton,' says Mr. Loudon, 'is, if possible, more interesting to us than even the new mansion and gardens. We have seen many ornamented villages both at home and abroad, but none so original and so much to our taste as this of Mr. Gregory's. Some of old date are too like rows of street houses, such as those of Newnham Courtenay, near Oxford; and Harewood, near Leeds; others are too affectedly varied and picturesque, such as that at Blaize Castle, near Bristol; and some have the houses bedaubed with ornaments that have not sufficient relation to use, as when rosettes and sculptures are stuck on the walls, instead of applying facings to the windows, porches to the doors, and characteristic shafts to the chimney tops. We recollect one near Warsaw, which is a repetition of the Grecian temple, with a portico at each end; and one at Peckra, near Moscow, every opening in which has a pediment over it, with highly enriched barge-boards. In some villages the attempt is made to ornament every house with trellis-work round the doors and windows, which produces great sameness of appearance, and if ornamental, is so at the expense of comfort, the creepers by which the trellis-work is covered darkening the rooms, and encouraging insects; while, in other villages, the cottages are so low and so small, that it is obvious to a passing spectator they cannot contain a single wholesome room. However, though we find fault with villages ornamented in these ways, we are still glad to see them, because any kind of alteration in the dwellings and gardens of country labourers can hardly fail to be an improvement, both with reference to the occupiers and to the country at large.'

The external condition of the residence, and the apparent rank it holds, is not without a beneficial moral effect on the occupants, by increasing their self-respect and pride in the decencies of life. Mr. Loudon's enumeration of the requisites for cottage building are given in the Appendix,[2] together with views of the groups of cottages Mr.

---

1. *Local Reps. E. & W.*, pp. 136–8. 2. *San. Rep.*, App. 9, pp. 396–9.

Gregory has erected; contrasted with these is a group of hind's cottages, as described by Dr. Gilly, in his appeal in behalf of the border peasantry,[1] from which a conception may be formed of the great difference in morals as well as in health that may be anticipated from the effects of the different order of residences on the population.

I have been favoured by the Earl of Roseberry with plans of the new labourers' cottages he has built on his property in Scotland, which have been highly approved by the Highland Society, who have inserted the plans for publication in their 'Transactions,' *vide* Appendix.[2] I have been favoured by James Monteath, Esq., with a model of the cottages erected by his father, Sir Stewart Monteath, Bart., for his labourers at Closeburn. The plan of these cottages presents an important improvement, by which one fire-place is made to warm two apartments on the same floor, and by means of an air pipe warms the air in the two rooms above them. I was informed that it admits of a further improvement in practice, namely, of some means of closing the access of the warm air to the sleeping-rooms during summer.

The best plans I have obtained of tenements in actual occupation of the rural manufacturing population appear to be those at Turton, and those erected at Bollington. The best plans of labourers' tenements in towns are those supplied by Mr. Hodgson, and the Committee of Physicians and Surgeons at Birmingham; the drawings and working plans of which I have appended.

In several of the plans for the rural districts there is one appendage of the cottage of which the best-informed witnesses consider they ought invariably to be divested, namely, a pigsty. The medical witnesses strongly object that it is injurious to the health, especially in rows of cottages, as it occasions accumulations of filthy refuse. Other witnesses, such as the Rev. Thomas Whately, object that the pig is not economical to the labourer, and that it furnishes a temptation to dishonesty. His evidence on that subject, and on the other more important question of large cottage allotments, will be found in the Appendix.[3]

Mr. Loudon has favoured me with two drawings and plans of model cottages, which need no other explanation than the specification. These comprise the best examples that have come under observation during the present inquiry of tenements in occupation that are well approved on trial.

Every detail, however, of the materials with which the cottage is constructed, and the mode of its construction, deserve, and there is little doubt will obtain, most careful attention, for it is only by considering their comforts in detail that they can be improved, or the aggregate effect on the immense masses of the community can be analyzed and estimated. For example, it has been mentioned that a decided difference is perceptible in the health and condition of workmen of the same class who live in houses made of brick as compared with those living in houses made of stone.

---

1. W. S. Gilly, *The Peasantry of the Border* (Berwick-upon-Tweed 1841).
2. Chadwick appears to be mistaken here, for there is no reference to these plans in any of the appendices to the *Sanitary Report*.
3. *San. Rep.*, App. 12, pp. 403-5.

A gentleman who has attentively observed the condition of the working classes in the north of Lancashire, and the north of Cheshire, states that the general health of the labourers in the north of Lancashire is decidedly inferior.[1] This inferiority he ascribes to several causes, and, amongst others, to damp cottages, and:

'Wood and wattled houses, such as our forefathers built, are the driest and warmest of all; brick is inferior in both these requisites of a comfortable house; but stone, especially the unhewn stone as it is necessarily employed for cottages, is the very worst material possible for the purpose. I prefer the Irish mud cottages. The evil arises from two causes. The stone is not impervious to water, especially when the rain is accompanied by high winds; and it sucks up the moisture of the ground, and gives it out into the rooms; but principally, stone is a good conductor of heat and cold, so that the walls cooled down by the outer air are continually condensing the moisture contained in the warmer air of the cottage, just as the windows steam on a frosty morning; besides, the abstraction of heat in stone houses must be a serious inconvenience. The effect of this condensation must be, and is, to make clothes, bedding, &c., damp, whenever they are placed near the wall, and therefore extremely prejudicial to those who wear the clothes or sleep in the beds. Of course I do not attribute all the damp of our cottages in this neighbourhood to the stone; much of it is due to the wet climate, wet soil, and building so near the ground; but the stone, as a material of building, must bear a considerable share of the blame. I believe, too, it is partly the cause of the very great difference of cleanliness of the Cheshire farming people and ours of the same class.

'Indeed the Cheshire people were brought up to wooden cottages: brick was of later introduction. The greater facilities and inducements to cleanliness in a dry house would, in the course of time, form a more cleanly people, and superior healthiness would follow.'

Mr. Parker observes, that the construction of the cottages in Buckinghamshire is frequently unwholesome:—

'The improper materials of which cottages are built, and their defective construction, are also the frequent cause of the serious indisposition of the inmates. The cottages at Waddesdon, and some of the surrounding parishes in the Vale of Aylesbury, are constructed of mud, with earth floors and thatched roofs. The vegetable substances mixed with the mud to make it bind, rapidly decompose, leaving the walls porous. The earth of the floor is full of vegetable matter, and from there being nothing to cut off its contact with the surrounding mould, it is peculiarly liable to damp. The floor is frequently charged with animal matter thrown upon it by the inmates, and this rapidly decomposes by the alternate action of heat and moisture. Thatch placed in contact with such walls speedily decays, yielding a gas of the most deleterious quality. Fever of every type and diarrhœa are endemic diseases in the parish and neighbourhood. Next to good drainage and thorough ventilation, the foundation of a cottage is the most important consideration. A foundation, to be good, must not only be sufficiently strong to bear the superstructure, and of sufficient depth to cut off all connexion with the surrounding vegetable mould and that beneath the floor, but also be constructed of materials calculated to resist moisture. The best materials for this purpose are concrete and sound bricks, partially vitrified in the kiln or clamp. If such bricks be well laid with mortar composed of sharp sand, containing no vegetable substances, and the concrete be free from earthy particles, well mixed and firmly thrown together, the

---

1. This probably relates, in fact, to the *South* of Lancashire, and the *North* of Cheshire. See p. 195, n. 1, above.

admission of damp will be entirely avoided. Stone, chalk, bricks which are not thoroughly burnt, impure mortar, and wood, have all a tendency to absorb moisture, which, if once received by such materials, ascends, or "creeps up," as it is technically called by builders, and thus affects the whole building. To avoid this "creeping up," builders are in the habit of placing a tire of slate in foundations above the surface mould, a remedy of a temporary character only, for the action of damp entirely destroys slate. Roman cement has also been used for this purpose, but the sand mixed with this material renders it in some degree porous. It has lately been suggested that a course of well-burnt bricks set in asphalte would effectually prevent this absorption of surface-water, and a favourable opinion of this plan has been expressed by two intelligent architects.'[1]

He adds that:

'In Berkshire the floors of the cottages are laid with red tiles, called "flats," or with bricks of a remarkable porous quality, and as each of these tiles or bricks will absorb half a pint of water, so do they become the means by which vapour is generated. The cleanly housewife, who prides herself upon the neat and fresh appearance of her cottage, pours several pails of water upon the floor, and when she has completed her task with the besom, she proceeds to remove with a mop or flannel so much of the water as the bricks have not absorbed.

'After having cleansed the cottage, the fire is usually made up to prepare the evening meal, and vapour is created by the action of the heat upon the saturated floor. Thus the means adopted to purify the apartment are equally as injurious to the health of the inmates as the filth and dirt frequently too abundant in the cottages of labouring persons.

'It is usual to insert in local Acts for the regulation of towns a clause prohibiting the use of straw and similar vegetable substances for roofing; and it appears to me to be desirable that some provision should be made for the rural districts, by which the thatch of cottages, when in a decomposed state, might be required to be removed. In the parishes of Binton, Dorsington, and Long Marston, in the neighbourhood of Stratford-on-Avon, simple continued fever, described to be similar in character to the form of fever which frequently occurs in the autumn and beginning of winter throughout England, prevailed very extensively in the winter of 1839. Of 31 patients attacked by it, seven died. Dr. Thompson of Stratford-on-Avon, the physician who visited all the cases by the desire of the Board of Guardians of the Stratford-on-Avon union, observes:—"As almost all the cottages in which there has been fever are thatched, and the thatch in many of them is in a very rotten and insufficient condition, it is not improbable that slow decomposition in the thatch, from the unusual quantities of rain which has fallen, may have been going on, and contributed to the production and continuance of fever. It has been observed by others, I believe, that it is more difficult to get rid of fever in thatched than in slated cottages." Dr. Thompson also remarks, that in thatched cottages it is not usual to ceil or plaster the inside of the roof; and he recommends that this should be done, and that the plaster should be lime-washed once-a-year.'[2]

In the course of some observations made on the construction of the cottages of the labouring classes in France, it is observed that:

'It is in vain that the workman breathes a pure air out of doors, if on his return to his home he finds an infected atmosphere. Air, which is so necessary to life and health, and which it is of the last importance to renew often,

---

1. *Local Reps. E. & W.*, pp. 91-2.
2. *Ibid.*, pp. 90, 94.

especially in small rooms, remains thick and loaded in the abode of the workman, because no currents can exist in consequence of the window being almost always placed alongside the door. The form of the chimney is another great evil in the construction of country cottages. With a shaft very short and very large, it is impossible for the room to get warm, and the heat produced is almost entirely lost. This form of the chimney is only explicable by the ignorance of the constructors. However large a fire may be required by the diverse needs of the family, it does not involve the necessity to make the chimney shaft of a corresponding size; on the contrary, the facility with which the smoke ascends is altogether proportioned to the smallness of the latter, as may be seen in the chimneys of stoves, which are always extremely narrow.'

The *Rev. C. Walkey*, of Collumpton, gives instances of the want of provision for ventilation in the cottages of the labouring classes:

'Cottages for the most part are without sufficient ventilation, particularly in the up-stairs apartment, this being almost invariably without a chimney, with a low window, commonly about two feet from the floor, and having no ceiling, therefore the thatched roof, lofty in itself, and full of cobwebs, contains the foul air; and in several instances I have been the means of restoring health apparently by blowing gunpowder in cases where fever has raged for months, the ground-floors being often damp—very seldom above the level of the land.'

The proceedings of the Highland Society for the improvement of the material condition of the labourer, especially on the subject of cottage economy, appear to be extremely well directed. They have sought to make improvements in detail, which are thus described in one of the reports of a committee appointed to inquire into the subject:

'Medals have been offered by the society to proprietors for building cottages of a good construction; and these medals are already in demand. The subject was again brought forward by the Marquis of Tweeddale, who filled the chair at the last general meeting; and throughout the whole of Scotland it is attracting increasing attention. The style of such buildings is everywhere improving, and the measures of the society will make the country acquainted with the best models. Still, without a considerable diminution of the expense, the rapid introduction of a better system is hardly to be expected. To that point, accordingly, the directors have turned their serious attention.

'Their first object has been the improvement of the windows, which always form one of the principal items of charge, and have been generally one of the worst constructed parts of the building. In many districts of the Highlands the huts of the peasantry have nothing of the kind, nor are there tradesmen within reach from whom they can be obtained; and even in many of the more improved parts of the country the cottage windows are seldom large enough to admit a sufficiency of light; they are almost never provided with the means of ventilation; and in a few instances can they be repaired without applying to a tradesman. This is always attended with considerable expense; and, in remote situations, skilful workmen are hardly to be obtained on any terms. Accordingly, when glass is broken, recourse is had to the most unseemly substitutes. These may annoy the inmate at first, but he soon becomes habituated to them; one eyesore prepares him for another, and in a short time the same slovenliness and disorder spread over the whole establishment.

'It appeared to the directors that much of this would be avoided if the public could be made acquainted with the best description of a cottage window. The demand would necessarily lead to their being extensively manufactured, and consequently supplied at a moderate price; and, what is of still more consequence, the general adoption of such windows would lead to glass of the proper size being kept in every village, and labourers would then be enabled to repair their own windows. A premium was accordingly offered last year for the best cottage window, not so much in the expectation of bringing forward anything altogether new, as of enabling the directors to select the best of the forms now in use.

'Various specimens were sent in. Some were made of zinc; but these were rejected, on the advice of tradesmen, as being too weak to admit of repair by an unpractised hand. Wood and lead are, for the same reason, equally unsuitable. One was constructed with astragals of malleable iron, so thin as very little to impede the light, and consequently admitting of glass of a very small size; but the astragals not being provided with flanges for the glass to rest upon, the repair must necessarily be a work of some difficulty; and these also were consequently deemed unfit for the purpose. Cast-iron appears to be the material least liable to objection; but astragals of cast-metal must be of considerable thickness; and such frames, therefore, could not be adapted to a very small size of glass without materially obscuring the light. It was made by Messrs. Moses M'Culloch and Co., Gallowgate, Glasgow; and, without the wooden frame, it costs 5s. Glass for such a window may be purchased at $2\frac{3}{4}d.$ per square. These windows would appear adapted for farm-houses and workshops as well as for cottages. They admit of being made of every variety of size, and, in most cases, they may thus be fitted with ease to houses already built. In many situations, it will thus deserve consideration whether it may be better to repair the glass of old frames, or to adopt windows of this construction, which may be purchased and kept up at so very moderate an expense. It is understood that Messrs. M'Culloch intend to establish agencies in all parts of the country, and light and pure air will thus be supplied to the humbler classes everywhere at a much cheaper rate than they have hitherto been obtained.

The directors have next turned their attention to the means of economizing fuel; and a premium for the best mode of accomplishing this will be found in the list of this year. It will be observed, that the object of the premium is not to obtain plans merely from Scottish tradesmen, but to ascertain the devices which are practised in foreign countries. In America, and several of the continental states, it is understood that stoves are generally used for this purpose, and some of these are said to be so perfect that no one who has been accustomed to them would tolerate the fire-places of the Scottish cottages. There may be a difficulty in introducing a novelty of this kind here; but if it should promise to be beneficial, it would be at least deserving of a trial; and if it should be generally adopted, this also would become the subject of an extensive manufacture, and be obtained at a cheap rate.

'It appears to the committee, that still further facilities would be afforded, both for the construction of new cottages and the improvement of those already built, were doors, shelving, and the other wooden work of the building manufactured in the same way as the windows. The committee do not at present see any means of contributing to the establishment of such works by the offer of premiums; but it occurs to them that extensive proprietors might find it worth their while to try the experiment, as an addition to the work of saw-mills. If it should succeed with them, it could not fail in the hands of tradesmen devoting their whole attention to the subject: and there would be no want of men ready to embark in such undertakings. Should an experiment of this kind be made, the committee hope that the directors will be made acquainted with the result.

'Such a supply of the leading materials would not only greatly facilitate the work of proprietors both in the erection of new cottages and the improvement of old ones, but labourers who have the prospect of being permanent tenants would likewise be induced, at their own expense, to make improvements, which they would at present find quite impracticable. As the reduction of the price of every article of dress now enables the humblest labourer to appear respectably clothed, so the reduction of the expense of so many of the essentials in the construction of a house would bring comfortable lodging equally within his reach.'

To the above-recited measures of the Highland Society, which are so well directed to the improvement of the structure of cottages in the important points of economy as well as of efficiency, they have added prizes for the best-kept cottages and the best cottage gardens, which have everywhere excited competition, and have been attended with beneficial results.

I have as yet met with no similar instance of attention given by large and influential public bodies, to the improvement of the residences of the working-classes in towns. I have, however, been favoured with one communication from *Mr. Sydney Smirke*, the architect[1], who has had experience in planning and superintending the erection of residences for the men of the coast-guard service, and who, in some suggestions for the improvement of the metropolis, has endeavoured to direct public attention to the improvement of the structure of the residences of the labouring classes. He states that:

'The course that has been adopted by great manufacturers and others in some rural districts, of erecting ranges of distinct cottages for their labourers, is plainly inapplicable to large towns. If there were no other obstacle to this arrangement, the value of land would alone be fatal to it in such places; but my belief is that, without ultimate pecuniary loss, and with the utmost direct and indirect benefit, buildings, placed under some public control, might be erected for the joint occupation of many families or individuals, and so arranged that each tenant might feel that he had the exclusive enjoyment of a home in the room or rooms which he occupied, and yet might partake, in common with his neighbours, of many important comforts and advantages now utterly unknown to him.

'I propose that there should be erected buildings, in various parts of the suburbs, consisting of perhaps 50 or 60 rooms, high, airy, dry, well ventilated, light and warm, comfortably filled up, fire-proof, abundantly supplied with water and thoroughly drained; such regulations might be laid down for the conduct of the inmates as may be necessary for the common good, without undue rigour or interference with natural and proper feelings of independence.

'Another class of structures should be raised, perhaps rather as dormitories than for permanent residence, from which families would be excluded; these should be arranged like some of the wards of Chelsea Hospital, with separate compartments appropriated to each tenant. Unlike the frail and worthless tenements that rise in great profusion around London, these buildings should be studiously planned and strongly constructed; all that the builder's art can contribute towards the safety, health, and comfort of each individual, should here be found. In the former class of buildings, a room or rooms should

---

1. Sydney Smirke (1798-1877), architect, who worked principally in London (restoration of the Temple Church, extension of British Museum, and exhibition galleries at Burlington House). Author of *Suggestions for the Architectural Improvement of the Western Part of London* (1834).

be let at a low weekly rent to any decent family that should apply: in the latter, each compartment should be let by the night.

'The exterior of these locanda, or public lodging-houses, should have a cheerful, inviting appearance, not entirely without architectural character, although free, of course, from the mere ornament and frippery of architecture.

'In throwing out these suggestions for such consideration as they may deserve, it seems superfluous at present to trouble you with explanatory plans and other details; it may be enough for me to assure you that buildings can be erected, affording all the accommodations above described, and offering to their inmates the luxury of a decent, cleanly, and healthy abode, at a cost less than is usually required by them for the purchase of the squalid resting-places they now resort to, and yet enough to repay a fair interest on the original expense of the new building.

'It may be said that in providing these commodious dwellings for their needy inmates, we shall be furnishing them with that which they do not desire; that habitual and long acquaintance with privation has taught them to regard and to endure, without any lively distaste, much of that misery from which others, more delicately educated, would shrink with disgust; but I consider this objection quite unfounded. A tainted atmosphere cannot be less injurious because by long habit it is breathed without nausea. If these deplorable habits have really acquired so much force, it should be our part to make corresponding efforts to teach the victims of them to become more sensible of their misery, not indeed by inculcating lessons of discontent, but by affording to them facilities for providing themselves with healthier and happier abodes.

'It is the true saying of an eloquent writer, that "les esclaves perdent tout dans leur esclavage, jusqu'au désir d'en sortir;" yet surely no benevolent person would think himself idly or unprofitably employed in loosing from bondage those whom long endurance has caused to forget the blessings of freedom. I am, however, unwilling to believe, even now, that the classes of whom I am speaking are insensible to the comforts of cleanliness, or unable to appreciate the benefit to be derived from improved habitations.

'I confess I cannot discover any objection to the adoption of such a plan for ameliorating the dwellings of the poorest classes of our fellow creatures that would not be counter-balanced by many direct and indirect advantages.'

I beg leave to submit this communication and the plans[1] with which Mr. Smirke has favoured me, that it may be made known and considered. Much importance will be attached to the testimony received from him as well as from other professional men, that it is possible to afford to the labouring classes the luxury of 'a decent, cleanly, and healthy abode at a cost less than is usually required from them for the squalid resting-places they now resort to, and yet enough to repay a fair interest on the original expense of the new building.'

I see no reason to doubt the applicability of Mr. Smirke's plan to such places as those where ranges of buildings are now required as lodgings for workmen, and, without questioning the applicability of the proposition last cited, to all classes of residences. It is proper to mention, that in the course of this inquiry frequent instances have arisen of much social disorder arising from the too close contiguity of residences, or from the want of some control over the inmates. In the instances noticed

---

1. Smirke's drawings of 'a plan for a public lodging house', which were inserted opposite p. 274 of the *Sanitary Report*, have not been reproduced in this edition.

of lodging-houses, or of one building, inhabited by different families, living as in the apartments of the same dwelling, the conclusion afforded by experience seems to be, that a power and discipline almost as strong as that of a man-of-war, is requisite to preserve order in such communities; and that until a degree of education of the lower classes is attained, which is hopeless for the present generation at least, it is desirable to avoid any arrangement which brings *families* into close contact with each other. A large proportion of the cases of assault and brawls which occupy the attention of the petty sessions and sessions in towns, arise from contentions amongst the inhabitants of courts and alleys, which are clearly ascribable to too close contiguity; and these effects have frequently given rise to the suggestion that if a city were rebuilt, the preservation of peace would be much easier if such places were entirely removed and the inhabitants separated. A common pump has gone far to furnish practice to a petty attorney. All the females wanted to use it at the same time, and perpetual quarrels and frequent assaults arose to get the first supplies. Several attempts have been made by benevolent landlords to get their labourers to make use of common bakehouses, common washhouses, to join for one common brewing, and have offered them the use of utensils; but they never could be got to agree upon it, and I have met with no instance in which such plans have succeeded. Unless the walls of contiguous cottages are very thick, detached cottages have social comforts and moral advantages superior to those houses built in rows; and persons even of the middle class pay a higher rent for detached tenements for the sake of the comparative freedom which they allow from disturbance by their neighbours. The information I received in Scotland respecting the assemblages of single men, farm-servants, in houses called boothies, showed that the effect was also extremely unfavourable to their moral habits.

In some of the new towns in Germany it is considered advantageous, for the sake of the circulation of air as well as for comfort and for security against fire, to have each house detached by a small space from its neighbours.

Effects of Public Walks and Gardens on the Health and Morals of the Lower Classes of the Population

Whilst separation rather than aggregation, more especially for families, is the course of policy suggested by experience for the places of residence of the working-classes, accommodation is called for from every part of the country for public walks or places of recreation. The committee of physicians and surgeons of Birmingham state, in the course of their report on the sanitary condition of the population of that town:

'The want of some place of recreation for the mechanic is an evil which presses very heavily upon these people, and to which many of their bad habits may be traced. There are no public walks in or near this town; no places where the working-people can resort for recreation. The consequence is that they frequent the ale-houses and skittle-alleys for amusement. Within the last half century the town was surrounded by land which was divided into gardens, which were rented by the mechanic at one guinea or half a guinea per annum. Here the mechanic was generally seen after his day's labour spending his evening in a healthy and simple occupation, in which he took great delight.

This ground is now for the most part built over, and the mechanics of the town are gradually losing this source of useful and healthy recreation.'[1]

Mr. Mott, in his report on the condition of the labouring population of his district, observes, in respect to that in Manchester:

'There are circumstances attending the local position of Manchester which might be urged in palliation of some of the habits of the working classes.

'There are no public walks or places of recreation by which the thousands of labourers or families can relieve the tedium of their monotonous employment. Pent up in a close, dusty atmosphere from half-past five or six o'clock in the morning till seven or eight o'clock at night, from week to week, without change, without intermission, it is not to be wondered at that they fly to the spirit and beer-shops, and the dancing-houses, on the Saturday nights to seek those, to them, pleasures and comforts which their own destitute and comfortless homes deny.

'Manchester is singularly destitute of those resources which conduce at once to health and recreation. With a teeming population, literally overflowing her boundaries, she has no public walks or resorts, either for the youthful or the adult portion of the community to snatch an hour's enjoyment.

'The prospect of obtaining any wide area to be appropriated as a public walk or otherwise for the use of the labouring classes, becomes more remote each year, as the value of the land within and in the neighbourhood of the town increases.[2]

Mr. Joseph Strutt, of Derby, has presented to that town a public garden of eleven acres, which has been so laid out by Mr. Loudon as to give the advantages of a walk of two miles, and the interest afforded by an arboretum, displaying the specimens of 1,000 shrubs and plants.[3] The plan of laying out this public ground so as to make the most of the space, appears to be one deserving of peculiar attention; and I have appended to this report a copy with which I have been favoured.[4] I am informed that his Grace the Duke of Norfolk has expressed an intention, as soon as some leases are out, to bestow 50 acres for the use of Sheffield as a public garden.[5]

Much evidence might be adduced from the experience of the effects of the parks and other places of public resort in the metropolis, to prove the importance of such provision for recreation, not less for the pleasure they afford in themselves, than for their rivalry to pleasures that are expensive, demoralizing, and injurious to the health. A benevolent gentleman near Cambridge, who wished to arrest the debauchery and demoralization promoted by a fair, and, if possible, to put an end to the fair itself, instituted on the days when it was held, and at a distance

---

1. *Local Reps E. & W.*, p. 213.
2. This passage is not in the version of Mott's report printed in *Local Reps. E. & W.*, but for the compilation of Mott's report, see Introduction, p. 50.
3. The Arboretum was presented to the town of Derby in 1840 by William Strutt, son of the industrialist Jedediah Strutt. See John C. Loudon, *The Derby Arboretum* (1840); and R. S. Fitton and A. P. Wadsworth, *The Strutts and the Arkwrights, 1758-1830* (Manchester 1958), pp. 187-8.
4. John C. Loudon, 'Arrangement of public walks in towns: plan of the Arboretum at Derby', *San. Rep.*, Appendix 13, pp. 405-8.
5. For the presentation of the 'Park' to the City of Sheffield, see S. Pollard, *A History of Labour in Sheffield* (Liverpool 1959), p. 98.

from it, a grand ploughing match, at which all persons of respectability were invited to attend. This brought from the fair all the young men whom it was desired to lead from it to a regulated and a rational and beneficial entertainment, and thus, without force and at a very trivial expense, the fair was suppressed by the quiet mode of drawing away its profit.

On the holiday given at Manchester in celebration of Her Majesty's marriage, extensive arrangements were made for holding a chartist meeting, and for getting up what was called a demonstration of the working classes, which greatly alarmed the municipal magistrates. Sir Charles Shaw, the Chief Commissioner of Police, induced the mayor to get the Botanical Gardens, Zoological Gardens, and Museum of that town, and other institutions thrown open to the working classes at the hour they were urgently invited to attend the chartist meeting. The mayor undertook to be personally answerable for any damage that occurred from throwing open the gardens and institutions to the classes who had never before entered them. The effect was that not more than 200 or 300 people attended the political meeting, which entirely failed, and scarcely 5s. worth of damage was done in the gardens or in the public institutions by the workpeople, who were highly pleased. A further effect produced was, that the charges before the police of drunkenness and riot were on that day less than the average of cases on ordinary days.

I have been informed of other instances of similar effects produced by the spread of temperate pleasures on ordinary occasions, and their rivalry to habits of drunkenness and gross excitement, whether mental or sensual.

But want of open spaces for recreation is not confined to the town population. In the rural districts the children and young persons of the villages have frequently no other places for recreation than the dusty road before their houses or the narrow and dirty lanes, and accidents frequently take place from the playing of children on the public highways. If they go into the fields they are trespassers, and injure the farmer. The want of proper spaces as play-grounds for children is detrimental to the morals as well as to the health in the towns, and it probably is so generally. The very scanty spaces which the children, both of the middle and the lower classes, the ill as well as the respectably educated, can obtain, force all into one company to the detriment of the better children, for it is the rude and boisterous who obtain predominance. In the course of some investigations which I had occasion to make into the causes of juvenile delinquency,[6] there appeared several cases of children of honest and industrious parents, who had been entrapped by boys of bad character; I inquired how the more respectable children became acquainted with the depraved; when it was shown that in the present state of many crowded neighbourhoods all the children of a court or of a street were forced to play, if they had any play whatsoever, on such scraps of ground as they could get, and all were brought into acquain-

---

1. *First Report of the Constabulary Force Commission*, P.P. 1839, XIX, pp. 12, 24-30.

tanceship, and the range of influence of the depraved was extended. The condition of the children in large districts where there are no squares, no gardens attached to the houses, and no play-grounds even to their day schools, and where they are of a condition in life to be withheld from playing in the streets, is pronounced to be a condition very injurious to their bodily development. The progress of the evil in the rural districts has been, to some extent, arrested by a beneficent standing order of the House of Commons, that all Enclosure Bills shall include provision for a reserve of land for the public use for recreation. For children, however, the most important reservations would be those which could be made for play-grounds in front of their homes, on plots where they may be under the eye of their mothers or their neighbours. Where the cottages are near a road, they should be some distance from it, with the gardens or play-ground in front. The separate or distant playgrounds have many inconveniences besides their being out of sight; and where they are far distant, they are comparatively useless. I have great pleasure in being enabled to testify that the instances are frequent where the regulated resort to private pleasure-grounds, and parks has been indulgently given for the recreation of the labouring population.

Amongst the instances of practical attention to the improvement of the physical condition of labouring classes in the agricultural districts, I may notice the following statement made to me by the late *Mr. Monck* of Coley House, Reading, who had bestowed much care upon the cottages on his own estate. It comprehends the provision adverted to:

'The care taken of these cottages and gardens,' said he, 'afford an excellent criterion of the character of the labourers. I have paid especial attention to those labourers who have displayed cleanliness and order; and I pay the most respect to those who have achieved a situation of the greatest comfort, and keep themselves and their houses cleanly, and their children tidy. Formerly the cottages were in bad order, their pavements and windows were broken; I had them all paved, and their windows glazed. I told the cottagers that I did not like to see shabby, broken windows, with patches of paper and things stuffed in, or broken pavements which they could not clean; and that I disliked Irish filth and all Irish habits of living. I engaged, after the cottages were thoroughly repaired, to pay 1*l*. a-year for repairing them. I undertook to make the repairs myself, and deduct the expense from this 1*l*.; but if no repairs were wanted, they were to have the whole 1*l*. themselves. This course has, I find, formed habits of care; and their cottages are now so well taken care of that very little deduction is made annually from the 1*l*. Formerly they used to chop wood carelessly on their pavements, and break them; now they abstain from the practice, or do it in a careful manner, to avoid losing the money. In the winter, I give them two score of fagots towards their fuel. I have found that by this means I save my hedges and fences, and am pecuniarily no loser, whilst pilfering habits are repressed. Since the enclosures have been made, I think some place should be provided for the exercise and recreation of the working-classes, and especially for their children. I have set out four acres at Oldworth as a play-ground for the children, or whoever likes to play. They have now their cricket-matches, their quoit-playing, and their revels there. Sheep and cows feed on it; so that it is no great loss to me. I let it for 4*l*. a-year to a man, on condition that he cuts the hedges and keeps it neat. I have surrounded it with a double avenue of trees. The sheep and cows do good to the ground, as they keep the grass under, which allows the ball to run. I give prizes to the boys at the school, which is maintained by the cottagers themselves, and to which I contribute nothing but the prizes for reading, writing, and knitting.

'Many persons accuse the poor of ingratitude, but I find them the most grateful people alive for these little attentions; and what do they all cost me? why not more altogether than the keep of one fat coach-horse.'

VII

RECOGNISED PRINCIPLES OF LEGISLATION AND STATE OF THE EXISTING LAW FOR THE PROTECTION OF THE PUBLIC HEALTH

The evidence already given will, to some extent, have furnished answers to the question—how far the physical evils by which the health, and strength, and morals of the labouring classes are depressed may be removed, or can reasonably be expected to be removed by private and voluntary exertions. I now submit for consideration the facts which serve to show how far the aid of the legislature, and of administrative arrangements are requisite for the attainment of the objects in question.

It will have been perceived, that the first great remedies, external arrangements, *i.e.* efficient drainage, sewerage and cleansing of towns, come within the acknowledged province of the legislature. Public opinion has of late required legislative interference for the regulation of some points of the internal economy of certain places of work, and the appointment of special agents to protect young children engaged in certain classes of manufactures from mental deterioration from the privation of the advantages of education, and from permanent bodily deterioration from an excess of labour beyond their strength. Claims are now before Parliament for an extension of the like remedies to other classes of children and to young persons, who are deemed to be in the same need of protection[1]. The legislature has interfered to put an end to one description of employment which was deemed afflicting and degrading, *i.e.* that of climbing-boys for sweeping chimneys, and to force a better means of performing by machinery the same work[2]. It will be seen that it has been the policy of the legislature to interfere for the public protection by regulating the structure of private dwellings to prevent the extension of fires[3]; and the common law has also interposed to protect the public health by preventing overcrowding in private tenements. The legislature has recently interfered to direct the poorer description of tenements in the metropolis to be properly cleansed. On considering the evidence before given with relation to the effects of different classes of buildings, the suggestion immediately arises as to the extent to which it is practicable to protect the health of the labouring classes by measures for the amendment of the existing buildings, and for the regulation of new buildings in towns in the great proportion of cases where neither private benevolence nor enlightened views can be expected to prevail extensively.

---

1. Lord Ashley's bill, introduced on 7 June 1842, became the Mines Act of that year (5 & 6 Vic., c. 99).
2. 3 & 4 Vic., c. 85 of 1840 prohibited anyone under 21 climbing chimneys as well as the apprenticing of children under sixteen to chimney-sweeps.
3. For Building Acts, see Introduction, p. 16.

It will have been perceived how much of the existing evils originate from the defects of the external arrangements for drainage, and for cleansing, and for obtaining supplies of water. Until these are completed, therefore, the force of the evils arising from the construction of the houses could scarcely be ascertained.

The experience of legislation available for England for the regulation of buildings is chiefly confined to the Metropolitan Building Act.[1] The provisions of that Act were directed simply to the prevention of the spread of fires by requiring that party-walls should be built so as to prevent the spread of fires, by confining them to the houses where the fires occur. In this object it is in most instances successful. Wherever a fire spreads beyond the single dwelling in the metropolis, it is usually found either that the provisions of the Act have been evaded, the walls being of the required thickness but rotten in substance, or that omissions have occurred from default of notice, or from neglect of the district surveyor. Out of the jurisdiction of the Act, the instances are frequent where fires spread from the want of party-walls. The erection of party-walls is good economy as a matter of insurance, for each house is thereby confined to its own risks, instead of having the additional risks of each of the contiguous houses, and perhaps of two or three houses beyond them. If there were any point on which *a priori* legislative interference might be thought unnecessary it would be this, on which the self-interest of the parties, for their own protection, would ensure attention. Yet the immediate interest of the builder in getting buildings erected at the lowest cost, or the want of foresight on the part of the owner himself, has caused extensive masses of buildings to be run up in the suburbs of the metropolis, and in provincial towns, without any such protection. Whilst this Report was in preparation I was informed of the destruction by fire of several contiguous houses at Oxford that were without party-walls. But party-walls are only one provision against fire; the omissions of other necessary precautions are fearfully extensive, especially in warehouses and buildings of a magnitude too great for the fire to be restrained by party-walls, or to prevent fire catching the adjacent buildings whenever it occurs.

One, however, I may advert to, as connected with the provisions necessary for the improvement of the sanitary condition of a town population. It has been shown that the cheapest mode of street cleansing is by supplies of water, which it would be necessary to use from standing pipes. By the Street Act[2], the parish officers are directed to provide standing pipes for the supply of engines in case of fire. This regulation is declared to be almost a dead letter. The only means to obtain supplies of water in the case of fire are from the plugs provided by the water companies themselves for cleansing the pipes by occasionally allowing the water to flow into the streets. It has been proved to be practicable without any considerable cost to keep up, at all times, such a pressure of water as on putting on a hose on any standing pipe connected with the service, to enable the water to be thrown over the highest houses. The

---

1. 50 Geo. III, c. 75, of 1810.
2. 57 Geo. III, c. 29, of 1817, 'For paving, improving and regulating the streets of the Metropolis'.

VII. Recognised Principles of Legislation 341

fronts of houses in London have, in some instances, been washed by this means, and in one instance it was immediately and successfully applied to extinguish a fire. A large proportion of houses are destroyed or seriously injured before engines can be brought to the spot or water obtained. During the last four years the fires in London have been more than 600 per annum. If each fire on the average incurred a loss of 500*l.*, the total loss annually would exceed the total cost of the supplies of water for the whole of the metropolis to the inhabitants, which, according to returns made to Parliament in the year 1834, amounted to 276,200*l*.[1] The superintendent of the police at Liverpool estimated the average loss by fires in that town during eight years at a much greater amount before a better system of prevention was established. The cost of keeping the water always on in the mains is so inconsiderable that it was voluntarily proferred by a competing company in the metropolis, as an advantageous arrangement to save the expense of water-tanks in private houses. I have high practical authority for stating that the arrangement for keeping the water on the mains for street cleansing, for washing the foot-ways as well as the carriage-ways, and, when necessary, for washing the fronts of the houses, would also serve, at an inconsiderable expense, as the most efficient means of extinguishing fires. Instead of the general loss of a considerable part of an hour's time before intelligence can be dispatched and the distant fire-engines be got to the spot, in a few minutes, or as soon as the flexible pipe in daily use could be screwed on the main, a supply of water as powerful as that from any engine might be brought to bear upon the fire. An extensive saving of life and property, and of well-grounded alarm, might thus be added to the train of benefits derivable from systematised arrangements for the cleansing of towns and the prevention of epidemics.

The provisions of the old Building Acts afford no sanitary securities, but in connexion with the provisions respecting sewerage they afford examples of what would be the effect of any measure which shall be either unequally applied as to the jurisdiction, or unequally administered.

The attention of the Board has several times been directed to the sickness prevalent amongst the working classes in various parts of the Kensington union. Having had occasion to inquire into the subject, I found that nearly all the illness occurred in premises run up by inferior speculating builders out of the jurisdiction of the commissions of sewers, or of the district surveyors; that they were built on undrained spots, with walls not more than one brick thick; and that the immediate expenditure for protective or sanitary purposes had thus been extensively evaded. On carrying the inquiry further, it became apparent that the limits of the jurisdiction of the commissioners of sewers, and the limits of the jurisdiction of the district surveyors around the metropolis, mark the commencement of buildings of an inferior character, built without drains, without the security from party-walls, and without proper means of cleansing. (*Vide* Appendix, the evidence of Mr. Gutch, district

---

1. This figure is derived from returns submitted to the *Select Committee on Metropolis Water*, and published as Apps. 1-8 of the *Report* of that Committee, *P.P.* 1834, XV, pp. 181-96.

surveyor.)[1] Under the peculiar circumstances of the country, towns may arise and the old evils may be implanted before any old district would probably be taken to include them. For example, the town of Old Kingston is tolerably well drained and healthy; on the completion of the railway a new town was suddenly run up by building speculators, called New Kingston, built out of the jurisdiction of Old Kingston, but without any adequate under-drainage, on a soil retentive of moisture, and with streets unpaved and covered with mud; it is reported as a consequence that fever has been rife in New Kingston, whilst Old Kingston is comparatively free from it.

If any one had to erect forty or fifty fourth-rate tenements near the metropolis, by shifting them beyond the limits of the jurisdiction of the district surveyor, he would nearly gain one house by the saving of fees alone in the ordinary mode of remunerating such officers.

All the information as to the actual condition of the most crowded districts is corroborative of the apprehensions entertained by witnesses of practical experience, such as Mr. Thomas Cubitt and other builders, who are favourable to measures for the improvement of the condition of the labouring classes, that anything of the nature of a Building Act that is not equally and skillfully administered will aggravate the evils intended to be remedied. To whatever districts regulations are confined, the effect proved to be likely to follow will be, that the builder of tenements which stand most in need of regulation will be driven over the boundary, and will run up his habitations before measures can be taken to include them. The condition of the workman will be aggravated by the increased fatigue and exposure to weather in traversing greater distances to sleep in a badly-built, thin, and damp house. An increase of distance from his place of work will have the more serious effect upon his habits by rendering it impracticable to take his dinner with his family, compelling him either to take it in some shed or at the beer shop. It is also apprehended that anything that may be done to increase unnecessarily or seriously the cost of new buildings, or discourage their erection, will aggravate the horrors of the overcrowding of the older tenements; at the same time, the certain effect of an immediate and unprepared dislodgement of a cellar population, would be to overcrowd the upper portions of the houses where they reside. It would indeed often be practicable to make those cellars as habitable as are the cellars inhabited by servants in the houses of the middle and higher classes of society. The difficulties which beset such regulations do not arise from the want of means to pay any necessary increase of rents for increased accommodation, but in the very habits which afford evidence of the existence of the sufficiency of the means of payment.

For practical legislation on the subject of increased charges on tenements, the labourers must be considered to be in a state of penury, and ready to shift from bad to worse for the avoidance of the slightest charges, and therefore to be approached with the greatest caution.

---

1. 'Evidence of Mr. George Gutch, district surveyor, on shifting and building inferior tenements in the suburbs, to avoid the provisions of the Metropolis Building Act', *San. Rep.*, Appendix 6, p. 394.

VII. Recognised Principles of Legislation 343

But there are other elements which it is proper to note as increasing the tendency to evade immediate charges even for benefits.

The increasing tendency to carry on manufacturing as well as commercial operations for small profits on large outlays will probably occasion the subject of the rents of labourers' tenements in manufacturing districts to be more closely considered as part of the cost of production than it has hitherto been. The whole of the consequences cannot distinctly be foreseen, further than that it will probably occasion a reduction of high ground-rents, or the abandonment of particular districts which are now the seats of some descriptions of manufacture. In the course of an examination of the condition of the working population of Macclesfield, which I was requested to aid, it was complained that much work was put out to a rural district at a few miles distance from the town. On inquiring as to the cause, it was answered, that the weavers in the rural district were enabled to do the work at a reduced price, but at the same real wages in consequence of reduced rents. The following examination, however, displays the element indicated:

Mr. Shatwell, relieving officer, examined:

'What is the common amount of rent paid by weavers in Macclesfield and the adjacent districts?—A weaver cannot get, in Macclesfield, a proper house for his loom, with due lights, for less than 10*l*. a-year. In Hazel Grove and other places, he may get them for 2*l*. or 3*l*. less—for about 7*l*.—with a small garden attached, worth at least 20*s*. a-year more.

'What difference in price do you think would induce a manufacturer to send goods to Hazel Grove in preference to Macclesfield?—A farthing a yard, as that difference might make the difference in his profit.

'How many yards will a weaver weave in the week?—They calculate that a good weaver will weave 12 yards a-day, or an average of 60 yards a-week.

'Since 1*s*. 3*d*. a-week, or a farthing a yard, will make the difference in profit, will not the difference in rent enable the weaver to make that difference in price and yet obtain the same net amount of wages?—Precisely so.

'So that a manufacturer who employs 1000 hands at a low-rented place, 3*l*. or 4*l*. a-year cheaper, such as Hazel Grove, if he obtain the difference of rent as profit, will obtain a profit of 3,000*l*. or 4,000*l*. per annum?—Certainly.

'The cost of building and building materials being nearly the same in Macclesfield and such a place as Hazel Grove, does not the difference in rent consist chiefly in the difference of ground-rent?—Yes.'

If in all instances, as in the last, better as well as cheaper residences, with gardens attached, were likely to be the result of the commercial operation to the workmen, the change were, of course, to be desired. But it is to be feared that it may often be otherwise than a competition of comforts, unless timely security be taken against its being otherwise by appropriate legislative measures, which indeed were necessary for the due protection of the rate-payers against the pecuniary consequences of the disease and destitution undoubtedly occasioned by such tenements as are thus described by *Mr. Mott*:

'An immense number of the small houses occupied by the poorer classes in the suburbs of Manchester are of the most superficial character; they are built by the members of building clubs, and other individuals, and new cottages are erected with a rapidity that astonishes persons who are unacquainted with their flimsy structure. They have certainly avoided the objectionable mode of forming under-ground dwellings, but have run into the opposite extreme, having neither cellar nor foundation. The walls are only half brick thick, or what the bricklayers call "brick noggin," and the whole of the materials are slight and unfit for the purpose. I have been told of a man who had built a row of these houses; and on visiting them one morning after a storm, found the whole of them levelled with the ground; and in another part of Manchester, a place with houses even of a better order has obtained the appellation of "Pick-pocket-row," from the known insecure and unsubstantial nature of the buildings. I recollect a bricklayer near London complaining loudly of having to risk his credit by building a house with nine-inch walls, and declared it would be like "Jack Straw's House," neither "wind nor water tight:" his astonishment would have been great had he been told that thousands of houses occupied by the labouring classes are erected with walls of $4\frac{1}{2}$ inch thickness. The chief rents differ materially according to the situation, but are in all cases high; and thus arises the inducement to pack the houses so close. They are built back to back, without ventilation or drainage; and, like a honeycomb, every particle of space is occupied. Double rows of these houses form courts, with, perhaps, a pump at one end and a privy at the other, common to the occupants of about twenty houses.'[1]

Whilst there is the new element of this extreme rapidity of construction to accommodate demands for labour, the increasing rapidity of the conveyance of goods and information is manifestly loosening the ties of the manufacturer to particular neighbourhoods. Whilst looms have been idle in Spitalfields on disputes on scale-prices, or from hesitation as to comply with the requisite changes of modes of working, I am informed that large quantities of work have been taken away, executed in the new neighbourhoods, and returned at reduced prices to the London markets. In the instance of Macclesfield, it is shown that neither foresight nor considerations of the expediency of a reduction operates on the speculating owners of tenements occupied by workmen in towns, or even on the other ratepayers, (who bear the burdens of the sickness and mortality, and pay extravagant rates, which are incident to them); nor can the operation of a wise self-interest be relied upon to avert the tendency to the dispersion of work, and the multiplication of ill-conditioned and ultimately burdensome tenements. The following evidence supplies additional illustration of this state of things:

John Wilson, relieving officer.

Are you acquainted with the cottage property in Macclesfield?—Yes, I am; as an assistant overseer, I see that the rates are collected.

Are there in Macclesfield many large owners of cottage tenements?—The number of owners of property in Macclesfield is about 1000; of these about 300 receive incomes from cottage property, some of those only one, others only two. The chief owner owns about 200 cottages; the next owns about two streets or 45 cottages. One man owns about 180.

Do you receive rates from these cottages?—From the cottages belonging to these large holders we get no rates.

How is it that you obtain no rates from these classes of cottages?—Because they are tenanted by the lowest class of persons who have nothing in their houses from which we could recover the rates.

---

1. *Local Reps. E. & W.*, pp. 240-1.

VII. Recognised Principles of Legislation 345

What are the rents paid from these cottages?—The rents vary from 1s. to 2s. 8d. each house. The average would be about 2s. a-week.

What would be the amount of rates on this cottage property if payment were enforced?—From the 1s. a-week cottages the rates would be 6s. per annum; from the others, 12s. per annum. Last quarter there were nearly 300 people excused; and the total amount lost for rates excused and houses empty was 900l.

What proportion does that bear to the whole rates for the quarter or for the year?—The loss for the year would be 1800l., and the rate last year was 8726l.; the amount collected was 5900l.; but the arrear of the former year would be in round numbers about 2000l. more.

Is the tenantry of these cottages a fluctuating tenantry?—Yes, very much so.

Are these tenements taken on the expectation that the rates will be excused? —Yes; in many cases they are told when objecting to the payment of the rent that they will have no rates to pay.

Considering the qualities of the tenements, are the rents charged really high rents?—Yes, they are.

Are they such rents as would justify the levy or the deduction of rates from the proprietor, comparing them with the rents paid for good property?—Yes, they are such rents; the house which I live in, and for which I pay rates, and pay 8l. a-year rent, is a house of three rooms on a floor, two floors, detached yard, and every convenience; whilst cottages of a very inferior description, with two rooms only on a floor, are as high rented and pay no rates.

Are the rents from the inferior tenements rigorously exacted?—Yes, they are.

Are the occupants of these houses frequently applicants for parochial relief? —Yes, they are.

Do any numbers of them receive relief?—Yes, they do.

What is the average amount of weekly out-door relief given to the recipients? —Perhaps about 3s.

Then the average relief is of the average amount of the rent of the tenements you describe?—Yes; and I have no doubt that much of the relief has gone to pay rent.

If the rates were duly exacted, do you think it must follow that the unduly high rents must be lowered in proportion?—Yes, they must.

If the landlords were compelled to pay the rates, what would be the saving to the town?—1s. in the pound.

And no additional burden cast on the labouring classes?—No material additional burden.

Of course the diminution of out-door relief would diminish the means of unduly paying high rents?—Certainly, it would.

The sanitary condition of many of these dwellings is described in the reports of Mr. Bland, the medical officer already quoted.

It may hereafter excite surprise, that the labouring classes have hitherto been left exposed to such influences as those described in the last evidence, and in the evidence previously cited, as to the pernicious operation of exemptions from payments of rates on the parties intended to be benefited.

My inquiries into the effects of the administration of the old poor law brought before me numerous instances of such devastation, the effects of which would not be obliterated during the lives of a generation. Examples might also be presented of the deterioration of property by the irruptions of an ill-regulated population by the running up of undrained and badly-constructed dwellings in the finest suburbs of the metropolis, and other towns throughout the country. Any regulations of the nature of Building Acts confined to towns, or to particular districts, or that were unequally or oppressively administered, must powerfully tend to increase such evils to the labouring classes, to the ratepayers, and to the owners of all suburban property.

Frequent opportunities are, however, presented and commonly lost for the erection of improved tenements for the use of the labouring classes, on the occasion of taking down old tenements and erecting new ones to form new streets, under the authority of Buildings' and Towns' Improvement Acts. It is usually assumed that the general effect of the 'clearances,' as they are called, occasioned by the formation of new streets, though attended with the present inconvenience of disturbing the occupants, is ultimately of unmixed advantage, by driving them into new and better tenements in the suburbs. I have endeavoured to ascertain by inquiries, with the aid of the relieving officers, how far the assumption is justified by the experience of such alterations as have been already made in some of the crowded districts of the metropolis, by taking down inferior tenements to form new streets.

It is found to be difficult to trace the individuals of a population so removed, and the inquiries on the subject are incomplete; but they tend to show that the working people make considerable sacrifices to avoid being driven to a distance from their places of work; that the poorest struggle against removal to a distance from the opportunities of charitable donations; and that where new habitations are not opened to them in the immediate vicinity, every effort is made by biddings of rent to gain lodgings in the nearest and poorest of the old tenements. To the extent to which the displaced labourers succeed in getting lodgings in the same neighbourhood, as a large proportion of them certainly do, the existing evils are merely shifted, and, by being shifted, they are aggravated. On a survey of the newly-built houses in the suburbs to which displaced labourers can go, it appears that the labourer, to use the expression of Dr. Ferriar, is almost 'driven to hire disease,' for if he do not find any lodging near his place of work, he is driven to a choice amongst tenements of the character of those found in the parts of Kensington out of the jurisdiction of the Metropolitan Building Act, without sewers or drains, without water or proper conveniences on the premises, without pavements or means of cleansing the streets; where exorbitant rents are levied, where adequate means of moral or religious instruction are yet unprovided, and where they will neither gain in health nor in morals.

On reference to such past experience it appears to suggest itself as an expedient arrangement, that on the removal of old tenements and the occupation of the old ground by building new houses and streets for a superior class of tenants, or for public buildings, some provision should be made against the aggravation of the existing evils as respects the old occupants; that it should be required to be shown, for example, that appropriate unoccupied tenements are in the market, and on failure to do so, provisions might be made (on the principle of those provided for preserving accommodation for the labouring classes in enclosure bills) for the construction of appropriate tenements, in which qualities of the

VII. Recognised Principles of Legislation

nature of those described by Mr. Sydney Smirke might be ensured.[1] If the attention and power by which large public alterations are obtained were, at the same time, directed to the construction of new dwellings for the labouring classes, instead of spreading existing evils, all such alterations might certainly, and at remunerative though not at increased rents, be made the means of greatly improving the condition of those who stand in the greatest need of attention and aid for improvement.

The most important immediate general measure of the nature of a Building Act, subsidiary to measures for drainage, would be a measure for regulating the increments of towns, and preventing the continued reproduction in new districts of the evils which have depressed the health and the condition of whole generations in the older districts. Regulations of the *sites* of town buildings have comparatively little effect on the cost of construction, and it may in general be said that a Building Act would effect what any enlightened owner of a district would effect for himself, of laying it out with a view to the most permanent advantage; or what the separate owners would effect for themselves if they had the power of co-operation, or if each piece of work were governed by enlarged public and private views. Had Sir Christopher Wren been permitted to carry out his plan for the rebuilding of London after the great fire, there is little doubt that it would have been the most advantageous arrangement for rendering the whole space more productive, as a property to the great mass of the separate interests, by whom the improvement was defeated. The most successful improvements effected in the metropolis by opening new lines of street, and the greater number of the openings projected are approximations at an enormous expense to the plan which he laid down. The larger towns present instances of obstructions of the free current of air even through the principal streets, and of deteriorations which a little foresight and the exercise of an impartial authority would have prevented. In one increasing town, a builder made a successful money speculation by purchasing such plots of ground as would enable him to erect impediments and extort compensation for their removal from the path of improvements in building. The improvements affecting whole towns are also frequently frustrated by the active jealousies of the occupants of rival streets. It would appear to be possible to provide an impartial authority to obtain and, on consultation with the parties locally interested, to settle plans for regulating the future growth of towns, by laying down the most advantageous lines for occupation with due protection of the landowners' interest. The most serious omissions in the building of common houses are so frequently oversights as to make it probable, that if it were required that a plan of any proposed building should be deposited with a trustworthy officer, with a specification of the arrangements intended for the attainment of the essential objects, such as cleansing and ventilation, the mere preparation of the document would of itself frequently lead to the detection of grievous defects. An examination of Mr. Loudon's specification of the requisites of cottages will show that a large proportion of the most important of these are independent of the cost of construction.

---

1. For Smirke, see above, p. 333, n. 1.

VII. Recognised Principles of Legislation

General State of the Law for the Protection of the Public Health

In a work which is considered in Germany the chief authority in respect to the extensive administrative duties comprehended under the term police,* the author, Professor Mohl, of Tubingen, in speaking of the sanitary police of towns, observes, that 'Medical police is both in theory and practice essentially German. In German states only, as Austria and Prussia, has anything been done in it systematically; the literature also of medical police[2] is almost entirely German. Other states either do nothing at all, as England, the United States of America, or only very imperfectly, as France; where anything is done, German principles and arrangements are closely imitated.'

It is stated that some of the new towns and the new parts of the old towns in Germany, as in Stuttgard, Manheim, Darmstadt, exhibit striking marks of this care in the comparative structure and arrangements of the houses, and in the general administration, with a view to the health and pleasure of the population, which is sometimes impressively displayed in the superior condition of the public walks and gardens, as at Frankfort and Baden-Baden. The professor's reproach is, however, scarcely applicable to the substantive English law, or to the early constitutional arrangements in which are found extensive and useful provisions, and complete principles for the protection of the public health.

1st. So much of the structural arrangements as depended on drainage was provided for by the Commissions of Sewers, who were invested with valuable powers by the statute 23d Hen. VIII. cap. 5, s. 1[3]; the authority of these Commissions 'to be directed into all parts within this realm where need shall require, according to the form ensuing, to such substantial persons as shall be named by the Lord Chancellor and Lord Treasurer, and the two chief justices, or by three of them, whereof the Lord Chancellor to be one,' to cause 'to be made, corrected or repaired, amended, put down or reformed, as the case shall require, walls, ditches, banks, gutters, sewers, gates, cullices, bridges, streams, and other defences by the coasts of the sea and marsh ground.'

2dly. The ancillary arrangements as to road cleansing as well as road structure, were provided for by the highway laws, including the provisions of the 5th Eliz. c. 13, s. 7[4], for the cleansing of the ditches, &c.

The common law provided general remedies for the redress of injuries, under the comprehensive title nuisance (*nocumentum*), meaning anything by which the health or the personal safety, or the conveniences of the

---

* Mohl. Polizei-Wissenschaft, vol. i. page 135, Note.[1]

---

1. Robert von Mohl, *Die Polizei-Wissenchaft nach den Grundsätzen des Reichstaates* (Tübingen, 2nd. edition, 3 vols., 1844).
2. The word 'police' is used in this context to mean 'regulation', a sense in which it was commonly used at this time, e.g. John Roberton, *A Treatise on Medical Police* (Edinburgh 2 vols. 1809).
3. 23 Hen. VIII, c. 5, of 1532, 'Concerning Commissions of Sewers'.
4. 5 Eliz. I, c. 13, of 1563, 'For the amending of highways' (confirming 2 & 3 Philip & Mary, c. 8, of 1555).

subject might be endangered or affected injuriously. By the law as it now stands, the subject is entitled to protection against things which are offensive to the senses, from which no injury to the health or other injury can be proved than the often overlooked but serious injury of discomfort, of daily annoyance, as by matters offensive to the sight, as by allowing blood to flow in the streets; by filth, by offensive smells, and by noises. The injuries termed nuisances were three-fold,—first, public or general; second, common; third, private. 'Public is that which is a nuisance to the whole realm; common is that which is to the common nuisance of all passing by; private is that which is to a house or mill, &c.' 2 Institute, 406. A common nuisance is defined to be an offence against the public 'either by doing a thing which tends to the annoyance of all the king's subjects, or by neglecting to do a thing which the common good requires.' Hawk, p. 1. c. 107, c. 75, f. 1. For the private injury there was the remedy by civil action; for the common and the public injuries, the remedy was by indictment.

The common-law obligation upon all owners of property has, in general, been adhered to by the superior courts. '*Prohibetur ne quis faciet in suo quod nocere possit alieno; et sic utere tuo ut alienum non lædas.*' 9 Co. Rep. 58.

Thus, it is held to be a common nuisance and indictable to divide a messuage in a town for poor people to inhabit, by which it will be more dangerous in time of infection. 2 Roll's Abridgment, 139. Such indictment of one Brown for dividing a messuage in the village of Hertford was held good, and he was put to plead to it; and it was then said that such indictments are frequent in London for dividing of messuages.

The policy of the common law was endeavoured to be enforced by the statute of the 31st of Eliz. c. 7[1], which provided that there should not be any inmate or more families or households than one dwelling or inhabiting in any one cottage, made or to be made or created, upon pain that every owner or occupier of such cottage, placing or wilfully suffering any such inmate or other family than one, should forfeit 10*s*. for every month that such inmate or other family than one should dwell in it. The statute provided that no cottage should for the future be built without four acres at the least of land attached to it. But this provision did not extend to cottages in towns, or for mineral works, navigation, sheep cotes, &c. From the number of decisions in the books, it would appear that the provisions of the statute were extensively enforced against the overcrowding of the tenements, but the obligation for attaching the four acres of land impeded the erection of new tenements, and occasioned inconvenience and led to the repeal of the whole statute, by the 15th Geo. III. cap. 32.

In a temporary Act passed in the 35th of Eliz. cap. c., for the reforming of the great mischiefs and inconveniences that 'daily grow and increase by reason of the pestering of houses with divers families harbouring of inmates,' that occurred in the city of London and Westminster, it is recited that the practice had been productive of 'great

---

1. 31 Eliz. I, c. 7, of 1589, 'Against erecting and maintaining of cottages'.

infection of sickness.'[2] This effect could scarcely have failed to be perceived when the plague was so frequent and dreadful in its visitations. The exemption from it is ascribed to such widening of the streets and improvements of the houses as took place after the Fire of London.

But we apprehend that the common-law remedy still remains in force as against the owners of tenements which are a nuisance. It was decided in the case of the King v. Pedley, temp. 1834, 1st Adolphus and Ellis, 822:

'That if the owner of land erect a building which is a nuisance, or of which the occupation is likely to produce a nuisance, and let the land, he is liable to an indictment for such nuisance being continued or created during the term.

'So he is if he let a building which requires particular care to prevent the occupation from being a nuisance, and the nuisance occur for want of such care on the part of the tenant.

'That if a party buy the reversion during a tenancy, and the tenant afterwards during his term erect a nuisance, the reversioner is not liable for it; but if such reversioner relet, or having an opportunity to determine the tenancy omit to do so, allowing the nuisance to continue, he is liable for such continuance. Per Littledale, J.

'And such purchaser is liable to be indicted for the continuing of the nuisance if the original reversioner would have been liable, though the purchaser has had no opportunity of putting an end to the tenant's interest or abating the nuisance.'

The stopping of wholesome air is held to be a nuisance as well as the stopping of the light. Co. 9 Will., Aldred, 57. In the case of Lewes v. Keene, Trin. Term. Jac. Rex, it was held by the court—'that the light which cometh in by the windowes, being an essential part of the house, by which he hath three great commodities, that is to say, air for his health, light for his profit, prospect for his pleasure, may not be taken away no more than a part of his house may be pulled down, whereby to erect the next house adjoining. And with this resolution agreeth the case of Eldred, reported by Sir Edw. Coke, in his Ninth Report, fol. 58, where he showeth the ancient form of the action upon the case to be *quod messuagium horrida tenebritate obscuratum facit;* but if there be hinderance only of the prospect by the new erected house, and not of the air, not of the light, then an action of the case will not lye, insomuch that the prospect is only a matter of delight, and not of necessity.'

The corruption of the water is an offence at common law, and was early the subject of a statutory provision. In the earlier periods the power of the legislature was directly exercised for the abatement of nuisances. I am favoured by the following illustrations from a collection of records upon the subject made by *Mr. T. D. Hardy*, of the Record Office in the Tower:

The first extract shows that sea-coal was in use in London much earlier than is commonly supposed:

'*Patent Roll*, 16 Edw. I.—The king to his beloved and faithful Thomas de Weylaund, John de Luvetot, John de Cobeham, and Ralph de Sandwico,

---

1. 35 Eliz. I, c. 6, of 1593.

General State of the Law 351

custos of his city of London, greeting: From the complaint of many persons, we understand that many people are dangerously aggrieved by the furnaces of lime which are built in the said city and its suburbs, and in Southwark; because the lime which formerly used to be burnt with wood, is now burnt with sea coal, by which the air there is affected and corrupted, to the great danger of persons frequenting those parts and dwelling around them: we, therefore, being willing to afford a fitting remedy for this, have appointed you to see those furnaces, and remove the danger and nuisances which threaten from them in these days, and to order further concerning them according to your discretion, as you shall see most expedient for the common use and safety; and therefore we command you, that taking with you our sheriffs of London and our bailiffs of Southwark, you perform the premises with diligence. We have also commanded the same sheriffs and bailiffs that at a certain day, which you shall make known to them, they attend to this with you, in form aforesaid. Witness, Edmund Earl of Cornwall, at Westminster, on the 26th day of May.'

'A.D. 1290, 18 Edw. I.—The Carmelite Friars of London, the Friars-preachers, the Bishop of Salisbury, and others, petition Parliament to abate a nuisance (viz. a great stench) near them which they cannot endure, and which prevents them from performing their religious duties, and from which several of the monks had died. (Petit. in Parl. 18 Edw. I.)

'35 Edw. I.—The mayor of London is commanded to prevent persons from lighting furnaces near the Tower of London during the stay of the Queen and the nobles at the tower, because the air is corrupted and infection generated by the insalubrity of the air on account of the said furnaces. (Rot. claus. 35 Edw. I.)

'A.D. 1320, 14 Edw. II.—The inhabitants of the neighbourhood of Smithfield complain to Parliament that wells and ditches are dug there without the king's license, to the annoyance of the inhabitants and passengers. The mayor and corporation of London are thereupon ordered to see that such nuisances are abated. (Petit. in Parl. 14 Edw. II.)

'A.D. 1330, 4 Edw. III.—The chancellor and University of Cambridge petition Parliament that the mayor and corporation of Cambridge may be constrained to scour the ditch of the town, which is injurious to the health of the inhabitants of the town. (Petit. in Parl. 4 Edw. III.)

'44 Edw. III.—The butchers of London are forbidden to slaughter cattle within that city, or throw entrails into the river Thames, on forfeiture of the carcase and imprisonment. (Rot. claus. 44 Edw. III.)

'A.D. 1370, 3 Rich. II.—The inhabitants of Smithfield and Holborn complain of the infection of the air from butchers slaughtering cattle, &c., and casting entrails into the ditches. (Petit. in Parl. 3 Rich. II.)

'By stat. 12th Rich. II. c. 13.—None shall cast any garbage or dung or filth into ditches, waters, or other places within or near any city or town, on pain of punishment by the Lord Chancellor at his discretion.

'Butchers of London shall erect a slaughter-house on the banks of the Thames, and thither carry off their offals, which, when cut into pieces, shall be carried in boats, and at the commencement of the ebb cast into the river. (Rot. Parl. 16 Rich. II.)

'A.D. 1392, 16 Rich. II.—It is enacted that the butchers of London shall not slaughter therein any swine or other beasts for sale. (Rot. Parl. 16 Rich. II.)

'Same date.—All filth, &c. ordered by Parliament to be removed from both banks of the Thames between the palace of Westminster and the power of London; and butchers or others are prohibited from casting entrails, &c. into the river on penalty of 40*l*. (Ibid.)

'Parliament forbids all persons from throwing dung, garbage, or entrails of slaughtered beasts into rivers or waters near cities or towns to corrupt the air and cause infection. (Rot. claus. 4 Hen. IV.)

'The Chancellor is authorized to treat touching the non-rebuilding of two forges in Fleet-street, London, demolished in a riot, as straitening the said street.' (Rot. Parl. 18 Hen. VI.)

We find the authority of Parliament exercised in the reign of Henry VII. to restrain a nuisance. In the 4th of his reign, c. 3.

'Item, it was shewed by a petition put to the king, our said sovereign lord, in the said Parliament, by his subjects and parishioners of the parish of St. Faith's and St. Gregory's in London, near adjoining unto the cathedral church of St. Paul's that whereas great concourse of people as well of his royal person as of other great lords and states with other his true subjects, oftentimes was had unto the said cathedral church, and that for the most part throughout the parishes aforesaid the which often-times been greatly annoyed and distempered by corrupt airs engendered in the said parishes, by occasion of blood and other foulis things by reason of the slaughter of beasts and scalding of swine, had and done in the butchery of St. Nicholas's flesh shambles, whose corruption and foul ordure by violence of unclean, corrupt, and putrefied waters is borne down through the said parishes, &c., complaint whereof at many and divers seasons also by the space of sixteen years continually, as well by canons and petty canons of the said cathedral church, landlords there, as also by many other of the king's subjects, of right honest behaviour, hath been made unto divers mayors and aldermen of the City of London and no remedy had been found; that it may please our said sovereign lord of his abundant grace, to provide for the conservation as well of his most royal person, as to succour his poor subjects and suppliants in this behalf, considering that in few noble cities and town, or none within Christendon, whereat travelling men have laboured, the common slaughter-house of beasts should be kept in any special part within the walls of the same, lest it might engender sickness unto the destruction of the people.'

Therefore it is enacted that butchers shall not slay beasts within the walls of London; and that this law be observed in every walled town 'except Berwick and Carlisle.'

The courts, however, have always had regard to the convenience of trade: thus it was held:

'Si homme fait candells deins un vill, per qui il cause un noysom sent al inhabitants, uncore ceo nest ascun nusans car le *needfulness* de eux dispensera ove le noisomness del *smell*.' (2 Roll's Abr. 139.)

But this decision has been doubted, 'Because,' says Serjeant Hawkins, Pl. Cor. 190, c. 75, 'whatever necessity there may be that candles be made, it cannot be pretended to be necessary to make them in a town, and that the trade of a brewer is as necessary as that of a chandler; and yet it seems to be agreed that a brewhouse erected in such an inconvenient place where the business cannot be carried on without incommoding greatly the neighbourhood may be indicted as a common nuisance. A presentment was made to a Leet for erecting a glass-house; and Twisden, J., said he had known an information adjudged against one for erecting a brewhouse near Serjeants' Inn; but it was insisted that a man ought not to be punished for erecting anything necessary for the exercise of his lawful trade; and it being answered that it ought to be in convenient places where it may not be a nuisance, the other justices

General State of the Law

doubted, and agreed that it was unlawful only to erect such things near the King's palace.' Vent. 26, Pasch. 21, Car. 2. Recently, however, when some architects and medical gentlemen went to the top of Buckingham Palace to examine it preparatory to its occupation by Her Majesty, they were assailed by a cloud of smoke from the chimney of the furnace of a neighbouring brewery; and the nuisance remains to the present time in full force, notwithstanding the statutory provisions against it.

Where the defendant in his business as a printer employed a steam-engine, which produced a continued noise and vibration in the plaintiff's apartment which adjoined the premises of the defendant, this was held to be a nuisance. The Duke of Northumberland *v.* Clowes, C. P., at Westminster, A.D., 1824.

The earlier sanitary regulations were frequently set forth in the provisions of the local Acts for the regulation of the streets. From the early street regulations of the city of London, we find that the purity of the river and of the contributary streams was zealously regarded; the ward inquests were specially charged to inquire:

'If any manner of person cast or lay dung, ordure, rubbish, sea-coal dust, rushes, or any other noiant, in the river of Thames, Walbrook, Fleet, or other ditches of this city, or in the open streets, ways, or lanes within this city.

'Also, if any person in or after a great rain falleth, or at any other time, sweep any dung, ordure, rubbish, rushes, sea-coal dust, or any other thing noiant down into the channel of any street or lane, whereby the common course there is let, and the same things noiant driven down into the said water of Thames.'

But when it is considered how few of the streets were paved, or sewered, or drained, the following regulation indicates what must have been their condition and the habits of the inhabitants:

'No man shall cast any urine-boles or ordure-boles into the street by day or night, afore the hour of nine in the night: and also he shall not cast it out, but bring it down, and lay it in the channel, under the pain of three shillings and four-pence; and if he do cast it upon any person's head, the party to have a lawful recompense, if he have hurt thereby.'

The state in which the streets were under such regulations is indicated in the proclamations issued at the time of the Plague, 1569, to 'warne all inhabitants against their houses to keep channels clear from filth, (by onlie turning yt) aside, that the water may have passage.'

The prominent provisions of the modern Sewers' and Street Acts are those which contain penalties against the most effectual means of street-cleansing,—that by discharging the street refuse through the sewers; but whilst the local legislation was deficient in principle in the main provisions, it is distinguished by a multitude of particular provisions against nuisances and obstructions, which would argue the most extensive foresight. The nature of the provisions habitually resorted to are illustrated in the statute of 4th Geo. IV, c. 50, s. 1[1], for building the new London Bridge.*

---

* 'Or shall on the said bridge, or in any street or place within the distance aforesaid (all the legislation was restricted to "fifty yards") from either end

1. 4 Geo. IV, c. 50, of 1824, 'for the rebuilding of London Bridge'.

'Every man may abate a common nuisance.' Br. Nuisance. 'The nuisance may be abated, that is, taken away or removed by the agrieved thereby, so as he commits no riot in doing it.' 'And the reason,' says Blackstone, 'why the law allows this private and summary method of doing one's-self justice, is because injuries of this kind which obstruct or annoy such things as are of daily convenience and use require an immediate remedy, and cannot wait for the slow progress of the ordinary forms of justice.' Com. B. iii. 6. And the annotator adds, 'The security of the lives and property may sometimes require so speedy a remedy as not to allow time to call on the person on whose property the mischief has arisen to remedy it. Pardon for a nuisance is void as for the continuance thereof.' 3 Cro. Jac. 492. Dewell *v.* Saunders.

State of the Special Authorities for reclaiming the Execution of the Laws for the Protection of the Public Health

The most important, perhaps, because the most cheap and accessible authority for reclaiming the execution of the law for the protection of the subject against nuisances, for punishing particular violations of it, was vested in the Courts Leet. The statute of the view of Frankpledge, 13 Edw. II., directs inquiry to be made of waters turned, or stopped, or brought from their right course, and obstructions in ditches were presentable at the Leet; but the stopping up a watering-place for cattle was held not to be presentible as a common nuisance. (40 Lit. 56 *a*.) The juries, commonly called 'annoyance juries,' impanelled to serve on Courts Leet in towns, are accustomed to perambulate their districts to judge of nuisances upon the view. But the state of this machinery will be seen in the state of the evils which come within its jurisdiction.

With all this legal strength, however, there is scarcely one town in England which we have found in a low sanitary condition, nor scarcely one village marked as the abode of fever, that does not present an example of standing violations of the law, and of the infliction of public

---

* *contd.:*

thereof, hoop, fire, cleanse, wash, or scald any cask or tub; or hew, saw, or cut any stone, wood or timber; or bore any timber; or make or repair, or wash or clean any coach, chaise, waggon, sledge or other carriage, or the wheel, body, springs, or other part of any coach, chaise, waggon, sledge, or other carriage (except such as may want immediate repair from any sudden accident on the spot, and which cannot be conveniently removed for that purpose); or wet, slack, or mix any lime; or wet, mix or make any mortar; or shoe, bleed, or farry any horse or other beast, unless in case of sudden accident; or clean, dress, drive, or turn loose any horse, or other beast, or cattle; or show or expose any stallion or stonehorse; or show or expose, or exercise or expose to sale any horse or other beast; or kill or slaughter, or scald, singe, dress or cut up any animal, either wholly or in part; or cause or permit any blood to run from any slaughter-house, butcher's-shop or shamble into any of the streets or places within the distance aforesaid from the said bridge; or shall sell or assist in selling by auction or public sale, any cattle, goods, wares, merchandize, or thing or things whatsoever; or hang up or expose to sale, or cause or permit to be hanged up, placed or exposed to sale, any goods, wares, or merchandize whatever, or any fruit, vegetables, or garden-stuff, butchers' meat, or other matter or thing upon the said bridge; or in, or upon, or so as to and common as well as of private injuries, the tenements overcrowded, streets replete with injurious nuisances, the streams of pure water polluted, and the air rendered noisome.

The chimneys of the furnaces which darken the atmospheres, and pour out volumes of smoke and soot upon the inhabitants of populous towns, afford most frequent examples of the inefficiency of the local administration, and the contempt of the law for the protection of the public against nuisances which are specially provided for.

Most modern private Acts contain penalties on gas companies permitting their washings to contaminate streams, or using for steam-engines furnaces which do not consume their own smoke. The general statute, 1 and 2 Geo. IV, c. 41, empowers the court to award costs to the prosecutor of those who use such furnaces. Where the grievance may be remedied by altering the construction of the furnace employed in the working of engines by steam, the court may make an order for preventing the nuisance in future.

The specific effects of an excess of smoke on the general health of a town population has not been distinguished, but from the comparatively high average of mortality amongst the middle classes in situations undistinguished by confined residences, or defective drainage, or anything but an excessively smoky atmosphere; from the comparatively rapid improvement of convalescents on removal to purer atmospheres, there is strong reason to believe that the prejudicial effect is much more considerable than is commonly apprehended even by medical practitioners. As the smoke in Manchester and other towns becomes more dense, the vegetation declines; and even in the suburbs the more delicate species die. *Dr. Baker*, in his report on the sanitary condition of the town of Derby, after adverting to the state of the places of work as affecting the health of the operations, proceeds to notice the effects of the smoke:

'The next general cause of injury to public health, and connected with the foregoing, is the corruption of the air caused by the torrents of black smoke

---

* *contd.:*
project over or upon the footway or carriageway of the said streets or places within the distance aforesaid, or beyond the line, or on the outside of the window or windows of the house, shop, or place at which the same shall be so hanged up, placed, or exposed to sale, or so as to obstruct or incommode the passage of any person or carriage: or leave open after sunset the door or window of any cellar, or other underground room or apartment, without having placed or left a sufficient light therein to warn and prevent persons passing in the streets and public places within the distance aforesaid from the said bridge, from falling into such cellars or other underground rooms or apartments; or bait, or cause to be baited any bull or other animal; or throw at any cock or fowl in the manner called cock-throwing, or set up any fowl to be thrown at in such manner; or play at foot-ball, or at any other game on the said bridge, or within such distance as aforesaid, to the annoyance of any inhabitant or inhabitants, or passenger or passengers,' * * * * 'or wilfully permit or suffer any horse, or other beast or cattle which such person may be riding or driving, or leading, to go thereon; or shall tie or fasten any horse or other cattle to any house, wall, fence, post, tree, or other thing whatsoever, across any of the highways, footways, or foot-pavements of the said bridge, or within the distance aforesaid.'

that issue from the manufactory chimneys, the nuisance from which is much augmented in heavy and moist states of the atmosphere. There is a law by which those who most offend, as regards their chimneys, can be punished; but of course the magistrates are not also prosecutors, whilst private individuals, being unwilling to become informers, little is done to check this nuisance; and such is the state of the air, that in gardens in the town none but deciduous shrubs can be kept alive.'[1]

Besides the prejudicial effects on the health of the population by the deterioration of the quality of the air that is breathed, a serious effect is created by its operation as an impediment to the formation and maintenance of habits of personal and household cleanliness amongst the working classes. Even upon the middle and higher classes the nuisance of an excess of smoke, occasioned by ignorance and culpable carelessness, operates as a tax increasing the wear and tear of linen and the expense of washing, to all who live within the range of the mismanaged chimneys. In the suburbs of Manchester, for example, linen will be as dirty in two or three days as it would be even in the suburbs of London in a week. One person stated that, on the Isle of Arran, a shirt was cleaner at the end of a week's wear than at Manchester at the end of a day's.

Nor is this the only oppressive tax occasioned by the carelessness; Mr. *Thomas Cubitt*, the eminent builder, when examined before the Committee of the House of Commons, was asked:

'Suppose it were intended to build a row of houses, would you not suffer them to be built unless there was a sewer provided?—I would not allow a house to be built anywhere unless it could be shown that there was a good drainage, and a good way to get rid of water. I think that there should be some public officer responsible for that; that there should be surveys of every district, so that the officer should be aware whether the sewers were provided or not. I think there should be an officer paid at the public expense, who should be responsible for that. I think they should not be appointed by the district; there should be no favouritism of that kind; but public officers, changed from point to point, to take care of all public nuisances. With respect to manufactories, here are a great number driven by competition to work in the cheapest way they can. A man puts up a steam-engine, and send out an immense quantity of smoke; perhaps he creates a great deal of foul and bad gas; that is all let loose. Where his returns are 1000*l*. a-month, if he would spend 5*l*. a-month more he would make that completely harmless; but he says, "I am not bound to do that," and therefore he works as cheaply as he can, and the public suffer to an extent beyond all calculation. I look upon it it has this effect: a gentleman comes to London, and lives in London; I will suppose he fits up his house in the best style he can; he has a taste for good pictures and upholstery, and so on. After a time the smoke has destroyed them, and he is disappointed and annoyed, and the effect is he is brought down in his feelings in a degree from the state in which he was accustomed to have things.'[2]

The appearance of the towns on the Sunday, when nearly all the furnaces are stopped, when there is little more than the smoke from the dwelling-houses, when everything is comparatively bright, and the distant hills and surrounding country that are never visible though the atmosphere of the town in the week-days may be seen across it, presents

---

1. *Local Reps. E. & W.*, p. 163.
2. *Report of Select Committee on the Health of Towns*, P.P. 1840, XI, Q. 3428.

nearly the appearance which such towns would assume on the working days, if the laws were duly executed, and the excessive smoke of the furnaces prevented. On inquiry of a peace-officer acting where redress is provided for under a local Act, how it was that the dereliction of duty occurred that was visible in the dense black clouds that darkened the town, he replied that the chief members of the Board were the persons whose furnace-chimneys were most in fault, and he appealed whether a man in his condition was to be expected to prosecute his patrons?

The greater part, if not the whole, of the excess of smoke and of unconsumed gas by which the metropolis and the neighbourhoods of manufactories are oppressed, is preventible by the exercise of care in the management of the fires of the furnaces. And here also the measures for the prevention of the nuisance are measures of economy.

Many witnesses whose opinions are enforced by practical examples, state confidently that such nuisances are generally the result of ignorance or carelessness. Amongst others we may cite the authority of Mr. Ewart, the inspector of machinery to the Admiralty, residing at Her Majesty's Dock-yard at Woolwich, where the chimney of the manufactory under his immediate superintendence, regulated according to his directions, offers an example of the little smoke that need be occasioned from steam-engine furnaces if care be exercised. He states that no peculiar machinery is used; the stoker or fire-keeper is only required to exercise care in not throwing on too much coal at once, and to open the furnace door in such slight degree as to admit occasionally the small proportion of atmospheric air requisite to effect complete combustion. Mr. Ewart also states that if the fire be properly managed, there will be a saving of fuel. The extent of smoke denotes the extent to which the combustion is incomplete. The chimney belonging to the manufactory of Mr. Peter Fairbairn, engineer at Leeds, also presents an example and a contrast to the chimneys of nearly all the other manufactories which overcast that town. On each side of it is a chimney belonging to another manufactory, pouring out dense clouds of smoke; whilst the chimney at Mr. Fairbairn's manufactory presents the appearance of no greater quantity of smoke than of some private houses. Mr. Fairbairn stated, in answer to inquiries upon this subject, that he uses what is called Stanley's feeding machinery, which graduates the supply of coal so as to produce nearly complete combustion. After the fire is once lighted, little remains to the ignorance or the carelessness of the stoker. Mr. Fairbairn also states that his consumption of fuel in his steam-engine furnaces, in comparison with that of his immediate neighbours, is proportionately less. The engine belonging to the cotton-mills of Mr. Thomas Ashton, of Hyde, near Stockport, affords to the people of that town an example of the extent to which, by a little care, they might be relieved of the thick cloud of smoke by which the district is oppressed.

At a meeting of manufacturers and others, held at Leeds, for the suppression of the nuisance of the smoke of furnaces, and to discuss the various plans for abating it, the resolution was unanimously adopted, 'that in the opinion of this meeting the smoke arising from steam-engine fires and furnaces can be consumed, and that, too, without injury to the boilers, and with a saving of fuel.' Notice of legal proceedings being given against Messrs. Meux, the brewers in London, for a nuisance arising from the chimneys of two furnaces, they found that by using anthracite coal they abated the nuisance to the neighbourhood, and saved 200*l*. per annum. The West Middlesex Water Company, by diminishing the smoke of their furnaces saved 1000*l*. per annum.

The gas-companies in the city of London were indicted for throwing their refuse into the Thames, and compelled to dispose of it otherwise; and they found out that they had been guilty of waste as well as of nuisance; and it is stated that the whole of what was formerly cast away has now become an important article of commerce.

In the rural districts the Courts Leet have generally fallen into desuetude. In illustration of the feeble tenure on which they were held, I may mention that in some instances, where it has been necessary to disallow payments of fees paid to the officers of those courts from the poor's rates, the stewards have stated that they should hereafter discontinue the courts; and it is probable that they did so. In the towns, Courts Leet are sometimes held, and inquest juries appointed; but it is objected to these bodies, and frequently to the bodies constituted under local acts, that they are usually composed of tradesmen who attend unwillingly and at an inconvenient sacrifice of time; who can have little or no information in respect to the evils in question; who have no arrangements to bring the evils in question before them; no time to master such information as may be brought before them casually; little interest and scarcely any real responsibility imposed for ensuring any mastery of it; and neither time nor adequate means at their disposal for the removal of such evils as those in question when they are presented to them, and proved to exist. Thus: two persons of respectability who were unexpectedly called upon to serve on a jury of this description in the metropolis, state that, as they had no properly qualified officer to instruct them, they were only directed to the performance of their duties by the accidental presence of a builder.

'When we were sworn in, we went over the district: we went through many places which were disgustingly filthy, that I have since learned were places where there is always fever, but we were not told about it; the afflicted knew nothing of our coming, and we had no medical officer, or means to enable us to detect the presence of any nuisances which would endanger the public health.

'The number of persons sworn in was twenty-four, of whom I can remember six were publicans (at one or other of whose houses we dined on the days of meeting), one or two cheesemongers, three or four tailors or drapers, one builder, and one bricklayer; the trades or occupations of the remainder I cannot remember. Of the twenty-four sworn in, twelve only served, and the duties were performed in rotation. An allowance of 2*s*. 6*d*. was given to each juryman for his expenses on the days of acting, with the exception of the foreman and the secretary, who had been unfortunate enough, or who, for some purpose of their own, managed to be sworn in on three or four previous occasions. None of the jury knew the nature of the duties further than that they were to examine weights and measures; that part of their duty respecting the removal of nuisances, or of things affecting the health or the lives of the inhabitants of the district which we perambulated, was entirely neglected or lost sight of; the only instance that I remember of any attention being paid to the subject, was that of the condemnation of an old house in a disgusting neighbourhood of houses; and in this case, although the house certainly looked in a bad condition, the jury were quite unable to come to a decision until the bricklayer and builder pronounced its condemnation, when the jury at once became unanimous, and condemned the house forthwith. My own impression was, that the house was not in a safe condition, but I felt, in common with others, (the tailors, drapers, and cheesemongers,) that however anxious we might be to discharge our duties faithfully, that the nature of our occupations did not at all qualify us to express an opinion upon the subject, and hence we were all guided and determined by the opinion of the bricklayer and builder who happened to be present. Had they not been present, we should probably have done nothing. It is only necessary for any sensible person to serve on such a body in a town to be convinced of its entire inefficiency.'

The district over which this jury perambulated was one in which contagious disease often prevails in its worst forms; and it is quite clear that, without appropriate arrangements, such a body would continue to walk over the ground, equally unconscious of the evil and impotent to effect its removal.

A civil engineer and surveyor of very high acquirements in the metropolis thus describes the qualifications of persons serving on these inquests:

'I speak from experience, having personally attended one of these inquests, with a view to give them the benefit of my practical knowledge: I did not find one of them amongst the twelve competent to perform usefully to the parish or the public the duties imposed upon them. I have known repeated instances in these united parishes, where ruinous houses have been permitted to remain for years without receiving any attention from the authorities, to the great danger of the occupiers and also to the public. I would instance two houses that to my certain knowledge have for ten or a dozen years inclined over in the street from the pavement upwards of eighteen inches, without being noticed by an Inquest Jury. My attention was lately directed professionally by the owner of the houses in question to their state and condition; upon a careful examination I found them so dangerous that I immediately gave directions to have them shored up, and recommended the tenant to vacate them in the meanwhile: to my great surprise, at the expiration of three or four days after the houses had been properly secured, the freeholders were served with a notice from the Inquest Jury to do what had already been done, viz., secure the houses from danger.'

A gentleman who has acted as one of the Commissioners under the Act for Bolton, thus describes the operation of its provisions:

'We have an Act in Little Bolton with extensive powers for the preservation of the public health.[1]

'I was appointed in 1837 one of the Trustees or Commissioners under this Act; they are elected by the rate-payers, and one-third go out annually; party political feeling has created a strife as to whether Whigs or Tories shall expend the public funds (the same is the case in Manchester), and hence a strife as to the economy of management. The streets are badly lighted, and sometimes not at all, to save the expense of gas. A surveyor is appointed in Little Bolton, whose duties are to see after the lighting, paving, cleansing, sewering, fire-engines, and firemen, the prevention of nuisances, encroachments, &c., &c.; to hiring and paying all the workmen, and buying the materials for repairing

---

1. 11 Geo. IV & 1 Wm. IV, c. 46, of 1830. For a discussion of this act, see *Local Reps. E. & W.*, pp. 278-81.

the roads and streets over a district containing about 15,000 inhabitants, for all of which service he receives 80*l.* a-year.

'With such talent as 80*l.* a-year will command, and such duties to perform, it may readily be supposed that sewerages and nuisances are liable to be overlooked.

'I once called the surveyor before a Board of about twenty Trustees, to draw attention to a pool of stagnant water lying in front of or betwixt two rows of cottages about 60 feet apart from each other, and about 150 feet long, covering nearly the whole of this vacant space of ground from one to two feet deep; dead dogs, kittens, and other impurities in the height of summer were floating in it, yet I was unable to obtain an order for the surveyor to expend a few pounds in draining it off, or to compel the owner to do it, although situate in the centre of a very populous district; and it continued in the same state till built over by cottages the following year.'

The nuisances which favoured the introduction and spread of the cholera were for the most part evils within the cognizance of the Leets, and could not have existed had their powers been properly exercised, yet so complete was the desuetude of the machinery of these Courts that it appeared nowhere to be thought of as applicable, and the new and special machinery of the Boards of Health were created for the purpose of meeting the pestilence.[1] There are no funds provided by which the common remedy by indictment could now be prosecuted: and since the most offensive and injurious nuisances are those supported by large capital, redress for the private injury is practically available only to persons who can afford to risk large sums in litigation. In one instance in Scotland, where the stream which supplied a village was discoloured and rendered disagreeable to the taste by some dye-works, a gentleman who took up the defence of the villagers, who were mostly his tenants, stated to me that the litigation incurred by an obstinate defence involved an expenditure of no less a sum than 4,000*l.*, the whole of which he did not recover, and that from his own experience he was clearly of opinion no one who had not most inflexible determination, as well as ample means, would be warranted in entering upon such a contest. Powerful influence was used to induce him to stay the suit, and he was by persons of his own class regarded as the persecutor of the author of the nuisance.

The complication of various nuisances in some of the larger manufacturing districts has frequently become so great as to put them beyond any existing legal remedy, whether private of public, by placing out of the apparent possibility of distinct technical proof any injury or particular effect arising from any one. An instance of this is stated by Messrs. Paris and Fonblanque[2], where two indictments were preferred; the one preferred against the proprietor of a Prussian-blue manufactory; the other against a black-ash manufacturer; both of these works were situated in Seward-street, Goswell-street, London. The counsel for the defendant, in his cross-examination of the witnesses for the prosecution of the Prussian-blue maker, drew from them an account of the noisome

---

1. For an account of these local boards of health, see Fraser Brockington, 'Public Health at the Privy Council, 1831-34', *Journal of Medical History*, XVI (1961), 61-85.
2. J. A. Paris and J. S. M. Fonblanque, *Medical Jurisprudence* (1823).

vapours of the black-ash manufactory; while in the latter trial the same barrister made the witnesses declare the extreme stench of the Prussian-blue manufactory; so that in both cases the defendants obtained a verdict, because in neither case could the witnesses for the Crown unequivocally prove from which of the manufactories the nuisance complained of arose.

State of the Local Executive Authorities for the Erection and Maintenance of Drains and other Works for the Protection of the Public Health

Having shown the state of the existing local authority for reclaiming the execution of the law, for *causing* that to be done 'which the common good requires,' and those things not to be done which tend 'to the annoyance of all the king's subjects,' I proceed to describe the general state of the executive authority, charged with the *doing* of so much of these things as is comprehended in town and road drainage; the sewerage for house and street drainage, and the provisions for the surface cleansing of streets.

The extent of the areas to be drained determines arbitrarily the extent of the operations of drainage, whether public or private, which shall combine efficiency and economy. If these areas are occupied by different parties, they cannot be cleared separately at an expense proportioned to the extent cleared. In general they are only to be won by agreement amongst the parties holding the property, to place the operations under the guidance of science; these labours will then be rewarded by production, whilst disease and pestilence, as well as sterility, are the effects of the ignorance and selfish rapacity which impede such union for the common advantage. The early history of the attempts of the separate owners of portions of the tract of country included in the Bedford Level to drain their property separately, is a history of expensive failures, of attempts to get rid of the surplus water only by flooding the lands of neighbours, and scenes of wretched animosities. These continued until the whole tract was put under one strong authority and scientific guidance, when productiveness and health arose as described in the account of the sanitary condition of the Isle of Ely. Had the natural district formed by the geological basin of that level been subdivided for drainage operations into districts co-extensive with districts for municipal, ecclesiastical, or parochial and civil administrative purposes; or had it been divided into districts according to property or occupation; had the commissions charged with the drainage of these subdivisions acted independently by ill-paid and ill-qualified officers, without any competent control, instead of acting on one comprehensive plan in subordination to an engineer of science adequate to its design and execution, vast sums of money might have been spent, and the land would still have remained a pestilential marsh occupied by a miserable population.

The amount of surface-water on those lands made the expediency of enlarged operations obvious, and their necessity pressing. Besides the towns and tracts of country oppressed with surface-water, as described in such evidence as that cited from the sanitary reports from populous districts, the extent of country which is unhealthy as well as comparatively unproductive, from the want of systematic under-drainage, appears to be extensive and immense beyond any conception that could be formed *a priori*, from the more conspicuous instances of enterprize, intelligence, and science manifest amongst the population. What the tract of country belonging to the Bedford Level, so subdivided and inefficiently and expensively managed once was, large urban and rural districts are now found to be in degree. The circumstances which govern what is called the private drainage will illustrate the nature of the administrative obstacles to efficient public drainage, and it is necessary to consider them in connexion, for they are inseparably connected by nature.

Although the larger share of the land-drainage redounds to the pecuniary profit of private individuals, yet it is proved so far to affect the public health beneficially, and contribute to the productive employment of the labouring classes, and to other general public advantages, that such works fairly come within the description of *publicum in privato*, and as such entitled to collective and legislative care. Drainage appears to be the primary, and in many cases the principal, operation for the efficient construction and economical maintenance of roads. But an efficient system of sewerage, and general town and road-drainage, has an additional value as removing serious impediments to the general land drainage. The following portion of the evidence of *Mr. Roe* affords an exemplification of the extent to which the private land-drainage is commonly affected by such operations:

'Have you found the sewerage produce any effect in the drainage of the surrounding land?—Yes, we have found it lower the water in the wells, often at great distances. For instance, in forming a sewer in the City-road, we found that it lowered by four feet a well nearly a quarter of a mile distance. The only remedy we could advise to the parties was to lower the well: they did so. We afterwards had occasion to lower the same sewer three feet, when the well was lowered again in proportion; so that the construction of the sewer, in this instance, drained an area of 40 or 50 acres on that side, and perhaps further. The water is sometimes in such quantities, and so strong in the land-springs, as to require openings to be left in the side of the sewer for its passage.'[1]

The first obstacles to the general land-drainage have already been adverted to in the small occupancies. To these must be added the want of capital. The legislature has recently given to the owners of life estates the power of charging the inheritance with the contributions to the cost of permanent improvements by drainage. This power does not meet the case of the smaller holdings; and drainage operations to be effectual must, in general, be on a scale too large to be within the habits of thought or action of small owners or occupiers, of varying interests, and wanting confidence in each other to combine, make, or manage immediate outlays for such purposes. But above all these is to be added the circumstance of the power which the possession of a small part of a district gives to one individual, to thwart those operations of the majority which are for the common advantage, and consequently the temptation which the possession of such power gives and almost ensures, of its use to exact unjust and exorbitant conditions. When

---

1. *San. Rep.*, Appendix 1, p. 377.

expressing to a gentleman who has actively promoted improvements in agricultural production in Scotland, my surprise at the large extent of marshy district allowed to continue in a state of comparative sterility, sources of rheumatism, and fevers and other diseases, he directed my attention to the following among other exemplifications:

About a mile and a half distant from one of the towns in Scotland, there is a moss about seven miles long, with a small stream running through it, with a fall of about 25 feet. At the outlet of this stream there is an old corn-mill, which yields a rental of about 25*l.* per annum. By the water being dammed up to turn this mill, the whole run is impeded; and the consequent sluggishness of the stream occasions it to be choked up with weeds. Whenever a fall of rain takes place, the banks are overflowed, and not only is every improvement rendered impracticable, but on several harvests as much as 500*l.* worth of hay has been destroyed at a time when a heavy fall of rain has occurred and occasioned an overflow.

It so happens that the proprietor of the mills would himself clearly gain more than the value of the mill from the drainage that would be effected on his own lands by the removal of the dam. The other proprietors, however, offered to him for its removal the full rental that he now derives from the mill. The property is in the hands of a factor, who is ignorant and obstinate, and the offer was refused. Now the land which would be affected beneficially by the removal of the dam, is a tract of seven or eight miles long, with an average width of two miles and a half. The expense of an Act of Parliament, if it were resisted, as it most probably would be, renders an appeal to the legislature valueless. Thus one individual is enabled to exercise a despotic caprice against the health and prosperity of the surrounding population, to inflict an extensive loss of labour and wages on the working man, the loss of produce and profit to the occupiers, the loss of rent to the other owners, and at the same time to inflict on all who may live on the spot, or come within reach of the marsh, the ill health and hazards of disease from the miasma which it emits!

The like despotic powers are found in every district in the way of the public health, as well as of the private advantage.

The passenger who enters Birmingham from the London railway may perceive, just before the terminus, a black sluggish stream, which is the river Rea, made the receptacle of the sewers of the town. *Mr. Hodgson*, and the committee of physicians of that town, state, in their sanitary report, that:

'The stream is sluggish, and the quantity of water which it supplies is not sufficient to dilute and wash away the refuse which it receives in passing through the town, and that in hot weather it is consequently very offensive, and in some situations in these seasons is covered with a thick scum of decomposing matters; and this filthy condition of the river near the railway station is a subject of constant and merited animadversions, and that it requires especial attention lest it should become a source of disease, &c.'[1]

The fatally dangerous sluggishness of this river is occasioned by the diversion and abstraction of its water to turn a mill, 'a fact which will

---

1. *Local Reps. E. & W.*, pp. 193-4.

amply account for the deficiency and sluggishness of the current in the very places where the contrary condition is the most wanted.' *Captain Vetch*,[1] who has been engaged in engineering operations in that part of the country which have led him to observe the spot, states that:

'The remedy is as easy as the evil is great; all obstruction being removed from the course of the brook, and the water restored to its original bed, the object would be effected; as to the value of the mill-power which would thus be subverted, it cannot be a matter of much amount, in a place where coals and steam-engines are so cheap, and where the constant and regular work of the mill must be an object of some importance.'[2]

After describing the means of the removal, he states:

'In this manner, and by reserving the whole body of the water of the Rea for cleansing its own bed, I have no doubt that this main sewer of Birmingham would become as conspicuous for its wholesome and efficient action as it now is for the contrary.'[3]

Birmingham presents an example such as indeed is common in most towns, of the stoppage of a main current of air by a private building carried across one end of a main street. The effects likely to result from the obstruction to the invisible current are not dissimilar to those which result from the obstruction to the stream of water, and the cost and difficulty of relief from them are perhaps much greater. *Captain Vetch* refers, as another example of the condition of many of the towns in respect to these chief streams, as described in the sanitary reports, to the case of Haddington:

'In the town of Haddington a mill-dam crosses the river Tyne in its passage through the place, and into the mill-pool the main sewer is discharged with a diminished and sluggish descent; and on occasion of floods in the river, the water passes up the sewers and occasionally lays the lowest part of the town under water. It would not be difficult to direct the main sewer into the bed of the river below the dam or weir, and by the additional declivity give some current to the water of the sewer, which, from the pending up of the river at its present outlet, has rendered it almost stagnant, so much so, that in hot weather, and where it is not covered over, the exhalations are very offensive; but was the sewer improved by the alteration mentioned, still the pooling up of the river for the mill keeps the lower part of the town damp, and even subjects it to partial inundations.

'One of the medical officers reports, that when "fever has been at any time prevalent in the town, it has been most so in a portion of it called the Nungate, lying close by the river, when during the summer and autumn it is occasionally almost stagnant, and where there is a considerable decomposition of vegetable matter.

'Another medical gentleman, speaking of the main sewer, says, "this small burn is a receptacle of the privies and refuse of vegetable matters from the houses near which it passes; and in those parts where it is uncovered, it forms an excellent index of the weather; previous to rain the smell is intolerable."

'The same gentleman proposes, as a remedy, that another small burn having a parallel course at a short distance, should be turned into the sewer to aid the sewerage. From my knowledge of the locality, the recommendation,

---

1. For James Vetch, see above, p. 124, n. 1.
2. *San. Rep.*, App. 5, p. 387.
3. *Ibid.*

I should say, is judicious; but in this manner, though the supply of water would be increased, the declivity or rather want of declivity of the sewer would remain the same, and could only be improved by removing the milldam, or directing the sewer into the bed of the river below it, as already mentioned. Unquestionably from the penning up of the river, the lower part of the town is at present very ill drained, and it is somewhat remarkable that it was the first site in Scotland visited by the Asiatic cholera.

'In reference to the two cases cited, and to others of a similar nature, it should be remarked, that the vicinities of the nuisances are chiefly inhabited by the poorer classes, and who, from want of influence in their own parts, are the more necessarily thrown under the protection of state regulations.'[1]

It does not appear that any improvements have been suggested to the inhabitants, or any question raised in respect to the compensation to the owners of these obstructions. They are, however, enabled to refuse a liberal compensation for removing from their property, and discontinuing proceedings so injurious by the agency of invisible miasma, that if the miseries were brought about by direct manual or visible operations, it would be deemed the most horrible tyranny. In many, if not in most such cases, the use of the property, with such attendant consequences, would be found to be in contravention of the existing public rights; but the expense and delay and uncertainty of the legal procedure practically sustain such invasions on the surrounding property and on the public health.

The powers of continuing such evils amidst large masses of the population, and against specific representations of the attendant evils, are terrible when the extent of those evils are examined. For example, it is stated in the records of the proceedings before adverted to, with which *Dr. Currie*, of Liverpool, was connected, that:

'In the beginning of the year 1802, the corporation of Liverpool, being about to apply to Parliament for powers to improve the streets and the police of the town, requested the physicians of the infirmary and dispensary to suggest to them "such alterations as might contribute to the health and comfort of the inhabitants," in order that, where necessary, they might include in the Bill about to be brought into Parliament the powers requisite to carry such alterations into effect. The physicians took this request into serious consideration, and presented a report of considerable extent, including a view of the causes of the uncommon sickliness of the two preceding years, and of the measures requisite to prevent its recurrence, and to remove the frequency of contagion in the habitations of the poor. To lessen as much as possible the contamination of the atmosphere, they recommended that lime should be prevented from being burnt within a certain distance of inhabited houses; that soaperies, tan-yards, and other offensive manufactories, should in future be prevented from being established in the town; and where now established, and authorized by usage, that they should, whenever practicable, be purchased by the body corporate, and the space they occupy be converted to other purposes. The same recommendation they extended to slaughter-houses, and to all other offensive trades or manufactories. They recommend, that in all cases where fire-engines, or steam-engines, are necessarily employed in the town or its vicinity, the burning of smoke should be enforced, as well as in all other practicable cases where large volumes of smoke are emitted.

'They pointed out the necessity of enforcing cleanliness in the streets, to

---

1. *San. Rep.*, App. 5, p. 388.

which end an improvement of the pavement was represented to be essential; and they particularly advised a general review of the common sewers, and an improvement of their structure, on the principles of a report on this particular subject addressed by them to the mayor and magistrates in 1788. They further advised that effectual provision should be made for draining the grounds within the liberties, and particularly to the north of the town. "Repeated remonstrances (I quote the words of the report) have been made for the last twenty years on the collections of standing water, including filth of every kind, which are suffered to remain in the district which extends along the termination of the streets from St. Paul's-square to Byrom-street, and to which the low fevers which, in the autumnal months especially, infest these streets, are principally to be imputed. These remonstrances have been passed over, on the ground, as we are informed, that the proprietors of the lands will not agree to the plan necessary for draining them." '

Some of the most important improvements that might be accomplished in the poorer and most infected districts of the larger towns by pulling down the present tenements and erecting tenements of a superior order, would, there is little doubt, amply repay any large capitalist or single proprietor. In the course of our examination of the most wretched and overcrowded wynds of Glasgow and Edinburgh, we were informed by persons apparently of competent local information that, if they could be purchased at a fair price for the public to be pulled down, there would be a gain in the prevention of the charges of sickness and crime arising from them; and that if they were simply rebuilt on a good plan, the necessary outlay would be repaid by the improved rental from the superior order of tenements. Each flat or story, however, frequently belonged to a different owner, and the property in which the most afflicted classes lived appeared to be extensively subdivided amongst persons of different interests, of different degrees of permanency, and with no power of co-operation, and with little or no capital.

Now the class of persons whose feelings, state of intelligence, and modes of action are displayed in the evidence on the drainage redounding to private profit, are the class from amongst whom are necessarily taken the members of the local boards, to whose uncontrolled direction and choice of officer the structural works essential to the public health are confided.

The natural districts for public drainage are so capriciously subdivided and departed from, as frequently to render economical and efficient drainage impracticable.

The municipal authorities who obtained powers for drainage, only thought of the surface drainage of their own jurisdictions. Some towns are at the bottom of basins and others on elevations, and the operations for effectual drainage must often be commenced at a distance. It is stated by persons of competent skill in drainage, as an example, a town situate on one side of a hill will be drained dry by tapping or opening a spring on the other side. The manifest defect in the areas of operations for drainage is noticed in the report of the Committee of the House of Commons, which in the year 1834 inquired into the administration of the sewers' rate in the metropolis, where perhaps the most money has been expended in imperfect sewerage and cleansing of any part of the kingdom. They reported that a primary defect of their constitution:

'Is the want of system or combination between the different trusts which have now, as before observed, each an independent action. The inconveniences in this are palpable, for where the line of communication with the Thames is not complete within each district, the very improvements in the one trust may prove injurious to the others. It appears by the evidence that a case of this kind occurred not long ago in the city of London, through which a part of the Holborn and Finsbury sewerage is conducted to the river. The sewers of the Holborn and Finsbury division having been greatly improved and enlarged, the city sewers became inadequate to carry off their contents, and a number of houses in the vicinity of the river were inundated after each fall of rain, the contents of their own drains, in addition to the waters from the high lands of the neighbouring trust, being actually forced back into their houses from the volume of water which occupied the main sewer. This has now been remedied at a great expense to the city of London district, and by dint of much labour and time; but if anything like combination had existed previously, the improvements would have been carried on simultaneously, and the inconvenience would never have occurred.'[1]

The surveyor of the City sewers under the management of the corporation, speaks in a tone of grievance and oppression, that the waters of the county would run into the municipal jurisdiction. Speaking of the formation of a particular sewer, he says:

'The commissioners under the power of the Act of Parliament carried the sewer, in the first instance, along their own pavement and for their own drainage. It was thence continued up to Finsbury-place to Bunhill-fields, then called Tyndal's burial-ground, and is so described in the Act; the county then communicated with it, and sent their surplus water, or an immense run of it, into that sewer. The city for its own drainage also built a sewer in Whitecross-street; the county somehow or other got possession of that, and the water that runs down Whitecross street is quite overpowering.'[2]

He speaks of some other drains which were formed by the city, and the effects of the waters let in upon them from the county.

'The commissioners find themselves very much annoyed by the quantity of water poured in from the county, which water communicates with the city in Bishopsgate-street, through Shoreditch. * * * The county then made another sewer, which takes water from the Tower Hamlets, and is continued up the Kingsland-road, so that a very large portion of that water has been thrown into that sewer, and annoyed this Irongate sewer (the only communication with the Thames) very sorely; and the Commissioners had been put to an enormous expense in rebuilding it, and that was increased by houses being built over it with very high stacks of chimneys. In consequence of the immense flood of water that pours down all those different sewers from the county, the inhabitants of the city, in the neighbourhood of Moorfields especially, have been most dreadfully annoyed, so much so that their cellars became useless.

'By the county, you mean the Holborn and Finsbury division?—Yes; everything out of the boundary of the city. In order to meet the difficulty for which there was no other cure, the commissioners have built a sewer for the New London Bridge, which is ten feet by eight feet at the mouth; they are continuing it up to the new street, eight feet six inches by seven feet, and it is intended to take it up the New Road to Moorfields, to continue the sewer along Princes-street and up that new street; and I confidently expect I shall

---

1. *Report of the Select Committee on Metropolis Sewers*, P.P. 1834, XV, p. v.
2. *Ibid.*, evidence of Richard Kelsey, Q. 604.

get from eight to ten feet additional depth, and that then the whole of Moorfields will be effectually relieved.

'The necessity for this new sewer of this large dimension, arises from the large quantity of water which flows in upon you from the county?—Certainly.

'You conceive yourself on the other side to derive some benefit from these waters, because they cleanse and scour your sewers down?—Yes, as far as the direct run goes they do, but beyond that they do an injury that is incalculable; in this way the water runs right a-head, and an immense quantity is brought in, it fills it, and the collateral sewers cannot bear up against it, they are driven back and the sediment is deposited, and when it falls that is left behind.'[1]

It need scarcely be pointed out that this municipal division had, until they chose to drain, operated as a barrier to all the water described, which was kept back to the injury of the county; to the injury indeed of the health of those merchants and traders, clerks and men of business, the population whose private residences are in the county, and beyond their residences to the injury of the city, in so far as their obstructions to drainage injured the pasturage and land cultivated for the supply of the city.

But a considerable portion of the city was itself imperfectly drained. The chairman was asked:

'539. Do you conceive there is any large portion of the City left without deriving direct advantage from the sewerage,—meaning, by direct advantage, some under-ground communication with the sewers so as to carry off the soil of the house?—There is a large part of the City of London in that state.'[2]

It was stated, as an example, that Cheapside had no sewer. This was accounted for from the circumstance, that the

'whole form of that part of the city is like a tortoise's back. Cheapside and Leadenhall-street are the back-bone; and that accounts for Cheapside, being the highest ground, never having had occasion for a sewer for the surface drainage; the water all flows northward and southward, so that accounts for the apparent contradiction of Cheapside, a main street, having no sewer in it.

'As far as *surface* drainage is concerned?—Yes; the inhabitants of Cheapside, generally speaking, have got cesspools: they perforated the yellow clay or loam and got into the gravel, and whatever is thrown into the cesspool mixes with the water and the earth: that is for the benefit of the water-drinkers!'[3]

Thirty old streets in Westminster had no sewers. Other considerable and ancient streets were also without sewers, although the inhabitants contributed to the rates.

Nor does there appear to be any conception as to the objects of the service; and illegal fees, that must operate as exclusions to the poorer inhabitants from the advantages which it is more desirable to confer, were allowed to be exacted by the officers. Thus the chairman of the City Commission was asked:

'574. Your clerks at the office take no fees?—I cannot say that they take no fees; there is an ancient fee allowed, that any person who communicates with

---

1. *Report of the Select Committee on Metropolis Sewers*, P.P. 1834, XV, p. v; evidence of Richard Kelsey, Qs. 602, 612-5.
2. *Ibid.*, evidence of Joseph Daw, Q. 539.
3. *Ibid.*, evidence of Richard Kelsey, Qs. 603-4.

the sewer shall pay a guinea; that is divided among the clerks, the surveyor, and inspector, who see that the communication is properly made: they pay a guinea for that purpose.

'575. Are your clerks paid by those fees?—No, by fixed salary; the fees are very trifling, for till lately they did not amount to 100*l*. a-year.

'576. The aggregate of the fees?—Yes, nor to 50*l*. a-year: if a party applies to communicate with a sewer, and the Commissioners have no objection, they call upon him to pay the estimate of the surveyor, and the charges are made at the contract price, and in addition to that they pay one guinea as a fee.'[1]

In another Commission the surveyor's fee for the privilege is stated to be one guinea.

Before the Committee *Mr. James Peake*, the surveyor of the Commissioners for the Tower Hamlets, states (Committee on Health of Towns), 'that in making a communication to the common sewers, the parties who have to make the drain, besides doing it at their own expense, have to pay 17*s*. 6*d*. for the first three feet of sewer. And they,' the Commissioners of Sewers, 'do that for this reason:—if they were not to resort to that measure, the sewers would be destroyed. *Every one would make a hole in the sewer*,' i.e., every one would *use* the sewer.[2]

Mr. Samuel Byles, another witness examined before the same Committee, was asked:

'193. You state that a great deal of disease is generated by the want of ventilation and sewerage; is there any power in the Sewer Commissioners to oblige the parties inhabiting the district to communicate with the sewer if they made one?—No; and there is unfortunately a paradox; there is a penalty on any person communicating from his house into the common sewer.

'194. If they are assessed to it that is not the case, is it?—Yes; it appears to be a complete paradox; if privies are known to empty themselves into the common sewer, the person is liable to a penalty.'

No arrangements are made to bring the effects of the absence of drainage to the knowledge of those bodies for their guidance in the performance of their duties, nor does it appear to enter into their conception that the protection of the public health forms any part of the objects of their service. *Mr. James Peake*, the surveyor of the Commissioners of the Tower Hamlets, was questioned on this point:

'2012. It is stated to the Committee, that "in a direct line from Virginia-row to Shoreditch, a mile in extent, all the lanes, courts, and alleys in the neighbourhood pour their contents into the centre of the main street, where they stagnate and putrefy;" is that the case?—I perceive by an inspection of the plan that there is no sewer about Virginia-row; there is none nearer to it than Princes-street.

'2013. It is stated that in some or other of those houses fever is always prevalent; do you know the district so as to be aware whether that is the case? —I cannot speak as to the state of the inhabitants; I know it is very wretched. The whole of this land was excavated for brick-making, and has been reduced to an unnatural level, so that the sewers are hardly available. I believe many of those houses have ditches round their gardens, and flowers and roots and stems are thrown into the ditches, where they remain and stagnate; we are

---

1. *Ibid.*, evidence of Joseph Daw, Qs. 574-6.
2. *Report of Select Committee on the Health of Towns*, P.P. 1840, XI, evidence of James Peeke (not Peake), Q. 2036.

working up, and shall be able to get the sewer in some parts five feet lower than it was.

'2014. It is stated to the Commissioners that in Whitechapel parish, Essex-street and its numerous courts, as Martin's-court, Moor's-court, Essex-court, Elgar-square, George-yard, and New-court, Crown-court, Wentworth-street, and many parts of that street, there is no sewer passes up?—There is none.

'2015. Are the people very much in want of some mode of cleansing in consequence?—It is the filthiest place which can be imagined.

'2016. Is it thickly inhabited?—Yes, very densely populated.

'2028. Do you not think that the want of such provision is very injurious to the health of the inhabitants?—I do not think that sewers have the effect which is attributed to them.

'2029. You disagree with the medical men who think that the neglect of this underground drainage is prejudicial to the health of the community?—I cannot see how, if they have a good surface drainage, they can be improved by an underground drainage, in nine cases out of ten.

'2064. Do you consider it your duty to alter a sewer, or carry up a sewer, with reference to the health of the inhabitants?—Certainly not.

'2065. Any alteration in the form of the sewerage, or any change respecting it, is with reference to property, not with reference to the health of the inhabitants?—Certainly.'

Mr. Unwin, the clerk to the Commissioners of Sewers for the Tower Hamlets, was thus examined before the Committee:

'1433. Do you know Hare-street-fields?—I do; that is not very densely populated: there are a number of houses, but very few persons living in them.

'1434. Do you know that in wet weather a large portion of that neighbourhood is completely inundated; that in all the houses forming the square, and in the neighbouring streets, fever is constantly breaking out, and that the character of the fever in the neighbourhood has lately been very malignant?—I never heard that before.

'1435. Then if that has occurred in the midst of your district, it is a matter you never heard of?—Just so.

'1436. Do you know Baker's-Arms-alley?—That is in the parish of Hackney; that is in our district; but it is a very open place.

'1437. If it is the fact that there is a narrow court with a dead wall about two yards from the houses, as high as the houses; that the principal court is intersected by other courts extremely narrow, in which it is scarcely possible for air to penetrate close to the dead wall; that between the wall and the houses there is a gutter, in which is always present a quantity of stagnant fluid full of all sorts of putrefying matter, the effluvia from which are most offensive, and the sense of closeness extreme; that all the houses are dark, gloomy, and extremely filthy; that at the top of the innermost courts are the privies, which are open and uncovered, the soil of which is seldom removed, and the stench of which is abominable; you have not heard of that?—No, I have not heard of any of those circumstances; I have heard of very few complaints of fever in the Tower Hamlets.

'1440. Do you not recollect that there are most fearful accounts of fever prevailing in that district?—No, I had a report sent to me, which I understood came from Dr. Southwood Smith, and there was a communication I think from the Secretary of State upon it.'

At the very time that this witness had heard of few complaints of fever in the Tower Hamlets, the Board found themselves compelled, on account of the appalling prevalence of fever amongst the poor resident in that district, to direct the special inquiry by Dr. Arnott, Dr. Kay, and Dr. Southwood Smith, as to the causes of the fever which led to the present extended inquiry.[1] The description given in the question of the narrow court with the dead wall about two yards from the houses was taken from one of those reports. That self-same court was the Bakers'-Arms alley, named in the preceding question; but instead of being situate, as described by the witness, in the parish of Hackney, two or three miles from the office of the Commissioners of Sewers, it is in Rosemary-lane, distant from that office only the length of a street, and that not a very long one—Leman-street.

On the subject of the escapes of gas from the sewers there is no one point on which medical men are so clearly agreed, as on the connexion of exposure of persons to the miasma from sewers, and of fever as a consequence.[2] It appears that the evils of these escapes, on which several medical men to whose testimony we have alluded gave evidence before the Committee of 1834, may be prevented, and one of them prepared a plan for this purpose. He states that the Commissioners having expressed their doubts as to whether they were justified in trying the experiment at the public expense, he said:

'Very well, gentlemen, I suppose you are quite right there; I will enter into an undertaking with you to do it at my own expense, to a limited extent, in any part that the surveyor of the sewers will say he thinks it will fail; at the worst part that he can point out I will try it; and moreover, in that undertaking I engaged to replace the things in *statu quo* if they failed. I entered into that understanding, and, as I was given to understand, the parish sent their bond, with a copy of the request, to the Commissioners. Some time elapsed and I heard nothing of it, and in fact I thought the thing was so simple, and as I heard nothing to the contrary, I began to make inquiries as to getting these traps cast, when one morning the parish surveyor brought me the model back, with a verbal message, which was, that "whether it would answer or not, it should not be tried;" the Commissioners had made up their minds that the stink should not be kept down.'[3]

The reply made to this before the Committee on behalf of the Commissioners, by one of the officers, was, 'The sewers must have vent somewhere; if you stop the vent in the street, it will penetrate into the houses; also the danger from the gas-explosions are continually taking place, and our people are frequently sent to the hospital. Our surveyor can show a specimen of an entire new skin to his hand, and he had an entire new skin to his face, and laid up in a very dangerous state. This was from an explosion in the sewers. This is a danger the Commissioners must of necessity look to.' 'The gas always ascends from its lightness. If the air-trap was put at the upper end of the gully-drain, that would be the place where the gas would lodge, and any candle brought near to this outlet into the upper part would occasion an explosion.'

---

1. For the reports by Arnott, Kay and Southwood Smith, see Introduction, pp. 43-4.
2. For the miasmatic theory of the generation of fever, see Introduction, pp. 62-4.
3. *Report of Select Committee on Metropolis Sewers*, P.P. 1834, XV, evidence of Peter Fuller, Q. 879.

VII. Recognised Principles of Legislation

Now it is precisely because 'the gas always ascends from its lightness' that men of competent science declare, without reference to the particular plan proposed in this instance, that by means of a shaft or chimney properly placed, private houses as well as the workmen may be relieved from the dangers of the escapes of this gas, which is becoming more deleterious from the increasing drainage from private houses as well as from the escapes of gas from the gas-pipes, into the sewers of which very strong instances are stated in the evidence.

In the map of Leeds,[1] where the cholera track is pourtrayed, it will be observed that it followed closely the fever track; and were such maps so far improved as to show at a view the condition of a district in respect to dwelling and drainage, the marks to denote sites where the drainage was imperfect would at the same time denote the seats of epidemic disease. This had been so far observed by medical men that there was, perhaps, no point on which they were more anxious and urgent than that increased sewerage and cleansing should be adopted as preventives of the cholera. Yet in one extensive densely populated district, the Commissioners, because they had observed no effects on their own men, who were accustomed to the sewers, took upon themselves to disregard all the precautions advised by persons of complete knowledge. 'At the time of the cholera the arching over the sewers was very much applied for' in the Ravensbourne Commission; 'but,' says the officer of the commission, 'I do not think there was anything done on account of the cholera, because the court held a different feeling on that point. Out of all the men employed by the Commissioners of Sewers, and who were constantly in those sewers, there was not one of those attacked by the cholera.'[2]

All this incompleteness as to the extent of the districts drained, and the imperfection in the mode of executing the works, appears from the complaints and evidence given before the Committee to be accompanied by disproportionate and oppressive assessments and extravagant expenditure.

The rates were complained of as levied on property which was undrained, and derived no benefit from them; and by equal assessments on houses which derive benefit by direct communications with the sewers, and on houses which have no communication with them, and only derive benefit from the surface drainage, and in some cases on houses which were unoccupied. These unequal charges, sometimes for long periods, and for large and permanent works, fell upon a fluctuating tenancy. 'We should claim,' says one witness, '20 years' rate from the incoming tenant (122), or we might have sold the premises' (129).[3]

In respect to the existing expenditure, very strong statements of mismanagement were made in the majority of the town districts; but I prefer referring on this topic to the evidence taken before the Committee of the House of Commons. One marked character of the expenditure is

---

1. For Baker's sanitary map of Leeds, see Introduction, p. 50.
2. *Report of Select Committee on Metropolis Sewers*, P.P. 1834, XV, evidence of Beriah Drew, Qs. 1402, 1404.
3. *Ibid.*, evidence of J. Houseman, Qs. 122, 129.

the greater amount paid to the clerk of the Board, and for office expenses, than for any skill or science in the superintendence of the work. Thus in the district where the Commissioners, on the example of their own workmen, adjudged that the applications for arching over the sewers on the ground that they created a predisposition to the spread of the epidemic were unfounded, the payments to the clerk of the Board for his salary and office was 750*l*., assistant-clerk 100*l*., and three surveyors were paid each 50*l*. (besides commission on works executed, and a fee of a guinea for communicating with the drain.) In another subdivision the expenses of the clerks, messengers, &c., exclusive of collection, were 15,737*l*. for 20 years, while for the same period the expense of surveyors, inspectors, and clerks of the works was 14,928*l*. In another division the tavern expenses for 20 years were 7,935*l*. In one district the cost of the commission, compared with the beneficial outlay on the works, appeared to be 200 per cent. In regard to another level, it is stated that there was laid out on works the sum of 17,455*l*. 18*s*. 10*d*.; and:

	£	*s.*	*d.*
In working the commission	9,003	18	7
Commission on collection	1,635	10	9½
Total	£10,639	9	4½

The proportion of the cost of management to the expenditure on work appears to have been similar in others of these administrative bodies. The Committee stated as a principal defect of these bodies—'The want of publicity and responsibility systematically enforced.' There were several of the trusts in which the Courts have not been open to the public, the right of the rate-payers to inspect the accounts not admitted, and 'where consequently a real responsibility in money matters can hardly be said to exist.'

Mr. W. Fowler, a Commissioner, says:

'If they are to go from year's end to year's end without being subject to any control, I feel the money will be expended as I believe it now is, and dribbled away, not expended fairly in carrying the ostensible works into execution.'[1]

Another defect resulting from the capricious constitution of these trusts, on which the Committee reported, was the want of uniformity.

'There are no two districts in which the law does not vary, or where, if the law be the same, the commissioners do not interpret some parts of in a different manner.

'Thus, a man having property in Finsbury and in Westminster, or in the City and in the Tower Hamlets, may find himself placed under different systems, and may be led by his knowledge of the regulations of the one district to violate the regulations of the other.'[2]

Such being the unfavourable constitution of these bodies as described in the Parliamentary Reports, and the evidence taken before the Committees, the accounts given of the qualifications of many of the officers of these trusts for the execution of any work of magnitude

---

1. *Ibid.*, evidence of W. Fowler, Q. 1841.
2. *Ibid.*, p. iv.

requiring scientific attainments are equally unfavourable. The following general account of them is given by an architect of eminence, who has conducted large works in the metropolis and in various parts of the country, and is corroborated by several other engineers of extensive practice.

'In the rural districts, the men appointed as surveyors by the local Commissioners are very little better than common labourers, men with no idea of construction or of management; that is the description of men I have met with in the country places: they are commonly a sort of foremen of the labourers who are called "ditch casters." In the towns the men appointed are frequently decayed builders, or tradesmen whose knowledge is limited to common artificers' work, such as bricklayers' and carpenters' work. Some may be capable of drawing: only a few. They have neither education, nor salary, nor station, to place them above bribery, and the consequences are notoriously such as might be expected of public services performed by such an agency. In some instances there are very good exceptions; that is, where the remuneration is adequate to ensure the service of a respectable person, and where, as occasionally happens, a person of respectability has the local influence to obtain the appointment. The district surveyors in the metropolis are in general respectable and well-qualified public officers. In local matters no thought is ever had of combining duties. The chief concern of the Commissioner of sewers, where he holds property of his own, is to drain his own property.'

Another description of the persons usually appointed as surveyors is given in the following terms by a gentleman who is himself a surveyor of extensive practice:

'As regards the appointment of surveyors to the Commissioners of Sewers, I would observe that, in my opinion, very few of them are properly qualified by education or otherwise to perform the important duties entrusted to them in an effective and proper manner. A man to be a good surveyor of sewers should be a practical civil engineer, in which science is comprehended levelling in all its branches, and other matters requisite and necessary in the construction of drains and sewers: in proof of this, an instance recently occurred in one of the divisions (which I need not particularize) in the construction of a sewer, that after it had proceeded for a considerable distance, from an error in taking the levels, was found to be below the level of the outlet, and was in consequence obliged to be all destroyed, and another sewer constructed upon a proper level. This error was so clearly traced to the want of practical knowledge on the part of the surveyor, or the application of it, that he was amerced in the greater part of the cost.'

A builder of extensive experience in the wealthy districts of the metropolis states, that in making drains and executing works which communicate with the sewers on which large sums have been expended, he has not found one main sewer in three properly made; and the strongest statements of the extravagant nature of the expenditure was made by witnesses who had themselves acted as members of the bodies directing it.

The office business of two of the commissions appeared to me to be very respectably conducted. But in the structural arrangements, in only one commission do any of the works executed approach the existing state of science. In that one, the Holborn and Finsbury trust, they happened to obtain a surveyor, having science and practical experience as an engineer, whose advice was acted upon, and that officer effected the only considerable improvements of a scientific character that have been made in the sewerage of the metropolis. These improvements for preventing the accumulations of deposits in the sewers, and the generation of malaria, and at the same time reducing the expenses of cleansing more than one-half, must be considered improvements of a very high order. But though they are demonstrated, and in full and successful action, they appear to have been imitated only in one other adjacent district. In the others they go on constructing sewers which are the latent sources of pestilence and death. This officer was asked the following questions:

'If the public, who may be ignorant of the science of sewerage and of what it may accomplish, make no complaints, and do not call for the adoption of any improved system, in how long a time do you think the improvements demonstrated in the Holborn and Finsbury divisions would reach the other ends of the metropolis by the force of imitation and voluntary adoption?— From the apathy shown and prejudice against anything new, however valuable it may be as an improvement, and the various interests affected, such as the contractors for cleansing, I do not expect that they would become general in the metropolis during my life-time. The public are passive, and the adverse interests are active.

'You know the description of persons engaged as surveyors of various descriptions in the rural districts and in the smaller towns?—Yes, I do.

'Unless care be taken, is it to be apprehended that any new expenditure will be made on imperfect and unwholesome drains with flat bottoms and on false principles at a disproportionate expense?—Undoubtedly, except they have to act on rule, it will certainly be so throughout the country. The drainage that I have seen in the country districts is worse than in the metropolis.'

The consideration of these circumstances, in respect to the past expenditure in this branch of local administration, appears to be necessary for meeting the objections and opposition to any future expenditure, and especially of any apparent increase required for the successful removal of the physical causes of bodily suffering, and the moral degradation of the labouring classes. In the towns and districts where the chief evils in question are admitted, but where anything wearing the appearance of a new expenditure for any purpose is unpopular, and will be thwarted or yielded unwillingly, the objections when examined are found to consist mainly of a rooted distrust of the money being equally levied, or carefully and efficiently expended for the attainment of the professed objects of public advantage. From such evidence as that already adduced from the Report of the Committee of the House of Commons, but presented in greater extent and strength in the course of the present inquiry—of instances of disease and death occasioned by miasma from badly made and sluggish or stagnant drains that pervade whole towns, it will be seen that it cannot fairly be said that the distrust is not well founded.

A due examination, however, of the experience even of voluntary and private expenditure on the wealthy districts where water is laid on, and the main drainage is complete for the removal of refuse, appears to establish the conclusion that only a part of the work is then attained, and that for the economical attainment of the general objects of protecting the least protected classes, that which is generally deemed the private and subordinate work, namely, the house drainage, must form part of the same general system, and be executed under the same general superintendence.

It appears to be partly a defect in legislation, and partly a defect in the constitution of the existing authorities for the direction of public drainage, that their agency is never thought of for the superintendence even of work which can seldom be cheaply and efficiently executed by private individuals, and that can only be so executed and kept in order by the systematic application of science and skill. An order, that the landlords of all houses which have no drains communicating with the main drains shall make them, is an order, when viewed in its operation in a street or district where there are 50 or 100 different owners, that those 50 or 100 persons shall separately get plans possibly from as many different builders, and enter into contracts with them, and procure capital which, to poor owners, will be a serious amount of several hundred pounds in the aggregate, to be applied as a permanent investment on property in which a large proportion of them will only have various transitory interests. Viewed in its aggregate operation on all places requiring amendment, the simple compulsory enactment for house drainage, and without any previous care as to the means, would be, in effect, an order for the expenditure of several millions of money in the manner described by *Mr. Charles Oldfield*, a practical witness of great experience, whose evidence (corroborated by the testimony of other witnesses of extensive experience) has already been referred to on this important topic:

'Have you as a builder had much experience in the drainage of houses? — Very considerable experience, and I pay particular attention to it; there is no part of a building to which I pay more attention than to the drainage. I seldom allow the drains to be covered in without seeing to them myself.

'Do you think it desirable that legislative provision should be made for the drainage of the tenements of the labouring classes?—I think it most necessary; but merely ordering the drains to be made will not do. Drains made for the tenements of the working classes, if left to the parties, are almost sure to be badly constructed, and badly constructed drains might merely carry away the soil; they might not do that; and they would probably let in as great an evil, namely, the foul air from the sewer. In general, unless care be taken, what is called making drains will be opening conduits for the escape of foul air from the sewers into the houses. This is frequently so with the houses of the better classes of persons, where the drains are not made perfectly air-tight, and are not properly trapped at all the apertures. I am frequently called upon to examine houses where they say they are oppressed by unpleasant smells. Some time ago I was called upon to examine a house in one of the principal streets in London, belonging to a gentleman of distinction, who was about to abandon it in consequence of the unpleasant smells which were continually arising. He was particularly annoyed that this smell arose in the greatest strength whenever he had parties; the drains had been opened, and there was no lodgement of soil in them. People commonly imagine that when they get rid of the soil they have got rid of the stench; they do not see and do not conceive the effect of the foul air, which is so much lighter than atmospheric air that it escapes where the atmospheric air would not. On examining the

State of the Local Executive Authorities

drains at his house, I found that they were imperfect, and that the foul air filtered through them. Whenever he had a party there was a stronger fire in the kitchen, and stronger fires in other parts of the house, and the windows and the external doors being shut, and a greater draught created, larger quantities of the foul air from the sewers rose up. These stenches arise in the greatest strength in the private houses when the doors and windows are closed, the fire and column of light air in the chimney being at work. So it would be with drains made from the house to the sewer, or from the sewer to the house of the poor man, unless care were taken in the construction of the drains. When the door was shut, and he sat down to enjoy his fire-side, he would have a stench. This would be the effect of merely ordering the drains to be made by the owners of such tenements, who would get the work done in the way they thought to be the least expensive. You would have them made in a row of tenements with every difference in faults,—different forms, different sizes, different falls, bad materials, without traps at the apertures, and not air-tight; therefore constantly conducting a stream of polluted air from the sewers into the houses; and there will be faults which an inspector will not easily remedy when work is done in this manner.

'In what way, then, would you recommend them to be done, for efficiency? —They should be done entirely by the persons in charge of the sewers, or under the control of officers of competent skill, who should have power to enter upon the premises, and see that the whole of the work was properly done. Neither should private persons have power to make any alteration without giving notice, and making the alteration according to well-tried and approved plans. I confine my observations, however, to tenements of certain size,—to those for the labouring man, who has no power to protect himself, and who stands in need of protection. It might be deemed objectionable to exercise any control over the higher class of tenements, and the wealthier people are able to protect themselves; but all those things that are out of sight are done in the worst manner in the smaller tenements.

'If such an authority were to contract for the drainage of a whole street, how much more cheaply do you conceive the work might be done under one contract than if the labour were to be done separately, by perhaps as many different occupiers or owners as there are houses, each employing his own bricklayer?—At the least, from 10 to 15 per cent. difference. Serving a notice in writing on a poor occupier, perhaps a shifting one, that he is to get a drain made, would be of no use. Proceeding by serving notices on the owners of such tenements, is a course beset with difficulties. Many of the small owners are not readily to be found; the ownership to some of the poorest plots are in dispute. Then, when the owners are found, every owner has to seek and bargain with a bricklayer for what he does unwillingly, and whom he tells to do the work in the cheapest way he can. The owner does not usually know what instructions to give; and in nine cases out of ten the work will be badly, and at the same time expensively done. It is with the greatest difficulty that I can get the drains to my own houses properly done. Frequent complaints are made of the state of the sewers by occupants in some districts, but when they are examined it is found, in many cases, that the cause of complaint arises from their own drain not being properly made. The poorer or reluctant owner would seek a cheap or needy bricklayer, and will get an expensive one. Everything ordered of this kind may be made a job of; the bricklayer may do more than is wanted, or may make larger drains than necessary, and thereby incur useless expense. If it be done by the public authorities, leaving to the private parties to do it if they please within a limited period, under the inspection of a proper officer, it can hardly fail to be much less expensively done for the private individual himself, and it is very sure to be better done for the poor owner. The certain obstacles to any mere general enactments to have the work done by a multitude of persons will be immense, and the work will certainly be badly done, whilst, if it is well done, it will be of the greatest public advantage.'

Mr. Roe, the engineer, was asked, with reference to house drainage:

'Have you found the system of cleansing the large drains by flushing with proper supplies of water equally applicable to small drains?—Yes, equally applicable. A gentleman has tried it on a private drain of 18-inch capacity, and 1200 feet length, and it answers equally well. It is cleansed by the collection of refuse water from 30 or 40 houses.

'Might not the drains from private houses be also cleansed in the same mode?—Yes, they might have a small and cheap apparatus for carrying away all ordinary refuse. If in the small drain a brick fell in, it could not be removed by the force of the small quantity of water which could be obtained in such a situation. In our large sewers the heads of water are in some cases strong enough to sweep away loose bricks.

'Would it not be of advantage to the occupier if the private drains were under the same general superintendence?—I conceive it would in management. They are frequently put to great expense by getting persons to attend to them who really do not understand them. They are often now obliged to have recourse to the contractor's men. Private property is often drained through other private property, and when the drains are choked, if the parties are not on good terms, they will not allow each other facilities for cleansing. Under the Finsbury Local Act there is a power to enforce the cleansing of private drains, and by way of appeal that power is sometimes resorted to by private individuals.

'May we not presume that the same principles of hydraulics, as to the advantages of a flow over a semicircular bottom, are as applicable to small drains as to large ones?—More so from the flow of water being smaller; the greater necessity for keeping it in a body to enable it to carry away the common deposit.

'Then there is a proportionate loss in having the private drainage made with flat-bottomed bricks or boards?—Yes, there is proportionate loss from the extra cost of cleansing. Semicircular drains of tiles would be better, and cheaper than brick for private houses.'[1]

Supposing that only one-third of the existing tenements require drainage, the saving of 15 per cent. on the expenditure by the execution of the work by contract under the superintendence of a responsible engineer would be more than 1,500,000*l*. sterling on the outlay, independently of the difference in efficiency.

The necessity has previously been suggested of spreading the immediate cost over a number of years to make the charge coincident with the benefit. Were it left to the option of individuals to repay the cost at intervals of 20 or 30 years, and charge their tenants, as described in a supposed form of notice to them, which I have appended to illustrate the practical working of such a provision, (allowing them either to defray the whole cost at once, or execute the work themselves, under proper superintendence; if they thought they could execute it cheaper), the immediate advantages of such improvements would then have some

---

1. *San. Rep.*, App. 1, pp. 375-6,

chance of being fairly estimated as against the immediate cost and inconveniences of a change, and resistance from latent motives of hostility would be obviated.

But however the charge may be diffused, and to whatever extent opposition on the part of the smaller owners may be obviated by care, it cannot safely be overlooked that in the poorest districts where it is most important that the works should be well executed, the superior direction of such expenditure will, in the ordinary course, fall into the hands of the owners of the worst-conditioned tenements, who have the greatest dread of immediate expenses, and who are under the strongest influence of petty jealousies; for in such districts it is precisely the class of persons who cannot agree to profitable measures of private drainage, who are the owners of the worst tenements, who, having leisure during the intervals of their weekly collections, and from other causes, are most frequently found in honorary offices for the direction of local expenditure. One officer, when asked how it was that in a district where fever had been rife nothing had been done under the authority of the law, which authorized its being cleansed? replied, that the Board had made precisely the same objections that were made when the cholera appeared; when it was proposed to cleanse the district, the answer made at the Board was, that 'they did not believe it would do any good:' and those of the officers who were landlords of the weekly tenements said, 'Why should we disturb and drive away our tenants?' and those who were shopkeepers said, 'Why should we frighten away our customers by representing the neighbourhood as unhealthy?' Consequently nothing was done.

The legislature, in making demands for such honorary services, has usually proceeded on the theory which views all those who may be called upon to render them, as persons qualified to understand the whole subject intuitively, and having no other interest or views than to perform the services zealously for the common weal; whereas, in the locality they are viewed in a totally different light, not as public officers, but in their private capacities, as owners or tradesmen, competitors for advantages of various kinds. However unjust this impression may frequently be, it is the impression that commonly prevails; and since all of one class cannot have a share in the administration of such funds, others of the same class, whether owners or tradesmen, view the persons exercising the power as rivals, and distrust their administration accordingly. As an owner, one member of a local Board is strongly indisposed to any line of operations that will apparently improve the property of another; and as an owner, too, he is under the strongest jealousy if he proposes or does anything which may appear to benefit his own property at the public expense.

Neither is such distrust as to trustworthiness from skill and adverse private interests confined to the administration of the public works of sewerage and drainage; it is fortified by the example of the local administration of the works of road construction and repair, a branch of administration so inseparably connected with drainage operations, as to justify and require a joint consideration with them.

Witnesses of the most extensive practical experience lay the greatest stress on the necessity of lifting these important branches of administration out of the influence of petty and sinister interests, and of doing so by securing the appointment of officers of superior scientific attainments, who (subject to a proper local as well as general control) may be made responsible for directing any new expenditure on a scale of efficiency as well as of economy. A competent, scientific, and efficient management, let it be applied to what part of these works it may, can scarcely fail to be immediately as well as ultimately the most economical management. But it will be found on examination that the consolidation of all the structural arrangements, comprising under-drainage and surface-drainage, road structure and repair, under one service, is most required for the sake of efficiency. Division of labour in the arts derives its efficiency from combination, adaptation, and subordination to direction to one end; but that which appears to be a division of labour in local administration is, in fact, an insubordinate separation, weakening the means of procuring adequate skill and power, occasioning obstructions and defective execution, and enhancing expense. Were pins or machines made as sewers and roads are constructed; shafts of pins would be made without reference to heads,—in machines screws would be made without sockets, and, it may be confidently stated, there would not be a safe or perfect and well-working machine in the whole country.

Mr. Telford, in a report on the Holyhead road, makes the following observations:

'Perfect management must be guided by rules and regulations, and these must be carried into effect by the unceasing attention of a judicious and faithful surveyor who has by actual experience and attention acquired a thorough knowledge of all that is required, and applicable to the general and local state of particular districts, as regards soil, materials, and climate; likewise the sort of wear to which the surface is liable. A person possessed of all these requisites, and otherwise properly qualified to level and set out new lines, &c., where necessary, must receive the remuneration such a character merits, and may always obtain, in this active and industrious country. But however convinced and well-disposed trustees may be to give this remuneration, the tolls of five or six miles do not afford the means of giving it. The consequence is that the Shifnal Trust (four miles) has hitherto been under the management of a person so little acquainted with proper road business, that it becomes a serious consideration whether it will be prudent to suffer the extensive improvement at Priors Leigh to be entrusted to his care. Until the Parliamentary Commissioners interfered and showed a practical example, the Wellington Trust (seven miles) was managed almost wholly by the clerk; he had a sort of foreman, who appeared to be only partly employed on the road. And on the Shrewsbury Trust (seven miles), as has already been stated, the surveyor and contractor were united in the same person. All these managers proceeded, without regard to any rules and regulations whatever, receiving only occasional directions from some of the most active of the trustees, whose varying opinions served more to distract than benefit the practical operations of the workmen. I must beg leave to add that these observations are applicable to all trusts of similar extent, and are evidences of the propriety of establishing districts of a magnitude to justify a more perfect arrangement, and the employing of a properly qualified surveyor, whose sole occupation should be the road under his care, and who should also be enabled to keep constantly employed

State of the Local Executive Authorities

a set of workmen thoroughly conversant with road observations, and working chiefly by contract.'—*First Annual Report on the Holyhead Road*, May 4, 1824. p. 25.[1]

It need scarcely be necessary to observe that in the sense of that great engineer, care of the road implied the greatest care in respect to the drainage. In consequence of the limited areas of management, although great expense is incurred, the appointments of the surveyors to superintend works which are never well executed by any other than an experienced engineer, are inferior even to the appointments of the paid officers to superintend the sewerage. Sir Henry Parnell in his work, 'On the Formation and Management of the Public Roads,' thus compendiously describes the composition of the chief bodies by whom these officers are chosen and directed:

'According to the provisions of every Turnpike Act, a great number of persons are named as trustees; the practice is to make almost every one a trustee, residing in the vicinity of a road, who is an opulent farmer or tradesman, as well as all the nobility and persons of large landed property: so that a trust seldom consists of fewer than 100 persons, even if the length of the road to be maintained by them does not exceed a few miles. The result of this practice is, that in every set of trustees there are to be found persons who do not possess a single qualification for the office, persons who conceive they are raised by the title of a road trustee to a station of some importance, and who too often seek to show it by opposing their superiors in ability and integrity when valuable improvements are under consideration, taking care, too frequently, to turn their authority to account, by so directing the spending of the road money as may best promote the interests of themselves or their connexions.

'It sometimes happens that if one trustee, more intelligent and more public-spirited than the rest, attempts to take a lead, and proposes a measure in every way right and proper to be adopted, his ability to give advice is questioned, his presumption condemned, his motives suspected; and as every such measure will, almost always, have the effect of defeating some private object, it is commonly met either by direct rejection or some indirect contrivance for getting rid of it. In this way intelligent and public-spirited trustees become disgusted, and cease to attend meetings; for, besides frequently experiencing opposition and defeat at the hands of the least worthy of their associates, they are annoyed by the noise and language with which the discussions are carried on, and feel themselves placed in a situation in which they are exposed to insult and ill-usage.'[2]

He observes, that 'Although this turnpike system has led to the making of many new roads, and to the changing of many old ones into what may be called good roads in comparison with what they formerly were, this system has been carried into execution under such erroneous regulations, and the persons who have been entrusted with the administration of them have uniformly been either so negligent or so little acquainted with the business of making or repairing roads, that at this

---

1. 'Report of Mr. Telford for the further improvement of the road from London to Holyhead', *First Report of Commissioners for the Road from London to Holyhead*, P.P. 1824, IX, App. B, p. 25.
2. Sir Henry Parnell, *A Treatise on Roads* (1833), pp. 292-4.

moment it may be stated with the utmost correctness that there is not a road in England, except those recently made by some eminent civil engineers, which is not extremely defective in the most essential qualities of a perfect road.'[1] To the varying extent of these defects the public are forced to ascend unnecessary heights, travel unnecessary distances, employ more horse-labour than would be necessary in travelling over roads that are kept hard, dry, and level, instead of wet, soft, and rugged. From the Report of the Commissioners appointed to inquire into the subject,[2] it appears that for every 200 miles of turnpike road there are, on an average, ten surveyors: whereas, if the highways and turnpike trusts were consolidated, one properly qualified surveyor might perform much better the service with which the ten are charged. There are, it appears, 1,116 turnpike trusts, comprehending about 22,000 miles. The officers employed consist of 1,120 treasurers, 1,135 clerks, and 1,300 surveyors: total 3,555. The annual cost of the *repair* of the turnpike roads is 51*l*. per mile: total expenditure of 1,122,000*l*. per annum. The debts amounted to upwards of 9,000,000*l*., and they appeared to be rapidly increasing. The average expense of the *management* of the highway and the turnpike roads is estimated at 10*l*. per mile per annum; but it is calculated that if the management of the turnpikes and highways were consolidated, they might be better managed at an expense of from 30*s*. to 2*l*. per mile per annum. On comparing the actual expense of the repairs of roads under a scientific management of the highways with the common cost, it appears probable that by management on an extended and appropriate scale, upwards of 500,000*l*. per annum may be saved on that branch of administration alone.

The Committee of the House of Commons, which sat in 1834,[3] examined some of the most able engineers in the country, and a Commission subsequently appointed, at the head of which were the Duke of Richmond and the Marquis of Salisbury,[4] coincided in recommending the adoption of the principle of consolidation as the only means of retrieving that branch of administration.

I venture humbly to submit the grounds for the opinion in which I believe their Lordships would concur, that the principle of consolidation may be carried still further, and include all public works within the locality, as the best means of obtaining for each or for all, at the least expense, the most efficient scientific direction.

It has been shown, in respect to drainage as well as road construction, that the economy and efficiency of the works will be according to the qualifications, the powers, and responsibilities of the officers appointed

---

1. Sir Harry Parnell, *A Treatise on Roads* (1833), pp. 290-1, with some slight differences of wording.
2. *Report of Commission on the State of the Roads in England and Wales*, P.P. 1840, XXVII, pp. 8-9.
3. There was no committee on any aspect of turnpike trusts in 1834. This reference must be either to the *Second Report of the Select Committee of the House of Lords on Turnpike Returns*, P.P. 1833, XV, or to the *Report of the Select Committee on Turnpike Trusts and Tolls*, P.P. 1836, XIX, both of which came out strongly in favour of the consolidation of trusts.
4. The Commission on the State of Roads of 1840.

to execute them, secured by legislative means, and that new labour on the old condition, without skill, will be executed in the old manner, extravagantly and inefficiently. But engineers or properly qualified officers having the science of civil engineering could not be procured for every separate purpose in every part of the country, as is generally assumed in Acts of Parliament for effecting particular objects. When such connected work is divided and separated, the remuneration necessary to obtain properly qualified officers to attend to the fragment of service is too high; the separation, therefore, in most places, amounts to the exclusion of science from public work, or, in other words, to its degradation. It will be found, when the works of draining and road making and maintenance are examined, that the common practice of making sewers on plans independently of the construction of roads, and roads independently of the arrangements for cleansing and keeping them dry, is always to the disadvantage of the work and to the public. The same surface levels and surveys serve for drainage and for road construction. The construction of the drains for roads and streets, and the maintenance of them, are the primary and most important works; the construction and maintenance of the surface of the road is a connected work, subsequent in order, and can be best superintended by the same officer. In every part of the country inconveniences and losses are experienced from the separation of such work on almost every occasion where repair or new construction is needed. In the towns a road is broken up by the bursting of a sewer or the necessity of cleansing or repairing it; the sewer is repaired, but the road is left broken, because the road surveyor and his separate set of workmen are engaged in some other work. In the metropolis, the breaches left in the roads by the delay and want of concert amongst the various officers are a source not only of great obstruction but of frequent accidents. In replacing the pavements the water and the gaspipes are not unfrequently put out of order, and these again occasion another opening and another expense to the public, for repairs. In the rural districts a road is out of repair, but the first remedy is drainage; the road surveyor cannot proceed because the sewers' surveyor has his men elsewhere occupied. In various other particulars the consolidation of the same work under the same officer, acting with a combined staff of foremen and workmen, is attended with advantages in efficiency and economy to which it were unnecessary to advert, if the opposite arrangements were not the most frequent. In the few instances that have taken place of a combination of duties, the experience of the advantages of the combination would occasion a proposal for separating them to be viewed as an increase of trouble and expense, and a hinderance to the proper execution of the work.

In the districts where the greatest defects prevail, we find such an array of officers for the superintendence of public structures as would lead to the *a priori* conclusion of a high degree of perfection in the work from the apparent subdivision of labour in which it is distributed. In the same petty districts we have surveyors of sewers appointed by the commissioners of sewers, surveyors of turnpike-roads appointed by the trustees of the turnpike trusts, surveyors of highways appointed by the inhabitants in vestry, or by district boards under the Highway Act[1]; paid district surveyors appointed by the justices, surveyors of paving under local Acts, surveyors of building under the Building Act, surveyors of county bridges, &c.

The qualifications of a civil engineer involve the knowledge of the prices of the materials and labour used in construction, and also the preparation of surveys, and the general qualifications for valuations, which are usually enhanced by the extent of the range of different descriptions of property with which the valuator is conversant. The public demands for the services of such officers as valuators are often as mischievously separated and distributed as the services for the construction and maintenance of public works. Thus we have often, within the same districts, one set of persons appointed for the execution of valuations and surveys for the levy of the poor's rates; another set for the surveys and valuations for the assessed taxes; another for the land tax; another for the highway rates; another for the sewers' rates; another for the borough rates; another for the church rates; another for the county rates, where parishes neglect to pay, or are unequally assessed, and for extra-parochial places; another for tithe commutation. And these services are generally badly rendered separately at an undue expense.

It is in the ordinary course that local bodies would have the power of appointing surveyors for seeing to the execution of provisions for the regulation of buildings, on the precedent of the Metropolitan Building Act[2]; and these officers are paid by fees varying from 1*l*. to 3*l*. 10*s*. each building. In the towns, it is rare that one-story houses are erected where the ground is of much value; and it will be a low average to take all the new houses as of two stories, that is, fourth-rate houses, for which a fee of 2*l*. has been proposed to be paid. Before the building surveyor can proceed, the sewers' surveyor must have seen that the drains are properly laid, and the builder have obtained a certificate from him to that effect. The labour of the building surveyor, if properly performed, may require as much as an hour for the inspection of each new building. But the amount of the proposed fee would in general more than pay, in ordinary cases, for the construction of an efficient drain for such a tenement. Any speculating builder who is building a fourth-rate street of fifty houses, would, by removing out of the limits of the jurisdiction, save by the removal the means of erecting an additional house or drains for the whole of them.

No past or proposed legislative measures prescribe any securities for appropriate skill, or trustworthiness for the performance of such services. It is a matter of complaint in one extensive district in the metropolis, that the duty of examining the premises is performed by young men, junior clerks to the district surveyor.

In proportion as science is securely allied to local administration is its respectability enhanced and the attainment of its objects ensured. It is dangerous to legislate in detail, for the information is not usually

---

1. The General Highway Act of 1835 (5 & 6 Wm. IV, c. 50) set up Highway Boards in parishes with over 5,000 inhabitants, and authorised the appointment by these boards of salaried surveyors.
2. 50 Geo. III, c. 75, of 1810.

State of the Local Executive Authorities 385

available for legislative preparation against all existing local difficulties, still less all future important contingencies. Where detailed regulations are prescribed arbitrarily, the danger is incurred of creating an obstacle to the work intended to be forwarded. For example, it has been proposed that Parliament shall not only provide 'That every outer wall of every building shall be built of good, sound, well-burnt bricks, or good sound stone, and set in good mortar,' but shall direct and instruct the builders, and fix, against any alteration or improvement, the mode in which good mortar shall be made, viz., 'And the mortar and cement shall be *well* compounded in the proportion of *one* part of good fresh-burnt lime or cement, and *three* parts of clean sharp sand:' there, however, are large tracts of country where neither clean sand, nor sharp sand, nor sand of any sort is to be had, and where they use smiths' ashes for the purpose. But the use of this material is thenceforward illegal, and no new discovery can be adopted without the sanction of an Act of Parliament. In one large parish it was lately desired to try a pavement of wood, when it was discovered that the local Act prescribed the use of granite for pavement. In the impracticability of carrying out all such detail, or from default of defining the ends and prescribing the attainment instead of the means, or stating the means generally, as that a wall shall be built 'of incombustible materials,' it is in the usual course to require that important work shall be done in such manner as 'shall be satisfactory to the surveyor who shall inspect the same,' or 'according to the directions of the surveyor of the district,' *e.g.*, that no chimney shall be built more than six feet high, 'unless the same shall be secured by sufficient iron stays of such strength and dimensions, and to be fixed in such manner as shall be approved of by the surveyor who shall inspect the building.' The objections entertained by builders of respectability to the granting of such large powers, is founded on the certainty as to the character of the appointments of surveyors to be hereafter made if no other securities than mere general directions be taken in respect to them for the public protection. It may be a rival builder who is appointed, and it is very certain to be generally a person in trade by whom the power is exercised, whose dissatisfaction with work really fair and good may be governed by sinister considerations against which a fair builder will feel he has no defence; but the greater danger is to the public, that no dissatisfaction may be expressed with work that is cheap but unsound. The building covers bad drains, and hides rotten walls, and the effects in the calamities of spreading fires and falling houses, and calamities of sufferings, and deaths, occur in after years, when the original defect may not be detected by the closest examination, and when all concerned may have departed.

If the services of men of independent position, with the science and qualifications of engineers, were secured, their inspection of works would often be invited, and the notice they could not fail to take of unintentional and profitless errors, such as wrong levels, which detract from the convenience and value of tenements, would be of much value and be received cordially, and the exercise of discretionary authority in such hands would meet with comparatively respectful obedience.

No one can have had occasion to examine much of the business of local administration, without being aware of other evils entailed by the multiplication of badly appointed officers in addition to the evils of excessive cost and bad quality of the service to the ratepayers. One of the evils is the fuel they add to the flames of local parties, by which both parties are generally losers. Where special and scientific qualifications are not defined, or, if defined, not secured—where the most fatal errors, as in this instance, are shrouded by the nature of the work from detection—all the idle dependents of election committees who have time to spare, because they have failed in their own business for want of steady application, and because their time is worthless, are let in as candidates, and in proportion to the absence of security for qualifications is the extent of expectation created and disappointment ensured. The dreadful state of the labouring classes in the most important towns,—the entire neglect of existing sanitary regulations,—the apathy to repeated remonstrances that have been made by eminent medical practitioners, as by Dr. Ferriar in Manchester and by Dr. Currie of Liverpool,—the entire neglect of recommendations made by them, which, if carried out, would have protected those communities from immense burdens, from pestilence and slaughters worse than many wars, and from an enfeebled, diseased, and, by physical causes, a degraded generation of workpeople,—the resistance made from no other manifest cause than a blind jealousy of interference, to the exercise of powers that can have no other object than to prevent the like evils for the future,—all indicate the conclusion as to the nature of the arrangements to be expected from those who have by familiarity become insensible to the means of preventing the evils which fall with the greatest weight on the least protected classes.

Supposing population and new buildings for their accommodation to proceed at the rate at which they have hitherto done in the boroughs, and supposing all the new houses to be only fourth rate, the expense, at the ordinary rate of payment of surveyors' fees, would be about 30,000*l.* per annum for the new houses alone. Fees of half the amount required for every new building are allowed for every alteration of an old one, and the total expense of such structures would probably be near 50,000*l.* in the towns alone—an expense equal to the pay of the whole corps of Royal Engineers, or 240 men of science, for Great Britain and Ireland.*

---

* Pay of the corps of Royal Engineers for the United Kingdom of Great Britain and Ireland, consisting of 241 officers, viz.—5 colonels-commandant, at 2*l.* 14*s.* 9½*d.* per diem each; 10 colonels, at 1*l.* 6*s.* 3*d.* ditto; 20 lieutenant-colonels, at 18*s.* 1*d.* ditto; 5 lieutenant-colonels, at 16*s.* 1*d.* ditto; 40 captains, at 11*s.* 1*d.* ditto; 40 second captains, at 11*s.* 1*d.* ditto; 80 first lieutenants, at 6*s.* 10*d.* ditto; 40 second lieutenants, at 5*s.* 7*d.* ditto;—total, 48,093*l.*

Pay of the corps of Royal Sappers and Miners for general service, consisting of 961 men, officers included; viz.—Staff: 1 brigade-major, at 10*s.* per diem; 1 adjutant, at 10*s.* ditto; 1 quarter-master, at 8*s.* ditto; 2 serjeant-majors, at 4*s.* 6½*d.* ditto each; 3 quarter-master serjeants, at 4*s.* 0½*d.* ditto; 1 bugle-major, at 4*s.* 0½*d.* ditto;—total 972*l.* One company consisting of—1 colour serjeant, at 3*s.* 0½*d.* per diem; 3 serjeants, at 2*s.* 6½*d.* ditto each; 4 corporals, at 2*s.* 2½*d.* ditto; 4 second corporals, at 1*s.* 10¾*d.* ditto; 75 carpenters, masons, bricklayers, smiths, wheelers, coopers, collarmakers, painters, tailors, miners, and 2 buglers, at 1*s.* 2½*d.* per diem each;—total 3,465*l.*—*Ordnance Estimates* for 1841.

State of the Local Executive Authorities

But at the rate of increase of the population, of Great Britain, which is 230,000 per annum, (*i.e.* equal in population to the annual addition of a new county, such as Worcester or the North Riding of Yorkshire,* and to accommodate them 59,000 new tenements are required, or a number equal to that of two new towns annually such as Manchester proper, which has 32,310 houses, and Birmingham, which has 27,268 houses,) affording, if all that have equal need receive equal care, fees to the amount of no less than from 80,000*l*. to 100,000*l*. per annum. This would afford payment equal to that of the whole corps of sappers and miners, or nearly 1,000 trained men, in addition to the corps of engineers.

From a consideration of the science and skill now obtained for the public from these two corps for general service, some conception may be formed of the science and skill that might be obtained in appointments for local service, by pre-appointed securities for the possession of the like qualifications, but which are now thrown away in separate appointments at an enormous expense, where qualifications are entirely neglected.

The officers of the engineer corps have the execution and care of structural works, docks and dockyards, fortifications, military roads, and barracks, in addition to the ordinary military duties. One captain of engineers fills the office of hydraulic engineer to the Admiralty, and to his superintendence is intrusted the construction and repairs of all the docks, buildings, and other public works.

The officers of the engineers have been distinguished for their services on some of the most important civil commissions. As collateral services which they have rendered to the public, may be mentioned the trigonometrical survey of Ireland, and that now in progress for England under the Board of Ordnance, and also the geological survey. The levelling, however, and the whole of the detail of the trigonometrical survey in England, is taken by the privates, corporals, and sergeants of the corps of sappers and miners, who have been instructed in geometry, drawing, and mensuration at the school at Chatham. The triangulation for the detail of this work is executed by the engineer officers under the direction of the superintendent of the survey, Colonel Colby. The great majority of the surveys obtained under the Parochial Survey and Valuation Act from private surveyors have been inferior to the surveys executed under

---

* It may be of interest to observe that as the whole population grows in age, the annual increase in numbers may be deemed to be equivalent to an annual increase of numbers of the average ages of the community. If they were maintained on the existing average of territory to the population in England, the additional numbers would require an annual extension of one fifty-seventh of the present territory of Great Britain, possessing the average extent of roads, commons, hills, and unproductive land. The extent of new territory required annually would form a county larger than Surrey, or Leicester, or Nottingham, or Hereford, or Cambridge, and nearly as large as Warwick. To feed the annually increased population, supposing it to consume the same proportions of meat that is consumed by the population of Manchester and its vicinity, (a consumption which appears to me to be below the average of the consumption in the metropolis,) the influx of 230,000 of new population will require for their consumption an annual increase of 27,327 head of cattle,

superintendence by the privates and non-commissioned officers of the sappers and miners serving at a pay of from 1*s*. 2*d*. to 3*s*. per diem. Out of 1,700 first-class maps received under the Parochial Assessment and Tithe Acts, not more than one-half displayed qualifications for the execution of public surveys without superintendence. Amongst the most satisfactory maps of the first class of parochial surveys were those executed by a retired sergeant of sappers and miners. The Commissioners for the colonization of South Australia found it difficult to proceed satisfactorily with persons of the ordinary qualifications of surveyors or civil engineers for that country; and deemed it requisite to obtain the services of an engineer officer, with a suitable number of trained men, sappers and miners, under his command.

But for the construction and care of local works, sewers, roads, and drains and houses, no qualification whatsoever is usually conceived to be requisite. The chairman of the Holborn and Finsbury Commission of Sewers, where a change of management so beneficial to the health, and so economical of the funds of the ratepayers, was obtained by placing the work under the direction of an engineer, informed me that when that commission advertised for a person to act as surveyor to the works who understood the use of the spirit level, the candidates, who were nearly all common housebuilders, were greatly surprised at the novel demand, and several of them began to learn the use of that instrument in order to qualify them for the appointment. In the canvassing letters which I have seen for parochial or local surveyorships, I never observed qualifications for skill or science even adverted to; and where a special qualification happens to be prescribed by statute, it is not regarded. For example, the Act of the 5 and 6 Wm. IV enables the parochial vestries to appoint as surveyor a person of 'skill and experience' to serve the office of surveyor of such parish. As an example of this description of appointments, I may mention one where, in an important district, the person appointed was an illiterate tinman, a leading speaker at parish meetings, who, for a service occupying a part of his time, receives a salary of 150*l*. per annum, *i.e.*, as much as a lieutenant of engineers and a private, or as much as three sergeants of sappers and miners, whose whole time is devoted to the public service.

---

* *contd.:*
70,319 sheep, 64,715 lambs, and 7,894 calves, to raise which an annual increase of upwards of 81,000 acres of good pasture land would be required. Taking the consumption of wheat or bread to be on the scale of a common dietary, *i.e.*, 56 oz. daily for a family of a man, woman, and three children, then the annual addition of supply of wheat required will be about 105,000 quarters, requiring 28,058 acres of land, yielding 30 bushels of wheat to an acre; the total amount of good land requisite for raising the chief articles of food will therefore be in all about 109,000 acres of good pasture land annually. If the increase of production obtained by the use of the refuse of Edinburgh (that is, of 3,900 oxen from one quarter of the refuse of Edinburgh) be taken as the scale of production obtainable by appropriate measures, the refuse of the metropolis alone that is now thrown away would serve to feed no less than 218,288 oxen annually, which would be equivalent to the produce of double that number of acres of good pasture land.

State of the Local Executive Authorities

The mode in which such emoluments are at present wasted in the course of administration under the Building Acts, and the extent of science and skill that might be obtained for all purposes by the same amount of money, may be seen by the rate of surveyors' emoluments for a single town. I submit, for example, the town of Leeds. There the average rate of increase of houses having been 855 per annum, and of families 940, it may be assumed that they will continue to increase at the same rate, that is, of two new houses and three-tenths per diem, which, if they were only fourth-rate houses, would be required to pay in fees 4*l*. 12*s*. per diem for two or three hours' service at the ordinary rate of payment to private surveyors. If we bear in mind the evidence as to the character of the past appointments, and of the works themselves, and consider that, where no securities are taken for qualifications, none will be found except by accident, the contrast with the payment for the services of men of superior qualifications will be clearly perceived. Such an amount of emolument would defray the expense of a whole Board of superior officers at the rate of pay to the officers of the corps of engineers:

Board of Officers

	£	s.	d.
1 Colonel	1	6	3
1 Lieutenant-colonel	0	18	1
2 Captains, at 11*s*. 1*d*.	1	2	2
2 First lieutenants, at 6*s*. 10*d*.	0	13	8
2 Second ditto, at 5*s*. 7*d*.	0	11	2
	4	11	4

Or if unity of direction and execution were required, the staff of officers and men at the rate of pay for general service from the public would be as follows. The rate of pay therein stated is subsistence pay: the half-fees for every alteration made in a building would in most cases suffice for the extra pay given to officers and men in active service:

	£	s.	d.
1 Captain	0	11	1
2 First lieutenants	0	13	8
3 Second ditto	0	16	9
1 Colour-sergeant	0	3	0½
3 Sergeants, at 2*s*. 6½*d*.	0	7	7½
6 Corporals, at 2*s*. 2½*d*.	0	13	3
22 Privates, at 1*s*. 2½*d*.	1	6	7
	4	12	0

The high rates of remuneration ordinarily given for fragments of practically irresponsible service, would not only serve to defray the expense of direction by scientific officers, but of execution by trained subordinate officers.

The following return will afford a display of the comparative rate of emoluments in other towns from fees on the ordinary scale of surveyors' fees:

	Rate of Increase of Families per Annum	Rate of Increase of Houses per Annum	No. of New Houses per Diem	Rate of Surveyors' Fees per Diem for Fourth-class Houses £ s. d.
Liverpool	1205	638	$1\frac{7}{10}$	3 8 0
Leeds	940	855	$2\frac{3}{10}$	4 12 0
Manchester	590	589	$1\frac{6}{10}$	3 4 0
Birmingham	561	474	$1\frac{3}{10}$	2 12 0

For the construction of efficient works for drainage, it is shown that science is indispensable. If scientific officers be chosen for this one purpose, if the objectionable mode of remuneration by fees be preserved, since they are required to inspect the foundations of houses for the purpose of drainage, they might for one-fourth of the proposed fee be required to give inspection to the remainder of the work, and the process of double certificates and divided responsibility be saved. Even if the amount of work were in particular places too great to be performed by one person, it would be better, and less expensive, that it should be performed by him through an assistant, for whose defaults he should be responsible. A reduction of the accustomed fees to one-fourth, or of the aggregate emoluments obtainable under a general Building Act to 15,000*l*. or 20,000*l*. per annum would still entail the loss of so much money that might serve to secure superior scientific service; whilst in the less populous districts the payment for the separate duty of verifying the fact of compliance with the provisions of the Act would be too small to ensure the service of competent and responsible officers.

Besides the evils inherent in narrow districts, and the splitting of connected functions which prevent the application of science by preventing the appointment of scientific officers, there are other evils attendant on such small jurisdictions and separation of functions, namely, in the mode in which the money for such expenditure is levied. The popular jealousy is excited by the further multiplication of unnecessary offices, as of clerks and collectors, but real annoyance is given by the consequent increased expense of separate collections. The prevalent repugnance to direct taxation in any shape has hitherto been greatly owing to the cause of grievances experienced in the number and oppressiveness of the collections incidental to the ordinary local taxation. Those collections confuse and obstruct the rate payers' economy. Where there are a number of rates collected at different periods, some are forgotten and not provided for; and when demanded, they fall with the inconvenience and create the irritation of a new tax. The householder may have paid the collector of his poor's rates, then the collector of his assessed taxes, then the collector of the land tax, then the collector of the watch rates, then the collector of his paving rates, then his lighting rates, then his water rates, and then he thinks he has done, when a collector calls to demand the payment of the church rates; he may have paid him, when

State of the Local Executive Authorities

another collector appears to demand the payment of a sewers' rate for two years, probably for the period of a former tenant, and for which the tenant on whom the demand is levied receives no apparent advantage. A witness says (2231), 'In Limehouse there had not been a sewer built for 100 and odd years, and there are 2,000 houses, and not a sewer to them.' Another states (2066), 'In one case a sewer rate of 6d. in the pound was levied for 10 years, without even surface drainage;' and in that case the party paid another rate to a trust for paving, lighting, and making drainage. 'We could claim six years,' says another witness (860); 'three years' rates in arrear, as against former occupiers, were levied on the incoming tenants' (1798).

In a house receiving no benefit, the occupier, having refused to pay the rate ten years, and having paid it but once in 1827, the commissioners, when he left (1834) the house, 'distrained on the newcomer, and tore down the corn-bin,' &c. His solicitor previously wrote to them that the occupier was out of town, and wished them to abstain from taking any violent measures, at the same time offering on his part to refer the matter to any competent person (2328). In another case of aggravated proceeding, Mr. William Baker, who was clerk to a like commission, complained of the state of the sewerage, and of the rates in another commission. He did not resist the rate, 'for he knew very well what the powers of the commissioners are, and it was not worth his while to resist so strong a body.' The assessments of sewers' rates are seldom strictly legal.[1]

Such rates, being small in amount, they are levied at long intervals, for the collection at once of a sum sufficient to defray the expense of collection; and because they are collected at long intervals, the irritation and resistance and trouble is great, and an additional sum is paid by the public for the collector's share of the trouble of the collection. For the collection of the assessed taxes 3d. in the pound is paid; for the collection of the sewers' rates from 6d. to 1s. in the pound is usually paid. I venture to state, that by a consolidation of the collection of such charges, enough may be saved of money (independently of the saving of oppression and irritation) from the collection of the one local tax, the sewers' rate, to pay the expense of the services of scientific officers throughout the country. At present the high constable collects the county rate from every parish, and carries it to the county treasurer, in the county town, and charges for the expense of a journey. By an easy alteration, by payment by cheques from the union treasurer to the county treasurer, in one county (Kent) 1,000l. per annum might be saved, or enough to defray the immediate expense of constructing permanent drains for upwards of 500 tenements. What might be gained on this head for immediate expenditure, in most towns, will be shown in the following extract from the evidence of *Mr. Simkiss*, the auditor of the Wolverhampton union:

What are the amounts of the chief local rates collected, in round numbers? —The poor's rates are about 4,000l., the highway rates about 2,000l., and there are rates levied by commissioners under a local Act for lighting,

---

1. Evidence reported in *Report of Select Committee on Metropolis Sewers*, P.P. 1834, XV.

watching, and improving the town, amounting to about 3,000*l*. in round numbers.

On his admission of the practicability of combining with advantage the superintendence of all this expenditure by one Board in such a town, a combination of which there are several examples, he observes:

The greatest public advantage in having those duties united would be the collection of the whole of the rates in one sum by the same individual, and payment afterwards to the several purposes.

What are the present disadvantages of a separate collection of these rates?— First, that there are three collectors to pay instead of one. 1*s*. in the pound is paid to the collector of the highway rates, which is supposed to produce 100*l*. per annum. The collector of the poor's rates is paid by a fixed salary of 150*l*. per annum. The collector of the commissioners' rates is paid 8*d*. in the pound, and he gets upwards of 100*l*. per annum. If the collection of the rates were consolidated, they might be collected for 200*l*. per annum, and upwards of 150*l*. per annum might be saved in salaries alone; but a much larger sum might be saved by a more efficient collection of the smaller rates. The surveyor's rates and the commissioners' rates not being sufficient to occupy the whole time of separate individuals, they attend to other things, and consequently much money is lost by the delay in the operation. Parties remove, or die, or leave the town. Three times the amount has been lost in Wolverhampton on the collection of the highway rate as compared with the poor's rates. The highway rate and the commissioners' rates, each being made for twelve months, the collectors usually collect from the large rate payers first; considerable time elapses before the smaller payers are called upon, consequently much is lost by the delay. I have known it that the highway rate has not been demanded in some parts of the town for seven or eight months after it has been granted. The surveyors of highways, and the commissioners of improvements, not taking so much care in obtaining securities for the smaller rates, run greater risks of defalcation. I do not advert to the collectors of the smaller rates in our town, but the collectors of the smaller rates, being tradesmen, usually use the public money in their trades, and there is frequently much peculation. The accounts of the collection and expenditure of the smaller rates are generally badly kept.

What I have already submitted will, I hope, suffice to sustain the recommendation, that at the least nothing should be done to aggravate the existing state of complication and waste, by new divisions of service and the unnecessary additions of new and unqualified officers, and that everything should be done to guard against the continued reproduction of the evils in question in districts where there is clear ground. It would, I apprehend, be practicable in the old districts to superadd the appointments of officers, with proper qualifications, without any diminution of the emoluments of the existing paid officers or any material disturbance of them.

When the great importance of the general land drainage to the health of those who labour upon it and to their most productive employment is fully considered, it will, I conceive, be found entitled to all collateral aid, to which an additional title would be conferred by equal contribution of the owners and occupiers to the expenses of public drainage. If officers of proper qualifications and responsibilities were appointed, the works for sewerage branching from the towns, and the road drainage, could not fail to aid, as indeed I conceive it should be directed to aid, the

State of the Local Executive Authorities 393

private land drainage. The same surface levels and sewerage, if made on the scale proposed by the Poor Law and Tithe Commissioners (namely, of three chains to an inch) would serve for all civil purposes, whether of towns or general land drainage, or road drainage, for determining the descent of streams, for the application of the water of which it is desirable to rid the upland wastes, and would frequently be most beneficially applied for the use of the towns, and for the use of the poorer districts.

The appointment of persons having the scientific qualifications and position of civil engineers might serve to supply a want which is generally found to be the chief impediment to the drainage of land subdivided amongst numerous small holders, namely, the means of reference or appeal to some authority deriving confidence from skill and impartiality to determine on the need of works, and the mode of executing them, or to arbitrate; and on the compensation due from damage arising from them. Given such an authority, and in those small, but, from their great number, most important cases, where the expense of an application to Parliament is out of the question, it might be safe to say, by a general provision, that the inhabitants of a town may procure springs of water, and make, deepen, and scour drains through the circumjacent district; that regulations may be made for arching over or covering the sewers to proper distances from the towns; for the purchase of ground, and for the erection of works for rendering the refuse of the towns available for agricultural purposes: power might also be given to lay pipes in the highways, to put plugs for the supplies of water against fires, and for watering the roads.

On referring to the experience of the efforts made in Ireland for the drainage and reclaiming of bog lands, by which large tracts would be obtained, it appears that the working of legislative measures for those purposes have extensively failed, because the landowners had not sufficient security that the work would be properly planned and executed.*

---

* By the statute of 1 and 2 Wm. IV, c. 57, power was given to undertakers to contract for the improvement of land in Ireland, on condition that they should receive a profit which was in no case to exceed 15*l*. per cent. on the outlay. The undertakers, on the consent of two-thirds of the proprietors or of the lessees, were to apply to the Lord-lieutenant for a commission. Individual proprietors or lessees, not exceeding six in number, upon receiving the assent of two-thirds of the proprietors or lessees, might also apply for a commission. To the reason above assigned for the failure, these must be added—that the machinery of the Act is considered complicated; that it nevertheless contained no provisions for ascertaining boundaries, without which in Ireland it would be unsafe to raise any annuity upon the lands; that the mode of repayment, *i.e.*, that if the landlords did not within a certain time pay the gross sum assessed, the undertakers were entitled to a redeemable annuity upon the lands drained; but there was no provision to compel the landowners to pay the gross sum, and the annuities might be small and numerous.[1]

---

1. For this act and other Irish land improvement schemes of this period, see R. D. C. Black, *Economic Thought and the Irish Question, 1817-1870* (Cambridge 1960) pp. 173-5.

VII. Recognised Principles of Legislation

I would here beg leave to guard myself from an apparent inconsistency. In 1838, I was examined before a committee of the House of Commons on their resolution, 'That it is expedient that the parishes, townships, and extra-parochial places should be united in districts for the repair of the highways throughout England and Wales.' On that occasion I adverted to the evil of the unnecessary multiplication of new establishments as well as new officers, to their inevitable inefficiency and to the expense and obstruction to improvement which they created; and I submitted these, amongst other grounds, for proposing that the new duties should devolve on the boards of guardians of the new unions, as such duties had been in various instances combined under local Acts. The committee recommended the proposal for adoption. On the premises then placed before me, as to the expediency of establishing a new administrative body with new clerks and officers for the collection and management of the fund for repairs of the highways *alone*, and in small districts for which even the areas of unions were thought large, I should still adhere to the same conclusion.*[1]

The present inquiry, however, has shown the general primary importance of the works of sewerage and drainage throughout the country. The execution of those works would properly devolve upon the commissioners of sewers already in existence in the towns, or in the marsh

---

* Except in endeavouring to give more emphatic recommendations as to the importance of making all the paid officers really responsible, I should not vary the representation I had then the honour to make in respect to the means of giving efficiency to local administration. 'With respect to the allusion of Mr. Earle, as to the cry of centralization, I conceive that it is a cry to which the few who use it can attach no definite ideas, and it has certainly had little influence except with the most ignorant. The phrase has been used abroad against the destruction of the authority of local administrative bodies, and the substitution of an inefficient and *irresponsible* agency by the general government. But even abroad, all those who call themselves the friends of popular liberty do not declaim against centralization, but against *irresponsibility*. Here the phrase is used against a measure by which strong local administrative bodies of representatives have been created over the greater part of the country, where nothing deserving the name of systematised local administration has heretofore existed. The central board may be described as an agency necessary for consolidating and preserving the local administration, by communicating to each board the principles deducible from the experience of the whole; and, in cases such as those in which its intervention is now actually sought, acting so as to protect the administration being torn by disputes between members of the same local board; between a part or a minority of the inhabitants and the board, and between one local board and another, and in numerous other cases affording an appeal to a distant and locally disinterested, yet highly responsible authority, which may interpose to prevent the local administrative functions being torn or injured by local dissentions. I feel confident that the more the subject is examined, the more clearly it will be perceived that the great security for the purity and improvement of local administration must depend on a central agency.'[2]

---

1. *Report of the Select Committee on the Highways Act*, P.P. 1837-8, XXIII, Qs. 142-200, 293-306.
2. *Ibid.*, Q. 306.

districts, or upon commissions of sewers which it will be found necessary to issue to places where there has been no need of surface drainage, but which stand in need of under-drainage. These being the primary works for making the ground clear and keeping it clear for all other works, would necessarily require the highest science and skill, and the strongest establishment; and it would be only carrying farther the principle of consolidation, as the only means of obtaining the most efficient service, the most conveniently and at the lowest cost, now to recommend that the care of the roads should, of all structural works, be made to devolve upon that body which has the best means of executing them, namely, the commissions of sewers, revised as to jurisdiction, and amended and strengthened as to power and responsibility. What Colonel J. F. Burgoyne, the experienced chairman of the Board of Works in Ireland, stated in his evidence before the committee of the House Commons in 1836, (question 35,) on the consolidation of the turnpike trusts, may be applied to the consolidation of other local works:—'One office and account will then do for the whole; a superior superintendent could then be employed, and more perfect machinery; the means will be more generally available, and can be concentrated where required, by which the works will be carried on with more advantage, and a system of regular and rigid maintenance can be established so much more economical and beneficial than that of occasional and periodical repairs.'[1]

It is due to state that in petitions from ratepayers much dissatisfaction is expressed with the proceedings of the commissions of sewers, and their objectionable working is assigned to their irresponsibility, and a favourite remedy proposed is to make them elective; but if the administration of expenditure by elective vestries be examined, it is found to be no better; and of entirely open vestries, even worse; and the practical responsibility for injustice done to individuals, or to any one who cannot get up a party, still less. It may, however, be submitted for consideration, whether the commissions for sewers might not be so far modified as to admit some infusion of the representative principle in their composition, by including, as ex-officio members of the commission, the chairman and vice-chairmen for the time being of the Boards of Guardians of the poor law unions included within the jurisdiction of the commission. These officers are elected by the elected representatives of the ratepayers—the guardians. It will be seen that much of the evil which the preventive measures within the province of the commission of sewers must provide against, is presented, in the first instance, to the Board of Guardians, in the shape of claims to relief on the ground of destitution occasioned by sickness. The chairman or the vice-chairman, before whom the cases are thus brought, would form an efficient medium of communication. The measures of drainage and structural improvement are permanent improvements of the greatest importance to the labouring men, in common with other classes; but it is matter of fact that such improvements are the least supported by

---

1. *Report of the Select Committee on Turnpike Trusts and Tolls*, P.P. 1836, XIX, Q. 35.

those who have the least permanent interest—the smaller occupiers; or by those who have the least means and have the greatest dread of immediate expenses—the smaller owners. The chairmen and the vice-chairmen of the unions in the rural districts are, however, the chief landed proprietors, who are elected by the guardians for the interest they take in the improvement of local administration. The most important improvements in the residences of the labouring classes that have been brought to view by this inquiry have arisen from the spontaneous benevolence of the larger proprietors; and so much improvement must depend upon their voluntary exertion, that, for the sake of the labouring classes, it recommends itself as an important arrangement, that those who, as chairmen of the Boards, have the distribution of relief to the destitution attendant on sickness, should be placed in a position to represent the need of the means of prevention, and urge forward their execution.

When the extent of the removable causes of sickness and mortality are more clearly and extensively understood, as they will be, the Board of Guardians will of necessity occupy much of the position of the Leet, as a body fitted to act on complaints made, and to reclaim the execution of the law against omissions and infractions which occasion illness or injury to the most helpless classes.

Boards of Health, or Public Officers for the Prevention of Disease

In reports and communications, the institution of district Boards of Health is frequently recommended, but in general terms, and they nowhere specify what shall be their powers, how they shall seek out information or receive it, and how act upon it. The recommendation is also sanctioned by the committee which sat to inquire into the health of large towns; and the committee state that 'the principal duty and object of these boards of health would be precautionary and preventive, to turn the public attention to the causes of illness, and to suggest means by which the sources of contagion might be removed.' 'Such boards would probably have a clerk, paid for his services, whose duty it would be to make minutes of the proceedings, and give such returns in a short tabular form as might be useful for reference, and important, as affording easy information on a subject of such vital interest to the people.'[1]

I would submit that it is shown by the evidence collected in the present inquiry, that the great preventives—drainage, street and house cleansing by means of supplies of water and improved sewerage, and especially the introduction of cheaper and more efficient modes of removing all noxious refuse from the towns—are operations for which aid must be sought from the science of the civil engineer, not from the physician, who has done his work when he has pointed out the disease that results from the neglect of proper administrative measures, and has alleviated the sufferings of the victims. After the cholera had passed,[2] several of the

---

1. *Report of the Select Committee on the Health of Towns*, P.P. 1840, XI, p. xix.
2. The cholera epidemic of 1831-2, when the local Boards of Health were established.

Boards of Health for the Prevention of Disease

local boards of health that were appointed on its appearance continued their meetings and made representations; but the alarm had passed, and although the evils represented were often much greater than the cholera, the representations produced no effect, and the boards broke up. In Paris a Board of Health has been in operation during several years, but if their operations, as displayed in their reports, be considered, it will be evident that, although they have examined many important questions and have made representations, recommending for practical application some of the principles developed in the course of the present inquiry; still as they had no executive power, their representations have produced no effect, and the labouring population of Paris is shown to be, with all the advantages of climate, in a sanitary condition even worse than the labouring population of London. In the Appendix I have submitted a translation of a report descriptive of the labours of the Conseil de Salubrité, in Paris.[1] From this report it will be seen that they have few or no initiative functions, and that they are chiefly called into action by references made to them by the public authorities to examine and give their opinion on medical questions that may arise in the course of public administration as to what manufacturing or other operations are or are not injurious to the public health.

The action of a board of health upon such evils as those in question must depend upon the arrangements for bringing under its notice the evils to be remedied. A body of gentlemen sitting in a room will soon find themselves with few means of action if there be no agency to bring the subject matters before them; and an inquiring agency to seek out the evils from house to house, wherever those evils may be found, to follow on the footsteps of the private practitioner would be apparently attended with much practical difficulty.

The statements of the condition of considerable proportions of the labouring population of the towns into which the present inquiries have been carried have been received with surprise by persons of the wealthier classes living in the immediate vicinity, to whom the facts were as strange as if they related to foreigners or the natives of an unknown country. When Dr. Arnott with myself and others were examining the abodes of the poorest classes in Glasgow and Edinburgh, we were regarded with astonishment; and it was frequently declared by the inmates, that they had never for many years witnessed the approach or the presence of persons of that condition near them. We have found that the inhabitants of the front houses in many of the main streets of those towns and of the metropolis, have never entered the adjoining courts, or seen the interior of any of the tenements, situate at the backs of their own houses, in which their own workpeople or dependents reside.

The duty of visiting loathsome abodes, amidst close atmospheres compounded of smoke and offensive odours, and everything to revolt the senses, is a duty which can only be expected to be regularly performed under much stronger motives than can commonly be imposed on honorary officers, and cannot be depended upon even from paid officers where they are not subjected to strong checks. The examination of

---

1. *San. Rep.*, Appendix 14, pp. 409-23.

loathsome prisons has gained one individual a national and European celebrity. Yet we have seen that there are whole streets of houses, composing some of the wynds of Glasgow and Edinburgh, and great numbers of the courts in London, and the older towns in England, in which the condition of every inhabited room, and the physical condition of the inmates, is even more horrible than the worst of the dungeons that Howard ever visited. In Ireland provisions for the appointment of Boards of Health have been made, but they appear to have failed entirely. One of the medical practitioners examined before the Committee of the House of Commons was asked, in respect to the operation of these provisions:

'3297. But in ordinary times, when the fever is not of very great intensity, and is confined to the dwellings of the humbler classes, there is no such provision put into force?—No, but then there is another provision which may be put into force; this Act provides, that "whenever in any city, town, or district, any fever or contagious distemper shall prevail, or be known to exist, it shall and may be lawful for any one or more magistrates, upon the requisition of five respectable householders, to convene a meeting of the magistrates and householders of such city, town, or district, and of the medical practitioners within the same, in order to examine into the circumstances attending such fever or contagious distemper." There is another Act of 59 Geo. III., c. 41, which enables the parishes to appoint officers of health; that is, a permanent power. Those officers have very considerable authority; they can assess a rate.

'3298. Are they appointed?—They are appointed, I think, in all the parishes in Dublin except two; but they are inoperative: they are unpaid, and it is a very disgusting duty. They can be made to serve, but there is not control as to the amount of service they perform; so that the provision is quite inoperative, unless an alarm exists.

'3299. Do you not think the appointment of some such officers, properly appointed, properly paid, and having reasonable power, for the purpose of suggesting and enforcing such measures as shall be beneficial, would be highly valuable?—I am sure it would, and it would save an amazing quantity of expenditure to the country.'[1]

It has only been under the strong pressure of professional duties by the physicians and paid medical and relieving officers responsible for visiting the abodes of the persons reduced to destitution by disease that the condition of those abodes in the metropolis have of late been known; and I believe that it is only under continued pressure and strong responsibilities and interests in prevention that investigation will be carried into such places, and the extensive physical causes of disease be effectually eradicated.

Whilst experience gives little promise even of inquiries from such a body as Boards of Health without responsibilities, still less of any important results from the mere representations of such bodies separated from executive authority, I would submit for consideration what appears to me a more advantageous application of medical science, viz., by uniting it with boards having executive authority.

Now, the claim to relief on the ground of destitution created by sickness, which carries the medical officer of the union to the interior of

1. *Report of the Select Committee on the Health of Towns*, P.P. 1840, XI, evidence of Dr. H. Maunsell, Qs. 3297-9.

the abode of the sufferer, appears to be the means of carrying investigation precisely to the place where the evil is the most rife, and where the public intervention is most called for. In the metropolis the number of cases of fever alone on which the medical officers were required to visit the applicants for relief, at their own residences, amounted during one year to nearly 14,000. The number of medical officers attached to the new unions throughout the country, and engaged in visiting the claimants to relief on account of sickness, is at this time about 2,300.

Were it practicable to attach as numerous a body of paid officers to any local Boards of Health that could be established, it would scarcely be practicable to insure as certain and well directed an examination of the residences of the labouring classes as I conceive may be ensured from the medical officers of the unions. In support of these anticipations of the efficiency of the agency of the medical officers when directed to the formation of sanitary measures, I beg leave to refer to the experience of a partial trial of them under a clause of the recent Metropolitan Police Act[2], by which it is provided, that if the guardians of the poor of an union or parish, or the churchwardens and overseers of the poor of any parish within the Metropolitan Police district, together with the medical officer of any such parish or union, shall be of opinion, and shall certify under the hands of two or more of such guardians, churchwardens, and overseers, and of such medical officer, that any house, or part of any house, is in such a filthy unwholesome condition that the health of the inmates is thereby endangered, then the magistrates may, after due notice to the occupiers, cause the house to be cleansed at his expense.

The defects of the provision are, that it only authorizes cleansing and not providing for the means of cleansing and personal cleanliness, by directing supplies of water to be laid on; that it does not extend to the alterations of the external condition of the dwelling; that the immediate expense falls upon the occupier, who is usually in so abject a state of destitution as to serve as a barrier to any proceeding apparently tending to any penal infliction. With all these disadvantages, its working may be submitted to show the general eligibility of the medical officers of unions as officers for the execution of sanitary measures. The following account is given by the clerk to the Board of Guardians of Bethnal Green of the working of the provision in that part of the metropolis:

Mr. William Brutton.—We have taken prompt measures to execute the clause of the Metropolitan Police Act, and the Commissioners' recommendations upon it, in our parish, and the effect produced has already been beneficial. For example, the medical officer recently reported, through me, to the Board of Guardians, that fever had arisen in certain small tenements in a court called Nicholl's Court, and that it was likely to spread amongst the poorer classes in the district. He reported that others of the houses than those in which fever existed (and the inmates) were in a filthy condition, and that, unless measures were taken for cleansing them properly, fever must necessarily ensue. The Board, on receiving this communication, desired me to proceed instantly, and take such measures as appeared to me to be necessary for the abatement and prevention of the evil. I immediately obtained a summons

---

1. 2 & 3 Vic., c. 71, of 1839.

from the magistrates for the attendance of the owner of the houses. He came directly, and stated that he was not aware that the premises were in the condition in which our medical officer had found them; and he promised that measures should be taken for proper cleansing. Those measures were taken: the furniture of the houses was taken out and washed; the houses were limewashed. Some of those who were ill died, but the progress of the fever was certainly arrested.

The Board followed up these proceedings by circulating the Commissioners' instruction and form of notification in every part of the parish.

But the proceeding had a very good effect in the immediate neighbourhood. The proceeding was observed by the neighbours, and there is every reason to believe that they have set to work to cleanse and prevent a similar visitation. We have also learned that the landlords of some of these smaller tenements have been rather more particular than before: they have said we must see to the cleansing of these places lest we should be had up for it before the magistrates.

The guardians, considering the form of notifications useful, have directed that they should be issued periodically before the times when disease usually appears. In the course of a fortnight or three weeks hence, when the equinoctial gales prevail, and when we have usually much sickness and claims to relief, we shall probably have another issue of the notifications.

We have also given instructions to the relieving officer, as well as the medical officer, to report on the existence of any filth or things likely to be productive of disease that he may observe in the course of his visits to the houses where he is called by the claims to relief. The services of the relieving officer are highly important, as he has an opportunity of observing the state of filth and the obvious predisposition, and perhaps of causes of disease, preventing it before the visits of the medical officer, who is of course only called upon to attend when disease has arisen. The relieving officers visit more frequently than the medical officer, and give the tickets or orders requiring his attendance.

You are Commissioner of the Sewers in the Tower Hamlets, are you not?—Yes, I am.

And you are of course aware of their procedure?—Yes.

Do you think that body would be available for the execution of sanitary measures?—Certainly not as compared with the Board of Guardians: the Commissioners of Sewers meet only monthly, and have no medical officers and no relieving officers. The Board of Guardians meets weekly, and their officers are constantly at work, night and morning. We have not even waited for the landlords, where prompt measures appeared to be necessary for the removal of any active cause of disease. Where cesspools have overflowed, and where there has been a stoppage of water, we have directed the surveyor of the roads to ascertain the cause of the stoppage, and to remedy the mischief forthwith.

But what legal right have the guardians had to do that: they have no legal right to direct the road surveyor in the performance of his duties?—Strictly speaking, we have not, but we have forcibly suggested it as a matter of expediency.

Between the notification of the evil and the execution of the remedy, in the example you have cited by the Board of Guardians, what length of time elapsed?—From the Friday to the Monday following.

What time, so far as you have had experience, need ordinarily elapse if execution follow immediately on the report?—Execution would follow immediately on the order of the Board of Guardians. I think, however, that the union officers should, in case of emergency, have a summary acting power immediately for the preservation of life. The Guardians thought their examination of the spot unnecessary after the report of the medical officer.

The following is the examination of the clerk to the Strand union as to the practical working of the same measure in another district:

Mr. James Corder, clerk to the Strand union, examined:

What has been done in the Strand union in respect to the provisions of the Metropolitan Police Act, 2 and 3 Vict., c. 71, sec. 41, with respect to the powers conferred by that statute for the cleansing of houses which are in an unwholesome condition?

The attention of the medical officers was immediately drawn to the section of the Act, and the instructions of the Poor Law Commissioners relating thereto; and the result has been that proceedings have been had in several cases, in all of which the necessary cleansing has been performed by the owners, without the guardians being driven to the necessity of causing the requisite lime-whiting and cleansing to be done. The medical officer had frequently complained of the condition of the places into which the cleansing had been carried. Those places had for years been in the filthiest and most unwholesome condition: in some courts and alleys the pavements were covered with an accumulation of the most offensive matter, including the carcases of dead animals, such as dogs and cats, which the scavengers said formed no part of their contract to remove: their contract was only to cleanse the carriage ways. Some of these courts and alleys abound in the principal thoroughfares in the metropolis. The public, in passing through a thoroughfare like the Strand, would scarcely imagine that an evil of so much magnitude was close at hand.

The powers conferred by the clause in question appears to be restricted to the cleansing of the houses and the passages within the cartilage. What proceedings did the guardians take with relation to these external passages?

They directed the condition of the places to be represented to the Commissioners for paving and cleansing the district, who caused the filth complained of to be removed. The cleansing of the footways, however, forms no part of the duty of the Commissioners of Pavement, nor of their surveyor, nor of the scavenger appointed by them; and what was done was done extraofficially.

It cannot, therefore, be relied upon for the future?

No; and it is to be observed that the Metropolitan Paving Act evidently contemplates that the cleansing of the footways shall be done by the inmates of the houses. In the poorer districts, however, this is entirely omitted to be done; in addition to which these courts and alleys are frequently made, on account of their obscurity, a depository for most offensive matter. In the better neighbourhoods, the service of cleansing is performed by the servants; but the poor people, who rise before daylight, go to their work, and return at a late hour, have no time to cleanse their courts, and their earnings are too scanty to allow payment to others for the performance of the duty. In the better neighbourhoods, the cleansing does not always take place. The medical officers report, that there is a better average health in the streets that are well cleansed than in others where the people are otherwise in the same condition of life.

What are the main defects you have experienced in respect to the provision of the Metropolitan Police Act, empowering the guardians to take measures for cleansing houses?

First, the delay which must take place before the provisions of the Act can be put in operation. The medical officer has first to make his report to the Board of Guardians; several days elapse before the Board meets; then guardians have to inspect the premises in conjunction with the medical officer previously to certifying as to the state thereof: then application is made to the magistrate, who issues his summons, returnable in seven days; at the expiration of which, if the cleansing be not performed, the guardians are empowered to cause it to be done; but they must first obtain a magistrate's warrant for the purpose. All this engenders delay; in addition to which our guardians have, in the first instance, caused the landlord to be written to with a view to prevent further proceedings, which in some instances have been successful; but when it is not successful, it creates a further delay, during which disease may rapidly increase and spread. The second defect of the provision is, that the owners are not liable for the expenses incurred; and the occupiers are mostly of the poorest class, who have no effects on which a distraint could be made. With all these difficulties, however, this provision has been very beneficial in its operation; and it is very much to be desired that larger facilities should be afforded for carrying its intention more fully into effect. It may be added, that the medical officer should have remuneration for the trouble he entails upon himself, by a report, in attending before magistrates, until the object is effected.

Mr. John Smith, the clerk to the Whitechapel union:

Have you taken any proceedings under the 41st clause of the Metropolitan Police Act?

We have issued notifications to every house in the union of the necessity of cleansing the houses by whitewashing them inside and out, and that the owners and occupiers were amenable for any neglect. The relieving officers report to me, that these notifications have already been productive of very good effects, and that whitewashing has been actively practised. The relieving officers were instructed, wherever they found a case of neglect, to threaten the landlord that he would be proceeded against unless the tenement was duly cleansed. But as yet we have taken no legal proceedings, because we have advised with the magistrates, who do not consider that the owners can be proceeded against in the first instance, and the occupiers of the tenements, which are liable to be proceeded against, are most of them paupers and persons in extreme poverty.

With respect to the remedies, I find that the personal inconvenience to which the clause subjects the guardians of visiting the spot is a provision which will greatly obstruct its operations, and will at all events greatly delay proceedings from time to time. The guardians who, in our union, are men of business, consider that their time is full occupied at the Board, and they object to any attendance out of the Board, and would give it reluctantly. If the cases are taken before the magistrate, it appears desirable that the medical officer should not be compelled to attend unless it were absolutely requisite, and that the relieving officer should be allowed to prove the facts as to the state of the dwellings recited in the medical officer's certificate, which could rarely be disputed. If the point were disputed by the owner, then the medical officer or other witnesses might be forthcoming.

What is the number of houses in the union?—About 8,000.

How many cases on the average do your medical officers visit in the year?—About 4,000.

Those visits of course are sometimes to different rooms of the same tenement?—No doubt of that, and very frequently to the inmates of the same room.

Are the visits of the relieving officers to the dwellings of the labouring classes more extensive than the visits of the medical officers?—I should say more extensive.

Between the two, are any class of the poorer and otherwise neglected residences that would probably escape visitation?—I should say that they must visit every spot within the district.

Within such districts as that of Whitechapel, do you think the three present medical officers and the relieving officers would suffice to carry out sanitary measures actively and efficiently?—I think that for efficiency additional strength would be required; perhaps one officer, whose especial duty it should be to attend to the duties connected with sanitary measures, supposing them carried out by the agency of the existing establishments.

From the consideration of such practical evidence, it will be seen that the ordinary duties of the relieving officer in the first instance, and of the medical officer afterwards, ensure domiciliary inspection of large districts to an extent and with a degree of certainty that could scarcely be ensured or expected of any agents or members of a board of health unconnected with positive administrative duties. The inspection of these officers of the boards of guardians more than supplies the external inspection of inquests or of the leets; and it is submitted that in their position these boards may most beneficially exercise the functions of the leet in reclaiming the execution of the law, as against acts of omission and of commission, by which the poorest of the labouring classes are injured and the ratepayers burdened.

It may therefore be submitted as an eligible preliminary general arrangement, that it shall be required of the medical officer as an extra duty, for the due performance of which he should be fairly remunerated, that on visiting any person at that person's dwelling, on an order for medical relief, he shall, after having given such needful immediate relief as the case may require, examine or cause to be examined any such physical and removable causes as may have produced disease or acted as a predisposing cause to it; that he shall make out a particular statement of them, wherein he will specify any things that may be and are urgently required to be immediately removed. This statement should be given to the relieving officer, who should thereupon take measures for the removal of the nuisance at the expense of the owner of the tenement, unless he, upon notice which shall be given to him, forthwith proceed to direct their removal. Except in the way of appeal by the owner against the proceedings of either officer, or where a higher expense than 5*l*., or a year's rent of the tenement, were involved by the alterations directed by the medical officer, it appears to be recommended that no application to the Board of Guardians or the magistrates should be required in the first instance, as it frequently happens that the delay of a day in the adoption of measures may occasion the loss of life and the wide spread of contagious disease; and an application to the Board of Guardians or to the petty sessions would usually incur delay of a week or a fortnight. To repeat the words of Blackstone,—'The security of the lives and property may sometimes require so speedy a remedy, as not to allow time to call on the person on whose property the mischief has arisen to remedy it.' When any tenement is in a condition to endanger life from disease, as it comes within the principle of the law, so it should be included within its provisions, and should be placed in the same condition as a tenement condemned as being ruinous and endangering life from falling.

The instances above given of the working of the provisions of the Metropolitan Police Act for the cleansing of filthy tenements are, however, instances of zealous proceedings taken by competent officers in unions, where the attention of the guardians was specially called to the subject, and where there were no opposing interests. But several other instances might be presented, where the execution of the law is as much needed, but where it is already as dead as any of the older laws for the public protection, and the reason assigned is, that the local officers will not, for the sake of principle and without manifest compulsion, enter into conflicts by which their personal interests may be prejudiced. Medical officers, as private practitioners, are often dependent for their important private practice, and even for their office, on persons whom its strict performance might subject to expense or place in the position of defendants. Under such circumstances it is not unfrequent to hear the expression of a wish from these officers, that some person unconnected with the district may be sent to examine the afflicted place, and initiate the proper proceedings. The working of the provisions of the Factory Act for the limitation of the hours of labour of children has been much impeded by the difficulty of obtaining correct certificates of age and bodily strength from private medical practitioners. On this topic a large mass of evidence might be adduced, showing the unreasonableness of expecting private practitioners to compromise their own interests by conflicts for the public protection with persons on whom they are dependant.

Cases of difficulty requiring superior medical experience and skill occur frequently amongst the paupers. For general supervision as well as for the elucidation of particular questions, the Board have proved the practicability of obtaining for the public service the highest medical skill and science. They have availed themselves of more various acquirements than would be found in any standing *conseil de salubrité*. On questions respecting fever they have availed themselves of the services of the physician of the London Fever Hospital;[1] on questions of vaccination they have consulted the Vaccine Board of London,[2] and the authorities on the same question in Scotland. On questions as to ventilation they have availed themselves of the services of Dr. Arnott; and on the general questions affecting the sanitary condition of the population they have consulted that gentleman and Dr. Kay, and Dr. Southwood Smith, and others who could be found to have given special attention to the subject. When serious epidemics have broken out in particular unions the central Board has dispatched physicians to their aid, or suggested to the guardians that they should have recourse to the services of physicians in the neighbourhoods. The services of Dr. Arnott, Dr. Kay, and Dr. Southwood Smith were thus directed in aid of the medical officers of the eastern districts of the metropolis; and their reports first[3] developed to

1. Dr. Southwood Smith.
2. The National Vaccination Establishment was set up in 1808 with an income of £3,000 p.a. to provide free vaccination in London and elsewhere. See R. J. Lambert, 'A Victorian National Health Service. State vaccination, 1855-71', *Historical Journal*, V (1962), 2.
3. See Introduction, pp. 43-4.

Boards of Health for the Prevention of Disease

the public and the legislature the evils which form the subject of the extended inquiry, and that might otherwise have continued without chance of notice, or mitigation or removal, to have depressed the condition of the labouring classes of the population. But the results of such occasional visits appear to prove the necessity and economy of an increase of the permanent local medical service, and to establish a case for the appointment of a superior medical man for a wider district than an ordinary medical officer, for the special aid and supervision of the established medical relief.

It will frequently be found that there is the like need of immediate local inspection of the medical treatment of the destitute that there is of a grade of inspecting surgeons for the military hospitals. It cannot be otherwise than that amidst a numerous body of men there must be much error and neglect in the treatment of the destitute, in the absence of immediate securities against neglect. The most able of the guardians would confess that if they are not entirely incompetent to supervise medical service, they are at the best but imperfectly qualified for such a task, and the medical officers would act with more satisfaction to themselves from the supervision of officers from whom they might derive aid and confidence.

But besides the medical treatment of the inmates of the workhouses and prisons, there are other cases within most districts which need the preventive service of a superior medical officer for the protection of the public health.

First, in the cases where the poorer classes are assembled in such numbers as to make the assemblages *quasi* public, and afford facilities for medical inspection, as in schools.

Secondly, also in places of work and in workmen's lodging-houses. The occasional visits of a district officer, for the prevention of disease would lead to the maintenance of due ventilation, and to the protection of the workpeople on such points as are already specified as injurious to the health, and that arise simply from ignorance, and are not essential to the processes. An examination of such places, if only quarterly, would lead to the most beneficial results.

So far as I have observed the working of the Factory Act, it appears to me that the duties now performed by the sub-inspectors of factories might be more advantageously performed by superior medical officers, of the rank of army surgeons, who are independent of private practice.

I am confirmed in this view by the following evidence of *Mr. Baker*, surgeon of Leeds, the only factory inspector who has such qualifications:

'Have you, as a surgeon, whilst visiting the factories as an inspector, had occasion to exercise your professional knowledge?—Frequently; during my service I have turned out great numbers of children with scald-heads, which they were apt to propagate amongst the rest of the children; some with phthisis, whose subsequent death was more than probable; some with scrofulous ulcers; a great many with extreme cases of ophthalmia; probably I may have removed a thousand of these cases altogether. I rarely go to a mill where I do not see a case of scald-head.

'Have you ever had occasion to interpose in respect to ventilation?—

Frequently in extreme cases of variable temperature, also in cases of offensive privies, which I find attended by dysenteric affections; and also where there has been offensive water from neglected sewers. I have also endeavoured to enforce personal cleanliness on the children through the instrumentality of overlookers and parents. One practice amongst the children in all kinds of mills is to wear handkerchiefs on the head, by which the neglect of personal cleanliness was concealed. Under these handkerchiefs were most of the cases of scald-head, in a state of filthiness not easily describable. I have assured the operatives that by the Act I had the power to direct measures for the protection of their health as well as labour; and I have established in many places the rule that the children shall come with the faces clean, and the hair combed, and without handkerchiefs whilst at work.

'By such inspection of workpeople in the places of work do you conceive it would be practicable to influence largely the sanitary condition of the labouring population without inspection of the private houses?—Yes; for the ill health which was occasioned by the state of their houses or other places, would of course be visible on such inspection. If they were removed from their places of employment on the presentation of such appearances, the inattention which had occasioned it would be removed too.

'What length of time do you find such inspection would require each time, say in a mill of about 1000 persons, and how frequent should such inspection be?—On the average about two hours; to a practised eye the symptoms of indisposition are discernable almost in walking through a room. Under some circumstances an inspection of once in three months would suffice.

'Are there masters in your district who are aware of the interest they have in the health of the workpeople?—Yes; there are many who pay particular attention. I might mention two where a surgeon is specially employed to take care of their workpeople. When persons are ill, they are listless and sleepy, and negligent; there is also more waste made in the processes of manufacture.'

The superior economy of preventive services by such inspection as that above displayed will scarcely need elucidation.

From a consideration of such opportunities of inspection it will be perceived that the enforcement of sanitary regulations on such inspection by superior and independent officers, qualified by previous examination, as in the army, would be a wise economy. By such arrangements efficient medical superintendence would be provided for the independent labourer employed in crowded manufactures, as well as for the soldier and the sailor, not to speak of the pauper or the criminal. One such officer would be able so to inspect and keep under sanitary regulations the places of work, the schools and all the public establishments of such a town as Leeds, which would bring under view perhaps the greater proportion of the lower classes of the population. There would still remain, however, those of the labouring classes who do not work or lodge in large numbers, or work in a quasi-public manner, to bring them within the means of convenient inspection. There would also remain without protection the cases of persons of the middle classes.

To meet these cases, I would suggest that the information brought to the superintendent registrar as to the cause of death, imperfect and hearsay as it yet is, may serve as the most accurate index to the direction of the labours of a district officer appointed to investigate the means of protecting the health of all classes. Having suggested the registration of the causes of death (under medical superintendence), a head of information not contained in the original draught of the Deaths' Registration Bill, I would guard against an over-estimate of the importance of that provision; but I feel confident it would be found, when properly enforced, one of the most important means of guiding preventive services in an efficient direction. For example, wherever, on the examination of these registries, deaths from fever or other epidemics were found to recur regularly, and in numbers closely clustered together, there will be found, on examination, to be some common and generally removable cause in active operation within the locality. Amongst whatsoever class of persons engaged in the same occupation deaths from one disease occur in disproportionately high numbers or at low ages, the cause of that disease will generally be found to be removable, and not essential to the occupation itself. The cases of the tailors, miners, and dressmakers, and the removable circumstances which are found to govern the prevalence of consumption amongst them, I adduce, as examples of the importance of the practical suggestions to be gained from correct and trustworthy registries of the causes of death occurring in particular occupations as well as in particular places. When a death from fever or consumption occurs in a single family, in the state of isolation in which much of the population live in crowded neighbourhoods, they have rarely any means of knowing that it is not a death arising from some cause peculiar to the individual. Even medical practitioners who are not in very extensive practice may have only a few cases, and may be equally unable to see in them, in connexion with others, the operation of an extensive cause or a serious epidemic. The registration of the causes of death, however, presents to view the extent to which deaths, from the same disease, are common at the same age, at the same time, or at the same place, or in the same occupation.

One of the most important services, therefore, of a superior medical officer of a district would be to ensure the entries of the causes of death with the care proportioned to the important uses to be derived from them. The public should be taught to regard correct registration as being frequently of as much importance for the protection of the survivors as a post-mortem examination is often found to be.

The mortuary registries and the registration of the causes of death are not only valuable as necessary initiatives to the investigation of particular cases, but as checks for the performance of the duty. The system of registration in use at Geneva, combining the certificate and explanation of the private practitioners and the district physician, corresponds with a recommendation originally made for the organization of the mortuary registries in England, and the experience of that country might, perhaps, be advantageously consulted.

It would be found that the appointment of a superior medical officer independent of private practice, to superintend these various duties, would also be a measure of sound pecuniary economy.

The experience of the navy and the army and the prisons may be referred to for exemplifications of the economy in money, as well as in health and life, of such an arrangement. A portion only of the saving from an expensive and oppressive collection of the local rates would abundantly suffice to ensure for the public protection against common evils the science of a district physician, as well as the science of a district engineer. Indeed, the money now spent in comparatively fragmentitious and unsystematized local medical service for the public, would, if combined as it might be without disturbance on the occurrence of vacancies, afford advantages at each step of the combination. We have in the same towns public medical officers as inspectors of prisons, medical officers for the inspection of lunatic asylums, medical officers of the new unions, medical inspectors of recruits, medical service for the granting certificates for children under the provisions of the Factory Act[1], medical service for the post-mortem examinations of bodies, the subject of coroners' inquests, which it appears from the mortuary registries of violent deaths in England amount to between 11,000 and 12,000 annually, for which a fee of a guinea each is given. These and other services are divided in such portions as only to afford remuneration in such sums as 40*l*., 50*l*., 60*l*., or 80*l*. each; and many smaller and few larger amounts.

Whatever may be yet required for placing the union medical officers on a completely satisfactory footing, the combination of the services of several parish doctors in the service of fewer union medical officers will be found to be advances in a beneficial direction. The multiplication or the maintenance of such fragmentitious professional services is injurious to the public and the profession. It is injurious to the profession by multiplying poor, ill-paid, and ill-conditioned professional men.* Although each may be highly paid in comparison with the service rendered, the portions of service do not suffice for the maintenance of an officer without the aid of private practice; they only suffice, therefore, to sustain needy competitors for practice in narrow fields. Out of such competition the public derive no improvements in medical science, for

---

* The parish doctors in England were often paid only 20*l*. per annum for attendance in parishes of considerable extent. The payments to medical officers who have their private practice are generally quadrupled, as compared with the parish doctors. The medical arrangements in Glasgow will illustrate the frequent state of the existing arrangements in Scotland. The burgh of Glasgow, exclusive of the suburbs, is divided into 12 districts, to each of which a medical practitioner is appointed, who is paid for his services out of the poor's rates. Dr. Cowan stated of them in his report,—'The duties of the district surgeons are laborious and dangerous. Nearly all of them take fever, which involves a heavy pecuniary loss. Their salary is less than 21*l*. per annum, being less than 1*s*. for the treatment of each case.'[2] For an equivalent district in population under the New Poor Law in England, namely, in Lambeth, there are four out-door medical officers, at salaries of 107*l*. each, and two in-door medical officers, at salaries of 128*l*. each. They have in addition their private practice and fees for vaccination, and special cases. The usual rate of medical allowance to the resident medical officers of dispensaries, who are excluded from private practice, has been from 60*l*. to 70*l*. per annum.

---

1. The 1833 Factory Act required that the ages of all children, whose employment was subject to restriction, should be certified by a surgeon.
2. Robert Cowan, *Vital Statistics of Glasgow* (Glasgow 1838), p. 10.

science comes out of wide opportunities of knowledge and study, which are inconsistent with the study to make interests and the hunt for business in poor neighbourhoods.

A medical man who is restricted to the observation of only one establishment may be said to be excluded from an efficient knowledge even of that one. Medical men so restricted are generally found to possess an accurate knowledge of the morbid appearances, or of the effects amongst the people of the one establishment, but they are frequently found to be destitute of any knowledge of the pervading cause in which they are themselves enveloped, and have by familiarity lost the perception of it. Thus it was formerly in the navy that medical officers on board ship, amidst the causes of disease, the filth, and bad ventilation, and bad diet, were referring all the epidemic disease experienced exclusively to contagion from some one of the crew who was discovered to have been in a prison. We have seen that local reports present similar examples of similar conclusions from the observation of single establishments in towns, in which reports effects are attributed as essential to labour, of which effects that same labour is entirely divested in establishments in the county, or under other circumstances which the practitioners have had no means of observing and estimating. The various contradictory opinions on diet, and the older views on the innocuousness of miasma, are commonly referable to the circumstances under which the medical observers were placed; and examples abound in every district of the errors incidental to narrow ranges of observation in cases perplexed by idiosyncracies, and by numerous and varying antecedents. It should be understood by the public that the value of hospital and dispensary practice consists in the range of observation they give; and that the extent of observation or opportunities of medical knowledge are influenced or governed by administrative arrangements. In several of the medical schools of the metropolis, however, the opportunities of knowledge are dependent on the cases which may chance to arise there. Fortunate administrative arrangements have, in Paris, greatly advanced medical knowledge, by bringing large classes of cases under single observation. The most important discoveries made with respect to consumption, those made by M. Louis[1], were based on the results of the post-mortem examinations of nearly 1,300 cases by that one practitioner. Nearly all the important conclusions deduced from this extensive range of observations were at variance with his own previous opinions and the opinions that had prevailed for centuries. The later and better knowledge of the real nature of fever cases has been obtained by a similar range of observation gained from the cases in fever hospitals. Applications have been several times made to the Commissioners by medical men engaged in particular researches to aid them in the removal of the impediments to extended inquiry, by collecting the information to be derived from the sick-wards of the workhouses and the out-door medical relief lists.

The highest medical authorities would agree that, whatsoever administrative arrangements sustain narrow districts, and narrow practice,

---

1. For Louis, see above, p. 92, n. 1.

sustain at a great public expense barriers against the extension of knowledge by which the public would benefit, and that any arrangements by which such districts or confined practice is newly created, will aggravate existing evils. An examination of the state of medical practice divided amongst poor practitioners in the thinly populated districts shows that, but for the examinations, imperfect though they be, as arrangements which sustain skill and respectability, a large part of the population would be in the hands of ignorant bone-setters.

On a full examination of the duties which are suggested for a district physician, or officer of public health, that which will appear to be most serious is not the extent of new duties suggested, but the extent of the neglect of duties existing. The wants, however, which it is a duty to represent and repeat, as the most immediate and pressing, for the relief of the labouring population, are those of drainage, cleansing, and the exercise of the business of an engineer, connected with commissions of sewers, to which the services of a board of health would be auxiliary. The business of a district physician connects him more immediately with the boards of guardians, which, as having the distribution of medical relief, and the services of medical officers, I would submit, may be made, with additional aid, to do more than can be done by any local boards of health of the description given, separated from any executive authority or self-acting means of bring information before them.

I have submitted the chief grounds on which it appears to me that whatever additional force may be needed for the protection of the public health it would everywhere be obtained more economically with unity, and efficiency, and promptitude, by a single securely-qualified and well-appointed responsible local officer than by any new establishment applied in the creation of new local boards. Including, as sanitary measures, those for drainage and cleansing, and supplies of water as well as medical appliances, I would cite the remarks on provisions for the protection of the public health, made by Dr. Wilson at the conclusion of a report on the sanitary condition of the labouring population of Kelso. After having noted some particular improvements which had taken place, as it were, by chance, and independently of any particular aids of science directed to their furtherance, he remarks that 'it is impossible to avoid the conclusion that much more might still be accomplished, could we be induced to profit by a gradually extending knowledge, so as to found upon it a more wisely directed practice. When man shall be brought to acknowledge (as truth must finally constrain him to acknowledge) that it is by his own hand, through his neglect of a few obvious rules, that the seeds of disease are most lavishly sown within his frame, and diffused over communities; when he shall have required of medical science to occupy itself rather with the prevention of maladies than with their cure; when governments shall be induced to consider the preservation of a nation's health an object as important as the promotion of its commerce or the maintenance of its conquests, we may hope then to see the approach of those times when, after a life spent almost without sickness, we shall close the term of an unharassed existence by a peaceful euthanasia.'

VIII
COMMON LODGING-HOUSES

A town may be highly advanced in its own internal administration, its general drainage, and its arrangements for house and street-cleansing may be perfect, and they may be in complete action, and yet if the police of the common lodging-houses be neglected, it will be liable to the continued importation, if not the generation, of epidemic disease by the vagrant population who frequent them. I have reserved the evidence respecting them in order to submit it for separate consideration, because they may apparently be better considered independently of the administrative arrangements which affect the resident population of the labouring classes.

From almost every town from whence sanitary reports have been received that have been the results of careful examinations, the common lodging-houses are pointed out as *foci* of contagious disease within the district. These houses are stages for the various orders of tramps and mendicants who traverse the country from one end to the other, and spread physical pestilence, as well as moral depravation. The evidence everywhere received distinguishes them prominently as the subjects of immediate and decidedly strong legislative interference for the public protection.

The following extract from the Report of *Mr. E. W. Baines*, the medical officer of the Barnet union, is submitted as an example of the information received respecting them from the rural unions:

'The lodging-houses for trampers are a prolific source of disease, and productive of enormous expense to the parish in which they may be situate; from one I have within this week sent into the union workhouse six cases, namely, two of fever, three of itch and destitution, and one of inflammatory dropsy. These unhappy beings are boarded and bedded in an atmosphere of gin, brimstone, onions, and disease, until their last penny be spent, and their clothes pledged to the keeper of the house, when they are kicked out and left to the mercy of the relieving officer.'

The committee of physicians and surgeons, who have made a sanitary report on the condition of the labouring population in Birmingham, give the following account of the lodging-houses in that town:

'Lodging-houses for the lowest class of persons abound in Birmingham. They principally exist near the centre of the town, many of them in courts; but great numbers of front houses, in some of the old streets, are entirely occupied as lodging-houses. They are generally in a very filthy condition; and, being the resort of the most abandoned characters, they are sources of extreme misery and vice. These houses may be divided into three kinds,—mendicants' lodging-house, lodging-houses where Irish resort, and houses in which prostitutes live, or which they frequent.

'We find it stated in Mr. Burgess's return, that in 47 of these the sexes indiscriminately sleep together. In the day time the doors of these houses are generally thronged with dirty, half-dressed women and children; and if visited in an evening, the inmates are found to be eating, drinking, and smoking. Such houses are, for the most part, occupied by beggars and trampers, but many of them are the resort of thieves. Some idea may be formed of the description of persons who frequent some of these abodes, by stating that in two of them, one of which was situate in John-street and the

VIII. Common Lodging-Houses

other in Thomas-street, a chain, fastened at one end by a staple and at the other secured by a padlock, was placed on the outside of the door, at the foot of the staircase which led to the sleeping apartments. Upon asking the mistress of the house for what purpose that was required, she stated that she employed it to lock in the lodgers until she released them in the morning, as they would otherwise decamp, and take away whatever furniture or moveables they could carry with them. Some of these houses are occupied exclusively by foreigners. In a court in Park-street we visited one which was inhabited by Italians, men and women, with their stock of musical instruments, monkeys, and other small animals. We are informed that there is another Italian lodging-house in Lichfield-street, as well as one which is frequented only by the Flemish or German broom-girls.'[1]

In whatever part of the kingdom these receptacles are examined they exhibit common characteristics. *Dr. Jenks*, in his report on the sanitary condition of the labouring classes in Brighton, gives the following account of the lodging-houses:

'Nottingham-street is the well-known haunt of tramps and beggars; Egremont-street of the lowest prostitutes and thieves. Both streets are on elevated ground, with good surface drainage, sufficiently wide and commodious, and might easily be preserved in a decent state; but all manner of disgusting refuse is thrown out of doors, and but seldom removed by the scavengers. In Nottingham-street there are eight or nine lodging-houses. Lodging-keepers have commonly three or four houses, for each of which they pay 2s. 6d. per week. The following is a description of one of them, and may serve as an *instar omnium*:—The keeper of the lodging-house rented four of these small tenements. One room, common to the whole of the inmates, who amounted to 30, including the children, served both as kitchen and sitting-room. This room was crowded when I visited it in company with the chief police-officer, Mr. Solomons, with not less than 17 people covered with filth and rags. In the largest of the sleeping-rooms, 16 feet by 10 feet, by 7 feet high, there were six beds, five on bedsteads and one on the floor, to accommodate twelve people of both sexes, besides children. Each person paid 3d. per night. Those who could afford more could be accommodated with a small room with one bed. * * * In a word, the streets in this neighbourhood have for many years been an intolerable nuisance to the town at large. They are the resort of tramps, begging impostors, thieves, and prostitutes of the lowest description, who daily and nightly take their rounds through the town.'[2]

The following account of the lodging-houses in Manchester is from the report of *Dr. Baron Howard*:

'The pernicious effects resulting from the vitiation of the atmosphere by the congregation of many persons in a confined space are lamentably illustrated in the common *lodging-houses* of the poor; the crowded, dirty, and ill-ventilated state of which is, I conceive, without doubt one of the most prolific sources of fever in Manchester. To those who have not visited them, no description can convey anything like an accurate idea of the abominable state of these dens of filth, disease, and wretchedness.

'The great prevalence of fever in these houses during the severe epidemic of 1837-38 attracted the especial notice of the Board of the House of Recovery, who passed and transmitted the following resolution to the churchwardens on the 3d of January, 1838:—"It appearing that a great number of cases of fever originates in the common lodging-houses of the poor of the town, the Board

---

1. *Local Reps. E. & W.*, pp. 197-8.   2. *Local Reps. E. & W.*, pp. 63-4.

VIII. Common Lodging-Houses

begs to suggest to the churchwardens and sidesmen the desirableness of appointing proper persons to inspect the same, in order to prevent, as far as possible, by cleanliness and ventilation, the increase and spread of this malady." In consequence of this suggestion the parochial authorities did immediately cause some of the most filthy of these establishments to be cleansed and white-washed; but it is evident that temporary exertions of this kind, however praiseworthy, are quite inadequate to effect much permanent improvement.

'In some of these houses as many as six or eight beds are contained in a single room; in others, where the rooms are smaller, the number is necessarily less; but it seems to be the invariable practice in these "keepers of fever beds," as the proprietors were styled by Dr. Ferriar, to cram as many beds into each room as it can possibly be made to hold; and they are often placed so close to each other that there is scarcely room to pass between them. The scene which these places present at night is one of the most lamentable description; the crowded state of the beds, filled promiscuously with men, women, and children; the floor covered over with the filthy and ragged clothes they have just put off, and with their various bundles and packages, containing all the property they possess, mark the depraved and blunted state of their feelings, and the moral and social disorder which exists. The suffocating stench and heat of the atmosphere are almost intolerable to a person coming from the open air, and plainly indicate its insalubrity. Even if the place be inspected during the day, the state of things is not much better. Several persons will very commonly be found in bed; one is probably sick, a second is perhaps sleeping away the effects of the previous night's debauch, while another is possibly dozing away his time because he has no employment, or is taking his rest now because he obtains his living by some night work. In consequence of this occupation of the room during the day, the windows are kept constantly closed, ventilation is entirely neglected, and the vitiated atmosphere is ever ready to communicate its poisonous influence to the first fresh comer whom habit has not yet rendered insensible to its effects, an exemption which seems to be in some degree acquired by habitual exposure, and which accounts for the immunity frequently enjoyed by the keepers themselves of these houses, whilst their lodgers are attacked in succession. This circumstance, which was particularly noticed by Dr. Ferriar, I have often observed. Where cellars are occupied as lodging-houses, the back room is generally used as the sleeping apartment; and as this has often no window, and can only receive air and light through the door opening into the front room, the utter impossibility of ventilation renders the ravages of infectious fevers particularly destructive when they once find entrance.

'The beds and bedding, being seldom washed or changed, are generally in the most filthy condition, and consisting usually of those porous materials to which contagious vapours are especially liable to attach themselves, the danger of sleeping in them may be well conceived. Even if a bed has been occupied by a fever patient who has died, or been removed, it is often immediately used by fresh lodgers, without having undergone any purification.

'The disgraceful state of these lodging-houses has been dwelt upon at some length, because I consider their evils of a most serious and extensive nature, and I feel quite satisfied they are the most malignant *foci* of infectious fevers in Manchester. Indeed it is my decided opinion that the vitiation of the atmosphere by the living is much more injurious to the constitution than its impregnation with the effluvia from dead organic matter; and certainly all I have observed in Manchester induces me to consider the "human miasms" generated in over-crowded and ill-ventilated rooms as a far more frequent and efficient cause of fever than the malaria arising from collections of refuse and want of drainage. I have been led to this conclusion from having remarked that fever has generally prevailed more extensively in those houses where the greatest numbers were crowded together, and where ventilation was most deficient, although the streets in which they are situated may be well paved, drained, and tolerably free from filth, than in those where there was less crowding, notwithstanding their location in the midst of nuisances giving rise to malaria. This inference is also supported by the fact of the higher relative proportion of fever to other diseases which has been shown to exist in the collegiate church district, where the number of crowded lodging-houses and confined courts, the closely compacted state of the buildings, the narrowness of the streets, and consequent density of the population and absence of ventilations, are most remarkable.'[1]

Mr. John Rayner, medical officer of the Stockport union, gives the following account of the lodging-houses in that town:

'The lodging-houses in these districts, which are principally occupied by the Irish labourers, are for the most part very much crowded, and are in a remarkably filthy state. The beds and bedding are not only loathsome to the sight but are extremely offensive to the smell, and are so closely packed that several families may occupy the same room, each bed containing several persons. In such places the married and single often repose together, and the beds are so arranged, that in some instances there is not room for a person to walk between them. I have seen seven persons in the same bed, and last week removed to the infirmary a case of rheumatic fever, with translation of the disease to the heart, from a bed which every night contains *eight* persons. I have generally found that the lower order of Irish labourers occupy the most filthy districts, and that wherever they *colonize*, misery and wretchedness is sure to abound. They are the most common applicants for medical relief at our charity.'

'I lately had a case of inflammation of the absorbments of the legs, from a trifling injury to the foot, in an Irish boy, who was living in a dark, damp cellar, about four yards square, in which were two beds. The height of the ceiling was not more than six feet, and yet *seven* persons laid in it, together with a few rabbits. One of the beds had to be removed from the wall on account of its extreme dampness, and so dark was the dwelling at mid-day, that I had to make use of a candle whilst inspecting him.'

The following is the description of the lodging-houses at the next stage, by the relieving officer of the Macclesfield union:

Mr. James Bland, medical officer of the Macclesfield union:

'I beg to observe that the lodging-houses are a fruitful source of fever. The persons renting these tenements showed greater resistance than others in having their houses properly whitewashed at the time the epidemic cholera appeared. The vagrants who visit these houses are frequently attacked with fever: exposed during the day to the inclemency of the seasons, with their imperfect covering, ragged clothes, and naked feet, at night thrust into a room perhaps of 16 or 20 square yards, having perhaps five or six beds and three individuals in a bed, married and single, male and female, to all appearance indiscriminately lodged. When a case of illness occurs, the lodging-house keeper is most importunate and clamorous in demanding relief from the town; and when obtained, it is quite a question whether it will really be applied to the wants of the sufferer. I have never any confidence that the remedies given will be administered to the patient.'

---

1. *Local Reps. E. & W.*, pp. 318, 319-20, 321.

VIII. Common Lodging-Houses

The further stages of the lodging-houses on the northern roads are thus described in the reports:

Mr. Nicholas Oliver, the medical officer of Durham, thus describes the lodging-houses in that town:

'One fruitful source of generating and propagating contagious diseases is to be found in those common lodging-houses where vagrants and mendicants, or any one whatever, whether healthy or diseased, are for a trifling sum provided with lodgings. I have known 40 persons half clothed, lodged in one of those wretched dwellings, three or four lying in one bed upon straw, and only a single counterpane to cover them, which is never changed. Excrementitious matter was allowed to accumulate and be about the rooms in all directions, the stench being most revolting. In the beginning of summer fever of a typhoid type occurred in this house and affected a number of the inmates, but being in the other district, they came under the care of the other medical attendant.'

The medical officer of the Teesdale union gives the following description of the houses in that stage:

'In this court there are eight common lodging-houses, and the number of lodgers sometimes amounts to 100; at this time it is 50: eight or ten sleeping in a room, upon the most unwholesome straw. The buildings are in general good; but the wretched and filthy state of the houses can scarcely be conceived. From this part many of our applications arise. It is, indeed, a source of physical and moral disease.'

Mr. Gilbert Ward, the medical officer of the Tynemouth union, describes the lodging-houses there as sources of disease, of which one example may suffice:

'In a low, damp, dirty, ill-ventilated, miserable hovel, kept by the most filthy people I ever beheld, containing four beds seldom changed, and which I have witnessed filled with beggars of the lowest description, there have been the following cases:—A son and daughter died, another son and daughter had the disease, and the mother had two attacks, all within a period of 18 months. This family, in consequence of their filthy habits, was removed to the workhouse, but could not be induced to remain; and they again returned to their old quarters, and were afflicted as above described.

'The constable has several times visited these houses, to endeavour to prevent the nuisance of so many congregating in them; but his efforts have hitherto been ineffectual.'

Sir John Walsham thus exemplifies the descriptions he has received of the lodging-houses in Newcastle:

'There is a considerable number of lodging-houses in Newcastle, some of the rooms of which are frequently occupied by from 15 to 20 persons each. In these houses the most deplorable scenes of profligacy and depravity are met with, both sexes being crowded together in a manner injurious to both health and morals.

'A medical gentleman told me, in Stockton, this morning, that in the common lodging-houses where travelling vagrants are frequently attacked with fever, &c., and in many cases die, the beds are the very next night occupied by fresh inmates, who of course are infected with the same disorder.'[1]

And one of the relieving officers for the same town says:

'I have frequently had occasion to complain to the magistrates against the

---

1. *Local Reps. E. & W.*, p. 418.

lodging-houses taking in so many lodgers; but the law in this respect is so defective that they could render me no assistance. On a Sunday last July, I went to see a man (a travelling musician) who was very ill of the small-pox, and died a few days afterwards. The house contained four small rooms, and was situated in a back yard, in a very narrow, confined, dirty lane. There were 40 people in the house, and they were not all in that lodged there. Four months ago I went into a room in the same yard; the room was very dirty; it was 9 feet broad by 15 feet long, and contained four beds, in which slept two men, four women, and thirteen children. I found in one of the beds two children very ill of scarlet fever; in another, a child ill of the measles; in another, a child that had died of the measles the day before; and in a fourth, a woman and her infant, born two days before; and the only space between the four beds was occupied by a tinker, hard at work.'

The lodging-houses in Scotland are similarly characterized. *Dr. Scott Alison* states that:

'There are many regular lodging-houses in Tranent, perhaps from 15 to 20, in which paupers, vagrants, and a few labouring people live. The people reside there for a considerable time. I have known colliers in employment to live in these houses. They are crowded at all hours, but more especially at night. Men, women, and children live and sleep in the same apartment. In one of them I have seen an apartment, about 18 feet long and 10 feet wide, which contained four beds made up constantly; and when the house was "throng," another was added to the number. The lodging-houses are the head-quarters for beggars. The people go about during the day pursuing their avocations, and return home at night to regale themselves with their earnings. These people lie in bed till very late, and, if visited in the forenoon, may be seen sitting beside the fire, roasting herrings or frying meat. They live well amidst their wretchedness.'[1]

In the report of *Mr. James Cameron*, surgeon of Tain, there occurs the following description of the lodging-houses in that part of Scotland:

'There are three lodging-houses in Tain, which are chiefly occupied by beggars and hawkers. These places are kept in the filthiest condition imaginable: I have been credibly informed that the bed-clothes used in one of these houses have not been washed for the last five years! Summer being the season when these people are generally abroad, these low lodging are then often crowded to excess. During the week-days the beggars and hawkers perambulate the country, returning on Saturday night. They frequently, especially when collected in large numbers, drink to excess; and their conduct on such occasions is riotous and disgusting in the extreme. The general charge for such lodgings is 2*d*. per head for the night, with an ample allowance of whisky to the landlords by way of perquisite. These individuals are unfortunately the means of introducing infectious diseases, such as fever, small-pox, measles, &c.'[2]

In Edinburgh and Glasgow, as the confluence of vagrants, and especially of Irish vagrants, becomes greater, such receptacles become more numerous and crowded, and the evils attendant upon them more intense.

The injury done to the health of the public in general, and to the

1. *Local Reps. Scot.*, pp. 88-9.
2. *Ibid.*, p. 317.

VIII. Common Lodging-Houses

health of portions of the operative classes, by the generation or propagation of disease in such places, forms only one part of the evils which call for interference by preventive measures. These evils appear to require for their correction powers to be put in operation by the concurrent exertions of the officers charged with sanitary measures, or the prevention of disease; of the officers charged with the administration of relief to destitution and the prevention of mendicity, and of the officers charged with the protection of the public peace and the prevention of crime. Further, to complete the view of the chief evils arising from these receptacles, we may refer to the report and evidence for the state of them, collected by my colleagues and myself, on the inquiry as to the state of crime, under the Constabulary Force Commission on the state of the lodging-houses in respect to crime:

' § 35. We found only few of the magisterial divisions from which we obtained information that were not seriously afflicted by the existence of such receptacles, and in any arrangements for the prevention of crime within the rural districts the means of suppressing or controlling the common lodging-house must have a prominent place. The trampers' lodging-house is distinct from the beer-shop or the public-house, or any licensed place of public accommodation: it is not only the place of resort of the mendicant, but of the common thief; it is the "flash-house" of the rural district; it is the receiving-house for stolen goods; it is the most extensively-established school for juvenile delinquency, and commonly at the same time the most infamous brothel in the district.

'The magistrates of the division of Warwick state:

' "That in the borough of Warwick such houses are both numerous and a very general receptacle of petty offenders. Here the common vagrants and trading beggars assemble in great numbers at nightfall, or take up their quarters for very many days, making the lodging-house the common centre from whence they issue in the morning, traverse their several beats, and return at night. It is not unfrequent for such vagrants to make the immediate neighbourhood their regular walk even for some weeks, changing their beats, which are carefully arranged among themselves, and only quitting their quarters to avoid detection in some petty pilfering, or because, from becoming too well known, they can no longer successfully impose on the public in the quarter they have so long frequented."

'The magistrates of the Chelmsford division state:

' "There are several lodging-houses in the town of Chelmsford where in the course of the year it is supposed upwards of 2000 trampers or vagrants resort. The greater number of these persons shelter themselves from apprehension and punishment under the Vagrant Act, by professing to be match-sellers. This is made a cloak for begging alms, and the pretext for going from house to house, and pilfering, as opportunity offers. The lodging-houses at Chelmsford are made the centre of a kind of circuit which these people make almost periodically.

' "The system of lodging-houses for travellers, otherwise trampers, requires to be altogether revised: at present they are in the practice of lodging all the worst characters unquestioned, and are subject to no other control than an occasional visit of inspection from the parish officers, accompanied by the constables, whose power of interference, if they have a legal right of entry, does not extend to some of the most objectionable points connected with those houses, as they can merely take into custody such persons as they find in commission of some offence. The state in which those houses are found on the occasion of such visit proves how much they require interference. The houses are small, and yet as many as thirty travellers, or even thirty-five, have been found in one house; fifteen have been found sleeping in one room, three or four in one bed, men, women, and children promiscuously. Beds have been found occupied in a cellar. It is not necessary to urge the many opportunities of preparing for crime which such a state of things presents, or the actual evils arising from such a mode of harbouring crowds of low and vicious persons." [1]

In our First Report we observed that—'The mischiefs of these migratory streams of depredators and vagrants, and other bad characters, is not confined to the crimes which they commit, though those must be extremely extensive to furnish such numerous hordes with the means of subsistence; these characters, experienced in the crimes and vices of the criminal associations of the larger towns from whence they sally forth, form such large proportions of the population of the gaols in the rural districts, as are stated in the return of prisoners in Knutsford gaol. The other portion of the inmates of the gaol, chiefly agricultural labourers, natives of the country, confined for misdemeanours, may in such receptacles be considered pupils in these normal schools of crime, to learn and carry back to the rural villages the knowledge and the incitement to felonious practices.'[2]

It appears that, on the several grounds of public expediency, for the preservation of the public health, and for the preservation of the public peace, all common lodging-houses,—all places which are open for the reception of strangers, travellers, and wayfarers by the night, and houses laid out and provided for numbers of lodgers, should be subjected to regulations for the protection of the inmates as well as the public at large. This appears, indeed, to be consistent with the ancient police of the country. By narrowing the definition of the places for which licences were rendered necessary to those where spirits or fermented liquors are sold to be drunk on the premises, (as if a revenue were the only proper object of their government,) it appears that there has been a mischievous dereliction of the ancient and sound policy of the law which subjects the 'victualler' as well as the keeper of the hostel, inn, or lodging-house to responsibilities for the protection of the inmates, and the convenience of the inhabitants in the neighbourhood where such houses may be situate. The common lodging-house keeper is in fact an inferior victualler, but evading the licence and the responsibilities of the victualler, by sending out for the fermented liquors which are consumed by the lodgers.

It appears, from various portions of evidence, that the occupation of a lodging-house keeper is a profitable one: instances are given from various parts of the country where the keepers of such houses have accumulated property; and whilst the keepers of public-houses, however small, or of beer-shops, are subjected to the necessity of taking out licences, there is no apparent reason for the exemption of lodging-house keepers from that charge by reason of poverty; neither should I consider

---

1. *First Report of the Constabulary Force Commission*, *P.P.* 1839, XIX, pp. 34-5.
2. *Ibid.*, p. 37.

that it would be a disadvantage, but the contrary, if the proper regulation of such houses were effected at some increase of the price of the lodgings. On examination of the description of persons accommodated in such houses, (whilst there is a public provision for those who are really in a state of destitution, and means are provided for removing them to their places of settlement when it is necessary,) I find no class whose migration is entitled to any encouragement by any diminution of the charge of providing proper lodgings. Another topic of consideration in connexion with houses of this class, is the tendency of the degraded accommodation to degrade the classes of the population who have recourse to it. I would therefore submit for consideration, whether all common lodging-houses should not be required by law to take out licences in the same manner as public-houses; and that, as the condition of holding such licences, they be subjected to inspection by the medical officers of the union (or the district medical officer), and bound to conform to such sanitary regulations in respect to cleanliness, ventilation, and numbers proportioned to the space, as he may be authorized to prescribe for the protection of the health of the inmates: and also that all such lodging-houses shall be subjected to the regulations of the magistrates, and shall be open to the visits and inspection of the police, for the enforcement of duly authorized regulations, without any search-warrant or other authority than that necessary for their entrance into any house belonging to a licensed victualler.

It may further be submitted for consideration that, by the beneficial progress made in the habits of temperance in some districts, the disuse of spirituous or fermented liquors may enable the proprietors of houses of a higher order of resort than those in question to convert them into coffee-houses or victualling-houses, and at the same time dispense with the expense of the licence, and avoid also the responsibilities for the protection of the public which the law has attached to licensed houses of resort for travellers.

From the reports received from the more populous towns, it would appear that there are few houses which are let for the accommodation of large numbers of regular lodgers which might not be benefited by the inspection of a medical officer. I believe it would be more beneficial to the public to extend than to narrow the definition of the places which should be subjected to regulations as lodging-houses; and that a discretion as to the description of house which shall be included might be safely confided to the magistrates who have local charge of the public peace and the public economy of the towns.

The report received from *Mr. Charles R. Baird*[1], on the state of the law applicable to the sanitary regulation of Glasgow, and the condition of the labouring classes, as affected by the incompleteness or absence of such regulations, affords evidence of the practical effect of measures such as those recommended. Powers for the execution of such measures have been already obtained and put into operation by the magistrates and authorities of that city.

---

1. Charles R. Baird, 'Report on the sanitary condition of the working classes in the city of Glasgow', *Local Reps. Scot.*, pp. 159-203.

"The lodging-houses," said Dr. Cowan, "are the media through which the newly arrived immigrants find their way to the fever hospital; and it is remarkable how many of the inmates of that hospital, coming from lodging-houses, have not been six months in the city."[1] He might have added, these lodging-houses are the great *foci* of poverty, vice, and crime, as well as of disease. These houses are generally of a very wretched description, in low, unwholesome situations, exceedingly dirty and ill-ventilated, and are frequently crowded to excess, it being no uncommon thing to find 8, 10, and 12 persons in one small apartment, as 9 feet by 8, or 11 by 8. Some of them also have no beds whatever in them, the inmates lying on the bare floor, or with a few shavings below them, with their clothes on. A more particular description of them will be got in Captain Miller's Papers on Crime in the City Proper[2], Mr. Rutherglen's (one of the magistrates) on Calton, and Mr. Richardson on the Barony of Gorbals. It would appear from these published documents, and from what I have been able to learn otherwise, that the lodging-houses in the City Proper are decidedly of the worst description; but I am aware that the authorities are adopting means to have them in better order in future. In the burgh of Anderston they have for some time been under the surveillance of the police; and a record is kept of all lodging-houses for the accommodation of casual visitors in Gorbals (by which it appears that there were lately 92—50 kept by males, and 42 by females; only 25 of them entertain the lowest class of poor), so that they may be properly regulated. It is only in Calton, however, that they are attended to with that strict care which is requisite, and fortunately the last Police Act for that burgh gives ample powers for that purpose. It provides, by section 20, That no keeper of lodging-houses of an inferior description, for the accommodation of mendicant strangers and others, shall receive lodgers without the house having been inspected and approved of by the superintendent of police, and the superintendent is authorized to fix the number of lodgers who may be accommodated, and to order a ticket containing the number of lodgers for which each house is registered; and any rules or instructions of the commissioners of police regarding health, cleanliness, and ventilation, to be placed in a conspicuous part of each room in which lodgers are received. It also provides that the keepers of such lodgings offending against these regulations shall be liable in penalties. Section 21 enacts, That in the event of any person in such houses becoming ill of fever or other disease, the keepers shall be bound to give intimation thereof to the superintendent of police or inspector, so that the disease may be inquired into and treated, and the magistrates are authorized to order such persons to be removed. And section 22 further enacts, That on any contagious or infectious disease occurring in any such lodging-houses, or in any house or apartment in any house, or apartment in any common tenement, &c., where there is reasonable apprehension of such diseases spreading, the magistrates may cause the remaining lodgers to be removed, and measures to be taken for the disinfecting and cleaning of the houses and apartments, and for the washing and purifying of the persons and clothes of the inhabitants.

'In addition to these excellent provisions, the magistrates of Calton, in virtue of the powers in their police Act, have issued the following rules and instructions to be observed by all keepers of lodging-houses, viz.—1st. The floors are to be washed at least twice in each week, viz., on Wednesday and Saturday. 2nd. The walls are to be whitewashed, and the houses thoroughly cleaned, on the 1st day of each of the months of June, August, November and

---

1. Robert Cowan, *J.R.S.S.*, III (1840), 290.
2. H. Miller, *Papers relative to the State of Crime in the City of Glasgow* (Glasgow 1840).

March, or on the following day if any of these days fall on Sunday. And, 3rd. The blankets used in all lodging-houses are to be thoroughly cleaned and scoured on the 8th day of each of the months of June, August, November, and March, or on the following day if any of these days fall on Sunday; and if any person or persons in such house shall be affected with fever or other infectious disease, the blankets and bed-clothes used by such person or persons shall be thoroughly cleaned and scoured immediately after the removal of the diseased, and the bedding used by persons affected with contagious disease fumigated immediately after the removal of such person or persons. And where the bedding used is shavings or straw, the same shall be burnt immediately after such removal.

'These provisions and regulations have been very judiciously enforced by the magistrates of Calton and their superintendent of police, and have been productive of most beneficial results. In addition to what was formerly stated by Bailie Rutherglen, I have now before me a distinct statement, by Mr. Smart, regarding the lodging-houses and state of fever in Calton, which enables me to give the following information:—Between 1st September, 1840, and 1st February last, 319 persons were brought before the magistrates of Calton for keeping unregistered lodging-houses. Of these 216 were ordered to desist from keeping lodgers till houses registered, &c.; 91 were fined and ordained not to keep lodgers; 12 cases were dismissed. Of the 307 convicted for keeping unregistered lodging-houses, 90 got their houses inspected and registered, 30 removed from the burgh, and 189 gave over keeping lodgers, and were refused registration—refused principally on account of the want of proper accommodation, and a few for harbouring disreputable characters. Mr. Smart also informs me that several hundreds of the worst houses of the poorer classes have been whitewashed with Irish lime, and the lodging-houses having been put under wholesome regulations, a marked improvement has taken place. In Whisky-close, New-street, for several years past, as many as 30 cases of fever occurred annually. Lime-washed in September last, and the vagrants removed; only one case of fever has been known: and Mr. Smart concludes, "I believe there are 1000 fever cases less in Calton this day than there were on 1st September last." Why should not the same measures that have been so successfully enforced in Calton be introduced into the City Proper and the other suburban districts?'[1]

It were only a statement of the concurrent opinion of the commissioners of police, of magistrates, of medical officers, and of the guardians charged with the administration of the poor's rates, to represent the urgent necessity of legislative provisions for the general adoption of similar measures throughout the country.

IX

RECAPITULATION OF CONCLUSIONS

The last cited instance of the practical operation of measures for the abatement of the nuisances attendant on common lodging-houses may also be submitted as an instance of the advantages derivable from the extension of such fields of inquiries as the present. On each of the chief points included in it there would have been a loss of what I hope will be deemed valuable corroborative information, had the inquiry been

---

1. *Local Reps. Scot.*, pp. 182-4.

confined either to England or to Scotland. The observation of the important productive use of the refuse of the city of Edinburgh would have been of comparatively little value as evidence leading to practical applications, apart from the observation of what is accomplished by the practical application of science to sewerage and drainage for the immediate and cheapest removal of all the refuse of towns by water through closed drains afforded by the operation in the Holborn and Finsbury division of the metropolis. It may be stated confidently that, if the inquiry could conveniently have had still further extension as to time and place, the information would have been strengthened and rendered more complete. From incidental facts I have met with, I am led to believe that the whole of the effects which are the subject of the present report would have been still more strikingly displayed in many parts of Ireland.

After as careful an examination of the evidence collected as I have been enabled to make, I beg leave to recapitulate the chief conclusions which that evidence appears to me to establish.

First, as to the extent and operation of the evils which are the subject of the inquiry:—

That the various forms of epidemic, endemic, and other disease caused, or aggravated, or propagated chiefly amongst the labouring classes by atmospheric impurities produced by decomposing animal and vegetable substances, by damp and filth, and close and overcrowded dwellings prevail amongst the population in every part of the kingdom, whether dwelling in separate houses, in rural villages, in small towns, in the larger towns—as they have been found to prevail in the lowest districts of the metropolis.

That such disease, wherever its attacks are frequent, is always found in connexion with the physical circumstances above specified, and that where those circumstances are removed by drainage, proper cleansing, better ventilation, and other means of diminishing atmospheric impurity, the frequency and intensity of such disease is abated; and where the removal of the noxious agencies appears to be complete, such disease almost entirely disappears.

That high prosperity in respect to employment and wages, and various and abundant food, have afforded to the labouring classes no exemptions from attacks of epidemic disease, which have been as frequent and as fatal in periods of commercial and manufacturing prosperity as in any others.

That the formation of all habits of cleanliness is obstructed by defective supplies of water.

That the annual loss of life from filth and bad ventilation are greater than the loss from death or wounds in any wars in which the country has been engaged in modern times.

That of the 43,000 cases of widowhood, and 112,000 cases of destitute orphanage relieved from the poor's rates in England and Wales alone, it appears that the greatest proportion of deaths of the heads of families occurred from the above specified and other removable causes; that their ages were under 45 years; that is to say, 13 years below the natural

IX. Recapitulation of Conclusions 423

probabilities of life as shown by the experience of the whole population of Sweden.

That the public loss from the premature deaths of the heads of families is greater than can be represented by any enumeration of the pecuniary burdens consequent upon their sickness and death.

That, measuring the loss of working ability amongst large classes by the instances of gain, even from incomplete arrangements for the removal of noxious influences from places of work or from abodes, that this loss cannot be less than eight or ten years.

That the ravages of epidemics and other diseases do not diminish but tend to increase the pressure of population.

That in the districts where the mortality is the greatest the births are not only sufficient to replace the numbers removed by death, but to add to the population.

That the younger population, bred up under noxious physical agencies, is inferior in physical organization and general health to a population preserved from the presence of such agencies.

That the population so exposed is less susceptible of moral influences, and the effects of education are more transient than with a healthy population.

That these adverse circumstances tend to produce an adult population short-lived, improvident, reckless, and intemperate, and with habitual avidity for sensual gratifications.

That these habits lead to the abandonment of all the conveniences and decencies of life, and especially lead to the overcrowding of their homes, which is destructive to the morality as well as the health of large classes of both sexes.

That defective town cleansing fosters habits of the most abject degradation and tends to the demoralization of large numbers of human beings, who subsist by means of what they find amidst the noxious filth accumulated in neglected streets and bye-places.

That the expenses of local public works are in general unequally and unfairly assessed, oppressively and uneconomically collected, by separate collections, wastefully expended in separate and inefficient operations by unskilled and practically irresponsible officers.

That the existing law for the protection of the public health and the constitutional machinery for reclaiming its execution, such as the Courts Leet, have fallen into desuetude, and are in the state indicated by the prevalence of the evils they were intended to prevent.

Secondly. As to the means by which the present sanitary condition of the labouring classes may be improved:—

The primary and most important measures, and at the same time the most practicable, and within the recognized province of public administration, are drainage, the removal of all refuse of habitations, streets, and roads, and the improvement of the supplies of water.

That the chief obstacles to the immediate removal of decomposing refuse of towns and habitations have been the expense and annoyance of the hand labour and cartage requisite for the purpose.

That this expense may be reduced to one-twentieth or to one-thirtieth, or rendered inconsiderable, by the use of water and self-acting means of removal by improved and cheaper sewers and drains.

That refuse when thus held in suspension in water may be most cheaply and innoxiously conveyed to any distance out of towns, and also in the best form for productive use, and that the loss and injury by the pollution of natural streams may be avoided.

That for all these purposes, as well as for domestic use, better supplies of water are absolutely necessary.

That for successful and economical drainage the adoption of geological areas as the basis of operations is requisite.

That appropriate scientific arrangements for public drainage would afford important facilities for private land-drainage, which is important for the health as well as sustenance of the labouring classes.

That the expense of public drainage, of supplies of water laid on in houses, and of means of improved cleansing would be a pecuniary gain, by diminishing the existing charges attendant on sickness and premature mortality.

That for the protection of the labouring classes and of the ratepayers against inefficiency and waste in all new structural arrangements for the protection of the public health, and to ensure public confidence that the expenditure will be beneficial, securites should be taken that all new local public works are devised and conducted by responsible officers qualified by the possession of the science and skill of civil engineers.

That the oppressiveness and injustice of levies for the whole immediate outlay on such works upon persons who have only short interests in the benefits may be avoided by care in spreading the expense over periods coincident with the benefits.

That by appropriate arrangements, 10 or 15 per cent. on the ordinary outlay for drainage might be saved, which on an estimate of the expense of the necessary structural alterations of one-third only of the existing tenements would be a saving of one million and a half sterling, besides the reduction of the future expenses of management.

That for the prevention of the disease occasioned by defective ventilation, and other causes of impurity in places of work and other places where large numbers are assembled, and for the general promotion of the means necessary to prevent disease, that it would be good economy to appoint a district medical officer independent of private practice, and with the securities of special qualifications and responsibilities to initiate sanitary measures and reclaim the execution of the law.

That by the combinations of all these arrangements it is probable that the full ensurable period of life indicated by the Swedish tables; that is, an increase of 13 years at least, may be extended to the whole of the labouring classes.

That the attainment of these and the other collateral advantages of reducing existing charges and expenditure are within the power of the legislature, and are dependent mainly on the securities taken for the application of practical science, skill, and economy in the direction of local public works.

And that the removal of noxious physical circumstances, and the promotion of civic, household, and personal cleanliness, are necessary

IX. Recapitulation of Conclusions

to the improvement of the moral condition of the population; for that sound morality and refinement in manners and health are not long found co-existant with filthy habits amongst any class of the community.

I beg leave further to suggest, that the principles of amendment deduced from the inquiry will be found as applicable to Scotland as to England; and if so, it may be submitted for attention whether it might not be represented that the structural arrangements for drainage would be most conveniently carried out in the same form as in England, that is by commissions, of the nature of commissions of sewers adapted, as regards jurisdiction to natural or geological areas, and including in them the chief elected officers of municipalities, and other authorities now charged with the care of the streets and roads or connected with local public works.

The advantages of uniformity in legislation and in the executive machinery, and of doing the same things in the same way (choosing the best), and calling the same officers, proceedings, and things by the same names, will only be appreciated by those who have observed the extensive public loss occasioned by the legislation for towns which makes them independent of beneficent, as of what perhaps might have been deemed formerly aggressive legislation. There are various sanitary regulations, and especially those for cleansing, directed to be observed in 'every town except Berwick and Carlisle;' a course of legislation which, had it been efficient for England, would have left Berwick and Carlisle distinguished by the oppression of common evils intended to be remedied. It was the subject of public complaint, at Glasgow and in other parts of Scotland, that independence and separation in the form of general legislation separated the people from their share of the greatest amount of legislative attention, or excluded them from common interest and from the common advantages of protective measures. It was, for example, the subject of particular complaint, that whilst the labouring population of England and Ireland had received the advantages of public legislative provision for a general vaccination, the labouring classes in Scotland were still left exposed to the ravages of the small-pox. It was also complained by Dr. Cowan and other members of the medical profession, that Scotland had not been included in the provisions for the registration of the causes of death which they considered might, with improvements, be made highly conducive to the advancement of medical science and the means of protecting the public health.

I have the honour to be,
Gentlemen,
Your obedient servant,
EDWIN CHADWICK.

INDEX

INDEX

Aberdeen
 disease in, 225-6
 water supply of, 138
ablutions, 315-8
accidents
 death by, 181, 263
 in mines, 181, 270-1
 prevention of, 321
administration
 existing system of public health, 59, 339-410
 recommendations for improvement of public health, 62, 394-6, 423-5
 reform of, under Whig government, 30-1
administrators
 and reformers, 29-37
 propaganda of, 30-1
 reform and professional, 30-2
adulteration of food, 7
age
 at death, 255-7, 258-60
 mortality rates and, 220-32, 234
 of persons in various occupations, 265-6
agricultural labourers
 average age of, 295-6
 chances of life of, 226-7
 domestic economy of, 208
 drainage and health of, 108-9, 166
 houses of, 86-7, 196-7, 298, 323-35
 recreation of, 338-9
 wages of, 4, 253
Alexandria, 246n
Alison, Dr S. Scott, 49, 97, 107, 137, 189-90, 207, 208, 215, 265-6, 416
Alison, Sir Archibald, 5, 57, 199
Alison, William P., 15, 23, 27n, 48, 57, 63-4, 65, 72, 97, 189
Ampthill, housing conditions in, 86, 190-1
Angus, 153
Annales d'Hygiène, 52
apartments, want of separate, 190-204
Arbroath, water supplies of, 139, 140
Archbishop of Dublin, 55
army
 public health precautions, 20, 116-7, 150, 407
 sickness rate, 282, 287
Arnott, Dr Neil
 career of, 34
 contribution to public health reform, 21-2
 membership of Health of Towns Commission, 131
 Poor Law Commission Report of 1838, 3, 16, 32, 44, 63, 71, 370-1, 405
 reply to Alison, 64-5
 views on macadamised roads, 131

 visit to Scotland with Chadwick, 51-2, 75, 97-9, 120, 121, 198, 277, 397
artisans, mortality rate of, 220-32, 234-5
Ashley, Lord, 68, 73
Austin, Henry, 56
Ayr
 drainage in, 107
 economy of families in, 207-8
 housing conditions in, 97, 301-2
 intemperance in, 293
 water supply of, 139

Babbage, Charles, 54
back-to-back houses, 6, 91, 114
Baker, Dr Robert, 50-1, 103n, 111, 112-4, 116, 120, 193, 200, 225, 243, 263, 355-6, 405-6
Banff, drainage in, 153
Barham, Dr Charles F., 32, 49, 53, 81-2, 181, 262, 263, 317, 318
Barnard Castle, housing conditions in, 94-5
Barnet, lodging-houses in, 411
Bath
 birth-rate in, 243
 bone-pickers of, 164-5
 housing conditions in, 201
 mortality rates in, 228-31, 234-6, 241, 247, 255-7
 water supply of, 141-2, 145-7
baths, 316-8
Bateman, T., 24
Beccles, mortality rate in, 102-3
bedding, 21, 278, 413
Bedford Level, 361, 362
Bedfordshire
 deaths in, 76
 housing conditions in, 86-7, 323-4
 population increase in, 249
 rents in, 7
 water supply of, 137
Bentham, Jeremy
 friendship with public health reformers, 34-5, 37
 influence of, 38-40
 views on need for quantification, 26
Benthamism, influence of, on Chadwick, 38-9
Berkshire
 Chadwick's study of, 2n, 75
 deaths in, 76
 housing conditions in, 87, 330
 population increase in, 249
Bicester
 drainage in, 157-8
 housing conditions in, 191
bills of mortality, 11
Bilston, disease in, 89

Birmingham
 death-rate in, 13, 225
 domestic habits in, 205-6
 house building in, 390
 housing conditions in, 89
 Irish immigrants in, 15
 methods of wage payment in, 309-10
 park in, 335-6
 preparation of data for the *Report*, 51
 sewerage of, 105-6, 363-4
 state of lodging-houses in, 411-2
 water supply of, 135
birth-rate
 death-rates and, 12-13, 15, 65-6, 243-50, 264
 disease and, 423
 levels of income and, 65
 poverty and, 65-6
 Registration Act and, 27-8
births, illegitimate, 244
Bishop's Stortford
 housing conditions in, 87
 water supply of, 137
Blane, Sir Gilbert, 20-1, 110
Blomfield, Bishop, 45, 55
Board of Health of Paris, 171n, 183, 397
Boards of Guardians
 and the administration of public health, 43, 395, 403, 410
 authorisation of migration of labour, 41
 preparation of data for the *Report*, 47
Boards of Health
 establishment of local, 16-17, 360
 in Ireland, 398
 operation of, 396-9
 under the Public Health Act of 1848, 71, 73
Bolton
 chances of life in, 223, 241
 housing conditions in, 303-4
 Public Health Act, 359-60
bone-pickers, 164-5
Booth, Charles, 36
Bossi, M., 245
Bradford
 mortality rate in, 264
 population increase in, 4
Brighton
 drainage in, 105
 lodging-houses in, 412
British Association, 26-7
Bromley, drainage in, 88-9
Brougham, Lord, 22, 30
Brown, R. G., 19
Brownlee, J., 11
Brussels, 239
bubonic plague, 8
Buccleuch Commission, *see* Health of Towns Commission
Buckhamshire
 deaths in, 76
 housing conditions in, 87, 329
 population increase in, 249
Building Acts
 administration of, 389

control of buildings under, 16, 342, 346-7
 drainage under, 45
 limitations of local, 345-6
 Metropolitan, 340, 346, 382
 public health and, 37, 341, 346-7
 town-planning and, 346-7
Burgess, T., 49
burial-grounds
 metropolitan, 24
 situation of, 82
 urban, 68
burials, Chadwick's study of urban, 68
Burton, J. H., 48, 55, 106, 140
Bury, housing conditions in, 293

Cambridge Medical School, 18
Cambridgeshire
 deaths in, 76
 population increase in, 249
Carlisle
 death-rate in, 13
 housing conditions in, 95
 life tables, 255, 284
 studies on mortality in, 25
Carlyle, Thomas, 38, 39, 54, 70
Catrine, mill-workers' houses in, 301-2
cattle, effect of drainage on health of, 154-6, 158
cellar-dwellings
 condition of, 91, 92, 277
 health and, 6, 102, 215-6, 225
 improved houses and, 342
 Irish imigrants in, 92
 number of, 6n, 105
 numbers occupying, 105, 215, 225, 303
 overcrowding in, 91, 93, 206-7
census, 4n, 188-9
Central Board of Health, 71, 73
central government
 extension of powers of, 38
 views of Chadwick on local and, 42, 59, 71, 379-82
cesspools, 117, 119, 124, 136, 161
Chadwick, Edwin
 approaches to individuals in the compilation of the *Report*, 48-51
 as a professional administrator, 31
 as a sociologist, 36-7
 attitude to doctors, 60-1
 attitude to engineers, 60-1
 authorship of the *Report*, 1-2, 61
 axioms of the *Report*, 58-9
 Bentham and, 35, 37-8
 campaign for Health of Towns Association, 68-9
 compilation of the *Report*, 1-2, 35
 correction of the *Report*, 53-4
 disagreement with Lord Normanby, 45-6, 66
 early career of, 35
 history of the *Report*, 43-58
 membership of Central Board of Health, 73
 misconceptions regarding history of public health movement, 2-3

Index

on administration, 62
on food, prosperity and epidemics, 4
on local and central government, 42, 59, 71
on lodging-houses, 59
on refuse disposal, 61-2
on Registration Act, 27n, 28
on sewerage, 59-60, 61-2
on ventilation, 59
organisation of the *Report*, 46-8
part in factory reform, 35, 36-7
part in poor law reform, 35, 36-7, 39
part in public health reform, 35-7, 73
propaganda for *Report*, 55-8
publication of *Report*, 54-5
recommendations of the *Report*, 421-5
Report from London and Berkshire, 2n, 75
Report of 1834, 2
Report of the Health of Towns Commission, 67-8
Report on Interment in Towns, 68
Secretaryship of the Poor Law Commission, 1, 31, 45
services on inquiries and commissions, 31
studies in foreign public health literature, 52-3
subsidiary points of the *Report*, 59-60
visit to Edinburgh and Glasgow, 51-2, 75, 97-9, 135n, 277, 397
visits to other places, 51-2, 75
Chalmers, A. K., 9n, 10
Chambers, William, 48-9, 106
chances of life
correlation with other factors, 58
national, 219
occupations and, 219-54
preventive measures and, 276-339, 422-3
Chelmsford, lodging-houses in, 417-8
Cheshire
deaths in, 76
housing conditions in, 329
population increase in, 249
Chester, Haygarth's studies on, 25
Chesterfield, drainage in, 157
Chesterton, drainage in, 104
chiffonniers, 164-5
Chigwell, land drainage in, 151
children
mortality rates, 19-20, 223, 241, 244-5
recreation grounds for, 338
Chippenham, housing conditions in, 85-6
cholera
and the Public Health Act, 71
Boards of Health and, 396-7
courts leet and, 360
deaths from, 237
epidemics of, 8, 10
housing conditions and, 89, 95, 198

method of diffusion of, 63
street cleansing and, 111, 163-4, 372
ventilation and, 365
Chorlton-upon-Medlock, housing conditions in, 206
Church Lane, London, 5
Clapham, Sir John, 5n
Clark, John, 25n
Clarke, Sir James, 27
cleanliness
health and, 287, 424-5
housing conditions and, 329
improvements and, 299
in places of work, 318-20
in prisons, 49, 279, 282
intemperance and, 313-4
in the army, 117
in the navy, 21, 285
personal, 25, 87, 88, 90, 99, 315-8
smoke and, 356-7
water and, 422
Clitheroe
drainage in, 108
housing conditions in, 194
labour in the cotton-printing industry, 253
Commission of Sewers
incompetence of, 110, 372-4, 388, 393, 400
limitations on jurisdiction of, 341
responsibilities of, 348, 368-71
Commissioners of the Metropolitan Police, 164, 165
Coode, George, 45
Cornwall
deaths in, 76
housing conditions in, 81-2
mines in, 262-3
population increase in, 249
cotton-mills, 182, 253
courts leet, 354-61, 423
Cowan, Dr Robert, 5, 8, 9, 10n, 25n, 48, 27n, 78, 97, 176, 199, 214, 272, 420, 425
Creighton, Charles, 9
Cumberland
deaths in, 76
educational facilities in, 268-9
mortality rates in, 255-7
population increase in, 249
Currie, James, 9, 15-16, 25n, 215, 365-6, 386

d'Arcet, J.P., 183
Davies, Griffith, 53-4
Day, William, 47
death
average age of, 241, 255-7
causes of, 258-60
from fever, 78-9, 235-6
from old age, 78, 172, 256
from violence, 78, 256, 408
in Scotland, 78
in the year 1838, 76-7
investigation of the causes of, 406-7
mortality rates and, 220-32, 234
occupation and, 258-60

death (*continued*)
  premature, 256, 258-60, 270-1, 290, 320, 423
death-rate, *see* mortality rate
delinquency
  housing conditions and, 302, 325 335
  intemperance and, 308-9
  lodging-houses and, 417-19, 420
  pauperism and, 267-9
Denison, Captain, 67
Derby
  domestic habits in, 204-5
  drainage of streets and houses, 99-102
  mortality rates in, 220
  park in, 336
  smoke in, 355-6
Derbyshire
  deaths in, 76
  housing conditions in, 90-1
  population increase in, 249
d'Espine, Dr, 234
Devon
  deaths in, 76
  housing conditions in, 80-1
  population increase in, 249
Dicey, A. V., 38-9, 40, 42
Dickens, Charles, 38, 39, 56-7, 70
diet
  health and, 276, 311, 313, 314
  in prisons, 49, 279, 282, 309
  in the navy, 20-1, 287
  varied opinions on, 409
disease
  birth-rate and, 423
  cost of, 254-76
  death-rate and, 14-15, 79, 233, 423
  dirt and, 21, 25
  domestic management as predisposing cause of, 204-6
  drainage and, 58, 77, 79, 88-9, 101, 102-3, 130, 150, 155-9, 160-1, 203-4, 422
  early studies of, 24-5
  housing conditions and, 26, 58-9, 80-99, 217-8, 378-9
  insanitation and, 12n, 34, 58
  in Scotland, 272-6
  intemperance and, 203-4, 205, 210-11, 213-4, 216, 275-6, 423
  Irish immigrants and, 15, 64
  lodging-houses and, 411, 412, 414, 415, 416, 420
  method of diffusion of, 62-4, 72
  morality and, 423
  overcrowding and, 7-8, 10, 12, 15-16, 58, 79, 189-90
  physique and, 210-11
  poverty and, 9, 31-2, 63-5, 79, 210-19, 242-3, 276
  privies and, 116, 117
  refuse disposal and, 79
  sewerage and, 130, 217
  social attitudes and responses to, 10-11
  social origins of, 24-5
  urbanisation and, 12-13, 15-16, 43-4

ventilation and, 11, 15, 16, 21, 25, 49, 77, 79, 168-9, 171, 172, 174, 214, 215, 216, 422
wages and, 204-5, 212-13, 422
water supply and, 58, 79, 143, 148-9
diseases of
  brain, nerves, and senses, 76-7, 172, 181, 256
  digestive organs, 76-7, 172, 181, 256
  epidemic, endemic, and contagious, 76-7, 256
  respiratory organs, 172, 174n, 180, 181, 256, 261
disinfection, 20
dispensaries, 20
Ditchingham factory, 103
doctors
  availability of services of, 18
  Chadwick's attitude to, 60-1
  numbers and health, 19-20
  numbers trained, 18
  see also medical officers
domestic
  industry workers, 4
  mismanagement and public health, 204-6
Dore, drainage in, 157
Dorset
  deaths in, 76
  housing conditions in, 82-4
  population increase in, 249
drainage
  administration of, 372-96
  causes of defective, 87-8, 109-10, 287-98
  consequences of neglect of, 90, 99-109
  construction of, 98, 109-10
  cost of, 101, 104, 106, 151, 287-98, 363, 372-5, 378-9, 384, 386-90, 392
  difficulties of, 361-2
  disease and, 58, 77, 79, 88-9, 101, 102-3, 130, 150, 155-9, 160-1, 203-4, 422
  effects of good, 150-6
  effects on cattle, 154-6, 158
  health and, 299
  in foreign countries, 160-4
  in Ireland, 393-5
  in Italy, 160-1
  in rural areas, 108-9, 166
  in Scotland, 106-8, 115-6, 153-4, 282, 363
  legislative measures and, 110, 162-3, 340, 346, 347, 353
  local authorities and, 361-96
  mortality rates and, 100, 102-3, 151, 225
  natural, 135
  need for, 164-6
  of houses, 282, 375-8
  of towns, 423-4
  rural, 108-9, 158-9
  sanitary effects of, 150-66
  under Building Acts, 45
  water supply and, 135, 138, 139
drains, open, 80, 81, 102, 107, 115
dress, 319, 322-3

Index 433

dressmakers, 176-7, 407
Dublin
  Board of Health, 398
  Hospital Reports, 148, 165
  housing conditions in, 24
  typhus epidemic in, 16
Ducpetiaux, M., 239
Dukinfield, 4
Dumfries
  Chadwick's visit to, 75
  cholera epidemic in, 198
Duncan, Dr William, 32, 92, 104, 111, 225
Dundee
  deaths in, 78
  economy of families in, 209-10
  fever in, 273-6
  small-pox in, 8n
  water supply of, 138, 140
Dunfermline, water supply of, 139, 140
Dunmow
  drainage in, 152-3
  water supply of, 137
duration of life, 254; *see also* expectation of life
Durham
  deaths in, 76
  housing conditions in, 94, 95-6, 191-2
  lodging-houses in, 415
  population increase in, 249
dust, 318-9
dysentery, 116, 149

Eastry, land drainage in, 152
economists and state intervention, 39-41
economy of families, 206-19
Edinburgh
  Chadwick's visit to, 51-2, 75, 97-9, 397
  death rate in, 13, 233, 247
  deaths from fever, 78
  drainage of, 106, 282
  housing conditions in, 97-9, 198, 277, 281-2, 397
  lodging-houses in, 416
  overcrowding in, 366
  prison in, 279-80
  sewerage of, 59-60, 120-4, 135n, 282
  sickness tables, 291
  University, 18, 22-3, 48
  ventilation, 282
  water supply of, 138, 162
education
  and health, 7
  and pauperism, 33, 267-9
  and the rise of the professional administrator, 31
  habits and, 199, 200, 202
  inspectors, 22
Elgin, drainage in, 153
Elliot, T. F., 31
emigrant shipping, 30, 31
emigration, 41, 241, 250
Emigration Acts, 31
employers
  dress and, 322-3

influence on housing, 58, 298-308
  in rural areas, 323-35
  method of wage-payment, 308-15
  ownership of houses, 300-8
  promotion of cleanliness, 315-8
  ventilation of places of work, 318-22
engineers
  Chadwick's attitude to, 60-1
  qualifications of, 383-90, 393, 396, 424
epidemics
  Boards of Health and, 16-17, 360
  deaths from, 76-7, 256
  outbreaks of, 8-10
  prosperity and, 4
  Registry of, 43
epidemiology, 25-6
Epping
  drainage in, 152-3
  housing conditions in, 88
Essex
  deaths in, 76
  population increase in, 249
Ewell, Rev., 57-8
expectation of life
  correlation with other factors, 58
  national, 219
  occupations and, 219-54
  preventive measures and, 276-339, 422-3

factories
  design of, 304-8
  dress in, 319, 322-3
  inspection of, 22, 31, 271-2, 320, 403-6, 408
  mortality in, 263-4
  sickness in, 280-1
  ventilation of, 318-22
Factory Act of 1833
  and the rise of the professional adminstrator, 31
  inquiry, 182, 251, 271-2, 281, 290, 301, 302
  provisions of, 177, 320
  registration and, 27n
  state intervention and, 41, 339
factory reform
  Chadwick's part in, 35, 36-7
families, contrast in the economy of, 206-19
Farr, William
  contribution to public health reform, 21-2
  correspondence with Chadwick, 43
  creation of study of vital statistics, 27, 45
  effect of work at Registrar-General's office, 28-9, 31
  on births and mortality rates, 65-6, 231
  on incidence of disease, 75-7
  on urban and rural death-rates, 13, 14, 15
Ferriar, J., 22, 24, 62, 215, 346, 386
fever, the, *see* typhus
fever hospitals, 20, 25
fines, 118

2E

434　Index

Finlaison, Alexander, 227
Finlaison, John, 12, 14, 26, 27-8, 35, 81, 282, 283-4, 287, 290, 291
fires, 340-1
Foleshill, drainage in, 159
food
　adulteration of, 7
　economy of families and, 207 209, 218
　health and, 205, 213, 216, 276, 279, 282, 287, 311, 313, 314
　in prisons, 49, 279, 282, 309
　in the navy, 20-1, 287
　mortality rate and, 246-8
　ventilation and, 197-8
　wage-payment and, 309, 311, 313, 314
Fracator, Hieronymus, 62
France
　drainage in, 160, 162
　health precautions in, 319, 320-2
　housing conditions in, 330-1
　intemperance in, 294n
　mortality rates in, 236-7
　studies in public health, 52, 183
　ventilation in, 175
　water supply in, 149
Friendly Societies, 13, 25, 35
fumes, 320-1

gardens, public, 335-9
gas, 148-9
Gaskell, Mrs, 69-70
Gaskell, Peter, 22
Gateshead, housing conditions in, 95
Gavin, Hector, 1n, 22
Geneva
　civil registration in, 407
　mortality rates in, 234, 240-1, 250
Germany, public health in, 348
Gilbert, W. J., 47, 80
Glasgow
　Chadwick's visit to, 51-2, 75, 97-9, 135n, 277, 397
　death-rate in, 13-14, 18, 247
　deaths from fever, 78
　education of paupers, 268
　fever statistics of, 210-12, 272, 275
　housing conditions in, 5, 97-9, 198-9, 277, 397
　interest of the medical school in, 48
　lodging-houses in, 416, 419-21
　number of people per house, 5
　overcrowding in, 189, 366
　population increase in, 4
　poverty and disease in, 243
　prison in, 279, 280, 309
　sanitary reforms in, 66n
　small-pox in, 8
　studies on disease in, 25n
　typhus in, 10
　water charges in, 142
　water supply of, 138
　workshops in, 173, 175
Gloucestershire
　deaths in, 76
　population increase in, 249
Graham, Sir John, 46, 68

Gravesend, drainage in, 151-2
Greenock
　overcrowding in, 189
　refuse and disease in, 119-20
　water supply of, 139

habits
　housing conditions and, 86, 90-1, 190-204
　improvement of, 294, 296
　insanitation and, 58-9, 80, 84, 85
　overcrowding and, 190-204
　reformation of, 202-3
　ventilation of places of work and, 168-9
　wage payment and, 313
　water supply and, 141
Haddington, ventilation of, 364-5
handloom weavers, 4
Hawkins, Dr Bisset, 174, 247n, 255n
Haygarth, John, 20, 25
Head, R., 57
Head, Sir Edmund, 46, 295
health
　housing conditions and, 4, 329
　preventive measures and standard of, 276-339
Health of Towns Association, 1n, 56, 68-9
Health of Towns Commission
　establishment of, 67
　first report of, 67-8
　membership of, 34, 67, 122n
　propaganda for, 68-9
　role of, 67
　second report of, 70
Health of Towns Select Committee, 45-6
Herefordshire
　deaths in, 76
　population increase in, 249
Hertfordshire
　Chadwick's study of, 75
　deaths in, 76
　population increase in, 249
Heysham, John, 25
Highland Society, 298, 328, 331
Hill, Frederick, 31
Holyrood Palace, 60, 122-3
hooping cough, 76-7
Horner, Leonard, 22, 31
hospitals
　fever, 20, 272-4
　hygiene in, 20
　infection in, 19
　mortality in, 174-5
　ventilation in, 174-5
house-building
　and population, 188-9
　design in, 81, 96, 97, 115, 117, 326-30, 343-6
　in 19th century, 6
　replacement of old by new, 346-7, 366
　speculative, 113
house cleansing, 103, 399-403
houses
　back-to-back, 6, 91, 114

Building Acts and, 339-47
change of ownership of, 287-8
condition of, 75, 80-95, 264
drainage of, 282, 375-8
miners', 261-2
number of people per, 4
number of, per acre, 4, 6
overcrowding in, 82-84, 86, 88, 89, 91-5, 98, 114, 188-90, 366
ownership of, 298-308
sewage disposal from, 356
statistics of, 4n
town drainage of, 99-109
ventilation of, 81, 84, 85, 87, 90, 91, 97, 104, 105, 188-90, 262, 264, 282
housing conditions
benefits of improvement of, 300-8
delinquency and, 302, 325, 335
disease and, 26, 58-9, 80-99, 217-8, 398-9
employers' influence on, 298-308
health and, 4, 329
in France, 330-1
in rural districts, 323-35
in Scotland, 5, 96-9, 195, 198-9, 277, 281-2, 328, 331-2, 397
intemperance and, 58-9, 84, 85, 90, 314, 324, 325
local variations in, 80, 81
morals and, 58-9, 79, 84, 85, 90, 190-204, 327
mortality rates and, 221, 232, 239
social cost of bad, 58-9
typhus and, 8-10, 80-97
urbanisation and, 4-5
want of separate apartments, 190-204
housing density
ill-health and, 6
incomes and, 5
local variations in, 5-6
national, 4-5
urbanisation and, 4
Howard, John, 276, 279, 398
Howard, Richard, 8, 9, 23, 32, 50, 92, 111-2, 125, 215
Howell, Thomas, 31, 117-8, 120
Hull
housing conditions in, 192, 193 221
Huntingdonshire
deaths in, 76
population increase in, 249
hygiene, 20-1

illness
cost of, 254-76
non-fatal, 79
see also disease
Improvement Commissions, 16-17
improvements, cost of, 287-98
incomes
aggregate real, 3
average real, 3, 4
birth-rate and, 65
health and, 7
housing and, 5
of working classes in early 19th

2E*

Index 435

century, 3-4
see also wages
infant mortality, 19-20, 223, 241, 244-5
insurance, 283-4, 290, 292
intemperance
delinquency and, 308-9
disease and, 203-4, 205, 210-11, 213-4, 216, 275-6, 423
housing and, 58-9, 84, 85, 90, 314, 324, 325
improvement and, 292-4, 299
mode of wage-payment and, 308-15
overcrowding and, 197, 198, 199, 200, 201
prisons and, 279
recreation and, 337
ventilation and, 168, 169, 171
Inverness
sewerage in, 115-6
street-cleansing in, 116
Ireland
Board of Health of, 398
drainage in, 393-5
famine of 1845-6, 5-6
Irish immigrants
disease among, 15, 64
habits of, 199, 338
housing conditions of, 5-6, 89, 92 93
in lodging-houses, 411, 414, 416
overcrowding and, 5-6
typhus among, 212
Irish Poor Inquiry, 15
irrigation
cost of, 124-5
for sewage disposal, 59-60, 121-4
Isle of Ely, drainage in, 150-1
Italy, drainage in, 160-1

Jeffrey, Lord, 22

Kay, James Phillips
career of, 32-4
contribution to public health reform, 21-2
interest in education of the poor, 33, 267
on availability of medical services, 19
Poor Law Commission Report of 1838, 3, 16, 32, 44, 63, 71, 370-1, 404
studies on London, 32, 33
studies on Manchester, 26, 33, 215
Kelso, improvements in, 410
Kent
deaths in, 77
land drainage in, 152
population increase in, 249
Kingsley, Charles, 38
Kings Lynn, refuse in, 115
Kinross, drainage in, 153
Kirkwall, supply of water of, 139
Knutton, drainage in, 104

labourers, mortality rates among, 220-32, 234-5

436 Index

laissez-faire
  in economic policy, 40-1
  in social policy, 41-2
  or state intervention, 38-43
Lanark, water supplies of, 140
Lancashire
  deaths in, 77
  housing conditions in, 329
  improved accommodation in, 297
  population increase in, 249
Lancaster, wage-payment in, 313
Lancisi, G.M., 160
landlords
  cost of improvement in drainage to, 287-98
  drainage schemes and, 104
  in rural areas, 323-35
  negligence of, 82, 117
  water supplies and, 136, 139
Langport, land drainage in, 155-6
Langton, William, 50
Lansdowne, Lord, 22, 30
Leeds
  Chadwick's visit to, 75
  cost of local government in, 389-90
  data on, for *Report*, 50
  death-rate in, 13, 224, 225, 228-31, 232n, 241, 244, 245
  drainage in, 103, 372
  factories in, 307-8, 310-13, 405-6
  fever in, 372
  hospitals in, 174
  housing conditions in, 193, 200, 277, 390
  poverty and disease in, 243
  refuse disposal in, 120
  rents in, 7
  smoke abatement in, 357
  street cleansing in, 11, 112-4
  wage-payment in, 310-13
legislation
  and public health, 339-410
  uniformity of, 425
Leicester, sanitary reforms in, 66n
Leicestershire
  deaths in, 77
  population increase in, 249
Leighton Buzzard
  drainage in, 158
  housing conditions in, 191
Lettsom, J. C., 24
Lewis, Rev. G., 49
Leyden, medical graduates from, 18
Liebig, J., 121-2
lighting commission, 16
Lincolnshire
  deaths in, 77
  housing conditions in, 91, 327
  population increase in, 249
Lind, James, 20, 52, 278
Lister, Thomas, 27
literature and the public health movement, 69-70
Littlejohn, Henry, 28
Liverpool
  appointment of Medical Officer of Health to, 16
  back-to-back houses in, 6
  Building Acts for, 16
  cellar-dwellings in, 105, 277
  death-rate in, 13, 225, 228-231, 232n, 241, 284
  drainage in, 104-5
  fires in, 341
  housing conditions in, 92-3, 192, 221, 390
  number of people per house in, 5
  street cleansing in, 111, 365-6
  studies on, 25n, 215
  typhus in, 9
local acts, 359-60
local authorities
  action on the *Report*, 66
  apathy of, 117
  competence of, 99-109, 359-60, 372-96
  courts leet and, 354-61
  improvements and, 99-109, 288
  public health and, 361-96
local government
  Chadwick's attitude towards, 42, 59, 71, 379-82
  extension of powers of, 38, 41
  inadequacies of, 294-5
  reform of, 30
local investigators, 46-51
Lochmaben
  drainage in, 159
  housing conditions in, 97
lodging-houses
  as focus of disease, 2, 24, 411, 412, 414, 415, 416, 420
  bedding in, 413
  Chadwick's concern over, 59
  condition of, 85, 92, 201-2, 218-9, 261, 279, 334, 335, 411-21
  crime and, 417-9, 420
  in Scotland, 416
  Irish immigrants in, 411, 414, 416
  regulation of, 419-21
  vagrants in, 411, 416, 417
  ventilation of, 412-5
lodging-shops for miners, 177-81
London
  age of mobs, 267
  baths in, 317
  bills of mortality, 11
  bone-pickers in, 164
  Building Acts, 16, 340, 346, 384
  charge for water, 142
  Church Lane in, 5-6
  diseases in, 213-4, 237-8
  fires in, 341
  housing conditions in, 197-8, 202, 239, 277, 333-4, 339-403
  immigration into, 250
  local authorities, 359, 360-1
  mortality rates in, 28-9, 224, 226, 227, 228-31, 238, 241, 247, 255-7
  police aid, 399-404
  sewerage in, 16, 70-1, 118, 117-8, 127-30, 133-4, 161, 366-71, 374-5, 388, 391
  St Giles Parish in, 5-6, 118
  Statistical Society, 5
  studies on diseases in, 3, 16, 24, 32, 33, 44-5, 63

Index 437

tuberculosis in, 11
water supply of, 135-6, 144-5, 162
loss of earnings, 273-4, 280, 290, 292
Louis, P. C. A., 92, 409
Low, Lieutenant, 31
lying-in hospitals, 19

Macclesfield
Chadwick's visit to, 75
housing conditions in, 91, 343, 344-5
lodging-houses in, 414
street cleansing in, 110-11
McKeown, T., 19
Mackinnon, W. A., 68
Mackintosh, Sir James, 22
malaria
drainage and, 103, 152-3, 157-9
housing conditions and, 80, 85, 87-8, 90, 93-4
miasma and, 297
Mallet, Edward, 240, 242, 245, 250
Malthus, Rev. T. R., 26, 65
Malton, drainage in, 159
Manchester
Board of Health of, 16
bone-pickers in, 164
cellar population of, 6n, 225, 277
Chadwick's visit to, 75
charge for water, 142
data of, for *Report*, 50
death-rate in, 13, 28, 223-5, 228-31, 239, 241, 244-5, 255-7
gas supply of, 147-8
housing conditions in, 92, 192-3, 201-2, 221-87, 343-4, 390
lodging-houses in, 412-4
overcrowding in, 221
park in, 336, 337
population increase in, 4
poverty and disease in, 243
rent collection in, 300
rents in, 7
smoke in, 356
Statistical Society, 15, 331, 187, 220, 222, 243, 248, 293
street cleansing and paving, 111-2, 125-6
studies on, 25-6, 215
water supply of, 136-7
Martin, John, 134n
Martineau, Harriet, 55
Mead, James, 52
measles
deaths from, 76-8
street cleansing and, 115
mechanics, mortality rates among, 220-32, 234-5
medical officers
Boards of Health and, 398-410
in factories, 404, 405-6
in places of work, 319
of health, appointment of first, 16
studies of mortality rates, 28
to Poor Law Unions, 32, 47-8, 76, 403
to the police, 404
under the Public Health Act, 71
medical profession

Chadwick's attitude to, 60-1
concern over typhus, 10-11, 15-16
contribution to the public health movement, 18-19
involvement in social questions, 21-4
numbers of, 18-20, 21
professional skill of, 18, 20, 21
role under New Poor Law, 32
Metropolitan Building Act, 340, 346, 384
Metropolitan Police Act, 399-404
Mexico, 246-7
miasma, 62-4, 371, 375, 409, 422
middens, 116
Middlesex
deaths in, 77
housing conditions in, 6
population increase in, 249
military medicine, 20, 116-7, 150, 282, 287, 407
Mill, John Stuart, 34, 40, 41, 54
Millar, Richard, 9, 10n, 23
milliners, 176-7
Milne, Joshua, 12
Milroy, Gavin, 22
miners
accidents among, 270-1
average age of, 265-6
duration of life of, 261-2
education among, 268-9
houses of, 261-2
lodging-shops for, 177-81
mortality rates among, 180-2, 258-60, 261-3, 270
working conditions of, 204, 262-3, 316-8, 407
mines
baths at, 316-8
inspection of, 31
ventilation in, 262
Monmouthshire
deaths in, 77
population increase in, 249
morals
birth-rate and, 244-5
disease and, 423
domestic mismanagement and, 205
dress and, 323
housing conditions and, 58-9, 79, 84, 85, 90, 190-204, 327
insanitation and, 58-9
overcrowding and, 190-204
parks and, 335-9
places of work and, 306-7
poverty and, 267-9
Morell, J. D., 22, 31
Morpeth, Lord, 70, 71
mortality rate
age and, 220-32, 234
among miners, 180-2, 258-60, 261-3, 270
among typhus cases, 100n, 233, 273, 275
birth-rate and, 12-13, 15, 65-6, 243-50, 264, 282
burdens created by, 254-76
causes of high, 58
chances of life and, 129-54

mortality rate (*continued*)
  disease and, 14-15, 79, 233, 240-3, 423
  drainage and, 100, 102-3, 151, 225
  epidemics and, 13-14
  Farr's studies in, 28, 65-6, 231
  food and, 246-8
  housing conditions and, 221, 232, 239
  in drained and undrained areas, 100, 102-3
  in France, 236-7
  in hospitals, 174-5
  in places of work, 176
  in prisons, 282
  in the navy, 285, 287
  insurance tables and, 283-4
  local variations in, 28, 219-20, 224-7, 233-6
  national, 219
  occupations and, 219-32, 234-5
  public health improvement and, 236-40
  Registration Act and, 27-8
  rural, 13
  seasonal variation in, 231
  street cleansing and, 113
  urban, 12-14
  wages and, 222, 242-3
Moss, William, 25n
Mott, Charles, 50
Municipal Corporations Act of 1835, 17, 41, 42
Musselburgh, housing conditions in, 97

Napier, Macvey, 57-8
Nassau Senior, 2, 39
navy, the
  effects of preventive measures in, 284-7, 407
  mortality rates in, 285, 287
  sanitary regulations in, 20-1, 78-9, 278
  scurvy in, 20, 21, 286-7
Newcastle
  lodging-houses in, 415
  studies on, 25n
Newhaven, drainage in, 151
New Lanark, mill at, 302
New Statistical Account of Scotland, 49
Norfolk
  deaths in, 77
  housing conditions in, 326
  population increase in, 249
Normanby, Lord, 25, 46, 66, 68
Northampton
  life tables, 255, 284
  mortality rates in, 12
Northamptonshire
  deaths in, 77
  housing conditions in, 86-7
  population increase, 249
Northumberland
  deaths in, 77
  population increase in, 249
Nottingham
  back-to-back houses in, 6
  population changes in, 12n

Nottinghamshire
  deaths in, 77
  housing conditions in, 91, 193
  population increase in, 249
nuisances, 37, 43, 44, 80, 86, 87, 90, 93, 95, 348-50, 352, 354-61

old age, deaths from, 78, 256
open spaces, 7, 123
orphans, 254-6, 258-60, 269-70, 422
overcrowding
  disease and, 7-8, 10, 12, 15-16, 58, 79, 189-90, 218-9
  habits and, 190-204
  housing conditions and, 82-4, 86, 88, 91-5, 98, 114, 188-90, 366
  improvements and, 293-4
  in cellars, 91, 93, 105, 206
  in places of work, 167, 175, 176-7
  in schools, 187-8
  intemperance and, 197-201
  Irish and, 5-6
  legislation and, 342, 349-50
  morals and, 190-204
  special authorities and, 355
  urbanisation and, 4-6
Oxford Medical School, 18
Oxfordshire
  deaths in, 77
  housing conditions in, 87
  population increase in, 249

painters
  disease among, 319-20
  intemperance among, 203
Palmerston, Lord, 22, 30
Parent-Duchâtelet, A. J. P., 52, 149, 160, 162, 175, 183, 321
Paris
  charge for water in, 142
  drainage in, 161-4
  hospitals in, 174
  housing and disease in, 217-8, 238-9
  medical administration in, 409
  street cleansing in, 132-3
  studies of typhus in, 217-8
  tuberculosis in, 172-3n
  water supply of, 141, 149
parks, 335-9
Patissier, Ph., 184-6
pauperism, 264, 267-8, 270-1, 274
paving
  Board, 110
  Commission, 16
  legislation and, 346, 353
  of footpaths, 118
  of roads, 111, 130-2, 237, 365-6
  public health and, 4, 7, 299
Paxton, Joseph, 56
Pendleton, morals in, 192, 193
Percival, Dr, 22
Perrier, Casimir, 163-4
Perthshire, drainage in, 153
Petty, Sir William, 175
physique
  effects of pauperism on, 267-8
  mortality rates and, 250-4
  wages and, 253-4

pigsties, 88, 89, 100, 102, 103, 111, 112, 115, 196, 328
Playfair, Lyon, 67, 123
pneumonia, deaths from, 76-7
Police Commission, 16
police, sickness among, 282
political unrest
  neglect of public health and, 266-7
  wage-payment and, 312
Pollard, S., 3
pollution of water, 120, 134, 138-41, 350-2, 353, 355, 360
poor-houses, 84
Poor Law
  Amendment Act of 1834, 31, 32, 41, 46
  Commission and Commissioners, see below
  inquiry, 2, 36
  New, 39, 45-6, 138
  reform, Chadwick's interest in, 35, 36-7
  Unions, 32, 37, 43
Poor Law Commission
  and the *Report*, 1-3, 45
  Chadwick's Secretaryship of, 1, 31, 45
  public health reform and, 3, 31-2, 43-5
  use of material in the *Report*, 51
  water supplies and, 143
poor-rates
  exaction of, 344-5, 390-1, 421
  exemption from, 294-7, 303
  neglect of sanitary measures and, 254, 256, 264
  relief of orphans from, 256
  support of special authorities, 358
  support of public health improvement, 143, 422-3
poor-relief, cost of, 256, 264
Portsmouth, street cleansing in, 110
poverty
  birth-rate and, 65-6
  disease and, 9, 31-2, 63-5, 79, 210-219, 242-3, 276
  ill-health and, 2, 31-2
  insanitary conditions and, 2n
  morals and, 267-9
Power, Alfred, 47
Preston, economy of families in, 207
preventive measures, effects of, 276-339
Pringle, Sir John, 20, 52, 116
prisons
  condition of, 276-9, 397-8
  health in, 49-50, 150, 276-81, 407
  in France, 282
  medical inspection of, 405
  mortality rate in, 282
  reform of, interest in, 31
  sickness tables, 279-81, 282-3
  ventilation in, 277, 279, 282
privies
  cleansing of, 289
  condition of, 44, 88, 91, 101, 111, 112, 114, 197
  construction of, 120, 214
  disease and, 116, 117

  number of, 116
  number per population, 91, 94, 100, 112
  provision of, 91, 98, 326
  public, 115, 119
professional classes, mortality rates among, 220-32, 234-5
Public Health Act of 1848
  passing of, 1, 70-1
  provisions of, 71-2
  Report and, 1, 71-2, 421-5
  Scotland excluded from, 62, 72-3, 425
public health
  and sanitation in early 19th century, 3-4
  boards, 71, *see also* Boards of Health
  commissions, 71
  cost of improvement of, 424
  deterioration of, 2n, 3-18
  legislation and, 339-410
  local authorities and, 16-17, 71, 361-96
  machinery of administration of, 423
  protection of, 348-54
  special authorities for, 354-61

Quetelet, L. A. J., 245, 246

Reading, drainage in, 87
recreation, 325-9
reformers, and administrators, 28-37
refuse
  accumulation of, 80-4, 86, 87, 89, 90, 91-2, 93-6, 98, 104, 106, 118
  arrangements for disposal of, 423-4
  Boards of Health and, 396
  Chadwick's proposals for disposal of, 61-2
  cost of removal of, 117, 118, 125-6, 128-9, 134-5, 288-9
  defective drainage and, 109-10
  in streets, 113, 114, 115, 118, 131-2, 133, 297, 353, 355
  removal of, 79, 99-109, 117-8
  sale of, 119-20, 123-4
  value as manure, 118, 120-4, 166
Registrar General, office of the
  and the *Report*, 43, 51
  Annual Reports, 29, 31
  contribution to public health studies, 27-9, 31
  establishment of, 24, 27-8
  Farr's position in, 27
Registration Act, 28
registration, civil, 48, 62, 72
Reid, Peter, 22
Renfrew, water supply of, 139, 141
rents
  collection of, 299-300
  extent of, 299
  of old houses, 117-8, 136, 221
  of new houses, 326, 334, 343, 345, 346
  urban and rural, 6-7

Report on the Sanitary Condition of the Labouring Classes of Great Britain
approach to individuals, 48-51
axioms of, 58-9
Chadwick's visits in connection with, 51-2
character of, 46-7
commissioning of, 43-5
correction of, 53-4
distribution of, 55-6
effect of, 71-2
extension to Scotland, 47, 48-9
Health of Towns Commission and, 67
issues of, 58-60
making of, 43-58
method of collecting material, 47-9
points of controversy in, 62-6, 67
publication of, 54-5
questionnaires used for, 48
reception of, 56-8
reception of, in Parliament, 66
recommendations of, 61-2, 66, 422-5
subsidiary points of, 59-60
see also Chadwick
respiratory diseases, 76-7, 172, 174n, 180, 181, 256, 261
Rimmer, W. G., 7
roads
cleansing of, 109-35
commission of, 110
construction of, 81, 130-3, 379-82
drainage of, 110, 381-3
health and, 299
macadamised, 131
paving of, 109-35
Roberton, John, 25
Roe, John, 127-30, 132, 133, 378
Rome, drainage in, 160
Romilly, Sir Samuel, 22
Romsey, housing conditions in, 191
roots of the sanitary idea, 3-43
Ross and Cromarty, drainage in, 153
rural districts
age in occupations, 295-6
Chadwick's visits to, 75
courts leet in, 358-9
death rates in, 13, 220-32, 234-5, 241, 247-8
drainage of streets and houses in, 108-9, 166, 374
economy of families in, 207-8
general condition of residences in, 80-91, 96-7
habits in, 190-2
income in, 4, 253, 276
improved housing in, 297-8, 323-35
and drainage in, 150-9, 166
lodging-houses in, 417
organised migration from, 33
overcrowding in, 188, 190-2, 196-7
recreation in, 337-9
rents in, 6-7
Scottish, 96-7, 138, 153-4, 159, 207-8, 328, 331-3

survey of, for *Report*, 46-7
water supplies of, 136-8
Russell, Lord John, 22, 27, 30, 43, 45
Rutland
birth-rate in, 245
deaths in, 77
housing conditions in, 221
mortality rates in, 222-3, 228-30, 241, 247-8
population increase in, 249
poverty and disease in, 243
schools in, 223

St Helens, sanitary reforms in, 66n
Salford
population increase in, 4
prison in, 279-80
street cleansing in, 124-5
Salop
deaths in, 77
population increase in, 249
scarlatina
deaths from, 76-7, 78
housing conditions and, 85, 86, 89
in the army, 287
street cleansing and, 115
scavenging
as a means of employing the poor, 165
cost of, 118, 126, 165
lack of, 107, 159
negligence in, 108, 114
refuse disposal and, 98, 99
road paving and, 132
schools
for paupers, 267-8
mortality rates and, 222
ventilation of, 187-8
Scotland
deaths in, 78
disease in, cost of, 272-6
drainage in, 106-8, 115-6, 153-4, 282, 363
economy of families in, 207-12
housing conditions in, 5, 96-9, 195, 198-9, 277, 281-2, 298, 303-7, 328, 331-2, 397
lodging-houses in, 416
morals in, 195, 198-9
mortality rate in, 233
overcrowding in, 195, 198-9
Poor Law reform in, 64
Public Health Act and, 62, 72-3, 425
Report and, 48-9, 51, 62, 425
sewerage in, 59-60, 106-8, 120-4, 282
sickness in, 281, 291
street cleansing and paving in, 111, 115-6
university medical schools in, 18
water pollution in, 360
water supplies in, 138-41
scurvy, 20, 21, 286-7
sewage
disposal of, *see* sewerage
rates, 391-2
sale of, 119-20, 123-4
value as manure, 118, 120-4, 166

Index

sewerage
  Chadwick's scheme for, 59-60, 61-2
  construction of, 127-30, 375, 376-8
  costs of different methods of, 104, 106, 117-8, 124-51, 128-9, 134-5, 288-9, 372-5, 378-9, 384, 386-90, 392
  health and, 7, 16, 130, 217, 363-4, 396
  housing and, 81-2, 86, 91, 93, 95, 97, 98
  in foreign countries, 160-4
  in prisons, 278
  in Scotland, 59-60, 106-8, 120-4, 282
  irrigation scheme for, 59-60, 121-4, 133-5
  legislation and, 341, 346, 353, 356
  local authorities and, 113-4, 361-96
  of London, 16, 70-1, 117-8, 127-30, 133-4, 161, 366-71, 374-5, 388, 391
  provision of adequate, 99-109
  water supply and, 61-2, 124, 138, 396
sewers
  commissions of, 110, 341, 348, 368-71, 372-4, 388, 393, 400
  condition of, 81-2, 112
  open, 44, 80, 87, 88, 107, 115
Shaw, Sir Charles, 164, 201, 289n, 290n, 357
Sheffield, public garden in, 336
Shropshire, *see* Salop
sickness
  cost of, 254-76
  improvement of, 287-98
  reduction of, 291
  tables, 279-84, 291
Simon, John, 73
Slaney, R. A., 45, 67
slaughterhouses, 82, 108, 119, 352
Sleaford, housing conditions in, 190
smallpox
  cleanliness and, 316
  cost of, 275
  deaths from, 76-7, 78
  housing conditions and, 85, 86, 89
  street cleansing and, 111, 116
  vaccination and, 8, 62, 242n
Smith, Adam, 39
Smith, James, health inspector, 22
Smith of Deanston, James, 50, 52, 67, 122n, 124, 304-8
smoke
  abatement, 356-8, 365
  as a nuisance, 355-6
Snow, John, 8n, 63
soap, 21
social
  cost of ill-health and bad housing, 58-9, 254-76
  influence of Edinburgh University and reform, 22-3
  policy and state intervention, 41-2
  reform and public health reform, 29-30

Somerset
  deaths in, 77
  housing conditions in, 84-5
  population increase in, 249
Southampton
  deaths in, 77
  population increase in, 249
Southey, Robert, 4
Southwood Smith, Dr
  career of, 34-5
  contribution to public health reform, 21-2
  membership of Central Board of Health, 73
  membership of Health of Towns Commission, 67, 68
  part in compilation of the *Report*, 1-2, 61
  Poor Law Commission Report of 1838, 3, 16, 32, 44, 63, 370-1, 404
  report on health of London, 44
  report on sewerage of London, 71-2
  studies on disease, 9, 62, 273
  special authorities for public health, 354-61
spending and bad housing, 58-9
Spitalfields
  Chadwick's visit to, 75
  poverty and disease in, 243
  weavers of, 33, 251, 344
Stafford, housing conditions in, 89-90, 324-5
Staffordshire
  deaths in, 77
  population increase in, 249
  water supply of, 137
standard of living and public health, 4
state intervention
  classical economists and, 39-40
  factory legislation and, 339
  in economic policy, 40-1
  in social policy, 41-2, 73
  laissez-faire or, 38-43
  professional administrators and, 31
statistical
  data used in the *Report*, 45, 51
  nosology, 28
  studies and public health, 26-9
Statistical Society of London, 5, 27, 189
Statistical Society of Manchester, 15, 187, 220, 222, 243, 248, 293
Stephenson, Robert, 56, 57
Stewart, Dugald, 22-3
Stirling
  street cleansing in, 107
  water supply of, 138, 140
Stockport
  drainage in, 102
  housing conditions in, 91-2
  lodging-houses in 414
  smoke abatement in, 357
Street Act, 340
street cleansing
  cost of, 125-6
  diseases and, 4, 109-24
  in Paris, 132-3
  in Scotland, 111, 115-6

street cleansing (*continued*)
  legislation and, 340-1, 346, 348, 353, 355
  local authorities and, 361, 365-6
  mortality rates and, 113
  value of, 126, 237
streets
  surface of, 130-2
  town drainage of, 99-109
strikes
  neglect of public health and, 266-7
  wage-payment and, 312
Strutt, Anthony, 54
Stuart, James, 22, 199, 302
Suffolk
  deaths in, 77
  housing conditions in, 326
  population increase in, 249
superannuation, 254, 270
Surrey
  deaths in, 77
  population increase in, 249
Sussex
  Chadwick's study of, 75
  deaths in, 77
  population increase in, 249
Sutherland, drainage in, 153
Swedish life tables, 255, 284, 423

tailors
  average period of working ability, 254
  benevolent societies for, 170, 173
  conditions of work of, 167-74, 184-7, 407
  diseases of, 168-9, 171, 172
  habits of, 168-9
  savings of, 170, 171
  superannuation of, 169, 173
  wages of, 168, 170
Tain
  lodging-houses in, 416
  water supply of, 139
Tamworth, drainage in, 103
Teesdale, lodging-houses in, 415
tenants, costs of improvements to, 287-98
Tenbury, improvements in, 295-6
Thackrah, C. T., 24
Tiverton, housing conditions in, 80-1
tobacco, 183-4
town-planning, 347
towns, rate of increase of population in, 4, *see also* urbanisation
trade cycle and typhus, 9-10
trade unions, 267
tradesmen, mortality rates among, 220-32, 234-5
Tranent
  average age in occupations in, 265-6
  economy of families in, 207, 208
  housing conditions in, 49, 97, 199
  lodging-houses in, 416
  overcrowding in, 189-90
  town drainage in, 107
  water supply of, 139-40
Tremenheere, S., 31
Truro
  housing conditions in, 81-2
  mortality rates in, 220
  water supply of, 137
tuberculosis
  among animals, 172-3n
  as an urban disease, 11
  death rate from, 11, 76-7, 78, 176, 180, 261
  in 19th century, 8
  ventilation and, 168-9, 171, 172, 174, 181, 407
Tynemouth, lodging-houses in, 415
typhus
  as an endemic disease, 9-10
  cost of, 272-6
  deaths from, 10, 18, 76-7, 78-9, 100n, 233, 273, 275, 407
  drainage and, 100, 101, 103, 104, 151, 152, 185-7, 159, 166, 372
  economy of families and, 209, 210-19
  epidemics in 19th century, 8-9
  housing conditions and, 9-10, 80, 83, 85, 86, 87, 88, 90, 91, 92, 97, 330, 342
  in Ireland, 15, 16
  inquiry into, 370-1
  in the Army, 287
  Irish immigrants and, 15, 212
  local authorities and, 358
  poverty and, 9
  opinions on the causes of, 214-9
  overcrowding and, 15-16, 22-3, 190, 191
  statistics of, 213
  street cleansing and, 111, 113, 114, 115, 116, 119, 127
  trade cycle and, 9-10
  ventilation and, 174, 176-7, 364
  water supply and, 137-8

undernourishment and disease, 11
University College Medical School, 18
urban burials, 68
urbanisation
  death-rate and, 12-14
  disease and, 12-13, 15-16, 43-4
  effect on housing density, 4-5
  overcrowding and, 4-6
  rate of, in early 19th century, 4

vaccination, 8, 62, 242n
ventilation
  as a preventive measure, 287
  cholera and, 365
  disease and, 11, 15, 16, 21, 25, 49, 77, 79, 168, 171, 172, 174, 214, 215, 216, 422
  food and, 197-8
  habits and, 168-9
  intemperance and, 168, 169, 171
  in the navy, 285
  legislation and, 350
  of hospitals, 174-5
  of houses, 81, 84, 85, 87, 90, 91, 97, 104, 105, 188-90, 262, 264, 282, 331, 333, 424
  of lodging-houses, 350, 412-5
  of mines, 262

of places of work, 59, 167-74, 176, 181-7, 305, 307-8, 318-22, 424
of prisons, 277, 279, 282
of tailor's workshops, 167-74
of towns, 364-5
street cleansing and, 111, 112
tuberculosis and, 168-9, 171, 173, 174, 181, 407
wages and, 168, 170, 171
Vetch, James, 124, 364-5
Vienna, factory conditions in, 182
Villermé, Louis René, 52, 149, 161, 236, 238, 239, 250, 251
violence, deaths from, 78, 256, 270, 408

wages
 disease and, 204-5, 212-13, 422
 economy of families and, 206-10
 food and, 309, 311, 313, 314
 habits and, 313
 health and, 276
 housing and, 299
 intemperance and, 308-15
 methods of paying, 308-15
 mortality rates and, 222-3, 242-3
 of agricultural workers, 4, 253
 of tailors, 168, 170
 overcrowding and, 194, 197, 198, 199, 201
 physique and, 253-4
 political unrest and, 312
 preventive measures and, 290-1, 294, 297, see also income
Wales, deaths in, 77
Walker, G. A., 24, 68
Warwick, lodging-houses in, 417
Warwickshire
 deaths in, 77
 housing conditions in, 86
 population increase in, 249
water charges, 136, 142-3, 146, 289
water closets, 106, 115, 116, 120, 133, 165, 321-2
water companies, 136, 142, 143-7, 149-50, 340
water pollution, 120, 134, 138-41, 350-2, 353, 355, 360
water rate, 142
water supplies
 Boards of Health and, 396
 cholera and, 8, 10, 163
 cleanliness and, 422
 cost of, 142-3, 286-97, 341
 disease and, 58, 79, 143, 148-9
 domestic, 135-50, 289, 399
 drainage and, 135, 138, 139
 habits and, 141
 health and, 4, 7, 287
 improved, 277, 286-97
 in France, 141, 149, 162-3
 in Scotland, 138-41
 installation of, 288-9, 299-300
 landlords and, 136, 139, 143
 legislation and, 340-1
 methods of providing, 140-4
 Poor Law Commission and, 143
 provision of adequate, 99-109
 recommendations concerning, in the *Report*, 423-4
 sewerage and, 61-2, 124, 138, 396
 typhus and, 137-8
Weber, Dr, 186-7
West Bromwich, population increase in, 4
West Ham, drainage in, 88
West Middlesex Water Company, 124-5, 358
Westmorland
 deaths in, 77
 population increase in, 249
Whiggism and reform, 30-1
widowhood, 254-6, 258-60, 264, 269-70, 422-3
Wigan
 housing conditions in, 93
 street cleansing in, 114-5
Willan, Robert, 11, 24
Wiltshire
 deaths in, 77
 mortality rates in, 228-30, 234, 241
 population increase in, 249
Windsor, drainage in, 87-8
Witham, drainage in, 87
Wolverhampton, rate collection in, 391-2
Worcestershire
 deaths in, 77
 population increase in, 249
working ability, average period of, 254-5, 270, 423

York
 housing conditions in, 221
Yorkshire
 deaths in, 77
 mining population in, 261-2
 population increase in, 249
Yule, J., 16